Management of Money Holdings

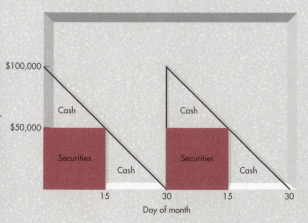

The Velo[...]

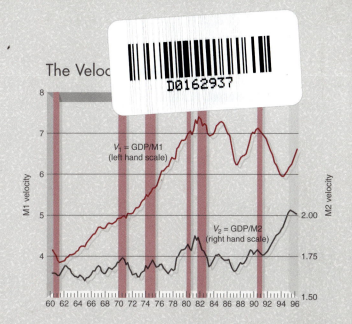

$V_1 = GDP/M1$
(left hand scale)

$V_2 = GDP/M2$
(right hand scale)

Actual and Potential Real GDP

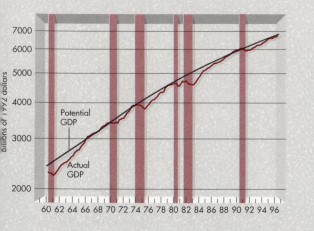

Potential GDP

Actual GDP

The Misery Index and Stock Prices

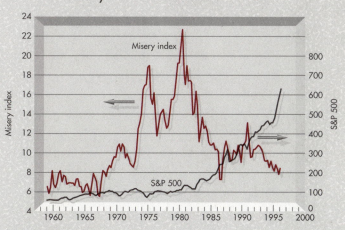

Misery index

S&P 500

Money, Banking, and Financial Markets

Money,
Banking, and
Financial Markets

Lloyd B. Thomas

Kansas State University

**Irwin
McGraw-Hill**

**Boston, Massachusetts · Burr Ridge, Illinois
Dubuque, Iowa · Madison, Wisconsin · New York, New York
San Francisco, California · St. Louis, Missouri**

Irwin/McGraw-Hill

A Division of The McGraw·Hill Companies

Money, Banking, and Financial Markets

This book is printed on acid-free paper.

Photo Credits:
Page 294 (Alan Greenspan): Gamma-Liaison; p. 407 (Allan Meltzer): Courtesy Allan Meltzer, Carnegie Mellon University, photo by Jonas Photography; p. 407 (Charles Plosser): Courtesy Charles Plosser, University of Rochester; p. 407 (William Poole): Courtesy William Poole, Brown University; p. 407 (Anna Schwartz): Courtesy Anna Schwartz, National Bureau of Economic Research; p. 495 (Irving Fisher): UPI/Corbis-Bettmann.

2 3 4 5 6 7 8 9 0 VNH VNH 9 0 9 8 7

ISBN 0-07-064436-5

This book was set in Times Roman by York Graphic Services, Inc.
The editors were Lucille Sutton and Peggy Rehberger;
the production supervisor was Paula Keller.
The design manager was Charles A. Carson;
interior design by Joseph Gillians.
Art by Fine Line Illustrations, Inc.
The photo editor was Anne Manning.
Von Hoffmann Press, Inc., was printer and binder.

Cover art: Hans Hofmann: *Yellow Burst,* 1956. Oil on canvas, 52-1/4 × 60-1/4″ (132.7 × 153 cm). Courtesy of the André Emmerich Gallery; Private collection.

Library of Congress Cataloging-in-Publication Data
Thomas, Lloyd Brewster,
    Money, banking, and financial markets / Lloyd B. Thomas.
        p.   cm.
    Includes bibliographical references and index.
    ISBN 0-07-064436-5
    1. Money.   2. Monetary policy.   3. Banks and banking.
    4. Securities.   I. Title.
HG221. T3986   1996
332. 1—dc20   96-32494

http://www.mhcollege.com

Cover: "Yellow Burst," by Hans Hofmann (1880–1966). Hofmann's work reflects a belief that all abstract art has its origin in nature. Through use of shapes and color and their relationships, he creates rhythm and movement—a dynamic tension among opposing forces. Such dynamism also characterizes a highly developed financial system.

About the Author

Lloyd B. Thomas, Jr., is Professor of Economics at Kansas State University. He received a B.A. and an M.A. in economics from the University of Missouri in 1963 and 1964 and a Ph.D. from Northwestern University in 1970.

Professor Thomas has published in numerous professional economic journals, primarily in the areas of his chief academic interests—macroeconomic policy, monetary economics, and international finance. He is the author or co-author of four previous textbooks, all of which have been published in multiple editions.

Recognized as an excellent teacher, Professor Thomas has won numerous teaching awards. His teaching interests lie chiefly in the areas of money and banking, monetary theory and policy, and principles of economics. Professor Thomas has taught at Northwestern University, the University of California at Berkeley, Florida State University, the University of Delaware, and the University of Idaho. For fun, he enjoys running and playing tennis.

For my mother,
Marianne Moon Thomas

CONTENTS

P R E F A C E

Students come to the undergraduate money and banking course with highly diverse backgrounds, interests, and majors. And instructors in this course place varying emphases on economic theory, institutions, monetary policy, finance, macroeconomic analysis, and microeconomics. This textbook reflects my view that the money and banking course should provide students with a solid grasp of the fundamental topics traditionally covered in courses on money, banking, and financial markets that are *not* thoroughly covered in other courses in the curriculum. For this reason, this text is designed to minimize the overlap with the intermediate macroeconomics course. Instead, it seeks to provide clear and up-to-date coverage of such fundamental topics as the nature and role of money, financial institutions and markets, banking structure and regulation, determinants of interest rates, money-supply analysis, the tools and intermediate targets of central bank policy, money demand and velocity, the transmission mechanism of monetary policy, the determinants of exchange rates, and the international monetary system.

This is a policy-oriented text. Its pages provide a thorough exposition of the relevant analytical framework, keyed closely to practical and specific issues of economic policy. Greater-than-normal attention is devoted to the tools of Fed policy and the difficulties involved in conducting monetary policy in an uncertain environment. Accordingly, this text provides an in-depth analysis of monetary policy. However, it does not skimp on economic theory. Chapter 20 presents the aggregate demand–aggregate supply framework, and Chapters 21 and 22 provide a thorough treatment of money demand and velocity. Results of a survey questionnaire sent by McGraw-Hill to hundreds of money and banking teachers indicate that some 30–40 percent cover the *IS-LM* model. However, those who do teach it demand thorough coverage in their textbook. Accordingly, the model is presented in Chapters 23 and 24, with emphasis on the use of the model to analyze such issues as deficit monetization, the crowding-out hypothesis, monetarist and Keynesian views on the effectiveness of monetary and fiscal policies, and the difficulties of conducting effective monetary policy under uncertainty. The text is structured so that the instructor can omit the *IS-LM* chapters and move on to Chapter 25 on the monetary policy transmission mechanism without loss of continuity. (The *Instructor's Manual* presents various suggested course assignments for courses with differing emphases.)

In this work, economic theory is used to shed light on real-world phenomena. Theory is not presented for its own sake, but rather is used to help students understand important economic events and policies. Theory is surrounded with examples from current events and economic history. For example, as soon as the theory of term structure of interest rates is presented, we use the analysis to evaluate the Clinton Administration proposal to issue only short-term government securities in order to save on interest expenditures. As soon as the monetary base-money supply multiplier framework is developed, it is used to analyze the collapse of the U.S. money supply in the early 1930s. Immediately after the aggregate demand–aggregate supply framework is developed, it is used to explain the key macroeconomics events of the past 30 years. Given this general approach, students quickly develop the attitude that economic theory is interesting and useful in explaining real-world phenomena.

Throughout the development of the macroeconomic analysis, we take the mainstream position that *both* monetary and fiscal policy strongly influence aggregate demand and economic activity. We do not emphasize extreme polar positions of Keynesianism, monetarism, or New Classical Macroeconomics from chapter to chapter. This would only serve to confuse students and lead them to believe the economics profession is in a state of disarray, unable to agree on almost anything. Instead, we discuss monetary and fiscal policies from a mainstream viewpoint and reserve one later chapter (Chapter 26) for the various polar positions (for example, that monetary policy has no effect on aggregate demand, that fiscal policy has no effect on aggregate demand, and that only *unanticipated* policies affect output and employment).

UNIQUE FEATURES OF THIS TEXT

Reviewers consistently remarked on the clarity of the writing style. Aside from its clear and unusually thorough coverage of financial institutions and markets, interest rates, money-supply analysis, the instruments of Fed policy, the velocity of money, the conduct of monetary policy, and exchange rates, instructors will note several distinguishing features of this book vis à vis alternative texts.

1 **Empirical Orientation.** One of the objectives of this text is to provide students with a feel for the key variables under discussion. Accordingly, this book goes beyond other textbooks in presenting real-world data. It features more than 85 graphs illustrating the behavior over time of important monetary and financial variables. More than a dozen of the boxed exhibits feature time-series graphs. Many of these illustrations are unique, having never appeared in other texts.

2 **Outstanding and Unique Exhibits.** This text features more than 50 boxed exhibits analyzing interesting and timely events. Most of these feature topics not covered in other texts. To mention only a few, these exhibits discuss the emergence of 100-year bonds, the bank merger craze of 1995–1996, derivatives and the demise of Barings Bank, the advent of the electronic purse, the explosion of U.S. currency held abroad, geographic implications of bank and S&L failures, salaries of Federal Reserve officials, the Shadow Open Market Committee, and the stock market.

3 **Introducing Students to Research.** Several exhibits give students a flavor of how empirical research is conducted in economics and finance. This is typically accomplished first by demonstrating graphically an important empirical relationship—for example, the relationship across countries between inflation rates and nominal interest rates. The exhibit then discusses the meaning of the intercept and slope of a line fit through the scatter of points. Similar analyses are presented for other relationships, such as budget deficits and monetization, discount-window borrowing and the incentive to borrow, and the estimation of money demand functions. Such exhibits can be skipped by instructors without loss of continuity. However, they will be appealing to many instructors, particularly those whose students intend to pursue further work in economics and finance.

4 **Unique Chapter on the Great Depression.** Partly because of a remarkable renaissance of interest in the Great Depression among economists and partly because the experience provides a unique case study of the determinants of the money supply and the conduct of Federal Reserve policy, we devote an entire chapter (16) to the role of the Federal Reserve in the Great Depression of the 1930s.

5 **Unifying Chapter on the Transmission Mechanism of Monetary Policy.** This chapter (25), widely cited by reviewers as a clear improvement upon the treatment in other texts, discusses the broad and complex mechanism through which Federal Reserve policy influences aggregate expenditures, GDP, and the nation's price level. The chapter emphasizes the changes that have occurred in recent years in the way that Fed policy influences economic activity.

PEDAGOGICAL FEATURES

This work contains a number of features designed to enhance the effectiveness of the book as a teaching instrument.

1 **Part Openers** for each of the seven sections of the text provide overviews outlining the importance of the topics covered in each section.

2 **From the Financial News** boxes introduce students to financial tables from daily newspapers, covering such information as stock prices, foreign exchange rates, Treasury bill yields, and weekly Federal Reserve data.

3 **International Perspectives** boxes provide a global perspective on key topics and empirical phenomena, allowing students to gain an appreciation for the integration of world financial markets and the global applicability of numerous concepts in the course.

4 More than 50 boxed **exhibits** provide interesting background on various concepts and events, emphasizing timely analyses of events in the 1990s.

5 **Key Terms** are printed in boldface when they are first defined, and are listed at the end of each chapter.

6 A **glossary** of all key terms, compiled in alphabetical order at the end of the book, includes the chapter number in which the term is introduced and defined.

7 **Chapter summaries** review key points developed in each chapter.

8 More than 130 **figures** are provided, with captions outlining the pertinent information conveyed in the figure. Approximately 70 figures involve time series plots indicating the behavior of key variables. In addition, many of the exhibits contain figures illustrating key points.

9 A **Your Turn** feature is designed to get students into an active mode by posing questions that test their understanding of important concepts and formulas.

10 **Study Questions** at the end of each chapter are carefully constructed to test students' understanding of the fundamental concepts discussed in the chapter.

11 **Suggestions for Additional Reading** at the end of each chapter guide instructors as well as students to classic literature as well as recent articles on major topics.

SUPPLEMENTARY MATERIALS

This text features a solid array of supplementary items.

1 The **Student Guide,** written by Prosper Raynold of Miami University of Ohio, includes a brief review of material, a variety of short-answer questions, and 15–18 multiple choice questions for each chapter.

2 The **Instructor's Manual,** prepared by the author and Alan Grant of Baker University, includes sample course outlines, explanations of key concepts in each chapter, and answers to questions and problems in the text.

3 The **Test Bank,** prepared by the author and Alan Grant, contains more than 1800 multiple choice exam questions—approximately 70 per chapter. The **Test Bank** is also available in computerized format for IBM PC's and Macintosh.

4 More than 100 **full-color transparencies** feature more than 80 percent of the figures included in the text.

Contact your local McGraw-Hill sales representative about obtaining these and other support materials.

ACKNOWLEDGMENTS

The efforts of many individuals were instrumental in making this final product possible. I am deeply grateful to Gary Burke, publisher of business and economics at McGraw-Hill, for the confidence he has shown in me, as well as his friendship over the years. Lucille Sutton, economics editor at McGraw-Hill has been a delight to work with. Her good humor, encouragement, and support have been greatly appreciated. Victoria Richardson, Adrienne D'Ambrosio, and Stephanie Cappiello of the economics editorial office have provided encouragement as well as efficient service in numerous ways on behalf of this project. Betty Morgan's chapter-by-chapter critique appreciably improved the clarity of the prose.

Peggy Rehberger expertly shepherded the manuscript through the editing and proofing process, and provided important encouragement while demonstrating uncommon patience with the author. I am also grateful to design manager Chuck Carson and designer Joe Gillians for their expertise in designing the book, and to Paula Keller for her skillful management of the production process. My greatest debt is to Alan Grant of Baker University. Without his able and conscientious daily efforts, this book simply could not have come to fruition in the timely fashion that it did. In addition to being responsible for Chapter 10, Al constructed all of the time-series graphs by computer, provided detailed suggestions and comments on two versions of every chapter, and developed many of the end-of-chapter study questions. My colleague, Patrick Gormely, graciously consented to write Chapter 27 on the International Monetary System. Other colleagues at Kansas State who contributed helpful suggestions include Michael Oldfather and Roger Trenary. Jim Butkiewicz of the University of Delaware provided an in-depth critique of Chapter 16 on the role of the Fed in the Great Depression. Velda Deutsch and Susan Koch provided outstanding secretarial expertise. Several of my graduate students also contributed to the project in various ways. These include Atanas Christev, David Ingram, Ilonka Lambeck, Danielle Lewis, and Pauline van der Sman-Archer. My long-time collaborators, Sally and Elizabeth, provided continuous encouragement and inspiration, and made the whole endeavor worthwhile.

McGraw-Hill obtained numerous reviews of each chapter of the text, and these were extremely beneficial in the transformation of early renditions of the chapters into the final products. I would like to thank the following individuals: Burton Abrams, University of Delaware; Peter Barger, North Central College; Charles R. Britton, University of Arkansas; Kevin Calandri, California State University-Sacramento; John A. Domonkos, Cleveland State University; Christopher A. Erickson, New Mexico State University; Bassam E. Harik, Western Michigan University; William G. Harris, Georgetown University; Julie A. Hewitt, Montana State University; Steven C. Hine, Lyon College; Arthur Janssen, Emporia State University; Eungmin Kang, St. Cloud State University; Dominique N. Khactu, University of North Dakota; Benjamin J. C. Kim, University of Nebraska-Lincoln; Stephen M. Miller, University of Connecticut; Raul Moncarz, Florida International University; Anthony O'Brien, Lehigh University; Peter A. O'Brien, Jr., Pace University; David Pate, St. John Fisher College; James E. Payne, Eastern Kentucky University; Douglas K. Pearce, North Carolina State University; Prosper Raynold, Miami University of Ohio; Edward Renshaw, State University of New York at Albany; Donald Sabbarese, Kennesaw State College; Bansi L. Sawhney, University of Baltimore; James Seal, University of Portland; Calvin D. Siebert, University of Iowa; and Robert Tokle, Idaho State University.

Lloyd B. Thomas

Money,
Banking, and
Financial Markets

P A R T

Introduction

1

In this opening section, we introduce several important concepts to be studied throughout this course. Chapter 1 overviews the role that money, banks, and financial markets play in a nation's economy. Crucial financial markets include the stock market, bond market, and foreign exchange market. The prices that are determined in these markets are powerfully influenced by current and expected future economic conditions. These prices, in turn, affect expenditure decisions, thereby influencing economic conditions. Chapter 2 examines the nature, functions, and evolution of money. Changes in the quantity of money typically lead to changes in a nation's output, employment, and price level. There are several alternative measures of money in the United States and other nations, and there is no clear concensus about which measure is best.

C H A P T E R

1

Money, Banking, and Financial Markets: An Overview

INTRODUCTION

As we approach the end of the twentieth century, it is difficult to imagine a more dynamic and exciting area of study than money, banking, and financial markets. In the past 15 years, we have witnessed the deregulation of the U.S. financial system, the development of many new financial markets and instruments, the increasing globalization of economic activity and financial markets, and a shocking rash of insolvencies among commercial banks and savings and loan associations. More recently, we have seen the beginnings of a major restructuring and consolidation of the U.S. banking system and the implementation of nationwide interstate banking. We have seen Congress pass the North American Free Trade Agreement (NAFTA), which promises to open up free trade among Canada, Mexico, and the United States. Federal budget deficits, which increased dramatically in the 1980s, are headed downward as we approach the year 2000. These events and many others continue to influence us all.

While you may be aware of these events, you probably do not fully understand them. During the course of carefully reading this text, you will become increasingly aware of the causes and consequences of important monetary, financial, and international economic phenomena. You will develop, for example, an understanding of the causes and consequences of changes in the supply of money, the level of interest rates, and the level of exchange rates. You will learn about financial institutions and markets and gain an appreciation of the nature and role of our central bank, the Federal Reserve System. Furthermore, you will emerge from this course with a grasp of the fundamental causes of such important developments as the savings and loan debacle, the changes in unemployment and inflation that occur over the course of the business cycle, and the problems of the European Monetary System.

This introductory chapter provides a brief overview of some of the key concepts, players, and events to be covered in depth in this course. You will quickly discover that, in addition to being interesting, this material has a direct bearing on your daily life and well-being.

MONEY AND BANKING: KEY CONCEPTS

Four key elements that play an important role in the U.S. economy are money, banks, interest rates, and federal budget deficits. Each element appears frequently in this book. Here, we briefly sketch the nature of each.

Money

Money is the stock of items used to make payment for goods and services. **Money,** or the **money supply,** is most commonly defined to include all currency and coin in circulation outside financial institutions and government coffers, together with the checkable accounts in depository institutions (commercial banks, savings and loan associations, mutual savings banks, and credit unions) owned by individuals and firms. A major objective of this text is to provide a clear explanation of the causes and consequences of changes in the quantity of money in the economy.

What Determines the Money Supply?

In Part 4, we will see that many factors can lead to short-run fluctuations in the money supply. The most important player in this process—indeed the player clearly responsible for the long-run or trend behavior of the money supply—is the **central bank,** known in the United States as the **Federal Reserve System,** or simply the **Fed.** By implementing certain policy tools, the Fed conducts **monetary policy**—measures that deliberately change the availability of credit, the level of interest rates, and the supply of money. For example, when the U.S. economy experiences a period of economic stagnation and rising unemployment, such as in 1990–1992, the Fed is likely to implement stimulative monetary policy measures. In this instance the Fed uses its policy tools to make bank loans more easily available to the public. This results in a decline in interest rates and an increase in the money supply—developments that boost aggregate expenditures for goods and services, thereby remedying the weakness in the economy.

Conversely, when the economy suffers from excessive spending and rising inflation, the Federal Reserve can implement measures that restrain aggregate spending. The Fed uses its policy tools to reduce the availability of credit and the money supply and push interest rates up. For example, in 1994, as the U.S. economy approached full employment and appeared to be on the threshold of an undesirable acceleration of inflation, the Fed acted on six occasions to boost interest rates and slow the growth of bank credit and the supply of money. Parts 4 and 5 of this book provide an in-depth analysis of U.S. monetary policy.

Figure 1-1 shows the behavior of the U.S. money supply in recent years. In mid-1996, it stood at roughly $1.2 trillion, or some $4500 per person (approximately $17,000 per family). If this seems too high a figure for the typical family, you are right! The figures are skewed by the fact that a considerable portion of the nation's money supply is held by firms. Just as you and I hold money to finance upcoming transactions, firms maintain money balances to pay for materials, meet payrolls, and so forth. Thousands of

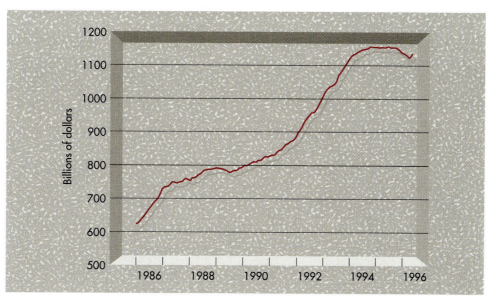

Figure 1-1   The U.S. Money Supply, 1986–1996. In mid-1996, the U.S. money supply (checking accounts and currency) approached $1.2 trillion. Its magnitude has increased at an average annual rate of roughly 6 percent per year in the past decade.   *Source:* Federal Reserve System.

business firms hold large checking accounts in depository institutions, all of which are included in the various measures of the nation's money supply. In addition, large amounts of cash are used to finance transactions in the U.S. underground economy—that is, to finance illegal activities. U.S. currency is coveted in Latin America and in the Eastern European nations currently in transition to capitalism.

Money and Inflation

When a nation's money supply increases more rapidly than its capacity to expand its output of goods and services, and does so for a sustained period, inflation occurs. **Inflation** is a persistent increase in a nation's general level of prices. The fundamental cause of inflation is excessive growth of expenditures for goods and services. Typically, rapid expansion of a nation's money supply leads to rapid growth in expenditures. If expenditures rise faster than the nation's capacity to produce goods and services, inflation occurs. History teaches us that no episode of severe and sustained inflation has ever occurred in the absence of accompanying rapid growth of the money supply.

Figure 1-2 illustrates the relationship between the average rate of money growth and the average rate of inflation for a cross section of nations in the period 1974–1994. Countries with high rates of money growth systematically experienced high rates of inflation. Note, however, that while the relationship is positive and relatively strong, it is far from perfect. Other factors besides money growth also influence price level behavior.

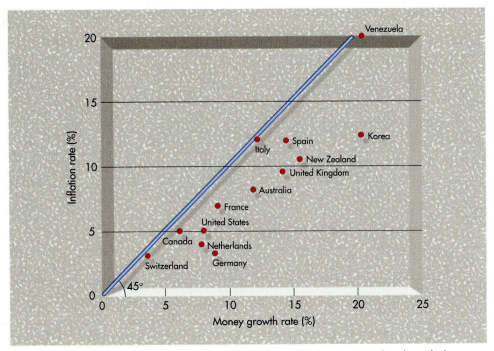

Figure 1-2   Money Growth and Inflation, 1974–1994. Countries with relatively low money growth rates (e.g., Switzerland) tend to experience modest inflation. Countries with rapid money growth (e.g., Italy, Spain, Venezuela) typically experience more severe inflation.   *Source:* Federal Reserve Bank of St. Louis.

Banks

Banks are institutions that accept various types of deposits and use the funds attracted primarily to grant loans. We use the term "banks" generically here to encompass not only the commercial banks where most people maintain checking accounts but other depository institutions such as savings and loan associations, mutual savings banks, and credit unions as well. Formerly, commercial banks were distinct from other depository institutions in their activities and functions, and differences still persist. However, as a result of deregulatory financial legislation in the 1980s, the distinctions have diminished—the depository institutions are today more homogeneous in nature. For example, all these institutions are authorized to issue checking accounts and make loans. We will therefore consider all of them to be "banks."

A key source of our interest in the behavior of banks flows from their intimate role in the money supply process. As we will see in Chapter 13, whenever banks extend new loans, money is created in the form of new checking accounts. And whenever banks reduce loans, the money supply declines as checks are written to pay off those loans (thereby reducing the amount of funds in checking accounts). The Federal Reserve System strongly influences the ability and willingness of banks to make loans by setting certain regulations and utilizing certain policy tools. In this way, the Fed retains full responsibility for the trend, or longer-run, behavior of the money supply, though not for its week-to-week gyrations. Because banks are the conduit through which the Fed implements monetary policy, we are particularly interested in studying banks.

But there are other reasons for our interest in banking. Banks are key **financial intermediaries**—institutions that serve as "middlemen" in the transfer of funds from savers to those who invest in real assets such as houses, equipment, and factories. Financial intermediaries promote economic efficiency by gathering the surplus funds of millions of individual savers and making them available to investors in these real assets. In performing this function, financial intermediaries improve the well-being of both savers and investors. By improving economic efficiency, they raise living standards.

Banks and other financial intermediaries have been an important source of financial innovations that have expanded the range of alternatives open to savers. Parts 2 and 3 of this text analyze the nature and role of financial institutions, the instruments with which they deal, the markets in which they operate, and the regulations by which they are governed.

Interest Rates

An **interest rate** is the cost of borrowing (or the return from lending), expressed as an annual percentage. It is a key variable in the economy, playing an important role in households' decisions to purchase durable goods such as cars and houses, and in influencing the construction of new business plants and commercial buildings. Especially significant is the **real interest rate,** the interest rate after adjusting for expected inflation. In addition to influencing consumption and investment expenditures, the real interest rate has major implications for the well-being of both borrowers and lenders, as it influences the way in which real wealth is redistributed among them.

The real interest rate also influences the **exchange rate** in the international market—for example, the value of the U.S. dollar expressed in units of foreign currency. By causing changes in exchange rates, changes in real interest rates help to determine the cost of imports. Given other factors, an increase in real interest rates at home attracts foreign funds, thereby raising the value of the dollar (the number of yen or deutsche marks per dollar). This increase in the value of the dollar raises the prices of domestic goods to foreigners and makes foreign goods cheaper in the United States. Because an increase in the value of the dollar makes competing in foreign markets more difficult for U.S. firms, it tends to increase the nation's *trade deficit*—the amount by which imports exceed exports.

Although we speak of "the" interest rate, there are of course a multitude of interest rates that prevail at any given time. Various financial instruments differ in their riskiness, length of time to maturity, tax treatment, and other characteristics. Hence, at any given time, we observe different rates on mortgages, corporate bonds, bank loans, savings accounts, certificates of deposit, municipal bonds, U.S. government bonds, and other financial instruments. Typically, these interest rates move in tandem, all of them being influenced by the business cycle, changes in expected inflation, and Federal Reserve policies.

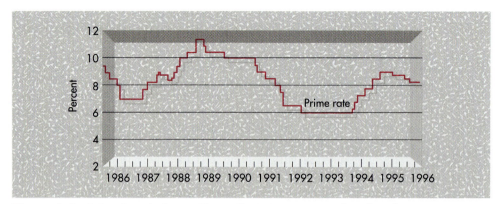

Figure 1-3   Prime Rate in Recent Years. The prime rate is a benchmark interest rate set by large U.S. banks. It changes frequently, triggering changes in the loan rates charged to customers whose rates are linked to the prime rate.   *Source:* Federal Reserve System.

The Federal Reserve can alter the level of interest rates by influencing the availability of loanable funds in banks. However, interest rates are also powerfully affected by factors other than Federal Reserve policy. There is sometimes a tendency for the media and the public to incorrectly attribute to the Fed responsibility for interest rate movements that are in reality caused by such factors as changes in inflation expectations or changes in business cycle conditions.

Figure 1-3 shows the movement in recent years of the **prime loan rate,** a key lending rate posted by large U.S. banks that is used as a benchmark for setting rates to small businesses, consumers, and other borrowers.[1]

Interest rates are established in competitive financial markets. They are among the most important variables encountered in this course. Chapters 5 to 7 provide a comprehensive analysis of interest rates. We will now examine one of the factors that economists believe influence interest rates, the federal budget deficit.

The Federal Budget Deficit

The government **budget deficit** is the amount by which government expenditures exceed tax receipts. Because the deficit must be financed by issuing debt—by borrowing—it has important economic ramifications.

Until the early 1980s, the United States did not experience large and persistent federal budget deficits except in time of war. But the implementation of the Economic Recovery Tax Act (ERTA) of 1981, coupled with a doubling of national defense expenditures

---

[1]The prime rate is sometimes defined as the rate banks charge their biggest and best customers. Technically, this definition is incorrect because large, highly stable corporations often are able to obtain big loans at rates below the prime rate. However, the overwhelming majority of bank borrowers are charged a rate above the prime. Home improvement loans, for example, may be set at 2 percentage points above the prime rate and auto loans 4 percentage points above the prime. When the prime rate is changed, these other loan rates typically change in lockstep.

between 1980 and 1987 and a failure to reduce entitlement expenditures (Social Se-curity, Medicare, and so forth), ushered in a new era of enlarged deficits. ERTA, the major policy initiative of the first Reagan administration, provided for successive in-come tax reductions of 10 percent in 1982, 10 percent in 1983, and 5 percent in 1984. Because these tax cuts were accompanied by increases in federal expenditures, the na-tion's budget deficit increased from an average rate of $57 billion per year between 1976 and 1980 to an average rate of $195 billion per year in the period 1982–1986.

The deficit declined somewhat in the late 1980s, disciplined temporarily by the Gramm-Rudman-Hollings Deficit Reduction Act of 1985. However, it increased sharply in the early 1990s in response to expanded entitlement expenditures, the recession of 1990–1991, and the sluggish recovery that followed. Since 1993, the Congress and the president have placed the deficit on a declining track, and there is some prospect for dra-matically reduced deficits by the year 2000. However, special efforts will be required to prevent the deficit from rising sharply in the early portion of the next century as a result of sharply increased entitlement expenditures stemming from demographic forces and in-flation in the health care sector.

Because of this string of annual deficits, the gross federal debt—the sum of all past deficits—increased more than 400 percent between 1980 and 1996. Today, it exceeds $5 trillion. Reducing the federal deficit and thereby slowing the growth of the national debt remains a difficult challenge. As federal programs and expenditures are reduced, there is likely to be a painful adjustment process.

Figure 1-4 shows the overall pattern of federal expenditures, receipts, and deficits since 1960.

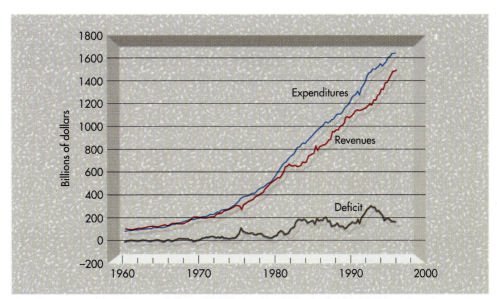

Figure 1-4   Federal Expenditures, Receipts, and Deficits, 1960–1996. Before the 1980s, federal budget deficits were small and transitory. In more recent years, they have become large and persistent.   *Source: Citibank Economic Database.*

Economists disagree about the economic consequences of government budget deficits. Most believe that larger deficits raise interest rates, although the empirical evidence from U.S. history is not decisive on this issue. If deficits do raise interest rates, investment spending on new plant, equipment, and technology may be compromised, thereby slowing the long-run growth in living standards. In this manner, large and persistent deficits may impose costs on future generations.

We have seen that higher interest rates attract funds from foreign countries, thereby driving up the dollar's value in foreign exchange markets and making it more difficult for American firms to compete in foreign trade. In the 1980s, persistent net lending to the United States by foreigners (as they took advantage of the high U.S. yields in this period) transformed the United States from the world's largest net creditor nation in international markets into its largest net debtor nation. Some observers fear that this transformation may produce a corresponding decline in U.S. prestige and influence in world affairs.[2]

An underlying concern is that the deficit, if not kept to a reasonably modest size in relation to the nation's economy, may ultimately lead to severe inflation. Because the government is a large debtor, and because inflation relieves the burden of debt (by allowing debtors to repay creditors with less valuable money), the government may eventually be tempted to get out from under the debt by fostering inflation. This could happen if the Federal Reserve were to assist the Treasury in financing the deficits by purchasing large amounts of government bonds, thereby increasing the nation's money supply. But while large budget deficits typically lead to severe inflation in less developed countries and nations with fragile political structures, this hasn't yet happened in the United States. Indeed, it need not happen. It is worth noting, however, that the savings and loan fiasco did not have to happen either—but it did! One good reason to reduce the federal budget deficit is to reduce our exposure to the possibility of a highly damaging episode of severe inflation.

Given the reluctance of elected officials to implement the painful measures required to eliminate the deficit—that is, tax hikes and cutbacks in government expenditures—the deficit may remain in the news for some time. Although economists disagree about the precise consequences of deficits, it seems clear that the persistence of a large U.S. budget deficit is one of the more important economic events of the past 15 years. Conversely, the successful phasing out of the deficit over the next 5 years would unleash significant economic consequences, many of them favorable.

KEY FINANCIAL MARKETS

Three crucial financial markets that cannot escape an overview of a money and banking course include the stock market, the bond market, and the foreign exchange market. These markets are important in part because the prices set in these markets have important effects on aggregate expenditures and therefore on real output, employment, and the price level. Let's look at the stock market first.

---

[2]This is a principal thesis of a book by Benjamin Friedman, an economist at Harvard University; see *Day of Reckoning: The Consequences of American Economic Policy under Reagan and After* (New York: Random House, 1988).

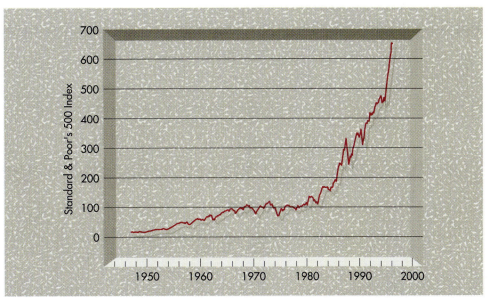

Figure 1-5   U.S. Stock Prices, 1947–1996 (the Standard & Poor's 500 Index). Stock prices tend to be volatile. Note the great bull markets of 1950–1965 and 1982–1996. In the latter period, an average bundle of stocks provided handsome returns—some 15 percent per year, including both price appreciation and dividends.   *Source: Citibank Economic Database.*

The Stock Market

In many ways, the most fascinating financial market is the stock market. In this market, **shares**—claims of ownership in individual corporations—are traded. Fluctuations in the price of an individual stock indicate the corporation's changing prospects. And movements in such indexes of stock prices as the Dow Jones Industrial Average (DJIA) and the Standard & Poor's 500 Index (S&P 500) reflect changing sentiments about the nation's economic future. Stock prices are an important barometer of perceptions about future economic prosperity.[3]

Stock prices are volatile, which helps to explain the public's fascination with the stock market. Individuals can make (or lose) a lot of money in this market in a hurry! Figure 1-5 shows the movements in the Standard & Poor's 500 Index in recent decades. As indicated in the figure, U.S. stock prices appreciated strongly from 1950–1965; fluctuated without a long-term trend from 1966 until 1982; and increased dramatically after 1982 (see Exhibit 1-1 for more on the stock market).

---

[3]However, the stock market is not a particularly good *predictor* of future economic conditions. Stock prices can sometimes change dramatically without foretelling any significant change in economic activity. The DJIA fell 522 points on October 19, 1987 (losing about 20 percent of its value in a single day), but its fall was not followed by a decline in economic activity. Economist Paul Samuelson, poking fun at the poor predictive performance of stock prices, once quipped that the stock market had "correctly signaled nine of the last five recessions."

EXHIBIT 1-1

The Stock Market—Is It for You?

Considering that more than 50 million Americans own stock in American corporations, it is clear that owning stock appeals to many people. You don't have to be rich to own stock. When you purchase stock in a company, you own a piece of the company and participate directly in the future success or failure of the firm.

Suppose you are thinking about buying a few shares of Wal-Mart, the remarkably successful discount chain whose founder, Sam Walton, was for many years reputed to be the wealthiest person in the United States (Walton had a net worth of roughly $15 billion when he died in 1992). To find the current price of Wal-Mart as well as other pertinent information, turn to the financial pages of any major newspaper (*The New York Times, USA Today, The Wall Street Journal*). On Feb. 26, 1996, the following information was printed in newspapers across the country in a table with other stock quotations.

52 Weeks					Yld		Vol				Net
Hi	Lo	Stock	Sym	Div	%	PE	100s	Hi	Lo	Close	Chg
27⅝	**19 1/16**	**WalMart**	**WMT**	**.20**	**.9**	**18**	**39402**	**22¾**	**21⅝**	**22¼**	**−⅛**
22⅛	17⅜	♣ WaldnResdntl	WDN	1.86f	8.6	27	497	21⅞	21½	21⅝	−⅛
s 36⅜	22⅝	Walgreen	WAG	.44	1.3	26	5415	35¾	34⅜	35	−⅜
60	30	WallaceCS	WCS	.86	1.5	19	2706	55⅞	55½	55⅞	+¼
26⅞	14⅞	Warnaco	WAC	.21e	.9	16	1422	24⅝	24	24⅝	+¾
3½	15/16	WarnerIns	WCP		...	dd	176	2⅞	2¾	2⅞	...
103	74½	WarnerLamb	WLA	2.76f	2.7	18	5362	101½	99⅛	100⅞	−⅞
20⅝	13	WashnEngy	WEG	1.00	4.9	dd	502	20⅜	20⅛	20¼	+⅛
s 22½	17⅝	WashGasLt	WGL	1.12	5.0	13	899	22⅜	22¼	22¼	...
6⅜	3¼	WashHomes	WHI	.15	2.9	9	11	5¼	5¼	5¼	+⅛

From left to right, the first two columns show the highest and lowest prices at which Wal-Mart traded during the past 52 weeks: a high of $27⅝ and a low of $19 1/16. The stock paid an annual dividend of 20 cents per share, which produced an annual yield of 0.9 percent (columns five and six). It was selling at a price/earnings ratio (PE) of 18, meaning that the price was 18 times its annual earnings, or profits per share. The next column indicates the number of Wal-Mart shares traded on the most recent day, measured in hundreds of shares. On Feb. 23, 1996, 3,940,200 shares were traded. The next three columns indicate the high, low, and closing prices for the day. Wal-Mart ranged from a high of $22¾ to a low of $21⅝ and closed at $22¼, down one-eighth of a dollar on the day.

The price of any stock is closely related to its current and expected future profits. Wal-Mart's moderately high PE (18) indicated that market participants expected the company to experience fairly solid growth of sales and profits in the future. By comparison, in early 1993 Wal-Mart stock had sold at a PE near 40. Apparently, investors revised their projections downward as the company approached completion of its expansion across the United States. To see the range of PEs, check the financial pages of your newspaper.

Because investors' sentiments about future earnings of a corporation are built into the current price of a stock, one cannot make money in the stock market simply by buying shares in companies that are growing rapidly. And because easily available information is already incorporated into stock prices, it is extremely difficult to make a profit through short-term trading (unless you have inside information unavailable to others, which is illegal to employ for personal gain). To determine whether a stock is a wise investment choice, you would be well advised to obtain as much information about the company as possible, emphasizing its prospects for the next few years. Select stocks that your intuition and research tell you should have a good future, and hang onto them for a period of years or even decades. Over the past 10, 50, and 100 years, a strategy of purchasing and holding an average bundle of stocks has yielded returns that sharply outstripped the returns from bonds and other debt instruments over the same period.

Stock prices have important macroeconomic ramifications. For one thing, stocks constitute an important portion of people's wealth. When the stock market plummeted in October 1987, hundreds of billions of dollars of wealth simply evaporated. Conversely, the long bull market that began in 1982 dramatically increased the wealth of some 50 million Americans who owned stocks either directly or through retirement and pension funds. Such changes in wealth induce changes in consumer expenditures, thereby influencing such crucial economic variables as gross domestic product (GDP) and the unemployment rate. One reason the United States avoided a recession during the long economic expansion of 1982 to 1990 was the support provided to consumer spending by the dramatic increase in stock values.

Stock prices may also influence investment spending on plant and equipment. The level of stock prices determines the amount of funds firms may obtain by issuing new shares of stock. When stock prices are relatively high, firms are inclined to issue new shares and use the proceeds to finance expansion of new plant and equipment.

Thus, one of the channels through which the Federal Reserve influences the economy is the stock market. This channel of influence runs from Fed policy to the money supply and interest rates, to stock prices, to consumption and investment spending, to output and employment. Of course, monetary policy is only one of a multitude of forces that influence stock prices.

The Bond Market

A **bond** is a debt instrument—an IOU—issued by a firm, a government, or a government agency. It involves a contractual agreement by the issuer to make a stream of payments to the lender at specified future dates and to return the principal at maturity. Unlike stocks, which are claims of ownership or equity, bonds are instruments by which lenders (or creditors) make funds available to borrowers (or debtors). Bondholders are *lenders,* not *owners.*

In the bond market, interest rates are determined by the market forces of supply and demand. A very active market, the bond market is of special interest in money and banking because the Federal Reserve conducts its monetary policy chiefly by purchasing and selling U.S. government bonds. Figure 1-6 illustrates the **yields,** or interest rates, on a variety of bonds in the period since 1950.

The Foreign Exchange Market

An American importer of Sony VCRs from Japan must pay for the equipment in Japanese currency—that is, yen. A U.S. mutual fund specializing in Mexican stocks must purchase its portfolio of stocks with pesos. By the same token, an Italian importer of IBM's mainframe computers made in the United States must settle up in dollars. Thus, foreign trade in goods and services and real and financial assets gives rise to trade in national currencies. The market in which foreign currencies such as dollars, deutsche marks, yen, and pesos are traded is called the **foreign exchange market.** The price at which one country's currency exchanges for another's is called the **foreign exchange rate.**

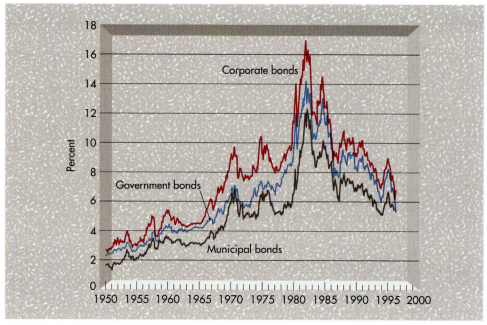

Figure 1-6 Yields on U.S. Government, Municipal, and Corporate Bonds, 1950–1996. Bond yields fluctuate over time, sometimes dramatically. From the 1950s to the early 1980s, these yields trended strongly upward. Since then, they have declined considerably. *Source: Citibank Economic Database.*

The foreign exchange market is an excellent example of a highly competitive market. This market contains a large number of buyers and sellers of a range of homogeneous products—national currencies. For many years, exchange rates were fixed. They were pegged, or held constant, by direct government intervention in the foreign exchange market. World trade was based on a system of **fixed exchange rates.** For the past quarter century, however, international exchange rates have been allowed to change continuously in response to the market forces of supply and demand, albeit with occasional government intervention intended to influence them. This is known as a **floating exchange rate system.**

Figure 1-7 shows the exchange rate of the U.S. dollar against a basket of foreign currencies. The exchange rate, expressed as units of foreign currency per dollar, has fluctuated dramatically in recent years. When the dollar **appreciates,** or rises in value, as during 1980–1985—the cost to foreign buyers of U.S.-made goods rises. Foreign products become cheaper in the United States, making it more difficult for domestic agricultural and manufacturing firms to compete in world markets. The U.S. **trade deficit**—the excess of imports over exports—rises.

Given other factors, when the dollar **depreciates** (declines in value), the tables are turned. U.S. exports expand and U.S. imports decline as domestic goods become more affordable in foreign markets and foreign products become more expensive at home. The U.S. trade deficit then decreases—that is, moves in the direction of a surplus.

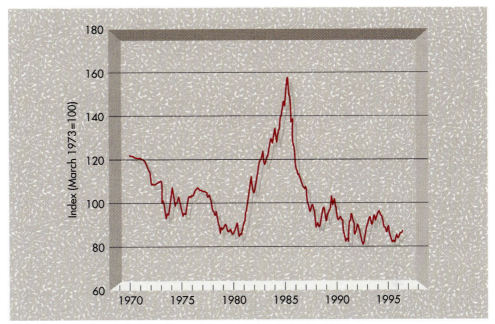

Figure 1-7   The Exchange Rate of the U.S. Dollar, 1970–1996. Exchange rates fluctuate continuously. The U.S. dollar depreciated in the 1970s, appreciated sharply during 1980–1985, and depreciated after early 1985. These changes have important consequences for Americans.   *Source: Federal Reserve Bulletin.*

It is clear that fluctuations in the exchange rate have important consequences for the U.S. economy. In Chapter 8, we will analyze the causes and consequences of exchange rate changes in depth. However, international economic and financial considerations are of pervasive significance throughout this course. Therefore, international considerations are woven into almost every chapter of this book.

CONCLUSION

Money, banking, and financial markets are exciting subjects characterized by dynamic change. In this course, we will focus on a multitude of issues that have an immediate impact on your well-being. Developments such as trade and banking legislation, financial innovations, the business cycle, budget deficits, and Federal Reserve monetary policy actions influence your job prospects, the cost of your loans, and the returns you earn on your savings. As you study these phenomena, your ability to digest and interpret economic news will increase, and you will be in a much better position to understand contemporary monetary, financial, and international economic developments. For these reasons, this course stands to be of considerable value to you. Work hard, and enjoy!

KEY TERMS

money (money supply)

central bank

Federal Reserve System (Fed)

monetary policy

inflation

banks

financial intermediary

interest rate

real interest rate

exchange rate

prime loan rate

budget deficit

share

bond

yield

foreign exchange market

foreign exchange rate

fixed exchange rates

floating exchange rate system

appreciate

trade deficit

depreciate

NOTE TO STUDENTS AND INSTRUCTOR

Each remaining chapter of this book is followed by a list of study questions as well as a discussion of recommended readings that provide additional perspective on the topics discussed in the chapter. Here, at the end of the first chapter, we simply list some of the sources of important data and other information which you may wish to tap throughout the course. Your library will have most of these sources, and those periodicals that are published by the Board of Governors of the Federal Reserve System and the 12 district Federal Reserve Banks are often available on request at little or no charge.

The Board of Governors publishes a monthly *Federal Reserve Bulletin,* which includes much data and information on recent monetary policy and financial developments. A convenient summary of the year's monetary policy deliberations and actions can be found in the *Annual Report* of the Board of Governors. An excellent discussion of each year's monetary and financial developments is also contained in the *Annual Report* of the Federal Reserve Bank of New York. Each of the 12 district Federal Reserve Banks publishes semimonthly or quarterly *Reviews* which contain interesting and timely articles. Other publications which you will find informative include the *Economic Report of the President,* published annually in February (U.S. Government Printing Office), and the *Annual Reports* issued by the Federal Deposit Insurance Corporation and the International Monetary Fund. The U.S. Trea-

sury publication *Treasury Bulletin* contains a wealth of statistical information on various aspects of public debt, fiscal operations, and international finance. Major sources of international financial data include *International Financial Statistics,* published monthly by the International Monetary Fund, and *International Economic Conditions,* published quarterly by the Federal Reserve Bank of St. Louis. Other good sources of data relevant to this course include *Monetary Trends, National Economic Trends,* and *U.S. Financial Data,* all published by the St. Louis Fed.

For timely and well-written articles on recent developments, see *Current Issues in Economics and Finance,* initiated in 1995 by the Federal Reserve Bank of New York. In general, one can find articles on financial and monetary developments in *The Wall Street Journal* almost every day. In particular, the *Journal* contains extensive daily stock, bond, Treasury bill, and foreign exchange rate quotations and also contains an article each Friday which outlines recent movements in monetary variables and Federal Reserve actions. For additional depth on hundreds of subjects covered in this book, an outstanding source is *The New Palgrave Dictionary of Money and Finance,* published in 1992. To glimpse the kind of research that occupies the frontiers of monetary economics and finance, pick up a recent issue of *Journal of Money, Credit, and Banking, Journal of Monetary Economics, Journal of Finance,* or *The Journal of International Money and Finance.*

Money: Its Nature, Functions, and Evolution

George Bernard Shaw once remarked that the lack of money is the root of all evil. While this is clearly an overstatement, there have been periods, like the Great Depression of the 1930s, for which the statement rings true. But there have also been numerous episodes in history in which too *much* money has been the root of all evil. The runaway inflation experienced in Russia in the 1990s is an example.

In one sense, money is unimportant. What determines a nation's living standard is the capacity of its people to produce goods and services. If we were suddenly to double the amount of goods and services that we collectively produce, our real incomes and standard of living would collectively double. If instead we were to double the amount of money (currency, coins, and checking accounts) existing in the nation, we would not be better off. Our ability to produce goods and services would not be enhanced, and our living standard would not rise. Indeed, the inflation unleashed by excessive expansion of the money supply would be highly damaging to the nation's well-being.

In another sense, money is extremely important. Money facilitates the process of exchange. It allows an economy to operate more efficiently, thereby raising the living standard. Supplied in appropriate quantity, money enables a society to avoid the extremes of depression and severe inflation and to maintain an environment in which economic activity can flourish. While irresponsibly managed money can do enormous damage to a society, prudently managed money can be a positive force which contributes to the stability of the economic variables that affect each of us—prices, income, and employment. In this chapter, we examine the nature, functions, and evolution of money and look at the various money measures employed by the Federal Reserve System.

THE NATURE AND FUNCTIONS OF MONEY

Money is a fascinating subject. It has occupied the minds of profound thinkers as well as crackpots. The management of the nation's money constitutes an important portion of this book. Who determines its amount and how? Why does excessive growth of money cause inflation? How does a severe contraction of the supply of money cause depression? These are questions to be covered later. But first, some preliminaries are in order. In this section we will address the questions of what money is and what its functions are.

The Meaning of Money

Money is most commonly defined as anything that is generally acceptable as payment for goods or services or for the discharge of debt. This is not a legal definition of money but a behavioral one. It emphasizes the element of confidence, the psychological factor involved in the concept of money. Money is what we believe others will accept as payment. Our willingness to accept a given item as payment is contingent on our belief that the item will retain its value, or purchasing power, and will continue to be acceptable. This confidence relies, in turn, on the assurance of reasonably strict limits on the supply of the item to be used as money. Historically, many different items—whales' teeth in Fiji, leather in France, stones on the island of Yap, tobacco and whiskey in the American colonies, and numerous types of metallic coins—have served as money because people had confidence in their value and were willing to accept them as payment.

Traditionally, most economists have defined as money all currency and coins held by the public, together with demand deposits and other checkable deposits in commercial banks and savings institutions. Since practically all payments are made by the exchange of coins and paper currency or by the transfer of deposit balances via checks or electronic transfer (wire), this definition fits our conceptual notion of money as those items which are "generally acceptable" in making payment.

What about credit cards? The use of credit cards is essentially a method of postponing payment—that is, entering into a credit arrangement—and therefore credit cards do not constitute money. Actual payment is made later, when a customer issues a check to pay a credit card bill by transferring a demand deposit balance. Credit cards do reduce the need to hold money balances at any given time by helping to synchronize the receipt of income with the expenditure of funds. Rather than influencing the *supply* of money, then, credit cards alter the need or willingness to hold money—or what economists call the *demand* for money.

The U.S. government has decreed coins and paper currency to be **legal tender.** The status of legal tender simply means that coins and paper currency cannot lawfully be refused in payment for goods and services and for debts. No creditor can demand payment in another form if the debtor wishes to make payment in legal tender. Checkable accounts in commercial banks and other depository institutions are *not* classified as legal tender. However, banks are required to redeem such deposits in legal tender (currency) on request by the depositor. Though the status of legal tender obviously enhances the acceptability of an item as money, historically many items have served as money without having the status of legal tender. Today, the transfer of checking account balances is the most important means of making transactions. Of the total dollar value of all transactions made in the United States, an estimated 1 percent is made with currency and an overwhelming 99 percent by transferring balances in checking accounts (via checks or wire transfer).

Distinctions among Money, Wealth, and Income

Misstatements about money are pervasive. You may ask a friend if she has any money. In reality, you want to know if your friend is carrying *currency,* a specific type or component of money. It is also commonplace in everyday conversation to confuse money with *wealth* or *income.*[1] Even professional economists are prone to state that someone has a lot of "money" (instead of wealth) or that major league baseball players are paid too much "money" (instead of income). While the concepts of money, wealth, and income are all expressed in terms of dollars, each has a distinctly different meaning.

Money consists of certain assets which people hold because they have certain properties. It is a *stock* of assets which exhibits certain characteristics and is measured at a given point in time. The items included in this stock are somewhat arbitrary and controversial. The most traditional definition limits them to currency and coins outside the banking system plus deposits of the nonbank public which may be transferred by check or wire.

Wealth is also a stock concept measured at a given time. Wealth encompasses the money stock as well as many other financial and real assets. The money stock—currency and demand deposits—constitutes less than 2 percent of the nation's total wealth. Even the broader definitions of money, discussed later in this chapter, make up less than 10 percent of all wealth. The bulk of our wealth is made up of our homes, autos, furniture, common stocks and bonds, and life insurance.

In contrast, **income** is a flow of dollars per unit of time—for example, $1000 per month or $12,000 per year. Income is made up of payments in the form of wages and salaries, dividends, rent, profits, and transfer payments. Because income is paid in dollars, an individual's money balances may roughly equal the paycheck-period income for a brief period, when the paycheck is first deposited in the bank. However, at other times, most individuals hold only a small portion of their income in the form of currency, coins, and demand deposits.

The amount of money an individual holds is a matter of individual discretion and can be varied at will within the constraints of one's assets or wealth. The decision as to what portion of one's wealth to hold in the form of money depends on the rate of return expected from nonmoney assets, as well as on other factors. An individual may hold a very small stock of money at any given time even if he or she earns a million dollars a year. In fact, it is possible for a blue-collar worker to have more money than a Texas oil magnate does.

An important and intriguing aspect of money is that while an *individual* may increase money holdings (within the limits of his or her wealth) at will, the total supply of money is controlled not by individuals but by the Federal Reserve System, the U.S. central bank.

Functions of Money

The role of money seems so obvious that we tend to take it for granted. In fact, the contribution to society associated with the use of money includes many benefits which you may never have considered. Money serves three functions: as a medium of exchange or

---

[1] In fact, look at the opening statement in this chapter by George Bernard Shaw. He appears to be confusing money with something else. Can you identify what it is that he is confusing money with?

means of payment; as a standard of value or unit of account; and as a store of value. To understand the role and functions of money, it will be useful to consider the operation of an economic system in the absence of money—that is, in a barter economy.

Medium of Exchange or Means of Payment

Consider the process of exchange in a barter economy. An individual attempting to purchase a given commodity (say, a personal computer) requires the following information:

1 Who is offering PCs, in what quantities, and at what prices?

2 Of those offering PCs at acceptable prices, which of them desires to purchase the commodity we offer, say, wheat?

The major obstacle in this barter situation is that the individual who produces wheat and wants to purchase a personal computer must locate a PC producer who happens to want wheat. This requirement of a *double coincidence of wants* implies a time-consuming search process. In a primitive society such as a self-sufficient farming community, in which each family produces its own food, clothing, and shelter, no medium of exchange is needed. In such a situation money is unlikely to exist, because none is needed. However, as society evolves and people become more specialized (less self-sufficient) and more dependent on goods and services produced by others, the amount of time devoted to the process of exchange becomes a huge drag on the society, imposing large losses. It is conceivable that the time and effort devoted to the *exchange* of goods and services could exceed the time allocated to their *production.*

The introduction of money as a medium of exchange effectively eliminates the requirement of a "double coincidence of wants"—item 2 above. The buyer of the personal computer doesn't care whether the PC producer wants wheat or not. The wheat can be sold for dollars, which can then be used to purchase a personal computer. The use of money thus allows purchases and sales to be conducted independently of one another. The purchase of one good no longer requires a simultaneous sale of another, as is the situation in a barter economy. As a medium of exchange, money greatly increases the efficiency of the economic system and the scope of specialization and division of labor—a process which raises living standards. Indeed, the existence of money to serve this function is a necessary precondition for the transformation of a primitive society of relatively self-sufficient families into an industrial society of interdependent, highly specialized units.

Historically, primitive societies have introduced money at an early stage in their development. While an increase in the degree of specialization and division of labor usually brings about the introduction of money to serve as a medium of exchange, the use of money in turn reduces the time and resources devoted to exchange, further expanding the specialization and division of labor. Clearly, the use of money as a medium of exchange is a precondition for supporting the population size and living standards that exist today. Table 2-1 lists some items that have been used by societies as media of exchange.

Standard of Value or Unit of Account

Another of the key functions money fulfills is that of a measuring rod or yardstick in assessing the value of goods and services. This unit-of-account function allows us to assess the relative values of various items. Just as one uses pounds, meters, or miles per hour to measure weight, distance, and speed, we employ the dollar, franc, or lira to measure the value of a pizza, a soda, a gallon of gasoline, or a haircut.[2] Each of us keeps in mind the

Table 2-1

Some Items That Have Served as Money

Tobacco	Corn	Copper
Whales' teeth	Salt	Brass
Tortoise shells	Leather	Iron
Woodpecker scalps	Knives	Bronze
Cigarettes	Whiskey	Nickel
Cattle	Stone	Silver
Horses	Iron	Gold

dollar price of dozens or even hundreds of items we regularly purchase. By expressing the value of society's many goods and services in terms of one common denominator, we greatly simplify economic life.

Consider a barter economy. Without money to serve as a unit of account, each item brought to market would bear a certain value in relation to *each* of the other items. Even with a relatively limited number of commodities, the number of rates of exchange (prices) between different items would become cumbersome. Suppose there are four goods in a primitive society: A, B, C, and D. Without money to serve as a unit of account, the value of each good would have to be expressed relative to *each other good*. So we would have the following exchange rates or prices: A:B, A:C, A:D, B:C, B:D, and C:D. With four goods, we would have six rates of exchange (prices). Such a rudimentary society can get by nicely without the use of money. However, the number of prices would increase rapidly as the number of goods in a society increased. This is illustrated by the following expression:

(2-1)
$$R_B = \frac{N(N-1)}{2}$$

where

R_B = the number of different prices or rates of exchange in a barter economy and

N = the number of goods and services in the economy.[3]

---

[2]There is one significant difference between the nature of the "yardsticks" used to measure weight, distance, speed, and so on, and those used to measure the value of goods and services: the units of account for the first group of items are absolute constants; they do not change over time. One liter represents exactly the same volume today as it did a hundred years ago. The same cannot be said for the U.S. dollar, the Japanese yen, the Mexican peso, or any other national currency. The value of a unit of currency in terms of goods and services fluctuates over time as the price level changes. Nevertheless, at any point in time, a nation's currency serves as a measuring rod in ascertaining the value of thousands of goods and services.

[3]In this case, there are N different items and each one has a price in terms of each of the other $(N-1)$ items. Hence, we obtain the numerator of our expression, $(N)(N-1)$. Because half of these prices are redundant (A:B being the reciprocal of B:A, for example), it is clear that, in a barter economy, there are $N(N-1)/2$ prices.

Table 2-2		

The Number of Prices in Barter versus Money Economies

Number of Commodities (N)	Number of Prices	
	Barter Economy (R_B)	Money Economy (R_M)
3	3	3
10	45	10
1,000	499,500	1,000
1,000,000	499,999,500,000	1,000,000

Table 2-2 shows how the number of prices or exchange rates in a barter economy escalates as the number of goods increases. The table thus indicates the complexity and inefficiency of such an exchange system for a society with a multitude of goods and services.

The first two columns illustrate the relationship between the number of items (N) and the number of different price ratios in a barter economy (R_B), as calculated using Equation 2-1. The third column indicates the number of prices for the same number of items in a money economy. In a primitive society with only a few commodities, the barter system is manageable. With 10 commodities, we would need to keep in mind 45 exchange ratios, or prices. But when the number of goods and services reaches 1000—still an extremely unsophisticated economy by twentieth-century standards—the number of exchange ratios reaches nearly half a million! Imagine entering a general store that offers each of the 1000 different items available in the (relatively primitive) nation for sale. The price tag for each item would contain 999 different prices—one exchange ratio for each other item.

In a barter economy, one needs to be aware not only of the exchange ratio between the item offered and the item needed but of a host of other exchange ratios as well.[4] With the introduction of money into an economy of 1000 commodities, only 1000 prices would exist—one for each of the 1000 commodities quoted in terms of the common denominator or unit of account, for example, dollars. This greatly reduces information costs and therefore the transactions costs of exchange. As a result, the production, exchange, and per capita income would rise. Money is a highly productive social innovation!

---

[4]Suppose that, in a barter economy, an individual brings good A (axes) to the market, seeking to exchange them for good B (bread). It behooves the individual to check not only the exchange ratio between axes and bread but also a multitude of combinations of exchange ratios involving other goods. For example, one might find that by trading axes for lumber and lumber for bread, one would end up with more bread than by bartering axes directly for bread. The scenario could easily become much more complicated. Thus, to maximize one's material well-being, it pays to devote much attention and effort to the details of exchange. In this case, activities which are profitable for an individual are a huge waste of resources from society's point of view. In a money economy, the process is greatly simplified. The seller of axes merely searches out the buyer who gives him the most *units of currency* for the axes. He then locates the seller of bread who offers to sell it for the fewest units. With money to serve as a unit of account, one can focus on the items of direct interest and ignore the thousands of other commodities.

Your Turn

a. Suppose that in a primitive society there are only eight goods in existence. If the society is a barter economy, how many different prices or exchange ratios would there be? If it were a money economy? Name your eight goods and list each exchange rate to double-check the results you get using Equation 2-1.

b. Now suppose the same society produces 10,000 goods. How many prices would there be if the economy were based on barter? On money?

Store of Value

A function of money that is closely allied to the medium-of-exchange function is that of a temporary abode of purchasing power, called the store-of-value function. In a barter economy, the purchase of any item implies a simultaneous sale of another item. Likewise, the sale of any good or service necessitates a corresponding purchase of another good or service. But the use of money allows purchases and sales to be made independently of each other. Today, most of us sell our labor services for income. Because this income is received at discrete, rather lengthy intervals which do not coincide with our more continuous flow of expenditures, we have a need to store purchasing power over time. One way of storing purchasing power is by holding money.

Money is not unique as a store of value. In an economy with developed financial institutions, there exists a multitude of financial assets which serve as a means of storing wealth. These include various types of time and savings deposits, government and corporate bonds, various types of short-term securities, and common stocks. In addition, various "real" assets, such as land and other real estate, antiques, jewelry, paintings, and precious metals serve as vehicles for storing wealth over time. Many of these offer advantages over money as a means of storing wealth (see Exhibit 2-1). They may provide price appreciation over time, tax advantages, or a higher interest rate than is obtainable on money.[5] Table 2-3 indicates the inflation-adjusted rates of return (real rates of return) for money and various other assets over a long period of time.

The effectiveness of money as a store of value depends on the behavior of the price level. In a period of falling prices (deflation) such as the early 1930s, money serves its store-of-value function quite effectively. Because the real value of wealth held in the form of money rises in proportion to the decline in the level of prices, those who hold money benefit from the general redistribution of wealth from debtors to creditors wrought by deflation. In periods of substantial inflation such as the 1970s, however, money does not serve the store-of-value function well. Inflation imposes a tax on money; the annual tax rate is the difference between the inflation rate and the rate of interest paid on money, if any.

Referring to Table 2-3, note that, over the 70-year period 1926 to 1995, all the assets except money served effectively as a store of value. Common stocks were most effective, returning nearly 7 percent annually after inflation. Gold, long-term corporate and

---

[5]If one defines money to include currency and coins, demand deposits, and other checkable deposits in depository institutions, only the third category pays interest. Currency and coins obviously do not pay interest. Nor do regular demand deposits (though they may pay implicit interest in the form of reduced service charges). By this definition of money, then, less than one-third of money pays interest, and even that portion pays a relatively low rate.

EXHIBIT 2-1

Gold as a Store of Value

When the price level doubles over a period of years, the purchasing power of each unit of money is cut in half. Hence, inflation imposes a "tax" on money and the tax rate is the annual rate of inflation. The real value of money depreciates by the annual rate of inflation. Money is a poor store of value in periods of high inflation. For this reason, whenever inflation begins to accelerate significantly, people seek to exchange money for assets which are perceived to be reliable hedges against inflation. Historically, gold more than any other asset has been sought out for this purpose. Severely limited in quantity by the earth's natural bounty, attractive visually, and valuable in industrial uses, gold has for centuries had a powerful mystique. Historically, civilizations have always been eager to accumulate gold, confident that its value would hold up over the years.

In 1834, gold sold for approximately $20 per ounce. In fact, a coveted U.S. coin in the nineteenth century was the $20 gold piece, consisting of one ounce of fine gold. In 1996, the price of gold exceeded $400 per ounce. This long-term increase in the price of gold has kept pace with inflation. Over *long* periods of history, gold has been a good hedge against inflation.

In the past 30 years, however, gold has been a good investment only in periods in which inflation has been quite severe. The accompanying figure indicates the price of gold since 1970, along with the U.S. consumer price index. In the 1970s, when inflation twice moved into the double-digit range, gold prices escalated dramatically. Between 1972 and 1980, gold prices increased more than 10-fold and for a period in 1980 the speculative mania drove the price above $800 per ounce. However, as the inflation rate came down sharply after the early 1980s, so did the price of gold. In the period since 1982, gold has not kept pace with inflation. In the past 15 years, even such conservative investments as passbook savings accounts and U.S. government bonds have far outperformed gold.

Keep your eye on the price of gold. The next time inflation raises its ugly head, see if you observe an upward spurt in the price of gold.

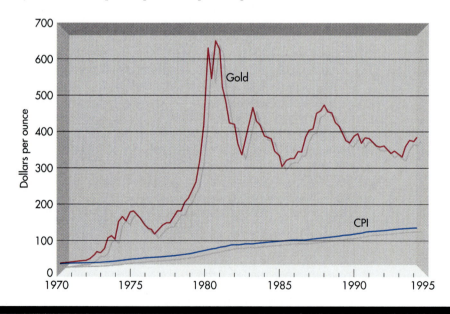

Table 2-3

Average Annual Inflation-Adjusted Rates of Return on Various Assets (in percent per year)

Period	Money*	Gold	Treasury Bills	Government Bonds	Corporate Bonds	Common Stocks
1926–1976	−2.4%	1.8%	0%	0.8%	1.5%	6.6%
1976–1995	−5.0	0.4	1.5	4.1	4.7	7.2
Total, 1926–1995	**−3.1**	**1.4**	**0.4**	**1.7**	**2.4**	**6.8**

*Assumes interest rate paid on money was zero throughout.

Sources: *Citibank Economic Database;* International Monetary Fund; Roger Ibbotson and Rex Sinquefield, *Stocks, Bonds, Bills, and Inflation: The Past (1926–1976) and the Future (1977–2000)* (Chicago: Financial Analysts Research Foundation, 1977).

government bonds, and short-term Treasury bills also served as reliable stores of value, although the returns from Treasury bills barely covered inflation. Money, however, depreciated in real terms at an average annual rate of approximately 3 percent over the whole period, and by 5 percent per year in the more recent 20-year period. With 3 percent inflation, money will lose half its value in approximately 24 years. If money does not retain value as well as other assets, why do people hold it as a store of value? The answer lies in the fact that there are significant costs associated with converting money into other assets and then converting these assets back into money.

The magnitude of the cost of converting an asset into money is an important concept known as **liquidity.** By liquidity, we mean the relative ease with which an asset may be converted into money (i.e., "liquidated") quickly without significant inconvenience, loss of time, commissions or other charges, or risk of loss of principal. Money, which is ready to spend at a moment's notice, is the ultimate in liquidity. Other financial assets, ranging from commercial bank savings accounts to common stocks, involve various inconveniences, transactions costs, and risks. Those assets therefore suffer from varying degrees of *illiquidity*—that is, lack of liquidity. For this reason, most people choose to hold some portion of their wealth in the form of money, to finance future transactions. As we shall see later (in Part 6), the nature of the decision-making process associated with holding money as a store of value has important implications for monetary theory and policy.

In a sense, the store-of-value function and the medium-of-exchange function of money are inseparable. This truth is illustrated by historical episodes of hyperinflation. In such instances, when the duration and rate of inflation advanced beyond certain thresholds, people desperately attempted to rid themselves of money because its value was deteriorating rapidly. That is, the store-of-value function of money had broken down. At the same time, sellers refused to accept payment in money, instead insisting on payment in goods and services. This breakdown in the store-of-value function then led to the collapse of the medium-of-exchange function. Soon the money economy broke down, and economic exchange reverted to a system of barter. Depression inevitably ensued. For money to be widely accepted as a medium of exchange, it must function reasonably effectively as a store of value.

THE EVOLUTION OF MONEY AND THE PAYMENTS SYSTEM

Our payments system has evolved over a period of centuries, and with it the nature and use of money. Very early, metallic coins circulated as money in numerous civilizations. Later, such coins were heavily supplemented with more convenient paper currency. Still later, the use of checks made it possible to pay for goods and services by transferring checking account balances in depository institutions. Today, our payments system continues to evolve. We are now moving toward supplementing our paper-oriented system with an electronic funds transfer system (EFTS).

In the following sections, we will trace the evolution of our payments system, beginning with the earliest coins.

Full-Bodied Money

In ancient civilizations, certain substances that were attractive, durable, divisible, and available in relatively small quantities naturally emerged as money, becoming widely used as media of exchange. Because of their ornamental qualities, durability, and convenient size, metallic substances such as bronze, iron, and copper emerged as money thousands of years ago. These early monies were **full-bodied monies,** or **commodity monies:** money whose value is the same whether used in exchange for goods and services (as money) or for nonmoney purposes (as a commodity). This approximate equality of value was ensured by the forces of supply and demand. If gold coins were initially worth more for their metallic content than as money, they would disappear from circulation and be melted down, to be used for nonmoney purposes. In time, this reallocation of use would tend to reduce gold's value as a commodity and increase its value as money, until the two values were equal. Conversely, if gold coins were initially worth more as money than as a commodity, gold would be withdrawn from industrial use and sold for use as coins. Thus, the forces of supply and demand ensured that the value of gold as money never deviated markedly from its value as a commodity. The fact that money had an alternative use as a commodity inspired confidence in coins and ensured their acceptability as media of exchange.

Metallic coins came to be widely used in ancient civilizations. At first, iron and copper predominated. However, major increases in their supply reduced the value of a given amount of the metals to the point where payment with coins became inconvenient because they were too heavy. Because silver was more scarce, it became popular as money. Until a couple of hundred years ago, gold was so scarce that it could not effectively serve as money; gold coins would have been too small. However, major worldwide gold discoveries in the nineteenth century sufficiently increased supplies to permit the use of gold coins of convenient size.

Representative Full-Bodied Money

With increasing specialization and division of labor, societies became more affluent, as well as more dependent on exchange. As these trends accelerated during the industrial revolution, which began in the eighteenth century, the exclusive use of coins as media of exchange became increasingly inconvenient. The weight and size of coins made them cumbersome to transport, store, and use in transactions involving relatively large amounts of money. Imagine paying for a new house with coins! For this reason, coins were supplemented with paper currency, initially backed 100 percent by the valuable metals. Paper money that attests to ownership of a commodity such as gold or silver is referred to as **representative full-bodied money.** The commodity itself is held in safekeeping, and the paper currency circulates in its place.

This form of money was first introduced in England during the sixteenth century. Originally, the notes were issued by private firms called *goldsmiths* and were essentially warehouse receipts acknowledging claim to a certain number of gold or silver coins, collectable on demand by the bearer of the note. Since these notes could be exchanged for a fixed quantity of metal coins on demand, they soon became as acceptable a means of payment as the coins themselves. This form of money circulated in the United States between 1900 and 1933 in the form of gold certificates. Bearers of gold certificates were entitled to redeem the certificates for gold coins at the U.S. Treasury. Silver certificates, a form of paper currency redeemable at the Treasury in silver, also circulated in the United States for many years.

Fiat Money, or Credit Money

Representative full-bodied money is 100 percent "backed"—that is, it is fully redeemable in some commodity such as gold or silver. But does money need to be backed 100 percent, or even 20 percent, by a commodity in order to perform its functions? Does it need to be backed by a commodity at all? Although some may disagree on the basis of historical experience, the logical answer to this question is no. If we are able to receive goods and services in exchange for our money, and if the monetary system is stable and functions effectively, who cares how much gold is available to back our money? The backing of our money today consists of an implicit faith and confidence that government will control the quantity of money in circulation, so that the purchasing power of a dollar does not depreciate significantly in a given week or month. Given this faith, money can serve its functions effectively without any commodity backing.

Money that derives its value by fiat or government decree rather than through its value as a commodity is called **fiat money,** or **credit money.** The evolution of this type of credit money can be traced back some four hundred years to English goldsmiths, who issued paper notes in exchange for gold or silver. They soon became aware that they didn't need to back their notes fully in gold. Normally, in any week or month, the demand to convert paper notes into gold amounted to only a small percentage of the total notes outstanding (and the total gold in storage). Therefore, it did not seem imprudent to issue notes in amounts above and beyond the value of gold and silver held. The goldsmiths loaned the extra notes to businesses and other worthy borrowers and earned a nice profit in the form of interest. Furthermore, some of the benefits were returned to gold owners in the form of reduced service charges for safeguarding the precious metals. These notes may be considered a forerunner of our modern fractional reserve banking system in the sense that whenever a goldsmith issued a note without receiving gold in exchange, money was created. The rigid link between precious metals and the money supply had been broken.

Today, all our currency and coins are fiat or credit monies. The link between gold and the money supply has been totally severed. The value of the dollar springs from its widespread acceptability (which, in turn, is based on the faith that government will not issue excessive amounts of money), not from the materials from which it is made. In fact, a $50 bill contains only a few cents' worth of paper, printing inks, and other materials. A quarter contains less than 10 cents' worth of nickel and copper. One important advantage of fiat money is that it costs the government a lot less to produce than full-bodied money. Fewer of the nation's resources are used to produce money, freeing the resources for more socially productive uses.[6] Another advantage of the fiat money system is that the quantity of money in circulation is determined by human judgment, not by the vagaries of mining discoveries.

Checking Accounts

An important innovation in the evolution of the payments process was the introduction of checks, which permit payment through the transfer of balances at depository institutions. Imagine the inconvenience that would ensue if the use of checks and checking accounts were abolished. People would be forced to carry large amounts of currency. To pay your bills, you might have to deliver currency by hand to the phone company, your landlord, the insurance company, and so forth because sending currency through the mail is risky. Occasional big-ticket purchases, such as a new automobile, would be even more awkward.

The use of checks permits us to make transactions without carrying around large amounts of currency and also avoids the transportation costs of moving currency, thereby increasing economic efficiency. Insured in amounts up to $100,000 by the Federal Deposit Insurance Corporation (FDIC), demand deposits are safer than currency, because currency has to be stored and can be lost or stolen. Because checks have no value until they are endorsed, they may be sent through the mail. They also provide a useful record of transactions.

A payments system based on checks is not without drawbacks, however. For one thing, it takes time for a check to be sent from one place to another. And you may have experienced the insult of being told by your bank that funds from a check you have

---

[6]To estimate the savings involved in a fiat money system, suppose our GDP is currently $8 trillion per year and our money supply is $1.4 trillion. Suppose that, in order to support 3 percent GDP growth, we require a 3 percent annual increase in the money supply. This would mean an increase of $42 billion in the first year (3% of $1.4 trillion), or approximately 0.5 percent of our nation's GDP. In a commodity money system, to produce $42 billion of new money costs approximately $42 billion. We would therefore produce $42 billion less of other goods and services. This illustrates the waste of resources in a commodity money system. In a fiat money system, it costs very little to produce $42 billion of money.

FED CONTROL will be shaped by the next president.

In his first year in office, Bush or Gore could fill as many as four of the Federal Reserve's seven board seats. Two of the 14-year seats are vacant. Vice Chairman Ferguson's term expired in January, and board member Laurence Meyer's term ends in January 2002.

Bush adviser Lawrence Lindsey, a former Fed member, says Bush is aware of "the need to fill these vacancies quickly." Bush's short list probably includes Stanford economist John Taylor. David Hale, a Zurich Financial economist, predicts a "clash between fiscal and monetary policy," especially if Bush wins and pushes tax cuts.

But Greenspan's term as Fed chairman doesn't expire until the end of the next administration, in 2004.

SENATE TEARS: U2 rock star Bono says that in a meeting with GOP Sen. Helms to urge debt relief for poor countries, Helms—a critic of foreign aid—wept over the plight of African children. "It was really quite extraordinary," says Bono. A spokesman says Helms was touched.

TAXING DEBATE: New York Democratic Rep. Rangel accuses Congress's Joint Committee on Taxation of sitting on an analysis of whether Bush's tax cut would bump more middle-class people into paying the alternative minimum tax. A Bush spokesman contends Gore's tax plan would be more likely to do so.

mon address of four more customers identified by L&H. This office, above a lamp shop, houses a notary public, with a list of about 30 companies outside the door. Not one is a customer named by L&H.

Interviews with L&H officials and a review of regulatory filings and documents provided by the company reveal that nearly all of L&H's revenue in the Asian city-state have come from the 19 companies. All of the companies started operation just last year, and L&H helped create all of them. L&H also recruited and trained their intial employees. None of the putative customers has any revenue, according to an outside L&H spokesman. In addition to sharing addresses, many of the customers have the same officers and nominee shareholders.

Under pressure from critics and short sellers—investors who bet on a company's stock falling—L&H yesterday issued a short statement saying that it is cooperating fully with the SEC investigation. "We are determined to resolve these matters," Messrs. Jo Lernout and Pol Hauspie, co-founders and co-chairmen of the company, said in the statement.

The company has directed all specific inquiries to the outside spokesman, who himself insisted on not being named. As L&H's stock price fell 29% yesterday, the spokesman said that all of the company's revenue

Asian Explosion

Lernout & Hauspie revenue, in millions

Asia

	$151.6

come of a meeting of the Organization of Petroleum Exporting Countries next week in Caracas, Venezuela.

Mr. Gore's proposal may serve as a clear signal to OPEC oil producers of the administration's willingness to use the reserve to move markets—instead of its primary mission of providing reserves in case oil supplies are disrupted. Yesterday, news of Mr. Gore's proposal sent oil prices down sharply, with West Texas intermediate crude down $2.80 to $34.40 a barrel.

Politically, Mr. Gore is hoping to capitalize on the growing public anger over steep gas prices and head off complaints of skyrocketing home heating-oil prices before the November election. But his actions may have the opposite effect: reinforcing the image that he would take any political step necessary to win the White House.

"The strategic reserve is an insurance policy meant for sudden disruption of oil supplies or for war," GOP presidential candidate George W. Bush said during a campaign stop in Cleveland. "The strategic reserve should not be used as an attempt to drive down oil prices right before an election."

Before yesterday, Mr. Bush has been slow to seize on the gas-price issue. That has left Democrats to allege that the former independent Texas oilman and his running mate Dick Cheney, head of oil-services company Halliburton Corp. until his selection, are in cahoots with "Big Oil."

Mr. Gore's vice presidential staff has worked closely with other White House officials in formulating a response to the rising price of oil. Over the past few wee-

For an ex-dissident, Czech President Vaclav Havel has a surprising perspective on IMF protests. Article on page A19.

on a career in the IMF because they want to be more popular."

But the IMF's 1,100 economists are dismayed to discover it is much worse than being unpopular. It turns out that many youths in the new millennium view the IMF the same way antiwar protesters viewed the Pentagon in the 1960s: evil.

As with the U.S. military during the Vietnam War, people inside the IMF are bewildered, resentful and frustrated, and don't feel like suffering in silence any longer. "At the end of the day, we all work for one goal, which is to improve economic growth in the countries that we work on and improve peoples' standards of living," says George C. Tsibouris, deputy chief of the IMF division that aids South Africa and Swaziland. "To have these efforts trivialized by some people who are unaware or misinformed or just plain wrong—it's more than just frustrating. It's difficult to take."

But Mr. Tsibouris, a Greek economist, and his colleagues will have to take more of it very soon. Starting this weekend, perhaps 20,000 demonstrators plan to descend on Prague to disrupt the annual meetings of the IMF and its sister organization, the World Bank—institutions the protesters see as promoting the interests of multinational corporations to the detriment of the world's poor.

It is hard to miss the message of www.destroyimf.org an antiglobalization Web site that discusses the planned Prague pro-

deposited in your account will not be available to spend for a couple of days. Most importantly, the checking system is expensive; processing checks in the United States costs more than $5 billion per year.

Electronic Money

In the long span of time since exchange was based on barter, there have been three major innovations in payments media: full-bodied money, including metal coins; fiat paper money and token coins; and checking accounts. A fourth innovation is now in progress: an **electronic funds transfer system (EFTS).** An EFTS has the potential to substantially reduce and perhaps even eliminate the use of currency, coins, checks, and credit cards.

The transition to an EFTS is well under way. Today, many payments are made electronically. For example, the Federal Reserve has a payments system known as **Fedwire.** Through this telecommunications system, all financial institutions that maintain accounts at Federal Reserve banks can wire funds to one another, permitting huge transfers to be made instantaneously. A private telecommunications system known as **Clearing House Interbank Payments System (CHIPS)** allows banks to transfer funds internationally via electronic impulse. Banks, corporations, securities dealers, money market mutual funds, and other major players can wire funds through these systems. While less than 1 percent of the *number* of transactions in the United States is conducted by wire, more than 90 percent of the *dollar value* of total transactions is carried out this way. In other words, almost all multimillion-dollar transactions are made electronically.

Several other examples of electronic payment are already in place. Many employers pay salaries by wiring funds directly into employees' checking accounts. And for years, individuals have been able to make certain recurring payments (utility bills, mortgage payments, etc.) electronically, by preauthorized agreement with their bank. Many students and others use debit cards to transfer payments from their own accounts to payee's accounts electronically. Debit cards are currently limited in their uses, however.

Technological advances in electronic data processing, information retrieval, and communications systems have made it technically feasible to implement a comprehensive EFTS, in which bank deposit balances can be transferred instantaneously to any part of the nation. In a fully implemented EFTS, a nationwide computer network would monitor the credits and debits of individuals, firms, and government units as transactions occur. Individuals would use electronically coded cards, and retail establishments would be equipped with on-line terminals capable of reading the cards and transmitting information to the EFTS computer center. Exhibit 2-2 examines the "electronic purse," an innovation that is moving us closer to a comprehensive EFTS.

The potential benefits of a comprehensive EFTS lie in the efficiency of such a system. The huge and rapidly growing costs associated with our current paper-oriented checking system would be reduced. Billions of dollars now spent handling checks could be eliminated. To the extent that the EFTS replaces credit cards, further gains would accrue. Credit cards are a highly inefficient system, involving excessive paperwork in the transfer of information and in billing. Such costs are not billed directly to credit card users but are paid by the merchants who accept the cards. Ultimately, the costs are shifted to consumers through higher prices. Because the costs imposed on the users of credit cards

EXHIBIT 2-2

The "Electronic Purse": Will Currency Become Obsolete?

Today, consumers can pay for goods and services with at least four media: cash, checks, credit cards, and debit cards. In 1995, major financial institutions announced plans to develop a new instrument, the stored-value card, or "electronic purse." Similar in size to a credit card, the electronic purse may soon replace currency in many transactions.

Prepaid cards have been used in the United States for more than a decade in a variety of *single-purpose* transactions; such cards are commonplace on college campuses, for example. Students use them in cafeterias, bookstores, and copying machines. The mass transit systems of several U.S. cities also use prepaid cards. In contrast to such "closed systems," in which a card has limited applicability, the electronic purse is to be an "open system," usable for a wide range of purchases.

Banks will issue the stored-value cards. Customers will then be able to transfer funds from their checking accounts to their cards at an ATM, via a personal computer, or by telephone. In making a purchase, a customer will pass the card through a point-of-sale terminal. No credit check or signature will be needed; funds will be deducted directly from the card and transferred to the seller's terminal. Merchants will then transfer the funds to their bank accounts by telephone whenever they choose.

The success of the electronic purse will depend on its benefits to consumers, merchants, and card issuers. Consumers would benefit from the convenience of using the card instead of checks for small transactions; from reduced loss owing to theft (the card would require use of a personal identification number, or PIN, known only to its owner); and from the card's acceptability in vending machines (people won't need to carry change). Merchants would benefit from a reduction in the handling of cash and from assured payment. Card issuers (banks) would benefit from a reduced need to hold cash and a possible reduction in the number of tellers needed, and would gain a new source of fee income. Banks would also earn interest on the "float"—the unspent balances customers hold in their electronic purses.

To the extent that the electronic purse is used, much of the outstanding currency (see the table below) will be redeposited in banks and disappear from circulation. Like the $20 gold piece and the privately issued bank note, currency and coins may someday be relegated to the role of an interesting artifact of monetary history.

Composition of U.S. Currency Outstanding as of December 31, 1994

	Number of Units (in billions)	Percentage of Total Number	Dollar Value (in billions)	Percentage of Total Value
Coins	N.A.	N.A.	$ 21.8	5.4%
$1 bills	6.1	36.7%	6.1	1.5
$2 bills	0.5	3.0	1.0	0.2
$5 bills	1.5	8.8	7.3	1.8
$10 bills	1.4	8.3	13.8	3.4
$20 bills	4.0	24.2	80.5	19.9
$50 bills	0.9	5.3	43.9	10.9
$100 bills	2.3	13.8	229.1	56.8
Total	**16.6**	**100.0**	**$403.5**	**100.0**

are below the true costs to society, excessive and inefficient use is made of these instruments. The same consideration applies to checks. In a fully implemented EFTS, the true cost of transferring funds would be greatly reduced; the increase in efficiency would manifest itself in higher living standards.

While an EFTS may be more efficient than our paper-oriented checking system, the public is likely to resist rapid implementation of an EFTS. The use of checks provides both a receipt and a record of payment, which people find useful. And unlike checks, an electronic system does not provide the option of delaying payment if one's bank account is low. Third, certain legal and security problems inherent in an EFTS must still be worked out. Who is responsible if someone gets access to your card and secret code? Widely publicized stories of computer fraud raise the possibility of unscrupulous individuals transferring money from others' accounts to their own. Thus, widespread implementation of an EFTS is probably contingent on further breakthroughs in the rapidly developing field of computer security.

MODERN MEASURES OF MONEY

Today, industrial nations employ fairly standard measures of money that include the volume of currency in circulation and the volume of deposits at any point in time. Typically, several measures of money are reported, differentiated by the type of deposits (and close substitutes for deposits) they include. One measure of money, sometimes known as the transactions or "narrow" measure, consists of currency and checking accounts used for everyday expenditures. Broader measures of money add checkable accounts that are used predominantly as savings vehicles (rather than transactions vehicles) and certain other liquid financial assets.

The Federal Reserve currently publishes several different measures of the U.S. money supply, including M1, M2, and M3. Table 2-4 shows these U.S. *monetary aggregates* and their components.

The Narrow Definition of Money: M1

Traditionally, most economists have preferred the "narrow," or transactions, measure of money, **M1,** which includes only currency, demand deposits, other checkable deposits, and traveler's checks. This measure of money is most appropriate if one emphasizes the medium-of-exchange function of money—that is, if one views money as consisting strictly of those things widely used as a means of payment. Even if one defines money in this way, however, some judgment calls must be made. What about balances in money market mutual funds (MMMFs)? Such balances may be transferred by check, albeit only in amounts above some minimum such as $250 or $500. What about brokerage accounts such as the Merrill Lynch Cash Management Account, which permit account holders to write checks against the value of stocks and bonds in their accounts? Such lines of credit can be used to make payments at will. The Federal Reserve has judged that MMMF shares are used more as a savings vehicle than a means of payment and has therefore excluded them from M1 but not from the

Table 2-4

The Federal Reserve's Measures of the Money Supply, April 1996

Aggregate and Component	Dollar Value (in billions)
M1:	***$1125.5***
Currency[1]	375.7
Demand deposits[2]	407.2
Other checkable deposits[3]	333.7
Traveler's checks	8.9
M2:	***3731.3***
M1	1125.5
Overnight repurchase agreements (RPs) issued by commercial banks plus overnight Eurodollar deposits	115.0
Money market mutual fund shares (general purpose)	487.9
Savings deposits at all depository institutions and money market deposit accounts (MMDAs)[4]	1078.7
Small time deposits at all depository institutions[5]	924.2
M3:	***4690.1***
M2	3731.3
Large time deposits at all depository institutions[6]	433.5
Term RPs and term Eurodollars	279.9
Money market mutual funds shares (institutions)	245.4

[1]Coins and paper currency outside the Treasury, Federal Reserve banks, and depository institutions.
[2]Non-interest-bearing checking accounts at banks.
[3]Interest-bearing checking accounts of the following types: NOW (negotiable order of withdrawal accounts), super-NOW accounts, ATS (automatic transfer from savings) accounts, and credit union share drafts.
[4]MMDAs (money market deposit accounts) are interest-bearing accounts at depository institutions, on which a limited number of checks can be written each month.
[5]Time deposits issued in denominations of less than $100,000.
[6]Time deposits issued in denominations of $100,000 or more.

Source: *Federal Reserve Bulletin* and Flow of Funds Accounts.

broader money supply measures. The Fed excludes credit lines in brokerage accounts from all measures of money. One can see, however, that the line of demarcation between those items to be included in money supply measures and those to be excluded is fuzzy.

Until the 1980s, the narrow measure of money consisted only of currency, non-interest-bearing demand deposits, and traveler's checks. However, financial innovations and deregulation made that definition obsolete. Before the 1980s, banks were generally prohibited from paying interest on checking accounts. As interest rates increased in the 1970s in response to rising inflation, savings institutions in New England developed a new instrument known as a negotiable order of withdrawal (NOW) account. NOW accounts are interest-bearing savings accounts on which a limited number of checks may be written. In 1981, Congress legalized nationwide issuance of NOW and automatic transfer from savings (ATS) accounts. ATS accounts are savings accounts that may be transferred to checking accounts by the bank's computer to prevent overdrafts.

Today, "other checkable deposits" consist of interest-bearing checking accounts held in depository institutions by individuals and nonprofit organizations. Corporations and other profit-oriented firms are prohibited from owning interest-bearing checking accounts in depository institutions. As indicated in Table 2-4, currency, demand deposits, and other checkable deposits each equals approximately one-third of M1; traveler's checks constitute less than 1 percent of the total. Hereafter, we will ignore traveler's checks when we discuss the composition of M1. M1 will be defined as *DDO + C^p:* demand deposits and other checkable deposits *(DDO)* plus currency held by the nonbank public *(C^p)*.

Broader Measures of Money: M2, M3

Although traditionally the majority of economists have preferred the M1 money supply measure, others have preferred the broader measures of money. In conducting monetary policy over the past decade, the Federal Reserve has placed higher priority on these broad measures than on M1. If one is inclined to emphasize the store-of-value function of money rather than the medium-of-exchange function, broader measures are appropriate. However, once one admits items into the measure of money that are not media of exchange, the line of demarcation between money and nonmoney assets becomes quite difficult to ascertain.

We have seen that assets may be classified on the basis of *liquidity,* or the ease and convenience with which they may be converted into a medium of exchange. Three considerations determine an asset's liquidity: how easily and quickly it can be sold; the costs of selling it; and the stability and predictability of its price. An asset that can be sold quickly at a low transactions cost may not be considered very liquid if the price has changed significantly since it was purchased. There is a continuum of liquidity among assets, ranging from highly liquid passbook savings accounts to highly illiquid real estate and antique cars.

Passbook savings accounts are extremely liquid. One can convert them to media of exchange (cash or checking accounts) quickly, without significant transactions costs, through a trip to the bank or ATM machine. Their price is known in advance with certainty. At the other extreme are houses and vintage automobiles. Selling such real assets at a price near fair market value typically requires several months, and significantly large commissions are likely to be involved. What about bonds and common stocks? Bonds are considered relatively liquid. An active market exists for bonds, transactions costs are fairly low, and bond prices are relatively stable—especially for short-term bonds.[7] Common stocks are less liquid than bonds. While both can be sold quickly and easily, stock prices are more variable than bond prices and sales commissions (transactions costs) for stocks are significantly higher than those for bonds.[8]

The Fed now publishes two broad measures of money, M2 and M3.[9] The principle involved in constructing these monetary aggregates is to combine assets of comparable levels of liquidity in each measure of money. Hence, in constructing **M2,** certain highly liquid assets are added to M1. Overnight repurchase agreements (RPs), Eurodollar deposits, and money market mutual fund shares (to be discussed in detail in Chapter 3) are extremely close substitutes for demand deposits. In fact, some economists would include them in M1. Savings deposits, small time deposits, and money market deposit accounts (MMDAs) in banks are quite liquid and are also included in M2.[10] **M3** is constructed by adding certain slightly less liquid financial assets to M2. M3 includes M2 plus large time deposits ($100,000 and above), certain repurchase agreements and Eurodollar deposits, and money market mutual fund shares held by institutions.

Those who emphasize the broader money measures point out that many highly liquid financial assets are easily substitutable for the narrow money measure, M1. As we have seen, savings and time deposits in banks can easily be converted to cash or demand deposits at a relatively low cost in terms of inconvenience and forgone interest. Even though such deposits cannot be used to make payments directly, the public seems to regard them as being almost equivalent to the narrow measures of money. Several other financial instruments may also be converted to money with minimal cost and effort.

Which Measure Is Most Useful?

Economists who advocate the broader measures of money are inclined to argue that the paramount motive for defining and measuring the money supply is to monitor and control it in order to stabilize economic activity, or at least to prevent abrupt changes in the money supply from causing damage to the economy. Rather than defining money as those items used to make payment, they feel, one should define it on the basis of empirical criteria, including in the money supply measure those items having a causal relationship with aggregate economic activity. The best measure of money is that measure

---

[7]We will demonstrate in Chapter 7 that, for any change in market yields, the relative change in a bond's price varies directly with its length of time to maturity. Longer-term bonds exhibit larger price fluctuations than shorter-term bonds and are therefore less liquid.

[8]Other things equal, assets with greater price variability are less liquid because people are less likely to be willing to sell them. If an asset's price has risen since its purchase, its sale would necessitate payment of a capital gains tax. If an asset's price has fallen, an individual may not be willing to acknowledge a mistake and accept a loss.

[9]In addition, the Fed publishes L, a measure of liquid assets not shown in Table 2-4. L includes M3 plus short-term Treasury securities and certain other liquid financial assets held by the public.

[10]Money market deposit accounts (MMDAs) are interest-bearing accounts in depository institutions on which a limited number of checks may be written each month.

which best predicts nominal GDP, real output, and the price level. And the medium-of-exchange measure of money is not necessarily the measure most closely associated with economic activity.

Furthermore, because many liquid assets are easily convertible to the medium of exchange, definitions of money should not be regarded as fixed and immutable. To a large extent they are a matter of judgment. Milton Friedman and Anna Schwartz, leading exponents of this view, have made the point eloquently:

The definition of money is to be sought for not on grounds of principle but on grounds of usefulness in organizing our knowledge of economic relationships. "Money" is that to which we choose to assign a number by specified operations; it is not something in existence to be discovered, like the American continent; it is a tentative scientific construct to be invented, like "length" or "temperature" or "force" in physics.[11]

This concept of money raises the strong possibility that the group of assets which constitute our measure of money today is likely to evolve over time. In the late 1970s and early 1980s, innovative financial practices ushered in by record-level interest rates and liberalization of regulatory practices caused the Fed to replace older money measures with the current ones. As long as new financial developments continue to loosen the link between traditional money measures and economic activity, we will need to revamp our measures of the money supply periodically.

Though economists agree that the behavior of M1, M2, and M3 has important implications for aggregate demand, nominal GDP, and the price level, there is no consensus about which measure is best. If the three measures always moved together over time (were scalar multiples of one another), the Fed would not be forced to choose among them. Unfortunately, as Figure 2-1 shows, that is not always the case. While the growth rates of all three measures were higher in the 1970s than in the 1960s, they have sometimes differed significantly. As the growth of M1 accelerated dramatically in the early 1990s, for example, the growth rates of M2 and M3 slowed appreciably. Such differences in the behavior of the monetary aggregates pose a problem for the Federal Reserve.

Weighted Measures of Money

M1, M2, and M3 are simple-sum weights: they give equal weight to each of the items they include. For example, M2 gives the same weight to passbook savings accounts and money market mutual fund shares as to currency held by the public and demand deposits in banks. Because different financial assets have differing degrees of "moneyness" and are therefore likely to influence expenditures differently, this lack of discrimination is a shortcoming. Just as the consumer price index places a higher weight on houses than on candy bars, our money measures should probably place more weight on items that strongly influence aggregate expenditures, such as demand deposits and currency, than on items less closely linked to aggregate expenditures (for instance, small time deposits in banks).

---

[11]Milton Friedman and Anna Schwartz, *Monetary Statistics of the United States* (New York: National Bureau of Economic Research, 1970), p. 137.

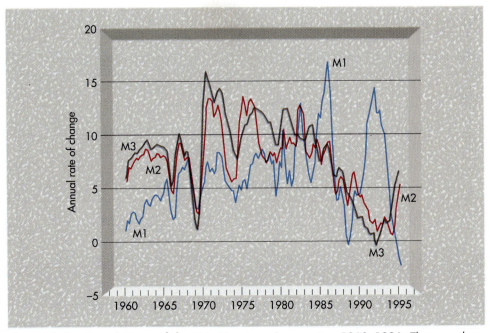

Figure 2-1   Growth Rates of the U.S. Monetary Aggregates, 1960–1996. The growth rates of the three monetary aggregates often differ significantly. There is no clear consensus on which aggregate is "best."   *Source:* Federal Reserve System.

If we knew that DDO and currency possessed twice the "moneyness," or impact on economic activity, of money market mutual fund shares and four times the "moneyness" of passbook savings accounts (*SD*) and small time deposits (*TD*), we might define the money supply as

$$M = DDO + C^p + 0.50(\text{MMMF}) + 0.25(SD + TD)$$

Given the current state of knowledge, however, economists are unsure of the appropriate weights to place on the various items in our money measure. The Federal Reserve is working on the problem. In experimenting with **divisia aggregates**—weighted measures of money—it has sometimes found them superior to existing monetary aggregates in predicting future changes in the nation's price level and output of goods and services. In the future, the Fed may replace the current measures of money with new measures based on weighted averages.

SUMMARY

Money is defined as anything that is widely acceptable as payment for goods and services or repayment of debt. Today, this measure of money consists of the public's holdings of currency and coins, and demand

deposits and other checkable deposits in banks and other depository institutions. The use of money benefits society by reducing transactions costs and stimulating the specialization and division of labor—that is, by increasing economic efficiency. Money serves as a medium of exchange or means of payment, a standard of value or measuring rod in assessing the worth of tens of thousands of items, and a store of value or means of preserving wealth over time. In primitive societies, money consisted only of substances that were highly esteemed and possessed significant value as a commodity. For centuries, such precious metals as copper, bronze, silver, and gold served as money. Transactions costs were lowered first by introducing paper money, then checks, and finally electronic payments. Today, societies use fiat or credit money—money that derives its value not by the substance from which it is

made, but by government decree. A fiat monetary system allows the money supply to be the product of human decision rather than the bounty of nature. Changes in the quantity of money have important implications for key economic variables such as output, employment, and the price level. Too rapid an expansion of the money supply leads to inflation while too slow an increase typically results in recession. Today the Federal Reserve publishes several measures of money and there is no consensus about which measure is best. The Fed is currently experimenting with measures of money that employ different weights for its different components.

Answers to Your Turn (p. 23)

a. *In a barter economy, each good must be expressed in units of each other good. Hence, there are 8 × 7 = 56 rates of exchange. However, half of those rates of exchange are redundant, being the reciprocal of another rate of exchange (if 10 loaves of bread = 1 bushel of wheat, then 1 loaf of bread = 0.1 bushel of wheat). Hence, there are (8 × 7)/2, or 28 different price ratios in this barter economy. In a money economy there would be only eight prices, because the price of each good would be expressed in units of the nation's standard of value, for example, dollars.*

b. *In a barter economy with 10,000 different goods, there would be (10,000 × 9,999)/2 different rates of exchange, or 49,995,000 prices. In a money economy, there would be only 10,000 prices.*

KEY TERMS

legal tender
money
wealth
income
liquidity
full-bodied money (commodity money)
representative full-bodied money
fiat money (credit money)

electronic funds transfer system (EFTS)
Fedwire
Clearing House Interbank Payments
   System (CHIPS)
M1
M2
M3
divisia aggregate

STUDY QUESTIONS

1 Explain in detail the meaning of the following concepts: money, income, and wealth.

2 Critique the following statements: "Doctors earn more money than engineers" and "Bill Gates has more money than Bill Clinton."

3 Are credit cards money? Explain why or why not.

4 What do we mean by "legal tender"? Is all money legal tender? Is all legal tender money?

5 By focusing on the standard-of-value and medium-of-exchange functions of money, analyze the benefits which accrue to society when money is introduced into a barter economy.

6 "At any point in time, money can effectively serve as a standard of value, or yardstick, to measure the relative values of various goods." Does this conclusion change if we allow time to vary?

7 "When the store-of-value function of money collapses, so does the medium-of-exchange function." Do you agree or disagree? Explain.

8 In 1980, the U.S. consumer price index increased by 12.5 percent. Which function of money was most jeopardized at that time? Explain by examining the effects of this event on the usefulness of money in each of its three functions.

9 Explain how the introduction of money eliminates the requirement of a double coincidence of wants in order for exchange to take place.

10 Why does the Fed publish three different measures of the money supply? Why have economists developed three different measures of the money supply? Why, for that matter, do we care about the money supply at all?

11 Historically, which of the following assets— money, gold, Treasury bills, U.S. government bonds, corporate bonds, and common stocks— has been most effective as a store of value? Which has been least effective?

12 Explain the distinction between full-bodied money and fiat or credit money.

13 Give three examples of the transfer of electronic funds in the United States today. What would be the benefits of a comprehensive electronic funds transfer system (EFTS)? What obstacles inhibit the implementation of a comprehensive EFTS?

14 Both money market mutual funds (MMMFs) and money market deposit accounts (MMDAs) permit transfer of funds by check, yet neither is included in the Federal Reserve's narrow money measure, M1. Should those items be included in M1? Explain.

15 Calculate your personal M1 holdings today. Are they larger or smaller than your monthly income?

16 Define the concept of liquidity. Rank the following assets according to their liquidity (most liquid to least liquid):

a A used car

b Funds in Dreyfus Liquid Assets (a money market mutual fund)

c $1000 in a passbook savings account

d $1000 in a certificate of deposit at your bank

e 400 shares of IBM stock

f An expected inheritance from your 75-year-old grandfather

17 A trip to Wal-Mart reveals 122,000 different products on the shelves. In a barter economy, how many different exchange rates would be necessary to determine the value of each good in terms of all the others? How would your answer change if money were introduced into the economy?

18 Why have economists developed divisia measures of money?

SUGGESTIONS FOR ADDITIONAL READING

Good general discussions of money are found in the two New Palgrave Dictionaries (*The New Palgrave Dictionary of Money and Finance* and *The New Palgrave Dictionary of Economics*). On the history of money, see Arthur Nussbaum, *A History of Money* (New York: Columbia University Press, 1957), and Paul Einzig, *Primitive Money,* 2d ed. (New York: Oxford University Press, 1966). A classic article outlining the development of money in a prisoner-of-war camp is R. A. Radford, "The Economic Organization of a Prisoner of War Camp," *Economica,* November 1945, pp. 189–201. An early discussion on measuring money is William Barnett, Edward Offenbacher, and Paul Spindt, "New Concepts of Aggregate Money," *Journal of Finance,* May 1981, pp. 497–505. A more recent paper on the same subject is K. Alec Chrystal and Ronald MacDonald, "Empirical Evidence on the Recent Behavior and Usefulness of Simple Sum and Weighted Measures of the Money Stock," Federal Reserve Bank of St. Louis *Review,* March–April 1994, pp. 73–109 (see also the comments by Charles Nelson that follow). On the use of various instruments in financing expenditures by families, see Robert Avery et al., "The Uses of Cash and Transactions Accounts by American Families," *Federal Reserve Bulletin,* February 1986, pp. 87–108. On the electronic funds transfer system, see Dennis W. Richardson, *Electric Money: Evolution of an Electronic Funds-Transfer System* (Cambridge, Mass.: MIT Press, 1970), and Mark Flannery and Dwight Jaffee, *The Economic Implications of an Electronic Monetary Transfer System* (Lexington, Mass.: Lexington Books, 1973). A more recent article on this subject is James McAndrews, "The Automated Clearinghouse System: Moving toward Electronic Payments," Federal Reserve Bank of Philadelphia *Business Review,* July–August, 1994, pp. 15–23. On the electronic purse, see John Wenninger and David Laster, "The Electronic Purse," *Current Issues in Economics and Finance,* Federal Reserve Bank of New York, April 1995.

P A R T

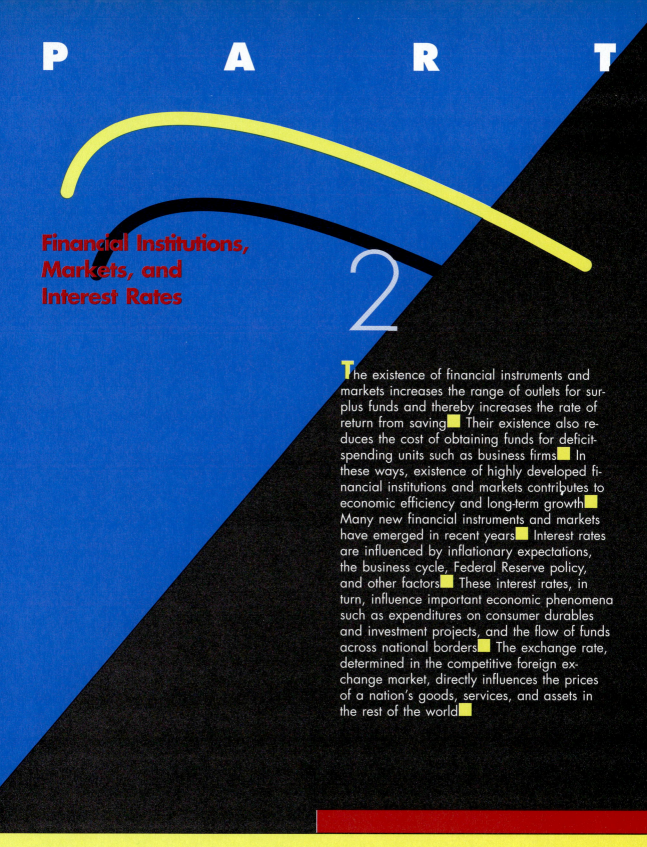

2

Financial Institutions, Markets, and Interest Rates

The existence of financial instruments and markets increases the range of outlets for surplus funds and thereby increases the rate of return from saving■ Their existence also reduces the cost of obtaining funds for deficit-spending units such as business firms■ In these ways, existence of highly developed financial institutions and markets contributes to economic efficiency and long-term growth■ Many new financial instruments and markets have emerged in recent years■ Interest rates are influenced by inflationary expectations, the business cycle, Federal Reserve policy, and other factors■ These interest rates, in turn, influence important economic phenomena such as expenditures on consumer durables and investment projects, and the flow of funds across national borders■ The exchange rate, determined in the competitive foreign exchange market, directly influences the prices of a nation's goods, services, and assets in the rest of the world■

CHAPTER

3

■ ## Financial Markets
and Instruments

A basic principle of introductory economics is the fundamental role of saving and investment. Consider the primitive world of Robinson Crusoe and his friend Friday. Marooned on a deserted island, these characters from the pages of Daniel Defoe were confronted with a basic fact of economic life—a shortage of goods and services relative to wants. Without adequate equipment, Crusoe and Friday were forced to obtain food by the most primitive techniques. Their method of catching fish was so inefficient that obtaining adequate nourishment occupied almost their entire day. In order to extricate themselves from their hand-to-mouth existence, Crusoe and Friday decided to invest in capital equipment—a fishing net. Such an investment might enhance their productivity, allowing them to produce nonfood items and possibly even to enjoy some leisure time. The investment would boost their standard of living.

To accomplish the production of the capital good (the fishing net), Crusoe and Friday had to catch more fish than they consumed. This act of *saving* allowed them to transfer economic resources (in this case labor resources) from the production of *consumer goods* (fish) to the production of *capital goods* (the fishing net). Once they had made their investment in capital goods, Crusoe and Friday were on their way toward the "good life."

This elementary example illustrates the importance of the saving and investment process in economic development. Because capital goods depreciate over time, a significant flow of saving must be generated and transferred into productive investment just to maintain a nation's capital stock and preserve existing living standards. For living standards to rise, a healthy flow of saving and investment must be sustained. As a general proposition, the greater the proportion of current output saved and invested, the more rapid the rate of economic growth.

In a modern society, contrary to the Robinson Crusoe story, the process of investment is separated from the savings process. While millions of households and thousands of firms engage in saving, decisions to purchase capital goods are made by a relatively small group of individuals and firms. In order for these investment intentions to be realized, the savings of the masses must be transferred to those seeking to invest. It is the function of financial institutions and markets to provide the mechanism

43

Saving Rates, Real Interest Rates, and Economic Growth

Given other factors, nations with higher saving rates should experience more rapid rates of economic growth over a long span of years. The act of saving, by depressing production of consumption goods, is the fundamental mechanism that allows greater production of investment goods. From a financial perspective, greater saving leads to lower interest rates and more funds available to finance investment. Thus, one would expect that countries with higher saving rates should generally tend to exhibit higher investment rates and more rapid long-term economic growth.

The accompanying figure shows the simple relationship in 10 nations—nine Asian economies, including several rapidly growing Pacific Rim nations, plus Turkey—between the saving rate and the average rate of long-term real GDP growth over a 25-year period. Note the positive, albeit somewhat loose relationship. On average, countries with relatively high saving rates (Singapore, Taiwan, Korea) experienced extremely high rates of growth. Countries with relatively low saving rates (Indonesia, Burma) experienced much more modest rates of growth.

Of course, causation may be running both ways in this statistical relationship. That is, rapid economic growth attributable to other factors may contribute to high saving rates. Also, low-saving nations sometimes avoid a rigid link between domestic saving and investment by borrowing abroad to finance a high level of investment at home. However, to the extent that the relationship in the figure reflects the fundamental process of high saving rates leading to high investment and robust economic growth, the policy implications for countries suffering from sluggish growth are clear: measures that stimulate the incentive to save are likely to result ultimately in a more rapid rate of economic growth.

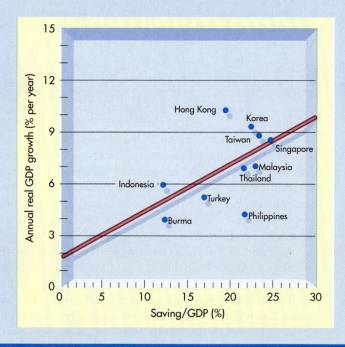

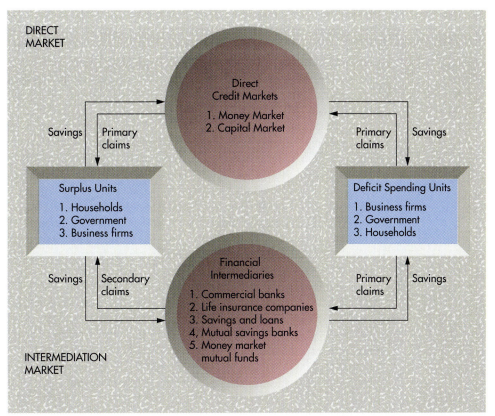

Figure 3-1   The Transfer of Funds from Surplus to Deficit Spending Units via Direct Credit Markets and Financial Intermediaries. Households and other surplus units (box at left) make funds available to deficit-spending units (box at right) either directly, by purchasing instruments issued by deficit spenders (circle at top), or indirectly, by purchasing secondary claims issued by financial intermediaries (circle at bottom).

for the transfer of funds from savers to investors. Figure 3-1 illustrates the basic principles and characters involved in this process. Basically, financial institutions and markets assist in funneling funds from surplus units (savers) to deficit spending units (dissavers).

The deficit spending units—those units whose annual revenues are insufficient to cover their expenditures—are shown in the right-hand portion of the figure. They include certain households, state and local governments in some periods, the federal government in most periods, and large numbers of business firms. Though practically all individuals, firms, and governments borrow at one time or another, taken collectively, firms and governments are deficit spenders; individuals are not.

The savers, or surplus units, are positioned in the left-hand portion of the figure. This sector includes millions of households, some firms, and on rare occasions the government. Collectively, only households qualify as net savers; firms and governments are deficit spenders.

The diagram shows that the savings generated by the surplus units are made available to the deficit spending units through two avenues: direct credit markets and financial intermediaries. In the direct credit market channel, claims such as stocks, bonds, and other debt instruments are issued by deficit spending units and are typically sold through brokers and dealers to the savings units.[1] The top part of the figure illustrates this flow of claims, called *primary claims,* from deficit spenders to savers by way of the direct credit markets.

The other channel used to transfer funds from savers to deficit spenders involves financial intermediaries. These are financial middlemen (hence the term "intermediary"), positioned at the bottom of the figure. Some of the primary claims issued by deficit spending units (bonds, mortgages, and so forth) are sold to these financial intermediaries instead of being sold directly to savers. The financial intermediaries hold these primary claims as investments; they obtain funds to pay for them by issuing *secondary claims* on themselves. The secondary claims—savings deposits, life insurance policies, money market mutual fund shares, and so forth—are sold to the surplus units (savers). In the United States, the predominant portion of the flow of funds from savers to deficit spenders is channeled through financial intermediaries.

In this chapter, we focus on the top part of the figure. We will examine the direct credit markets—the money market and the capital market—and the financial instruments traded in them. We will devote special attention to the U.S. government securities market, one of the largest financial markets in the world. Chapter 4 provides an analysis of financial intermediation, along with a discussion of the various types of financial intermediaries in the United States. We will begin this chapter with a discussion of three key attributes of financial instruments: liquidity, risk, and yield.

ATTRIBUTES OF FINANCIAL INSTRUMENTS

Three of the most important characteristics of financial instruments are the related concepts of liquidity, risk, and yield. These characteristics have important implications in the decision-making process in which individuals and firms allocate financial wealth among money ($DDO + C^p$), savings accounts, stocks, bonds, and various other financial assets.

Liquidity

As defined in Chapter 2, **liquidity** refers to the ease and willingness with which an asset may be converted into money on short notice. There are three prerequisites for a financial instrument to be considered highly liquid. First, the instrument must be easily converted

---

[1]The distinction between a broker and a dealer is as follows: a broker acts as the customer's agent in locating a buyer or seller and works on a commission basis, while a dealer makes markets in securities by maintaining an inventory of securities. Dealers stand ready to buy or sell securities to the general public from their inventory.

to cash. Second, the transactions costs of doing so must be low. Third, the principal must remain relatively stable over time. The existence of highly developed markets in which financial instruments can be bought and sold contributes strongly to the liquidity of these instruments.

Common stocks are considered less liquid than short-term U.S. government securities. While easily accessible markets make the sale of both instruments convenient, transactions costs are higher for common stocks. Stocks also exhibit appreciably greater price variation over time than government securities do. What about passbook savings accounts and U.S. government Series H bonds? Passbook savings accounts score very high on all three criteria and are therefore extremely liquid. But because Series H bonds are redeemable for cash without penalty only at a specified future date, they are considered relatively illiquid.

Risk

The risk inherent in financial instruments derives from the possibility of not recovering the full value of funds originally invested. Risks may be divided into two types: default risk and market risk.

Default risk refers to the possibility of not receiving the contractual interest payments or of not recovering the principal due to the insolvency of the instrument's issuer. U.S. government bonds and commercial bank savings accounts carry a lower default risk than corporate and municipal bonds and corporate stocks do, because the U.S. government has the constitutional authority to tax or print money to meet its financial obligations and because savings deposits in commercial banks are insured by the Federal Deposit Insurance Corporation. Such safety features are not offered by corporate and municipal bonds or common stocks.

Market risk refers to the risk of fluctuation in the price or market value of the financial instrument. In the event one is forced to sell, one may not be able to recover the original principal. A savings deposit in a commercial bank or savings and loan association has less market risk than a long-term marketable U.S. government bond. One can cash in the savings account on short notice without risking loss of principal. Such is not the case for marketable bonds, whose prices fluctuate daily because of changes in inflationary expectations and other factors that influence interest rates and the outlook for business earnings.

Yield

The **yield** is the rate of return on an asset, expressed as a percentage per year. Most commonly, the yield is computed as the yearly return on the instrument (in dollars) divided by the price, or initial principal. This concept is sometimes known as the **current yield.** An alternative measure, known as the **yield to maturity,** is sometimes employed for bonds. The yield to maturity takes into consideration any capital gain or loss realized at maturity, when the face value of the bond (usually $1000 or $10,000) is redeemed. If the bond was purchased at a price below its face value, the yield to maturity, which is the average rate of return over the life of the instrument, exceeds the current yield. If the bond was purchased at a price above its face value, its holder will suffer a capital loss at maturity, and the yield to maturity will fall short of the current yield. We will illustrate these yield concepts shortly, when we discuss the market for U.S. government securities.

Liquidity, Risk, and Yield: Their Relationship

The three attributes of a financial instrument (liquidity, risk, and yield) are systematically linked. Investors will normally accept a lower yield in order to obtain increased liquidity. Thus, passbook savings accounts have lower yields than 3-year certificates of deposit. Risk and yield are positively related because most investors are risk averse and must be compensated with higher returns for accepting a higher degree of risk. Thus, corporate bonds have higher yields than U.S. Treasury bonds. Risk and liquidity are also inherently related. More liquid financial instruments are less risky, because they may be cashed in at short notice, at a price not significantly lower than the original purchase price. Thus, because long-term bonds exhibit greater price fluctuation than short-term bonds, they are less liquid and more risky than short-term bonds.

Ranking Financial Claims by Their Liquidity

We may reinforce our discussion of risk, liquidity, and yield by ranking a sample of financial claims on the basis of their relative liquidity. Table 3-1 lists several financial claims commonly held by individuals, arranged in the approximate order of their liquidity from most liquid to least liquid. The order is not intended to be exact or definitive; depending on one's income level, occupation, or other considerations, one might argue

Table 3-1

Financial Claims Ranked by Degree of Liquidity

1. Currency, demand deposits, and other checkable deposits (M1)
2. Noncheckable savings deposits in commercial banks and thrift institutions
3. Money market mutual fund shares
4. Time deposits and certificates of deposit in banks and thrift institutions
5. U.S. Treasury bills (marketable)
6. U.S. Treasury notes (marketable)
7. U.S. Treasury bonds (marketable)
8. Municipal bonds
9. Corporate bonds
10. Corporate stocks

for a slightly different order. For example, an aggressive manager of an upper-income family's finances may consider money market mutual fund shares to be more liquid than a savings account. Nevertheless, Table 3-1 illustrates the general concept of liquidity.

Currency, demand deposits, and other checkable deposits top the list in Table 3-1 because they constitute money (M1) and are therefore perfectly liquid by definition. Savings deposits in commercial banks and nonbank financial institutions (item 2) are also considered highly liquid because they can easily be converted into money on short notice without risk of loss.[2] With savings accounts, there is no fluctuation in principal. Therefore, they have no market risk. The same holds for money market mutual fund shares, which can be withdrawn by check. Time deposits and certificates of deposit (CDs) are similar to savings accounts in that their owners have the authority to convert a known and fixed principal amount into cash. However, they are less liquid than savings accounts, because the terms on which they may be cashed in are less attractive. (Depositors who withdraw time deposits and CDs prior to maturity typically forgo accrued interest.)

The remaining claims on the list—U.S. Treasury bills through corporate stocks—offer decreasing liquidity because of their increasing degree of market risk and risk of insolvency. In the case of U.S. Treasury bills, notes, and bonds, the risk involved is purely market risk—that is, the risk of fluctuating market prices. In the case of municipal bonds, corporate bonds, and corporate stock, one must add to their significant market risk an increasing element of default risk. As we will demonstrate later, the degree of market risk of a security generally increases with its length of time to maturity. For this reason, U.S. Treasury bills (which have maturities of 1 year or less) are considered more liquid than U.S. Treasury notes and bonds (which are longer-term instruments). U.S. Treasury bonds, municipal bonds, and corporate bonds are roughly similar in their element of market risk. We may rationalize their ranking on the basis of default risk, which increases as we move down the list. While U.S. Treasury bonds are essentially free of default risk, that is not the case with municipal bonds. Corporate bonds and stocks possess a significant element of default risk, though bonds are less risky than stocks since bondholders have a prior claim on corporate income and assets. (Stockholders are reimbursed only after bondholders' claims have been satisfied.)

CLASSIFICATION OF FINANCIAL MARKETS

There are several possible criteria for classifying financial markets. One may distinguish between debt and equity markets, between primary and secondary markets, between organized and over-the-counter markets, and between money and capital markets. We will emphasize the distinction between money and capital markets. To provide important institutional information, however, we will briefly discuss the other classification schemes.

---

[2]Technically, depository institutions reserve the right to require advance notice of withdrawal of deposits. In practice, passbook savings accounts may generally be withdrawn on demand.

Debt versus Equity Markets

A **debt instrument** involves a contractual agreement by the borrowing party to pay a specific amount of money (the principal, or face value) at some specified future date. Included in most arrangements is an agreement to make a specified annual interest payment. Examples of debt instruments include all forms of U.S. government securities (bills, notes, and bonds), corporate bonds, municipal bonds, mortgages, and several short-term money market instruments issued by banks and other businesses. These debt instruments are actively traded in financial markets. **Equities** are claims which give the owner a right to share the net income of the instrument's issuer. The main equity instruments are common stocks.

From the point of view of investors, debt instruments tend to be safer than equities, because they involve a contractual claim on the issuer. In the event of extreme financial problems (insolvency), owners of corporate debt instruments have a prior claim over stockholders on the income and assets of the corporation. On the other hand, stockholders stand to benefit from growth in a firm's earnings because they possess ownership claims, while holders of bonds and other debt instruments do not. At the middle of 1996, the value of equities outstanding in the United States was approximately $9 trillion. The total value of debt instruments outstanding was even larger, approximately $14 trillion in early 1996. Figure 3-2 indicates the amount outstanding of several of the most prominent debt instruments.

Primary versus Secondary Markets

A **primary market** is a market for new issues; a **secondary market** is a market for the exchange of previously issued securities. The New York Stock Exchange and the U.S. government securities markets are examples of secondary markets. When an individual calls her broker to buy stocks, or when a money market mutual fund purchases marketable

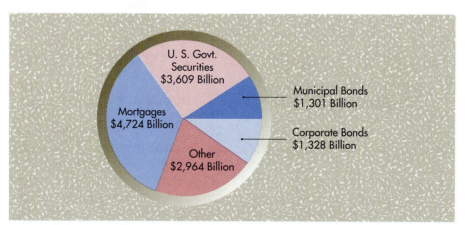

Figure 3-2   Composition of Outstanding Debt Instruments, June 1995. In terms of magnitude, the most important debt instruments are mortgages, U.S. government securities, corporate bonds, and municipal bonds.   *Source:* Federal Reserve System, *Flow of Funds Accounts.*

government securities, new funds are not supplied to corporations or the government. That occurs only when securities are first offered in the primary market. Instead, the buyer simply swaps claims with other parties. The secondary market serves the important economic function of providing liquidity to financial instruments, enhancing the ability of firms and governments to attract funds through new issues. Few individuals or firms would purchase newly issued stocks and bonds if viable secondary markets did not exist.

To issue new debt or equity, a corporation often retains the services of an *investment banker* that specializes in providing information and advice on new issues, including the choice between debt and equity. If the firm issues a debt instrument, the investment banker will provide counsel regarding the appropriate coupon rate, the maturity, and other matters. Often an investment banker will *underwrite* the new securities, agreeing to purchase the entire issue and resell it to the public. In the event of a relatively large offering, several investment banking firms may pool their resources and jointly underwrite the new issue, in order to spread the risk.

Organized versus Over-the-Counter Markets

Once issued, a security may be traded in a secondary market, either "on the floor" of an organized exchange or "over the counter," a term which refers to an informal system of telephone contacts among brokers and dealers. The New York Stock Exchange, American Stock Exchange, and numerous other organized exchanges provide a physical meeting place in which brokers and dealers who are members of the exchange may conduct transactions. Those brokers and dealers are linked through various communications devices to other brokers, dealers, firms, and individuals throughout the nation. Buy and sell orders are transmitted through this network to the floor of the exchange, where transactions are carried out. The great bulk of the trading on organized exchanges is in stocks issued by relatively large corporations.

Though corporate stocks tradeable on the exchanges make up the dominant portion of the *value* of all corporate stock, the number of firms whose shares are traded constitutes a small minority of all corporations. The equities issued by the great majority of corporations, as well as most of the debt instruments issued by corporations, the U.S. government, and state and local governments, are traded over the counter. Unlike the organized stock exchanges, in which agents meet face to face, the over-the-counter market is a communications arrangement in which brokers and dealers throughout the United States maintain contact with one another in order to "make markets" in securities. Some dealers and brokers specialize in specific types of securities. For example, U.S. government securities are traded by dealers who specialize in those instruments. Over-the-counter markets include those in municipal bonds, negotiable certificates of deposit, federal funds, and bankers' acceptances.

Money versus Capital Markets

The **money market** is one in which short-term debt instruments—those with maturities of less than 1 year—are traded in massive quantities. Money market instruments, which are issued by governments, banks, and other private firms, are characterized by their high liquidity and relatively low default risk. The **capital market** is one in which long-term securities issued by government and private concerns are exchanged. Both debt and equity instruments are traded in the capital market, and they often carry greater default and market risks than the instruments of the money market. As compensation, however, these long-term instruments frequently return a relatively high yield.

Typically, business firms use the money market to obtain working capital—that is, funds to cover short-term operating expenses. To finance long-term investment in plant, equipment, and technology, firms normally obtain their funds in the capital market. That is, they issue bonds and equities to finance projects with long-term payoffs.

As far as banks and the Federal Reserve System are concerned, the most important financial market is the U.S. government securities market. It is one of the most active and efficient markets in the world. We will now take a detailed look at that market.

THE U.S. GOVERNMENT SECURITIES MARKET

The market in securities issued by the U.S. government is so intimately involved in both commercial banking and Federal Reserve policy that it merits special attention. The Federal Reserve implements its monetary policy mainly by purchasing and selling U.S. government securities through a network of government securities dealers. Other active participants in this market include both financial and nonfinancial firms, pension and retirement funds, individuals, and foreigners. The volume of transactions conducted in the U.S. government securities market is enormous, typically exceeding $100 billion on any given day.

Kinds of U.S. Government Securities

Table 3-2 shows the composition of the U.S. government debt at the end of 1995. Of the gross public debt, approximately $5 trillion in early 1996, about two-thirds is marketable and is actively traded, with prices and transactions quoted daily in the major newspapers. About 40 government securities dealers associated with New York commercial or investment banks hold inventories and stand ready to buy or sell these securities. These dealers do not charge a commission or brokerage fee for their service. Instead, they earn a living by maintaining a slightly higher price received (the ask price) than the price they pay (the bid price). Due to the enormous volume of government securities transacted daily, dealers are able to earn a handsome income on the basis of a remarkably small spread between their bid and ask prices.

Dealers buy and sell three types of marketable U.S. government securities: Treasury bills, Treasury notes, and Treasury bonds. **Treasury bills** are short-term debt instruments with a maturity of 3 months to 1 year when issued. **Treasury notes** are generally of 1 to 10 years' maturity when issued. **Treasury bonds** have original maturity dates of 10 to 40 years. As Table 3-2 shows, more than 80 percent of marketable U.S. government debt is in the form of Treasury bills and notes.

Table 3-2

U.S. Government Debt Outstanding, by Type of Security, December 31, 1995

Security	Amount of Debt (in billions)
Marketable:	*$3292.2*
Treasury bills	760.7
Treasury notes	2010.3
Treasury bonds	521.2
Nonmarketable:	*1696.5*
Government account series*	1299.6
Savings bonds and notes	181.9
State and local government series	104.5
Other	110.5
Total public debt	**$4988.7**

*Held only by U.S. government agencies and trust funds.

Source: *Federal Reserve Bulletin.*

The U.S. Treasury is responsible for federal **debt management**—decision making regarding the maturity structure of newly issued government debt. Because large amounts of federal debt mature each month and because the federal government is currently operating at a deficit, the U.S. Treasury is constantly issuing new debt. We will discuss several types of marketable and nonmarketable U.S. government securities.

Treasury Bills

These popular instruments are issued in 91-day, 182-day, and 1-year maturities. The large number of these securities outstanding implies a correspondingly large runoff (number of bills maturing) each month. In fact, the U.S. Treasury auctions off large quantities of newly issued Treasury bills each week. They are sold on a competitive basis via sealed bids. Once issued, Treasury bills are traded in a highly competitive secondary market. The entire market in Treasury bills is quoted daily in *The Wall Street Journal, The New York Times,* and many other major newspapers. Figure 3-3 shows the spectrum of Treasury bills outstanding as of Feb. 26, 1996. These securities mature at the specific dates indicated, at which time the purchaser (lender) receives the specified principal, or face value, for example, $10,000.

Note that, on Feb. 26, 1996, a prospective investor could choose from at least four different maturity dates in each month from March 1996 through August 1996, and from at least one maturity date in each month from September 1996 through February 1997. A distinguishing feature of this market is that potential buyers can tailor their purchases so that their securities reach maturity when the proceeds are needed to meet planned expenditures.

Treasury bills are conventionally quoted in annual rates of return—*discount rates* and *yields*—rather than prices. This form of quotation is convenient for the thousands of

Maturity	Days to Mat.	Bid	Asked	Chg.	Ask Yld.
TREASURY BILLS					
Feb 29 '96	1	4.13	4.03	+0.11	4.10
Mar 07 '96	8	4.63	4.53	....	4.61
Mar 14 '96	15	4.55	4.45	+0.03	4.53
Mar 21 '96	22	4.06	3.96	−0.03	4.04
Mar 28 '96	29	4.52	4.48	+0.05	4.57
Apr 04 '96	36	4.85	4.81	+0.03	4.91
Apr 11 '96	43	4.81	4.77	+0.03	4.88
Apr 18 '96	50	4.99	4.95	+0.01	5.07
Apr 25 '96	57	4.71	4.69	+0.04	4.80
May 02 '96	64	4.86	4.84	+0.04	4.96
May 09 '96	71	4.85	4.83	+0.02	4.96
May 16 '96	78	4.85	4.83	+0.03	4.96
May 23 '96	85	4.85	4.83	+0.02	4.97
May 30 '96	92	4.85	4.83	+0.02	4.97
Jun 06 '96	99	4.80	4.78	+0.03	4.92
Jun 13 '96	106	4.76	4.74	+0.01	4.89
Jun 20 '96	113	4.76	4.74	....	4.89
Jun 27 '96	120	4.78	4.76	+0.02	4.92
Jul 05 '96	128	4.78	4.76	....	4.92
Jul 11 '96	134	4.77	4.75	....	4.92
Jul 18 '96	141	4.77	4.75	−0.01	4.92
Jul 25 '96	148	4.78	4.76	−0.01	4.94
Aug 01 '96	155	4.79	4.77	+0.01	4.95
Aug 08 '96	162	4.79	4.77	+0.01	4.96
Aug 15 '96	169	4.79	4.77	−0.01	4.96
Aug 22 '96	176	4.79	4.77	....	4.97
Sep 19 '96	204	4.79	4.77	+0.01	4.97
Oct 17 '96	232	4.81	4.79	+0.04	5.00
Nov 14 '96	260	4.82	4.80	+0.03	5.02
Dec 12 '96	288	4.78	4.76	+0.02	4.99
Jan 09 '97	316	4.80	4.78	+0.02	5.02
Feb 06 '97	344	4.79	4.77	+0.03	5.02

Figure 3-3 The Market for U.S. Treasury Bills, Feb. 26, 1996. *Source:* Reprinted by permission of *The Wall Street Journal,* Feb. 27, 1996. Copyright © 1996 Dow Jones & Company, Inc. All rights reserved Worldwide.

Treasury bill market participants, who can quickly size up the returns available on Treasury bills for comparison with alternative investments. Consider the first security listed in Figure 3-3: the Treasury bill maturing in three days (on Feb. 29, 1996) quoted as bid 4.13 percent, asked 4.03 percent, and ask yield 4.10 percent. Treasury bills are sold at a discount from face value of $1000. Their return arises from the difference between the price paid and the $1000 guaranteed at maturity. We may set down the relationship among the discount rate (r), the price (P), and the number of days to maturity as follows:

$$(3\text{-}1) \qquad r = \frac{1000 - P}{1000} \times \frac{360}{\text{days to maturity}}$$

This formula states that the rate of return, known as the discount rate (r), is equal to the gain on the asset relative to its face value of $1000—that is, $(1000 - P)/1000$—times a factor which annualizes that gain (360/days to maturity). If a U.S. Treasury bill that matures in 60 days sells for $990, its discount rate is $10/$1000 × 360/60, or 6 percent.[3]

---

[3]The alert reader will note two peculiarities in this calculation and Equation 3-1. First, contrary to the conventions of financial terminology, we know there are 365 days in a year. Second, it seems more natural to compute the rate of return on the basis of P, the purchase price of the Treasury bill, instead of its face value of $1000. Incorporating these considerations, we can compute the *yield* on a Treasury bill as $Y = [(1000 - P)/P] \times 365/\text{days to}$ maturity. This is, in fact, the procedure used in calculating the yield column in Figure 3-3. The quoted yield of 4.10 percent on the February 29 Treasury bill applies this procedure, using the asked price of the bill.

Equation 3-1 allows us to compute the discount rate, given the price of the Treasury bill and the number of days to maturity. Since Treasury bills are conventionally quoted in discount rates, we would like to be able to calculate the price. We can rearrange Equation 3-1 to solve for the price of the Treasury bill, as follows:

$$(3\text{-}2) \qquad P = \$1000 - \frac{\$1000(r)(\text{days to maturity})}{360}$$

Solving for the asked price of the first Treasury bill quoted in Figure 3-3 at an asked discount of 4.03 percent, we obtain:

$$P = \$1000 - [1000(0.0403)(3)]/360 = \$999.664$$

We can easily check the validity of our calculation by substituting the answer of $999.664 back into Equation 3-1 and ascertaining whether we obtain the quoted return of 4.03 percent. Check this out!

To get an idea about the transactions costs for U.S. Treasury bills, let's compute the dealer's price using the *bid* discount rate quoted on this same security—that is, 4.13 percent. Doing so, we obtain a price of slightly more than $999.65. On a $1000 transaction, the spread between the dealer's bid and asked price is only 1 cent! Transactions costs in U.S. Treasury bills are virtually nil, a factor that contributes to their high liquidity and popularity.[4] Players who conduct multimillion-dollar transactions in this market experience phenomenally low transactions costs.

Your Turn

a. A Treasury bill with 36 days to maturity is priced at $995. Calculate its discount rate.

b. A Treasury bill with 80 days to maturity is quoted at a discount rate of 0.062, or 6.2 percent. Calculate its price.

One more demonstration will help to explain the great liquidity and desirability of Treasury bills. Based on the data in Figure 3-3, let's construct a graph that relates the price of Treasury bills to the number of days remaining to maturity. The result is illustrated in Figure 3-4.

The length of time to maturity, measured in months, is shown on the horizontal axis. The market price, computed from the asked discount rates quoted in Figure 3-3, is shown on the vertical axis. Note that at any point in time (in this case, Feb. 26, 1996), the market price of a Treasury bill is closely and inversely related to the length of time to maturity. The nearer the maturity date, the higher the price. A Treasury bill *must* continually

---

[4]The bid-to-ask price spread increases somewhat as the maturity date lengthens, probably because the market is thinner—i.e., the trading volume is lower. For example, the bid and ask prices on the Feb. 6, 1997, maturity Treasury bill are $954.23 and $954.42. In this case, the spread is 19 cents on the $1000 transaction. Check the spread on the August 22, 1996, issue.

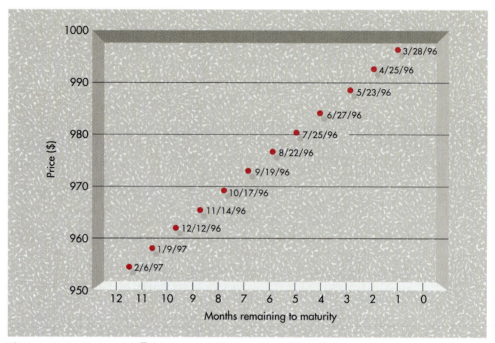

Figure 3-4   Treasury Bill Price versus Time to Maturity, Feb. 26, 1996. Treasury bills with shorter times to maturity sell at higher prices. This means that, once issued, a Treasury bill gradually appreciates in price until it reaches face value at maturity.   *Source:* Calculated from the data in Figure 3-3.

rise in price as the maturity date approaches, to provide a given yield (say, 6 percent). Otherwise, the yield would rise continually as the maturity date approached.[5]

Because the price of any 91-day or 182-day U.S. Treasury bill almost inevitably rises each week as it approaches maturity, the risks involved to owners of Treasury bills are about as close to zero as possible. The default risk is nil, because the U.S. government can tax, borrow, or print money to pay off its creditors. Market risk is also extremely low, owing to the mechanism illustrated in Figure 3-4. Should one purchase a newly issued 91-day Treasury bill and then be forced to sell it 30 days later, the odds are extremely high that it will have appreciated in price. Only a phenomenal upsurge in market interest rates in the 30 days following its purchase would prevent its appreciation in price. This virtual absence of risk, together with the respectable yield and extremely low transactions costs, explains the popularity of Treasury bills as a source of investment income for commercial banks, money market mutual funds, and firms with excess funds to invest. Individuals may purchase Treasury bills in minimum denominations of $10,000 through their district Federal Reserve Bank.

---

[5]Suppose a U.S. Treasury bill with 60 days to maturity is priced at $990. Using the formula in footnote 3, its yield would therefore be about 6 percent, that is $10/990 × 365/60). Suppose that, after 30 days pass, the same Treasury bill remains priced at $990. Its yield would then be about 12 percent $10/990 × 365/30). The forces of supply and demand tend to prevent such an occurrence by bidding the price up toward $995.

Treasury Notes and Bonds

As has been stated, Treasury notes are of 1 to 10 years' maturity when issued; bonds are longer-term instruments. Notes and bonds are issued through three methods: auction, exchange, and subscription. Some are auctioned off in the same way as Treasury bills. In an exchange, the Treasury offers existing owners of maturing notes and bonds a choice of several new issues. In a subscription, the public is first notified of the **coupon rate** (the annual yield, based on its face value—that is, its value at maturity) and other pertinent features of a new issue. By a specified date, investors must subscribe for their desired amounts, which are to be sold to them at face value. If, as is commonly the case, the amount subscribed for by the public exceeds the amount offered by the Treasury, each subscriber is allocated a pro rata share of the amount requested. Commercial banks often subscribe to newly issued securities.

Once issued, U.S. Treasury notes and bonds are actively traded by dealers in U.S. government securities. End-of-the-day quotations on all outstanding U.S. Treasury notes and bonds (more than 200 issues) are printed daily in major newspapers. For purposes of illustration, Table 3-3 lists a small sample of quotations from Feb. 26, 1996.

The coupon rate is given in the first column. The first issue quoted, the 6s of June 1996, pays $6 a year per $100 of face value (or maturity value). Thus, an individual who owns $10,000 (face value) worth of the 6s of 1996 will receive payments totaling $600 a year. Payments are made semiannually. The Treasury selects a coupon rate that will allow the note or bond to be initially auctioned at a price close to the face value ($100). Thus, if long-term government bond yields on actively traded bonds are 6.5 percent, currently issued Treasury bonds will have a coupon rate of 6.5 percent. We may infer that the $11\frac{5}{8}$s of November 2004

Table 3-3

Selected U.S. Treasury Notes and Bonds, Feb. 26, 1996

Coupon Rate	Maturity Date (month/year)	Bid*	Asked*	Bid Change[†]	Ask Yield
6	June 96n[‡]	100:10	100:12	—	4.83
$6\frac{1}{2}$	Aug 97n	101:28	101:30	−2	5.11
$4\frac{3}{4}$	Aug 98n	98:25	98:27	−3	5.25
$11\frac{5}{8}$	Nov 04	137:27	137:31	−9	5.97
$6\frac{1}{2}$	Aug 05n	103:07	103:09	−3	6.04
10	May 05–10	126:24	126:28	−11	6.14
$6\frac{1}{4}$	Aug 23	95:18	95:20	−15	6.60
6	Feb 26	94:03	94:05	−12	6.44

*Figures immediately following colons represent 32ds. Thus, 100:12 means $100\frac{12}{32}$.
[†]Change in bid price from previous day's closing price, in 32ds.
[‡]An *n* following the maturity date indicates issue is a note. All other issues are bonds.

Source: Reprinted by permission of *The Wall Street Journal,* Feb. 27, 1996. Copyright © 1996 Dow Jones & Company, Inc. All rights reserved Worldwide.

were issued at a time when yields were considerably higher than they are today. The 4¾s of August 1998 were issued at a time of very low market yields—probably August 1993.

The second column of the table gives the maturity date. Treasury notes are designated by the letter *n* following the maturity date. If the date is not followed by an *n*, the issue is a bond. Notice the 10s of May 2005–2010. This particular bond is "callable," a special feature that gives the government the option to redeem the bond and pay off the face amount on any interest payment date between the year 2005 and the year 2010. In the event that interest rates drop well below those that prevailed when the bond was issued (10 percent), the Treasury may decide to exercise the call option.

The third and fourth columns list the dealers' bid and ask prices. In a convention of the bond markets, the figures to the right of the colon refer to 32ds rather than 100ths. The 95:18 bid price for the 6¼s of August 2023 indicates a price of $95¹⁸⁄₃₂, or $95.56 per $100 face amount. Column 5 indicates the change in the bid price relative to the previous day's closing bid price, measured in 32ds of a dollar.

Note that five of the eight securities in Table 3-3 are quoted at prices above the face value payable at maturity. These bonds sell at a *premium* because the market yields on the day their prices were quoted (Feb. 26, 1996) were significantly lower than the coupon rates the bonds carried. In early 1996, market yields were lower than the average rates of recent years. Buyers were willing to pay (and sellers insisted on receiving) more than the face value for the right to receive these attractive annual coupon payments, which had been established in times of high market yields. Conversely, if interest rates are higher than those in force at the time a security was issued, the market dictates a price below the $100 face value and the bond sells at a *discount*. The 6¼s of August 2023 and the 4¾s of August 1998 commanded a market price below $100 in February 1996 because their $6.25 and $4.75 coupon rates (per $100 face value) were relatively unattractive.

This brings us to the concept of yields on U.S. Treasury notes and bonds. The two relevant yield concepts mentioned earlier in this chapter, the current yield and yield to maturity, apply to all types of notes and bonds—government, corporate, and municipal. The *current yield* refers simply to the annual return divided by the price. Stated algebraically, it is

$$(3\text{-}3) \qquad Y_c = \frac{R}{P}$$

where

Y_c = the current yield

R = the annual coupon payment in dollars, and

P = the market price

Illustrating with the 11⅝s of November 2004 in the table and using the asked quotation, we obtain a current yield of $11.625/$137.97, or 8.43 percent.[6] Since the market

---

[6]Here we use the ask price to compute the yield, because that is the relevant price to a potential buyer. Some analysts prefer to compute the yield using a price midway between the bid and ask prices.

price is above face value ($100), the current yield is clearly below the coupon rate of 11.625 percent. The current yield may be the relevant yield for an individual who is considering purchasing a security for income only. Such an individual may not be particularly concerned about a potential capital gain or loss to be realized at a distant maturity date. Because the current yield neglects to take account of the gain or loss that will accrue at maturity, however, it is a poor measure of the average return earned when an instrument is held to maturity.

To take into account the capital gain or loss realized at maturity, one must use the *yield to maturity*—the average yield over the life of the security. In some cases, appreciation or depreciation in the market price of a security constitutes a significant portion of the average annual yield earned over the life of an asset. Investors in high tax brackets may prefer to purchase "discount bonds," such as the 4¾s of 1998, so that a significant portion of the total return they earn on an instrument will be taxed at the favorable capital gains tax rate.[7] One crude measure of the yield to maturity is expressed as follows:

$$(3\text{-}4) \qquad\qquad Y_m = \frac{R + (C/N)}{P}$$

where

Y_m = yield to maturity

R = the annual coupon payment in dollars

C = the capital gain (+) or loss (−) realized at maturity

N = the number of years remaining to maturity, and

P = the current price of the security

The distinguishing consideration in this formulation is the C/N component, which indicates the average annual capital gain (or loss, if negative) received over the remaining life of the security. Let us illustrate by returning to the 4¾s of 1998, quoted at an ask price of $98²⁷⁄₃₂, or $98.84 per $100 face value. In this case, a gain of $1.16 per $100 face value will be realized at maturity, about 2½ years in the future (measured from Feb. 26, 1996). Using Equation 3-4, we obtain

$$Y_m = [4.75 + (+1.16/2.5)]/\$98.84 = 5.27 \text{ percent}$$

Because the owner who holds this security to maturity receives an average annual capital gain of $0.46 (per $100 face value) in addition to the annual coupon of $4.75, the calculated yield to maturity comes to 5.27 percent per year. Note that the yield to maturity is greater than the current yield, which is 4.80 percent. This should be

---

[7]Suppose you purchase $100,000 worth of the 4¾s of August 1998 for $98,843. You will be taxed by the IRS (though not by your state or local government) at your regular marginal income tax rate on the $4750 worth of annual income from the note. In 1998, when the note matures, you will be taxed on a capital gain of $1157 (that is, $100,000 − $98,843). Capital gains are taxed at a lower rate than other forms of income.

obvious, since a capital gain will be realized at maturity. On the other hand, any note or bond which is purchased at a price above face value ($100) will exhibit a yield to maturity that is lower than its current yield, because a capital loss will be realized at maturity.

Your Turn

The U.S. Treasury 8s of November 2021 are quoted at an asked price of 120:08. Assuming the bond matures exactly 24 years from today, compute both its current yield and its yield to maturity. Why is the yield to maturity lower than the current yield?

Nonmarketable Government Debt

As indicated earlier in Table 3-2, a substantial portion of government debt has been issued in forms other than marketable bills, notes, and bonds. The dominant portion of the nonmarketable debt is the government account series, of which more than $1.3 trillion was outstanding in 1996. These securities are sold only to the approximately 120 government agencies and trust funds, such as the Federal Old-Age and Survivors Insurance Trust Fund, the Federal Employee Retirement Fund, and the Bank Insurance Fund. Such government trust funds are legally required to invest only in U.S. government securities. (Exhibit 3-1 provides a breakdown of ownership of the U.S. government debt.)

U.S. savings bonds, designed for individual investors, are nonmarketable in the sense that they cannot be traded to others through financial markets. However, they may be redeemed for cash prior to maturity through commercial banks and other financial institutions. Two types of U.S. savings bonds are currently offered by the U.S. Treasury: Series EE and HH. Series EE bonds are offered in denominations ranging from $25 to $10,000. Like U.S. Treasury bills, they are *appreciation bonds;* a $25 bond appreciates to $50 after several years, for example. A series EE bond may be cashed in 6 months after it is issued; its redeemable cash value is based on the length of time it is held. Series HH bonds are *income bonds;* they are sold in denominations of $500, $1000, $5000, and $10,000 and pay interest only; that is, they do not experience appreciation. Interest on Series EE and HH savings bonds is not subject to state or local income tax.

Having completed our detailed examination of the U.S. government securities market, we now turn to the instruments of the money and capital markets, including those issued by the private sector and those issued by government.

INSTRUMENTS OF THE MONEY AND CAPITAL MARKETS

Instruments of the Money Market

The chief instruments traded in the money market include U.S. Treasury bills, commercial paper, banker's acceptances, negotiable certificates of deposit, federal funds, repurchase agreements, and Eurodollars.

Who Holds the National Debt?

Because of large and persistent budget deficits, the U.S. national debt has increased more than fivefold since 1980. At the beginning of 1996, it reached the level of $5 trillion. Who owns these bonds, notes, and bills? The accompanying figure indicates that the national debt is owned partly by the government itself (federal agencies, state and local governments, and the Federal Reserve), by the American private sector (banks, other businesses, and individuals), and by foreigners. The largest holder is the federal government itself. Together, the Federal Reserve and federal government agencies hold 35 percent of the national debt. Government trust funds and agencies, legally bound to invest only in U.S. government securities, hold more than one-fourth of the federal debt. The Federal Reserve buys and sells U.S. government securities for the purpose of influencing financial conditions. Over time, the Fed accumulates government securities in order to increase the money supply. In early 1996, the Fed owned almost $400 billion worth of government securities.

American individuals own 7 percent of the federal debt *directly* in the form of U.S. savings bonds and other government securities. *Indirectly,* by holding claims issued by money market mutual funds, life insurance companies, and other financial intermediaries, individuals own a much larger share of the federal debt. Foreign investors, including governments, banks, nonbank firms, and individuals, own approximately 16 percent of the U.S. national debt. Foreign buyers are attracted to U.S. government securities because of their attractive yield and perceived safety, as well as the worldwide acceptability of dollars. The portion of the national debt owned by foreigners has increased from less than 3 percent in the 1950s to around 16 percent today.

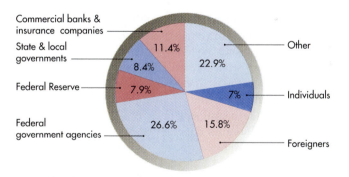

U.S. Treasury Bills

We have already discussed this form of short-term government debt. Highly popular owing to their safety, liquidity, and respectable yield, Treasury bills constitute approximately 25 percent of the marketable federal debt. The Treasury issues new Treasury bills at regular weekly auctions both to refinance maturing issues and to help finance ongoing budget deficits. The principal bidders are government securities dealers, banks, money market mutual funds, other corporations, and individuals willing to invest $10,000 or more. More than $30 billion worth of Treasury bills are "rolled over," or refinanced, in an average week. Once issued, they are traded in an active, efficient secondary market. The volume of daily trading activity in this market is enormous—approximately 10 times that of the New York Stock Exchange.

Commercial Paper

Commercial paper is a short-term, unsecured promissory note (IOU) issued by a corporation to attract funds for day-to-day business activities.[8] The main issuers of commercial paper are industrial firms, finance companies, public utilities, and bank holding companies. Only well-known firms with impeccable credit ratings—about 1200 of the nation's 2 million business firms—find it feasible to borrow in this market. The magnitude of the average issue is approximately $100 million. Commercial paper is sold directly or through dealers to a considerable range of investors with large amounts to invest for brief periods. Primary buyers include various financial institutions and nonfinancial corporations.

Commercial paper is a very old instrument of the money market in England and Europe; it has become popular in the United States in recent decades. From the point of view of major corporations, issuing commercial paper may be regarded as an alternative to borrowing from banks. Hence, when bank loans are in short supply or relatively high in cost, the volume of commercial paper outstanding is likely to increase. In 1996, it stood at more than $700 billion; it has grown at an average rate of approximately 12 percent per year over the past quarter century.

Banker's Acceptances

Banker's acceptances are a form of credit that has been used for centuries in other countries and for roughly 75 years in the United States. A **banker's acceptance** is simply a bank draft (check), generally written by a business firm, that is payable at some specified date in the future and is marked "accepted" by the bank on which it is drawn. Such an instrument might be used, for example, by a little-known U.S. firm desiring to import foreign products to be sold at retail in the United States. Because the firm is not well known to foreign exporters, it draws a bank draft and has it marked "accepted" by a well-known U.S. bank, thus substituting the bank's higher credit rating for that of its own. The bank charges the U.S. importer a modest fee for this service and requires the firm to deposit the funds stipulated on the draft no later than the date on which the instrument matures. The U.S. importer then sends the banker's acceptance to the foreign concern, thereby providing assurance of payment on the date the instrument matures.

Since a banker's acceptance has been stamped "accepted" by a reputable bank, it is virtually risk free and therefore highly marketable. Thus, a foreign exporter may choose to sell a banker's acceptance rather than wait until its maturity date to be paid. Because these instruments constitute an agreement to pay a specified amount *in the future,* they are sold at a discount from face value, like U.S. Treasury bills. Banker's acceptances are traded through dealers in a secondary market; some investors regard them as substitutes for commercial paper and U.S. Treasury bills. In early 1996, some $20 billion of banker's acceptances were outstanding in the United States.

---

[8]In the conventional language of finance, "paper" refers to marketable short-term claims issued by various entities in the private sector.

**Negotiable
Certificates
of Deposit**

A **certificate of deposit (CD)** is a receipt issued by a commercial bank for the deposit of funds. The receipt stipulates that the bearer will receive annual interest payments of a specified magnitude, plus, at maturity, a lump sum equal to the original principal. Banks do not ordinarily redeem such certificates prior to maturity. However, beginning in the early 1960s, a secondary market was established in which CDs in denominations of $100,000 or more could be traded prior to maturity. Because these CDs are "negotiable," that is, tradeable, they are called **negotiable CDs.**

Banks issue negotiable CDs to attract additional funds to make additional loans or to counteract the restrictive effect of deposit withdrawals.[9] The volume of negotiable CDs outstanding is volatile and tends to expand significantly when credit demand escalates and the Federal Reserve adopts restrictive policies. Negotiable CDs are held by lenders with a need for temporary investment outlets for large amounts of funds, typically $1 million or more. Thus, the primary buyers of negotiable CDs are corporations, money market mutual funds, government institutions, charitable organizations, and foreign buyers. Over the past 20 years, the volume of negotiable CDs outstanding has varied from $150 billion to $550 billion.

**Federal
Funds**

Federal funds are unsecured, usually overnight loans by depository institutions of deposits at the Federal Reserve Banks. Banks and thrift institutions are required to maintain a certain portion of their deposit liabilities in the form of either cash or deposits at a Federal Reserve Bank. Depository institutions which fail to meet the requirements are penalized. On the other hand, banks which keep excess funds on deposit at the Federal Reserve penalize themselves, because deposits at the Fed do not earn interest.

A very active market in federal funds developed after World War II. In this market, banks, generally large ones, trade their deposit balances at the Federal Reserve. Banks whose reserves are insufficient to meet the Fed's requirements borrow or "buy" federal funds; banks which have more than enough reserves to meet requirements lend or "sell" federal funds.[10] It should be noted that federal funds are traded through the Fed's wire system, generally for only one day or a weekend. The minimum unit is $1 million. The interest rate involved—the federal funds rate—is a highly sensitive and widely quoted money market yield.

**Repurchase
Agreements**

A **repurchase agreement (RP)** is a short-term loan (often overnight) from a corporation, state or local government, or other large entity that has idle funds to a commercial bank, securities dealer, or other financial institution. The borrower provides collateral in the form of U.S. government securities, making the loan free of default risk. In the most common

---

[9]The impetus for the establishment of negotiable CDs by Citibank in 1961 was an increase in money market interest rates, which, in conjunction with the statutory interest rate ceilings on regular CDs and other time deposits, caused some corporations to withdraw funds from banks in order to purchase high-yielding commercial paper, Treasury bills, and other money market instruments. Banks began issuing negotiable CDs, which were not subject to statutory interest rate ceilings, in an effort to halt the withdrawal of deposits.

[10]Large commercial banks operate in the federal funds market to profit from yield differentials. For example, when the federal funds rate is below the Treasury bill yield, a large commercial bank has an incentive to borrow federal funds and use the proceeds to buy Treasury bills. This sort of arbitrage activity contributes to the high correlation among yields of various money market instruments.

case, a large corporation with $100 million or more that will not be needed for a few days "buys" a large block of government securities from a major bank.[11] The bank agrees to "repurchase" the securities on the date the corporation needs the funds (often the next day), at a price sufficiently above the price the company paid for the securities to provide a rate of return about one-quarter of 1 percent below the current federal funds rate. Thus, rather than holding large checking account balances, which earn no interest, the corporation makes a safe, convenient investment at a competitive yield.

Banks, dealers, and others who borrow in this market find it a useful source of funds. Because aggressive management of cash positions by corporations, state and local governments, and other large organizations has become widespread, the RP market has grown dramatically in the past 25 years. The amount of RPs outstanding reached $200 billion in 1996.

Eurodollars   The term **Eurodollar** refers to deposits (generally time deposits) in foreign banks or U.S. bank branches located in foreign countries but denominated in U.S. dollars rather than in local currencies, such as francs or deutsche marks. Eurodollars developed after World War II, when the dollar became widely accepted in international markets. To the extent that dollars are accepted abroad, merchants and others can avoid costly foreign exchange transactions by maintaining Eurodollar deposits for use in foreign transactions. Eurodollars are considered a money market instrument because U.S. banks in need of funds may borrow Eurodollars from foreign banks or branches of U.S. banks located in foreign cities. Likewise, U.S. firms seeking an investment outlet may lend in this market when rates payable on Eurodollars are relatively attractive.

In the late 1960s, U.S. banks began turning to the Eurodollar market for funds when they had difficulty obtaining funds through traditional channels. This phenomenon was stimulated by the legal interest rate ceilings on various time deposits (including CDs) in the United States, which were later abolished. The amount of Eurodollars outstanding reached $100 billion in early 1996.

Instruments of the Capital Market

The main capital market instruments include common stocks, corporate bonds, state and local government bonds, U.S. government notes and bonds, and mortgages.

Stocks   **Common stocks** are ownership claims on a firm's real capital assets. Unlike debt instruments, stocks have no maturity date. They are outstanding for as long as the corporation is in business. For this reason, the existence of well-developed secondary markets in stocks is imperative. Secondary markets provide liquidity and enhance the marketability of new issues of stock, thus reducing the real costs of financing to business firms and expanding the possibilities for raising funds. Stocks are traded by brokers in organized stock exchanges and over-the-counter markets. Any corporation having more than 300 stockholders may have its stock traded over the counter. Large corpo-

---

[11]The term "*repurchase agreement*" is a misnomer in the sense that ownership of the securities never actually changes hands. The bank retains ownership and uses the securities as collateral for the loan.

rations that meet certain standards of size and stability may apply to the Securities and Exchange Commission for listing on an organized stock exchange, such as the New York Stock Exchange or the American Stock Exchange.

The preponderant portion of stock transactions is carried out in secondary markets. The annual magnitude of new issues of stock (approximately $50 billion per year during 1990 to 1995) is typically less than 1 percent of the existing supply of stock (more than $9 trillion in 1996). The annual volume of new issues varies considerably with economic and financial conditions. When stock prices are depressed, firms shy away from issuing new stock and may in fact buy up some of the existing shares. As stock prices rise, raising funds through new issues becomes more attractive to firms. The increasing valuation of real capital assets, reflected by rising share prices, may also induce firms to expand investment expenditures. (For this reason, a healthy stock market is an important ingredient in capital formation and economic growth.)

Corporate Bonds

Corporate bonds are debt claims against a corporation's assets, claims which may or may not be secured by mortgages and other assets. Unsecured corporate bonds, or *debentures,* are generally issued only by firms of high credit rating. Each year, new corporate bond issues exceed new stock issues substantially, in spite of the fact that the total value of corporate bonds outstanding is less than one-third the value of stocks. This puzzle is explained by the rollover factor in bonds and the fact that many bonds are called in (bought back) by the issuer prior to maturity. As previously indicated, corporate stocks are perpetual issues.

The behavior of the bond market is very important to firms' financing decisions. A corporation contemplating investment in new plant and equipment may consider several alternatives, including issuing equities or bonds, borrowing from banks, or deferring the project. Because profit-maximizing firms undertake only those investment projects whose expected returns exceed the cost of borrowing—that is, the interest rate—the bond yield is a major consideration. Hence, when bond yields are high, many investment projects are postponed.

Corporate bonds generally have original maturities of 10 to 30 years and are traded over the counter in a market which is "thin" compared to the major stock exchanges and the U.S. government securities market. Many corporate bonds have call features, inserted for the benefit of the issuing corporation. Some are convertible into common stock, a feature which "sweetens" the bond for potential buyers, allowing the corporation to borrow at a lower interest rate. Buyers of corporate bonds are primarily institutions that do not require highly liquid financial assets. These buyers include life insurance companies, private pension funds, state and local government retirement funds, and nonprofit organizations.

Municipal Bonds

Like corporations, state and local governments and other political subdivisions must finance capital investment projects, such as schools, bridges, sewage plants, airports, subways, and so forth. Roughly two-thirds of these capital expenditures are financed by issuing **municipal bonds.**[12] In 1996, some $1.3 trillion of municipal bonds was outstanding, including more than 1 million different bonds issued by 90,000 political

---

[12]Municipal bonds include bonds issued not only by local governments and municipalities but also by states and various political subdivisions, such as school and water districts.

subdivisions in the United States. New issues of municipal bonds are generally purchased by investment bankers and resold to commercial banks, property and casualty insurance firms, and high-income individuals. The market in municipal bonds is thin because of the limited number of participants. The number of dealers handling a given issue is also quite limited, and many hold small inventories.

Years ago, a ruling was made that interest on municipal bonds would not be taxable by the Internal Revenue Service. As a result of this tax-free interest status, municipal bond yields tend to be slightly lower than U.S. government bond yields and considerably lower than yields on high-grade corporate bonds. Consequently, only investors in high tax brackets prefer to purchase municipal bonds. Commercial banks, typically in the 34 percent corporate income tax bracket, have traditionally been important buyers.

U.S. Government Notes and Bonds

The nature of U.S. government notes and bonds was discussed in detail earlier in this chapter. U.S. Treasury notes and bonds are popular instruments because of their absence of default risk and the efficient, well-organized market in which they are traded. Major purchasers include individuals, life insurance companies, private pension funds, and state and local government retirement funds.

Mortgages

A **mortgage** is a long-term loan to finance the purchase of real property, secured by a lien on that property. Traditionally, interest rates have been fixed over the life of the mortgage. Since the 1930s, mortgage payments have been *amortized,* meaning that part of each regular payment covers interest and part contributes to repayment of the principal. At maturity the debt is extinguished, and the property is owned free and clear.

The mortgage market is the largest debt market in the U.S. capital market. As of 1996, some $4.8 trillion in mortgages was outstanding, 60 percent of them for one- to four-family homes. Other mortgages finance business property, apartment buildings, and farms. Savings and loan associations, mutual savings banks, commercial banks, and life insurance companies are the chief mortgage lenders, that is, buyers of mortgages.

Largely because of the belief that home ownership should be accorded a high social priority, the federal government became heavily involved in the mortgage market after World War II. Three government agencies have helped to improve the market in mortgages, with a view toward assisting the market in periods when credit is tight and interest rates are high. The Federal National Mortgage Association (FNMA, or "Fannie Mae"), the Government National Mortgage Association (GNMA, or "Ginnie Mae"), and the Federal Home Loan Mortgage Company (FHLMC, or "Freddie Mac") issue bonds and use the proceeds to provide funds to the mortgage market.

Mortgage-Backed Securities

Because individual mortgages have different risks, maturities, and interest rates, they are neither liquid nor suited to trading on secondary markets. As a result, prior to the 1980s, savings and loan associations (S&Ls), mutual savings banks, and commercial banks held more than 80 percent of the mortgages. However, a new instrument originated and guaranteed by Ginnie Mae in the 1960s, known as the **mortgage-backed security,** has come to dominate the residential mortgage market. In this instrument, the financing and servicing of mortgages are split apart. A commercial bank or S&L packages a group of mortgages into a standard $1 million or $10 million block and sells it to a large investor, typically a pension fund or life insurance company. The bank or S&L continues to collect the payments on the mortgages and passes them on to the owner of the security.

Today, more than two-thirds of mortgages made by banks and S&Ls are packaged and sold as mortgage-backed securities. This revolutionary development has improved the efficiency of the mortgage market, contributing to lower mortgage rates for home-owners.

SUMMARY

Financial markets facilitate the transfer of funds from savers (those with an excess of funds) to spenders who have a shortage of funds. Such funds may be transferred directly from savers to spenders through the purchase by the savers of instruments issued by the spenders (for example, when a saver purchases a newly issued corporate bond or stock). Alternatively, the funds may be transferred from the savers to the spenders indirectly, through financial intermediaries (for example, when a saver deposits funds into a bank or savings and loan association, which uses the funds to issue a mortgage to a new homebuyer). Whether direct or indirect, such transfers benefit both savers and borrowers because they transfer funds from people without investment alternatives to those with such opportunities. In this way, financial institutions and markets increase economic efficiency and enhance living standards. Financial markets may be classified in sev-

eral ways: money and capital markets, debt and equity markets, and primary and secondary markets. The money market is the market in which debt instruments of less than one year maturity are traded, and money market instruments include U.S. Treasury bills, commercial paper, banker's acceptances, negotiable CDs, federal funds, repurchase agreements, and Eurodollars. The capital market is the market in which debt instruments of more than one year maturity and equities (stocks) are traded. Important capital market instruments include corporate stocks and bonds, municipal bonds, U.S. government notes and bonds, mortgages, and mortgage-backed securities. In debt markets, savers *lend* money to spenders by purchasing their IOUs, whereas in equity markets, *ownership* claims are traded. A primary market involves the trading of newly issued securities, while a secondary market involves trading of second-hand (previously issued) securities.

Answers to Your Turn *(p. 55)*

a. *The discount rate is ($1000 − $995)/$1000 × 360/36 = 0.05, or 5 percent.*

b. *The price is $1000 − [$1000(0.062)(80)]/360 = $986.22.*

Answer to Your Turn *(p. 60)*

The current yield is $8/$120.25, or 6.65 percent. The yield to maturity is ($8 − $20.25/24)/$120.25 = 5.95 percent. The yield to maturity is lower than the current yield because the principal will decline from its purchase price of $120.25 to $100 at maturity. A capital loss will accrue.

KEY TERMS

liquidity
default risk
market risk
yield
current yield
yield to maturity
debt instrument
equity
primary market
secondary market
money market
capital market
Treasury bills
Treasury notes
Treasury bonds

debt management
coupon rate
commercial paper
banker's acceptance
certificate of deposit (CD)
negotiable CD
federal funds
repurchase agreement (RP)
Eurodollar
common stock
corporate bond
municipal bond
mortgage
mortgage-backed security

STUDY QUESTIONS

1   Explain the distinction between the direct credit market and financial intermediation.

2   Discuss the relationship between liquidity and risk in a financial instrument; between risk and yield; and between liquidity and yield.

3   Why is a corporate bond less liquid than a U.S. Treasury bill? Why are common stocks less liquid than long-term U.S. government bonds?

4   Explain why U.S. Treasury bills are popular short-term investments for banks and other corporations.

5   "If you buy a 91-day Treasury bill and sell it 30 days later, the odds are better than 20 to 1 that you will sell it for more than you paid for it." Do you agree or disagree? Explain.

6   What is the distinction between the current yield and the yield to maturity of a bond?

7   List and define five instruments of the U.S. money market.

8   Explain why the gap between "ask yield" (right-hand column) and the asked discount rate in Figure 3-3 widens as time to maturity increases. (*Hint:* See footnote 3.)

9   What is the price of a Treasury bill with a discount rate of 8 percent if it matures in 30 days? 90 days? 360 days?

10   Calculate the price of a Treasury bill that matures in 30 days if it has an asked discount rate of 7 percent. How would your answer change if the asked discount rate were 9 percent? Can you explain the difference in price intuitively?

11   Consider your answer to question 10. Your friend Richard "The Brain" tells you that the bid rate on a given Treasury bill is 6 percent and the asked rate is 6.2 percent. Is your friend as bright as his name suggests? Why?

12   A corporate bond that has a coupon rate of 6 percent will mature in 5 years. Its price is currently $115 ($100 face amount).

a   Calculate the current yield on this bond.

b   If this bond is held to maturity, will its holder realize a gain or loss at maturity? How much will that gain or loss be? Divide the gain or loss by the number of years to maturity to calculate the average annual gain or loss.

c   Calculate the yield to maturity on this bond.

13   You are considering the purchase of an IBM coupon bond and want to look up relevant price and yield information. However, your friend Elmo has spilled ketchup on the price quotation. All you can see is that the coupon rate is 6.5 percent and the asked yield is 5.3 percent.

a Will this bond sell at a premium or discount to face value? Explain.

b Will the current yield be higher or lower than 6.5 percent? Explain.

14 Suppose a Texaco coupon bond sells at a discount from face value.

a Will the coupon rate be greater or less than the current yield? Why?

b Will the yield to maturity be greater or less than the current yield? Why?

c How will your answers change if the bond sells for a premium?

15 "Secondary markets simply trade *already existing* securities. The original issuer receives nothing in this process. Therefore, secondary markets play no role in the capital formation process. They are simply a sideshow." Evaluate this statement.

16 Is it a coincidence that the 10 most highly developed countries in the world all have well-developed secondary markets for securities while the 10 poorest do not? Explain your reasoning.

17 Rank the following on the basis of liquidity (most liquid to least liquid):

a Stock in a newly formed biotech company

b IBM stock

c AT&T 20-year bonds

d Commercial paper issued by Motorola

e Money market mutual fund shares

Now rank the same assets by the rate of return required to induce you to purchase each, from highest to lowest. Is your ranking correlated with your ranking for the first part of this question? Explain.

18 Two corporate bonds carry identical yields to maturity. However, their coupon rates differ— one has a coupon rate of 4 percent and the other a coupon rate of 9 percent. Which do you expect to sell for a higher price? Why?

19 What is the function of government-sponsored agencies in the American housing market? Is this government activity justifiable? On what grounds?

SUGGESTIONS FOR ADDITIONAL READING

On the money market and the instruments traded therein, see Timothy Cook and Robert LaRoche (ed.), *Instruments of the Money Market,* 7th ed., Federal Reserve Bank of Richmond, 1993, and Marcia Stigum, *The Money Market,* 3d ed. (Homewood, Ill.: Dow Jones Irwin, 1990). A study of the U.S. government securities market is U.S. Treasury, *Joint Report on the Government Securities Market* (Washington, D.C.: U.S. Government Printing Office, 1992). Also, for a wealth of data on both marketable and nonmarketable U.S. government securities, see *The Treasury Bulletin,* published quarterly by the U.S. Treasury. On the commercial paper market, see Mitchell Post, "Evolution of the Commercial Paper Market since 1980," *Federal Reserve Bulletin,* December 1992, pp. 879–891. A good general source on financial markets is Robert Kolb, *The Financial Institutions and Markets Reader,* 2d ed. (Miami: Kolb Publishing, 1993).

C H A P T E R

4

■ ## Financial Intermediation

The beginning of Chapter 3 included a diagram illustrating the flow of funds from surplus units (savers) to deficit spending units (borrowers). Figure 3-1 indicated that funds may be channeled from surplus units to deficit spending units either directly, via money and capital market instruments, or indirectly, through financial intermediaries. This chapter is devoted to the subject of **financial intermediation,** or the flow of funds from savers to deficit spenders by way of financial intermediaries.

The money and capital market instruments discussed in Chapter 3—U.S. government securities, commercial paper, corporate and municipal bonds, mortgages, and common stocks—are known as **primary claims** because they are issued by the ultimate deficit spending units, chiefly businesses and government. Financial intermediaries—banks, life insurance companies, and mutual funds—issue claims of their own, called **secondary claims,** to attract the funds of individuals and firms. Examples of these claims include savings deposits, life insurance policies, and shares in mutual funds. Financial intermediaries use the funds attracted through these claims to purchase the primary claims issued by deficit spending units.

THE ECONOMIC BASIS FOR FINANCIAL INTERMEDIATION

To understand the economic role of financial intermediaries, try to imagine a world without them. Begin by assuming there are no financial institutions or markets—no banks, stock markets, money market mutual funds, and so forth. Now suppose you have $10,000 cash that you have saved for a rainy day. You would like to earn a return on your money so the principal will grow. Unfortunately, because there are no financial institutions or markets, you are denied the opportunity.

Meanwhile your neighbor Joe, an enterprising recent high school graduate, is embarking on his second year in his lawn care service. Last year he earned $8000 from the business, using only an inexpensive, residential-grade lawn mower and a few other inexpensive tools. If he could get his hands on $10,000 to purchase a commercial-grade 42-inch Snapper mower, he could take on several large projects, earn 20 percent per year on his investment, and boost his income appreciably. Unfortunately, because there are no financial institutions, there is no way Joe can get a loan. He is prevented from moving up the ladder of economic success by the absence of developed financial institutions and markets.

You, Joe, and society at large are penalized by the absence of financial institutions. If you (the surplus unit) could somehow get your funds to Joe (the prospective deficit unit), you and Joe could both benefit. You could split the 20 percent return from his purchase of a state-of-the-art lawn mower. In a world without financial intermediaries, however, that kind of arrangement is risky and unlikely to occur.

Risks and Costs without Intermediation

Joe, learning of your desire to earn interest on your savings, may approach you for a direct loan. He may offer to pay you 10 percent per year on the loan, suggesting that the two of you split the 20 percent return on the lawn mower down the middle. But you may be reluctant to lend the money to Joe because of **asymmetric information,** meaning that Joe has a better understanding of his intentions and the likely risks and returns associated with the lawn-mowing business than you do. Asymmetric information gives rise to two problems that reduce your willingness to lend to Joe: adverse selection and moral hazard.

Adverse Selection and Moral Hazard

Adverse selection is the tendency for those persons with the highest probability of experiencing financial problems to seek out and be granted loans. (Such individuals are more likely to need to borrow and are willing to pay relatively high interest rates to obtain funds.) Not knowing Joe's financial history or personal characteristics, and being aware of the principle of adverse selection, you may be unwilling to make the loan.

The second problem associated with asymmetric information, **moral hazard,** occurs *after* a loan is made. Moral hazard arises because the debt contract allows the borrower to keep any and all returns that exceed the fixed payments called for in the loan agreement. The borrower therefore has an incentive to take on more risk than is consistent with the best interests of the lender, in an attempt to reap a high return. Once you make the loan to Joe, how can you be sure he won't catch the next plane to Las Vegas and roll the dice in an effort to run your $10,000 up to $1 million? Because Joe stands to lose only *your* $10,000 but to gross $1,000,000 from this risky venture, he has an incentive to engage in "immoral" activities (from your perspective) with your money. Because you are not well equipped to monitor Joe's activities after you make the loan to see that he does not take undue risk with your funds, you may not be willing to loan him your hard-earned money.

A major rationale for the existence of financial intermediaries is their superior ability to deal with asymmetric information and the associated problems of adverse selection and moral hazard. Depository institutions such as commercial banks, thrift institutions, and finance companies specialize in assessing the credit risks of potential borrowers. Because they have access to private information, such as the loan applicant's deposit history, income, assets, liabilities, and credit history, and because they are equipped to monitor the borrower's activities, financial institutions are in a better position to make rational loan decisions.

Now consider a world with financial intermediaries. You deposit your funds in a bank or thrift institution or buy commercial paper issued by a finance company, earning 8 percent interest in the process. Joe approaches the bank or the finance company for a loan and is granted one at 12 percent interest. Because Joe earns 20 percent on his new Snapper and pays 12 percent on his loan, he comes out ahead. You earn an 8 percent return on your savings, so you are happy too. (While the 8 percent rate is lower than the 10 percent rate you might have earned directly from Joe, the lower default risk on your loan more than compensates you for your lower rate of return.)

The financial intermediary has facilitated the flow of funds from a surplus unit (you) to a deficit spending unit (Joe), improving economic efficiency in the process. From society's viewpoint, welfare has been enhanced. Capital expenditures have increased (the new mower is purchased), boosting productivity and living standards. A net gain to society accrues from the existence of the intermediary. Viewed in this light, financial intermediaries are not greedy middlemen but are useful organizations that contribute materially to the economic process.

Transactions Costs

Another problem associated with asymmetric information, **transactions costs,** involves the money and time spent carrying out financial transactions. One important element of transactions cost is search cost. In the absence of financial intermediaries, Joe must spend considerable time searching for someone who will lend him $10,000 at a reasonable interest rate. Another type of transactions cost is the time and money you would likely have to spend before deciding to lend to Joe. For example, you might have to spend considerable time evaluating the viability of the lawn mower venture. To protect yourself, you might spend $300 to hire a lawyer to draw up a viable loan contract. By pooling the funds of many savers, financial intermediaries take advantage of economies of scale and permit diversification, as well as specialization and division of labor. For instance, a bank or finance company can use a standard loan contract drawn up by its attorney for use in hundreds of loans. By reducing transactions costs, financial intermediaries benefit both savers and deficit spenders.

The problem of matching individual borrowers' needs with those of lenders cannot be overestimated. Many features of the financial instruments that deficit spending units issue to obtain funds are incompatible with the preferences of surplus units. In other words, borrowers and lenders have different needs. One borrower might need access to $20 million for 25 years to build a new high school. Another might need a 30-year, $80,000 loan to purchase a new home. On the other hand, an individual saver might have $600 to lend for one year. Another (a large firm) might have $80 million to lend out for 60 days. In some instances, brokers, dealers, and investment bankers are able to mesh the needs of borrowers and lenders directly, through money and capital market transactions. But the predominant portion of funds transferred today is channeled through financial intermediaries.

Benefits of Intermediation

Financial intermediation benefits both surplus and deficit spending units. By doing so, the process of intermediation benefits society at large—that is, it increases economic efficiency and raises living standards.

Benefits to Surplus Units

From the point of view of surplus units (savers), financial intermediaries provide certain obvious benefits. By pooling the funds of thousands of individuals, intermediaries can overcome the obstacles that stop savers from purchasing primary claims directly. Some of these obstacles are lack of financial expertise, lack of information, limited access to financial markets, the absence of many financial instruments in small denominations, and regressive transactions costs.[1]

An extremely important consideration for the individual saver is *diversification,* the spreading of risk made possible by the pooling of funds. Financial intermediaries have the funds to acquire the large variety of claims needed to spread risk. While an individual may be unwilling to purchase an individual stock with a 2 percent probability of default, he or she may be quite willing to invest in a mutual fund or pension fund that holds 200 stocks, each having a 2 percent default probability. Likewise, an individual may be unwilling to invest in a single mortgage but quite willing to own a share of a large package of mortgages or a CD in a bank or savings and loan association that holds thousands of similar mortgages.

Benefits to Deficit Units

From the perspective of deficit spenders, financial intermediaries also broaden the range of instruments, denominations, and maturities an institution can issue, which significantly reduces transactions costs. Municipalities and corporations would be greatly inconvenienced if they had to issue bonds in $50 and $100 units in order to attract funds directly from hundreds of thousands of individual savers. If, in the absence of financial intermediaries, they found it impossible to market securities in maturities of more than 5 years, they would also suffer. And imagine the chaotic state of affairs that would exist if each household seeking to take out a mortgage on a new home had to first locate an individual or business that would lend the desired amount at an acceptable interest rate. By reducing transactions costs and dealing more effectively with the problem of asymmetric information, financial intermediaries increase economic efficiency, boost economic activity, and elevate living standards.

We now turn to an analysis of the specific types of financial intermediaries in the United States.

CLASSIFICATION OF FINANCIAL INTERMEDIARIES

Though there are several types of financial intermediaries in the United States, each with unique characteristics, all financial intermediaries have one characteristic in common. All issue secondary claims against themselves to the public in order to purchase the primary

---

[1]Brokerage fees for common stocks are highly regressive, in the sense that such fees may amount to 3 percent or more of the principal for transactions of $5000 or less but only about 0.2 percent for transactions in excess of $10,000,000. Most bonds cannot be purchased in units of less than $1000, and short-term marketable U.S. securities are generally issued in minimum denominations of $10,000. Negotiable CDs and commercial paper come in denominations of $100,000 and $1,000,000, respectively. Viewed from the perspective of the typical American household, many of these denominations are prohibitively large.

Table 4-1

Principal Assets and Liabilities of Financial Intermediaries

Type of Intermediary	Principal Liabilities (Sources of Funds)	Principal Assets (Uses of Funds)
Depository institutions:		
Commercial banks	Deposits	Mortgages, loans, government securities
Savings and loan associations	Deposits	Mortgages, government securities
Mutual savings banks	Deposits	Mortgages, government securities
Credit unions	Deposits	Consumer loans
Contractual savings institutions:		
Life insurance companies	Premiums	Corporate bonds, mortgages
Fire and casualty insurance companies	Premiums	Bonds, stocks, government securities
Private pension funds and government retirement funds	Employee and employer contributions	Corporate stocks and bonds
Investment intermediaries:		
Mutual funds	Shares	Stocks, bonds
Finance companies	Stocks, bonds, commercial paper	Consumer and business loans
Money market mutual funds	Shares	Money market instruments

claims issued by deficit spending units. Financial intermediaries may be classified into three categories: depository institutions, contractual savings institutions, and investment-type intermediaries. Table 4-1 lists the sources of funds (liabilities) of each type of intermediary and the primary uses to which funds are put (that is, the assets of each type of intermediary).

Depository Institutions

In terms of size, depository institutions are still the dominant financial intermediary, although their share of total assets of all intermediaries has declined sharply. Included within the depository institutions category are commercial banks, savings and loan associations, mutual savings banks, and credit unions. The latter three are sometimes lumped together and referred to as "thrift institutions," or "thrifts."

Depository institutions issue checking, savings, and time deposits; they use the funds obtained to make various types of loans and to purchase securities. The deposits issued by these institutions are devoid of market risk, because the principal does not fluctuate in nominal value the way stocks and bonds do. (Your savings account, for example, never declines in nominal value—if you have $1000 in the account now, you will have $1000 plus interest

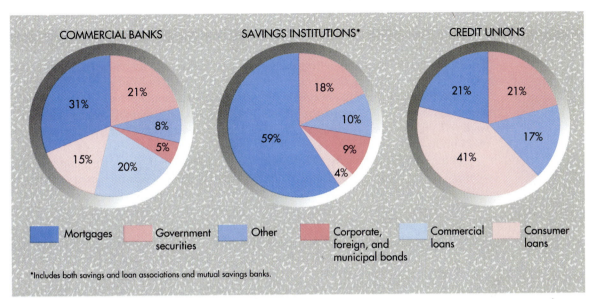

Figure 4-1   Allocation of Funds (Assets) of Depository Institutions, 1995. Depository institutions use their funds principally to make business, consumer, and mortgage loans and to purchase securities. Of the depository institutions, commercial banks are the largest and most diversified.   *Source:* Federal Reserve System, *Flow of Funds Accounts.*

later.) In practice, these deposits may be withdrawn on very short notice, in most instances on demand. As a result of their high liquidity, most deposits issued by these institutions are included in the various measures of the U.S. money supply (see Chapter 2). Figure 4-1 shows the uses to which the funds attracted by depository institutions are put. (You may want to refer back to this figure as we outline the nature of each of the deposit-type intermediaries.)

Commercial Banks

Commercial banks are the largest and most important of all financial intermediaries. Compared to other intermediaries, banks have historically been the most diversified in their activities. Their liabilities are predominantly demand deposits, savings accounts, and time deposits. Their assets are fairly evenly spread among mortgages, government securities, business (commercial) loans, consumer loans, and other items (see Figure 4-1). In recent years, the share of commercial bank assets constituted by mortgages has increased, while the share allocated to consumer and business loans has fallen as bank customers have turned to other sources of funds.

Banks that are members of the Federal Reserve System are governed primarily by that organization; nonmember banks are regulated by the states. However, legislation enacted in 1980 requires nonmember banks to abide by standards set by the Federal Reserve regarding the proportion of demand deposit liabilities that must be held as reserves—that is, as cash and deposits at the Federal Reserve. Because of the important role of commercial banks in the money supply process, this text places special emphasis on the nature and behavior of commercial banks. Chapter 9 is devoted to commercial banking, and Chapter 10 examines the structure of the banking industry and how it is regulated.

Savings and Loan Associations

Originally known as "building-and-loan associations," savings and loan associations (S&Ls) were first formed on the East Coast in the 1830s by groups of people seeking to foster homeownership. The group would pool its savings and make loans to a few members (sometimes selected by lottery) to finance the purchase of a home. Beginning in the 1930s, the federal government contributed to this effort by establishing the Federal Housing Administration (FHA) to insure mortgages and by encouraging the issue of amortized mortgages by S&Ls. In an *amortized* mortgage, part of each monthly payment goes toward reduction of the principal, so that the home is owned free and clear after a period of 25 or 30 years.[2]

In the years immediately after World War II, expansion of homeownership was particularly rapid. Between 1945 and 1965, the total assets of S&Ls increased 20-fold. In 1930, only about one-third of American households were homeowners; today, approximately two-thirds of households own their own home. S&Ls grew with the postwar boom in homeownership.

Traditionally, S&Ls have been highly specialized. They obtain funds by issuing passbook savings accounts or time deposits and use them mostly to grant long-term mortgage loans. Because S&Ls borrow short term to finance long-term mortgages, they are vulnerable in periods in which market forces drive interest rates sharply higher. That scenario occurred in the United States in the late 1970s and early 1980s as a sustained increase in inflation (followed by restrictive monetary actions designed to combat it) produced dramatically higher interest rates. To retain depositors, S&Ls were forced to sharply increase the interest rates paid on their savings accounts. But they were unable to increase the rates they earned on the fixed-rate mortgages still outstanding in their portfolios. They thus suffered major operating losses in the late 1970s and early 1980s, and many became insolvent. A dramatic shakeout of the industry occurred from the 1980s through the early 1990s, and the number of S&Ls, which had stood at more than 6000 in the 1960s, declined to approximately 1900 by early 1996. (These events and issues will be discussed further in Chapters 10 and 11.)

S&Ls may be chartered by the federal government or by the state in which they reside. Most S&Ls are members of the Federal Home Loan Bank System (FHLBS), established in the 1930s. The FHLBS has 12 district banks and is supervised by the Office of Thrift Supervision (OTS), the federal chartering agency for S&Ls. The OTS sets minimum capital requirements and keeps tabs on federally chartered S&Ls.

As a result of the thrift industry crisis of the 1980s, a number of changes in the industry were legislated in 1989. The Federal Home Loan Bank Board (the predecessor of the Office of Thrift Supervision) was abolished and replaced by the OTS. The Federal Savings and Loan Insurance Fund, which was bankrupt, was abolished and replaced with a new insurance agency, the Savings Association Insurance Fund (a branch of the Federal Deposit Insurance Corporation). The Resolution Trust Corporation (RTC) was established for the purpose of administering the closing and merging of insolvent thrift institutions. To avoid paying for S&Ls' losses out of general tax revenues, Congress established the

---

[2]Previous types of mortgages involved periodic payment of interest only. At the end of the loan period, the homeowner had failed to increase his or her equity in the home. Such arrangements made it difficult for most American households ever to own their home free of debt.

Resolution Funding Corporation for the purpose of issuing government-insured bonds to finance the cleanup. The total cost of the S&L bailout was estimated at approximately $140 billion. (Chapter 11 examines the S&L fiasco in more detail.)

Mutual Savings Banks

Mutual savings banks (MSBs) were established in the early nineteenth century for the purpose of encouraging savings by working-class Americans. Like savings and loan associations, these institutions obtain funds by issuing savings accounts and use them primarily to invest in mortgages. Unlike S&Ls, mutual savings banks exist in only 16 of the 50 states; only 3 of those states are west of the Mississippi River. In fact, more than 90 percent of all MSB assets are held in New York, Massachusetts, and the New England states (half are in Massachusetts alone). At one time, the total assets of MSBs were far greater than those of S&Ls. But because MSBs did not join S&Ls in the westward expansion of the U.S. economy, MSB assets today are only about one-fourth those of S&Ls. Approximately 90 percent of the roughly 400 MSBs operating today were established before 1900.

All mutual savings banks are chartered by the 16 states that permit these organizations. The authorities in those states have traditionally imposed stringent limitations on the types of assets MSBs may acquire. Eligible assets include mortgages, U.S. government securities, and high-grade corporate securities. Legislation passed in 1980 allowed MSBs, as well as S&Ls and credit unions, to diversify their asset holdings and required them to abide by reserve requirements set by the Federal Reserve System. The deposits of the majority of MSBs are insured by the FDIC for up to $100,000 per account. Deposits in those institutions not insured by the FDIC are typically insured by state insurance funds.

Credit Unions

Credit unions (CUs)—relatively small, consumer-oriented savings and lending institutions—were first established in the early 1900s to provide loans for working-class people and help them avoid loan sharks. Credit unions are organized by particular groups, such as unions, universities, or members of a particular firm or occupation. They issue time deposits (known as "shares") to members and use the funds to lend to other members. Loans are usually granted for the purpose of home improvements or purchases of durable goods. Credit unions also issue mortgages and have achieved modest diversification by investing about one-fifth of their assets in U.S. government securities. The profits earned by CUs are exempt from federal income taxes, allowing them to offer attractive rates relative to banks and other thrift institutions. Because their assets are predominantly short term, CUs avoided the severe financial problems experienced by S&Ls and MSBs in the 1980s.

Like MSBs, credit unions are "mutuals"—that is, they are owned and run by the members (depositors). CUs generally have low overhead expenses; members sometimes work for the institution without pay, and office time and space are commonly furnished by the employer. Credit unions can be chartered either by the federal government or by the states. The National Credit Union Administration (NCUA) issues federal charters, keeps tabs on credit unions, and sets minimum capital requirements. The deposits of approximately 97 percent of the nation's 13,000 credit unions are insured for up to $100,000 per account by the National Credit Union Share Insurance Fund. Although credit unions tend to be quite small—more than half of CUs currently have less than $20 million each in deposits—they have grown more rapidly than other depository institutions during the past 15 years.

Contractual Savings Institutions

Contractual savings institutions obtain funds under long-term contractual arrangements and invest them predominantly in the capital market—that is, in long-term equity and debt instruments. Included in this category are insurance companies, private pension funds, and state and local government retirement funds. These institutions enjoy relatively stable inflows of funds because of agreements which require regular payments from policyholders and pension fund participants. Because both the inflows and outflows are relatively stable and predictable, liquidity is typically not a high priority in the asset management of these institutions. Figure 4-2 shows the uses of funds (that is, the assets) of four types of contractual savings institutions.

A fundamental source of the growth of contractual intermediaries has been a desire on the part of the public to provide for old age. Increasing life expectancy, rising medical care costs, and the widespread perception that Social Security benefits will be insufficient to cover retirement needs have raised the demand for various types of retirement funds and life insurance policies.

Life Insurance Companies

Life insurance companies issue life insurance policies and invest more than two-thirds of the proceeds in corporate and government bonds and mortgages. On the surface, they might appear to be totally different from depository institutions such as S&Ls and MSBs, but there are similarities. Life insurance premiums constitute a continuing source of funds, as do savings inflows for savings institutions. And the owner of a typical life insurance policy owns a potentially liquid asset with a fixed nominal value, which is legally convertible to cash on demand. That is, most life insurance policies have a specified cash surrender value which increases over time; policyholders can obtain that cash on request.

The fundamental difference between life insurance companies and depository institutions lies in their customers' perception of their products. Policyholders regard their insurance more as a source of protection than as a source of liquidity. Consequently, they tend to view the cash value of their policies as untouchable except in extreme emergency. Such is not the case with savings accounts in depository institutions, which are often raided to purchase a new stereo or finance a family vacation. For this reason, the asset structure of life insurance companies requires less liquidity than that of depository institutions. Life insurance companies, typically regulated by the state insurance commissioner, hold only a tiny portion of their assets in cash and demand deposits. In 1996, there were some 2000 life insurance companies in the United States, with assets totaling $2.1 trillion.

Fire and Casualty Insurance Companies

Fire and casualty insurance companies sell protection against loss resulting from fire, theft, accident, natural disaster, malpractice suits, and other events. Most of the funds are obtained from premiums, although a significant portion is obtained through retained earnings and the issue of new stock. These companies invest heavily in municipal bonds because of the nontaxability of their interest payments (see Figure 4-2). They also invest heavily in corporate stocks and bonds and in U.S. government securities. Because

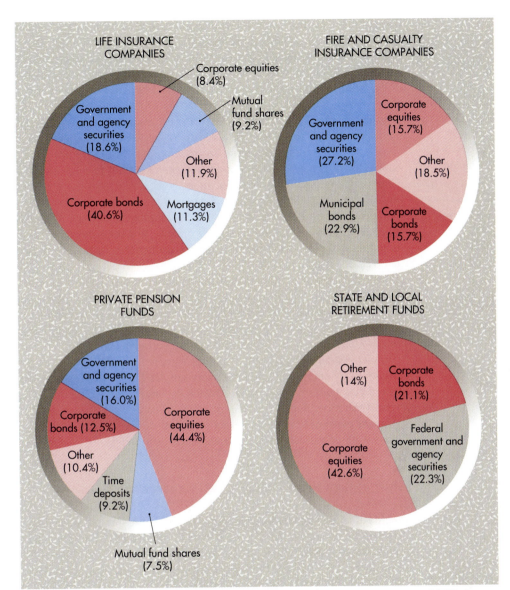

Figure 4-2   Allocation of Funds (Assets) of Contractual Savings Institutions, 1995. Because long-term income growth is a higher priority than liquidity for contractual savings institutions, they invest heavily in stocks and bonds.   *Source:* Federal Reserve System, *Flow of Funds Accounts.*

property losses are more difficult to predict than human deaths and can vary significantly from year to year, these institutions keep a significantly more liquid asset structure than life insurance companies do. In 1996, there were approximately 3900 fire and casualty insurance companies in the United States, with total assets of approximately $750 billion. These companies are regulated by state insurance commissioners.

Private Pension Funds and Government Retirement Funds

The desire to achieve financial security in retirement has led to remarkable growth in various types of retirement funds. Saving for retirement may be accomplished in two ways: through personal saving initiatives and through employer-sponsored pension plans. There are several distinct advantages of saving through employer-provided funds. First, pension funds may be able to manage a portfolio more efficiently than an individual can. They provide diversification, reduced transactions costs, and financial expertise. Second, the tax code encourages employees as well as employers to contribute to pension plans. Income contributed directly to a retirement fund is nontaxable when it is earned—that is, contributions are tax deductible. Instead, it is taxed when it is distributed at retirement.[3]

Today, the great majority of major corporations as well as state and local governments and other organizations offer retirement programs to their employees. Employers deduct the funds from workers' paychecks and send them—sometimes with matching contributions—to a pension fund or retirement fund. The funds invest the contributions in corporate stocks and bonds and U.S. government bonds, and the employee receives a contract guaranteeing a regular monthly income at retirement. Because the monthly contributions by employees and employers substantially exceed the monthly benefits paid out to retirees, pension funds have a relatively large and stable pool of funds to invest each year. With more than $4 trillion in assets in early 1996, private and state and local government pension funds held nearly one-third of the value of publicly traded equities and one-fourth of the value of corporate bonds outstanding.

Investment-Type Financial Intermediaries

Included among investment-type intermediaries are mutual funds, finance companies, and money market mutual funds. The benefits provided by these investment intermediaries include lower transactions costs (obtained by buying in large blocks); the financial expertise supplied by mutual fund management; and increased diversification relative to that feasible for an individual. In recent years, the growth of investment-type intermediaries has been explosive.

---

[3]A major advantage of saving through private pension funds and government retirement funds is that income that accrues (contributions and earnings therefrom) is nontaxable by federal and state governments. That is, income which would be taxed as earned if put into a personal saving program is permitted to compound tax free in private pension plans and government retirement programs. In addition, an employer's matching contribution is tax deductible to the employer. Hence, the tax code not only provides terrific incentives to save through pension programs, it also provides incentives for employers to expand retirement benefits in lieu of giving wage and salary increases.

Mutual Funds

Mutual funds pool the funds of many individuals in order to purchase a diversified portfolio of stocks and/or bonds. One may choose from mutual funds with various objectives, such as long-term growth of capital or high current income. Particular mutual funds may emphasize technology, natural resource, utility, or emerging growth stocks. Others specialize in international stocks, including stocks of firms in China, Brazil, Latin America, Europe, and the former Soviet bloc nations.

There are two broad categories of mutual funds specializing in common stocks: *open-end funds* and *closed-end funds.* An open-end fund has the right to issue additional shares at its discretion. In buying an open-end fund, one purchases a pro rata share of a portfolio. Shares can be redeemed at any time at their net asset value—the value of the shareholder's portion of the portfolio. A closed-end fund is closed in the sense that it cannot issue additional shares and the owner cannot redeem the shares at their market value from the fund itself. Instead, the shares are traded like common stock on a secondary market (over the counter or through one of the stock exchanges).

Open-end funds may be further classified as *no-load* or *load* funds. A no-load fund imposes no up-front charge, although such funds typically charge an annual fee in the amount of 0.5 to 1 percent of total assets. A load fund charges a fairly stiff fee up front—typically 4 to 8 percent of the total value of the transaction. No annual fee is charged thereafter.

Mutual funds were quite popular in the 1950s and 1960s. They fell on hard times in the prolonged bear market of the 1970s and early 1980s, though funds specializing in debt instruments such as corporate bonds expanded sharply in the 1970s. Tax-exempt bond funds emerged after 1976, when Congress passed legislation making income earned from such funds nontaxable by the Internal Revenue Service. Mutual funds have experienced a terrific increase in popularity in the past 15 years. Both the number and total value of mutual fund shares have escalated dramatically in the booming stock market of the 1990s. Figure 4-3 indicates the growth in the number of mutual funds as well as their total assets, together with the allocation of those assets between stocks and bonds.

Mutual funds are regulated by the *Securities and Exchange Commission* (SEC) in Washington, D.C. The SEC enforces reporting and disclosure regulations for mutual funds and guards investors against fraudulent practices by mutual fund managers.

Finance Companies

Finance companies obtain funds by issuing commercial paper or stocks or by borrowing from banks. They use the funds to make small loans to individuals and businesses. They also gather and monitor information that allows them to estimate potential borrowers' default risk. Because customers of finance companies tend to have higher default risks than do borrowers from banks, finance companies typically charge higher interest rates than banks do. Unlike commercial banks, finance companies obtain funds in large blocks and lend in small amounts. The growth of the commercial paper market has given finance companies an advantage over commercial banks. As a result, finance companies have maintained their share of the intermediation market, while the commercial banks' share has declined significantly. Because finance companies do not issue deposits, regulatory authorities have imposed few regulations on them beyond

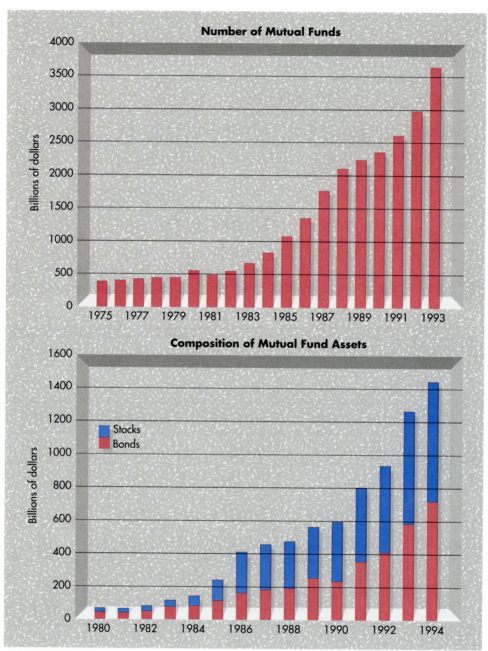

Figure 4-3 The Recent Growth of Mutual Funds. Mutual funds have grown dramatically since the early 1980s, both in number and in total assets. Today, mutual fund assets are divided approximately equally between stocks and bonds.   *Source:* Federal Reserve System, *Flow of Funds Accounts.*

disclosure requirements and efforts to prevent fraud. The asset structure of finance companies is basically unregulated.

Finance companies may be divided into three categories. *Sales finance companies,* which are usually associated with a large corporation, exist to finance the sale of the corporation's products. For example, General Motors Acceptance Corporation conveniently provides auto loans for cars sold by General Motors. *Consumer finance companies,* such as Household Finance Corporation, make small loans to households for the purpose of financing furniture, household appliances, and home improvements. *Business finance companies* make loans to small businesses, often by purchasing their accounts receivable at a discount from face value. These companies are also active in purchasing expensive equipment (such as airplanes) and leasing it to businesses. The total assets of all finance companies stood at approximately $850 billion in early 1996.

Money Market Mutual Funds

Money market mutual funds (MMMFs) are relatively new institutions that blossomed during the period of escalating interest rates in the late 1970s (see Exhibit 4-1). These funds issue "shares," which are actually interest-bearing deposits. The yield payable on MMMF shares changes daily in response to market forces.[4] Customers may write checks on their deposits, although MMMFs typically require that checks be in amounts of at least $250 or $500. A minimum deposit of anywhere from $1000 to $20,000 is usually required to open an account.

MMMFs pool the funds of thousands of depositors and purchase large blocks of liquid money market instruments, such as commercial paper, U.S. Treasury bills, repurchase agreements, and negotiable CDs. Unlike deposits in banks and thrift institutions, MMMF shares are not insured. However, they are relatively safe because MMMFs invest in instruments of very low default risk. Some MMMFs invest entirely in U.S. Treasury bills, making them virtually free of default risk.

While we have listed MMMFs among investment-type intermediaries, they clearly have some of the characteristics of depository institutions. Indeed, MMMF shares outstanding are included in M2 and M3, the broader measures of the U.S. money supply. In early 1996 there were more than 650 taxable MMMFs in the United States, along with approximately 250 tax-exempt MMMFs, which purchase short-term municipal bonds. The total assets of MMMFs in early 1996 were approximately $750 billion, with more than 80 percent being held by taxable MMMFs. Figure 4-4 shows the allocation of money market mutual fund assets at the time. Yields currently payable by each of the approximately 900 MMMFs, along with total assets and average maturity of assets of each MMMF, are published regularly in major newspapers such as *The Wall Street Journal.*

---

[4]Because the prices of securities fluctuate with interest rates, the value of an MMMF's portfolio also fluctuates with interest rates. For example, an increase in interest rates reduces Treasury bill prices. However, because the securities held by MMMFs are of short-term maturity, such price fluctuations are modest. The Securities and Exchange Commission permits MMMFs to redeem shares at a fixed value ($1 dollar per share) if the average maturity of the fund portfolio is less than 90 days. Price fluctuations are incorporated into the daily yields rather than the principal. Hence, if you invest $10,000 by purchasing 10,000 shares in a MMMF, you can withdraw the full $10,000 (plus accumulated interest) via check at any time.

EXHIBIT 4-1

A Brief History of Money Market Mutual Funds

The development of money market mutual funds (MMMFs) in the 1970s is an excellent example of how market incentives produce financial innovations. Before the 1980s, banks and thrift institutions were governed by statutory interest rate ceilings which limited the interest rates they were allowed to pay depositors on savings and time deposits. In addition, banks are subject to reserve requirements which require them to hold a portion of their deposit liabilities in the form of cash and non-interest-bearing deposits at the Federal Reserve. These two regulations led to the emergence of MMMFs.

The first MMMF was established in 1971 as an alternative to bank deposits. Total shares outstanding were quite limited for several years, because market interest rates generally stayed below the ceiling interest rates payable by depository institutions. But in the late 1970s, in response to years of escalating inflation, yields on such money market instruments as Treasury bills and commercial paper moved above 10 percent. That was far above the 5.5 percent ceiling imposed on savings and time deposits in banks and thrift institutions. As depository institution customers pulled funds from savings and time deposits to invest in high-yielding money market mutual funds, the total assets of MMMFs ballooned from less than $4 billion in 1977 to more than $230 billion by November 1982. By 1982, the explosive growth in MMMFs placed them far above stock and bond mutual funds in total assets.

The first reaction of depository institutions was to lobby Congress to put reserve requirements and other restrictions on MMMFs. But because MMMFs had become so popular with the public, that proposal proved politically unpopular. Instead, Congress granted depository institutions the authority to issue a new instrument, the *money market deposit account* (MMDA). Similar to MMMF shares, MMDAs offer limited check-writing privileges and are not subject to reserve requirements. The new instrument enabled banks to stem the flow of funds into MMMFs temporarily, as indicated by the contraction in MMMF assets in 1984, as shown in the accompanying figure. But MMMFs remained a viable and permanent player in U.S. financial markets. Today, MMMF shares account for over 4 percent of the total assets of all financial intermediaries and over one-fourth of the total assets of all mutual funds combined (stock funds, bond funds, and MMMFs).

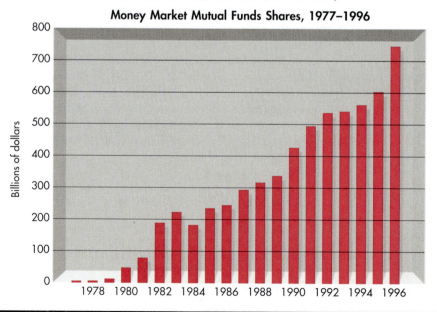

Money Market Mutual Funds Shares, 1977–1996

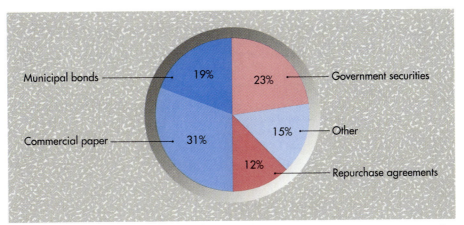

Figure 4-4   Allocation of Money Market Mutual Fund Assets, 1996. Money market mutual funds invest in highly liquid short-term assets such as commercial paper, U.S. Treasury bills, and short-term municipal bonds.   *Source:* Federal Reserve System, *Flow of Funds Accounts.*

We conclude this chapter by analyzing the consequences of several important changes that have taken place in the financial intermediation process in recent decades.

THE CHANGING NATURE OF FINANCIAL INTERMEDIATION

After the Great Depression of the 1930s, Congress implemented a host of measures to promote a highly specialized financial system. Those measures locked financial intermediaries into specific activities, protected them from economic hardship, and generally reduced competition both within and among industries. Banks were set up to take in deposits and issue short-term loans. Interest ceilings and legal restrictions on creating branches reduced the scope of competition. Thrift institutions were prohibited from making business or consumer loans and were forced to specialize in long-term fixed-rate mortgages. Life insurance companies were to issue policies and purchase corporate bonds; they were forbidden to hold significant amounts of corporate stock. In 1933, the Glass-Steagall Act separated commercial banking from investment banking. Commercial banks were forbidden to underwrite corporate stocks and bonds or to hold common stocks in their portfolios. Investment banks were forbidden to accept household deposits or make commercial loans.

For these reasons, financial institutions were traditionally highly specialized. Families would go to one institution to get a mortgage, another to establish a checking account, another to obtain brokerage services, and yet another to get a car loan. In the 1950s, the typical family held a savings account in a bank or thrift institution and a life insurance policy that contained saving provisions (that is, a whole life policy). Only 15 percent of the labor force was covered by a private pension plan. Only well-to-do families held stocks and bonds.

Table 4-2

Share of Total Assets of all Financial Intermediaries, 1960–1995 (in percent)

	1960	1980	1995
Depository institutions:			
Commercial banks	38.6%	36.7%	28.8%
S&Ls and mutual savings banks	19.0	19.6	7.0
Credit unions	1.1	1.6	2.0
	58.7	57.9	37.8
Contractual savings institutions:			
Life insurance companies	19.6	11.5	13.1
Property and casualty insurance companies	4.4	4.5	4.6
Private pension funds	6.4	12.5	16.3
State and local government retirement funds	3.3	4.9	8.1
	33.7	33.4	42.1
Investment intermediaries:			
Mutual funds	2.9	1.7	10.8
Finance companies	4.7	5.1	5.1
Money market mutual funds	0.0	1.9	4.2
	7.6	8.7	20.1
Total	100	100	100

Source: Federal Reserve System, *Flow of Funds Accounts.*

Since then, financial innovations, changing regulations, and changing preferences on the part of the public have produced major changes in the nature of financial intermediation. Table 4-2 summarizes the structural changes in the share of total assets held by each type of intermediary over the past 3 or 4 decades.

Especially prominent are the sharp decline in the relative importance of depository institutions in the intermediation process and the corresponding increase in the relative importance of both contractual savings institutions and investment intermediaries. Specifically, the asset shares of commercial banks and savings institutions have declined, while the asset shares of retirement and pension funds and of mutual funds have increased sharply. The life insurance share of total assets, which declined sharply from 1960–1980, has stabilized and rebounded slightly since 1980. In the next two sections, we examine these changes in detail.

The Emergence of Retirement Funds and Mutual Funds

Most noteworthy in Table 4-2 is the rapid growth of private pension funds, state and local government retirement funds, mutual funds, and money market mutual funds. Altogether, the share of total financial intermediary assets contributed by these four types of institutions increased from less than 13 percent in 1960 to more than 39 percent in 1995. In recent years, these institutions have dramatically stepped up competition for household savings, a phenomenon that has reduced the profitability of some types of financial intermediaries and increased the profitability of others. Their phenomenal growth has forced many financial institutions to adapt and engage in new activities in order to survive.

Private pension plans, state and local government retirement plans, and mutual funds have dramatically altered the allocation of household savings. In the early 1950s, households held only 6 percent of their financial assets in pension funds and only 1 percent in mutual funds. By 1995, those figures stood at 31 percent and 10 percent, respectively.

The same period saw a major shift of household assets away from direct ownership of stocks, life insurance, and savings deposits and toward indirect ownership of stocks and bonds through mutual funds and pension funds. In the period 1952–1995, the portion of household financial assets made up of direct holdings of equities declined from 32 percent to 21 percent and the life insurance portion declined from 12 percent to 3 percent. Households also reduced their relative holdings of bonds and savings deposits in this period.

Ironically, life insurance companies have benefitted from the increased role of private pension programs. As the growth of demand for life insurance policies began to be crowded out by the increasing role of pension and mutual funds, life insurance companies adapted by moving heavily into management of pension fund assets.

The dramatic increase in the relative importance of pension funds and mutual funds has hurt commercial banks, thrift institutions, and investment banks. And the declining role of individuals in the stock market (individuals held 91 percent of corporate stocks in 1952 and only 50 percent in 1995) has hurt brokerage houses that traditionally catered to individual investors. Wholesale brokerage houses have been less affected by this development. In the next section we will examine the effects of these changing events on commercial banks and thrifts.

The Decline of Commercial Banks and Thrifts

The phenomenal growth of pension and mutual funds has adversely affected commercial banks and thrifts in several ways. The emergence of money market mutual funds has squeezed bank profitability by raising the costs of and reducing the returns on bank funds. First, the added competition for depositors has forced banks to increase the interest rates paid on deposits to prevent an exodus of funds. And the growth of MMMFs has given a big boost to the commercial paper market (note in Figure 4-4 that MMMFs hold more commercial paper than any other asset). By providing a major outlet for commercial paper, MMMFs have encouraged large corporations to issue this paper instead of borrowing from banks. Furthermore, small businesses increasingly borrow from finance companies, which in turn issue commercial paper to obtain loanable funds. In short, the rise of the commercial paper market has reduced business demand for bank loans, thereby lowering the rate of return banks are able to earn on assets.

The emergence of mutual funds, private pension funds, and state and local government retirement funds also created a large demand for high-yielding mortgage-backed securities (see discussion at end of Chapter 3). And the successful marketing of securitized mortgages in the 1970s led to the securitization of consumer loans in the mid-1980s. In other words, loans made by banks and finance companies were securitized and sold off in large blocks. This confluence of events put downward pressure on bank profits in the 1980s and early 1990s, although they have recovered strongly since then.

Squeezed by higher costs of funds, lower returns, and declining market share, banks have been forced to turn to new endeavors. They have placed an increasing share of their funds into mortgages and have moved into underwriting and distributing securities, sponsoring mutual funds, and selling insurance products. For a time, thrift institutions were given the authority to expand into consumer and business loans, but the large losses they suffered in the late 1980s led to new restrictions and a renewed emphasis on mortgage lending. In part because of recent financial problems in the thrift and banking industries, Congress has hesitated to expand the range of permissible bank activities. For example, Congress has refused to repeal the Glass-Steagall Act.

Benefits and Costs of Institutional Change

The remarkable growth in the role of pension funds and mutual funds in the intermediation process must be regarded, on balance, as a positive development. It has simultaneously stimulated the range of investment outlets for individuals and firms and expanded the range of alternatives open to deficit spenders. Hence, it has enhanced the efficiency of financial intermediation.

However, the growth of pension and mutual funds created transitional costs in the form of increased financial instability, experienced in the late 1980s and early 1990s. The increased competition reduced the profitability of banks and thrifts, increasing their exposure to adverse shocks such as the collapse of oil prices in the mid-1980s. But though many banks and thrifts failed in the late 1980s and early 1990s, depository institutions' earnings and balance sheets have strengthened dramatically since the recession of 1990–1991. Today these institutions are relatively healthy, and bank failures are running at 20-year lows.

Though the financial system established in the early post-Depression era was designed to stabilize financial intermediaries, it inhibited competition and prevented household funds from flowing to the most profitable investment areas. Ultimately, it raised the economic cost of intermediation. Today, many legal restraints have been removed, and competition from MMMFs, the commercial paper market, and securitization has tied depository institutions' loan rates more closely to money and capital market rates. Household savings flow more readily to the most profitable investment areas, thus improving the efficiency of the intermediation process.

SUMMARY

Financial intermediaries obtain funds by issuing liabilities, and use the funds to make loans and purchase securities. By reducing transactions costs, and overcoming the problems of adverse selection and moral hazard created by informational problems in financial markets, they provide benefits to both savers and borrowers, thereby increasing economic efficiency. Financial intermediaries benefit lenders by providing diversification and financial expertise and by overcoming the problems of regressive transactions costs and lack of information.

They benefit borrowers by reducing transactions costs through broadening the range of instruments, denominations, and maturities that deficit-spenders can issue. There are three types of financial intermediaries: depository institutions such as commercial banks, savings and loan associations, mutual savings banks, and credit unions; contractual savings institutions such as insurance companies, private pension plans, and government retirement programs; and investment-type intermediaries such as stock and bond mutual funds, finance companies, and money market mutual funds. Because of financial innovations and other factors, the relative importance of depository institutions in the intermediation process has declined since 1960, while that of contractual savings institutions and investment-type intermediaries has correspondingly increased.

KEY TERMS

financial intermediation
primary claim
secondary claim
asymmetric information

adverse selection
moral hazard
transactions cost

STUDY QUESTIONS

1 If information between lender and borrower were not asymmetric, would the problem of adverse selection still exist? Could a moral hazard problem still exist? Explain.

2 In a world with no financial markets, why might you be unwilling to lend to your neighbor? Why might you be more willing to lend to your neighbor than to a lawn-mowing enterprise in another city?

3 Explain how the emergence of financial intermediaries reduces the problems of adverse selection and moral hazard. Does it *eliminate* those problems? Could it *create* such problems?

4 Tom Wolfe's *Bonfire of the Vanities* describes financial middlemen as little more than butlers who follow the money around and pick up the crumbs, borrowing at 3 percent and lending at 5 percent. Is that unflattering description accurate, or do financial intermediaries serve an important purpose in society?

5 Joe Average has an average life—an average job, an average home, 2.5 kids, a dog, and a Dodge in the garage. He dreams of becoming rich some day and is secretly withholding a portion of his income to invest each month. Describe the difficulties and potential problems Joe will encounter if he tries to invest his funds in the direct credit market. Explain how financial intermediaries can reduce those problems.

6 As a small saver, it probably makes little difference whether you take your money to a commercial bank, an S&L, or a credit union. But as a borrower, the institution you approach may make a big difference. Examine Figure 4-1 and explain the sense in which these depository institutions are different from one another.

7 Explain the fundamental reasons why private pension funds have experienced rapid growth in the past 15 years.

8 Explain why Aetna Crop Insurance Company has a more liquid asset structure than Northwestern Mutual Life Assurance Company.

9 Explain why the tremendous growth of pension funds has actually aided rather than harmed life insurance companies.

10 Framing your discussion in the context of the advantages of transferring funds through intermediaries rather than directly to deficit spending units, discuss the factors that have contributed to

the rapid growth of stock mutual funds over the last 10 years. What are some of the implications of this rapid growth?

11 Explain the circumstances that triggered the dramatic growth of money market mutual funds in the late 1970s and early 1980s.

12 From your personal vantage point as a lender of funds, what are the advantages of placing your funds in a money market mutual fund instead of a bank? The disadvantages?

13 "Because they are not subject to reserve requirements, money market mutual funds have been granted an unfair advantage over banks." Do you agree or disagree? Explain.

14 Could money market mutual funds be categorized as depository institutions rather than as investment intermediaries? Explain your reasoning.

15 Explain the effects of financial intermediation on market efficiency and overall social welfare.

SUGGESTIONS FOR ADDITIONAL READING

For more in-depth treatments of the various financial intermediaries, see George G. Kaufman, *The U.S. Financial Systems: Money, Markets, and Institutions* (New York: Prentice Hall, 1995), 6th ed. For an analysis of the evolution of financial institutions, see Benjamin Friedman, "Postwar Changes in American Financial Markets," in Martin Feldstein, ed., *The American Economy in Transition* (Chicago: Univ. of Chicago Press, 1980). An excellent source on recent changes in financial intermediaries and their implications is Fed-eral Reserve Bank of Kansas City, *Changing Capital Markets: Implications for Monetary Policy,* 1993 (see particularly the lead article by Franklin Edwards and the comments of the symposium participants). A lucid analysis of the causes and consequences of the increasing role of pension and mutual funds in the intermediation process is Gordon Sellon, "Changes in Financial Intermediation: The Role of Pension and Mutual Funds," Federal Reserve Bank of Kansas City *Economic Review,* 3d quarter, 1992, pp. 53–70.

C H A P T E R

5

The Behavior of
Interest Rates

In Chapters 3 and 4, we outlined the instruments and markets involved in the transfer of funds from surplus units (lenders) to deficit spending units (borrowers). We also looked at the role of financial intermediaries in the U.S. economy. In this chapter and the two to follow, we analyze the forces that determine the level and structure of interest rates in financial markets.

Interest rates rank among the most crucial of variables in macroeconomics as well as in the practical world of finance. Changes in interest rates have important implications for a multitude of phenomena, including the level of investment spending, consumer expenditures on durable goods, the redistribution of wealth between borrowers and lenders (debtors and creditors), and the prices of such key financial assets as stocks, bonds, and foreign currencies.

An interest rate may be thought of as the price of borrowing or renting the use of funds. Alternatively, it may be regarded as the price or cost of credit. There are many different interest rates—for example, those on mortgages, U.S. Treasury bills, commercial paper, bank certificates of deposit, and bonds issued by corporations, municipalities, and the U.S. government. If investors regarded all these instruments as perfect substitutes for one another, the interest rate, or yield, would be the same for each one. Clearly that is not the case. The multitude of yields existing at any given time is accounted for by differences in default risk, tax considerations, marketability and liquidity, and length of time to maturity among various instruments.

For purposes of analysis, we often speak of "the" interest rate. We take the behavior of the yield on a hypothetical debt instrument devoid of both market risk and default risk as being representative of interest rates in general. In the United States, the U.S. Treasury bill most closely approximates this ideal. Various other debt instruments are less liquid and marketable and involve greater default risk than Treasury bills. Yields on these other securities typically move in tandem with the Treasury bill yield, differing from it by a margin sufficient to compensate lenders for greater default risk and inferior liquidity.

In this chapter, we begin by discussing the importance of the interest rate in determining the present value (and price) of a financial asset such as a bond or a U.S. Treasury bill. We will then employ a simple analytical framework to explain the behavior of

"the" interest rate. We will use this framework to analyze the effects of expected inflation, Federal Reserve policy, the business cycle, and federal budget deficits on interest
rates. Then we will sketch the causes of major swings in U.S. interest rates over the past
45 years. In Chapter 6 we discuss the measurement of inflation expectations and analyze
the behavior of *real,* or inflation-adjusted, interest rates. Chapter 7 explores the effect of
term to maturity on the level of interest rates, a concept known as the term structure of
interest rates.

PRESENT VALUE, INTEREST RATES, AND SECURITY PRICES

We now present a general framework for understanding how financial markets place a
specific price on any financial or real asset that is expected to yield a flow of income in
the future. This framework helps one understand intuitively why bonds, Treasury bills,
stocks, and other financial assets fluctuate in price.

The Concept of Present Value

Consider the present value formula, expressed in Equation 5-1.

$$(5\text{-}1) \qquad \textbf{PV (or price)} = \frac{R_1}{1+i} + \frac{R_2}{(1+i)^2} + \frac{R_3}{(1+i)^3} + \cdots + \frac{R_n}{(1+i)^n}$$

In the equation, PV represents the present value (or price) of the asset; $R_1, R_2, \dots, R_n$
indicate the annual returns currently expected from the asset in years 1, 2, ... , n; i
represents the interest rate used to discount these expected future returns (discussed
shortly).

Every financial asset holds the promise of yielding a stream of returns in future years
$(R_1, R_2 \dots, R_n)$. For some securities the promise may involve only one return, to be received in one year (R_1), or perhaps in 30 years (R_{30}). An example of the former is a one-
year U.S. Treasury bill. An example of the latter is a 30-year *zero-coupon bond*—that is,
a bond that makes no annual payments, but merely agrees to return a specific principal
(say $1000) at maturity in 30 years. Most corporate, municipal, and U.S. government
bonds promise a finite series of returns, involving constant annual or semiannual payments for 10, 20, or 30 years.

Because bonds and other debt-instruments involve payments to be made in the *future,* the face amount of these payments must be discounted if we are to properly evaluate their **present value**—that is, the value *today* of payments to be received in the future. An instrument calling for a one-time payment of $1000 in one year is worth less
than $1000, since an individual with $1000 today could place the funds in a savings
account (or other interest-bearing asset) and come out with more than $1000 in one
year.

Money Rates

Each day, *The Wall Street Journal* publishes a column entitled "Money Rates," which reports the current interest rates, or yields, on a large number of debt instruments. Included are the prime rate, the federal funds rate, and the rates on commercial paper, certificates of deposit, Treasury bills, banker's acceptances, and money market mutual fund shares (the Merrill Lynch Ready Assets Trust). A quick glance at this column gives the interested reader an overview of the yields currently available to potential lenders. The following column shows the yields available on May 23, 1996.

MONEY RATES

Thursday, May 23, 1996

The key U.S. and foreign annual interest rates below are a guide to general levels but don't always represent actual transactions.

PRIME RATE: 8.25%. The base rate on corporate loans posted by at least 75% of the nation's 30 largest banks.

DISCOUNT RATE: 5%. The charge on loans to depository institutions by the Federal Reserve Banks.

FEDERAL FUNDS: 5 5/16% high, 5 1/8% low, 5 1/8% near closing bid, 5 3/16% offered. Reserves traded among commercial banks for overnight use in amounts of $1 million or more. Source: Prebon Yamane (U.S.A.) Inc.

CALL MONEY: 7%. The charge on loans to brokers on stock exchange collateral. Source: Dow Jones Telerate Inc.

COMMERCIAL PAPER placed directly by General Electric Capital Corp.: 5.27% 30 to 149 days; 5.29% 150 to 179 days; 5.27% 180 to 239 days; 5.35% 240 to 270 days.

COMMERCIAL PAPER: High-grade unsecured notes sold through dealers by major corporations: 5.37% 30 days; 5.37% 60 days; 5.37% 90 days.

CERTIFICATES OF DEPOSIT: 4.69% one month; 4.72% two months; 4.81% three months; 5.00% six months; 5.23% one year. Average of top rates paid by major New York banks on primary new issues of negotiable C.D.s, usually on amounts of $1 million and more. The minimum unit is $100,000. Typical rates in the secondary market: 5.34% one month; 5.37% three months; 5.49% six months.

BANKERS ACCEPTANCES: 5.25% 30 days; 5.25% 60 days; 5.25% 90 days; 5.27% 120 days; 5.27% 150 days; 5.27% 180 days. Offered rates of negotiable, bank-backed business credit instruments typically financing an import order.

LONDON LATE EURODOLLARS: 5 13/32% - 5 9/32% one month; 5 13/32% - 5 9/32% two months; 5 15/32% - 5 11/32% three months; 5 1/2% - 5 3/8% four months; 5 17/32% - 5 13/32% five months; 5 9/16% - 5 7/16% six months.

LONDON INTERBANK OFFERED RATES (LIBOR): 5 7/16% one month; 5 1/2% three months; 5 19/32% six months; 5 7/8% one year. The average of interbank offered rates for dollar deposits in the London market based on quotations at five major banks. Effective rate for contracts entered into two days from date appearing at top of this column.

FOREIGN PRIME RATES: Canada 6.50%; Germany 3.30%; Japan 1.625%; Switzerland 4.50%; Britain 6.00%. These rate indications aren't directly comparable; lending practices vary widely by location.

TREASURY BILLS: Results of the Monday, May 20, 1996, auction of short-term U.S. government bills, sold at a discount from face value in units of $10,000 to $1 million: 5.03% 13 weeks; 5.11% 26 weeks.

OVERNIGHT REPURCHASE RATE: 5.21%. Dealer financing rate for overnight sale and repurchase of Treasury securities. Source: Dow Jones Telerate Inc.

FEDERAL HOME LOAN MORTGAGE CORP. (Freddie Mac): Posted yields on 30-year mortgage commitments. Delivery within 30 days 8.18%, 60 days 8.23%, standard conventional fixed-rate mortgages; 5.125%, 2% rate capped one-year adjustable rate mortgages. Source: Dow Jones Telerate Inc.

FEDERAL NATIONAL MORTGAGE ASSOCIATION (Fannie Mae): Posted yields on 30 year mortgage commitments (priced at par) for delivery within 30 days 8.11%, 60 days 8.17%, standard conventional fixed-rate mortgages; 6.70%, 6/2 rate capped one-year adjustable rate mortgages. Source: Dow Jones Telerate Inc.

MERRILL LYNCH READY ASSETS TRUST: 4.78%. Annualized average rate of return after expenses for the past 30 days; not a forecast of future returns.

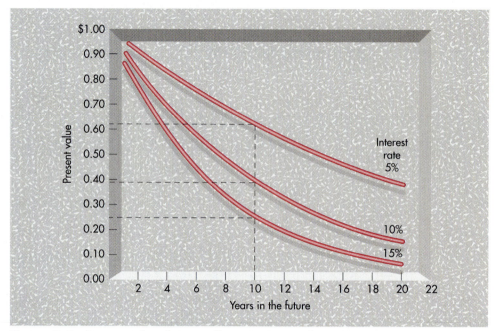

Figure 5-1   Present Value of One Dollar to Be Received in *N* Years. The value today (present value) of the promise of $1 in the future declines as the length of time before the dollar is to be received increases. It also declines as the interest rate rises.

Figure 5-1 shows how the present value of a fixed claim of one dollar payable in the future depends both on the level of the interest rate used to discount the dollar and on the number of years in the future the dollar is to be received. The figure indicates, for example, that the present value of one dollar to be received in 10 years drops from 61 cents to 39 cents to 25 cents as the interest rate rises from 5 percent to 10 percent to 15 percent. Note also that if one uses a 15 percent interest rate to discount future payments, the present value of one dollar to be received in 20 years is only about 6 cents.

Your Turn

A U.S. government zero-coupon bond agrees to pay $1,000 at maturity in 30 years.

a.   If competitive yields on such instruments are 7 percent, calculate the current price of the bond.

b.   If yields rise to 8 percent, what happens to the price of the bond?

Interest Rates and Security Prices

Note in the "Your Turn" problem that an increase in market yields (interest rates) is associated with a decline in the price of the zero-coupon bonds. This inverse relationship between interest rates and prices applies to all debt instruments. An increase in yields reduces security prices; a decrease in yields increases security prices. Consider a bond that pays a series of annual "coupons" or annual payments, designated as C's, and also pays back the principal, or face value at maturity, designated as F. The general present value formula expressed in Equation 5-1 now becomes a bit more specific, as indicated in Equation 5-2.

$$(5\text{-}2) \qquad PV = \frac{C_1}{(1+i)} + \frac{C_2}{(1+i)^2} + \cdots + \frac{(C_n + F)}{(1+i)^n}$$

$C_1, C_2, \ldots, C_n$ represent the returns (annual "coupons") to be obtained at the end of years $1, 2, \ldots, n$. F represents the face value of the instrument, to be redeemed when the bond matures at the end of year n. The i in the denominators represents the going interest rate on comparable securities.

The above formulation may be used to calculate the market price of a bond, given the coupon payments and the market yield. Suppose that a bond having four years to maturity provides an annual coupon payment of $50, and that yields on comparable instruments are 5 percent. Assume the bond will also repay the principal of $1000 at maturity. Then the market valuation of this instrument may be approximated as follows:

$$PV = \frac{\$50}{1.05} + \frac{\$50}{(1.05)^2} + \frac{\$50}{(1.05)^3} + \frac{\$50}{(1.05)^4} + \frac{\$1000}{(1.05)^4} = \$1000$$

If yields on comparable instruments are 5 percent, the market will dictate that the rights to this instrument will be priced at $1000. If this bond were priced at less than $1000, other securities would be sold in order to purchase this one, bidding its price up. If this bond were priced at more than $1000, market participants would sell it in order to buy the alternative securities yielding 5 percent. This action would bid the price back down to $1000.

Suppose, instead, that yields on comparable instruments are 6 percent. Then no one would be interested in this asset at a price of $1000. The present value and price of the security would be less than $1000. Specifically,

$$PV = \frac{\$50}{1.06} + \frac{\$50}{(1.06)^2} + \frac{\$50}{(1.06)^3} + \frac{\$50}{(1.06)^4} + \frac{\$1000}{(1.06)^4} = \$965.34$$

Because the market interest rate is used to discount the fixed stream of returns from a debt instrument to place a value or price on it, it should be clear that the price and yield of a debt instrument are inversely related. The higher the price, the lower the yield, and vice versa. The lower the price, the higher the yield, and vice versa. Falling interest rates mean that bond prices are rising. Rising interest rates are associated with falling bond prices.

THE LOANABLE FUNDS MODEL

To analyze the behavior of interest rates, we will develop a relatively simple and highly useful framework called the **loanable funds model.** This model is often used by economists and financial analysts for purposes of forecasting interest rates. In this model, the

Table 5-1

Sources of Supply of and Demand for Loanable Funds

Sources of Supply	Sources of Demand
Personal savings	Household credit buying
Business savings	Business investment
Government budget surplus	Government budget deficit
Increase in the money supply	Foreign borrowing in the United States
Foreign lending in the United States	

interest rate is defined as the price paid for the right to borrow or use loanable funds.[1] Borrowers—society's deficit spending units—issue claims, or IOUs, to finance expenditures that exceed their receipts or funds currently on hand. These IOUs constitute a demand for loanable funds, or a demand for credit, by borrowers. On the other side of the market, lenders seek to purchase financial claims—that is, to supply loanable funds to the market. Table 5-1 lists the sources of supply of and demand for loanable funds.

Table 5-1 indicates that households, firms, government units, and foreign entities contribute to both sides of the market for loanable funds. Households are a major source of loanable funds through personal savings; yet they are also demanders of funds through consumer credit purchases and home mortgages. Business savings are a source of funds, while business investment in plant, equipment, and inventories creates a demand for funds. Federal, state, and local governments often use idle cash to supply funds to the market, purchasing bonds and other IOUs with their surplus funds. On the other hand, government budget deficits produce a demand for loanable funds. Finally, foreign lending is a source of funds in the United States, while foreign borrowing represents a demand for U.S. funds.

If we look at the loanable funds market on a *net* basis, however, the supply of loanable funds comes from three sources: personal savings, increases in the money supply, and foreign lending. Personal saving currently exceeds consumer credit buying, while business saving is outstripped by business investment spending. And any budget surpluses accruing to state or local governments are generally more than offset by the large federal budget deficit. In recent years, foreign lending in the United States has exceeded foreign borrowing. On a *net* basis, therefore, demanders of loanable funds (the issuers of debt instruments) include the federal government, municipalities, and business firms. Net buyers of these claims—suppliers of funds—include principally the household sector and foreign lenders.

---

[1]In an alternative model, known as the liquidity preference theory, the interest rate is determined by the supply and demand for *money*. The choice between the two theories may be governed by their usefulness in various purposes. The loanable funds framework is more popular among financial market practitioners and seems more convenient for forecasting.

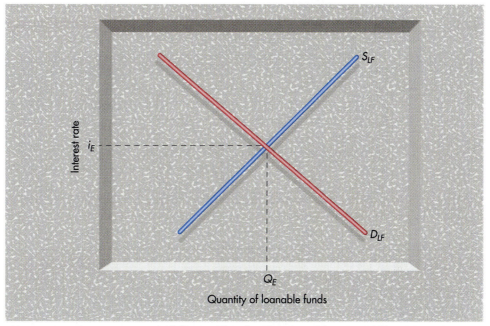

Figure 5-2   Interest Rates and the Supply of and Demand for Loanable Funds. Interest rates are determined in financial markets by the supply of and demand for loanable funds. Changes in interest rates are produced by shifts in these supply and demand curves.

Just as the quantity of wheat supplied and demanded in the market is responsive to the price of wheat, the quantity of loanable funds supplied and demanded depends on the price of loanable funds—that is, the interest rate. This principle is illustrated in Figure 5-2. In the figure, S_{LF} and D_{LF} represent the supply and demand curves for loanable funds. The appearance (slope) of these curves may be explained intuitively by assessing the interest rate responsiveness of the individual sources of the supply and demand for funds.

The supply curve of loanable funds (S_{LF}) is drawn as an upward-sloping function of the interest rate. Classical economists regarded the interest rate as a measure of the incentive to abstain from current consumption—that is, to save. In making the decision to save, individuals substitute future consumption for current consumption. The higher the interest rate, the greater the amount of future consumption that can be gained by abstaining from current consumption—that is, by saving. In this way, a high interest rate works to overcome the human trait of **time preference**—the preference for current consumption over future consumption—and therefore encourages saving.

Generally speaking, econometric studies have not found that saving responds strongly to changes in the interest rate. By itself, this finding might indicate a very steep or nearly vertical supply curve in Figure 5-2. However, other forces are at work which tend to make the quantity of funds supplied responsive to the interest rate. For example, the money supply tends to vary directly with the interest rate because banks grant loans more aggressively as rates rise. Also, an increase in U.S. interest rates attracts additional funds to U.S.

financial markets because an enormous pool of financial capital can be transferred instantaneously from one country to another in response to yield advantages. Hence, we draw the S_{LF} curve as upward sloping.

The demand curve for loanable funds is downward sloping. This is attributable largely to the fact that a decline in the level of interest rates stimulates expenditures on items financed through borrowing—durable goods purchases, new home buying, and investment in plant, equipment, inventory, and nonresidential real estate. Also, holding other factors constant, lower U.S. interest rates induce foreigners to step up borrowing here.

According to the loanable funds model, the interest rate moves to the level that equates the quantity of loanable funds supplied with the quantity of loanable funds demanded. In Figure 5-2, equilibrium occurs at i_E. Any factor that produces a shift in the position of the supply curve or demand curve will change the equilibrium interest rate. An increase in demand (a rightward shift of the demand curve) or a reduction in supply (a leftward shift of the supply curve) will cause an increase in interest rates. An increase in supply (a rightward shift of the supply curve) or a decrease in demand (a leftward shift of the demand curve) will cause a decline in interest rates.

Return to the list of factors in Table 5-1. What factors would exert downward pressure on interest rates? An increase in personal saving resulting from a greater emphasis on the virtues of thrift would increase the supply of loanable funds, causing interest rates to decline. So would an increase in business saving resulting from cost-cutting measures. Federal Reserve actions which increase the money supply would also boost the supply of available funds and reduce interest rates, as would an increased preference for U.S. securities worldwide due to increased political instability in foreign nations.

On the demand side of the market, reduced business investment and household credit buying resulting from a decline in business and consumer confidence would reduce the demand for loanable funds and exert downward pressure on interest rates. Likewise, an income tax hike or a reduction in government expenditures that trims the magnitude of the federal budget deficit would reduce the government's demand for funds, shifting D_{LF} leftward and pulling down interest rates. Table 5-2 illustrates the effects of several events that will shift the supply and demand curves for loanable funds, thereby altering interest rates.

Given this analysis, which views changes in interest rates as being driven by shifts in the supply and demand curves for loanable funds, we now examine the general forces which determine the level of interest rates.

Your Turn

In early 1996, during a heated budget battle with President Clinton, the U.S. Congress threatened to default on interest payments on the government debt. Assume that foreign lenders, perhaps not being wise to the ways of U.S. politics, take this threat seriously. Analyze the effect of Congress's threat on yields on U.S. government bonds.

Table 5-2

Some Factors Shifting the Supply of and Demand for Loanable Funds

Factors shifting S_{LF}:		Impact on interest rate
1. Household thriftiness increases (S_{LF} shifts right)	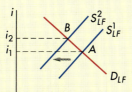	−
2. Banks tighten their lending standards (S_{LF} shifts left)	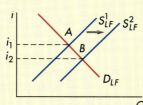	+
3. Federal Reserve increases money supply (S_{LF} shifts right)	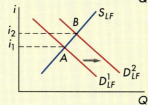	−

Factors shifting D_{LF}:		
1. Consumer confidence improves (D_{LF} shifts right)	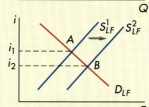	+
2. Congress eliminates federal budget deficit (D_{LF} shifts left)	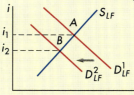	−
3. Stock market declines, impairing business confidence (D_{LF} shifts left)	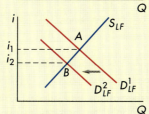	−

MAJOR DETERMINANTS OF INTEREST RATES

We have seen that a multitude of forces can initiate shifts in the supply of or demand for loanable funds, thereby triggering changes in interest rates. Four particularly important forces are inflation expectations, Federal Reserve policy, the business cycle, and federal budget deficits.

Inflation Expectations

The level of interest rates strongly tends to rise in periods in which the expected rate of inflation increases. Interest rates typically fall when expected inflation declines. The loanable funds framework can explain this phenomenon. Suppose that inflation has been relatively subdued for several years—approximately 3 percent per year for the past decade. Given this environment, the supply and demand curves for loanable funds are represented by S_{LF}^1 and D_{LF}^1 in Figure 5-3, with equilibrium at A. The equilibrium interest rate is i_1.

Now suppose that the inflation rate escalates to around 6 percent per year and the public comes to expect this higher rate of inflation to continue for some time. Given this event, we will demonstrate that the supply curve of loanable funds shifts leftward, the demand curves shifts rightward, and the equilibrium interest rate increases.

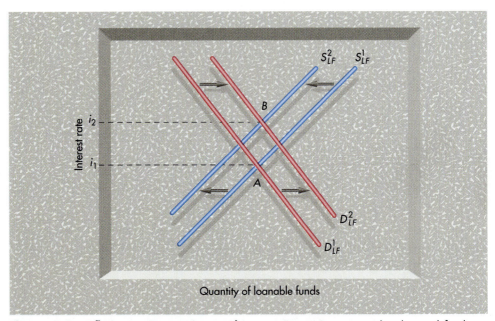

Figure 5-3 **Inflationary Expectations and Interest Rates.** By raising the demand for loanable funds and reducing the supply, an increase in expected inflation raises interest rates.

The development of prospects for continuing inflation of 6 percent reduces the supply of loanable funds, shifting the supply curve leftward from S^1_{LF} to S^2_{LF}. At each and every interest rate, the willingness to lend money is reduced because the real value of the principal is expected to erode more rapidly. Lenders reconsider the alternatives to lending. Some former lenders may elect instead to purchase common stocks, gold and other precious metals, real estate, or other real assets that are believed to be more effective hedges against inflation than debt instruments. For these reasons, the supply of loanable funds decreases (shifts leftward). At any given interest rate, lending is less attractive now that expected inflation has increased.

At the same time, the increase in expected inflation raises the demand for loanable funds. At each and every interest rate, the willingness to borrow is stimulated, shifting the demand curve rightward from D^1_{LF} to D^2_{LF}. This follows from the fact that the price, or nominal value, of goods or assets purchased with borrowed funds is expected to rise with inflation while the nominal value of the principal borrowed is not. Alternatively stated, the *real* value of the projects built or goods purchased with borrowed funds remains constant during inflation, while the real burden of the debt incurred is reduced. Therefore an increase in expected inflation tends to increase the rate of homebuilding activity, household credit purchases, and investment in plant, equipment, and inventories at each possible interest rate. The demand curve for loanable funds in Figure 5-3 shifts rightward when expected inflation increases.

Given the reduction in supply and the increase in demand for loanable funds induced by the increase in expected inflation, the equilibrium moves to B in the figure. The equilibrium price of loanable funds—the interest rate—rises. Assuming the existence of competitive financial markets unrestricted by controls, the interest rate in Figure 5-3 rises from i_1 to i_2. The effect that a change in expected inflation exerts on the level of interest rates is known as the **Fisher effect,** named for the great American economist, Irving Fisher, who pioneered the theory linking interest rates and expected inflation.

The Fisher Hypothesis   A formulation linking the behavior of nominal (actual) interest rates and expected inflation is given in Equation 5-3.

(5-3) $$i = r + \beta p^e$$

where

i = the nominal (actual) interest rate

r = the real interest rate, the interest rate that would prevail in a sustained era of zero inflation

p^e = the expected rate of inflation, and

β = the extent to which nominal interest rates adjust to changes in expected inflation.

If the real interest rate (r) remains constant over time and β equals 1.0, movements in actual interest rates (i) would be entirely accounted for by changes in expected inflation (p^e). The **Fisher hypothesis,** in its strong version, asserts that β is equal to one—that is, that interest rates move in a one-for-one fashion with the magnitude of expected inflation.

(The weak version of the Fisher hypothesis merely states that β is positive and significant—that is, that expected inflation significantly influences interest rates.) If the real rate (r) remains constant at 2 percent and expected inflation increases from 3 percent to 8 percent in the strong version of the Fisher hypothesis, for example, interest rates would increase from 5 percent to 10 percent. This is known as the **inflation neutrality** case because in this event the increase in interest rates neutralizes the potential effect that higher inflation exerts in redistributing wealth between lenders and borrowers.

In reality, the real interest rate changes over time because of changes in factors such as the productivity of capital and time preference.[2] Therefore, changes in nominal (actual) interest rates reflect other factors in addition to changes in expected inflation. Furthermore, few empirical studies have estimated the magnitude of β to be equal to 1.0.[3] Nevertheless, economists agree that inflation expectations powerfully influence the level of interest rates. If not equal to 1.0, β is certainly positive and not very far from 1.0 in magnitude. Few economists would question the validity of the weak version of the Fisher hypothesis.

Because inflation expectations are strongly influenced by the recent course of inflation, interest rates are positively correlated with the rate of inflation. Figure 5-4 illustrates the yield on 10-year U.S. government notes, along with the inflation rate (in the prior 12-month period) for the period since 1959. The dramatic upward surge of U.S. interest rates in the period from 1965–1980 was attributable primarily to the upward ratcheting of inflation (and inflation expectations) in that period. Furthermore, the decline in inflation in the 1980s and early 1990s accounted for much of the decline in interest rates that followed. If the inflation rate should increase significantly in, say, the next 2 years, it is an almost sure bet that the level of interest rates will also increase.

Empirical Evidence on the Fisher Hypothesis

Empirical research designed to measure the size of β in Equation 5-3—that is, research designed to measure the response of interest rates to a change in expected inflation—indicates that the sensitivity of interest rates to inflation expectations increased sharply in the post–World War II era. Before the war, financial markets do not appear to have responded to inflation in the systematic manner suggested by the Fisher hypothesis. But in the inflation-conscious era of the past 50 years, interest rates have shown a definite sensitivity to the outlook for inflation.

---

[2]There is reason to believe that real interest rates declined in the 1970s and increased in the 1980s. Dramatic increases in oil prices in the 1970s reduced the returns expected from investment in capital goods, which are energy intensive—that is, they require a considerable use of energy per unit of output. As investment declined, the demand for loanable funds decreased, lowering the real interest rate. This trend was reversed in the 1980s as real energy prices came down sharply.

[3]β, the coefficient that relates the expected inflation rate to the interest rate, may not be precisely 1.0. Its value depends on the elasticities of the supply and demand curves for loanable funds (Figure 5-3) and the magnitude of the shifts in those curves in response to a change in expected inflation. There is reason to argue that β should be greater than 1.0, because nominal interest income is taxable to the lender and tax deductible to the borrower. That is, to preserve a given aftertax return, the lender must receive an increase in pretax yield in excess of the increase in the inflation rate. And the borrower can afford to pay an increase in the pretax interest rate in excess of the increase in the inflation rate and still preserve a given real aftertax interest cost.

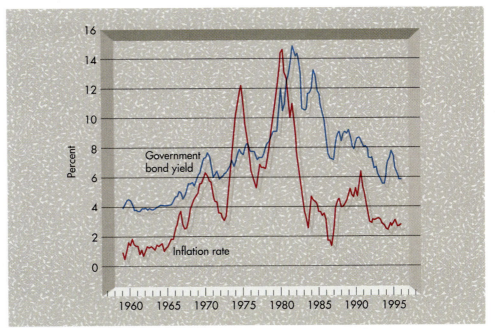

Figure 5-4   Inflation and Government Security Yields since 1959. As inflation ratcheted upward from the mid-1960s to 1980, so did yields on government securities. As inflation came down after 1980, interest rates followed. This evidence is consistent with the hypothesis that interest rates are strongly influenced by inflation expectations.   *Source: Citibank Economic Database.*

The majority of empirical studies estimate that β is less than 1.0, although it has increased since the 1940s.[4] However, some studies which make allowance for changes in the real rate of interest (r) over time have estimated β at around 1.0 or slightly higher. This finding implies that interest rates are extremely responsive to changes in expected inflation and may adjust in a way that approximately neutralizes the redistributive effects of inflation between debtors and creditors.[5]

---

[4]Two major problems confront these studies. First, it is very difficult to estimate the magnitude of the real interest rate (r), since it is unobservable. Many empirical studies simply assume it is constant. Second, inflation expectations are difficult to measure, and the various measures of expected inflation are subject to shortcomings, as we will see in the next chapter.

[5]Two important studies of the relationship between inflation expectations and interest rates, by Lawrence Summers and James Wilcox, are cited in "Suggestions for Additional Reading" at the end of this chapter. Summers estimates that β was approximately 0 before World War II and was still significantly less than 1.0 after the war. He attributes this finding to "money illusion"; that is, he believes the financial markets were fooled by inflation. Wilcox reports that if one allows for the fact that supply shocks such as major oil price hikes reduced real interest rates in the 1970s, β is estimated to be at least 1.0, as most economists believe it should be. Wilcox points out that most previous studies that attempted to measure β assumed that the real interest rate (r) remains constant over time. Some studies therefore produced inaccurate estimates of β.

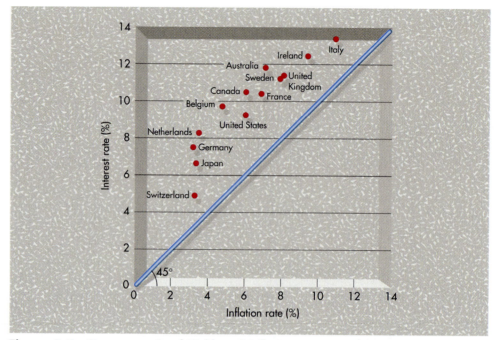

Figure 5-5   Government Bond Yields and Inflation Rates in 13 Nations, 1975–1994.
Countries that experience high inflation tend to have high interest rates; countries that experience modest inflation typically have low interest rates.   *Sources:* Computed from data in *Federal Reserve Bulletin* and Federal Reserve Bank of St. Louis, *International Financial Conditions.*

Figure 5-5 illustrates the relationship between inflation rates and interest rates in 13 nations in the period 1975–1994. For each country, the average inflation rate and the average government bond yield during the period 1975–1994 are plotted. This graph constitutes a crude international test of the strong version of the Fisher hypothesis that interest rates move on a one-for-one basis with expected inflation. The figure clearly shows that countries that experience high inflation also experience high interest rates. Nations with the highest inflation rates during 1975 to 1994 (Italy, Ireland, the United Kingdom) exhibited very high interest rates. Countries with relatively low inflation during this period (Switzerland, Japan, Germany) enjoyed relatively low interest rates. In the figure, the vertical distance between each point plotted and the 45-degree line indicates the average real interest rate experienced by the country during the period. In all instances, the nominal interest rate exceeds the inflation rate—that is, the real interest rate is positive. This real rate ranges from about 1 percent in Switzerland to more than 4 percent in Germany, Canada, Australia, and the Netherlands. In general, the graph strongly supports the view that expected inflation exerts a powerful effect on interest rates. (See Exhibit 5-1 for an econometric analysis of the relationship illustrated in the figure.) As we will see, however, inflation expectations are only one of several major forces that influence interest rates.

EXHIBIT 5-1

Estimating the Relationship between Expected Inflation and Interest Rates

The data illustrated in Figure 5-5 permit us to conduct a very simple, crude test of the Fisher hypothesis. Suppose we wish to estimate the simple model of the form $i = r + \beta p^e$ for this cross section of nations. If we fit a regression line to the points in the figure, we obtain the following equation for the relationship:

$$i = 4.28 + 0.89p^e, \qquad R^2 = 0.84$$
$$(7.4)$$

How should we interpret these findings? First, the *intercept* of the equation is 4.28 percent. This is the estimate of the average real interest rate of the 13 countries in the sample. This suggests that if a nation had zero expected inflation, its nominal (and real) government bond yield would be 4.28 percent.

Second, note the *slope* of the regression line, the estimated coefficient on the p^e term—that is, the estimate of β of our Fisher equation. This coefficient of 0.89 is fairly close to 1.0. The figure in parentheses in the estimated equation is the *t*-statistic associated with the estimate of β. The high *t*-statistic indicates that inflation expectations are statistically highly significant in influencing interest rates. At conventional levels of significance, we cannot reject the hypothesis that β is 1.0. This evidence suggests that, in this case, we are unable to reject either the weak or the strong version of the Fisher hypothesis.

Third, note that R^2 is 0.84. This means that variation in inflation rates across countries accounts statistically for 84 percent of the variation in government bond yields across these same countries. The points cluster fairly closely around the regression line.

Of course, this model is overly simplistic and naive. Additional variables that influence nominal interest rates besides expected inflation need to be added to the model. However, even the simple model serves to remind us of the powerful role that inflation expectations play in interest rate determination.

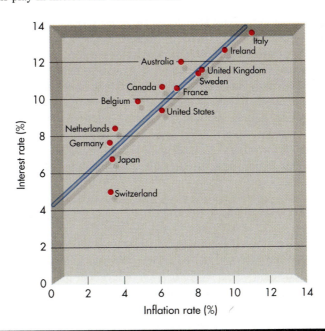

Federal Reserve Policy

The Federal Reserve uses certain policy tools to influence the availability of loans through banks. This process is analyzed in depth in Parts 4 and 5. Because bank loans are an important component of the supply of loanable funds, we may view Federal Reserve policy actions as triggering shifts in the supply curve of loanable funds (S_{LF} in Figure 5-3).

When the Fed wishes to stimulate the economy, it takes measures that encourage banks to expand the amount of loans they grant. The supply curve of loanable funds shifts rightward, reducing interest rates and stimulating expenditures on interest-sensitive items such as houses and business plant and equipment. When the Fed desires to restrain economic activity, it implements actions that force banks to reduce their lending. The supply curve of loanable funds shifts leftward, driving up interest rates and inhibiting household and business spending.

Money and Interest Rates

The effect of an increase in the money supply on the level of interest rates may be divided into three channels: a *liquidity effect,* an *income effect,* and an *inflation expectations effect.* Initially, an increase in the money supply increases liquidity in the economy, triggering a decline in interest rates (the **liquidity effect**). As the economy begins to respond to the economic stimulus, output and income rise, boosting the demand for funds and pushing interest rates back up at least partially (the **income effect**). Finally, to the extent that the *announcement* of the increase in the money supply raises expected inflation, interest rates will be boosted via the Fisher effect (the **inflation expectations effect**). If financial markets are highly sensitized to inflation, and if they attribute inflation principally to the money growth rate, the evidence of more rapid money growth may push long-term interest rates up quickly. That is, the inflation expectations effect may sometimes outweigh the liquidity effect, resulting in higher interest rates. The inflation expectations effect may show up more strongly in long-term interest rates than short-term rates, which are more heavily influenced by other factors such as business cycle conditions and the liquidity of the banking system.

In sum, the Fed has more influence on short-term interest rates than on long-term interest rates, which are more sensitive to expected inflation. When the Fed first pumps funds into banks in an effort to stimulate bank lending and reduce interest rates, most of the effect is manifested in short-term interest rates. Because the resulting increase in the money supply may boost expected inflation, the Fisher effect may lead to an *increase* in long-term interest rates. In an era in which financial markets are highly attuned to the outlook for inflation, one cannot assume the Fed is always capable of lowering long-term rates significantly through stimulative policy actions.

The Business Cycle

Interest rates have historically exhibited a strong procyclical pattern, rising during the expansion phase of the business cycle and falling during periods of economic contraction (recession or depression). This procyclical pattern is most evident in short-term interest rates and is illustrated in Figure 5-6.

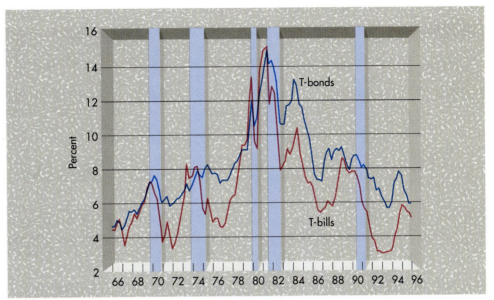

Figure 5-6 **The Procyclical Behavior of Interest Rates.** Interest rates tend to rise during periods of economic expansion and decline during periods of contraction (shaded areas). The tendency is especially pronounced for short-term interest rates.   *Source: Citibank Economic Database.*

Figure 5-6 shows the pattern of yields on short-term and long-term U.S. government securities in the period from 1966 to the present, a period encompassing five full business cycles (recessions are shaded in the figure). As can be seen, recessions occurred in 1969–1970, 1973–1975, the first half of 1980, 1981–1982, and 1990–1991. Note that interest rates typically decline during recessions and increase during economic expansions. The cyclical pattern is especially pronounced for short-term yields (Treasury bills). Though long-term interest rates also exhibit a procyclical pattern, they are less volatile than short-term yields, exhibiting considerably less amplitude over the course of the business cycle.

The loanable funds framework may be used to explain the procyclical behavior of interest rates. During periods of economic expansion, the demand for funds grows rapidly as business and consumer borrowing escalates. In addition, inflationary pressures tend to increase, pushing interest rates up through the Fisher effect. Also, the Federal Reserve may work to restrict the availability of funds to counteract inflation as the economy strengthens. All three forces tend to push interest rates up. During business recessions, the opposite occurs. The demand for funds drops as businesses and consumers retrench, and inflationary pressures diminish. Also, the Fed begins to increase the supply of loanable funds. These three forces combine to bring interest rates down.

This overview, while broadly valid, simplifies a somewhat more complex process. In the early phase of recovery—the first year or two—the upward pressure on interest rates is typically very mild. The demand for credit may rise somewhat as firms borrow to build up inventories and bolster working capital. Bond issues by municipalities may increase. But several forces work to hold down and perhaps even depress interest rates in the first year or two of economic recovery. The federal budget deficit declines because of rising tax receipts. And on the supply side of the loanable funds market, the reduction in unemployment and the growth in income increase personal saving. Business profits and retained earnings also respond positively to economic expansion. And because the economy continues to exhibit considerable unemployment and excess capacity in the early years of the cyclical expansion, the Federal Reserve may be working to increase the supply of funds through stimulative monetary policy measures. Finally, the state of inflation expectations typically reaches a cyclical low in the early phase of the recovery. On balance, therefore, there may be very little upward pressure on interest rates in the first year or two of a recovery.

In the later phase of the cyclical expansion, the upward pressure on interest rates becomes more pronounced. Business investment (and the concurrent demand for funds) is likely to pick up significantly because of the high and rising rate of capacity utilization and the natural feeling of optimism resulting from a healthy growth in sales and profits. Consumer confidence also increases as unemployment declines and job stability improves. This leads to an increase in household buying on credit and therefore to an increase in the demand for loanable funds. The Fed may begin taking steps to reduce the supply of funds. Finally, expected inflation typically increases during the latter portion of the expansion, as inflationary pressure picks up steam. All these forces overwhelm the favorable influences resulting from a continued growth in personal and corporate saving and a declining federal government budget deficit. Thus, interest rates rise strongly in the later phase of the cyclical expansion.

Federal Budget Deficits

Intuitively, it may seem clear that, other things being equal, an increase in the federal budget deficit should raise interest rates. An increase in borrowing by the federal government implies a rightward shift in the demand curve for loanable funds. Other things being equal, interest rates must rise. Moreover, a larger budget deficit may arouse inflation expectations, thereby pulling up interest rates via the Fisher effect.

Most economists agree that an increase in the budget deficit does raise interest rates. However, there is some disagreement on this issue in the profession. At least for periods before the 1980s, there is surprisingly little evidence that interest rates are positively related to budget deficits. (This may be due in part to the fact that pre-1980 budget deficits were typically much smaller than more recent deficits.) Economists who do not believe that budget deficits significantly affect interest rates have advanced two explanations in support of their view. One involves the worldwide scope of the market for loanable funds. The other concerns the alleged tendency for larger budget deficits to stimulate the nation's private saving rate.

The first reason for questioning the view that deficits strongly influence interest rates is that the size of the U.S. budget deficit, though enormous in an absolute sense, is rather small in relation to the total worldwide pool of financial capital. In recent decades, financial markets in various nations have become increasingly integrated, so that the market is now worldwide in scope. As interest rates in the United States begin to rise in response to heavier federal borrowing, the quantity of funds available to meet the government's demand rises as foreign institutions step up their lending in the United States. In other words, the supply curve for loanable funds in the United States is thought to be quite elastic—almost horizontal—with respect to the interest rate. This sensitive supply response tends to limit the upward pressure on U.S. interest rates caused by increased federal borrowing.

The second explanation advanced by economists involves the alleged relationship between the federal budget deficit and individuals' saving behavior. Suppose the public is "forward looking" and recognizes that today's larger budget deficits imply either higher future taxes or lower future living standards. To protect themselves and their heirs from this expected future belt-tightening, they step up their current saving rates. In this event, the supply of loanable funds shifts rightward, tending to neutralize the effect on interest rates of the increased demand for funds by the government. Given certain strong assumptions about rational behavior and foresight, interest rates will be unaffected by larger budget deficits.

Supporters of this position, which is known as the **Ricardian Equivalence Proposition,** point out that it is consistent with rational behavior. Because a larger budget deficit today implies greater future interest expenditures to finance the enlarged deficit and therefore higher future tax rates, it makes sense for perceptive individuals to increase their saving rates. Critics of this view regard it as unrealistic. They point out that most measures of private saving rates declined significantly in the 1980s while deficits were growing larger. How many of your acquaintances have raised their saving rates in the past 15 years in response to enlarged deficits? While this evidence by no means invalidates the Ricardian Equivalence Proposition, it would seem to throw the burden of proof upon supporters of the proposition.

Professional financial market participants believe almost uniformly that larger deficits or expected future deficits raise interest rates significantly. Academic economists are currently divided on this issue. Ultimately, the issue is likely to be resolved by empirical investigation. See Exhibit 5-2 for a discussion of the relationship between budget deficits and interest rates in the United States in the early 1990s.

MAJOR INTEREST RATE MOVEMENTS, 1950–1996

We will now use our loanable funds framework to sketch the forces that have produced the major swings in U.S. interest rates over the past 45 years. Figure 5-7 illustrates the behavior of yields on corporate, municipal, and U.S. government bonds from 1950 through early 1996. It shows that the period from the early 1950s through the early 1960s was a stable one for U.S. financial markets. Inflation was subdued and interest rates were relatively low, increasing slowly from their artificially depressed levels during World War II. This interlude of relatively stable interest rates was followed by a long period of dramatic fluctuations in rates. Why?

First, as discussed, the period 1965–1981 witnessed a persistent upward ratcheting of interest rates, as strong growth in the demand for funds outstripped the growth in the supply of funds. A large increase in borrowing by consumers and businesses to finance

---

EXHIBIT 5-2

Large Budget Deficits and Low Interest Rates—A Paradox?

Analysts who dispute the view that larger deficits cause higher interest rates point to the 1991–1993 period in support of their view. In this period, federal budget deficits were at all-time highs (around $300 billion in 1992), while short-term interest rates reached their lowest levels in 30 years. If budget deficits have such a strong effect on interest rates, they ask, why were interest rates at their lowest level in 3 decades?

To refute this assertion, one needs to recall that interest rates are influenced not just by budget deficits but by expected inflation, Federal Reserve policy, and the business cycle as well. All three of these considerations were working strongly to produce low interest rates in the early 1990s, possibly obscuring the role of budget deficits.

First, the magnitude of expected inflation was low and falling lower in the early 1990s. The sustained reduction of actual inflation after the early 1980s had steadily reduced the public's expectations of future inflation. By 1992 and 1993, it appeared that the nation might be entering an era like the 1950s and early 1960s, when annual inflation had been 1 or 2 percent.

Second, Federal Reserve policy in the early 1990s was quite stimulative. Bank reserves and the money supply (M1) expanded at annual rates of approximately 12 percent in 1992 and 1993, far above the norm. In mid-1992, the Federal Reserve reduced its discount rate to 3 percent, the lowest level in 30 years, and left it there throughout 1993.

Finally, both the U.S. and world economies were in a sluggish state in 1992 and 1993. The U.S. economic recovery that followed the 1990–1991 recession was unusually anemic; in the first two years of recovery, the rate of output growth was insufficient to prevent an increase in the unemployment rate. Many European nations remained mired in recession throughout 1992 and 1993. Such sluggish economic activity holds down the demand for credit, keeping interest rates low.

In short, those who point to the low interest rates of the early 1990s as evidence that larger deficits do not raise interest rates are guilty of neglecting the concept of *ceteris paribus. If* everything else remains constant, an increase in the budget deficit *will* raise interest rates. But in the early 1990s, everything else did not remain constant; several forces worked powerfully to depress interest rates. Because the real-world economics laboratory of actual experience does not permit other factors to be held constant, disentangling the true effect of budget deficits is extremely difficult.

---

consumer durables, residential and nonresidential construction activity, and business investment in plant and equipment was not matched by growth in household saving.

But most important, the powerful acceleration of inflation during the 1965–1980 period pulled up interest rates through the Fisher effect. An economic boom fueled by the natural forces of the business cycle and excessive monetary stimulus by the Federal Reserve caused the great increase in inflation and interest rates in the late 1970s. Finally, dramatic increases in oil prices in 1973 and 1979 contributed to the most severe episode of inflation in U.S. peacetime history. It was followed by a steep spike in yields

Figure 5-7   Yields on Bonds in the United States, 1950–1996. In the United States, bond yields trended strongly upward from 1950 to 1981. Since then they have declined significantly.   *Source: Citibank Economic Database.*

in 1980 and 1981. Partly responsible for this final surge in interest rates was a dramatic shift in Federal Reserve policy procedures implemented near the end of 1979. This shift in procedures permitted the Fed to slow the growth of the money supply and allow interest rates to move dramatically higher in order to reduce inflation.

In the 1980s and early 1990s, interest rates came down a long way from their peaks of the early 1980s. First and foremost, the rate of inflation (and therefore expected inflation) declined sharply after 1981. In fact, inflation came down much faster in the 1980s than either the Reagan administration or professional economists thought possible. The eradication of severe inflation gradually pulled down interest rates as inflation expectations lagged behind the actual (declining) rate of inflation. Economic activity remained somewhat depressed both in the United States and worldwide for several years following the severe 1981–1982 recession. Oil prices collapsed in late 1985 and have remained relatively low ever since. The U.S. inflation rate has hovered around 3 percent for a decade or more.

Most recently, the 1990–1991 recession and the unusually sluggish economic recovery that followed, accompanied by an aggressive easing of monetary policy by the Federal Reserve during 1992 and 1993, resulted in significant further declines in interest rates. In 1993, short-term interest rates were as low as at any time since the early 1960s. In 1995 and early

The International Synchronization of Interest Rate Movements

Major interest rate movements in the United States are typically accompanied by similar movements in other nations. For example, the illustration below shows the parallel movements of yields on short-term government securities in the United States and Japan for the period after 1973. Note that, in both nations, interest rates spiked in 1979–1980, trended downward through 1987, increased in the late 1980s, and came down sharply in the early 1990s. A similar pattern occurred in England, Germany, and other nations. What causes interest rate movements to be synchronized across countries?

First, many of the major forces that influence interest rates are experienced simultaneously by other nations. For example, the 1979 oil price shock that pushed up inflation in the United States had a similar effect on Japan and other nations. Also, business cycles tend to be transmitted internationally. For example, a contraction in economic activity in one nation reduces its demand for imported products and thereby spills over to dampen economic activity abroad. Because the business cycle has an important influence on interest rates and because business cycles are often worldwide in scope, one would expect interest rate movements to be synchronized across nations. Also, because inflation pressures in one nation are transmitted at least in part to other countries, the Fisher effect frequently works to produce similar interest rate movements in many countries.

Also, because a huge worldwide pool of funds can be quickly transferred internationally to the money center offering the most competitive yields, interest rate movements are propagated across countries. Given other factors, an increase in interest rates in the United States will reduce the supply of loanable funds available in Japan as funds flow to the United States. This means that interest rates in Tokyo tend to rise in sympathy with those in New York. A decline in New York rates pulls down Tokyo rates as the supply curve of loanable funds in Tokyo shifts rightward. For all these reasons, interest rate movements in the United States are highly correlated with interest rate movements abroad.

Interest rate comovements

EXHIBIT 5-3

The Emergence of 100-Year Bonds

Throughout the period of economic expansion during 1992–1996, inflation in the United States remained unusually subdued. As the prospect of an accord between Congress and the president on the elimination of the federal budget deficit emerged in 1995, long-term interest rates declined sharply. In December 1995, the bellwether 30-year Treasury bond yield dipped below 6 percent, just shy of its all-time low in late 1993 (30-year Treasury bonds were first issued in 1977). Sensing that interest rates were unlikely to fall much further, several large U.S. corporations issued bonds with 100-year maturities—a highly unusual event in the United States, where bond maturities have seldom exceeded 40 years. Between 1954 and 1993, no 100-year bonds were issued, and only a few were issued in late 1993, when yields reached very low levels.

Included among the companies issuing 100-year bonds were BellSouth, Wisconsin Electric, and Columbia/HCA Healthcare, the largest for-profit hospital organization in the United States. In late November 1995, Columbia/HCA Healthcare issued $200 million worth of 100-year bonds at an interest rate of 7.5 percent. Two weeks later, the $500 million BellSouth issue sold at a price representing a 7 percent yield—a surprisingly modest premium relative to the 6.3 percent yield on 30-year Treasury bonds that prevailed that same day.

What is the thinking behind the decision to issue or purchase a 100-year bond? Would you buy a 100-year bond? If so, at what yield would you be interested? Clearly, in such a transaction there are risks to both parties. To the borrower (for example, Bell-South), the risk involves the possibility that the United States might be embarking on an extended era of nearly zero inflation or perhaps even deflation. In such an environment, interest rates would move even lower than those in late 1995, causing corporations to regret their commitment to paying 7 percent interest over the next century.

Two risks confronted purchasers of the 100-year bonds: default risk and market risk. One hundred years ago, telephones did not exist. Who can be sure they will exist 100 years from now? In other words, there is a possibility that the heirs of the buyers of Bell-South's 100-year bonds will not be repaid the principal at maturity in the year 2095. Perhaps more threatening was the possibility that the quiescent inflation of the mid-1990s might give way to significantly higher inflation in the future. If that were to happen, market interest rates would move to higher levels and the price of the 100-year bond would decline. If inflation were to average more than 5 percent annually over the 100-year life of the bond, the bond's long-term owner would likely not quite break even after considering taxes and inflation. Even if inflation were to average only 3 percent annually, the bond would be a mediocre investment at best. The fact that BellSouth was able to issue a 100-year bond at a yield of 7 percent meant the market was betting on a lower average inflation rate over the next century than the rates that have prevailed in the past 40 years.

1996, long-term interest rates also moved down sharply in response to developing prospects for lower budget deficits and lower inflation. By 1996, then, the interest rate cycle had almost come full circle over a 30-year period! Exhibit 5-3 discusses how economic conditions in the mid-1990s led to an unusual phenomenon—the issuance of 100-year bonds.

SUMMARY

Interest rates are influenced by many forces, and the loanable funds model is a useful framework for analyzing those forces. Factors that increase the demand for loanable funds or reduce the supply of funds result in higher interest rates. Factors that reduce the demand for loanable funds or increase the supply of funds lead to lower interest rates. The outlook for future inflation exerts a major influence on interest rates, and much of the upward movement of interest rates from the mid-1960s through the end of the 1970s is attributable to rising in-

flation expectations. Much of the decline in interest rates after 1980 is explained by the major decline in inflation (and inflation expectations) after 1980. Other major forces that influence interest rates include Federal Reserve policy actions, the business cycle, and the size of the federal budget deficit. Restrictive Fed policy initiatives, more robust economic activity, and larger federal budget deficits tend to increase interest rates, while stimulative Fed policy actions, weaker economic activity, and smaller budget deficits work to reduce interest rates.

Answers to Your Turn (p. 94)

a. *The expression for the present value (and price) of the bond is $PV = \$1000/(1 + .07)^{30}$. The price of this bond is $131.37.*

b. *The price of the bond is now given by $PV = \$1000/(1 + .08)^{30}$. The price of the bond falls to $99.38.*

Answer to Your Turn (p. 98)

The threat of default reduces the willingness of foreigners to purchase U.S. government bonds. The supply curve of loanable funds in the U.S. government bond market shifts leftward, increasing the yield on these bonds.

KEY TERMS

present value
loanable funds model
time preference
Fisher effect
Fisher hypothesis

inflation neutrality
liquidity effect
income effect
inflation expectations effect
Ricardian Equivalence Proposition

STUDY QUESTIONS

1 Explain the sources of supply of and demand for loanable funds.

2 Explain in detail how a decrease in expected inflation would produce a decrease in the level of interest rates.

3 Suppose that the expected returns from real estate investment decline sharply due to enactment of tax legislation unfavorable to real estate. Other things being equal, what will this do to interest rates?

4 A corporate bond with face value of $1000 pays an annual coupon of $80, and comes due exactly three years from today. Using the present value formula developed in this chapter, calculate the price of this bond if market yields on similar bonds are 6 percent. Now, assume that market yields on such bonds increase to 7 percent. Calculate the new price of the bond, and explain intuitively why the price of the bond decreased.

5 In October 1979, with inflation raging at rates in excess of 10 percent per annum, the Federal Reserve adopted a set of procedures that amounted to a movement toward a less accommodative, or more restrictive, monetary policy. What effect would you expect this move to have on short-term interest rates? Long-term rates?

6 Analyze the debate over whether the size of federal budget deficits influences the level of interest rates. Take a position in the debate and defend it analytically.

7 Name and explain the forces that typically operate to produce a reduction in the level of interest rates during the contraction (recession) phase of the business cycle.

8 Explain why the announcement of a large increase in the U.S. money supply may actually result in an *increase* in long-term bond yields.

9 The 1980s saw the demise of numerous political regimes in Latin America. Explain the effects this instability would have on the loanable funds market and interest rates in the United States.

10 Why do interest rates fall more slowly in the first half of a recession than in the second half? Explain by examining business and consumer confidence, inflationary expectations, government budget deficits, and Federal Reserve policy.

11 Interest rates tend to move procyclically, rising during periods of cyclical expansion. A major business cycle trough occurred in late 1982, and economic expansion followed until the cyclical peak occurred in mid-1990. Yet during this nearly 8-year-long economic expansion, long-term interest rates trended downward (review Figure 5-7). Explain how this could have occurred.

SUGGESTIONS FOR ADDITIONAL READING

The most comprehensive treatment of all aspects of interest rates, together with up-to-date citations of relevant literature, is provided in James C. Van Horne, *Financial Market Rates and Flows,* 4th ed. (Englewood Cliffs, N.J.; Prentice Hall, 1994). On the theory of interest rates, a good place to start is the classic by Irving Fisher, *The Theory of Interest Rates* (New York: Macmillan, 1930), reprinted by Augustus M. Kelley in 1955 and 1961. An analysis of the various theories, including the loanable funds model, is found in Alvin Hansen, *A Guide to Keynes* (New York: McGraw-Hill, 1953), chaps. 6 and 7. For discussions of the effect of inflation on interest rates, see James Wilcox, "Why Were Interest Rates So Low in the 1970s?," *American Economic Review,* March 1983, pp. 44–53, and Lawrence Summers, "The Nonadjustment of Nominal Interest Rates: A Study of the Fisher Effect," in James

Tobin, ed., *Macroeconomics, Prices and Quantities* (Washington: Brookings Institution, 1983), pp. 201–241. Another important paper on the Fisher effect is Frederic Mishkin, "Is the Fisher Effect for Real?," *Journal of Monetary Economics,* 1992, pp. 195–215. On the impact of budget deficits on the level of interest rates, see Paul Evans, "Do Large Deficits Produce High Interest Rates?," *American Economic Review,* March 1985, pp. 68–87. For an opposing viewpoint, see Lloyd B. Thomas and Ali Abderrezak, "Anticipated Future Budget Deficits and the Term Structure of Interest Rates," *Southern Economic Journal,* July 1988, pp. 150–161. A review of the various studies on this issue is provided in Preston J. Miller and William Roberds, "How Little We Know about Deficit Policy Effects," *Federal Reserve Bank of Minneapolis Quarterly Review,* Winter 1992, pp. 2–11.

C H A P T E R

6

Real Interest Rates

In Chapter 5 we developed the loanable funds model, a general framework for analyzing the behavior of interest rates. We used that model to examine the role of such key interest rate determinants as expected inflation, Federal Reserve policy, the business cycle, and federal budget deficits. In this chapter we probe deeper by looking into the meaning and measurement of *real* interest rates—that is, actual interest rates corrected for expected inflation. In order to do this, we discuss the methods economists employ to measure expected inflation. In addition, we analyze some of the fundamental forces which account for the changes in real interest rates during the past 35 years.

THE MEANING AND IMPORTANCE OF REAL INTEREST RATES

The *real interest rate* is the rate of interest that would prevail in a hypothetical world of zero permanent inflation. Such a rate would be positive—probably in the 1 to 3 percent range most of the time—because of the *productivity of capital* and *time preference* (that is, the preference for current goods over future goods). This real interest rate is not constant but changes over time in response to various phenomena.

Why the Real Interest Rate Is Positive

Because of the **productivity of capital,** a society that allocates a larger portion of its current output to capital goods (as opposed to consumer goods) increases its capacity to produce goods—both capital goods and consumer goods—in the future. By forgoing current consumption and instead producing more capital goods, a nation can shift its production possibilities curve outward more rapidly. It can enjoy higher *future* living standards. And because

Table 6-1

Growth of $20,000 Principal at Various Real Interest Rates

Real Interest Rate (%)	Principal Today	Principal in 10 Years	Principal in 20 Years	Principal in 40 Years
0%	$20,000	$20,000	$20,000	$20,000
3	20,000	26,878	36,122	65,241
6	20,000	35,817	64,143	205,714
10	20,000	51,875	134,550	905,185

capital is productive, borrowers—those who undertake the real economic investment—are willing to pay a positive real interest rate to obtain the use of funds with which to purchase capital goods. Since the rate of return from investment in capital goods varies over time, one would expect the real interest rate to fluctuate as well.

Classical economists also regarded the rate of interest as a reward for postponing consumption—that is, a reward for saving. Because people plan for current and future consumption, they normally spend only part of their income, saving the rest. Typically, they prefer present consumption over future consumption, a human trait known as **time preference.** People would prefer to have a new car today rather than a year from now. However, if an individual consumes more today, he or she must consume less in the future. Furthermore, the amount of future consumption that can be gained per dollar of current saving varies directly and exponentially with the real rate of interest. This is demonstrated in Table 6-1, which shows how an initial principal of $20,000 (accumulated through saving) grows in buying power over the years, given various real rates of interest.

If the real interest rate is 3 percent, note that $20,000 today will grow in buying power to $26,878 in 10 years and $65,241 in 40 years. The opportunity cost of buying the $20,000 car today rather than postponing its purchase for a decade is a loss of $6,878 in additional real buying power 10 years from now. (And of course the opportunity cost is much larger if one is looking 20 to 40 years into the future.) If the real interest rate were 6 percent, the $20,000 principal would grow in real terms to $35,817 in 10 years and $205,714 in 40 years. At 6 percent, the opportunity cost of buying the car today rather than postponing its purchase for a decade is the loss of $15,817 of additional buying power 10 years from now. As the real interest rate rises, the opportunity cost of consuming today rises. The higher the real interest rate, the greater the amount of future consumption that can be enjoyed by abstaining from a dollar's worth of consumption today. In theory, by enticing them with the prospect of greater *future* consumption, an increase in interest rates tends to cause people to postpone consumption—that is, to increase saving. Higher interest rates work to overcome the human trait of time preference. Classical economists viewed the real interest rate as the reward for saving.

Ex Ante and Ex Post Real Interest Rates

Because we do not live in the hypothetical world of zero inflation, we cannot observe real interest rates. We can estimate them, though. The **expected** or **ex ante real interest rate** is the difference between the actual interest rate and the expected rate of inflation. If the actual interest rate is 8 percent and the expected inflation rate is 5 percent, the ex ante or expected real interest rate must be 3 percent. To estimate the ex ante real interest rate, we obtain some measure of expected inflation and subtract it from the actual, or nominal, interest rate. Because many important economic decisions are based on expectations, the ex ante real interest rate is an important factor influencing such decisions.

Quite often, actual inflation differs from the rate that was expected. Suppose in the above example, in which the nominal interest rate was 8 percent and the expected inflation rate was 5 percent, that inflation turns out actually to be 7 percent. This means the **realized** or **ex post real interest rate** turns out to be 1 percent rather than 3 percent. Whenever expected inflation is not realized, the ex ante and ex post real interest rates will differ. When inflation turns out higher than expected, the ex post real interest rate is lower than the ex ante real interest rate. Whenever inflation turns out to be lower than was anticipated, the ex post real rate is higher than the ex ante real rate. Table 6-2 illustrates average ex ante and ex post real yields on U.S. Treasury bills in 5-year intervals beginning in 1961.

In the period 1961 to 1965, yields on U.S. Treasury bills averaged 3.5 percent. Because expected inflation averaged 2.3 percent per year in this period, the ex ante real yield was 1.2 percent. However, because inflation came in lower than expected at 1.7 percent

Table 6-2

Ex Ante and Ex Post Real Interest Rates in the United States

	Treasury Bill Yield (%)*	Expected Inflation (%)†	Ex Ante Real Interest Rate (%)	Actual Inflation (%)‡	Ex Post Real Interest Rate (%)
1961–1965	3.5%	2.3%	1.2%	1.7%	1.8%
1966–1970	5.9	4.6	1.3	4.4	1.5
1971–1975	6.5	6.3	0.2	7.3	−0.8
1976–1980	8.6	8.2	0.4	10.4	−1.8
1981–1985	11.1	5.3	5.8	3.8	7.3
1986–1990	7.5	4.6	2.9	4.5	3.0
1991–1995	4.7	3.9	0.8	3.1	1.6
Average	**6.9**	**5.0**	**1.9**	**5.1**	**1.8**

*Average 1-year Treasury bill yield.
†Expected inflation rate (CPI) from Michigan Survey.
‡Actual (CPI) inflation rate.

Source: *Citibank Economic Database* and University of Michigan.

per year, the ex post real Treasury bill yield (1.8 percent) was higher than the ex ante real rate. Buyers of Treasury bills reaped a higher real yield than they had expected to.

Conversely, in the period 1976–1980, actual inflation (10.4 percent per year) ran significantly higher than expected (8.2 percent per year). Therefore, the realized or ex post real yield earned from Treasury bills (−1.8 percent per year) was even lower than the ex ante real rate (0.4 percent per year). The 1980s witnessed a return to unexpectedly low inflation, so that ex post real yields exceeded the real rates that had been anticipated. Note that, over the entire period after 1961, nominal Treasury bill yields averaged 6.9 percent. With expected inflation averaging 5 percent, the ex ante real Treasury bill yield averaged 1.9 percent. Because inflation turned out to be 0.1 percent higher than expected, the ex post real Treasury bill yield averaged 1.8 percent.

The Importance of the Ex Ante Real Rate

Business firms base investment decisions in part on the ex ante real interest rate. Also, flows of financial capital among nations are powerfully influenced by ex ante real interest rates. Because the expected, or ex ante, real interest rate is crucial in determining such important economic phenomena as investment spending and exchange rate behavior, we will focus most of our attention on this rate. In the remainder of this chapter, we will take "real interest rate" to mean the ex ante, or expected, real rate unless explicitly stated otherwise.

In computing the (ex ante) real interest rate, it is essential to use the average inflation rate expected over the life of a particular loan contract or debt instrument. In other words, to compute the real interest rate on a 90-day Treasury bill, we would subtract the annual inflation rate expected over the next 90 days from the current yield on 90-day Treasury bills. To compute the real interest rate on a new 30-year mortgage, we would first have to tackle the difficult task of estimating the average inflation rate expected over the next 30 years. We would then subtract that figure from the actual mortgage rate.

The longer the time horizon, the greater the uncertainty and the more difficulty one encounters in measuring the expected inflation rate. This point may be intuitively confirmed by asking yourself what you believe the average inflation rate will be over the next 3 months and the next 30 years. You are probably confident that the inflation rate in the next 3 months is not likely to deviate markedly from the recent inflation rate (the inflation rate in the past year, for example), but you will have only a vague notion concerning the average inflation rate that will be experienced over the next 30 years. There are simply too many unpredictable events that could affect long-term price level behavior for you to feel confident about your prediction. Future political and military developments, future oil supply conditions, future weather conditions (for example, the magnitude of global warming)—these and many other unforeseeable factors will influence the inflation rate you experience over the next 30 years.

Yet measuring expected inflation rates is crucial. In the economic environment of the past 30 to 40 years, laypersons as well as professional economists have become much more conscious of the distinction between nominal and real interest rates and of the overriding importance of the latter concept. Real, not nominal, interest rates most strongly influence investment in plant and equipment, the flow of financial capital among nations, and the redistribution of income and wealth between lenders and borrowers. Given other factors, for example, an increase in real interest rates reduces investment expenditures and attracts foreign capital, thereby driving up the nation's exchange rate.

THE ESTIMATION OF REAL INTEREST RATES

In order to estimate real interest rates, economists must first measure the rate of inflation expected by the public. This rate is then subtracted from the nominal or actual interest rate in order to obtain the (ex ante) real interest rate.

Measuring Inflation Expectations

Economists have generally used three procedures to estimate expected inflation: simple measures based solely on recent inflation, forecasts derived from macroeconomic models of inflation, and results obtained from surveys of expected inflation. In most early studies, researchers constructed proxies for expected inflation by taking some sort of weighted average of actual recent inflation.[1] However, this process implies that people are entirely "backward looking"—that they ignore current information and form their expectations strictly on the basis of past experience, an assumption that seems naive and unrealistic.

More recently, with the emergence of the **rational expectations theory** as an integral concept in macroeconomics, economists have begun to assume that people use a more sophisticated method of forming expectations. In forecasting inflation, people are assumed to consider all information about variables that influence price level behavior: current government budget policy, recent growth rates of the monetary aggregates (M1, M2, etc.), recent exchange rate developments, prospects for oil and food prices, military and political developments, and other considerations that are known to affect price levels. In the rational expectations world, people are assumed to behave as if they were tuned in to the state-of-the-art model of inflation. Thus, as new information on key determinants of inflation becomes available, they quickly plug it into their inflation model and revise their outlook accordingly. Economists sometimes employ inflation rates forecasted by macroeconomic models as measures of expected inflation. The Board of Governors of the Federal Reserve System and Data Resources Incorporated (DRI), for example, have built macroeconomic models for the purpose of forecasting inflation. Also, economists frequently use measures of expected inflation obtained through surveys of professional economists and households.

Surveys of Inflation Expectations

Increasingly, survey data on individuals' inflation expectations have replaced the older measures of weighted averages of past inflation in economists' studies. Unfortunately, measures of long-term inflation expectations have only recently become available. However, measures of short-term expected inflation have been available for several decades. One of the most popular is the Livingston Survey, which tracks the 6-month and 12-month forward price level forecasts of approximately 40 professional economists.

---

[1]If, for example, we construct a measure of expected inflation for 1998 by using a weighted average of actual 1995 inflation (say, 2.5 percent), actual 1996 inflation (assume 4 percent), and actual 1997 inflation (say, 5 percent), and if the weights are set (arbitrarily) at 0.2, 0.3, and 0.5, respectively, our measure of expected inflation for 1998 is 4.2 percent, that is, $0.2 \times 2.5\% + 0.3 \times 4\% + 0.5 \times 5\%$.

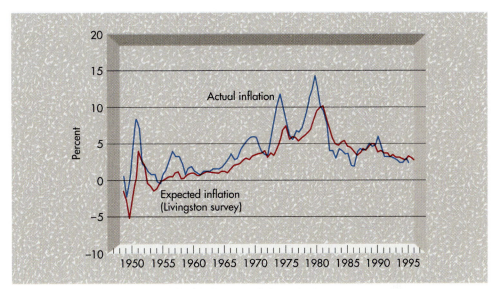

Figure 6-1   Inflation-Tracking Performance of the Livingston Survey Data, 1948–1995.
The professional economists polled in the Livingston Survey have done a reasonably good job of forecasting inflation. On average, however, note that they underpredicted inflation; also, their forecasts lagged behind the actual inflation rate.   *Source:* Federal Reserve Bank of Philadelphia.

Figure 6-1 shows the expected consumer price inflation rate predicted by the Livingston Survey for 1948–1995, along with the inflation rate that actually occurred (measured after the fact). As is clear in the figure, the Livingston Survey does a respectable job of tracking the actual inflation rate. The accuracy of a survey is judged by its *average absolute error*—that is, the average of the absolute values of the differences between the actual inflation rate and the rate that had been expected. The average absolute error during the 47-year period was 1.55 percentage points; since 1986, it has been considerably smaller.

A survey of expected inflation is *unbiased* if it correctly predicts inflation *on average*—that is, if all of the positive and negative prediction errors sum to zero. A survey may be highly inaccurate and still be unbiased. Contrary to the implications of the rational expectations theory, for the entire 47-year period (1948–1995) the survey results were *biased,* underpredicting inflation by 0.94 percentage points on average. This finding is inconsistent with a strict version of rational expectations, which assumes that the public's expectations of inflation are unbiased predictors of actual inflation.

Furthermore, during the period 1965–1980, when U.S. inflation was ratcheting higher and higher, the economists in the survey consistently underpredicted the inflation rate. Then, as inflation came down in the 1980–1986 period, they persistently overpredicted the inflation rate. Note that both the *level* and the *turning points* of the expected inflation rate persistently lagged behind movements in the actual inflation rate. This result is contrary to the assumptions of a strong form of rational expectations theory. In that theory, economic agents do not persistently make one-sided forecast errors—that is, they do not overestimate or underestimate inflation for many consecutive periods.[2]

Another survey of inflation expectations, conducted by the University of Michigan, is based on the opinions of U.S. households. Over the period 1948–1995, household predictions of inflation were more accurate and less biased than those of professional economists (see Exhibit 6-1 for an evaluation of the performance of the Livingston and Michigan Surveys). Recently, however, the economists have begun to outperform the households.

Computing the Real Interest Rate

There are two formulations for computing the real interest rate. One ignores income tax considerations; the other takes them into account. The simpler and more popular approach is stated in Equation 6-1.

(6-1)
$$r = i - p^e$$

This formula defines the real interest rate (r) as the difference between the nominal or actual interest rate (i) and the annual inflation rate expected to prevail over the life of the security or loan (p^e). Hence, if the yield on a 1-year Treasury bill is 10 percent and the expected inflation rate for the next year is 4 percent, the real Treasury bill yield is 6 percent. If a 5-year Treasury note yields 6 percent and the expected inflation rate for the next 5 years is 3 percent, the real yield on the Treasury note is 3 percent.

This approach ignores the fact that, in the United States, interest earned is taxable to the recipient and interest paid is tax deductible for the borrower.[3] Clearly, rational borrowers and lenders will focus on *aftertax* considerations. A formula that expresses the real aftertax interest rate is

(6-2)
$$r_{at} = i(1 - t) - p^e$$

---

[2] Consider an equation of the form $p = a + bp^e + e$, where p is the actual inflation rate for the period and p^e is the rate which had (earlier) been predicted for that period. In the formulation, a and b are parameters, with a being the intercept—that is, the amount of inflation that occurs on average when expected inflation is zero—and b being the slope term showing the average response of actual inflation to each 1 percent of additional expected inflation. The term e is the error term, indicating the deviation between actual inflation and the amount predicted by the equation. If $a = 0$ and $b = 1$, the survey forecasts are *unbiased* predictors of actual inflation. This means that, while the survey may not predict inflation in a precise or accurate way at any point in time, it does not *systematically* overpredict or underpredict inflation. In other words, it predicts accurately *on the average*. Also, if the residual terms (e's) are random or serially uncorrelated, economic agents do not overestimate or underestimate inflation for many consecutive periods. The implication is that all available past information is incorporated into the forecasts. One could not improve one's forecast of future inflation by knowing past prediction errors. (For a statistical analysis of surveys of expected inflation, see the article by M. A. Akhtar, Cornelius Los, and Robert Stoddard cited in "Suggestions for Additional Reading" at the end of this chapter.)

[3] To a limited extent, the Tax Reform Act of 1986 changed this. Interest expenses incurred through consumer credit purchases were made nondeductible by the act, as Congress acted to remove tax incentives for dissaving by consumers. Other forms of interest expenditures, such as mortgage interest and business interest expenses remain deductible under the current tax law, however.

EXHIBIT 6-1

Performance of the Various Measures of Inflation Expectations

In evaluating various measures of expected inflation, two criteria are particularly useful: bias and average absolute error. *Bias* is the extent to which the measure tends to overpredict (+) or underpredict (−) inflation *on average*. The *average absolute error* is simply the sum of the absolute values of the differences between actual inflation and the rate that had been expected each period, divided by the number of periods. This indicates how *accurately* the measure tracks actual inflation. A measure might exhibit zero bias (thus being correct on average), yet exhibit enormous overprediction and underprediction errors each period which cancel out over the entire period. Over the period 1948–1995, the bias and average absolute error for three alternative measures of expected inflation are shown in the following table.

	Bias	Average Absolute Error
Livingston Survey	−0.94	1.55
Michigan Survey	−0.19	1.22
Naive expectations formulation*	+0.13	1.77

*Assumes expected inflation over the next 12 months equals actual inflation over the previous 12 months.

Both the Livingston and the Michigan Surveys exhibited a downward bias—that is, on average, they *underpredicted* inflation over the 47-year period. A naive expectations measure, which simply assumes that the expected inflation rate for the next 12 months will equal the actual inflation rate experienced in the most recent 12 months, is also evaluated. Surprisingly, the naive expectations measure exhibited the least bias over the period, although it ranked last in accuracy. Note that the Michigan Survey was the most accurate, exhibiting the lowest average absolute error of the three measures. Because the Michigan Survey also exhibited less bias than the Livingston Survey, it may be considered the most reliable. In more recent years, however, the Livingston Survey has outperformed the Michigan Survey on both criteria (not shown in table).

Source: Livingston Survey data from Federal Reserve Bank of Philadelphia; Michigan Survey data from Richard Curtin, University of Michigan.

In this equation, the **real aftertax interest rate** (r_{at}) equals the actual or nominal aftertax interest rate $i(1 - t)$ (where t is the marginal income tax rate) minus the expected inflation rate. Thus, if the owner of a 1-year Treasury bill yielding 10 percent is in a marginal income tax bracket of 30 percent, and if expected inflation in the next year is 4 percent, the real aftertax interest rate is only 3 percent, that is $10\% \times (1 - .30) - 4\%$. Because of the 30 percent marginal income tax rate, the owner gets to keep only 70 percent of the 10 percent yield; hence, the *nominal* aftertax yield is 7 percent. By subtracting the expected inflation rate of 4 percent, we obtain the real aftertax yield of 3 percent. The real aftertax rate, which is always lower than the simple real interest rate of Equation 6-1 if

Table 6-3		
Relationship between Nominal Interest Rate (i) and Two Measures of Real Interest Rate*		
Nominal Interest Rate (i) (%)	Real Interest Rate (r) (%)	Real Aftertax Interest Rate (r_{at}) (%)
5%	1%	−0.5%
8	4	1.6
10	6	3
14	10	5.8

*Assumes that expected inflation is 4 percent and the marginal income tax rate is 30 percent.

the marginal income tax rate is positive, would seem to be the more relevant measure of the real interest rate.[4] Table 6-3 shows the relationship between the nominal interest rate and the two measures of real interest rates (r and r_{at}) under the assumption that expected inflation is 4 percent and the marginal income tax rate is 30 percent.

Your Turn

Suppose you are interested in buying a 3-year U.S. Treasury note that pays 6 percent interest. Assuming you are in a 25 percent marginal income tax bracket (federal and state combined) and you expect inflation to average 3 percent annually over the next 3 years, calculate your real aftertax yield on the Treasury note.

THE HISTORICAL BEHAVIOR OF REAL INTEREST RATES

Figure 6-2 shows the behavior of the 90-day Treasury bill yield during the period 1964–1996, along with two measures of the real Treasury bill yield (r and r_{at}) calculated using Equations 6-1 and 6-2. The top line represents the nominal Treasury bill yield (i). The middle line represents the simple real Treasury bill yield (r) and the bottom line indicates the real aftertax yield for an individual in a 30 percent marginal income tax bracket (r_{at}). The shaded areas depict periods of recession—that is, periods of falling output and income.

---

[4]Viewed from the vantage point of borrowers, real rates appear much less burdensome if one uses real aftertax interest rates. For example, a borrower in a 40 percent marginal tax bracket (federal, state, and local tax rates combined) who pays 15 percent interest during a period of 6 percent expected inflation experiences a real aftertax interest cost of 3 percent. (Contrast this with the ostensibly punitive 9 percent real rate calculated using Equation 6-1.)

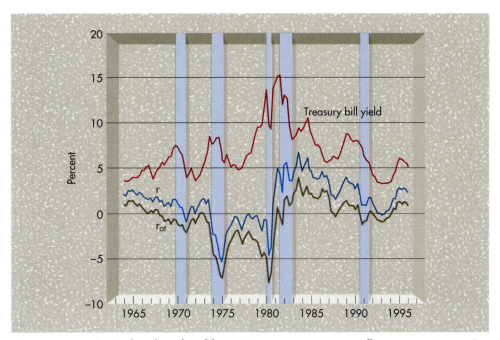

Figure 6-2   Nominal and Real Yields on 90-Day U.S. Treasury Bills, 1964–1996. Real yields on U.S. Treasury bills drifted downward from the mid-1960s–1980 and were negative throughout much of the 1970s. From 1981–1986, real yields were unusually high but recently have returned to more typical levels. (*Note:* Real yields were computed with Equations 6-1 and 6-2 using a rolling 12-month actual inflation rate [Consumer Price Index] as a proxy for expected inflation and a 30 percent marginal income tax rate.) *Source:* Constructed with data from *Citibank Economic Database.*

Both nominal and real yields tend to move procyclically—that is, they typically rise during the latter portions of an economic expansion and fall during a recession. (Note, for example, the decline in real yields in both the 1974–1975 and 1990–1991 recession.)[5] The procyclical pattern of real interest rates is partly attributable to sluggishness in the inflation process, that is, the tendency for the underlying inflation to persist for a considerable period.[6] In recessions, while nominal yields fall quickly, the inflation rate (and inflation expectations) are slower to come down. Hence, real yields decline. When nominal interest

---

[5]The increase in real interest rates during the 1981–1982 recession was atypical and therefore requires special explanation. Inflation had accelerated during the late 1970s and was running at double-digit levels in 1979 and 1980. The Federal Reserve pursued restrictive monetary actions, maintaining nominal interest rates at unusually high levels during the recession in a determined effort to knock out the severe inflation that had developed over the previous 15 years. As it turned out, inflation came down much faster than economists or the Fed expected, and the result was that (ex post) real interest rates *increased* significantly during 1981 and 1982.

[6]Labor contracts which fix wages at specific levels for fairly lengthy periods of time cause average wages to respond sluggishly and with a lag to business cycle conditions. Also, other institutional factors tend to impart inertia into the inflation process, thereby inhibiting the responsiveness of actual inflation to changes in business cycle conditions.

An International Comparison of Real Interest Rates

The figure below indicates the average ex post real interest rates in a sample of industrial nations over the period 1975–1994. The real rates are calculated by subtracting the average inflation rate over the period from the average yield on short-term government securities in the same period. Note that average real yields range from a high of about 4 percent in Australia, Canada, and the Netherlands to a low of 1 percent in Switzerland.

Because a huge worldwide pool of financial capital is poised to flow to nations exhibiting the highest expected real returns, a powerful force exists to equalize expected (ex ante) real yields across countries. How, then, can we account for the pattern shown below? Several factors may contribute. Income tax rates, for example, differ sharply across countries. The Netherlands had extremely high income tax rates in this period. This suggests that higher simple real yields (r) are required in the Netherlands than in the United States if real after-tertax yields (r_{at}) are to be equalized. Switzerland is known to be a safe haven where individuals can stash their wealth to avoid high taxes elsewhere. This suggests an abnormally large demand for bank deposits in Switzerland. Because banks typically pump excess funds into government securities, this may explain why Swiss short-term yields have been so low. The United States was also a safe haven for international funds during much of this period and experienced relatively low real Treasury bill yields.

Because the figure shows ex post rather than ex ante real yields, another possible explanation for the large range of real yields involves possible discrepancies between inflation expectations and actual inflation. If such discrepancies differ across countries, one would expect ex post real interest rates to differ also.

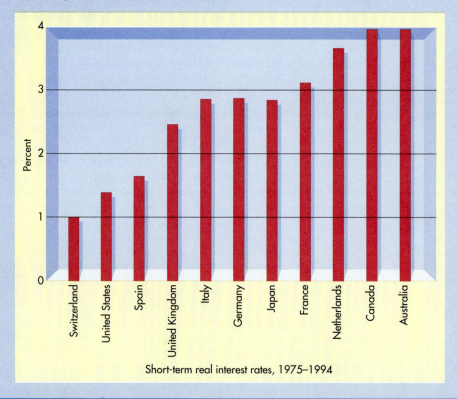

Short-term real interest rates, 1975–1994

rates are pulled up during the latter portion of a cyclical expansion, inflation and inflation expectations again tend to lag behind. Real interest rates typically (but not always) rise.

It should be pointed out that the Treasury bill market, like most financial markets, is a highly competitive one in which thousands of buyers and sellers interact to determine yields. It is interesting in this connection to contemplate the behavior of actual and real yields during this period of recent history. Note, for example, that during most of the 1970s, both measures of real Treasury bill yields were negative. This result is not unique to Treasury bill yields; a similar result is obtained if one uses the real prime loan rate, the real mortgage rate, or practically any other measure of real interest rates during that period. The negative real interest rate implies that debtors (borrowers) benefitted at the expense of creditors (lenders) during the period.[7] See Exhibit 6-2 for a discussion of one important implication of negative real interest rates.

What causes real interest rates to rise and fall? In the next section we will look at five factors that can influence the level of real interest rates.

FACTORS THAT INFLUENCE REAL INTEREST RATES

We have already discussed two major forces governing the level of real interest rates. These forces are the expected rate of return from new investment in capital goods and the rate of time preference, the extent to which people prefer present goods over future goods. An increase in the marginal productivity of capital and an increase in the rate of time preference, for example, will increase ex ante real interest rates. Also, high real interest rates are transmitted across countries. The large increase in demand for capital in China and Eastern Europe in the 1980s likely contributed to high real interest rates in the United States. And we know that central bank policies have considerable influence over nominal interest rates. Because ours is an economy in which inflation and inflation expectations develop momentum and are characterized by considerable short-run sluggishness, the Fed can influence real short-term interest rates for extended periods of time. Before we discuss Federal Reserve policies, however, we will examine some other factors that influence real interest rates—factors the Federal Reserve is incapable of controlling.

Supply Shocks: Changes in Energy Prices

When energy prices rise sharply, real interest rates should decline. This follows from the fact that the **marginal productivity of capital**—the return expected from net investment in new capital goods—declines when energy prices rise. Capital goods are relatively en-

---

[7]In the 15-year period from the mid-1960s through the 1970s, almost everyone in the United States who purchased a new home financed by a long-term mortgage experienced a *negative* real aftertax interest rate, which made the house a terrific investment. After 1980, real aftertax mortgage rates swung sharply into positive territory, contributing to a major slowdown of inflation of home prices.

EXHIBIT 6-2

Real Interest Rates, House Prices, and the Accumulation of Personal Wealth

The behavior of real interest rates has important implications for the redistribution of wealth between borrowers and lenders. One of the most dramatic examples of this phenomenon was experienced during the period from roughly 1965–1980 by those who owned homes financed by relatively low-interest-rate mortgages taken out in the 1960s or before.

Suppose your parents purchased a nice home in 1966 for $50,000, paying for it by making a $5,000 down payment and taking out a then typical 30-year fixed-rate mortgage for the remainder at 6 percent interest. Suppose too that in the inflationary environment that ensued, their home appreciated in value by an average of 10 percent per year over the 14-year period ending in 1980. What kind of investment would this home have turned out to be?

By 1980, the house would have appreciated in value to $189,875. The balance of the mortgage after 14 years would have been $33,249. By making monthly payments of $269.80 over a 14-year period (perhaps about the same amount that would have been required initially to *rent* the home), your parents would have parlayed $5,000 into $156,626. That works out to an average rate of return of about 28 percent per year.

In terms of Equation 6-1, the simple real interest rate in this example is −4 percent. Assuming a 25 percent marginal income tax bracket, the real aftertax interest rate is negative 5.5 percent (6% × .75) − 10%. Therefore, it is not surprising that your parents came out ahead on the investment. The power of compound interest, given the significantly large negative real interest rate, can produce surprisingly large gains for the borrower over a period of years.

For millions of American families, the home purchased in the 1950s, 1960s, or early 1970s, financed by a relatively low fixed-rate mortgage, was the best investment they ever made. The home became a major source of the family's wealth or net worth. By the mid-1970s, the euphoria produced by such gains was encouraging many families to purchase larger and more expensive homes than would formerly have been considered prudent. In many regions, speculation resulted in the bidding up of house prices to unrealistic levels by the late 1970s. Later on the bubble burst in some areas, producing significant declines in home prices.

Because mortgage rates are higher today than they were 30 years ago and the inflation rate of housing prices has decreased sharply, real mortgage rates are positive and relatively high. New homebuyers can no longer count on their house being the terrific investment it was for their parents.

---

ergy intensive: they require a relatively large amount of energy to operate. A sharp increase in energy prices (a negative "supply shock") signals a decline in the optimal amount of capital desired by firms per unit of output. This decline in the desired capital-to-output ratio means that real economic investment is less profitable. The rate of return on investment declines. The demand for investment goods by firms and therefore the demand for loanable funds falls. The demand curve for loanable funds shifts leftward or downward. This should pull down the real interest rate. Indeed, the pattern of rates shown in Figure 6-2 is consistent with this hypothesis. Note the extremely low level of real rates in the 1970s, the decade in which the negative supply shocks occurred.[8] When the real price of energy *declined* sharply in the 1980s, the *positive* supply shock worked to push up the returns on investment, raising the real interest rate. Note that the figure shows a far different pattern of real interest rates for the 1980s than for the 1970s.

Changes in Federal Tax Policy and the Regulatory Environment

Changes in tax policy and the regulatory environment can affect the profitability of business investment, altering the real interest rate. When the tax environment for business worsens, as it did in the 1970s, the returns expected from new investment decline.[9] Such a change should pull down the real interest rate. The decline in real interest rates from the mid-1960s through the 1970s (depicted in Figure 6-2) is consistent with this view (note the behavior of real rates in the 1970s as the burden of business taxation increased). On the other hand, the favorable tax policy, deregulatory measures, and probusiness climate ushered in with the implementation of the Reagan administration policies of the early 1980s would tend to increase the returns from investment and pull up real interest rates. A glance at Figure 6-2 indicates that the data are consistent with this hypothesis—that is, real interest rates were higher in the period of reduced tax rates and lower regulatory burdens on businesses than in the 1970s.

Changes in Federal Budget Deficits

As we saw in Chapter 5, an increase in the federal budget deficit directly increases the demand for loanable funds. The demand curve for loanable funds shifts rightward or upward. This means that interest rates (both nominal and real) must increase unless the supply curve of loanable funds is horizontal or unless the nation's private savings rate is directly boosted by the announcement of larger deficits (that is, unless the supply curve of loanable funds shifts significantly rightward). The expectation of a larger future deficit may also boost the premium in long-term interest rates by fostering uncertainty about the future. Large budget deficits have been experienced since the early 1980s; for political reasons, they have proven almost intractable. It is likely they have contributed to the maintenance of real interest rates above the levels that would otherwise have prevailed. Real

---

[8]In an article cited in "Suggestions for Additional Reading" at the end of this chapter, James Wilcox demonstrates that the negative supply shocks of the 1970s helped to account for the unusually low real interest rates of the 1970s.

[9]Before the indexation of the tax system for inflation, inflation and the tax system conspired to work a hardship against firms and create a bias against business investment. Because depreciation allowances were based on historic costs instead of replacement costs of capital goods, firms could recover through tax savings only a small portion of the funds required to replace worn-out capital. Contemporary accounting practices also overstated business profits for income tax purposes; firms were essentially paying taxes on fictitious profits. These biases against firms were removed in the 1980s by the comprehensive indexation of the tax system for inflation implemented in the Economic Recovery Tax Act of 1981.

interest rates (both long term and short term) increased sharply in the early 1980s as the large deficits emerged, while long-term real rates decreased sharply in 1995 and early 1996 as proposals for a major reduction in or elimination of the federal budget deficit by the year 2002 were discussed seriously by Congress and the president.

Deregulation of the Financial System

Prior to the 1980s, statutory interest rate ceilings (known as Regulation Q) put an effective lid on the interest rates financial institutions could pay depositors. Lenders regard bank deposits and money market instruments (Treasury bills, commercial paper, and so forth) as substitutes. The regulation may have increased the relative demand for Treasury bills and other instruments not subject to interest rate ceilings. If so, we may infer that security prices were higher and yields (interest rates) lower than those that would have prevailed in an unregulated financial environment. When the statutory ceilings were phased out in the 1980s, security prices dropped and yields moved up.

In the old, closely regulated financial system, the Fed could slow economic activity and stem inflation with only a modest increase in nominal interest rates. The movement of security yields to a point or two above the statutory interest rate levels precipitated **disintermediation,** the withdrawal of deposits from banks and thrift institutions. That in turn produced a quick slowdown in homebuilding activity, together with a contraction of demand for all the products that go into new homes. This meant that a modest increase in interest rates sufficed to achieve the Federal Reserve's aim of slowing aggregate spending and cooling off inflation. In the absence of statutory interest rate ceilings, nominal interest rates must increase by a considerably larger amount to cool off spending. Over the course of the business cycle as a whole, then, interest rates will tend to be higher in the absence of statutory ceilings.

Thus, an important structural change in the economy—financial deregulation—may have altered the relationship between expected inflation and the average level of nominal interest rates. Deregulation may have increased real interest rates, which have been higher in the 1980s and 1990s on average than in the 1970s.

Federal Reserve Policy

We have seen that the Fed has a strong influence on short-term nominal interest rates. Because inflation (and expected inflation) do not respond immediately to Federal Reserve actions, the Fed also influences real interest rates in the short run. Typically, the Fed conducts monetary policy by setting a specific target for short-term interest rates and leaving that target unchanged for a significant period. In the 1970s, for example, as inflation was escalating, the Fed held nominal rates at levels that turned out to be low relative to the inflation rate. In this way, the Fed contributed to the low ex post real interest rates of the 1970s (review Table 6-2); in the same table, note the high real interest rates of 1981 to 1985. By pursuing a relatively tight monetary posture in this period, the Federal Reserve likely contributed to the unusually high levels of ex post real interest rates in the early 1980s.

ARE FINANCIAL MARKETS SUBJECT TO MONEY ILLUSION?

We have provided several explanations to account for the pattern of real interest rates illustrated in Table 6-2 and Figure 6-2. Broadly speaking, real interest rates were significantly higher after 1980 than before. The year 1980 thus emerges as a sort of watershed. One interesting hypothesis views the period after 1980 as the normal time and the period before 1980 as an aberration requiring special explanation. Some economists believe that, for many decades, financial markets were subject to "money illusion" or "tax illusion," which they finally shed after the 1970s episode of severe inflation. The terms **money illusion** and **tax illusion** mean that economic agents (individuals and firms) fail to account fully for inflation and taxes in their behavior. In the case of money illusion, for example, individuals and firms (irrationally) base their decisions on nominal interest rates rather than real rates. In the case of tax illusion, individuals and firms (irrationally) base their decisions on the simple real interest rate (r) rather than the real aftertax rate (r_{at}).

Suppose we assume a 33 percent marginal income tax rate (federal, state, and local tax rates combined) and that inflation is expected to be 5 percent in the near term. In this case, a 12 percent nominal interest rate is equivalent to a real aftertax rate of only 3 percent, that is (12 percent $\times$ .66) $-$ 5 percent. This is within the range of real interest rates normally assumed to prevail as a result of the fundamental forces of productivity of capital and time preference. One could argue that the upward surge of real interest rates after the 1970s (shown in Figure 6-2) is attributable to the shedding of money illusion or tax illusion.[10] That is, after the 1970s, economic agents learned from the severe experience of the 1970s and finally began to think in terms of real (r) or aftertax real (r_{at}) interest rates rather than nominal interest rates (i). The real mystery, in this view, is not why real interest rates were so high in the 1980s but rather why they were so low in the 1960s and 1970s. Why did it take so long for real interest rates to reach the levels dictated by the fundamental forces of time preference and the productivity of capital?

Economists differ in the credibility they accord to the various explanations we have outlined for the behavior of real interest rates over the past 3 decades. If the hypotheses emphasizing financial deregulation and the shedding of money and tax illusion are the most important or true explanations, we can expect that higher real interest rates than those that prevailed before 1980 will be the norm for the future. If budget deficits play a major role in the determination of real interest rates, we can expect high real rates to be the norm until our elected officials come to grips with the deficit. (In this connection, eliminating the deficit in the next few years could lead to significantly lower nominal and real interest rates.) To the extent that energy prices and federal tax and regulatory policies hold the key, we can expect to observe significant changes in real interest rates over time as energy prices change and tax and regulatory policies are altered.

---

[10]This is the hypothesis advanced by Lawrence Summers in his comprehensive study of the impact of inflation on interest rates, cited in "Suggestions for Additional Reading" at the end of this chapter.

SUMMARY

Real interest rates adjust nominal interest rates for inflation. The expected, or ex ante, real rate is the difference between the nominal interest rate and expected inflation and is observed in advance. The realized, or ex post, real interest rate is the difference between the nominal interest rate and actual inflation and is observed only after the fact. Because actual inflation often differs from the rate that had been expected, ex ante and ex post real interest rates frequently differ. Economists estimate the ex ante real interest rate by employing the forecasts from macroeconomic models of inflation or the findings from surveys of expected inflation, and subtracting these estimates of expected inflation rates from nominal interest rates. These model forecasts and surveys of ex-

pected inflation do a reasonably good job of tracking actual inflation. Over the past 50 years, the surveys have exhibited a slight downward bias—that is, they have underpredicted inflation on average. Both ex ante and ex post real interest rates trended downward in the 1970s, increased to very high levels in the early 1980s, and returned to more typical levels after the mid-1980s. Fundamental forces that influence real interest rates are the marginal productivity of capital and the public's rate of time preference. Some of the other forces that influence real interest rates are energy prices, the tax and regulatory environment, Federal Reserve policies, and the federal budget deficit. Also, the deregulation of the financial system after 1980 may have boosted real interest rates.

Answer to Your Turn (p. 124)

The aftertax real yield is (6 percent × 0.75) − 3 percent, or 1.5 percent. Given the 6 percent pretax nominal return, the aftertax nominal return is 4.5 percent. Subtracting the 3 percent expected inflation from that figure gives us the aftertax real yield of 1.5 percent.

KEY TERMS

productivity of capital
time preference
expected or ex ante real interest rate
realized or ex post real interest rate
rational expectations theory

real aftertax interest rate
marginal productivity of capital
disintermediation
money illusion
tax illusion

STUDY QUESTIONS

1 Due to cultural differences, the Japanese seem to have a lower rate of time preference than Americans. In other words, the Japanese care less about current consumption and more about the future well-being of their society. Given other factors, would you expect the real interest rate in Japan to be higher or lower than that in America? Explain.

2 Suppose you form your expectations for future inflation solely by using a weighted average of recent past inflation. Specifically, suppose you employ the following formula: $p_t = .6p_{t-1} + .3p_{t-2} + .1p_{t-3}$, where the p's indicate the inflation rates experienced in the year indicated by the subscript (p_{t-1} represents last year, and so forth). If inflation in the last 3 years measured

6 percent, 5 percent, and 4 percent, respectively, what do you expect the inflation rate to be this year?

3 Using the formula in question 2, demonstrate that in a period of consistently rising inflation, your forecasts will consistently underpredict inflation. What will happen in a period of falling inflation? Is it rational to base inflation forecasts only on past inflation? Explain. (*Hint:* Study footnote 2 of this chapter, on p.122.)

4 Graph the results of question 3. Then examine Figure 6-1. Can you detect any similarities in the two graphs? Why do we say that the Livingston Survey is backward looking?

5 Suppose the current yield on 1-year Treasury bills is 8 percent. If you expect 4 percent inflation over the next year and are in a 25 percent marginal income tax bracket, what is your real aftertax rate of return? How does it compare with the simple real return (calculated by Equation 6-1)?

6 Interest earned from municipal bonds is nontaxable. Compare the real aftertax rates of return from a corporate bond yielding 10 percent and an equally safe municipal bond hypothetically yielding 10 percent, when expected inflation is 4 percent and the relevant income tax bracket is 20 percent. Why will market forces in reality prevent the stated scenario from occurring? If in fact the corporate bond yields 10 percent, what must the nominal rate of return on the municipal bond be in order to match the aftertax real return?

7 One of the first things the Clinton administration accomplished in 1993 was the enactment of an income tax hike and a reduction in government spending. These measures reduced the federal budget deficit. Analyze the impact of these actions on the level of real interest rates, as well as real aftertax rates. Do both of these measures of real rates change by the same amount? Explain.

8 Suppose next January the administration and Congress target major tax initiatives at corporations in an effort to spur investment spending. Given other factors, analyze the impact of these initiatives on the level of the ex ante real interest rate.

9 Suppose OPEC engineers a dramatic hike in oil prices in 1998, pushing the price of crude oil to $50 per barrel. Analyze the impact of this action on real interest rates.

10 In the United States, the "baby boomers" (born during 1946–1964) are rapidly moving into middle age (the age group with the highest saving rate). When this population bubble reaches retirement age, what will be the effect on real interest rates? Why?

11 Suppose you have wealth of exactly $100, which you can save or spend now on candy bars. The price of a candy bar is 50 cents, so you could purchase 200 candy bars today.

   a If you can earn a nominal rate of interest of 10 percent on a savings account, how much (nominal) wealth will you have in 1 year if you abstain from candy bars?

   b If the price of a candy bar increases to 52 cents in the next year, in line with other prices, what is the measured rate of inflation?

   c How many candy bars will you be able to afford 1 year from now if you decide to save your $100 now? What is your real return from saving? Have you benefitted materially or been hurt by saving?

   d How would your answers to part *c* change if the price of a candy bar increases to 55 cents in 1 year? To 60 cents?

12 On average, real interest rates were considerably higher during the 1980s than during the 1970s (review Table 6-2 and Figure 6-2). Outline *three* explanations you think might help to account for this fact.

13 In 1996, presidential candidate Steve Forbes campaigned on a platform that included a flat tax on earned income and a tax *exemption* on all income earned from financial assets. If this policy were enacted, what would be its implications for the real interest rate? The real aftertax rate?

SUGGESTIONS FOR ADDITIONAL READING

Important sources of information about real interest rates are included in the works by James C. Van Horne, Lawrence Summers, and James Wilcox cited in "Suggestions for Additional Reading" at the end of Chapter 5. Studies of the various surveys of expected inflation are reported in M. A. Akhtar, Cornelius Los, and Robert Stoddard, "Surveys of Inflation Expectations: Forward or Backward Looking?," Federal Reserve Bank of New York *Quarterly Review,* Winter 1983 to 1984, pp. 63–66, and Frederic Mishkin, "Are Market Forecasts Rational?," *American Economic Review,* 1981, pp. 295–306. An excellent recent article on measuring the real interest rate is Robert Darin and Robert Hetzel, "An Empirical Measure of the Real Rate of Interest," Federal Reserve Bank of Richmond *Economic Quarterly,* Winter 1995, pp. 17–47. A widely cited work on the role of income taxes in interest rate determination is Michael Darby, "The Finan-cial and Tax Effects of Monetary Policy on Interest Rates," *Economic Inquiry,* June 1975, pp. 266–276. A long-term historical study of real rates is Jeremy Siegel, "The Real Rate of Interest, 1800–1990," *Journal of Monetary Economics,* 1992, pp. 227–252. Inter-country comparisons of real interest rates are reported in Howard Howe and Charles Pigott, "Determinants of Long-Term Interest Rates: An Empirical Study of Several Industrial Counties," Federal Reserve Bank of New York *Quarterly Review,* Winter 1991–1992, pp. 12–28. Articles evaluating world real interest rates include O. J. Blanchard and L. H. Summers, "Perspectives on High World Real Interest Rates," *Brookings Papers on Economic Activity,* 1984:2, pp. 273–324, and Robert J. Barro and Xavier Sala-i-Martin, "World Real Interest Rates," *Macroeconomics Annual,* National Bureau of Economic Research (Cambridge, Mass.: MIT Press), 1990, pp. 15–61.

CHAPTER 7

The Term Structure and Risk Structure of Interest Rates

In Chapters 5 and 6 we developed a framework for analyzing the behavior of nominal and real interest rates. We examined the effect of such factors as expected inflation, the business cycle, government budget deficits, and Federal Reserve policy on the level of interest rates. We also examined the distinction between nominal and real interest rates, emphasizing the importance of real rates in many economic processes. Two other factors have significant bearing on both nominal and real interest rates: the length of time to maturity of a financial instrument and its default risk, the risk that the lender may not recover the original principal. The role of both these factors in interest rate determination is examined in some depth in this chapter.

THE TERM STRUCTURE OF INTEREST RATES

The length of time to maturity of a financial instrument contributes significantly to its yield. For purposes of analysis, suppose we hold constant all other factors that govern yields. In other words, suppose we choose securities of equal default risk, tax treatment, and marketability—that is, securities differing only in time to maturity—and compare their yields. The relationship that exists *at a given point in time* between the length of time to maturity and the yield on a security is known as the **term structure of interest rates.** The graphic illustration of this relationship is often referred to as the **yield curve.**

Figure 7-1 shows the yield curves for U.S. government securities on several dates. A set of points is plotted corresponding to the yields existing on a given day on various maturities of a particular type of bond. The graph indicates that, on May 15, 1981, 1-year bonds were yielding approximately 17 percent, 5-year bonds were yielding about 15 percent, and 30-year bonds were yielding roughly 14 percent. The yield curve, or term structure of interest rates, is thus a snapshot rather than a moving picture. The yields shown in Figure 7-1 are for U.S. government securities; a similar figure could be

135

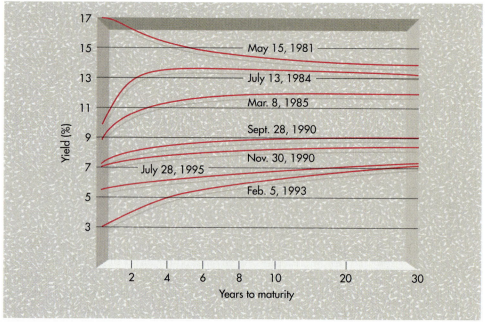

Figure 7-1 Yield Curves Prevailing on Selected Dates. The yield curve indicates the yields available on securities of differing maturities at a given point in time. The shape and position of the yield curve change continuously. *Source:* Constructed with data from *Citibank Economic Database.*

constructed for corporate or municipal bonds. By confining our graph to U.S. government securities, however, we can eliminate default risk and focus our attention on securities that are relatively marketable.[1]

We can see from the figure that both the level and the shape of the yield curve change significantly over time. Historically, upward-sloping, or ascending, yield curves have been much more common than downward-sloping, or descending, patterns. In the period 1979–1981, when yields were exceptionally high, the downward-sloping pattern prevailed. And in late 1994 and early 1995, the yield curve was almost flat for maturities beyond 2 years. In general, the differential between long-term and short-term yields diminishes or becomes negative as the level of interest rates rises. That is, the yield curve is typically flatter (and sometimes even downward sloping) when the general level of interest rates is relatively high. The yield curve is normally steeper when interest rates are relatively low. Note the strongly upward-sloping yield curve of Feb. 5, 1993, when interest rates were unusually low, and the descending yield curve of May 15, 1981, when interest rates were extremely high. We will provide explanations for these tendencies as we discuss the theories of term structure.

---

[1]U.S. government securities are considered to be free of default risk because the U.S. government has the constitutional authority to tax or, if necessary, to print money to meet its financial obligations. All maturities of U.S. government securities are highly liquid, although the short end of the market is more active and involves somewhat lower transactions costs than the long end.

⟩ FROM THE FINANCIAL PAGES ⟨

The Treasury Yield Curve

Each issue of *The Wall Street Journal* contains a graph showing the yield curves for U.S. Treasury securities the previous day, 1 week earlier, and 4 weeks earlier. The graph shown here was published on Friday, Feb. 16, 1996.

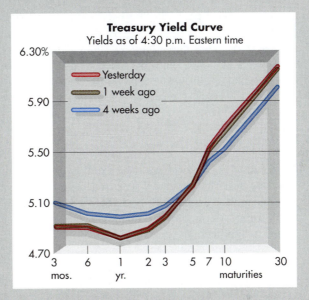

Treasury Yield Curve
Yields as of 4:30 p.m. Eastern time

A quick look at the graph allows potential lenders to compare the returns available on safe securities of various maturities. For example, on Feb. 15 (the red line) lenders could earn approximately 4.9 percent on 3- and 6-month Treasury maturities, 5.6 percent on 7-year maturities, and 6.2 percent on 30-year bonds. The yield curve was quite flat for the first 2 years of maturity and fairly steep beyond that.

Note the change in the shape of the yield curve for Feb. 15, 1996, in relation to the curve of 4 weeks earlier. In the past 4 weeks, short-term rates had declined significantly while long-term yields had increased. By the time you finish this chapter, you will have a good understanding of why the yield curve changed shape.

Figure 7-2 shows the various patterns the yield curve may take. The perfectly flat yield curve in panel *A* is highly improbable, although curves approaching it have occurred from time to time (note the curve for Nov. 30, 1990, in Figure 7-1). The ascending or upward-sloping yield curve in panel *B* is most common. While the downward-sloping, or inverted, yield curve in panel *C* sometimes occurs when interest rates are considerably higher than normal, the humped yield curve in panel *D* is more common. What determines the shape of the yield curve?

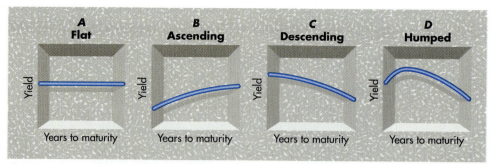

Figure 7-2   Yield Curve Patterns. The yield curve may assume any of four general shapes: flat (*A*), ascending (*B*), descending (*C*), or humped (*D*). The most common shape is the ascending, or upward-sloping, pattern (*B*).

THEORIES OF TERM STRUCTURE

To answer this question, we must examine four different theories of the term structure of interest rates. These theories seek to account for the shape of the yield curve at any point in time and for changes in its shape over time. These theories include the pure expectations theory, the liquidity premium theory, the segmented markets theory, and the preferred habitat theory.

The Pure Expectations Theory

The **pure expectations theory** singles out the role of current expectations about future interest rates as the crucial determinant of the current term structure of interest rates. According to this theory, market forces dictate that the yield on a long-term security of any particular maturity is equal to the geometric mean (the average) of the current short-term yield and the successive future short-term yields currently expected to prevail over the life of the long-term security. If that is the case, and if the transactions costs of buying and selling securities are assumed to be zero, an investor would expect to earn the same average return over the long run by purchasing a long-term bond and holding it to maturity as by purchasing a short-term bond and "rolling it over"—that is, reinvesting the proceeds each year in a new short-term security. In this theory, market forces operate to produce a yield curve, or term structure, that equalizes expected returns among alternative maturities for any planning period or investment horizon.

The pure expectations theory is based on the following assumptions:

1   Investors desire to maximize holding period returns, that is, the returns earned over their relevant time horizon.

2   Investors have no institutional preference for particular maturities. They regard various maturities as perfect substitutes for one another.

3 There are no transactions costs associated with buying and selling securities. Hence, investors will always swap maturities in response to perceived yield advantages.

4 Large numbers of investors form expectations about the future course of interest rates and act aggressively on those expectations.

If these assumptions are valid, the term structure of interest rates will reflect only the expectations about future interest rates. Nothing else will affect the shape of the yield curve.

The intuition underlying the pure expectations theory can be understood through a simple example. Suppose you have $10,000 in savings and you are hoping to buy a late-model used car in 2 years, when you graduate from college. You are a conservative investor and are unwilling to risk losing this wealth, so you are committed to investing in U.S. government securities, which have no default risk. You desire to maximize your returns over the 2-year period. Suppose you read in *The Wall Street Journal* that 1-year Treasury securities currently yield 4 percent, while 2-year Treasury securities yield 6 percent. Suppose further that the transactions fees of buying and selling Treasury securities are negligible. You face a choice between investing your $10,000 in the 2-year security and holding it until maturity (strategy 1) and investing in the 1-year security and reinvesting the proceeds a year from now, when the security matures (strategy 2).

The optimal choice depends on what you think the yield on 1-year Treasury securities will be a year from now. Suppose you think it will be the same as it is today—4 percent. Then clearly you are better off buying the 2-year bond, which yields 6 percent. Suppose, however, you expect 1-year Treasury yields to move up to 10 percent in the next year. In that case, you are better off employing the second strategy. By doing so, your return would average approximately 7 percent annually (4% plus 10%)/2 rather than the 6 percent per year currently available on the 2-year bond. That would give you more funds in 2 years than the first strategy, permitting you to purchase a nicer car.

The Implicit Forward Interest Rate: Two-Year Investment Horizon

There is some implicit **forward interest rate**—a rate on 1-year securities 1 year in the future—that would leave you indifferent between the two strategies. Consider the following expression:

$$R_1 + {}_{t+1}r_1 = 2R_2$$

R_1 and R_2 are the yields available today on 1- and 2-year Treasury securities, respectively. The term ${}_{t+1}r_1$ is the implicit forward rate that would balance the equation—the hypothetical 1-year rate which, if it prevails a year from now, would make your two investments produce the same average return over the 2-year period. Given that both R_1 and R_2 are known today (4 percent and 6 percent, respectively), it is easy to calculate this implicit forward rate:

$$_{t+1}r_1 = 2R_2 - R_1$$

Thus, in the example of the college student saving for a car, the implicit forward rate that would equalize returns for the two strategies is 8 percent—that is, $2 \times 6\% - 4\%$. The average return earned via the second strategy is the simple arithmetic mean of 4 percent and 8 percent—that is, 6 percent, which matches the return one earns by purchasing the 2-year bond and holding it to maturity.

In the case of *compounding*—in which both the principal and interest are reinvested each year—we need to modify the analysis somewhat. Consider the following expression:

(7-1)
$$(1 + R_1)(1 + {}_{t+1}r_1) = (1 + R_2)^2$$

In this formula, each dollar invested in a 1-year bond at yield R_1 is compounded after one year at the implicit 1-year forward rate $({}_{t+1}r_1)$ to earn the same rate of return available on 2-year bonds, R_2. Solving for the implicit forward rate, we obtain

(7-2)
$${}_{t+1}r_1 = \frac{(1 + R_2)^2}{(1 + R_1)} - 1 = \frac{(1.06)^2}{(1.04)} - 1 = 1.0804 - 1$$
$$= .0804, \text{ or } 8.04\%$$

Thus, the 1-year forward rate that would make you indifferent between the two strategies is slightly more than 8 percent. According to the pure expectations theory of term structure, this implicit rate is the market's expectation of the yield that will prevail a year from now on 1-year Treasury securities.[2]

To see that this is so, assume instead that the consensus in the market is that interest rates on 1-year securities will be less than 8 percent a year from now. Thus investors could accumulate more wealth over the 2-year period via the first strategy—that is, buying and holding the 2-year bond. If so, investors like yourself would sell their 1-year securities in order to purchase 2-year securities. In the process, the price of the 1-year bond would be bid down, raising its yield, while the price of the 2-year bond would be bid up, reducing its yield. R_1 would rise above 4 percent, and R_2 would fall below 6 percent. Such behavior would continue to boost 1-year yields and reduce 2-year yields until the expected returns from the two strategies were equalized.

If investors believe that a year from now 1-year yields will exceed 8 percent, they will sell 2-year bonds and purchase 1-year bonds. Such activity would drive up R_2 and drive down R_1 until the returns expected over the 2-year period were equalized. The pure expectations theory is based on the intuitively plausible notion that market forces will produce a term structure that leaves investors who are motivated to maximize returns indifferent among maturities. Such a term structure is the *only* equilibrium term structure; any other

---

[2]Economists evaluate this theory by testing whether the forward rate is an unbiased measure of the market's expectation of future short-term rates. The theory hypothesizes that the forward rate is equal to the expected future interest rate. For this reason, the pure expectations theory is sometimes known as the unbiased expectations theory. Consider the regression equation $i^e = a + bi^f$, where i^e is the expected future interest rate, i^f is the forward rate prevailing today, and a and b are parameters. In a regression model, if a and b are estimated to be 0 and 1, respectively, then i^f is said to be an unbiased estimate of i^e; that is, on average, the forward rate is equal to the expected future rate. Such an empirical finding would support the pure expectations theory. However, the theory is difficult to test because existing measures of the market's expectations of future interest rates are subject to shortcomings.

term structure produces incentives for investors and borrowers to switch maturities, thereby altering the shape of the yield curve.

In looking at Equation 7-1, you can see that if expected future short-term rates ($_{t+1}r_1$) exceed current short-term rates (R_1), then R_2 must exceed R_1. In other words, if interest rates are expected to rise, longer-term interest rates will exceed shorter-term interest rates—that is, the yield curve will be upward sloping. Conversely, if R_2 exceeds R_1, then $_{t+1}r_1$ must also exceed R_1. If the yield curve is upward sloping, there is a consensus that yields are going to increase.

On the other hand, if $_{t+1}r_1$ is lower than R_1, then R_2 is lower than R_1. This indicates that if the market expects rates to fall, the yield curve is downward sloping. Conversely, if R_1 exceeds R_2, then $_{t+1}r_1$ is smaller than R_1. If the yield curve is downward sloping, there is a consensus that interest rates are going to fall.

Implicit Forward Rate: 20-Year Investment Horizon

As we extend the planning period and the range of maturities beyond 2 years, we must use the formula expressed in the following equation to obtain the implicit forward rate:

$$(7\text{-}3) \qquad (1 + {}_tR_L)^n = (1 + {}_tR_1)(1 + {}_{t+1}r_1)(1 + {}_{t+2}r_1) \cdots (1 + {}_{t+(n-1)}r_1)$$

In this equation, the R's represent the yields actually available *today* on long-term bonds ($_tR_L$) and short-term (1-year) bonds ($_tR_1$). The investor has the option of buying a long-term bond and holding it or buying a short-term security and reinvesting the proceeds each year. The r's again represent the implicit forward interest rates—that is, the hypothetical interest rates that would balance the equation. The subscript preceding these actual and implied rates refers to the year (t being this year, $t + 1$ being 1 year from now, and so forth), while the subscripts following them refer to the number of years to maturity of the instrument (L being long term—that is, 20 years in this example—and 1 being 1 year). The variable n is the number of years in the planning horizon, or the investor's holding period.

Suppose an investor is considering investing in government securities over a 20-year period, beginning today. Equation 7-3 states that there is some implicit future pattern of short-term interest rates (r's) which, when combined with the yield existing today on 1-year bonds ($_tR_1$), would cause 1 dollar invested today to grow to the same sum in 20 years ($n = 20$) as one would accumulate by purchasing the 20-year bond today and holding on to it to maturity. According to the pure expectations theory, these implicit rates are *unbiased estimates* of the market's expectation of future interest rates.

The intuition underlying this theory is straightforward: rational investors desire to maximize their holding period returns. Suppose their holding period is 20 years. If a general consensus prevailed that investors could accumulate more wealth in a 20-year period by purchasing the 20-year bond and holding it to maturity, market participants would sell short-term bonds and buy long-term (20-year) bonds. Their action would push up short-term yields and bid down long-term yields until the advantage of the 20-year bond no longer existed. On the other hand, if the consensus were that more wealth could be accumulated over 20 years by buying the 1-year bond and reinvesting in 1-year bonds for 19 consecutive years, market participants would immediately begin selling their long-term bonds and purchasing short-term securities. Again, any initial advantage would be bid away as long-term yields were pushed up and short-term yields pressured downward. The pure expectations theory is appealing in that it is based on the rational notion that investors simply attempt to maximize their returns over their planning horizons.

If we rearrange Equation 7-3 to solve for $_tR_L$, we obtain the following expression:

$$(7\text{-}4) \qquad _tR_L = \sqrt[n]{(1 + {_tR_1})(1 + {_{t+1}r_1})(1 + {_{t+2}r_1}) \cdots (1 + {_{t+(n-1)}r_1})} - 1$$

This formula states that the current long-term bond yield ($_tR_L$) is the geometric mean, or average, of the current 1-year bond yield ($_tR_1$) and future 1-year bond yields (the r's) currently expected to prevail over the life of the long-term bond. This is the essential meaning of the pure expectations theory.

Note from Equation 7-4 that if the r's exceed $_tR_1$, then $_tR_L$ must exceed $_tR_1$. That is, if investors believe that interest rates will be higher in the future, the yield curve today is upward sloping; that is, long-term yields are higher than short-term yields. On the other hand, if the r's are lower than $_tR_1$, then $_tR_1$ must exceed $_tR_L$. If investors think interest rates will decline in the future, the yield curve is downward sloping or inverted. In the pure expectations theory, the existence of an ascending yield curve is evidence that the consensus in the market is that interest rates are headed upward. The existence of a downward-sloping or inverted yield curve implies that economic agents expect interest rates to be headed lower. A flat yield curve implies a consensus that future yields will remain the same as current yields.[3] In the pure expectations theory, *nothing* except the outlook for interest rates affects the shape of the yield curve.

Your Turn

Suppose the yield curve is currently perfectly flat, with yields being the same on U.S. securities of all maturities. At a time when the U.S. economy is operating very close to full employment, suppose the U.S. president unexpectedly announces a decision to become involved in a major foreign war. Assume you believe in the pure expectations theory.

a. As a personal investor in government securities with $100,000 to invest today, how would you allocate your funds between long- and short-term securities?

b. What would happen to the shape of the yield curve after the market digests the announcement of war?

The Liquidity Premium Theory

Another theory of term structure, the **liquidity premium theory,** accepts the basic intuition underlying the pure expectations theory of term structure, but with one major qualification. Because long-term bonds entail greater **market risk**—the risk of fluctuation in

---

[3]The humped yield curve illustrated in panel D of Figure 7-2 is rationalized by proponents of the pure expectations theory as follows: Suppose investors believe that interest rates are above normal and will come down, but not until they rise further in the near term. This belief would cause borrowers (issuers of debt instruments) to shy away from issuing both long-term and very-short-term debt instruments and concentrate their offerings in the intermediate range. Such behavior would produce the humped yield curve.

Table 7-1

Impact of Interest Rate Fluctuations on Zero-Coupon Bond Prices

Maturity	Price if *i* is 4%	Price if *i* is 6%	Price if *i* is 8%
1 year	$961	$943	$926
10 years	676	558	463
30 years	308	174	99

the value of the principal—than do short-term securities, long-term yields normally include a premium to compensate investors for that risk. The premium in longer-term bond yields for increased market risk is known as a **term premium.**

It is well known that the volatility of bond prices increases with the length of time to maturity. Long-term bonds are riskier than short-term bonds because investors may have to liquidate their assets before maturity, therefore exposing themselves to the possibility of big losses. Table 7-1 shows the prices for which 1-year, 10-year, and 30-year zero-coupon bonds (face value = $1000) will sell under three different interest rate scenarios.[4] The table documents the well-known fact that higher interest rates are synonymous with lower bond prices (read laterally across each row of the table). More importantly, note that for any given change in interest rates, long-term bond prices exhibit proportionally greater price fluctuations than do short-term bonds. For example, if yields rise from 6 percent to 8 percent, a 1-year zero-coupon bond declines in price from $943 to $926, a decline of less than 2 percent. On the other hand, the 30-year bond declines from $174 to $99, a decline of more than 40 percent. This demonstrates that the market risk in bonds increases with length of time to maturity.

If investors are risk averse, they must be compensated (through a premium in the yield) for the greater market risk inherent in long-term bonds.[5] According to the liquidity premium theory, the long-term interest rate is the average of the current and expected future short-term yields *plus* a term premium to compensate the investor for the additional market risk in long-term securities:

$$(7\text{-}5) \quad _tR_L = \sqrt[n]{(1 + {_tR_1})(1 + {_{t+1}r_1})(1 + {_{t+2}r_1}) \cdots (1 + {_{t+(n-1)}r_1})} - 1 + TP$$

[4]The general formula that relates the price of a zero-coupon bond to its yield is $PV = \$1000/(1 + i)^n$, where i is the yield, PV is the present value and price of the bond, and n is the number of years to maturity. The same principle relating price responsiveness to interest rate changes across maturities applies also to coupon bonds, but the formula relating price and yield is more complicated. Hence, we use zero-coupon bonds in this illustration.

[5]Conversely, if borrowers (issuers of debt) are risk averse, they will generally prefer to borrow in the long end of the market. Borrowing short term and refinancing frequently by issuing new debt exposes borrowers to the risk that interest rates may rise in the future. Thus, risk-averse borrowers prefer to borrow long term and lock in the interest rate. The predisposition to borrow long to avoid the risk of higher future interest rates contributes to the predominance of ascending yield curves. That is, the behavior of risk-averse borrowers reinforces the behavior of risk-averse lenders; both parties contribute to the general prevalence of an upward-sloping yield curve.

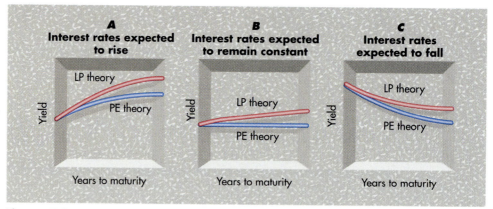

Figure 7-3   Term Structure in Pure Expectations Theory versus Liquidity Premium Theory. The liquidity premium theory implies a more steeply ascending (or less steeply descending) yield curve than the pure expectations theory does.

In this theory, the long-term rates *exceed* the average of current and expected future short-term rates by a term premium (*TP*) that is a positive function of the term to maturity of the longer-term bond. Because *TP* is positive and increases with the length of term, this theory asserts that the normal yield structure is ascending, or upward sloping. In other words, even if agents expect future interest rates to be the same as today's, the yield curve will slope upward. Only if market participants are in consensus that interest rates will come down *considerably* in the future will the yield curve slope downward.

Figure 7-3 illustrates the implications for the shape of the yield curve of the liquidity premium theory relative to the implications of the pure expectations theory. No matter what the outlook for interest rates, the liquidity premium theory implies higher long-term yields than the pure expectations theory does. When yields are expected to remain constant (implying a flat yield curve in the pure expectations theory), the liquidity premium theory implies a slightly upward-sloping yield curve. When yields are expected to rise (implying an upward-sloping yield curve in the pure expectations theory), the liquidity premium theory implies an even steeper yield curve. When yields are expected to fall (implying a downward-sloping yield curve in the pure expectations theory), the liquidity premium theory implies a more gently downward-sloping curve, or perhaps even a flat or modestly upward-sloping curve. Exhibit 7-1 illustrates the relevance of the theory of term structure for an important real-world policy issue—how the U.S. Treasury should manage the maturity structure of its debt.

The Segmented Markets Theory

Another theory of term structure, the **segmented markets theory,** asserts that securities of different maturities are very poor substitutes for one another. It disputes the second assumption underlying the pure expectations theory, asserting instead a strong preference for particular maturities. This assertion is held to be true for both suppliers

EXHIBIT 7-1

Managing the National Debt

One of the tasks of the U.S. Treasury is managing the federal debt. Because about one-third of the nation's marketable debt is in maturities of 1 year or less, each year the Treasury must issue at least $1.2 trillion of new debt to refinance maturing debt. The Treasury must also finance new borrowing resulting from the annual budget deficits, which have been running at approximately $200 billion per year in recent years.

In funding the national debt, the Treasury is confronted with decisions regarding its maturity. Should it issue short-term or long-term debt? An important consideration in making this decision is the desire to minimize the interest expense incurred by the government.

In 1993, shortly after taking office, the Clinton administration floated a proposal that the Treasury stop issuing long-term bonds and instead fund the debt entirely through short-term Treasury bills. At first blush, the proposal looked tempting. In late 1993 and early 1994, the yield curve was unusually steep. Short-term yields were around 3 percent, while 30-year bond yields were roughly 8 percent. There was no doubt that, in the near term, the Treasury could save money for taxpayers by issuing only short-term bills. Given such yields, if the Treasury issued $1.2 trillion of new debt, the government would incur $60 billion less interest expense in the first year alone by funding all its borrowing requirements in the short-term sector rather than in 30-year bonds.

But what about later years? Remember that the pure expectations theory states that the yield on long-term securities is simply the average of the current short-term yield and the short-term yields expected to prevail in the future. In this view, if market expectations are correct, the ultimate cost to the Treasury over a period of years will be the same regardless of the maturity of newly issued debt. This suggests that though the Treasury will initially save taxpayers money by shortening the maturity of the debt, it will lose later when it refinances in periods of higher interest rates. Only if the market is wrong about future interest rates and the Treasury is wiser than the market can the Clinton administration idea save money. Indeed, proponents of the pure expectations theory regard the proposal as arrogant, shortsighted, and politically motivated.

If the liquidity premium theory is valid, the Clinton administration's proposal would likely save taxpayers money over the long term. In this theory, because long-term rates are higher *on average* than short-term rates, it would pay to reduce the average maturity of the nation's debt. In 1996, the average maturity of the nation's marketable debt was approximately 5 years.

of loanable funds (lenders) and demanders of loanable funds (borrowers). From the vantage point of lenders, short-term securities possess liquidity and great stability of principal (that is, price stability). Thus, they have low market risk. On the other hand, long-term securities provide stability of income over time. By buying a long-term bond, a lender locks in a fixed income for many years. Thus, a lender who prefers stability of income over stability of principal would clearly prefer long-term bonds. And a lender who values protection of principal over stability of income would clearly prefer short-term securities.

Borrowers too are alleged to have fairly clear-cut preferences. Firms borrowing to finance inventories prefer short-term loans. Families buying homes prefer long-term fixed-rate mortgages to avoid the risk that monthly payments might rise with interest rates after the home is purchased. And municipalities and corporations, which finance long-term capital projects by issuing debt, prefer to borrow long term to ensure continuous access to funds and lock in interest costs in advance.

According to the segmented markets theory, institutions are strongly motivated to match the maturities of their assets with the maturities of their liabilities. For example, life insurance companies, whose liabilities (life insurance claims) are clearly long term and predictable on the basis of mortality tables, strongly prefer to invest in long-term assets such as corporate bonds and mortgages. They seek a stable and certain flow of income in the future. Allegedly, they cannot be tempted to invest in short-term securities. Commercial banks, on the other hand, have a short-term liability structure. Demand deposits and many savings deposits are essentially withdrawable on demand. Banks therefore find it prudent to maintain a substantial portion of their assets in a highly liquid form. That explains the popularity of U.S. Treasury bills and other short-term financial instruments in commercial bank portfolios. Similarly, because money market mutual funds issue "shares" that are cashable on demand, they strongly prefer short-term instruments with a low market risk, such as Treasury bills, commercial paper, and negotiable CDs.

The segmented markets theorists conclude from these assertions that there is little or no scope for substitution of securities of different maturities in response to yield differentials. Each maturity sector of the market is viewed as being almost totally walled off from other maturity sectors. Because of low substitutability, yields in any maturity sector are determined strictly by supply and demand conditions in that sector, with minimal influence from other maturity sectors. The flow of funds from one maturity to another in response to interest rate incentives is regarded as minimal and almost nonexistent.

According to this theory, corporate and U.S. Treasury debt-management decisions significantly influence the shape of the yield curve. If firms and the government are currently issuing predominantly long-term debt, the yield curve will be relatively steep. If they are issuing principally short-term debt, short-term yields will be high relative to long-term yields. Thus, in the segmented markets theory, Treasury debt management is a potential tool of economic policy. Suppose the Treasury would like to raise short-term interest rates to attract foreign capital to the U.S. and strengthen the dollar in foreign exchange markets. Suppose it also wants to reduce long-term interest rates in order to bolster domestic investment in plant, equipment, and new technology. By issuing only short-term debt, the Treasury could push up short-term yields and reduce long-term yields, effectively twisting the yield curve (see Figure 7-4). The Federal Reserve could contribute to the twisting of the yield curve by simultaneously selling short-term securities and buying long-term bonds.[6] Such influence over the yield

---

[6]The Fed and Treasury collaborated in the early 1960s in an attempt to twist the yield curve in this manner. In the empirical literature on that episode, there is no consensus as to whether the effort succeeded.

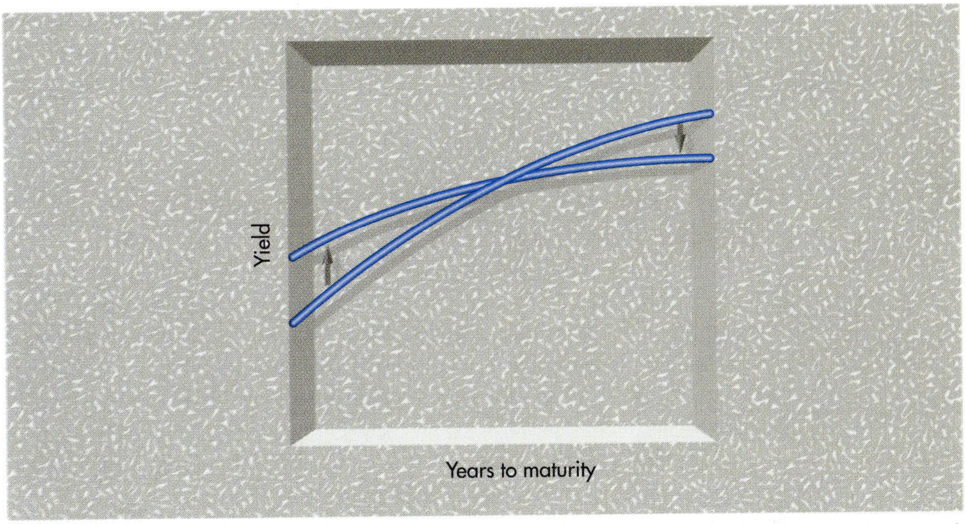

Figure 7-4   Twisting the Yield Curve. In the segmented markets theory, the Treasury and Federal Reserve can change the shape of the yield curve by altering the supply of and demand for securities of various maturities.

curve is not feasible if the pure expectations theory or its variant, the liquidity premium theory, is valid. In those theories, interest rate expectations determine the shape of the yield curve.

The Preferred Habitat Theory

The **preferred habitat theory** combines elements of the other three theories of term structure. Its proponents hypothesize that borrowers and lenders do have strong preferences for particular maturities. The yield curve will therefore not conform strictly to the predictions of the pure expectations and liquidity premium theories. However, if the expected additional returns to be gained by deviating from their preferred maturities or habitats become large enough, institutions will in fact deviate from their preferred maturities or habitats. For example, if the expected returns on long-term securities exceed those on short-term Treasury bills by a large enough margin, banks and money market mutual funds will lengthen the maturities of their assets. That is, they will purchase some intermediate- or long-term bonds. And if the excess returns expected from buying short-term securities become large enough, life insurance companies will stop limiting themselves to the long end of the market and will place a limited portion of their portfolio in shorter-term instruments.

The preferred habitat theory is based on the realistic notion that agents and institutions will accept additional risk in return for additional expected returns. In accepting elements of both the segmented markets and pure expectations theories, yet rejecting their extreme polar positions, the preferred habitat theory moves closer to explaining real-world phenomena. In this theory, both market expectations and the institutional factors emphasized in the segmented markets theory influence the term structure of interest rates.

TERM STRUCTURE THEORIES: HOW WELL DO THEY EXPLAIN THE FACTS?

The validity and usefulness of any theory hinges on its ability to explain real-world phenomena. The facts that any useful term structure theory must explain include the following empirical regularities in the term structure of interest rates:

1 The yield curve is upward sloping most of the time; on average, long-term yields have been significantly higher than short-term yields.

2 The yield curve typically shifts up and down over time rather than twisting or rotating. In other words, when short-term yields are rising, long-term yields are usually also rising; when short-term yields fall, long-term yields usually fall. Short- and long-term yields seldom move in opposite directions.

3 While both short-term and long-term interest rates exhibit a procyclical pattern, short-term yields exhibit much greater amplitude over the business cycle than long-term yields do. Short-term yields fall faster than long-term yields in a recession and rise faster than long-term yields during an economic expansion. Therefore, the yield curve exhibits a regular cyclical pattern, sloping steeply upward near the low point of the business cycle but flattening out as the expansion phase proceeds and frequently even inverting as the economy approaches the peak of the business cycle.

In the following sections we will examine each of these phenomena and explain how well each theory accounts for these empirical regularities.

Fact 1: The Upward-Sloping Yield Curve Predominates

Upward-sloping yield curves are much more prevalent than inverted yield curves. Furthermore, in periods when inverted yield curves do occur, short-term interest rates exceed long-term rates by a significantly smaller margin than the corresponding margins by which long-term yields exceed short-term yields when the yield curve is upward sloping. Table 7-2 documents the tendency for long-term rates to exceed short-term rates, on average, in the post–World War II era. The second column indicates the amount by which yields on 5-year Treasury securities exceeded yields on 90-day Treasury bills ("the spread"), on average, for each decade. The third column indicates the average size of this spread between 30-year Treasury bonds and 90-day Treasury bills for each decade. The

Table 7-2

Average Yield Spreads on U.S. Government Securities, 1950s–1990s

Decade	5-Year, 90-Day Spread (%)	30-Year, 90-Day Spread (%)	Months Ascending (%)*
1950s	+0.67%	+1.04%	98%
1960s	+0.59	+0.56	73
1970s	+0.92	+1.10	73
1980s	+1.20	+1.74	87
1990s†	+1.86	+2.72	100
1950–1995	+0.98%	+1.32%	85%

*Percentage of months in which the 30-year bond yield exceeded the 3-month Treasury bill yield.

†Includes 1990–1995.

Source: *Citibank Economic Database* and *Federal Reserve Bulletin,* various issues.

final column indicates the percentage of months during each decade in which this latter spread was positive—that is, the percentage of months during which the yield curve was upward sloping.

The predominance of the upward-sloping yield curve in this period is extremely difficult to reconcile with the pure expectations theory. If the theory were valid, upward-sloping and downward-sloping yield curves would occur with approximately equal frequency. Instead, the yield curve was upward sloping 85 percent of the time over the 46-year period (right-hand column of the Table 7-2). According to the pure expectations theory, this would occur only if people persistently regard interest rates as being below normal levels and therefore persistently expect them to be higher in the future. But such an asymmetrical and biased expectation is inconsistent with the theory of rational expectations, which asserts that people do not repeatedly make the same mistake—that is, *on average,* people do not expect interest rates to increase. Hence, the strong predominance of the upward-sloping yield curve is incompatible with the pure expectations theory.[7]

Also, the pure expectations theory implies that, over a long period of years, the yield spread should be zero on average. In each of the 5 decades listed, the average yields on both 5-year and 30-year bonds exceeded those on short-term Treasury bill yields. On average, the 5-year yield exceeded the bill yield by 0.98 percentage points, while the 30-year bond yield exceeded the bill yield by 1.32 percentage points. (Note that most of the upward slope in the yield curve typically comes in the first 5 years of the maturity structure.)

---

[7]A possible explanation consistent with the pure expectations theory is that transactions costs are higher for longer-term instruments. Also, longer-term markets are thinner and dealer bid-to-ask price spreads are larger for longer-term securities. These factors related to transactions costs may typically produce a modest yield premium in longer-term securities independent of market risk considerations. It is not possible, however, that this consideration could be sufficient to account for the relatively large average yield differentials shown in the table.

Because the liquidity premium theory predicts the existence of a premium in long-term yields to compensate for risk, it is consistent with the facts reported in Table 7-2. Indeed, this theory was developed in response to the observed propensity of the yield curve to be upward sloping most of the time. The segmented markets theory, because it emphasizes institutional preferences for various maturities by lenders and borrowers, is also consistent with the facts shown in the table. Because it accepts portions of all other term structure theories, the preferred habitat theory is also compatible with these facts.

Fact 2: The Yield Curve Typically Shifts Rather Than Rotates

Most of the time, when short-term yields are falling, long-term yields are declining as well. And when short-term rates are on the rise, long-term rates are usually rising also. In other words, the yield curve normally shifts upward or downward each week or month rather than twisting or rotating.

The pure expectations theory and its close relative, the liquidity premium theory, easily explain this empirical regularity. Suppose that short-term yields are pushed up by aggressive Federal Reserve sales of short-term securities or by large issues of new Treasury bills by the U.S. Treasury. Because the various maturities are regarded as close substitutes, this rise in short-term yields will trigger a chain of reactions. Lenders will be induced to sell some of their long-term bonds in order to purchase the newly attractive short-term securities. And borrowers will be induced to issue more longer-term securities to avoid the suddenly increased cost of borrowing in the short end of the market. These actions by lenders and borrowers will push up long-term yields and reduce short-term yields, quickly transmitting the increase in short-term rates to long-term maturities. Thus the yield curve shifts.

Because the liquidity premium theory and preferred habitat theory are essentially modifications of the pure expectations theory, they too explain the propensity of long- and short-term rates to move together over time. However, the segmented markets theory has problems accounting for the shifting yield curve. Because the theory regards the various maturities as poor substitutes for one another, its proponents would not expect the increase in short-term yields to be transmitted to other maturities. Instead, the yield curve would show an isolated blip (increase in yield) in the market sector in which the Fed is selling securities (or the sector in which the Treasury is issuing securities). Only by chance, in the segmented markets theory, would the yield curve shift—for example, if some event triggered a simultaneous increase in demand for all maturities (shifting the entire yield curve down). But the fact that the yield curve tends to be relatively smooth most of the time suggests a high degree of substitutability among maturities, casting doubt about the validity of the segmented markets theory.

Fact 3: The Yield Curve Exhibits a Regular Cyclical Pattern

Both short-term and long-term interest rates move procyclically over the course of the business cycle, rising during economic expansions and falling during recessions. But short-term rates exhibit much greater amplitude over the cycle. This fact implies that the yield curve also has a regular pattern over the course of the business cycle. Figure 7-5 illustrates these empirical regularities. The figure shows the yields on 30-year and 90-day U.S. government securities, together with the differential between them over the most recent 30-year period. Periods of recession are shaded.

Recall that, at the trough of a recession and in the early portion of a recovery, the yield curve is strongly ascending—that is, long-term yields substantially exceed short-term yields. But as a nation's output expands during the second half of the recovery, short-term interest rates increase more strongly than long-term rates do. Hence, the yield curve shows a flat pattern as the economy approaches the peak of a cycle. Typically, some months before the peak, the short-term rates move above the long-term rates and the yield curve becomes inverted, or downward sloping. During the ensuing recession, the pattern is reversed. As the economy moves toward the trough (low point) of the recession, the short-term interest rates move down faster than the long-term rates, and the yield curve resumes its strongly ascending pattern.

This cyclical pattern of the yield curve is easily explained by the pure expectations theory and its hybrids. Financial market agents are well aware of the historic propensity for interest rates to move procyclically—to rise during expansion and fall during recession. During an expansion, as the economy picks up steam and approaches full employment, interest rates rise. Wise participants in the market realize that this is a normal phenomenon and that interest rates are likely to fall as soon as the economy weakens again. They therefore take actions which tend to flatten or invert the yield curve. That is, investors sell short-term securities and use the proceeds to purchase long-term bonds to lock in their attractive yield. Later, as the economy moves into recession and then reaches a trough, savvy financial market participants recognize that interest rates are abnormally low and are likely to rise in the future. As they adjust their strategies accordingly (selling long-term bonds and purchasing short-term maturities), the yield curve takes a strongly ascending pattern.

Though the segmented markets theory's explanation for the cyclical pattern of the term structure is not as neat as that of the pure expectations theory, it is credible. According to this theory, as the economy expands in a cyclical upswing, bank loan demand increases. At the same time, however, the Fed tightens its monetary posture. To get the funds with which to accommodate the demand for loans, banks are forced to sell off short-term securities. Heavy selling of Treasury bills by banks pushes their prices down and yields up, flattening and possibly inverting the yield curve. In recessions, as the demand for loans at banks plummets and the Fed eases credit conditions, banks are awash with funds. Because they have an institutional bias against long-term bonds, they pump their excess funds into Treasury bills, pushing up their prices and lowering their yields. This action produces a strongly upward-sloping yield curve. Hence, in the segmented markets theory, the residual role of Treasury bills in bank portfolios can at least partially account for the cyclical behavior of the yield curve. Exhibit 7-2 discusses the potential usefulness of the yield curve for purposes of economic forecasting.

In sum, most theories of the term structure of interest rates encounter difficulty in explaining some of the empirical regularities experienced by economic phenomena. The pure expectations theory utterly fails to explain why yield curves are normally upward sloping. The segmented markets theory cannot account for the persistent tendency for

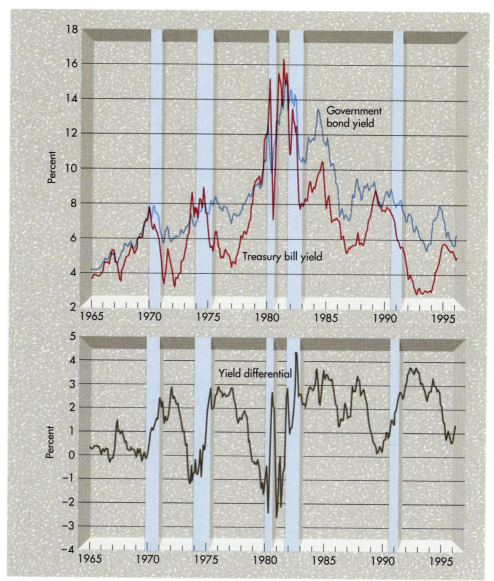

Figure 7-5   Long-Term versus Short-Term Yields, 1965–1996. Short-term yields exhibit greater cyclical amplitude than do long-term yields (top panel). The differential between long- and short-term rates tends to fall during periods of economic expansion and rise during recessions (bottom panel).   *Source: Citibank Economic Database.*

EXHIBIT 7-2

How Well Does the Term Structure of Interest Rates Forecast the Future?

Information about likely future economic conditions is of considerable value to both individuals and business firms. The latter shell out large sums of money to purchase economic forecasting services. Unfortunately, such services are notorious for their lack of accuracy. Some observers have suggested that a much cheaper (virtually free) yet equally reliable source of information about future economic conditions is contained in the term structure of interest rates. Can the term structure be used to forecast the future course of interest rates or real GDP?

Remember that a strongly upward-sloping yield curve indicates a consensus in the marketplace that interest rates are likely to move higher. A downward-sloping, or inverted, yield curve indicates that the market expects interest rates to fall. Because interest rates tend to fall during recessions, a downward-sloping yield curve may be a harbinger of recession.

Several conditions are necessary for the yield curve to function reliably as a forecasting tool. First, the shape of the yield curve must be heavily influenced by expectations about future interest rates, as is hypothesized in all term structure theories except the segmented markets approach. Second, people's expectations about the future direction of interest rates must be broadly correct. And if the yield curve is to be helpful in forecasting not just interest rates but economic activity as well, interest rates must be strongly correlated with economic activity—that is, they must move in a systematic fashion over the business cycle.

Assume under these conditions that interest rates and economic activity have both been very high in recent months. Suppose a widespread belief exists that the economy will go into recession soon and interest rates will fall. Through the forces discussed in this chapter (in all theories except the segmented markets theory), the yield curve will become inverted. If the economy does decline into recession next year and if interest rates do fall during the recession (as they almost always do), the inverted yield curve will have correctly signaled both the recession and the decline in interest rates.

Let's look at the historical record of the past 30 years to see how well the yield curve has signaled the future course of economic activity. The period 1964–1996 witnessed five recessions—periods in which real output declined for at least 2 consecutive quarters. In all five instances, the yield curve was inverted, with 1-year bond yields exceeding 30-year bond yields at some point in the *year* immediately preceding the recession. In four instances it was inverted in the *month* preceding the downturn. In one instance an inverted yield curve was *not* followed by a recession, but that episode (1966–1967) narrowly escaped meeting the criteria for a recession. The Federal Reserve Bank of Cleveland has reported that at least some segment of the yield curve was downward sloping in the year preceding 13 of the 17 cyclical downturns that have occurred since 1910.

Thus, while the term structure of interest rates is not a perfect indicator of future economic conditions, it is a useful and cost-free source of information.

short- and long-term yields to move in the same direction. The preferred habitat theory is more versatile in accounting for these empirical regularities. While it acknowledges certain institutional preferences for specific maturities on the part of borrowers and lenders, it also attributes a powerful influence to expectations in determining the term structure of interest rates.

Now that we have an understanding of the effect of term to maturity on the level of interest rates, we conclude our discussion of interest rates by examining the role of default risk on the level of yields.

THE RISK STRUCTURE OF INTEREST RATES

A default is a failure to meet the terms of a contractual agreement in full. In the case of a debt instrument such as a bond, default may refer to the borrower's failure to make the full interest payment as stipulated or to the failure to redeem the bond at face value at maturity. In a bond default there are varying degrees of loss to the lender, ranging from a delay in the payment of interest to a total loss of interest and principal.

Embedded in the yields of risky securities is a premium to compensate the lender for the risk of default. The magnitude of this premium varies widely among different securities. Conceptually, the magnitude of the premium may be estimated by taking the difference between the yield on a risky security and that on a security which is free of default risk but is similar in other respects (maturity, tax treatment, and so forth). For example, to estimate the default premium on 90-day commercial paper, one can look at the difference between its yield and the yield on 90-day Treasury bills. To estimate the premium on a corporate bond, one can calculate the difference between its yield and the yield on a U.S. government bond of comparable maturity.[8] This spread between the yields on securities with and without default risk is known as the **risk premium.** A bond with default risk will have a risk premium built into its yield, and an increase in this default risk will increase the risk premium.

Needless to say, potential bond buyers need information on the default risk of various bonds. Two investment advisory services, Moody's and Standard & Poor's, provide ratings of the quality of corporate and municipal bonds in the United States. Table 7-3 compares the rating schemes. Bonds with a Moody's rating of Baa or above are considered to be investment grade; bonds with lower ratings are considered **junk bonds.**

Figure 7-6 compares the yields on long-term U.S. government bonds and Moody's Baa-rated corporate bonds over the past 30 years. The yield differential between the two (bottom line in the figure) may be thought of as a measure of the default risk of the corporate bonds. Periods of recession are shaded.

---

[8]Actually, the tax treatment of the two bonds differs slightly. Interest earned on U.S. government bonds is nontaxable by state government and taxable by the federal government, while income earned on corporate bonds is taxable by both the federal and state governments. This consideration implies that even if a corporate bond had no default risk, the market would place a slight premium in its yield relative to that of U.S. government bonds to compensate for the modest difference in tax treatment.

Table 7-3

Bond Ratings of Investment Advisory Services

Moody's	Standard & Poor's	Interpretation
Aaa	AAA	Highest quality
Aa	AA	High quality
A	A	Upper medium quality
Baa	BBB	Medium quality
Ba	BB	Lower medium quality
B	B	Speculative grade
Caa	CCC	Poor quality
Ca	CC	Highly speculative grade
C		Extremely poor quality
	D	In default

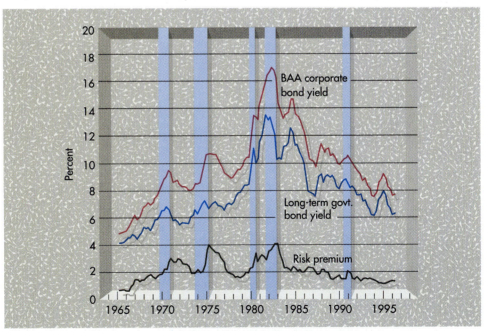

Figure 7-6   Yields on Corporate Baa Bonds versus Government Bonds, 1965–1996. The default risk of a bond is indicated by the difference between its yield and the yield on a risk-free bond. The difference widens during recessions and other periods of financial distress. *Source: Citibank Economic Database.*

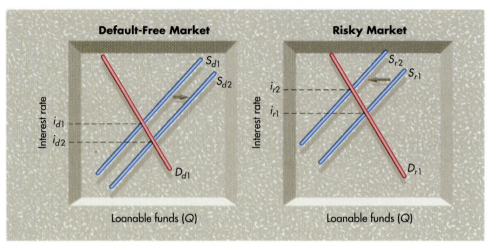

Figure 7-7 Analysis of Changing Risk Premiums. When default risk increases, lenders redirect funds from risky markets to risk-free markets. This increases the yield differential, that is, the risk premium in corporate bond yields.

Typically, the magnitude of the gap between the yields on these bonds increases in periods of recession and at other times when firms experience financial distress. For example, the risk premium was extremely high during the Great Depression of the 1930s and was low and relatively stable during the tranquil period of the 1950s and early 1960s (not shown). It rose again during the unstable 1970s and early 1980s, then trended downward in the more stable period of the past decade. The severe recessions of 1973–1975 and 1981–1982 saw risk premiums that were much higher than those experienced in the relatively mild recession of 1990–1991.

We can graph the behavior that produces a change in risk premiums. Figure 7-7 shows the initial supply and demand for loanable funds in both the risky and default-free bond markets. The left-hand portion of the figure shows the market in default-free securities (U.S. government bonds); the right-hand portion shows the risky market (corporate bonds). Remember that the supply curve originates from surplus units seeking to lend their funds in order to earn interest. The yields initially prevailing in the default-free and risky markets are i_{d1} and i_{r1}, respectively. The risk premium in corporate bonds is the difference, $i_{r1} - i_{d1}$.

Now suppose a major U.S. corporation shocks the financial markets by announcing a dramatic deterioration in its financial condition, raising the specter of insolvency. The psychological effect of the announcement is likely to have a significant impact on the bond markets, including an upward revision in the risk premium required on the yield on corporate bonds, especially those that do not have outstanding credit ratings. In Figure 7-7, we ignore any shifts in the demand for loanable funds (behavior by borrowers) and focus on the behavior of lenders.[9] Because lenders are now more conscious of the possibility of default, they will attempt to upgrade the quality of their portfolios. The supply of funds offered in the default-free market (government bonds) increases from

---

[9]Keep in mind that the supply of loanable funds corresponds to the demand for bonds: an increase in the supply of loanable funds implies an increase in the demand for bonds.

S_{d1} to S_{d2}, while the supply of funds offered in the risky market decreases from S_{r1} to S_{r2} as lenders reallocate their funds to safer markets. The result is a simultaneous increase in yields on corporate bonds and decrease in yields on government bonds; the risk premium increases to $i_{r2} - i_{d2}$.

This analysis explains the tendency for the risk premium to fluctuate over the course of the business cycle. Typically, the yield spread increases in recessions and decreases during economic recoveries. In recessions, business sales and profits decline and more firms are exposed to financial problems. As more firms go bankrupt, lenders divert their funds from corporate bonds to government bonds, and the default premium increases. During an economic recovery, firms' sales and profits increase, reducing their exposure to financial problems, and business failures decline. Lenders become more willing to purchase the higher-yielding corporate bonds, and the default premium narrows.

SUMMARY

The term structure of interest rates is the relationship between the length of time to maturity of a debt instrument and its yield, all other factors influencing yields being held constant. The graphic depiction of the term structure is known as the yield curve. There are several theories of term structure. The pure expectations theory singles out the role of expected future interest rates in explaining the term structure. The liquidity premium theory accepts the pure expectations theory with the added caveat that long-term yields contain a term premium to compensate lenders for illiquidity. The segmented markets theory emphasizes institutional factors that limit the substitutability among different maturities by borrowers and lenders. The preferred habitat theory accepts elements of the other theories but rejects the extreme viewpoints that only expectations or only institutional factors determine the term structure. Real-world empirical regularities that confront term structure theories include the fact that the yield curve is upward sloping most of the time, that long- and short-term yields usually move together over time, and that short-term yields exhibit greater amplitude over time than do long-term yields. The preferred habitat theory accords more closely with these facts than do the other three theories. Bonds and other debt instruments have varying degrees of default risk, and the yields on these instruments reflect the market's assessment of this default risk. The difference between the yields on a risky bond and a risk-free bond reflects the magnitude of this default risk. This difference typically increases during recessions and other periods of financial distress and decreases during periods of prosperity.

Answers to Your Turn (p. 142)

a. *Your expectation is that inflation will increase; the Fisher effect will take interest rates higher in the coming months and perhaps years. Bond prices are likely to fall significantly as time goes by. To avoid exposure to potential capital losses in long-term bonds, you will invest all your funds in the short end of the market.*

b. *The announcement of war will produce a consensus that interest rates are headed higher for the foreseeable future. Thousands of investors will sell long-term bonds, forcing their prices down and their yields up. Many of them will seek a safe haven in short-term Treasury securities, pushing their prices up and their yields down. The yield curve will quickly change from a flat to an upward-sloping pattern.*

KEY TERMS

term structure of interest rates
yield curve
pure expectations theory
forward interest rate
liquidity premium theory
market risk

term premium
segmented markets theory
preferred habitat theory
risk premium
junk bond

STUDY QUESTIONS

1   Look for the daily report entitled "Treasury Yield Curve" in the most recent *Wall Street Journal.* Note the change in the yield curve over the last 4 weeks (shown in same figure). What recent developments can you think of to explain this change?

2   Suppose a constitutional amendment outlawing budget deficits is passed by Congress and ratified by the states. Suppose the budget deficit is to be phased out over the next 5 years. What would be the implication of this announcement for the shape of the yield curve?

3   Suppose the Federal Reserve attempts to twist the yield curve by simultaneously selling Treasury bills and purchasing long-term bonds. In which theory will the Fed be successful? In which theory will the Fed be unsuccessful? Explain.

4   Suppose you notice in the paper that the yields available today on 1-year, 2-year, and 3-year Treasury bonds are 6 percent, 7 percent, and 6.5 percent, respectively. According to the pure expectations theory of term structure, what does the market believe 1-year bond yields will be 1 year from now? 2 years from now?

5   Why is the yield curve usually upward sloping?

6   Suppose that, instead of being risk averse, both borrowers and lenders are actually risk lovers— that is, they prefer risk. According to the liquidity premium theory, what would be the normal shape of the yield curve?

7   Suppose we relax the assumption of pure expectations theorists that large groups of agents form expectations about future interest rates and act

aggressively upon their expectations. What would be the implications for the validity of the pure expectations theory? The segmented markets theory?

8   Suppose competition among dealers in the financial markets drops off sharply, and as a result transactions costs rise sharply. What would this imply for

  a   The validity of the pure expectations theory?

  b   The shape of the yield curve?

9   Interest rates were much more volatile in the 1970s than in the 1990s. What is the implication for the average differential between long-term and short-term yields on Treasury securities in those decades

  a   According to the pure expectations theory?

  b   According to the liquidity premium theory?

10   Under what conditions would a flat yield curve exist in

  a   The pure expectations theory?

  b   The liquidity premium theory?

  c   The segmented markets theory?

11   Suppose short-term yields are currently 12 percent and long-term yields are 10 percent. Should the government aggressively lengthen the maturity structure of its newly issued debt? Explain.

12   Treasury bills are issued in minimum denominations of $10,000; longer-term government notes and bonds are issued in denominations of $1000. In the segmented markets theory, what would have been the impact on the term structure of interest rates of the advent of money market mutual funds? In the pure expectations theory?

13 Suppose the U.S. Treasury deems it essential to reduce short-term government security yields. How could the Treasury accomplish that goal? Do you think the Treasury would be successful? Explain.

14 On average, interest rates have been lower in the 1990s than in the 1980s. Yield spreads (long-term yield minus short-term yield) have been larger in the 1990s. Based on your knowledge of the theories of term structure, is there a connection between these two phenomena? How would you explain the increase in yield spreads in the 1990s?

15 Assume you are convinced of the validity of the pure expectations theory of term structure. Suppose you observe that yields on 1-year, 2-year,

and 20-year Treasury securities are currently 4 percent, 6 percent, and 9 percent, respectively. What are the likely implications for economic activity in the next couple of years? Explain.

16 If you knew a severe recession was coming next year, would you be better off holding 30-year U.S. Treasury bonds or 90-day Treasury bills? Would you be better off holding 30-year U.S. Treasury bonds or 30-year Baa corporate bonds? Explain.

17 Suppose a recession begins next year. What will happen to the yield spread between corporate Baa and U.S. government bonds of similar maturity?

18 Suppose yield spreads between corporate Baa bonds and U.S. Treasury bonds increase sharply in the next month. What information does this give about the market's opinion of the outlook for the economy?

SUGGESTIONS FOR ADDITIONAL READING

For an excellent survey of the theory of term structure, together with copious citations of the literature, read Chapter 5 of James C. Van Horne, *Financial Market Rates and Flows,* 3d ed. (Englewood Cliffs, N.J.: Prentice Hall, 1994). A rigorous and somewhat mathematical review of term structure is Robert Shiller, *Handbook of Monetary Economics,* Benjamin Friedman and Frank Hahn, eds. (Amsterdam: North-Holland, 1990), chap. 13. An enlightening historical discussion of the term structure in the United States, complete with voluminous data, is provided in Sidney Homer and Richard Sylla, *A History of Interest Rates,* 3d ed. (Rutgers, N.J.: Rutgers Univ. Press, 1991), pp. 394–409. The pure expectations theory was originally developed by Irving Fisher nearly one hundred years ago in "Appreciation and Interest," reprinted in *Publications of the American Economics Association,* 10, August 1986. Seminal papers setting forth the segmented markets theory and the preferred habitat theory, respectively, are J. M. Culbertson, "The Term Structure of Interest Rates," *Quarterly Journal of Economics,* November 1957, pp. 489–504, and Franco

Modigliani and Richard Sutch, "Innovations in Interest Rate Policy," *American Economic Review,* May 1966, pp. 178–197. Other useful papers on term structure include Alan Garner, "The Yield Curve and Inflation Expectations," Federal Reserve Bank of Kansas City *Review,* September–October 1987, and Peter Abken, "Innovations in Modeling the Term Structure of Interest Rates," Federal Reserve Bank of Atlanta *Economic Review,* July–August 1990, pp. 2–27. A study which reports that the yield curve is a good predictor of real economic activity is Arturo Estrella and Gikas Hardouvelis, "The Term Structure as a Predictor of Real Economic Activity," *The Journal of Finance,* June 1991, pp. 555–576. An excellent survey of the predictive power of the yield curve is contained in Ben Bernanke, "On the Predictive Power of Interest Rates and Interest Rate Spreads," *New England Economic Review,* November–December 1990, pp. 51–68. A widely cited early paper on default risk is Lawrence Fisher, "Determinants of Risk Premiums on Corporate Bonds," *Journal of Political Economy,* June 1959, pp. 217–237.

CHAPTER

8

■ ## The Foreign Exchange Market

Nations engage in international trade in goods, services, and financial and real assets for the same reason that individuals engage in domestic trade—that is, to expand their material well-being through the specialization and division of labor and to purchase the real and financial assets expected to yield the highest returns. Rather than trying to be self-sufficient and produce all the goods she needs, an individual can enhance her standard of living and that of her nation by specializing in the production of a narrow range of goods or services in which she is relatively most proficient, and trading for other goods and services. By extending this principle of comparative advantage beyond national borders, all nations can potentially emerge with higher levels of real income and consumption. The basic point is that specialization requires trade. Specialization and trade raise living standards. This holds true at all levels: individual, state, regional, and national.

Thus, just as there are incentives for individuals to engage in the exchange of goods and services and for geographic regions of a country to conduct interregional trade, a natural incentive exists for nations to engage in international economic transactions. Except for transportation costs, there are no natural barriers to international trade. However, various manmade barriers exist, causing the volume of world trade to fall short of the level that would maximize the living standards of the nations involved. Among these barriers are the existence of different national currencies, languages, and financial and legal institutions. In addition, various national economic policies impede the free flow of goods, services, and capital among nations. Tariffs, quotas, and foreign exchange controls are examples. To a limited extent, increasing awareness of the potential gains from trade has in recent years resulted in a movement to reduce these barriers. Examples include the North American Free Trade Agreement (NAFTA) and the formation and expansion of the European Monetary System (EMS).

FOREIGN EXCHANGE MARKETS AND RATES

When a Kansas City grocery store chain purchases a load of oranges from a Florida citrus grove owner, both parties to the transaction prefer to deal in the same currency—dollars. This conformity of preferences does not exist when a U.S. importer purchases a shipment of Japanese Nikon cameras. The U.S. importer would prefer to pay in dollars, while the Japanese producer would prefer to receive payment in yen. By the same token, a Japanese importer of U.S. lumber would prefer to make payment in yen, while the lumber producers would want dollars.

The Foreign Exchange Market

The **foreign exchange market** is the market in which such national currencies as dollars, pesos, deutsche marks, yen, francs, and others are exchanged. It is not an organized market with fixed hours and a physical meeting place, such as the New York Stock Exchange or the Chicago Board of Trade. The foreign exchange market is an over-the-counter market, the primary communications instruments being the telephone and the computer. The market has developed rapidly in the past quarter century, and the volume of activity has escalated dramatically in response to the growth in the volume of world trade in goods and services, and especially in response to the expansion of **international capital flows**—the acquisition of financial and real assets across national borders. Total worldwide foreign exchange market transactions in 1996 were approximately $1.2 trillion, or $1200 billion *per day*. More than 90 percent of these transactions are associated with capital flows. Among the most important financial centers are New York, London, Tokyo, Paris, Frankfurt, Hong Kong, and Zurich.

The *direct* participants in the foreign exchange market include U.S. commercial banks with deposits in foreign branch banks or foreign correspondent banks, and these foreign banks. Several hundred dealers (mostly banks) maintain inventories of major foreign currencies in the form of bank deposits denominated in foreign currencies. The Chase Manhattan bank, for example, maintains deposit balances in foreign correspondent banks in the form of yen in Tokyo, francs in Paris, deutsche marks in Frankfurt, and so on. When a dealer sells a foreign currency, it sells deposits it owns in a foreign commercial bank. When it buys foreign exchange, it acquires additional deposits in a foreign bank. In other words, the foreign exchange market involves buying and selling bank deposits rather than physical packages of currency and coins. Foreign exchange dealers do not charge a commission. Instead, as with dealers in U.S. government securities, a bid-to-ask price spread is the source of income.

But who are the *ultimate* participants in the foreign exchange market? First, consider the thousands of large and small import and export firms in the United States, together with their foreign counterparts, that must buy or sell foreign currencies in connection with their business. Second, consider all the tourists and other travelers around the world who want foreign currencies. For example, Americans want lire to finance vacations in Italy, and Japanese businessmen need dollars to travel in the United States. Third, consider financial entities such as banks, private pension and government retirement funds, and money market mutual funds in one country, which seek to purchase financial assets (relatively high-yielding CDs and other money market instruments, bonds, and stocks) in another country. In addition, the Federal Reserve and U.S. Treasury often have occasion to conduct transactions in the foreign exchange market, as do corresponding agencies in other countries.

Table 8-1

Foreign Exchange Rates versus the U.S. Dollar for Selected Currencies

Country	Currency Unit	Symbol	Units of Foreign Currency per Dollar in January			
			1966	1976	1986	1996
Austria	Schilling	S	25.9	18.4	17.2	10.2
Britain	Pound	£	0.36	0.49	0.70	0.65
Canada	Dollar	C$	1.07	1.01	1.41	1.37
France	Franc	Fr	4.90	4.48	7.48	4.98
Germany	Deutsche mark	DM	4.01	2.60	2.44	1.46
Italy	Lira	L	625	702	1633	1580
Japan	Yen	¥	361	305	200	106
Switzerland	Franc	SFr	4.33	2.60	2.0	1.17

Source: International Monetary Fund, *International Financial Statistics.*

The Foreign Exchange Rate

The price at which one nation's currency is exchanged for another's is the **foreign exchange rate.** An exchange rate exists between each pair of nations that engages in international commerce. Table 8-1 indicates the name and symbol of the currency unit for a sample of eight countries. It also indicates the exchange rates against the U.S. dollar of each country at the beginning of 1966, 1976, 1986, and 1996. Each exchange rate is quoted as the number of units of foreign currency per U.S. dollar. Thus the exchange rates in the table may be interpreted as the *value of one dollar* expressed in units of foreign currency. For example, in early 1996, $1.00 was exchangeable for 106 Japanese yen, 1.46 German marks, and 0.65 British pounds. With the exception of the dollar-pound exchange rate, this is the way exchange rates are conventionally quoted in the United States. Note, however, that international currency values are reciprocal in nature. If $1.00 is equivalent to 0.65 British pounds, the pound is equivalent to 1.54 dollars—that is, $1.54. The dollar-pound exchange rate is conventionally quoted in the United States as dollars per pound.

As Table 8-1 indicates, exchange rates vary considerably over time. In early 1996, for example, the dollar was worth fewer German marks and Japanese yen than in 1966, 1976, and 1986. Over the years, the dollar has **depreciated** against the deutsche mark and yen—that is, it has declined in value, or purchased fewer units of deutsche marks and yen. These foreign currencies **appreciated** against the dollar—that is, they increased in value and became worth more dollars. On the other hand, note in the table that the dollar appreciated against the Italian lira and the British pound in the period 1966–1986. In other words, over that 20-year period the lira and pound depreciated against the dollar.[1] Over the years, the *strong currencies* included in the table—those that have appreciated against most other currencies—have been the Austrian schilling, the German mark, the Japanese yen, and the Swiss franc. The Italian lira, British pound, and Canadian dollar have been *weak currencies,* depreciating vis-à-vis the U.S. dollar and most other major currencies. The U.S. dollar and French franc occupy an intermediate position, depreciating relative to the strong currencies but appreciating against the Italian, Canadian, and British currencies.

Figure 8-1 illustrates the exchange rate behavior of the U.S. dollar against two perennially strong currencies (the yen and deutsche mark) and two weak currencies (the lira and Canadian dollar) over the past 30 years. Because all these exchange rates are expressed as units of foreign currency per U.S. dollar, you may note through a glance at the figure that the dollar has trended downward (depreciated) against the yen and deutsche mark and trended upward (appreciated) vis-à-vis the lira and Canadian dollar. This, of course, is equivalent to stating that the yen and deutsche mark have appreciated against the dollar, while the lira and Canadian dollar have depreciated against it. Later in this chapter we will present a framework that helps explain why these exchange rate changes have occurred.

Fixed and Floating Exchange Rates

Since the early 1970s, international trade has been based on **floating exchange rates**—that is, most major nations have permitted exchange rates to change in the marketplace from day to day, sometimes by a rather significant amount. Before the 1970s, governments adhered to an agreement in which each one aggressively intervened in foreign exchange markets to *fix,* or *peg,* its exchange rate at a predetermined level. This fixed exchange rate was to be maintained by direct government foreign exchange market intervention until demonstrable evidence was presented to the **International Monetary Fund** that the level was inappropriate and unsustainable. Upon approval of the IMF, the exchange rate level might be adjusted and then repegged at a new level. This was dubbed the **adjustable-peg,** or **Bretton Woods, exchange rate system.**[2] For a variety of reasons, the most important of which was highly divergent rates of inflation among countries, this adjustable-peg exchange rate system collapsed in the early

---

[1]Because exchange rates are reciprocal in nature and can be quoted either as units of foreign currency per unit of domestic currency or as units of domestic currency per unit of foreign currency, it is easy to become confused. To minimize confusion, think first of the currency in the *denominator* of the quotation. If the U.S.-Japanese exchange rate moves from 106 yen per dollar to 115 yen per dollar, the dollar *appreciates*—that is, it becomes worth more yen. This means the yen *depreciates* against the dollar. If you read that the U.S.-British exchange rate moves from the $1.50/£ to $1.60/£, clearly the pound has appreciated as it has become worth more dollars. Thus, the dollar has depreciated vis-à-vis the British pound.

[2]This system was established at an important conference of major industrial nations held in 1944 at Bretton Woods, New Hampshire, for the purpose of establishing a new post–World War II international trade and monetary order. At this conference, the decision was made to implement the adjustable-peg exchange rate system, which is therefore commonly referred to as the Bretton Woods system. The International Monetary Fund was also created. (The Bretton Woods conference also led to the creation of the World Bank and, ultimately, to the formation of the General Agreement on Tariffs and Trade, or GATT.)

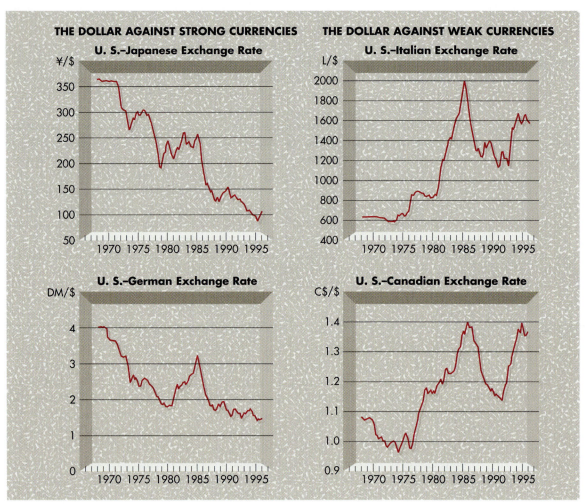

Figure 8-1   Trends in the U.S. Dollar, 1968–Present. In the past quarter century, the U.S. dollar has fallen against the Japanese yen and German mark but has risen against the Italian lira and the Canadian dollar. *Source: Citibank Economic Database.*

1970s, and world trade has since been based on floating exchange rates. (The merits of floating exchange rates versus those of the adjustable-peg system will be evaluated in Chapter 27.)

Spot and Forward Exchange Markets

Markets in foreign currencies may be divided into spot and forward markets. **Spot transactions** involve the exchange of currencies for immediate, or "on-the-spot," delivery and payment (actually, there is a 2-day settlement period). The exchange rate at which such transactions take place is called the **spot exchange rate.** The forward exchange market is similar to the futures market in commodities. **Forward transactions** involve the purchase and sale of foreign currencies for delivery and payment at some future date, at a price specified *in advance. The Wall Street Journal* carries daily quotations of **forward exchange rates** for the dollar against six major currencies for delivery in 30 days, 90 days, and 180 days, as well as spot quotations (see "From the Financial Pages"). Forward markets also exist for other maturities and other currencies.

The chief function of the forward exchange market is to provide hedging facilities through which the risk of an adverse movement in the spot exchange rate may be eliminated. Suppose a U.S. importer of Swiss watches agrees to purchase a shipment of watches for 100,000 Swiss francs, with payment to be made upon delivery of the shipment in 30 days. Suppose the spot exchange rate is 1.25 Swiss francs per dollar when the agreement is made, so that the importer expects the watches to cost $80,000—that is, 100,000 francs divided by 1.25 francs per dollar. Assume, however, that when the shipment arrives the dollar has depreciated to 1.00 Swiss francs. In this event, the importer ends up paying $100,000 for the watches rather than the hoped-for $80,000.[3]

A more prudent approach by the importer would be, immediately upon agreement to purchase the watches, to enter the foreign exchange market and purchase *forward* 100,000 Swiss francs for delivery and payment in 30 days, to coincide with the expected arrival of the watches, at an exchange rate known at the time of the agreement. This locks in the dollar cost of the watches, removing the risk of an adverse change in the exchange rate— that is, a depreciation of the dollar. Furthermore, the payment of dollars does not have to be made until the Swiss francs are delivered, 30 days later. Ordinarily, the spot and forward rates differ by a very small amount. Suppose the forward dollar sells at a discount to the spot rate of 0.004 francs per dollar.[4] That is, while the spot rate is 1.25 francs per dollar, suppose the forward rate is 1.246 francs per dollar. This means that, through a forward purchase of francs, the importer can lock in the cost of the watches at $80,257, that is, 100,000 francs divided by 1.246 francs per dollar. For $257, the importer can buy insurance against an adverse move in the dollar.[5]

Other market participants besides importers and exporters may find it useful to enter into forward exchange transactions. Any individual, firm, or organization intending to make payment or receive payment in foreign currency on a future date may be motivated to hedge against an adverse move in the dollar exchange rate through a forward transaction. A U.S. money market mutual fund expecting to receive interest payments on high-yielding German 90-day CDs may hedge by selling the expected deutsche mark interest

[3]Of course, the importer could purchase the 100,000 Swiss francs on the spot market immediately upon entering into the agreement to buy the watches and hold them until the watches arrive or invest them in time deposits in Swiss banks for 30 days. These choices are costly, however, because they involve either loss of interest on the funds or inconvenience and other transactions costs of having to make arrangements with Swiss banks in order to earn interest on the funds for 30 days.

[4]Note the table of exchange rate quotations in "From the Financial Pages." The 30-day forward exchange rate for the dollar against the Swiss franc indicates that the dollar sells at a forward discount of 0.0036 francs, or 0.36 percent of 1 franc. Our estimate here of the cost of hedging thus errs slightly on the high side.

[5]Actually, the true cost of this hedge is much lower than $257. The fact that the forward dollar sells at a discount to the spot dollar implies that U.S. interest rates are higher than those in Switzerland. By purchasing forward rather than spot francs, the importer can keep the funds invested in more attractive U.S. financial instruments for 30 days, offsetting much of the $257 cost mentioned above.

Exchange Rate Quotations

Each day in *The Wall Street Journal* and other major newspapers, U.S. exchange rates with more than 50 foreign nations are quoted. Exporters, importers and those responsible for investing funds—portfolio managers of banks, pension funds, mutual funds, etc.,—find this useful. In the table below, exchange rates for Wed., Apr. 3, and Thurs., Apr. 4, 1996, are shown. Note, in the case of the U.S.-Germany exchange rate, that Thursday's rate is quoted in two ways: $.6754 dollars per mark, and its reciprocal, 1.4805 marks per dollar. Since it is convenient to think in terms of the value of the *dollar*, we will use the latter quotation. Note that the dollar depreciated slightly on Thursday, falling from 1.4812 marks to 1.4805 marks. Besides these *spot* exchange rates, quotations of *forward* exchange rates—rates for future delivery of and payment for currency—are provided for six major U.S. trading partners (Britain, Canada, France, Germany, Japan, and Switzerland).

Most foreign exchange market participants obtain less favorable exchange rates than those quoted here. The rates below are for multimillion-dollar transactions conducted by dealers. They may be viewed as wholesale exchange rates. An individual or small business needing to buy or sell foreign currency will usually make such transactions through a hometown bank or a credit card company such as Visa or MasterCard. Such customers pay the retail rate—that is, they pay a premium to make foreign exchange transactions.

CURRENCY TRADING

EXCHANGE RATES

Thursday, April 4, 1996

The New York foreign exchange selling rates below apply to trading among banks in amounts of $1 million and more, as quoted at 3 p.m. Eastern time by Dow Jones Telerate Inc. and other sources. Retail transactions provide fewer units of foreign currency per dollar.

Country	U.S. $ equiv. Thu	Wed	Currency per U.S. $ Thu	Wed
Argentina (Peso)	1.0012	1.0012	.9988	.9988
Australia (Dollar)	.7822	.7810	1.2785	1.2804
Austria (Schilling)	.09605	.09614	10.411	10.401
Bahrain (Dinar)	2.6525	2.6525	.3770	.3770
Belgium (Franc)	.03289	.03290	30.400	30.394
Brazil (Real)	1.0137	1.0137	.9865	.9865
Britain (Pound)	1.5312	1.5265	.6531	.6551
30-Day Forward	1.5305	1.5251	.6534	.6557
90-Day Forward	1.5270	1.5244	.6549	.6560
180-Day Forward	1.5270	1.5170	.6549	.6592
Canada (Dollar)	.7364	.7364	1.3579	1.3579
30-Day Forward	.7367	.7367	1.3574	1.3574
90-Day Forward	.7370	.7370	1.3569	1.3568
180-Day Forward	.7422	.7378	1.3474	1.3554
Chile (Peso)	.002439	.002446	409.95	408.85
China (Renminbi)	.1197	.1197	8.3525	8.3538
Colombia (Peso)	.0009615	.0009615	1040.00	1040.00
Czech. Rep. (Koruna)	....	....	....	....
Commercial rate	.03674	.03670	27.219	27.248
Denmark (Krone)	holiday	.1753	holiday	5.7040
Ecuador (Sucre)	....	....	....	....
Floating rate	.0003306	.0003304	3025.00	3027.00
Finland (Markka)	holiday	.2163	holiday	4.6225
France (Franc)	.1985	.1979	5.0380	5.0525
30-Day Forward	.1987	.1981	5.0322	5.0468
90-Day Forward	.1992	.1986	5.0213	5.0361
180-Day Forward	.1998	.1991	5.0060	5.0215
Germany (Mark)	.6754	.6751	1.4805	1.4812
30-Day Forward	.6766	.6764	1.4780	1.4785
90-Day Forward	.6790	.6787	1.4728	1.4734
180-Day Forward	.6828	.6824	1.4646	1.4654
Greece (Drachma)	.004159	.004161	240.42	240.30
Hong Kong (Dollar)	holiday	.1293	holiday	7.7338
Hungary (Forint)	.006795	.006799	147.17	147.08
India (Rupee)	.02930	.02930	34.135	34.135
Indonesia (Rupiah)	.0004293	.0004294	2329.63	2329.00
Ireland (Punt)	1.5770	1.5738	.6341	.6354
Israel (Shekel)	.3194	.3192	3.1305	3.1325
Italy (Lira)	.0006409	.0006399	1560.25	1562.67

Country	U.S. $ equiv. Thu	Wed	Currency per U.S. $ Thu	Wed
Japan (Yen)	.009342	.009355	107.04	106.89
30-Day Forward	.009380	.009394	106.61	106.46
90-Day Forward	.009458	.009471	105.73	105.59
180-Day Forward	.009572	.009584	104.48	104.34
Jordan (Dinar)	1.4124	1.4124	.7080	.7080
Kuwait (Dinar)	3.3411	3.3411	.2993	.2993
Lebanon (Pound)	.0006319	.0006319	1582.50	1582.50
Malaysia (Ringgit)	.3952	.3952	2.5301	2.5305
Malta (Lira)	2.7778	2.7778	.3600	.3600
Mexico (Peso)	....	....	....	....
Floating rate	holiday	.1330	holiday	7.5200
Netherland (Guilder)	.6050	.6033	1.6529	1.6575
New Zealand (Dollar)	.6822	.6827	1.4658	1.4648
Norway (Krone)	holiday	.1563	holiday	6.3987
Pakistan (Rupee)	.02921	.02921	34.230	34.230
Peru (new Sol)	.4271	.4277	2.3412	2.3382
Philippines (Peso)	holiday	.03820	holiday	26.180
Poland (Zloty)	.3865	.3863	2.5872	2.5885
Portugal (Escudo)	.006559	.006566	152.47	152.29
Russia (Ruble) (a)	.0002049	.0002050	4881.00	4879.00
Saudi Arabia (Riyal)	.2666	.2666	3.7505	3.7505
Singapore (Dollar)	.7123	.7118	1.4039	1.4049
Slovak Rep. (Koruna)	.03319	.03319	30.131	30.131
South Africa (Rand)	.2430	.2426	4.1150	4.1220
South Korea (Won)	.001282	.001282	780.05	780.15
Spain (Peseta)	holiday	.008054	holiday	124.16
Sweden (Krona)	.1502	.1508	6.6596	6.6300
Switzerland (Franc)	.8381	.8364	1.1932	1.1956
30-Day Forward	.8406	.8389	1.1896	1.1920
90-Day Forward	.8457	.8440	1.1825	1.1848
180-Day Forward	.8534	.8519	1.1718	1.1739
Taiwan (Dollar)	holiday	.03673	holiday	27.227
Thailand (Baht)	.03962	.03961	25.241	25.245
Turkey (Lira)	.00001401	.00001404	71366.00	71247.50
United Arab (Dirham)	.2723	.2723	3.6730	3.6730
Uruguay (New Peso)	....	....	....	....
Financial	.1328	.1328	7.5300	7.5300
Venezuela (Bolivar)	.003448	.003448	290.00	290.00
Brady Rate	.002128	.002128	470.00	470.00
SDR	1.4590	1.4585	.6854	.6856
ECU	1.2565	1.2569	....	....

Special Drawing Rights (SDR) are based on exchange rates for the U.S., German, British, French, and Japanese currencies. Source: International Monetary Fund.

European Currency Unit (ECU) is based on a basket of community currencies.

a-fixing, Moscow Interbank Currency Exchange

proceeds forward for dollars. Foreign exchange speculators also find the forward market to their liking. Such speculators are typically firms that alter the timing of their foreign exchange transactions to profit from expected movements in exchange rates. Suppose the U.S.-French spot exchange rate is currently 5 francs per dollar and speculators expect it to move toward 5.10 francs per dollar—that is, they expect the dollar to appreciate over the next 6 months. A French speculator could buy dollars in the spot market and wait for them to appreciate, investing the funds in U.S. Treasury bills or CDs in the meantime. Alternatively, the speculator might purchase dollars for 180-day forward delivery and payment. Assuming that forward dollars can be purchased for approximately 5 francs, the speculator would anticipate immediately selling the dollars when delivered 180 days later in the spot market at a price significantly above the current spot and forward prices. In either case, the speculator will earn a profit. But the forward route is advantageous because no funds except a small "earnest money" deposit must be put up at the time the forward transaction is made. Successful speculation in the forward market can produce a positive return on the basis of little or no funds invested.

The Importance of the Exchange Rate

The level of a country's exchange rate is a matter of considerable national importance. In conjunction with domestic prices, the exchange rate determines the cost of U.S. products to buyers in foreign nations, thereby influencing U.S. exports. An IBM mainframe computer costs twice as much in France if the exchange rate is 10 francs per dollar than if it is 5 francs per dollar. By the same token, the exchange rate determines the cost of everything Americans purchase from the rest of the world: a 100-franc bottle of French wine costs $20 in the U.S. if the exchange rate is 5 francs per dollar but only $10 if the dollar exchanges for 10 francs. Largely because of such considerations, disputes between nations have sometimes arisen over governments' decisions to intervene in the floating system with the intention of influencing the exchange rate level. Later in this chapter, we will look in more detail at the consequences of exchange rate changes. Before we do so, however, let us examine the factors that determine the exchange rate level and the forces that cause it to change over time.

Your Turn

Suppose you want to purchase a Japanese-made Sony compact disc player. Assume its price in Japan is 30,000 yen. Neglecting transportation costs, taxes, and so forth, how would its cost to you differ if the exchange rate is 150 yen per dollar as compared to 100 yen per dollar? As a consumer, are you better off with a weak dollar or a strong dollar?

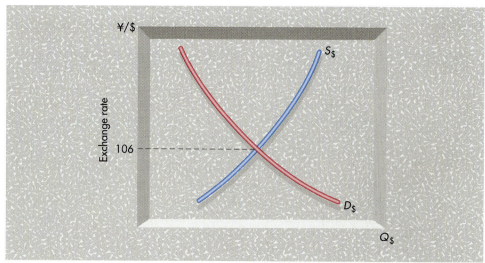

Figure 8-2   The U.S.-Japanese Exchange Rate. The foreign exchange market value of the U.S. dollar relative to the Japanese yen is determined by the forces of supply and demand. This exchange rate changes daily in response to shifts in the supply of and demand for dollars.

EXCHANGE RATE DETERMINATION

The foreign exchange market is an excellent example of a highly competitive market. In this market, there are many buyers and sellers of a homogeneous product—a national currency. Each buyer and seller is relatively small compared to the total market, so that no single buyer or seller can appreciably influence the exchange rate. In a system of *freely floating* exchange rates, governments abstain from intervention in the foreign exchange market and permit exchange rates to be driven entirely by the forces of the free market. Like prices in the soybean market and other auction markets, the impersonal forces of supply and demand determine the exchange rate. In a *managed float,* a government sometimes intervenes in an effort to prevent exchange rate movements perceived to be extreme or strongly at odds with the national interest. For example, the Federal Reserve intervened on several occasions in 1995 to support the dollar against the yen and deutsche mark. Today, even when governments occasionally intervene, the volume of such activity tends to be quite small relative to the total amount of private activity in foreign exchange markets.

Consider the determination of the U.S. exchange rate with Japan, illustrated in Figure 8-2. In this analysis, we are explaining the value of the U.S. dollar. If we wish to find the price of oranges, we determine the number of units of money per orange. Similarly, we express the value of the U.S. dollar in terms of the number of units of foreign currency, such as yen. Because the figure concerns the value or price of the U.S. dollar, the units on the vertical axis—the prices—are expressed as yen per dollar. The units on the horizontal axis are the quantity of dollars per period. The supply and demand curves indicate the flow of dollars supplied and demanded per period at each possible exchange rate. In the figure, the supply and demand curves for dollars intersect to determine an equilibrium exchange rate of 106 yen per dollar.

What are the forces that lie behind the supply and demand curves for dollars shown in the figure? The demand curve for dollars stems from Japanese buyers of American goods and services, U.S. financial assets such as stocks, bonds, and CDs, and real assets such as office buildings, banks, factories, and land. Because Japanese buyers must pay for these American items with dollars, they demand U.S. dollars, selling their yen in exchange. The demand curve in Figure 8-2 is downward sloping because, *given all other factors,* a decline in the U.S. dollar makes everything in the United States cheaper to potential Japanese buyers, thereby stimulating purchases. For example, if the dollar were to depreciate from 120 yen to 100 yen, a $4 U.S. bushel of wheat would decline in price in Japan from 480 yen to 400 yen (ignoring transportation costs, taxes, and so forth). For a Japanese tourist, a $100 San Francisco hotel room would drop from 12,000 yen to 10,000 yen.

The supply curve in Figure 8-2 originates from Americans seeking to purchase Japanese goods and services, financial assets, and real assets. Because Americans must pay for these items in yen, they must sell dollars to obtain yen and finance the transactions. The supply curve for dollars corresponds to a demand curve for yen.[6] The supply curve in the figure slopes upward because, *given other factors,* an increase in the value of the dollar (measured in yen) reduces the price of Japanese goods, services, and assets in the United States. A Nikon camera selling for 90,000 yen in Tokyo costs an American $600 if the dollar exchanges for 150 yen; it costs $900 if the dollar fetches only 100 yen. Because a stronger dollar reduces the cost of Japanese items to Americans, we tend to respond to it by supplying more dollars to finance increased purchases.[7]

Price changes in competitive markets are precipitated by shifts in supply and demand curves. Numerous factors may produce a shift in the supply or demand curve of Figure 8-2, and such factors thus produce a change in the U.S.-Japanese exchange rate. Fundamental factors that produce such exchange rate changes include changes in relative price levels, income levels, and real interest rates in the countries involved. Also, development of new products, changes in consumer preferences, and changes in productivity can initiate changes in supply and demand curves in foreign exchange markets, thereby producing a change in exchange rates. Imposition of tariffs, quotas, and other forms of trade barriers also produces exchange rates changes. Speculators' anticipation of forthcoming

---

[6]One could draw a corresponding figure to accompany Figure 8-2, in which the exchange rate is expressed as $/¥ rather than ¥/$. The horizontal axis would be labeled $Q_¥$ and the supply and demand curves would be in yen rather than in dollars. The $D_¥$ in such a figure would correspond to the $S_$$ in Figure 8-2—that is, Americans sell dollars to buy yen to make payment in Japan. The $S_¥$ in this hypothetical figure would be related to the $D_$$ in Figure 8-2, that is, Japanese sell yen to buy dollars to make payment in the United States. The equilibrium exchange rate in this hypothetical figure, given the equilibrium rate in Figure 8-2 of 106 ¥/$, would be its reciprocal, or $.0094/¥.

[7]Technically, this assumes that the U.S. demand for Japanese products is relatively elastic with respect to the price in dollars. If, instead, the demand is relatively inelastic and Americans continue to purchase approximately the same quantity of Japanese items in spite of a lower dollar price due to a stronger dollar, Americans would actually need to pay fewer dollars. In the short run, the supply curve may be "backward bending," or negatively sloped, because people do not respond immediately and fully to a more favorable price. In the long run, economists believe the supply curve is upward sloping as illustrated because U.S. demand for imported goods and services is believed to be highly responsive to their price in dollars.

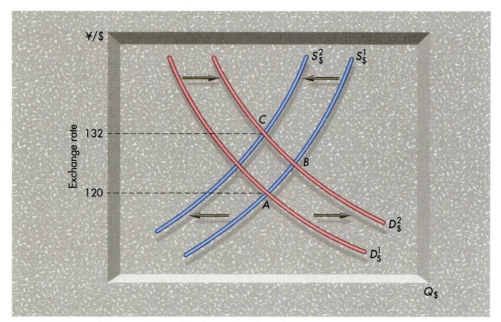

Figure 8-3   Relative Price Level Behavior and Exchange Rates. An increase in the price level in Japan relative to that in the United States increases the demand for dollars, reduces their supply, and causes the dollar to appreciate against the yen.

changes in fundamental factors strongly influences current exchange rates. For purposes of discussion, we will divide our analysis of exchange rate determinants into factors that influence exchange rates in the long run and those that exert a short-run influence.

LONG-RUN EXCHANGE RATE DETERMINANTS

In the long run, relative price level behavior in nations, along with preferences, product development, productivity growth, and trade restrictions are powerful forces that influence the exchange rate. We begin by examining the role of price level behavior. We will discover that nations with chronically high inflation are likely to be weak-currency nations—that is, they are likely to see their currency *depreciate* over a period of years.

Relative Price Level Behavior

Assume the U.S.-Japanese exchange rate is initially 120 yen per dollar, with the supply and demand curves for dollars ($S_\$^1$ and $D_\$^1$) intersecting at A in Figure 8-3.

Now assume the price level increases 10 percent in Japan but remains constant in the United States. Clearly, at each and every exchange rate, U.S. goods and services are now relatively more attractive to both Japanese and Americans. The increased desire of Japanese to purchase U.S. goods shifts the demand curve for dollars from $D_\$^1$ to $D_\$^2$, an *increase* in demand. This would move the equilibrium to B in the figure, indicating an appreciation of the dollar (a depreciation of the yen). Also, because U.S. goods now look relatively more attractive to Americans at each exchange rate, the desire to import from Japan is reduced and the supply curve of dollars shifts leftward from $S_\$^1$ to $S_\$^2$, a *decrease* in supply. This indicates a further appreciation of the dollar, the new equilibrium being at C in the figure; the exchange rate then reaches 132 yen per dollar. The Japanese inflation has produced a depreciation of the yen and a corresponding appreciation of the dollar.

This analysis suggests that countries with relatively high inflation can expect to experience depreciation of their currencies in the long run. Indeed, the two countries in Table 8-1 that exhibited the most rapid inflation from 1966–1996—Italy and Great Britain—also experienced the most severe depreciation of their currencies against the dollar in that period. Mexico (not shown in the table), which experienced extremely high inflation, saw the peso lose more than 99 percent of its value vis-à-vis the dollar. In other words, the dollar appreciated more than 100-fold against the peso.

The Purchasing Power Parity Theory (PPP)

Building on the preceding analysis, the **purchasing power parity theory (PPP)** postulates that exchange rates adjust fully to offset the effects of different rates of inflation in two countries. If the U.S.-Japanese exchange rate is initially in equilibrium at 106 yen per dollar and the U.S. price level then doubles relative to the price level in Japan, PPP theory predicts that the dollar will depreciate sufficiently to restore the original level of purchasing power. That is, PPP predicts the dollar exchange rate will fall by half (50 percent), to 53 yen per dollar. If the dollar were to fall by less than 50 percent, Japanese products would look more attractive relative to American products—to both Japanese and U.S. buyers—than was the case before the U.S. price level disturbance. U.S. imports from Japan would increase, and U.S. exports to Japan would decline, exerting downward pressure on the U.S. dollar until it had restored purchasing power parity by declining by 50 percent.[8]

Under certain highly restrictive and unrealistic conditions, PPP theory would always be valid. Suppose there exist only two countries, the United States and Turkey. Suppose these nations produce only one homogeneous, or identical, product for export—wheat. Suppose wheat costs $4 per bushel in the United States and 4000 lire per bushel in Turkey. Then the U.S.-Turkish exchange rate must be 1000 lire per dollar. *The wheat must cost the same to an American or a Turk whether purchased at home or abroad.* If American wheat were cheaper, increased Turkish demand for U.S. wheat (and dollars) would drive up the dollar (raising the price of U.S. wheat in Turkey) until the discrepancy was eliminated. If

---

[8]Hence, PPP theory implies that inflation does not impair a nation's long-run competitive position in world trade if freely floating exchange rates prevail. The exchange rate is predicted to move precisely to compensate for inflation differences among countries, thus leaving each nation's products relatively unchanged in price in foreign markets. If U.S. prices double, making the price of an American Buick increase from $30,000 to $60,000, and the dollar falls from 1.5 deutsche marks to 0.75 deutsche marks, the Buick continues to sell for 45,000 DM in Germany. Suppose in Germany, where the price level remains constant, a Mercedes-Benz sells for 90,000 DM. The depreciation in the U.S. dollar raises its price in the United States from $60,000 to $120,000—the same percentage price increase experienced by the Buick and other U.S. goods. According to PPP theory, floating exchange rates allow countries with chronically high inflation to remain competitive in world trade.

Turkish wheat were cheaper, U.S. demand for it would drive down the dollar, boosting the price of Turkish wheat in the United States until the discrepancy was eliminated. This principle is known as the **law of one price.** If American wheat were to rise to $8 per bushel while Turkish wheat remained at 4000 lire, the dollar would depreciate from 1000 lire to 500 lire, so that potential wheat buyers in both Turkey and the United States would be indifferent to where they purchased wheat. This example reflects the basic intuition behind PPP. (To gain an appreciation of the limited applicability of the law of one price, see Exhibit 8-1, which discusses the price of Big Macs around the world.)

Adapting this framework to the real world, we must recognize that many products are not homogeneous in nature. When the dollar falls and Toyotas become more expensive relative to Fords, Americans continue to purchase Toyotas (though presumably in somewhat reduced quantities) because of perceived quality differences, product loyalty, and habit, as well as for other reasons. Also, a nation's price level includes many nontradeable goods and services, whereas only tradeable items are strictly relevant to PPP. The prices of tradeable and nontradeable goods do not necessarily move together over time. In episodes of severe inflation, PPP theory seems to work well in accounting for exchange rate movements. For example, the U.S. dollar depreciated sharply against the deutsche mark and many other currencies in the late 1970s because the U.S. inflation rate considerably exceeded that of Germany and many other industrial nations. However, in the low-inflation environment that has existed in the past 15 years, PPP theory has pretty much collapsed as an explanation of exchange rate movements. This was especially true during 1981 to 1985, when the dollar staged a dramatic appreciation that was totally unmerited by price level behavior.

Figure 8-4 provides a test of the PPP theory by illustrating the actual U.S.-German exchange rate (DM/$) since 1973, together with the hypothetical exchange rate that would

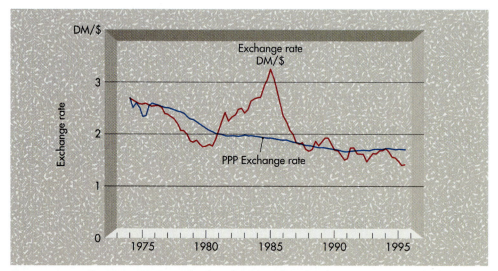

Figure 8-4   The U.S.-German Actual and PPP Exchange Rates. Over a period of many years, PPP theory describes the trend of exchange rates rather well. In the short run, however, exchange rates sometimes deviate sharply from the rates predicted by PPP.   *Source: Citibank Economic Database.*

EXHIBIT 8-1

The Price of Big Macs around the World

The law of one price states that, under conditions of free trade, an identical good that is produced and consumed in two countries should not differ in price by more than the cost of transportation. The exchange rate should gravitate to a level which makes the price of a good (when converted at that exchange rate) similar in the two countries. The accompanying table shows the price of a Big Mac in the United States and eight foreign countries in August 1995 (column 2). The table also indicates the exchange rate of each nation with the United States in August 1995, expressed as units of foreign currency per dollar (column 3).

    The price of a Big Mac abroad, together with the actual exchange rate, allows us to compare the 1995 dollar prices of foreign Big Macs with the 1995 U.S. price of $1.90 (column 4). Such prices ranged from a high of $3.98 in Switzerland to a low of $1.51 in Australia. Column 5 reports the implied purchasing power parity (PPP) exchange rate, calculated by dividing the foreign price of a Big Mac (shown in column 2) by the U.S. price of $1.90. Because the U.S. dollar prices of Big Macs differ considerably across countries, the implied PPP exchange rates deviate correspondingly from actual exchange rates. If Big Macs are cheaper abroad than in the United States, the actual exchange rate (foreign currency/$) is higher than the implied PPP rate, and the dollar is overvalued. If Big Macs are more expensive abroad, the actual exchange rate is below the PPP rate and the dollar is undervalued.

    This simple example suggests that, relative to the currencies of six of the eight important nations listed, the dollar was undervalued (too low) in August 1995. Big Macs were more expensive throughout Europe and Japan than in the United States. Indeed, this simple finding is consistent with sophisticated measures that reported an undervalued dollar in 1995 and 1996. Such findings indicate that, even if we neglect air fare, an American tourist would find that it was cheaper to travel in the United States than abroad (with the exception of countries such as Australia and Canada).

    To solidify your understanding of the law of one price, ask yourself why it does not apply to Big Macs.

Country	Price of Big Mac	Actual Exchange Rate (foreign currency/$)	Dollar Price of Big Mac	Implied PPP Exchange Rate (foreign currency/$)	Implied Percentage Overvaluation (+) or Undervaluation (−) of U.S. Dollar
Australia	A$2.06	1.36	$1.51	1.08	+26%
Britain	£1.45	0.65	$2.23	0.76	−15
Canada	C$2.27	1.36	$1.67	1.19	+14
France	Fr15.4	5.06	$3.04	8.10	−38
Germany	DM3.9	1.48	$2.64	2.05	−28
Italy	L3700	1623	$2.28	1947	−17
Japan	¥322	96.9	$3.32	169.5	−43
Switzerland	SFr4.89	1.23	$3.98	2.57	−52
United States	$1.90	—	—	—	—

have maintained purchasing power parity—that is, the PPP exchange rate. The figure assumes that the actual exchange rate reflected PPP in the beginning year (1973), and shows the extent to which changes in relative price level behavior since that date have accounted for changes in the exchange rate.

As indicated by the figure, a strict version of PPP is clearly rejected by the data. That is, the exchange rate does not move in a manner that precisely reflects different price level behavior in the United States and Germany. If it did, the actual exchange rate would always track the PPP rate perfectly, or at least move parallel to it over time.[9] Even though a strict version of PPP theory is easily rejected, note that relative price level behavior in the United States and Germany does a pretty good job of explaining the downward trend in the dollar vis-à-vis the mark over the long period from the early 1970s through the mid-1990s. Overall, the dollar depreciated against the deutsche mark because the United States experienced higher inflation than Germany did. Inspection of similar graphs (not shown) indicates that the long-term depreciation of the dollar against the Japanese yen and Swiss franc can be explained by the fact that Japan and Switzerland experienced lower inflation than did the United States. By the same token, the long-term *appreciation* of the dollar relative to the British pound and Italian lira can be explained largely by the fact that the United States had lower inflation than England and Italy over the period.

Other Long-Run Exchange Rate Determinants

Other factors that can affect long-term exchange rate developments include changes in preferences and product development, changes in productivity behavior, and imposition of tariffs and quotas. We briefly look at each factor.

Preferences and Product Development

Exchange rates are influenced by the demand for various products. This demand, in turn, depends on people's preferences. If Seattle's Boeing Company develops a worldwide reputation for producing the safest, most efficient aircraft, a strong preference for Boeing planes will develop worldwide. This will increase the demand for dollars (in order for foreigners to purchase more of the planes), thus causing the U.S. dollar to appreciate. By stimulating Americans' preference for French wine through advertising and other measures, French vintners cause the French franc to appreciate (and the dollar to depreciate) as Americans step up their purchases of francs.

By developing desirable new products, or by making major improvements in existing ones, nations induce an increase in demand for their products. This produces an appreciation of their currency. Hence, when Silicon Valley computer manufacturers initiated vast improvements in the power and efficiency of personal computers, they caused the dollar to become stronger than it would otherwise have been. By the same token, if the

---

[9]One problem with testing PPP is that because we use national price indexes to compute the PPP exchange rate, we have to select a base year (somewhat arbitrarily) in which it is assumed that the exchange rate accurately reflected PPP. The theory is then tested by seeing if relative changes in the exchange rate have tracked relative changes in the two nations' price levels. Here, we assumed that such an equilibrium prevailed shortly after the dollar was floated against the mark in 1973. Selection of a different base year would result in a shift in our PPP exchange rate in the figure, though over time this new PPP rate would move in parallel with the one illustrated.

United States lags behind other nations in innovation and product development, the dollar is likely to depreciate. In sum, by developing attractive new products and increasing worldwide preferences for a nation's existing products, entrepreneurs cause the nation's currency to appreciate in the long run.

Productivity Behavior

Productivity behavior—changes in output per hour of work—is a major factor influencing production costs and product prices. By holding down costs and prices, countries experiencing rapid productivity growth will become increasingly competitive in world markets and will therefore see their currencies appreciate. Countries that lag in productivity growth are likely to experience a long-run depreciation of their currencies. The long-term depreciation of the British pound against the deutsche mark, yen, and dollar is an example. The British pound has lost two-thirds of its value vis-à-vis the U.S. dollar in the past 50 years (in 1948, the dollar-pound exchange rate stood at $4.86 per pound, while today it is around $1.50 per pound).

Tariffs and Quotas

Tariffs are taxes on imported goods; **quotas** are restrictions on the volume of imports a nation permits. Under *free trade,* there are no tariffs or quotas. Returning to our basic supply and demand diagram (Figure 8-2) to illustrate, suppose the United States imposes a $1000 tax on each Japanese car imported into the United States. As imported autos thus become less attractive, U.S. buyers will want to purchase fewer cars and yen and therefore will sell fewer dollars. Thus, the imposition of such a tariff would shift the supply curve of dollars leftward, causing the dollar to appreciate in the long run. Similarly, if the United States places a quota on steel imports from Japan, the supply curve of dollars will shift left, causing the dollar to appreciate.

Long-Run Exchange Rate Developments: Summary

Table 8-2 summarizes the long-run determinants of exchange rates. As we will see, however, exchange-rate movements we observe from day to day are usually triggered by other factors.

Table 8-2

Long-Run Exchange Rate Determinants

Factor	Change in Factor	Impact on U.S. Dollar
Price level behavior	U.S. price level increases	Dollar depreciates
Preferences	Preference for U.S. goods increases	Dollar appreciates
Product development	Japan develops state-of-the-art high-resolution TV screen	Dollar depreciates
Productivity	U.S. productivity growth accelerates	Dollar appreciates
Tariffs	United States puts tariffs on imported cameras	Dollar appreciates
Quotas	United States puts quotas on imported steel	Dollar appreciates

SHORT-RUN EXCHANGE RATE DETERMINANTS

We have presented a theory of long-run exchange rate determination. This theory enables us to understand why the dollar today exchanges for less than one-half as many deutsche marks and yen as it did in 1966 and why it buys more than twice as many Italian lire (review Table 8-1). However, to understand why exchange rates can move sharply in a given week or day, we must look to other factors besides relative price level behavior, productivity trends, preferences, and international trade restrictions. Such factors cannot account for the daily and weekly swings in exchange rates that we observe. We need to develop a framework that is equipped to demonstrate why exchange rates change so much in the short run.

To understand short-term exchange rate behavior, it is important to recognize that foreign exchange market activity is dominated by asset demand—that is, demand for financial instruments and deposits in various countries—rather than by demand for goods and services. In 1996, the total value of world imports and exports of goods and services accounted for less than 2 percent of the total value of all foreign exchange transactions. This indicates that the bulk of international transactions is attributable to capital flows. In today's economy, capital is highly mobile. The currencies of the major industrial nations are very close substitutes for one another. With low foreign exchange transactions costs and computer technology, dollar deposits in New York can be transformed instantaneously and almost without cost into yen deposits in Tokyo, pound deposits in London, deutsche mark deposits in Frankfurt, and so forth. Any perceived advantage of investing funds in Frankfurt will trigger an immediate increase in the demand for German deposits.

Expected Returns from Investing at Home and Abroad

Consider a U.S. institutional investor with $100 million to invest in high-yielding bank CDs. The investor is willing to invest the funds in any major financial center—that is, New York, London, Frankfurt, Hong Kong, and so forth. Let us designate the interest rates available on domestic and foreign CDs as i_D and i_F, respectively. If the funds are invested in New York CDs, no foreign exchange transactions are involved, and the expected return is simply i_D. If the investor transfers the funds to a German bank in Frankfurt, however, the investor must deal with the fact that the exchange rate may change between the day the funds are invested and the later date on which the funds are returned to the United States. To calculate the returns expected from investing in Frankfurt, the investor must consider the prospective appreciation or depreciation of the U.S. dollar while the funds are earning interest in Germany. Suppose the institutional investor can earn 8 percent interest on 1-year German CDs but expects the dollar to appreciate (the deutsche mark to depreciate) by 3 percent during the year. Then when it comes time to convert the deutsche mark CD earnings back into dollars, a 3 percent exchange rate loss is expected because it is expected to cost 3 percent more marks to buy a dollar than a year earlier, when the funds were invested in Germany. Thus, the expected return from investing in German securities is only approximately 5 percent—that is, 8 percent minus 3 percent.[10] Consider the following expression:

$$(8\text{-}1) \qquad\qquad R_F = i_F - \frac{(ER_{t+1}^e - ER_t)}{ER_t}$$

where

R_F = the expected rate of return from investing abroad

i_F = the foreign interest rate—that is, the rate on 1-year German CDs

ER_t = the actual (spot) exchange rate in the current period (t), expressed as deutsche marks per dollar, and

ER_{t+1}^e = the exchange rate currently expected to prevail in 1 year, when the CD comes due and the German deposits are to be converted back into U.S. deposits

The expression simply states that the expected return from investing in foreign assets is equal to the foreign interest rate minus the expected percentage *appreciation* of the U.S. dollar (or depreciation of the deutsche mark) during the next year.[11] If one can earn 3 percent interest on the German CDs but the deutsche mark is expected to appreciate (dollar to depreciate) by 6 percent during the year, the expected return (R_F) is 9 percent. In this case, the U.S. investor expects to earn a 3 percent return in marks and gain another 6 percent from the fall in the dollar.

The Interest Parity Condition

Because capital is highly mobile and because investors seek to maximize their returns, interest rates and exchange rates align themselves so that expected returns are equalized across countries. In other words, in equilibrium, $i_D = R_F$; that is, expected returns in the United States and Germany are equalized. If we employ Equation 8-1 and set it equal to the expected return on domestic deposits (i_D), we obtain

$$(8\text{-}2) \qquad\qquad i_D = i_F - \frac{(ER_{t+1}^e - ER_t)}{ER_t}$$

This expression, known as the **interest parity condition,** is based on the simple notion that, in a world of capital mobility, expected returns on assets are equalized across

---

[10]Suppose the exchange rate is initially DM1.50/$ and the dollar is expected to appreciate by 3 percent during the year, to DM1.545/$. The $100 million will initially exchange for DM150 million and will earn DM12 million in interest income during the year (.08 × DM150 million). If the DM162 million are converted back to dollars a year later at DM1.545/$, they will fetch only $1,048,544. On the original $1,000,000 investment, the rate of return is thus 4.85 percent.

[11]Alternatively, R_F may be defined as the foreign interest rate *plus* the expected percentage *depreciation* of the dollar. Of course, appreciation of the dollar is the same as negative depreciation and vice versa.

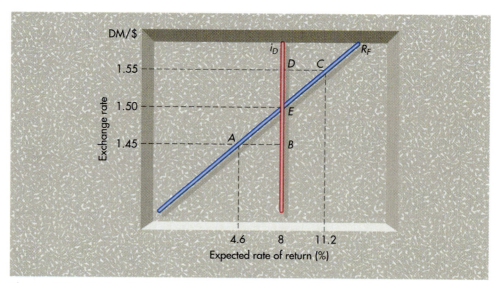

Figure 8-5   Foreign Exchange Market Equilibrium. Equilibrium in the foreign exchange market occurs at the exchange rate at which the expected returns from investing abroad (R_F) and the expected returns from investing at home (i_D) are equal. Shifts in these two schedules produce short-run exchange rate changes.

countries. In equilibrium, interest rates and exchange rates have aligned themselves so that traders cannot profit by switching currencies. This seems intuitively plausible. Suppose, hypothetically, that investors initially expect to receive a higher return in Germany than in the United States. The demand for German assets (and demand for deutsche marks) would then increase, causing the mark to appreciate and the dollar to depreciate. Given the expected future exchange rate, this decline in the dollar would increase the expected future appreciation of the dollar (or reduce its expected depreciation), reducing R_F—that is, the expected net return earned from German CDs. This depreciation of the dollar would continue until the expected advantage of investing in Germany was eliminated. If investors felt that they could earn more by investing in New York, the supply of dollars offered by Americans to purchase German marks would fall and the demand for dollars by foreigners would rise, causing the dollar to appreciate. Given the expected future exchange rate, this exchange rate appreciation reduces the expected future appreciation, thus boosting R_F. This process would continue until interest parity was achieved, that is, until $i_D = R_F$.

Equilibrium in the Foreign Exchange Market

Figure 8-5 illustrates how the interest parity condition works to determine the exchange rate in the short run. The vertical axis displays the exchange rate, expressed in units of foreign currency per dollar—in this case deutsche marks per dollar. The horizontal axis displays the expected rates of return from investing at home (i_D) and abroad (R_F). In the figure, the exchange rate (vertical axis) is the independent variable. The expected rate of return (horizontal axis) is the dependent variable.

Expected Return on Dollar Deposits

Because no foreign exchange transactions are involved, the expected return to a domestic (U.S.) investor on dollar deposits (i_D) is independent of the exchange rate and is therefore shown as the vertical line i_D. Suppose this return is 8 percent. The U.S. investor in U.S. deposits earns 8 percent, regardless of the exchange rate. An increase in domestic interest rates will shift the i_D schedule rightward; a decrease in domestic interest rates will shift it leftward.

Expected Return on Foreign Deposits

Equation 8-1 indicates that the expected rate of return on foreign deposits (R_F) depends on three factors: the interest rate paid on foreign deposits (i_F), the current exchange rate (ER_t), and the exchange rate expected to prevail in the next period, when the funds are to be returned home (ER_{t+1}^e). Holding constant the interest rate paid on foreign deposits, and holding constant the expected future exchange rate, this means that the returns expected from foreign deposits depend on the current exchange rate. A higher current exchange rate (more deutsche marks per dollar) implies a smaller expected appreciation (or larger expected depreciation) of the dollar and therefore a higher expected rate of return from German deposits, R_F. This explains the upward slope of the R_F function in Figure 8-5.

In the figure, suppose that the interest rate paid on German deposits is 8 percent and the expected future exchange rate is 1.50 deutsche marks per dollar. If the current exchange rate were 1.45 deutsche marks per dollar, the dollar would be expected to appreciate by 3.4 percent, that is, (DM1.50 − DM1.45)/DM1.45. This must be subtracted from the 8 percent rate on German deposits to derive an expected return (R_F) of 4.6 percent. This is shown as point A in the figure. The figure indicates that, at 1.45 deutsche marks per dollar, the returns expected by a U.S. investor from U.S. deposits (8 percent) exceed the returns expected by a U.S. investor from German deposits (4.6 percent). This is a disequilibrium situation that violates the interest parity condition. In the foreign exchange market, the supply of dollars would decrease as Americans purchase fewer German deposits, and the demand would increase as Germans buy more U.S. deposits. These forces would cause the dollar to appreciate.[12]

If the exchange rate were 1.55 deutsche marks per dollar, the dollar would be expected to *depreciate* by 3.2 percent, that is, (DM1.50 − DM1.55)/DM1.55. The returns expected by a U.S. investor from German deposits would now be 11.2 percent, that is, 8 percent + 3.2 percent. This is shown as point C in the figure. Because the returns expected from German deposits exceed the returns expected from U.S. deposits when the current exchange rate is 1.55 deutsche marks per dollar, this situation cannot persist. The supply of dollars by U.S. investors to purchase deutsche marks would increase, the demand for dollars by German investors to buy U.S. assets would decrease, and the dollar would depreciate.

---

[12]From the perspective of German investors, U.S. CDs yield 8 percent in dollars, as do German CDs in deutsche marks. However, because the deutsche mark is expected to depreciate, the returns expected from investing in the United States would exceed 8 percent. Such a situation would stimulate the buying of dollars by Germans. This would cause the dollar to appreciate and the mark to depreciate.

Finally, if the exchange rate is 1.5 deutsche marks per dollar, there is no expected change in the exchange rate, and the rate of return expected from German deposits is 8 percent (point E). Because the return available on U.S. deposits is also 8 percent, interest parity prevails and the market is in short-run equilibrium (point E); the expected returns from investing in Germany and the United States are thus equal. Given the situation depicted in Figure 8-5, the equilibrium exchange rate is 1.50 deutsche marks per dollar.

Your Turn

Suppose that yields on safe, 1-year government securities are 6 percent in the United States and 11 percent in Italy. Assuming that the current exchange rate is 1600 lire per dollar and that the interest parity condition holds, calculate the expected lira-dollar exchange rate a year from now.

Factors Causing Short-Run Exchange Rate Changes

If you understand the interest parity condition and the model presented in Figure 8-5, understanding the factors that cause short-run exchange rate changes will be straightforward. You can see that any factor that shifts the i_D function rightward or the R_F function leftward will cause the dollar to appreciate. Any factor that shifts the i_D function leftward or the R_F function rightward will cause the dollar to depreciate. Frequent shifts in these two functions account for the short-term exchange rate volatility that we observe.

The only factor that can shift the i_D function is a change in interest rates in the United States. An increase in U.S. interest rates shifts i_D rightward, while a decrease in U.S. interest rates shifts i_D leftward. Equation 8-1 indicates that there are three factors that influence R_F: the foreign interest rate (i_F), the expected future exchange rate (ER_{t+1}^e), and the current exchange rate (ER_t). Because a change in ER_t moves us *along* the R_F schedule in Figure 8-5, the two factors that *shift* R_F are changes in foreign interest rates and changes in the expected future exchange rate. In our example of the deutsche mark–dollar exchange rate, the two factors shifting R_F are changes in German interest rates and changes in the expected exchange rate. An increase in real interest rates in Germany increases the returns expected from investing in German deposits, shifting R_F rightward and causing the dollar to depreciate (and the mark to appreciate). A downward revision of the expected future value of the dollar (a decline in ER_{t+1}^e) increases the returns expected by a U.S. investor from German assets, shifting R_F rightward and causing the dollar to depreciate.

As foreign exchange dealers, managers of investment portfolios, and other major foreign exchange market participants receive new information each minute and hour of the day, they process this information and revise their outlook for future exchange rates. Such information produces continuing shifts in the R_F function, thus precipitating short-run

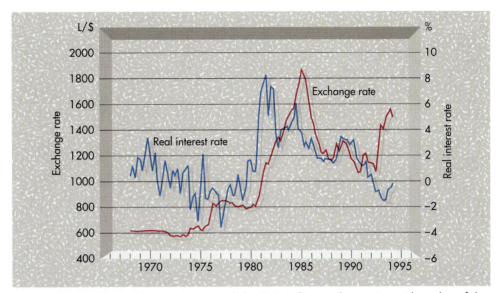

Figure 8-6   U.S. Real Interest Rates and the U.S.-Italian Exchange Rate. The value of the U.S. dollar (L/$) tracks the real U.S. Treasury bill yield remarkably well. This suggests that the Federal Reserve can influence exchange rates by altering real short-term yields. (*Note:* Real Treasury bill yield is calculated by subtracting the 1-year expected inflation rate indicated by the Michigan Survey of Expected Inflation from the 1-year U.S. Treasury bill yield.) *Sources:* University of Michigan and *Citibank Economic Database.*

exchange rate changes. By altering the expected future exchange rate, information bearing on the future behavior of the fundamental factors influencing exchange rates will shift R_F and thereby influence the exchange rate immediately.

Real versus Nominal Interest Rate Changes

Suppose U.S. interest rates rise while the outlook for U.S. inflation remains constant— that is, *real* U.S. interest rates rise. In Figure 8-5, the i_D schedule shifts right, the demand for U.S. assets increases, and the dollar appreciates. On the other hand, suppose U.S. interest rates rise due to an increase in expected U.S. inflation. Then i_D shifts right because of higher interest rates, but R_F also shifts right due to expectation of a longer-run depreciation of the dollar owing to higher expected U.S. inflation. The short-term impact on the exchange rate is ambiguous, depending on the relative magnitudes of the shifts of i_D and R_F.[13] Figure 8-6, which illustrates the real U.S. Treasury bill yield together with the U.S.-Italian exchange rate since 1970, indicates the importance of U.S. real interest rates in exchange rate determination. A similar pattern is obtained if one examines the U.S. exchange rate with Canada, France, Japan, and so forth (not shown).

---

[13]The exchange rate literature indicates that the dollar is likely to depreciate because the impact on international capital flows of the expected depreciation of the dollar due to higher expected inflation outweighs the effect of higher nominal U.S. interest rates. In part, this may be due to a consensus in the empirical interest rate literature that the Fisher coefficient is less than 1—that is, an increase in expected inflation exerts a less than one-for-one effect on nominal interest rates.

Examples of Forces Producing Short-Run Exchange Rate Changes

A few examples of the type of information that influences short-term exchange rate behavior will reinforce your understanding. We will look at the effects of information pertaining to the outlook for future inflation, information influencing the outlook for future interest rates, and information on current trade deficits.

Factors Indicating a Change in Outlook for Inflation

Suppose news is released indicating a likely sharp increase in OPEC oil prices. This oil price hike will tend to raise inflation in all countries but will especially impact those nations which rely strongly on imported oil. For example, the impact on the price level in Japan is likely to be stronger than the effect on U.S. prices. Because this will cause the dollar to appreciate against the yen in the long run, the expected return earned by American investors on Japanese deposits (R_F) will decline. The R_F function shifts leftward, and the dollar will appreciate on the announcement. Alternatively, suppose the Federal Reserve reports a sharp increase in the U.S. money supply. If investors interpret this as indicating an increase in future U.S. inflation, they will expect the dollar to depreciate. This shifts R_F rightward, causing the dollar to depreciate as soon as the announcement is made.

Factors Indicating a Change in Outlook for Real Interest Rates

Any news that leads to expected real interest rate changes in the United States or foreign nations leads to shifts in the R_F function, producing immediate changes in the exchange rate. For example, an announcement that consumer confidence in the United States has declined sharply will lead to expectations of a slowdown in U.S. economic activity and a decline in U.S. real interest rates. Because lower U.S. real interest rates will lead to a depreciation of the dollar, the expected return on foreign deposits increases (the R_F function shifts rightward), triggering an immediate decline in the dollar. Suppose, alternatively, that an announcement is made that the U.S. president has appointed two new members to the Board of Governors who are known to be hard-liners against inflation. This is likely to lead to expectations of more restrictive monetary policy actions and higher U.S. real interest rates in the near term, as well as lower U.S. inflation. These expectations cause agents to revise upward their projection for the future exchange rate (foreign currency/$). This revision shifts R_F leftward, causing the dollar to appreciate immediately.

Unanticipated Changes in the Trade Deficit

Given other factors, announcement of a larger U.S. trade deficit is likely to lead agents to expect the dollar to have to fall over the intermediate term in order to correct the deficit—that is, to stimulate U.S. exports and reduce imports. Such an announcement would thus increase the returns expected from foreign assets, shifting R_F rightward. Given other factors, the dollar would fall on the announcement of a larger trade deficit. (Exhibit 8-2 indicates some of the types of news that have resulted in short-term changes in the U.S. dollar exchange rate in recent years.)

EXHIBIT 8-2

Changes in Factors Driving Exchange Rate Speculation

Many factors can cause speculators to turn bullish or bearish on a currency. As pertinent economic and political information becomes available each hour, speculators estimate the likely effect on future exchange rates and make decisions about buying and selling a currency. It is interesting to note how the particular information deemed crucial by exchange rate speculators changes over time.

In the late 1970s, U.S. inflation was rampant, and many questioned the will of the U.S. government (including the Fed) to pay the price to defeat it. Each month, speculators would watch for the release of the official price indexes. In the 1970s, the purchasing power parity (PPP) theory provided a fairly reliable model of exchange rate determination. If the price indexes revealed that U.S. inflation was running higher than expected, speculators would sell dollars immediately in anticipation that import and export activity would later drive the dollar down.

During the 1980s, PPP broke down as a reliable tracker of exchange rates. Changes in real interest rate levels, by triggering international capital flows, played a larger role in explaining exchange rate changes. In late 1979, the Fed implemented a policy of targeting money supply growth, allowing interest rates to seek whatever levels were compatible with the modest growth of the money supply. Speculators would turn their attention to the weekly money supply announcement that flashed across the ticker at 2:00 P.M. EST each Thursday. If the announced money supply exceeded expectations, speculators would anticipate a tightening of Fed policy to get back onto the money target. This suggested that nominal and real interest rates would have to rise, thereby inducing a capital inflow and appreciation of the dollar. Hence, speculators would purchase dollars immediately on the announcement, causing the dollar to firm up within seconds.

By the mid-1980s, the Fed abandoned its experiment with money supply targeting and speculators abandoned their fascination with the money supply numbers. In this period (1983–1987), the U.S. trade deficit increased sharply—chiefly in response to the enormous 1981–1985 appreciation of the dollar and the robust U.S. economic expansion, which stimulated imports. After early 1985, the dollar began to depreciate, but the trade deficit continued to expand in 1986 and 1987. Speculators now focused their attention on the monthly release of the trade figures. If the trade deficit came in larger than expected, speculators would immediately dump dollars in anticipation that further depreciation of the dollar would be required in order to turn the burgeoning U.S. trade deficit around. In January 1988, when the trade figures revealed an unexpected and large decline in the deficit, the dollar rallied strongly as speculators turned bullish en masse.

Based on your reading of the daily newspaper and your observation of the evening news, what chief indicators are the foreign exchange market speculators watching this year?

CONSEQUENCES OF EXCHANGE RATE CHANGES

We have already discussed how the exchange rate level influences the cost of goods imported into the United States, as well as the price paid by foreign buyers of U.S. exports. If the U.S. dollar appreciates, the prices of U.S. imports fall, while the prices of U.S. products increase in other nations. Given other factors, when the dollar depreciates, we get the opposite effects. Imported products cost more in the United States, while U.S. goods become cheaper to the rest of the world. For this reason, an appreciation of the dollar tends to increase U.S. imports and reduce U.S. exports, thereby increasing the U.S. **trade deficit**—that is, the amount by which U.S. imports exceed U.S. exports. A depreciation of the dollar tends to reduce the trade deficit.

Exchange rate changes may significantly affect such key variables as inflation and unemployment rates and a nation's standard of living. Moreover, exchange rate changes may affect income distribution, simultaneously helping some groups and hurting others. For these reasons, nations are sometimes reluctant to accept exchange rate changes, even when they are dictated by fundamental forces such as changes in real interest rates. A government sometimes alters its conduct of monetary policy to prevent undesired changes in exchange rates, even though such monetary policy actions may have adverse consequences for domestic employment. Here, we will look at some of the more important consequences of exchange rate changes. We will focus on the effect of a change in a nation's exchange rate on its price level, distribution of real income, and standard of living.

Price Level Effects

When the U.S. dollar depreciates, it buys fewer units of foreign currency. This means that foreign products become more expensive in the United States. At the same time, U.S. products become cheaper abroad. After some time lag, the physical volume of U.S. exports increases and U.S. imports decline. The aggregate demand for U.S. goods and services increases, tending to push up U.S. prices as well as output. More important, to the extent that imported goods directly or indirectly affect the prices of goods consumed in the United States, the price level increases, independently of the effect of currency depreciation on aggregate demand already mentioned. Finally, by reducing the "discipline" imposed by foreign competition, pressure on U.S. industries to hold down wages and prices is reduced if the dollar falls more than is justified by purchasing power parity considerations. For all these reasons, depreciation of a nation's currency leads to an increase in its price level.

When the dollar appreciates, as it did dramatically during 1981–1985, strong disinflationary forces are unleashed. Aggregate demand for U.S. goods decreases as U.S. imports rise and exports fall. Reduced prices on imported cars, electronic equipment, and other products tend to directly lower the U.S. price level. Finally, the specter of a flood of cheap imports imposes great pressure on

U.S. manufacturing firms to hold the line on costs and prices to remain competitive. The fear of losing jobs because of cheap imports serves to inhibit workers' wage demands. In these ways, the powerful appreciation of the dollar during 1981–1985 significantly aided the effort to reduce U.S. inflation from the intolerable rates of the 1970s.

Income Distribution Effects

Because changes in exchange rates affect the prices U.S. consumers pay for foreign (and domestic) products as well as the ability of the United States to compete effectively in world markets, such changes affect different groups in society in different ways. A falling dollar, by stimulating exports and slowing imports, benefits U.S. workers and owners who are involved in the export sector and sectors competing with imported goods. Hence, a falling dollar benefits autoworkers in Detroit by making imported Hondas more expensive in the United States and Fords cheaper in Europe. On the other hand, by causing U.S. consumers to pay more for imported goods, a falling dollar imposes costs on the mass of U.S. consumers, directly lowering their living standards. A rising dollar turns the tables, hurting U.S. manufacturing firms subject to foreign competition but showering U.S. consumers with inexpensive imported goods.

Terms-of-Trade Effects

A nation's **terms of trade** is defined as the ratio of the price of its exports divided by the price of its imports, both measured in units of domestic currency. When the dollar appreciates as a result of factors other than relative price level behavior, the terms of trade increase or improve because the price of imports measured in dollars falls while the price of exports remains constant. This means the United States receives more imported items per, say, bushel of wheat exported. This net gain to society is reflected in the benefit that U.S. consumers experience through the availability of cheaper imported goods. A depreciation of the U.S. dollar caused by factors other than price level behavior means that while wheat may remain at $4 per bushel in the United States, the cost of an imported Swiss watch increases. More bushels of wheat must be yielded by the United States in order to obtain a Swiss watch. A net loss accrues to U.S. society at large because the depreciation of the dollar creates an adverse movement in the terms of trade.

SUMMARY

The exchange rate—the price at which one country's currency exchanges for another's—is a key variable because it plays an important role in determining the price of a nation's products in the rest of the world as well as the domestic price of goods imported from abroad. Today, world trade is conducted in a floating exchange rate system. In this system, exchange rates change continuously throughout the day. Factors determining exchange rates may be divided into short-run determinants and long-run determinants. A crucial long-run exchange rate determinant is price level behavior among nations. Countries that have relatively high inflation experience long-term depreciation of their currencies. Other long-run determinants of exchange rates include preferences and product development, productivity growth, and trade restrictions such as tariffs and quotas. The volume of foreign exchange market activity is dominated by transactions in financial assets—bank deposits and money market instruments—rather than transactions in goods and services. For this reason, short-term exchange rate movements—that is, daily, weekly, and monthly movements—are driven by changes in expected returns from investing in domestic and foreign financial assets. Any news that leads to higher expected returns from U.S. financial assets will cause an immediate appreciation of the dollar. Any news that produces expectations of higher returns abroad will produce an immediate depreciation of the dollar. As new information becomes available each hour of the day, major foreign exchange market participants project the likely influence on exchange rates in the weeks and months ahead. If they believe the net influence will be to cause a depreciation of the dollar, they immediately sell dollars in exchange for yen, deutsche marks, and other foreign currencies. As a result, the dollar declines within minutes of the announcement.

Answer to Your Turn (p. 167)

At an exchange rate of 150 yen per dollar, it will cost you $200 to purchase 30,000 yen and the CD player—that is, 30,000 yen divided by 150 yen per dollar. At an exchange rate of 100 yen per dollar, the cost of the CD player increases to $300. As a consumer, you prefer a strong dollar, because the cost to you of all imported goods falls as the dollar appreciates.

Answer to Your Turn (p. 180)

The interest parity condition states that expected returns on interest-bearing assets having the same characteristics must be equalized. This means that if U.S. investors can earn 6 percent on U.S. Treasury securities, they must expect to earn 6 percent on the Italian securities after converting the lira proceeds back into dollars. Because the yield on Italian securities in lire is 11 percent, we infer that the dollar is expected to appreciate against the lira by approximately 5 percent in the next year. This means that the expected exchange rate 1 year from now (ER^e_{t+1}) is approximately 1600 × 1.05, or 1680 lire per dollar. This is the result obtained by using Equation 8-2 and solving for ER^e_{t+1}. To be more precise, 1600 lire invested in Italy at 11 percent for 1 year will grow to 1776 lire. One dollar invested in the U.S. at 6 percent will grow to $1.06. To equalize returns, $1.06 must convert into exactly L1776 in one year, which means the exchange rate must be L1776/$1.06, or 1675.47 lire per dollar. This represents a 4.72 percent appreciation of the U.S. dollar.

KEY TERMS

foreign exchange market
international capital flows
foreign exchange rate
depreciate
appreciate
floating exchange rates

International Monetary Fund
adjustable-peg exchange rate system
Bretton Woods exchange rate system
spot transaction
spot exchange rate
forward transaction

forward exchange rate
purchasing power parity theory (PPP)
law of one price
tariff

quota
interest parity condition
trade deficit
terms of trade

STUDY QUESTIONS

1 Consider the exchange rate between the U.S. and France. Draw a demand curve for dollars and a supply curve for dollars. Label the vertical axis "French francs per dollar" and the horizontal axis "Quantity of dollars." Show the equilibrium U.S.-French exchange rate. Explain why the demand curve is downward sloping. Explain why the supply curve is upward sloping.

2 Return to the example of the U.S.-French exchange rate posed in question 1. Holding other factors constant, analyze the impact of each of the following events on the value of the dollar (expressed in French francs):

a The Federal Reserve increases U.S. interest rates.

b The U.S. price level rises by 5 percent.

c A French company introduces a highly attractive new line of tennis shoes.

d The United States imposes a new tariff on all French products sold in the United States.

e A new "buy American" ethic is promoted in the United States to protect American workers.

f U.S. federal budget deficits are eliminated.

g France goes into a severe recession, but interest rates remain constant.

h U.S. productivity growth accelerates to 4 percent per year.

3 Explain the purchasing power parity theory of foreign exchange rates and the intuition underlying it. Why do you suppose PPP has done a better job of tracking the U.S.-Mexican exchange rate in the past 15 years than the U.S.-Japanese exchange rate?

4 Under what conditions would the purchasing power parity theory always be valid? Explain. Why does the theory often fail to accurately predict exchange rate movements in the real world?

5 Return to your diagram for question 1. Now suppose the United States removes all taxes and tariffs on French wine. Explain whether this event would

a Shift the supply or demand curves for dollars (if so, explain in which direction).

b Cause the U.S. dollar to appreciate or depreciate.

6 You are interested in purchasing a beautiful hand-woven rug from an artist in Saudi Arabia. The price is quoted as 45,000 riyals. The money changer offers an exchange rate of 3.85 riyals per dollar. How much will your purchase cost? What will it cost if the quoted exchange rate is $.25974 per riyal? (*Hint:* Read the question very carefully.)

7 While digging through some old newspapers, you find that the exchange rate between the dollar and the Philippine peso was 20 pesos per dollar in 1987. Look up the 1996 exchange rate in "From the Financial Pages" on page 166. Did the dollar appreciate or depreciate between 1987 and 1996? Did the peso appreciate or depreciate?

8 In the same newspaper, you find that the exchange rate between the British pound and the dollar was 1.61 dollars per pound. Again, check the 1996 exchange rate. Did the dollar appreciate or depreciate between 1987 and 1996? The pound?

9 You are expecting a shipment of Swiss watches in 3 months. Upon delivery, you must pay the sum of 131,000 Swiss francs. What is the risk in waiting 3 months and buying the francs in the spot market at that time to pay for the watches? Explain two strategies that you might use to deal with this risk.

10 You have a $12,000 nest egg that you wish to invest. A confidential source at the Federal Reserve tells you the Fed will aggressively pursue a policy to drive the yen-dollar exchange rate to 125 yen within 6 months. Assume the current exchange rate is the one indicated in "From the Financial Pages." Explain how you can use (albeit illegally) the spot market for your own financial gain. How might you use the forward market?

11 Suppose the current exchange rate between the United States and India is 34 rupees per dollar. Assume that PPP theory holds. If the United States experiences 3 percent inflation and India experiences 7 percent inflation, what would you expect the exchange rate to be in 1 year?

12 What effect might the British "mad cow disease" scare of 1996 have had on the value of the pound in foreign exchange markets? Explain.

13 Look up the spot and 180-day forward rates for the German mark in "From the Financial Pages." Without making any calculations, indicate whether German interest rates were higher or lower than U.S. interest rates. If the yield on 6-month U.S. Treasury securities was 8 percent in April 1996, what was the yield on comparable German securities?

14 Suppose that the interest rates on comparable one-year U.S. and Japanese government securities are 4 percent and 6 percent, respectively, and the spot exchange rate is 110 yen per dollar. What must the expected exchange rate one year from now be?

15 Explain at least two ways in which an appreciation of the U.S. dollar works to reduce inflation in the United States.

16 Examine Figure 8-1 (all four components), with emphasis on the 1980–1985 period. Does the observed exchange rate pattern help account for the emergence of large U.S. trade deficits in the mid-1980s?

17 Glance at the left-hand portion of Figure 8-1. Note that the dollar generally trended downward against the yen and deutsche mark during the 1970s, appreciated strongly during 1980–1985, and depreciated again after 1985. Can you briefly explain the fundamental causes of these three movements in the dollar?

18 U.S. legislation during the 1980s prohibited investment in South African assets. Explain the likely consequences of this action on the rand-dollar exchange rate.

19 In the spring of 1994, Alan Blinder was appointed vice chairman of the Board of Governors of the Federal Reserve Board. Blinder was perceived as "soft on inflation."

a How would news of the appointment likely have affected expectations as to the future exchange rate?

b How would this revision of expectations affect the R_F schedule in Figure 8-5?

c How would this news affect the deutsche mark–dollar exchange rate?

20 In response to rising unemployment, the German central bank moved to reduce interest rates in the spring of 1996. Use the short-term exchange rate model to analyze the consequences of this announcement on the dollar–deutsche mark exchange rate.

21 Suppose the U.S. Department of Commerce announces a trade deficit figure that is substantially lower than expected. Explain, using the short-term exchange rate model, the effect of this announcement on the value of the dollar.

SUGGESTIONS FOR ADDITIONAL READING

For more in-depth analyses of the topics in this chapter, consult an undergraduate international economics textbook. Good examples include Paul Krugman and Maurice Obstfeld, *International Economics: Theory and Policy,* 3d ed. (New York: HarperCollins, 1995); and J. Orlin Grabbe, *International Financial Markets,* 3d ed. (Englewood Cliffs, N.J.: Prentice-Hall, 1996). Other important recent books covering many of the topics in this chapter include Bennett McCallum, *International Monetary Economics* (Oxford, England: Oxford University Press, 1996); and John Williamson (ed.) *Estimating Equilibrium Exchange Rates* (Washington, D.C.: Institute for International Economics, 1994). On foreign exchange markets, see K. Alec Chrystal, "A Guide to Foreign Exchange Markets," Federal Reserve Bank of St. Louis *Review,* March 1984, pp. 5–18. For an excellent review of the purchasing power parity theory, see Craig Hakkio, "Is Purchasing Power Parity a Useful Guide to the Dollar?," Federal Reserve Bank of Kansas City *Economic Review,* Third Quarter 1992. Many data on foreign exchange rates are available in International Monetary Fund, *International Financial Statistics,* published monthly. See also the quarterly publication by the Federal Reserve Bank of St. Louis, "International Economic Conditions." For an analysis of recent international economic conditions as they pertain to the U.S. economy, see the most recent *Economic Report of the President,* published in February each year by the U.S. Government Printing Office in Washington, D.C.

P A R T

3

Banking: Structure, Regulation, and Deposit Insurance

Banks and other depository institutions play a key role in the financial system■ They are intimately involved in the creation of money and credit■ They contribute importantly to economic efficiency and growth, and provide benefits to both borrowers and lenders■ The U.S. banking industry is unique■ While other nations have only a few huge banks with lots of branches, the United States has almost 10,000 separately owned banks■ However, a major consolidation is currently underway, and the number of banks has declined by nearly a third in the past decade■ First the savings and loan industry and then the banking industry went through very difficult times in the 1980s and early 1990s■ Insolvencies increased sharply and major costs were incurred by depository insurance agencies and U.S. taxpayers■ Much of the problem can be attributed to a flawed regulatory and insurance system■ As a result of this experience, new measures have been implemented to reduce incentives for risk taking by depository institutions■

Commercial Banking

Depository institutions, or "banks," play a key role in channeling funds from savers to borrowers and investors. Banks grant loans to students, homebuyers, consumers, and businesses and provide us with services such as checking and savings accounts. Among depository institutions, commercial banks are clearly the dominant players. They are also the oldest and most diversified of all financial intermediaries. In December 1996, commercial banks had some $4.7 trillion in total assets—more than 75 percent of the total assets of all depository institutions (commercial banks, savings and loan associations, mutual savings banks, and credit unions) combined.

However, our interest in banks stems not only from their dominant role among financial intermediaries but from the special role they play in the money supply process. A substantial portion of the claims banks issue (checking accounts) circulates as money. In fact, the dominant portion of our transactions measure of the money supply (M1) consists of commercial bank checking accounts. Through the process of lending and investing in securities, commercial banks create new money. Banking activity is the major conduit through which Federal Reserve monetary policy influences the nation's credit conditions and money supply. For all these reasons, commercial banking merits special attention.

Because of the key role banks play in the economy, a financially healthy banking sector is important to the nation's economic well-being. In the past 15 to 20 years, banks have been challenged by financial innovation, deregulation, and globalization. In the process, their profitability has fluctuated significantly. Banks went through hard times in the late 1980s and early 1990s, but since 1992 their financial condition has strengthened materially.

In this chapter we will look at the business of banking. We will examine the commercial bank balance sheet and the sources and uses of bank funds (liabilities and assets). We will study the principles and constraints governing the management of bank assets and liabilities. We will look at the concepts of bank liquidity and capital adequacy, and we will discuss the reasons banks sometimes become insolvent. Though much of the analysis of this chapter applies also to savings institutions and credit unions, we will concentrate primarily on commercial banks.

THE COMMERCIAL BANK BALANCE SHEET

Banks are in business to earn a profit. They do so by borrowing funds (issuing debt) at relatively low interest rates and lending or investing the funds at higher interest rates. The "spread" between the rate banks pay for funds and the rate they earn is the major determinant of bank profits, although in recent years service fees have increased in importance.

Perhaps the best way to learn about the business of banking is to examine a typical bank's balance sheet. The **balance sheet** of any entity (business firm, individual, government) is a statement of its assets, liabilities, and net worth at a given point in time. A bank's **assets** are indications of what the bank *owns,* or claims the bank has on external (nonbank) entities: individuals, firms, governments. A bank's **liabilities** are indications of what the bank *owes,* or claims on the bank that are held by external entities. A fundamental and simple accounting identity is the following:

$$\text{Assets} - \text{Liabilities} = \text{Net Worth}$$

or

$$\text{Assets} = \text{Liabilities} + \text{Net Worth}$$

Net worth is a residual term that is calculated by subtracting total liabilities from total assets. In banking, net worth is known as **capital accounts,** or simply **capital.** Capital accounts may be viewed as the value of the owners' residual claim on the bank's assets—that is, the owners' equity in the bank. This item is listed on the right-hand side of the balance sheet, below liabilities, so that the two sides of the balance sheet always balance.

Another way of viewing the balance sheet is as a statement of the sources of and uses for bank funds. Banks obtain funds by issuing debt (liabilities) in the form of demand deposits and savings and time deposits, by borrowing funds from other banks or the public, and by obtaining equity funds from the owners (shareholders) of the bank through the capital accounts. Banks use these funds to grant loans, invest in securities, purchase equipment and facilities, and hold cash items such as currency and deposits in other banks. These are the banks' assets. Loans and securities are the banks' *earning assets.* The interest earned from loans and securities generates the bulk of commercial banks' revenues. These revenues are used to cover the cost of bank operations and to provide a profit for the banks' owners. Figure 9-1 illustrates the sources of and uses for commercial bank funds.

Table 9-1 shows the collective balance sheet of all U.S. commercial banks in March 1996. Each item on the balance sheet is expressed as a percentage of total assets. We will examine bank liabilities—that is, the sources of bank funds—first, followed by bank assets and then by bank capital.

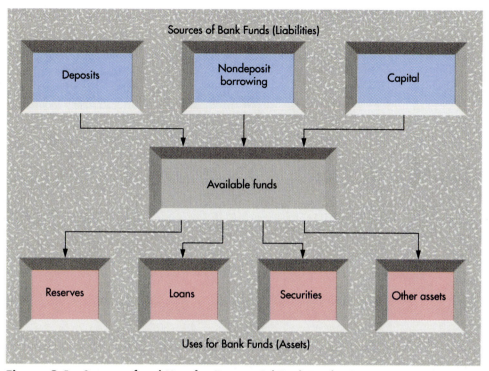

Figure 9-1   Sources of and Uses for Commercial Bank Funds. Commercial banks obtain funds by issuing deposits, borrowing from nondeposit sources, and issuing capital (equity claims). They use these funds principally to make loans and purchase securities.

COMMERCIAL BANK LIABILITIES

Bank liabilities are the funds banks obtain and the debts they incur, primarily to make loans and purchase securities. These bank liabilities include various types of deposits, borrowings, and other liabilities. Your bank deposit, which you regard as an asset, is regarded by your bank as a debt—that is, a liability. You have a claim on the bank: it owes you the amount in your account.

Bank deposits may be divided into two categories, transactions deposits and non-transactions deposits. We will examine the various types of deposit in each category, beginning with transactions deposits.

Transactions Deposits

Transactions deposits, also known as **checkable deposits,** are deposits against which checks may be written. Transactions deposits are payable on demand; you can walk into your bank and withdraw funds from your checking account at any time. You can also order

Table 9-1

Balance Sheet of U.S. Commercial Banks, March 1996 (as a percentage of total assets)

Assets (Uses of Funds)		Liabilities (Sources of Funds)	
Cash assets:	5.4%	*Deposits:*	64.7%
Vault cash	0.9	Transactions deposits	20.4
Deposits with Federal Reserve	0.6	Nontransactions deposits	44.3
Deposits with other banks and cash items in process of collection }	3.9	*Borrowings*	16.4
Loans:	61.7	*Other liabilities*	10.6
Real estate	26.0		
Business	17.0	*Capital accounts*	8.3
Consumer	11.7		
All other	7.0		
Securities:	23.9		
U.S. government	18.4		
State and local government and other	5.5		
Other assets	9.0		
Total assets	100.0%	Total liabilities and Capital	100.0%

Source: *Federal Reserve Bulletin.*

your bank to transfer funds to someone else simply by writing a check. Transactions deposits are the lowest-cost source of bank funds. Included in this category are **demand deposits,** which are non-interest-bearing checking accounts. Other types of checkable accounts do pay interest. Included are **negotiable order of withdrawal (NOW) accounts, automatic transfer service (ATS) accounts,** and **money market deposit (MMD) accounts.** While individuals and nonprofit organizations may hold both demand deposits and other types of checkable deposits, regulations prohibit banks from issuing NOW, ATS, or MMD accounts to business firms. That is, profit-oriented business firms are not allowed to hold interest-bearing checking accounts in banks.[1]

---

[1]Although banks are prohibited from paying explicit interest to business firms on checking accounts, it is a mistake to think of demand deposits as a free source of funds for banks. In reality, banks pay *implicit interest* on such funds. For example, banks routinely provide check-clearing services and send monthly bank statements to all depositors. For corporate depositors, banks frequently provide such services as payroll preparation and foreign currency transactions. For corporate customers that keep large demand deposit balances, many banks grant loans at below-market interest rates. Some banks even go so far as to calculate the total amount of free services they will provide to corporate customers. They do this by applying an appropriate interest rate to the average balance held by the customer.

NOW Accounts

From the 1930s to the early 1980s, federal law generally prohibited depository institutions from paying interest on checking accounts. Beginning in the late 1960s, and especially in the 1970s, as money market yields increased sharply, that prohibition began to cause problems for depository institutions. Banks witnessed the phenomenon of *disintermediation*—the active withdrawal of funds from depository institutions by customers in search of higher yields. In 1972, after 2 years of litigation, savings banks in Massachusetts were authorized to call a check a "negotiable order of withdrawal." Because the accounts on which such checks were written, called *NOW accounts,* were not considered demand deposits, they were not subject to the regulations that prohibited the payment of interest. Thus, a NOW account is essentially a savings account on which checks may be written. Though lobbyists for banks won an early ruling prohibiting the spread of NOW accounts beyond New England, in 1980 the Depository Institutions Deregulation and Monetary Control Act (DIDMCA) authorized nationwide issuance of NOW accounts.

ATS Accounts

At the same time that NOW accounts were legalized nationwide, a similar instrument, the ATS account (automatic transfer service), was authorized. With an ATS account, the customer maintains a minimal checking account balance and holds additional funds in an interest-bearing savings account. As checks drawn on the checking account are presented for clearance, the bank's computer automatically transfers sufficient funds from the individual's savings account to the checking account to permit checks to clear and maintain the minimum checking account balance. Like the NOW account, the ATS account is essentially an interest-bearing checking account.

MMD Accounts

Money market deposit (MMD) accounts are interest-bearing transactions deposits that were authorized in 1982 to permit banks to compete with money market mutual funds. MMD accounts offer only limited check-writing privileges; the yield payable fluctuates with market yields.[2] From the public's point of view, MMD accounts have an advantage over MMMF shares inasmuch as they are insured by the FDIC for up to $100,000 per account.

Because MMD accounts are less likely to be withdrawn, and because they are not subject to reserve requirements (a concept to be introduced shortly), banks can offer a higher interest rate on MMD accounts than on NOW and ATS accounts. And though demand deposits, NOW accounts, and ATS accounts are included in the Federal Reserve's narrow measure of money (M1), MMD accounts are not (they are included in M2). Despite their check-writing features, the Fed deems them more as a savings account than as a vehicle for financing everyday expenditures.

Figure 9-2 indicates the long-term growth of demand deposits and other types of checkable accounts. Note the rapid growth of the interest-bearing "other checkable deposits" since 1980, when deregulatory legislation authorized nationwide issuance of NOW and ATS accounts. The growth of demand deposits has been limited by the legal statute prohibiting the payment of interest on them, coupled with the development of close substitutes. Since 1950, the portion of total bank funds obtained through demand

---

[2]Money market deposit accounts permit no more than six transactions (preauthorized, automatic, or other transfers) per month. Of these six transactions, no more than three can involve the use of checks.

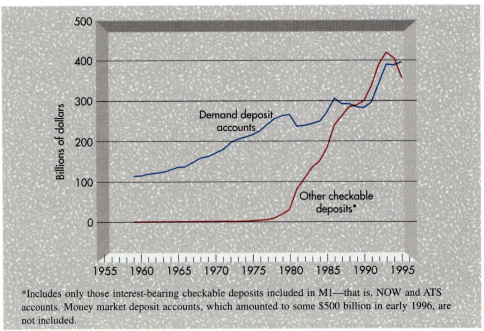

*Includes only those interest-bearing checkable deposits included in M1—that is, NOW and ATS accounts. Money market deposit accounts, which amounted to some $500 billion in early 1996, are not included.

Figure 9-2   Growth of Demand Deposits and NOW and ATS Accounts, 1960–1995.
Since they were first authorized nationwide in the early 1980s, newer types of checkable deposits have grown much more rapidly than traditional demand deposits.   *Source: Federal Reserve Bulletin.*

deposits has declined from approximately 75 percent to less than 25 percent. As a result of the declining role of demand deposits and the increasing role of time deposits, MMDs, and other sources of funds, banks are having to pay considerably more for deposits relative to money market yields than they did in the past.

Nontransactions Deposits

Nontransactions deposits are interest-bearing deposits on which checks cannot be written. Included within this category are passbook savings accounts, small consumer-type time deposits or certificates of deposit (CDs), and large negotiable CDs issued in minimum denominations of $100,000. Nontransactions deposits are currently the primary source of bank funds, accounting for more than twice as many funds as transactions deposits.

Passbook Savings Accounts

For generations, passbook savings accounts have been popular with middle-class Americans. They are symbolized by a little blue or green book (the passbook) in which transactions and accrued interest are recorded. Passbook savings accounts are a highly liquid vehicle for saving. Available in any denomination, they have no specific maturity date; funds may be added to the account at any time. In practice, savings may be withdrawn on demand, although technically a bank may require 30 days advance notice. Once a major source of bank funds, this type of deposit has declined in popularity, chiefly because of financial innovations that have made attractive new instruments available to the public.

Small Time Deposits (CDs)

Time deposits are issued in specific maturities, such as 3 months, 6 months, 1 year, and so forth. Fairly stiff penalties (in the form of loss of accrued interest) are levied for withdrawal prior to the maturity date. Because these instruments are less liquid and less likely to be withdrawn than passbook savings accounts and MMD accounts, banks pay a higher interest rate on them. They are therefore a more costly source of funds than passbook savings accounts and money market deposit accounts. The longer the maturity of a CD, the higher the interest rate paid by the bank. Over the years, CDs have become an increasingly important source of bank funds.

Negotiable CDs

Large negotiable CDs are issued in minimum denominations of $100,000 and are typically purchased by corporations and money market mutual funds as an alternative to short-term government securities. Issued in specific maturities, they provide a reliable source of funds for the large, well-known banks that issue them. While negotiable CDs are not redeemable prior to maturity by the bank, they may be traded in an active secondary market and are therefore highly liquid. The volume of negotiable CDs outstanding fluctuates with economic conditions. When credit demands escalate during an economic expansion and the Federal Reserve moves to restrain bank lending, the volume of negotiable CDs tends to escalate. From 1989–1992, as the U.S. economy softened and credit demand declined, the volume of negotiable CDs outstanding declined by more than 25 percent. As the economy strengthened in 1994 and 1995, the volume of negotiable CDs increased 25 percent.

Nondeposit Borrowing

In addition to borrowing from depositors, commercial banks borrow funds from the Federal Reserve System, from other banks, and from corporations. Loans made by the Fed to commercial banks are known as **discount loans;** the rate charged is called the **discount rate.** Such loans are typically made for only 1 day and cannot be granted for the purpose of extending additional loans to the public. Banks can also borrow funds overnight from other banks (in the form of deposits at the Federal Reserve) in the **federal funds market.** The interest rate payable is called the **federal funds rate.** Unlike borrowing from the Federal Reserve, banks may borrow continuously in the federal funds market and may use the funds to grant loans or purchase securities. Federal funds are classified as *immediately available funds*—banks that borrow in this market obtain immediate credit in their account at the Federal Reserve.

Banks also borrow from their parent companies (holding companies) through the latter's issuing of commercial paper, and from other corporations through repurchase agreements (RPs). In an RP, a bank essentially borrows its corporate customers' checking account, typically on an overnight basis, and pays a competitive interest rate for the privilege. Finally, U.S. banks borrow *Eurodollars,* dollar-denominated deposits held by foreign banks or foreign branches of U.S. banks. Nondeposit borrowing has emerged as an important source of bank funds. The ratio of borrowed funds to total bank assets has increased from 2 percent in 1960 to more than 15 percent today.

Other Liabilities

Among the other liabilities banks carry are notes and bonds issued by the banks, bills payable, and certain other items. This liability category is relatively small.

COMMERCIAL BANK ASSETS

Commercial banks use their funds primarily to purchase income-earning assets. On the aggregate commercial bank balance sheet shown in Table 9-1, bank assets are divided into four categories: cash assets, loans, securities, and other assets. Note that more than 85 percent of total bank assets are *income-earning assets*—that is, loans and securities.

The acquisition of earning assets by commercial banks is constrained by Federal Reserve regulations that require banks to maintain a certain percentage of their deposit liabilities in the non-interest-earning form of **legal reserves,** or simply **reserves.** Reserves include currency and coins in the bank plus the bank's deposit at the Federal Reserve. The regulations that mandate the holding of reserves are referred to as **reserve requirements,** or **required reserve ratios.** At the present time, reserve requirements apply only to demand deposits, NOW accounts, and ATS accounts, although they have sometimes been levied against savings and time deposits and certain other bank liabilities. Chapter 18 contains a detailed discussion of reserve requirements. Here we need only emphasize that reserve requirements limit the portion of a bank's funds that it can use to make loans and purchase securities.

Cash Assets

Cash assets provide a bank with the funds to meet reserve requirements and the liquidity to meet the withdrawal of deposits and accommodate new loan demand. Included in this category are currency and coins (called "vault cash" because the funds are placed in the bank vault after business hours); deposits with Federal Reserve banks; deposits with other commercial banks; and cash items in the process of collection (see Table 9-1). Banks keep currency and coins on hand to meet the public's demand for it, as well as to meet reserve requirements. Besides helping to meet reserve requirements, commercial bank deposits with Federal Reserve banks also facilitate the clearing of checks through the Federal Reserve's check collection system.

Collectively, commercial banks hold large demand deposit balances in other banks. Such deposits derive from the system of *correspondent banking,* in which banks in small towns deposit funds in larger banks in return for a variety of services. These services include the collection of checks, investment counsel, and assistance with transactions in securities and foreign currencies. Essentially, the correspondent banking system extends the expertise and economies of scale enjoyed by large banks to the nation's small banks. In compensation for the services received, the smaller banks maintain deposit balances with their larger correspondent banks.

"Cash items in process of collection" refers to the total value of checks recently deposited in banks that have not yet been credited to the banks' deposit accounts with the Federal Reserve. This technical item corresponds to an item included in "other liabilities" (on the liability side of the bank balance sheet) and is listed among bank assets to balance total assets with total liabilities.

As a share of total bank assets, cash assets have declined from approximately 20 percent to about 5 percent over the past 40 years, a phenomenon favorable to bank profitability. Reductions in reserve requirements, together with a large reduction in the portion of total bank liabilities made up by demand deposits and other checkable deposits subject to reserve requirements, have caused the decline.

Loans

Loans are the largest source of income for banks, providing nearly 50 percent of total bank revenue in 1995. Unlike securities, most bank loans involve a personal relationship between banker and borrower. There are several types of bank loans, including, in order of current magnitude, real estate loans (residential and nonresidential mortgages and other real estate loans); business loans (commercial and industrial loans); and consumer loans.

From the viewpoint of banks, loans are less liquid than other assets. Unlike securities, a loan cannot be cashed in before it comes due.[3] Loans also have a higher default risk than other assets do. In compensation for their lower liquidity and higher risk, loans yield the highest rate of return among bank assets. When economic activity strengthens, the ratio of bank loans to total bank assets increases and bank profits rise.

Real Estate Loans

Real estate loans include long-term mortgages on residential properties, farms, and business properties; short-term loans to building contractors, which are generally paid off when the property is completed and sold; and home equity loans. Real estate loans are relatively illiquid and involve both interest rate risk and default risk. Banks that issue fixed-rate mortgages are at risk in the event that interest rates rise significantly after the loans are made. The default risk in real estate loans is attributable to the fact that while most of these loans are collateralized by the property being financed, real estate values can change sharply. During 1990–1992, many U.S. banks suffered major losses on commercial real estate loans, and some became insolvent as a result. Banks have taken steps to reduce the risk involved in real estate loans by issuing variable-rate mortgages and by "securitizing" mortgages—that is, bundling individual mortgages into packages and selling them to large investors such as pension funds and life insurance companies.

---

[3]An exception is securitized loans—loans that banks have packaged and sold off in the form of securities.

Business Loans

Relative to other financial intermediaries such as life insurance companies, banks have a comparative advantage in making business loans. Their familiarity with business depositors allows them to do careful evaluation and monitoring of potential borrowers. Banks consider business loans to be high-priority items. Because a large portion of all demand deposits in banks are held by businesses, bankers feel a strong need to accommodate reasonable loan requests from established businesses in order to retain their deposit accounts and maintain a reputation as a reliable source of funds. Small and midsized banks lend heavily to local businesses.

Many banks extend a *line of credit* to their business customers. This arrangement enables a business firm to obtain frequent short-term loans. The bank makes a *loan commitment* to the firm, typically allowing the firm to borrow on demand. In exchange for this valuable privilege, the customer is commonly required to maintain a *compensating balance*—that is, a non-interest-bearing checking account averaging perhaps 10 percent of the line of credit. A compensating balance raises the cost of the arrangement to the business customer and compensates the bank for the risk involved in guaranteeing a ready source of funds at all times.

Business loan demand exhibits a marked *procyclical* pattern, rising during economic expansions and declining during recessions. During periods of economic expansion, banks obtain funds to accommodate rising business loan demand by selling short-term U.S. government securities, issuing negotiable CDs, and engaging in nondeposit borrowing. During economic downturns, as loan demand declines, banks use the proceeds of loan repayments to purchase government securities, redeem maturing negotiable CDs, and reduce other forms of bank borrowing.

Consumer Loans

Banks grant loans to individuals, commonly known as consumer loans, through several arrangements. Many consumer loans are for durable goods—automobiles, for example. Others are general-purpose loans—for example, credit card loans. From the bank's point of view, consumer loans are generally more liquid than other types of loans. They tend to be short term, and many are *amortized*—that is, part of each regular payment goes to reduce the principal.

Credit card loans and overdraft arrangements, which grant on-the-spot loans to individuals to prevent their checks from bouncing, are sometimes known as "instant credit privileges." Ushered in by the record-keeping efficiency of computers, these loans are essentially an automatic line of credit to consumers. The first bank credit card was issued in 1952 by the Franklin Bank of New York. A credit card, such as VISA or MasterCard, gives a customer a preauthorized line of credit from the bank that issues the card. The customer may also obtain cash advances from any of thousands of banks that honor the card. Overdraft privileges allow customers to obtain automatic credit when they write checks in excess of their demand deposit balances. The bank grants a loan to the customer in the amount of the overdraft, either by debiting the customer's credit card or by making an automatic direct loan.

Credit card loans are extremely profitable for banks. First, the bank that issues the card repays the merchant at a discount of anywhere from 2 to 5 percent of the value of merchandise purchased. In addition, the interest rates that are charged on credit card balances are often extremely high. As a result, banks typically earn a return on credit card

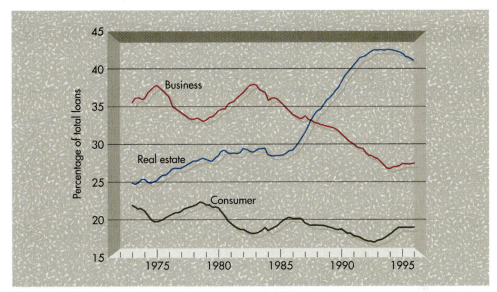

Figure 9-3   Composition of Loans, All Commercial Banks, 1973–1996. The relative importance of business and consumer loans among bank assets declined sharply after 1982. Real estate loans have expanded dramatically since 1985.   *Source:* Federal Reserve System.

loans more than 10 percentage points higher than the interest rates on U.S. Treasury bills. Given that loan losses on customer balances have averaged less than 3 percent in recent years, credit cards are a lucrative business for banks.

Other Loans

Other types of loans granted by banks include loans to financial institutions; loans to dealers, brokers, and individuals to purchase or carry stocks; loans to farmers; and federal funds sold. The latter item refers to commercial bank deposits at the Federal Reserve which have been loaned to other banks. (Its counterpart, "federal funds purchased," is included in the liability item "borrowings"—see Table 9-1.)

Figure 9-3 shows that the shares of bank loans constituted by business, real estate, and consumer loans have changed significantly over the past couple of decades. Note the sharp decrease in the relative magnitude of business (commercial) loans and the corresponding increase in the magnitude of real estate loans over the past 15 years. The decline in business loans is largely due to the emergence of the commercial paper market as an alternative source of funds for corporations. The recent expansion in real estate loans may be attributed in part to the decline in corporations' borrowing from banks, which stimulated a search by banks for alternative earning assets. Furthermore, the innovation of mortgage securitization—the packaging and selling of blocks of mortgages by banks—made mortgage lending more liquid, less risky, and more attractive to banks. In this way, the securitization phenomenon stimulated bank real estate lending. (Exhibit 9-1 explains how changes in financial technology and competitive forces have altered the way in which banks earn income.)

EXHIBIT 9-1

The Changing Sources of Bank Income

Banking is a rapidly evolving industry. Commercial banks have been squeezed by competitive pressures on both the asset side and the liability side of their balance sheets. On the asset side, corporate demand for bank loans—once a chief source of bank income—has been reduced by the development of the commercial paper market and the advent of junk bonds. And local banks, which used to have a major advantage in local mortgage lending because they were in a superior position to evaluate risk by obtaining information about prospective borrowers, have been hurt by the securitization of mortgages. Today, out-of-town lenders can largely eliminate the risks stemming from informational problems by packaging individual mortgages and selling them in blocks (securitization).

On the liability side, banks have experienced increasing competition for consumers' funds, as alternatives to checking, saving, and time deposits have become available to the public. Inroads were first made by money market mutual funds. More recently, stock and bond mutual funds have been in vogue. More and more young workers are having part of their paychecks deposited directly in such mutual funds. As a result, demand deposits, or non-interest-paying checking accounts—the cheapest source of banks funds—have grown very slowly.

To combat these pressures on their profitability, banks have added new services and have begun to collect fees for those services (see accompanying figure). Services that provide fee income include trust management, brokerage services, loan syndication services, and arrangement of swaps and other forms of sophisticated derivatives for business customers. Some banks have even gone so far as to charge customers a $3 fee for teller service. As a result of these trends, the portion of total commercial bank income generated by fees increased from less than 25 percent in 1985 to more than 35 percent in 1995. Simultaneously, the shares of bank income contributed by the interest earned on loans and securities have experienced corresponding declines. Given the pressures on commercial banks, don't be surprised if these trends continue.

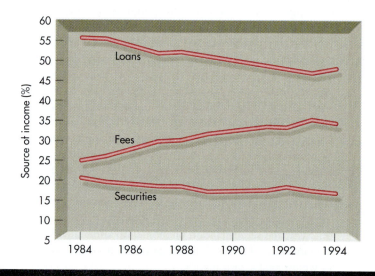

Securities

Securities are an important item on the bank balance sheet, accounting for almost one-fourth of bank assets and contributing approximately 15 percent of bank income. This item consists entirely of debt instruments because banks are not permitted to purchase corporate stocks.[4] Among the securities, or "investments," banks hold are U.S. government and government agency securities, and state and local government bonds.

U.S. government and agency securities are highly liquid because of the well-developed market in which they are traded. Because they are issued by the federal government, they are safe from the risk of default.[5] However, they are subject to market risk—the risk that interest rates may rise, causing a decline in the price of the securities. Some banks got into trouble in the late 1970s and early 1980s as interest rates rose dramatically and the prices of their bonds took a beating. However, most U.S. government securities held by banks today have short-term maturities and are therefore subject to only modest price fluctuations. The market risk of these securities is minimal.

State and local government securities have a tax advantage for banks: interest income earned on them is not taxable by the IRS. Another reason banks purchase them is that state and local governments are more likely to do business with banks that hold their securities. But these securities are riskier than U.S. government securities because state and local governments sometimes default on their obligations. For this reason, state and local government bonds have a higher aftertax return than U.S. government securities do. In recent years, the portion of total bank assets allocated to state and local government bonds has declined significantly.

Figure 9-4 compares the long-term trend in the ratio of bank security holdings to total bank assets with the long-term trend in the ratio of bank loans to total bank assets. In the late 1940s, government and agency securities made up nearly 50 percent of total commercial bank assets. By 1980, that figure stood at less than 20 percent. As securities declined in importance, loans assumed a more important role.

The long-term decline in the role of securities in bank assets is explained by the long-term increase in the demand for loans, together with the advent of alternative sources of liquidity available to banks other than short-term securities. In general, loans are more profitable than securities. In the 1940s and 1950s, banks held massive quantities of government securities, largely because loan demand was limited and because short-term securities are highly liquid—that is, they can be cashed in with minimal risk

---

[4]Many commercial banks are engaged in buying stocks, but only for the trusts, estates, and pension funds they manage for their clients. They are not permitted to purchase corporate stocks or bonds for the bank's own portfolio.

[5]In early 1996, some members of Congress threatened to refuse to increase the federal debt ceiling. This move was a tactical ploy intended to force the Clinton administration to propose expenditure cuts. If actually carried out, it would have been difficult for the government to meet its obligations, thus raising the possibility of a default on government debt. The U.S. financial markets, however, seemed to take the ploy in stride. Most observers believe that the default risk on U.S. government securities remains negligible.

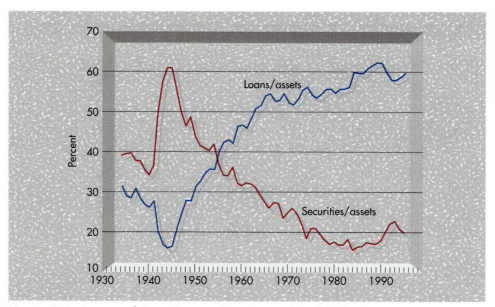

Figure 9-4 Loans and Securities as a Percentage of Total Bank Assets, 1935–1996.
Since the 1940s, commercial banks have sharply increased the amount of their loans relative to total bank assets. Banks' holdings of securities relative to total bank assets has correspondingly declined.   *Source: Citibank Database.*

of loss of principal when banks need funds for loans and other purposes. Since the 1950s, loan demand has risen, and banks have increasingly gained access to other sources of liquidity besides the sale of securities. They have borrowed federal funds, issued negotiable CDs, and adopted other innovative techniques to obtain funds as needed. These changes explain the declining role of securities in banks' asset structure. Note, however, that the long-term trends of the two asset ratios reversed direction in the late 1980s.

Besides their long-term trend, bank security holdings exhibit a distinct cyclical pattern. Government security purchases are a residual use of bank funds. During the expansion phase of the business cycle, when loan demand is rising, banks typically sell short-term government securities to obtain funds to lend to worthy borrowers. During economic contractions, as loan demand declines, banks purchase U.S. government securities for income.

Other Assets

Other bank assets include the physical assets of a bank—bank buildings, computers, automatic teller machines, and other equipment. Also included in this category is the collateral the bank has repossessed from borrowers in default.

COMMERCIAL BANK CAPITAL ACCOUNTS

Listed beneath "other liabilities" on the aggregate bank balance sheet (Table 9-1) is bank capital, or capital accounts. The difference between total assets and total liabilities, it is the bank's net worth—the equity stake the owners have in the bank. Bank capital derives from the issue of stock in the bank and from retained earnings—profits earned by the bank that are not paid out to the owners (stockholders). In March 1996, bank capital was reported to be 8.3 percent of total assets—on a historical basis, an exceptionally high figure, reflecting the robust financial condition of banks in the mid-1990s.

Bank capital provides a cushion against a contraction in the value of a bank's total assets, which could result in insolvency. A bank becomes **insolvent** when the value of its total assets drops below the value of its total liabilities. When that occurs, the regulatory authorities either close the bank or arrange for new owners and managers to come in. In this case the original owners lose their equity stake in the bank.

Consider the balance sheet of the Bank of Muddy Gap (Wyoming) before and after the regulatory authorities force the bank to write off $600,000 worth of bad loans to ranchers. Before the bad-loan write-off, the bank had $11 million of total assets and $10.5 million of total liabilities, so its capital was (positive) $0.5 million.

Bank of Muddy Gap (before loan write-off)

Assets		Liabilities	
Cash assets	1.0m	Deposits	10.0m
Loans	7.0m	Other liab.	0.5m
Securities	2.0m	Total liab.	10.5m
Other assets	1.0m	Capital	0.5m
Total assets	11.0m	Total liab. and capital	11.0m

Bank of Muddy Gap (after loan write-off)

Assets		Liabilities	
Cash assets	1.0m	Deposits	10.0m
Loans	6.4m	Other liab.	0.5m
Securities	2.0m	Total liab.	10.5m
Other assets	1.0m	Capital	−0.1m
Total assets	10.4m	Total liab. and capital	10.4m

Note that when the bank writes off the bad loans (right-hand balance sheet), its loans decrease by the amount of the write-off. Given that there is no change in the bank's total liabilities, the bank's capital account also decreases by the amount of the write-off ($0.6 million). Because the capital accounts are now negative ($0.1 million), the bad-loan write-off has forced the Bank of Muddy Gap into insolvency. The regulatory authorities will move in and close the bank or sell it to new owners. (Exhibit 9-2 discusses how banks handle loan loss reserves.)

Frequently, by the time the regulatory authorities have closed an insolvent bank, its net worth has become significantly negative.[6] Because the Federal Deposit Insurance

---

[6]In the 1990s, the FDIC implemented measures to identify banks that were likely to fail so that they could be closed while the capital accounts were still positive.

EXHIBIT 9-2

Loan Loss Reserves

Occasionally one reads about banks increasing their *loan loss reserves,* or their reserves for bad loans. Don't confuse this type of reserves with the reserves banks maintain on the asset side of their balance sheet—that is, cash plus deposits at the Federal Reserve. Loan loss reserves are totally different and are recorded on the right-hand side of the balance sheet, in the capital accounts.

Under U.S. tax law, banks are allowed to build up reserves for future loan losses from their flow of income. Loans declared to be uncollectable can be charged against this account so that bad-loan write-offs do not affect the bank's current income. When a bad loan is written off, the bank's balance sheet shows equal deductions to bank assets, in the form of loans, and to the capital accounts, in the form of loan loss reserves.

When a bank anticipates that it will have to write off an increased amount of bad loans over the next few years, it will typically set aside additional loan loss reserves from the current year's profits. There are several reasons for doing so. First, the bank signals the anticipated future losses in advance and seeks to assure the public that it can handle them. In doing so, it is hoping to gain credibility even as it acknowledges having used poor judgment in its lending decisions. Second, in setting aside additional loan loss reserves, a bank reduces its reported *current* profit, thereby reducing its current tax liability. Just as deferring taxes is advantageous, advancing tax write-offs is beneficial to the taxpayer. (The powerful incentive to build up excessive loan loss reserves has been reduced by recent tax provisions applying to banks with over $500 million in total assets.)

In the late 1980s and early 1990s, because of declining commercial real estate values, many bank loans turned into "bad" loans. As the accompanying figure shows, banks set aside large reserves for loan losses in 1989, 1990, and 1991. While the increased provisions for loan loss reserves penalized reported bank profits in those years, they provided the basis for robust profits in subsequent years. After 1992, as banks became aware that losses were not as severe as they had anticipated, reserves set aside for loan losses declined sharply, and reported bank profits surged. By mid-1996, the prices of many bank stocks were five times higher than they had been just a few years earlier.

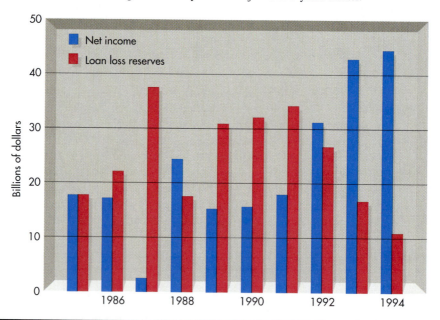

Corporation (FDIC) insures deposits up to $100,000, bank capital may be regarded as a cushion that protects depositors with accounts of more than $100,000 as well as the FDIC (and therefore taxpayers). We will discuss the management of bank capital later in this chapter.

COMMERCIAL BANK MANAGEMENT

Commercial banks are business firms; like all firms, they strive to earn a profit. The object of commercial bank management is therefore to maximize profits while maintaining a very low risk of becoming insolvent. To remain solvent, a commercial bank must take precautions to ensure that the value of its assets exceeds the value of its liabilities *at all times.* If at any time losses from securities, defaulted loans, or other investments force the value of the bank's assets below the value of its liabilities, the bank becomes insolvent.

A bank is considered *solvent* if it could, in an orderly manner—perhaps over several weeks—sell its assets and obtain sufficient revenues to meet its liabilities. Solvency must be distinguished from **liquidity,** which refers to a bank's immediate ability to meet currency withdrawals, check clearings, and new loan demand while abiding by the reserve requirements. To maintain bank solvency, banks must employ skillful *liquidity management* and *capital management.* In the remainder of this chapter, we will discuss those tools, along with the techniques of *liability management.*

Liquidity Management

Let's begin our discussion of liquidity management by illustrating the effect of the withdrawal of currency and the clearance of checks on the bank balance sheet and the bank's reserve position. To do this, we will use **T-accounts,** which are statements of the *change* in a balance sheet resulting from a given event. (Rather than showing the balance sheet both before and after the event, we will simply indicate the *change* in the balance sheet by using a T-account.)

Suppose a customer withdraws $200 in cash from a savings account at the Bank of Medicine Bow, Wyoming. The T-account would indicate the balance sheet change as follows:

Bank of Medicine Bow			
Cash	−200	Savings deposits	−200

The bank simply presents the customer with $200 worth of currency and debits the savings account by $200. The bank's *reserves* (cash plus deposits at the Fed) also decline by $200, because the withdrawal of currency from a bank reduces its reserves on a dollar-for-dollar basis. Unless the bank was initially holding **excess reserves**—reserves above and beyond the required amount—it is now short on reserves and will have to take measures to obtain more reserves in order to abide by the Fed's reserve requirements.

A similar result occurs when a check written by a bank customer is cleared. Suppose a customer of the Bank of Medicine Bow writes a check for $12,000 to a New York stockbroker to pay for newly purchased shares of stock. The Bank of Medicine Bow is a member of the Federal Reserve System, so the check is cleared through the Fed's check-processing facilities. When the check has been processed and cleared, the T-account for the Bank of Medicine Bow appears as follows:

Bank of Medicine Bow			
Deposit at Federal Reserve	−12,000	Demand deposits	−12,000

How does this happen? The stockbroker deposits the check in the brokerage firm's account in a New York commercial bank, which sends the check on to the Federal Reserve. The Fed deducts the reserve account of the Bank of Medicine Bow by $12,000; credits the reserve account of the New York bank by $12,000; and sends the check back to the Bank of Medicine Bow. At that point, the Bank of Medicine Bow deducts the customer's demand deposit account by $12,000. The important point to note is that the Bank of Medicine Bow loses reserves in the amount of the check—that is, $12,000. Unless it had excess reserves to begin with, it must take measures to replenish its reserve account.[7]

To summarize, withdrawal of currency and/or clearance of checks written on a bank reduces that bank's reserves by an equivalent amount. Conversely, the deposit of currency and/or clearance of checks deposited into a bank increases the bank's reserves on a dollar-for-dollar basis. According to the law of averages, one would expect withdrawals and deposits to be more or less equal, so that a bank's reserves would remain roughly constant over a given week or month. However, banks sometimes experience significant fluctuations in their reserve positions.

The crucial questions facing bank management are the following: How severe is the bank's exposure to significant reserve losses? What measures would the bank need to take to remedy a prospective loss of reserves? If a bank has minimal exposure to reserve losses or is in a position to recover a potential reserve loss easily without incurring significant costs, it is probably in sound financial condition, even with a relatively small capital account. On the other hand, if a bank is exposed to large deposit outflows and can obtain reserves only at substantial cost, it may find itself in serious trouble even if it has a large capital account. Banks that exhibit higher risk need larger capital accounts. We will now examine the trade-off between liquidity and risk.

---

[7]The dollar amount of required reserves also declines somewhat because of the reduction in demand deposits, so the bank will not need to recover the full $12,000 worth of reserves lost. With a 10 percent reserve requirement, required reserves would decline by $1,200. The bank would thus need to obtain only $10,800 worth of new reserves—that is, $12,000 minus $1,200.

The Liquidity/ Risk Trade-off

To see the importance of liquidity management, consider the following (simplified) balance sheet of Imprudent Bank. Assume the reserve requirement for deposits is 10 percent.

Imprudent Bank

Assets		Liabilities	
Reserves (cash + deposits at Federal Reserve)	40m	Deposits	400m
		Capital accounts	40m
Marketable securities	10m		
Loans	390m		
Total assets	440m	Total liabilities and capital	440m

Note that Imprudent Bank, with reserves of $40 million, just meets the 10 percent reserve requirement. It holds deposits (DDO) of $400 million, so its required reserves are $40 million (10% × $400 million). It has no excess reserves. In addition, it holds $10 million in marketable U.S. government securities and $390 million worth of loans. Because loans provide a higher rate of return than securities, Imprudent Bank has been tempted into allocating an extremely high proportion of its total assets to loans. The right-hand side of the balance sheet indicates that the bank has capital in the amount of $40 million, which represents a solid capital-to-assets ratio of 9.1 percent.

Now, suppose rumors circulate that a large portion of Imprudent Bank's loans are in trouble due to severe problems in the real estate sector, to which the bank has made large loans. Some depositors with more than $100,000 (the FDIC insurance ceiling) in their accounts are likely to withdraw their deposits. Suppose those depositors withdraw 5 percent of the bank's total deposits, or $20 million, by writing checks on their demand deposits. The new balance sheet for Imprudent Bank is as follows:

Imprudent Bank

Assets		Liabilities	
Reserves	20m	Deposits	380m
Marketable securities	10m	Capital accounts	40m
Loans	390m		
Total assets	420m	Total liabilities and capital	420m

Note that Imprudent Bank's reserves have dropped to $20 million, while its required reserves are now $38 million (10% × $380 million).[8] The bank is thus $18 million short on reserves. Though it can sell off its marketable securities to gain an additional $10 million of reserves, it will still be $8 million short of meeting the Fed's reserve requirement.

---

[8]When the customers of Imprudent Bank write checks for $20 million, the Federal Reserve clears the checks by deducting Imprudent Bank's reserve account at the Fed by $20 million (and crediting the reserve accounts of the banks in which the checks are deposited by $20 million).

The bank must now attempt to gain $8 million of additional reserves, either by reducing its loans or by borrowing funds through the liability side of its balance sheet. Both these options are likely to be difficult and costly. To the extent that the rumors are widespread, Imprudent Bank may have difficulty borrowing funds. Would you lend to a bank you suspect will fail? And bank loans are relatively illiquid assets—they are contractual agreements that typically cannot be called in before they come due. The bank has the option of selling its loans to other banks. However, because of informational problems, it is likely to have to sell the loans at prices significantly lower than their true value. If that is the case, the bank will take a loss—a dollar-for-dollar hit against its capital account. Such a loss, added to the bad loans (assuming the rumors were true), increases the likelihood that the bank will become insolvent and will be closed or sold to new owners.

Imprudent Bank was tempted to take big risks in order to achieve the greater profitability associated with allocating a high proportion of total assets to loans. In the next section, we will consider the trade-off between liquidity and profitability.

The Liquidity/ Profitability Trade-off

Now consider the balance sheet of Prudential Bank, a highly conservative, cautious institution:

Prudential Bank

Assets		Liabilities	
Reserves	50m	Deposits	400m
Marketable securities	190m	Capital accounts	40m
Loans	200m		
Total assets	440m	Total liabilities and capital	440m

This bank is probably excessively concerned about liquidity. It has exactly the same amount of liabilities and capital as Imprudent Bank but exhibits a much more liquid asset structure. Prudential Bank has $10 million worth of excess reserves ($50 million − 10% × $400 million) and a huge portfolio of marketable securities. In other words, it has lots of **secondary reserves,** or excess reserves and interest-bearing liquid assets that can quickly and conveniently be converted into actual reserves—that is, cash and deposits at the Federal Reserve.[9]

Now suppose the rumors about bad loans that brought down Imprudent Bank circulate about Prudential Bank as well. Depositors withdraw $20 million, but Prudential Bank still has $30 million in reserves. Since its required reserves are now $38 million, it is short only $8 million and can easily liquidate a small portion of its marketable

---

[9]Secondary reserves include excess reserves, short-term U.S. government securities, federal funds sold (loaned to other banks), and certain other highly liquid earning assets.

securities to obtain enough reserves to meet the reserve requirement. Prudential will not have to sell off any loans and is clearly in a better position to handle the rumors than Imprudent was. If necessary, Prudential could write off up to 20 percent of its loan portfolio and still remain solvent. In contrast, write-offs of slightly more than 10 percent of Imprudent Bank's loans would bankrupt that institution.

Prudential Bank, in its obsession to minimize risk, has limited its own profit by maintaining a large amount of excess reserves, which earn no interest, and an unusually low proportion of loans to total assets. (Remember that loans earn a higher rate of return than securities.) This example illustrates the trade-off between liquidity and profitability. Contrast this with Imprudent Bank, which in its single-minded quest for profit maintains an illiquid and highly risky asset structure, with almost 90 percent of its assets in loans. In normal and good times, Imprudent will earn a higher profit than Prudential Bank. However, it is perilously exposed to insolvency in the event that a significant portion of its loans turn sour. Most real-world banks maintain a balance sheet somewhere between the extremes exhibited by Imprudent Bank and Prudential Bank.

Indicators of Liquidity

There are several indicators of the liquidity of the commercial banking system. One is the ratio of bank loans to total assets, along with the corresponding ratio of securities to total assets. The higher the loans to total assets ratio, *given other factors,* the more *illiquid* is the banking system. (Review Figure 9-4, which shows the trend of this ratio.) Another indicator is the ratio of cash assets to total assets. The higher this ratio, *given other factors*, the more liquid the banking system.

Both these indicators point to a decline in bank liquidity over the past 50 years. Bank loans as a percentage of total assets have increased from 30 percent in the 1950s to approximately 60 percent today. Cash items have declined from about 20 percent of total assets in the 1950s to approximately 5 percent today.[10] On the other hand, the *need* for a highly liquid bank asset structure has also declined for at least two reasons. First, the share of total bank deposits constituted by demand deposits has declined sharply over the past 35 years, from approximately 70 percent in 1960 to roughly 30 percent today. With a larger share of bank funds coming from savings and time deposits, which have relatively low turnover rates, banks require less liquidity in their asset structure than formerly. Second, since 1960, banks have been able to turn to the liability side of the balance sheet to obtain liquidity when needed. In the next section, we turn to the topic of bank liability management.

---

[10]To the extent that the decline in cash assets reflects lower reserve requirements, however, bank liquidity is not reduced. The required portion of a bank's reserves cannot be used to meet currency withdrawals or adverse check clearings. It is not a source of liquidity but must be maintained at all times to meet reserve requirements. Only excess reserves and other items the bank can sell off willingly and easily to raise funds can be considered liquid assets. A significant portion of the decline in the ratio of cash items to total assets reflects periodic reductions in reserve requirements over the years.

Your Turn

Consider the balance sheets of two banks, HC Bank and LC Bank, and answer the following questions.

a. What is the capital to total assets ratio of each bank?

b. Which bank exhibits a more liquid asset structure?

c. Over time, which bank is likely to exhibit greater variance in its deposits and reserves?

d. Which bank do you suppose would cause more concern to the regulatory authorities?

HC (High-Capital) Bank

Assets		Liabilities	
Cash assets	10m	Demand deposits	80m
Short-term securities	5m	Savings deposits	15m
Long-term bonds	25m	Small time deposits	5m
Loans	70m	Capital accounts	10m
Total assets	110m	Total liabilities and capital accounts	110m

LC (Low-Capital) Bank

Assets		Liabilities	
Cash assets	20m	Demand deposits	30m
Short-term securities	25m	Savings deposits	20m
Long-term bonds	25m	Small time deposits	50m
Loans	35m	Capital accounts	5m
Total assets	105m	Total liabilities and capital accounts	105m

Liability Management

Before the 1960s, banks took their liabilities as essentially given. Prohibitions on the payment of interest on checking accounts, together with statutory ceilings on interest rates payable on savings and time deposits, prevented banks from competing aggressively for deposits. Furthermore, the federal funds market was relatively undeveloped, and negotiable CDs and repurchase agreements had not yet been conceived. Other than mounting advertising and marketing campaigns, there was little banks could do to gain additional funds at their own discretion. Banks pretty much passively accepted deposits and then made decisions on how to allocate these funds among cash assets, loans, and securities. Banks practiced asset management but not liability management.

Starting in the 1960s and accelerating more recently, banks began to look for good lending opportunities and then to search for the funds to finance these loans. Today, when a large bank finds a profitable loan opportunity, it can obtain funds through several techniques. One is to "buy" federal funds—that is, borrow the reserve deposits of other banks held by the Federal Reserve. Another is to issue negotiable CDs at whatever interest rate is required to attract funds. Banks can also issue repurchase agreements or borrow Eurodollars (dollar-denominated deposits in European or Caribbean banks or foreign branches of U.S. banks). Finally, banks can obtain funds via the commercial paper market, through their large bank holding companies. To a lesser extent, even midsized and relatively small banks can practice liability management, either through the federal funds market or by bidding for *brokered deposits*—pieces of large negotiable CDs that have been broken down into fully insurable $100,000 blocks for placement through money brokers.

Today, many large banks target a certain growth rate for total assets. They then search for profitable lending opportunities and practice aggressive liability management to obtain the funds to make the loans. Banks find liability management desirable inasmuch as it permits them to make profitable loans that they would otherwise have to turn down. This liability management contributes strongly to bank profits. The growth of liability management by banks is indicated by the fact that, between 1965 and 1996, the volume of negotiable CDs outstanding increased from $20 billion to more than $400 billion. In the same period, the volume of federal funds purchased and security repurchase agreements outstanding ballooned from less than $50 billion to more than $400 billion.

Yet there are dangers inherent in aggressive liability management. Because banks' assets typically have longer maturities than their liabilities, banks can suffer severe losses in the event that interest rates rise sharply. And if unfavorable rumors about a bank's financial condition begin to circulate, a bank's sources of funds may dry up quickly as large depositors cut and run. This phenomenon contributed to the failure of the Continental Bank of Illinois in 1984 (see Exhibit 9-3).

Despite Continental's experience, some banks act as if liquid funds can be borrowed as needed, almost without limit. They see little need to hold marketable short-term securities. But the huge cash shortages experienced in recent years by some banks make clear the fact that liquidity needs cannot be ignored. In fact, the regulatory authorities sometimes close a bank because of liquidity problems, even though it is technically solvent. In 1991, for example, the Federal Reserve closed the $10 billion Southeast Bank of Miami when it failed to come up with sufficient cash to repay loans it had taken out from the Fed.

The emergence of liability management has complicated the task of the Federal Reserve. For example, the Fed sometimes attempts to slow aggregate expenditures in periods of excessively strong economic activity by implementing restrictive monetary policy actions. If banks scramble to issue additional liabilities to fund surging loan demand, the Fed's ability to control aggregate expenditures is compromised. At such times, the Fed has sometimes imposed reserve requirements on certain managed liabilities in an effort to curb banks' attempts to circumvent its intentions.

Capital Management

As was indicated earlier, bank capital provides banks with a financial cushion, so that short-term setbacks will not cause them to become insolvent. Essentially, bank capital serves to protect large uninsured depositors and the FDIC. But bank capital also protects bank managers and owners from their own folly. Reasonable mistakes can be made without wiping out owners' equity and terminating managers' careers.

EXHIBIT 9-3

The Run on Continental Illinois Bank

In May 1984, there was a massive run on the huge, $42 billion Continental Illinois Bank. It was not an old-fashioned run, with customers lined up for blocks waiting to get their money. Continental Illinois, the largest bank in the midwest and the nation's eighth largest in 1984, was a money center bank, like Citibank and Chase Manhattan. Its financial base consisted of big deposits held by large corporations, money market mutual funds, and other multimillion-dollar accounts. Such funds may be transferred electronically in seconds.

What caused the run on Continental? In the late 1970s, Continental elected to target a very high rate of growth. From 1977 to 1981, its loans expanded at an annual rate of 22 percent. Unfortunately, because Illinois law prohibited banks from opening more than three branches, Continental lacked a rapidly growing, large-scale consumer deposit base. To finance its rapid loan growth, the bank chose to purchase funds through aggressive liability management. It issued a huge amount of negotiable CDs and other forms of "hot money," including more than $12 billion to foreign customers. In addition, the bank's asset structure was highly illiquid. Its loan-to-deposit ratio was 79 percent, contrasted with 67 percent for other money center banks and 56 percent for all U.S. banks at the time. Continental was taking big risks, using highly volatile sources of funds to finance an illiquid and risky asset structure.

Continental also had large problem loans outstanding in energy and agriculture, as well as major loans to troubled Latin American nations. The slide began when Continental was forced to absorb large losses on some energy-related loans it had purchased from the failed Penn Square Bank of Oklahoma City. Because most of Continental's deposits were in the form of huge CDs, only about $4 billion of its $29 billion of deposits were covered by FDIC insurance. As rumors circulated about other bad loans on Continental's books, large depositors panicked, and the stampede was on. When their large CDs matured, U.S. corporations, money market mutual funds, and foreign customers withdrew their funds. In a few weeks, the bank had lost $10 billion, or approximately one-third of its deposits.

Without massive aid, Continental would have failed immediately, perhaps triggering a run on many other banks. But the regulatory authorities did not wait. They moved in with an unprecedented relief scheme involving an infusion of $2 billion of capital from federal banking agencies, a credit line of $5.5 billion from a consortium of 24 major U.S. banks, and an extended loan of $5 billion from the Federal Reserve. The FDIC waived the $100,000 insurance ceiling, so that all depositors of the bank were fully covered (even this action failed to fully stem the run, as some depositors doubted the viability of the FDIC insurance fund). The authorities tried to find a merger partner, but no bank was willing to take on Continental Illinois on terms acceptable to the FDIC. Finally, the FDIC was forced to purchase about $5 billion of questionable loans from the bank at full face value, in exchange for 80 percent ownership of the bank. The FDIC later sold off all its stock in the bank, which today is a scaled-down version of its former self.

Banks are exposed to several types of risk. First is *default risk*—the risk that a loan (or the interest thereon) will not be repaid or that a municipality will default on its bonds. Second is *interest rate risk,* or the risk that interest rates may rise after securities have been purchased, depressing the prices of the securities. And because bank assets typically have longer maturities than bank liabilities, higher interest rates can increase the cost of funds without commensurately increasing the return earned on assets, impairing the bank's profits. Third, banks are subject to *liquidity risk,* the risk that depositors may pull their funds out. Fourth, the banks doing business across national borders are sometimes exposed to *foreign exchange rate risk*—the risk that exchange rates may move in a way that causes losses to banks. Fifth, large banks with loans and investments abroad assume *political,* or *country risk,* which involves the possibility that a bank's funds or assets outside the United States may be confiscated or otherwise prevented from being returned to the United States. Finally, as several recent scandals have attested, banks are increasingly subject to what might be called *management,* or *supervisory risk*—the risk that certain bank employees, in an era of almost incomprehensible financial technology, might, unknown to upper management and owners, engage in activities that involve enormous risk.[11]

Some of these risks can be hedged, at a cost, through derivatives and other financial instruments; other risks cannot. Banks knowingly take legitimate risks in order to earn an attractive rate of return. In fact, a fundamental principle of finance is that riskier investments bring higher expected rates of return. A bank that is exceedingly risk averse will earn a low profit and may alienate customers by denying them legitimate loans.

The predominant cause of bank insolvency stems from bad loans. Loans that appear sound when they were made are sometimes rendered bad by changing economic conditions. For example, when oil prices collapsed in late 1985, thousands of loans made by Texas banks went into default as the dramatic decline in oil revenues rippled through the Texas economy, closing businesses and throwing people out of work. Hundreds of Texas banks failed in the following few years.

Given other factors, the higher a bank's capital to total assets ratio, the lower its risk of insolvency. On the other hand, the higher its capital ratio, the lower the rate of return earned by the bank's owners (the owners' equity is the capital account). Consider the following identity:

$$(9\text{-}1) \qquad \frac{\textbf{Earnings}}{\textbf{Equity capital}} = \frac{\textbf{Earnings}}{\textbf{Total assets}} \times \frac{\textbf{Total assets}}{\textbf{Equity capital}}$$

The left-hand side of the expression is the percentage rate of return earned by the bank's owners on their capital, or owners' equity; it is known as the *rate of return on equity,* or *rate of return on capital.* The first expression on the right-hand side is the rate of return earned on total assets. It is an indicator of the bank's efficiency, because it shows the profit earned per dollar of assets. The final expression, the ratio of total

---

[11]Barings, a venerable British bank, became insolvent in 1995 because of the activities of one rogue trader employed by the bank. Nicholas Leeson, who essentially gambled in derivatives with the bank's funds, lost more than $1 billion before his activities were discovered. Because his losses exceeded the bank's capital, they bankrupted the institution. (On this episode, see Exhibit 10-2 on page 247.)

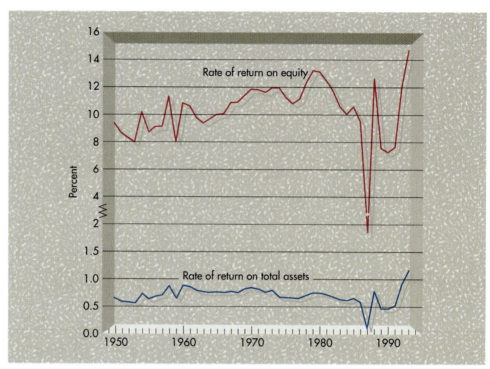

Figure 9-5 **Rates of Return Earned by All U.S. Banks, 1950–1995.** Since 1950, the rates of return on total bank assets and on bank equity have averaged approximately 0.7 percent and 11 percent, respectively. After 1992, these rates of return increased appreciably.   *Source:* Federal Deposit Insurance Corporation.

assets to equity capital, is sometimes known as the **equity multiplier.** It is simply the reciprocal of the bank's capital accounts to total assets ratio and expresses the amount of leverage that is applied to the rate of return on total assets. A high capital to total assets ratio represents a low equity multiplier; a low capital to total assets ratio implies a high equity multiplier.

Suppose a bank earns an annual profit of 1 percent of its total assets—approximately the average return earned by U.S. banks over the past 5 years. If the bank has a capital to total assets ratio of 5 percent (an equity multiplier of 20), Equation 9-1 indicates that it will earn a rate of return on equity of 20 percent per year ($1\% \times 20$). Alternatively, if the capital to total assets ratio is 10 percent, the rate of return on equity will be only 10 percent per year ($1\% \times 10$). A higher capital accounts ratio has both benefits and costs. Though it reduces the risk of insolvency, it also reduces the rate of return earned by the bank's owners. Clearly, there is a trade-off between short-run profitability and the risk of insolvency, a trade-off that every bank must grapple with. Figure 9-5 shows the rates of return U.S. banks have earned on total assets and equity capital over the years.

Our analysis suggests that for each bank there is some optimal ratio of capital to total assets. This optimal ratio depends on the nature of the bank's assets and liabilities

EXHIBIT 9-4

The Upgrading of U.S. Bank Balance Sheets, 1992–1996

The late 1980s and early 1990s were hard times for banks and other depository institutions. Banks had huge loans to developing countries, the commercial real estate sector, and the energy sector on their books. Changing economic conditions had rendered many of those loans uncollectable. As those loans were written off, bank insolvencies soared.

More recent events have contributed to a massive turnaround in the profits and balance sheets of commercial banks. Since the 1990–1991 recession, a general economic recovery in the United States has produced rising loan demand and a corresponding increase in bank revenues. The recovery has also contributed to a sharp decrease in bad-loan write-offs and a corresponding decline in provisions for loan loss reserves in 1993, 1994, and 1995. Rising fees for nontraditional bank services have also contributed to revenue growth, and cost-cutting measures have held down expenses.

As a result, the net income of all insured U.S. banks increased from less than $15 billion per year in 1989 and 1990 to more than $40 billion per year in 1993, 1994, and 1995. The rate of return on total assets earned by banks jumped from an average of less than 0.50 percent during 1989–1991 to more than 1 percent during 1993–1995. Banks plowed much of the additional profits into their capital accounts. Sharply rising bank stock prices also induced banks to issue additional equity—that is, shares of stock. The accompanying figure shows the improvement in bank capital positions. By 1996, the capital ratios of U.S. banks were the highest in decades.

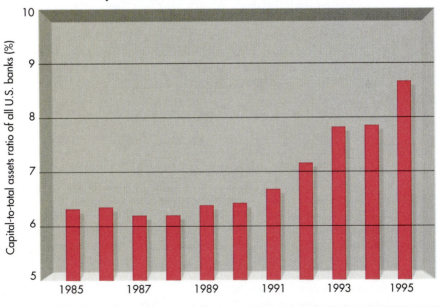

Capital Accounts Ratio of all U.S. Banks, 1985–1995

and may vary over time with economic conditions. For example, when a period of financial distress looms ahead, a prudent bank will take steps to increase its capital ratio. When a period of stability appears likely, a prudent bank may reduce its capital ratio.

A bank that wants to increase its capital to total assets ratio has three choices. First, it can increase retained earnings by reducing dividend payouts to the bank's owners. Second, it can issue new shares of stock. Third, it can shrink total assets by selling securities and reducing loans, and use the proceeds to reduce borrowings or other liabilities. Unlike the first two choices, the third does not increase bank capital. However, by reducing the total assets of the bank, it increases the capital to total assets ratio.

In the early 1990s, in the wake of anemic bank profits and depressed stock prices, many banks employed this third option. Major U.S. banks had suffered large loan losses in the late 1980s and early 1990s. Bank insolvencies had soared from an average of 6 per year during 1960–1979 to 150 per year during 1984–1992. Regulatory authorities reacted in part by imposing strict capital standards, which forced thousands of banks to increase their capital ratios. They reduced their lending in order to bolster their capital ratios and comply with tightened federal standards, creating what has been called a "capital credit crunch" in the process. Bank loans became unusually difficult to obtain, as thousands of banks tightened their lending standards. Since then, the robust profits earned by banks during the economic expansion of 1992–1996 have further raised the bank capital ratios. Today, U.S. banks are in much stronger financial condition than they were in the 1980s and early 1990s (see Exhibit 9-4 on p. 219).

In closing, we must note that the cost to society of a bank failure exceeds the cost borne by the failed bank. When a bank fails, large depositors and the FDIC insurance fund frequently incur losses (banks are seldom closed before the capital accounts become significantly negative). For this reason, the capital ratio deemed optimal by banks is lower than the ratio that is optimal from society's viewpoint. Many economists therefore support the imposition of binding capital standards on banks by regulatory authorities. We will have more to say on this issue in Chapter 11.

SUMMARY

Commercial banks, as the dominant type of financial intermediary, are key players in the U.S. financial system. They take in funds by issuing deposits, borrowing from sources other than depositors, and obtaining equity funds from their owners. They use these funds primarily to purchase federal, state, and local government securities and to extend loans to businesses, consumers, and other borrowers. A sound banking system is essential to the nation's economic health. To maintain solvency, banks practice liquidity management and capital management. Although highly liquid assets such as U.S. Treasury bills yield low rates of return, banks hold them to protect against the cost of adjusting to deposit and currency outflows and the accompanying loss of reserves. Although a higher ratio of capital to total assets reduces the rate of return on equity for bank owners, higher capital ratios provide a larger cushion to reduce the risk of bank insolvency. In the past 20 years, the nation's banks have been challenged by financial innovations, macroeconomic shocks, and other events. In the late 1980s and early 1990s, banks' financial conditions deteriorated and more than one thousand commercial banks failed. However, since the 1990–1991 recession, both the income statements and the balance sheets of the nation's commercial banks have strengthened dramatically.

Answers to Your Turn (p. 214)

a. *HC Bank has a capital ratio of 9.1 percent; LC Bank has a capital ratio of 4.8 percent.*

b. *LC Bank has a much more liquid asset structure. It holds twice as many cash assets and five times as many short-term securities as HC Bank. It has only half as many loans, which are relatively illiquid because banks cannot convert loans to cash until the loans come due.*

c. *HC Bank will likely exhibit a more variable deposit structure and greater variance in its reserves over time. Eighty percent of its total deposits are demand deposits, as opposed to 30 percent for LC Bank. HC Bank has only one-tenth the amount of small time deposits as LC Bank. (Small time deposits have much lower turnover, or withdrawal rates, than demand deposits do.)*

d. *Even though HC's capital ratio is nearly twice as high as LC's, the regulatory authorities are likely to be more critical of HC Bank. Its assets are much more heavily weighted with loans, and it finances those assets with a more volatile liability structure than LC Bank does. As a result, HC Bank is much more likely to encounter liquidity problems. (Its holdings of cash and short-term securities are only one-third that of LC Bank.) A much higher percentage of HC's assets is subject to either market risk or default risk. In fact, it has twice as many loans (which are subject to default risk) as LC Bank does.*

KEY TERMS

balance sheet	discount rate
assets	federal funds market
liabilities	federal funds rate
net worth	legal reserves (reserves)
capital accounts (capital)	reserve requirement (required reserve ratio)
transactions (checkable) deposits	insolvent
demand deposits	liquidity
negotiable order of withdrawal (NOW) account	T-account
automatic transfer system (ATS) account	excess reserves
money market deposit (MMD) account	secondary reserves
discount loan	equity multiplier

STUDY QUESTIONS

1 List three sources of and three uses for commercial bank funds.

2 Why have cash items and securities decreased as a proportion of total bank assets over the past 40 years? What has taken their place, and why?

3 What is meant by a commercial bank's capital accounts? Suppose a bank wants to increase its capital by $1 million. How could it do so?

4 This Christmas, you decide to buy your true love a partridge in a pear tree. After consulting with several garden centers, you make your purchase by writing a check for $150. The garden center promptly deposits your check in its bank.

a Using T-accounts, show the effects of this transaction on your bank and on the garden center's bank.

b What happens to your bank's reserves? To the reserves of the garden center's bank?

c Assuming the reserve requirement is 10 percent and your bank was holding no excess reserves initially, what is the level of excess reserves in your bank after the transaction?

d List four possible methods your bank can employ to remedy its reserve deficiency.

5 "The ratio of capital accounts to total assets is only one of many factors that indicate the financial condition of a commercial bank." Evaluate this statement.

6 Your bank has total assets of $220 million and a capital to total assets ratio of 7 percent. You learn that your bank's entire $20 million loan package to Central American nations will be written off as bad loans. Will your bank survive this crisis? Explain.

7 Distinguish bank solvency from bank liquidity.

8 From the point of view of an asset manager, discuss the trade-offs among the objectives of safety, liquidity, and profitability.

9 What is meant by liability management? Discuss the instruments that banks use in liability management. What are the advantages and potential pitfalls of liability management for commercial banks?

10 Explain the conditions that caused the emergence of NOW accounts, repurchase agreements, and ATS accounts. Why are such innovations more likely to occur in a period of high inflation and interest rates?

11 Why does the volume of negotiable CDs outstanding move procyclically?

12 The growth of several government agencies (FNMA, GNMA, and so forth) has produced a liquid secondary market in mortgages. What has been the impact of these developments on

a Mortgage rates?

b The risks borne by mortgage lenders?

c The composition of commercial bank loan portfolios?

13 Many banks in your community have been contacted about participating in a large syndicated loan arrangement. Your bank has been invited to participate but does not have enough excess reserves to meet the terms of the agreement. How might your bank raise the funds to participate in the deal?

a Through asset management?

b Through liability management?

14 Why might the FDIC and bank stockholders have different opinions of the merits of maintaining a high capital accounts ratio? Discuss the trade-offs involved. Can you illustrate those trade-offs with a numerical example?

15 Bill's bank and Ted's bank have dramatically different liability structures. Bill's bank, located in an affluent neighborhood, raises funds by issuing small time deposits to neighborhood residents. Ted's bank, located in a working-class neighborhood, issues mostly checking accounts to its customers. How might you expect the portfolio of assets held by Bill's bank to differ from that held by Ted's? Explain.

SUGGESTIONS FOR ADDITIONAL READING

Excellent texts that are devoted entirely to commercial banking are Peter Rose, *Commercial Bank Management,* 3d ed. (Homewood, Ill.: Irwin, 1996), and Joseph F. Sinkey, *Commercial Bank Financial Management,* 4th ed. (New York: Macmillan, 1992). See also Timothy Koch, *Bank Management,* 2d ed. (Fort Worth: Dryden Press, 1992). An article detailing the bottom-line financial performance of commercial banks in the most recent year appears annually in the June issue of *Federal Reserve Bulletin.* On bank failures and related issues, consult the Federal Deposit Insurance Corporation, *Annual Report of the FDIC,* published each year in April. A pertinent article on the banking industry in historical per-

spective is George Kaufman and Larry Mote, "Is Banking a Declining Industry? A Historical Perspective," Federal Reserve Bank of Chicago *Economic Perspectives,* May–June 1994, pp. 1–21. See also Franklin Edwards and Frederic Mishkin, "The Decline of Traditional Banking: Implications for Financial Stability and Regulatory Policy," Federal Reserve Bank of New York *Economic Policy Review,* July 1995, pp. 27–45. On bank liquidity practice, see Federal Reserve Bank of New York, "Recent Changes in Liquidity Practices at Commercial Banks and Securities Firms," 1990. A wealth of data on bank income and balance sheets is contained in Federal Deposit Insurance Corporation, *Statistics on Banking.*

CHAPTER

■ ## The Banking Industry: Structure and Regulation

In Chapter 9, we saw how an individual commercial bank operates. In this chapter, we will examine the banking industry as a whole—its structure and the laws it must obey to satisfy regulators. As you read, be alert for themes that have consistently influenced both bank and regulatory behavior over the last 2 centuries. In Chapter 11, we will take a closer look at the wave of bank and thrift failures that occurred in the 1980s and 1990s. Integral to that discussion will be the roles regulation and the deposit insurance system play in U.S. banking.

AN OVERVIEW OF MODERN U.S. BANKING

Among industrialized nations, the U.S. banking industry is unique. Without being aware of it, you have probably noticed the feature that makes the American system unique. In the United States, there is almost literally a different bank on every corner. This state of affairs differs sharply from that in other countries, where a few large banks are the norm. While the United States has some 10,000 banks, Germany has only about 250, Japan has fewer than 100, and England and Canada have fewer than 50.

While other countries rely on a small number of gigantic financial institutions with numerous branch offices to channel funds from savers to borrowers, the United States accomplishes the task with thousands of smaller, separately owned banks, most of which have few if any branches. But it would be a mistake to assume that the large number of banks in the United States indicates a highly competitive industry. Rather, it reflects a legal environment that has placed strict limitations on how and where a bank may operate. Historically, those limitations have prevented banks from branching out and may have effectively *reduced* competition.

If you are from a small town, you may be well acquainted with monopoly power in local banking. You probably bank at a small bank, one of only a few in town. The United States has fewer bank offices per person than any of the previously mentioned countries except Japan. Banks that are protected from competition do not have to aggressively seek business; instead, business has little choice but to go to them. A high ratio of bank offices per million population is evidence of greater consumer choice and a higher level of service, both of which reflect a competitive environment.

These disparities naturally prompt economists to ask a few questions. First, is the U.S. system more economically *efficient*? That is, do U.S. banks operate at a lower average cost per unit of service provided? Second, what are the implications of the U.S. system for the welfare of its customers? Both questions will be examined in detail in this chapter. But first we pose another interesting question: *Why* is the U.S. system so different from that of other nations?

U.S. BANKING HISTORY AND EVOLUTION

The forces that shaped the U.S. banking system can be traced to the struggle for independence from Great Britain in the late eighteenth century. In the early years of the nation, a heated debate took place over the form the federal government was to take. Under the Articles of Confederation the nation was organized as a loosely linked group of highly independent states. The federal government, which had little power, existed mainly to settle disputes among the states. When the weaknesses of the system became apparent, the struggle to redefine the role of the federal government began.

The Bank of the United States

One school of political thought, espoused by the Federalists, advocated a strong central government. Led by Alexander Hamilton, the Federalists envisioned a nation built on commerce and industry, and pushed for centralized power. In direct contrast, the Democratic-Republican Party (commonly referred to as the "Anti-Federalists") envisioned a nation based on the United States' most abundant and precious resource, land. Under the leadership of Thomas Jefferson, they fought for a rural, agricultural society with political power residing in the states.

Given the importance of commerce and industry in the United States today, one may have difficulty understanding why Jefferson and the Anti-Federalists so strongly desired an agrarian society. We must remember that, prior to the Revolution, Americans had suffered under Great Britain's concentrated political and economic power. Fear of the United States becoming another England fueled the fires of Anti-Federalist thought.

The debate between Federalists and Anti-Federalists had an enormous influence on the banking industry. Until the 1790s, banks were chartered by individual state legislatures and were forbidden to operate across state lines. Following passage of the Constitution (which was viewed as a compromise between the Federalist and Anti-Federalist positions) in 1789, Hamilton began a concentrated effort to form a nationally chartered bank, the **Bank of the United States.** His reasons were twofold. First, the states had accumulated large debts during the Revolutionary War. Those debts were to be assumed by the newly formed national government. Hamilton believed that a nationally chartered bank could best hold this debt and handle the federal government's financial operations. Second, an industrial society requires a strong, stable financial sector, and he believed the best way of achieving one was by creating a national bank.

Central to this assumption was the fact that the United States did not have a uniform official currency. At that time, money took the form of individual banknotes, similar to the currency issued by goldsmiths in England (see Chapter 2). By forming a large national enterprise to issue the nation's currency, Hamilton hoped to bring stability to the value of the dollar.

Jefferson, who favored a strict interpretation of the Constitution, was opposed to the federal government's assuming powers not specifically granted it. But Hamilton argued that the federal government could assume any powers not expressly denied it by the Constitution. After heated debate, Hamilton prevailed, and in 1791 the Bank of the United States was granted a 20-year charter.

As chartered, the Bank of the United States was a semigovernmental concern: the federal government owned one-fifth of the stock, and the remaining four-fifths was held by the public. The bank was given the exclusive right to branch across state lines. So widespread was its branching that by the time the charter for the **Second Bank of the United States** (the First Bank's successor) expired in 1836, the Second Bank controlled one-third of all deposits in the banking system.

It soon became apparent that Jefferson's mistrust of the concentration of financial power was well founded. The Bank of the United States quickly caused difficulty for state-chartered banks, either by refusing to accept their banknotes or by accumulating large masses of their notes and then redeeming them for gold all at once. Such an act could quickly drive an illiquid bank into insolvency. The Bank of the United States was also accused of playing politics by discriminating against Anti-Federalists in granting loans and by favoring industry over agriculture.

Many state-chartered banks had achieved virtual monopolies before the advent of national banking. Not surprisingly, when the Bank of the United States' charter came up for renewal in 1811, the banking sector mounted strong opposition. Appealing to popular sentiment, opponents claimed that national banking was drawing funds from the country to the city, aiding industry at the expense of agriculture. The charter was not renewed until 1816, when a new 20-year charter was granted in the hope that a national bank could repair the financial havoc that followed the War of 1812. By the time populist president Andrew Jackson refused to renew the Second Bank's charter in 1836, the lessons of national banking (true or otherwise) seemed apparent to the public: one should mistrust any concentration of financial power and take all steps possible to prevent it. As a result, many states adopted strict limits on branching both across and within their borders. Some states outlawed branching altogether, allowing banks to operate out of only one office. Such **unit banking** provisions remained on the books in several states until the 1980s.

The Free Banking Era

The dissolution of the Bank of the United States inaugurated a period known as the **Free Banking Era.** During this time, there was little supervision of banking activities. Anyone who was willing to meet certain lenient conditions could organize a bank. As a result, banks and banknotes proliferated.[1] While the new system relieved many of the problems associated with national banking, it brought its own set of problems. With so many banks issuing their own notes, supposedly redeemable in gold, differentiating between genuine and counterfeit currencies became difficult. Many banks, known as "wildcat banks," located their offices in obscure places to prevent redemption of their notes. Notes of faraway banks and banks considered unsafe often circulated at a discount from face value. Merchants were forced to keep books showing the currencies of different banks to establish the authenticity of notes received in trade and determine at what value they should pass. Bank failures were common, though many resulted from declining asset values rather than fraud or mismanagement.

The National Banking Act of 1863

The free banking era was brought to an abrupt halt with the **National Banking Act of 1863.** The impetus for this act stemmed from two sources. First, the problems with free banking prompted sentiment for some sort of legislative reform. And second, the federal government needed a market for the new debt issued to finance the Civil War.

Passage of the act allowed the federal government to charter national banks, which would issue a uniform currency. The national banks were required to back their banknotes more than 100 percent with interest-bearing federal government bonds, deposited with the Comptroller of the Currency. If a national bank failed, its noteholders were to be repaid in full from the bonds on deposit with the Comptroller. Because the notes were both uniform and safe, they were accepted at par value through the nation.[2] This greatly reduced the information costs associated with state banknotes.

As an additional source of revenue, Congress levied a high tax on state-issued banknotes. The hope was that the tax, coupled with the uniform acceptability of national banknotes, would drive state banks out of business, thus eliminating competition for national banks. But the response of the state banks was swift. As a substitute for banknotes, they developed demand deposit accounts, an innovation that helped them to maintain their deposit bases in the face of strong competition from national banks. As a result, the United

---

[1]At this time, the checking account had yet to be developed. Within specified limits similar to today's system of reserve requirements, banks were permitted to issue their own dollar-denominated banknotes whenever they made a loan. The system operated much as the English system, in which goldsmiths were permitted to issue gold certificates with fractional backing in gold. The effect of the issuance of such notes is the same as that which occurs today when banks make loans; that is, money is created.

[2]National banks were required by law to redeem notes of other national banks at par value. This enhanced the public's faith and confidence in the currency and helped maintain the value and acceptability of the notes.

States developed a **dual banking system,** a system which remains intact. Today, about one-third of all banks are national banks, chartered by the Comptroller of the Currency; the remaining two-thirds are chartered by the states.

The Glass-Steagall Act

During the First World War, commercial banks became heavily involved in the securities business. The banking system was responsible for distributing war bonds, and many banks held them in their investment portfolios. Gradually, commercial banks began to act as **investment banks**—institutions that are responsible for underwriting new securities issues and for trading existing issues.

Then, in the period from 1929–1933, some 10,000 banks—fully one-third of the nation's commercial banks—failed. With other influential politicians, Senator Carter Glass (who had helped draft the Federal Reserve Act of 1913) charged investment bankers with responsibility for the calamity. His attack on investment banking was two-pronged. First, he noted that banks that hold a large portion of their assets in securities are naturally vulnerable to a stock market collapse, such as the Crash of 1929. Second, he revealed that many banks had allowed customers to use securities as collateral for bank loans, further increasing banks' exposure to market risk.[3] Ultimately, Glass and supporters of what would become the **Banking Act of 1933**—better known as the **Glass-Steagall Act**—alleged widespread abuse of privilege that fueled speculation and destabilized the banking industry. Conflict of interest, stock price manipulation, and misrepresentation of facts to unwary customers were among the abuses.

Riding a wave of popular sentiment (most people suffered some kind of financial loss during the banking collapse), the Banking Act of 1933 was quickly passed into law. The act contained four major provisions:

1 Ownership of commercial and investment banking firms was separated. (After the act was passed, firms that were principally engaged in commercial banking generally chose to remain in commercial banking; investment banks most often chose to remain investment banks.)

2 Commercial banks were prohibited from underwriting and distributing stocks, bonds, and other securities, with the exception of government bonds, general-obligation municipal bonds, and certificates of deposit.

3 Banking was separated from other types of commercial activity, such as industry. (This provision stemmed from a fear of the concentration of financial power: were

---

[3]The stock market crash eroded the value of the securities that served as bank collateral. As the economic contraction deepened, loan defaults escalated. The decline in collateral value forced banks to absorb the difference between the outstanding value of the loan and the market value of the collateral as losses, which eroded their capital accounts.

they not separate, banks could favor their industrial affiliates and attempt to drive competitors out of the market.)

4 Banks were permitted to hold as assets only certain types of approved debt instruments.

The Glass-Steagall Act also contained provisions for federal deposit insurance (to be explored in Chapter 11); prohibited the payment of interest on demand deposits; set interest rate ceilings for time deposits; and established *margin requirements*—minimum cash requirements for the purchase of securities. Many of these provisions have been adopted in other countries as well. But economists disagree about the merits of such provisions. Many European countries allow investment banking activity by commercial banks, and Japan has forged a unique link between banking and industry. (See the "International Perspectives" box for more information.)

Recent Banking Legislation

In the 1970s, economic volatility and high inflation drove interest rates to unprecedented highs. At the same time, Regulation Q of the Glass-Steagall Act prohibited the payment of interest on demand deposits and set rigid ceilings for interest payable on time deposits. With statutory interest rate ceilings in place, banks and thrifts rapidly lost deposits to money market mutual funds and other investment alternatives. Particularly at risk during the period were thrift institutions that held long-term asset portfolios. With deposits flowing out, thrifts were forced to sell some of their assets, but high market interest rates had driven asset values down. Under Regulation Q, high interest rates were a double-edged sword to lending institutions.

Clearly, substantial change was required in the banking industry. The problems of disintermediation, coupled with the Fed's desire to obtain a tighter grip on the money supply in hopes of controlling inflation, led to passage of the Depository Institutions Deregulation and Monetary Control Act of 1980 (DIDMCA). Central to the act were three provisions. First, interest rate ceilings were to be phased out so that banks could compete for funds during periods of high interest rates. Second, interest-bearing checking accounts were authorized in the form of NOW, ATS, and share draft accounts. Thrifts were also allowed to diversify their assets by making consumer loans, issuing credit cards, and performing other previously forbidden activities. Third, all depository institutions were brought under the same set of reserve requirements.

DIDMCA was followed closely by another act which further deregulated banking, the Garn–St. Germain Act of 1982. This act, which was directed toward thrift institutions, allowed thrifts to behave more like commercial banks. For the first time, thrifts were allowed to make commercial loans and were given expanded opportunities to make consumer loans. The act also permitted interstate mergers of failing institutions and authorized the issuance of money market deposit accounts. As a result of DIDMCA and Garn–St. Germain, the distinction between banks and thrifts became fuzzy.

Two other pieces of recent legislation have proven significant. In the late 1980s, the failure rate of savings and loan associations skyrocketed, due in part to the deregulatory

The Link Between Banking and Commerce in Japan

In the United States, Glass-Steagall restrictions have drawn a dividing line between banking and other forms of business. But in other nations such arrangements are not forbidden; in fact, they are encouraged. Experts trace a good portion of the rapid postwar growth in Japan to the manner in which the banking system is structured to promote commerce and industry. A quick glance at the Japanese system illustrates why these links may be important.

To understand the role banking plays in Japanese industry, we must first examine the organization of industry itself. Unlike in the United States, where antitrust concerns have discouraged the formation of huge firms, Japan's economy is centered around six major industrial concerns, or *keiretsu.* These huge conglomerates are widely diversified and vertically integrated. Together, they account for almost half of the country's sales of primary products and industrial machinery. As is true with most industrial concerns worldwide, the six *keiretsu*—Mitsubishi, Mitsui, Sumitomo, Fuyo, Dai-ichi Kangyo, and Sanwa— rely heavily on a steady supply of credit to finance new projects and maintain existing operations.

Compare the names of the *keiretsu* with the names of the world's largest banks on page 238. Each of these megafirms is affiliated with a large banking concern. The banks serve as a long-term source of financing for the *keiretsu.* Additionally, the affiliated banks own substantial equity in the enterprises of the *keiretsu.* Partial ownership of the firm enables them to monitor the activities of the firm and, by playing a role in the appointment of directors and managers, help direct the path of the firm's development.

Economists point out several distinct advantages to such a symbiotic relationship. The bank–industry affiliation allows banks to establish a long-term relationship with their loan customers. Allowing equity ownership gives the bank increased access to information and the ability to guide the course of the company—important factors in reducing moral hazard and adverse selection. The firm has improved access to loans, permitting it to invest more and grow faster than a firm without a bank affiliation can. In cases of financial distress, an affiliated bank is much more likely to assist in a restructuring effort rather than initiating a foreclosure.

Should the United States implement such a system? There are clearly advantages in linking banking and commerce. The organization of Japanese banking is not perfect, however. The *keiretsu* often find themselves paying higher rates of interest in return for their ease of access to funds. Such a system may also leave small firms and households with an artificially low supply of credit. More than 70 percent of all bank deposits are controlled by the nation's 13 largest banks, which are naturally more inclined to lend to established industrial concerns with which they are affiliated. The geographical diversity of the United States would lead to the same problems of credit availability faced by rural Japan—that is, the funneling of cash from rural to commercial centers. Nevertheless, moral hazard and adverse selection problems alone may warrant removing the equity restrictions of the Glass-Steagall Act. Expect this topic to be at the forefront of continuing debate on the deregulation of banking.

provisions contained in Garn–St. Germain. At the same time, difficulties with the administration of federal deposit insurance exacerbated the ills of an already sick system. As the problem worsened, Congress passed the Financial Institutions Reform, Recovery, and Enforcement Act (FIRREA) of 1989 and the Federal Deposit Insurance Corporation Improvement Act (FDICIA) of 1991. Both of these acts will be examined in detail in Chapter 11.

REGULATION OF THE BANKING INDUSTRY

The structure of the U.S. banking industry is unique: the dual banking system has produced a large number of small banks. The business of banking is also very different from other forms of commerce, because bankers carry the nation's financial security with them in the form of our deposits, and their actions influence the condition of the nation's economy. It is only natural, then, to ask who is acting as watchdog over this powerful group of institutions.

Banks are subject to numerous restrictions that govern where they can operate, what kinds of assets they can purchase, what kinds of debt they can issue, and how closely they can associate with other types of businesses. These regulations spring from all levels of government and are ultimately directed toward three main goals. First, regulation is designed to prevent or at least limit bank failures. Because depositors have only limited information about the risk associated with a bank's asset structure, rumors about an institution's health can touch off a costly bank panic. Therefore, government regulators strive to ensure that banks meet acceptable standards of financial health.

Second, government regulation is designed to enhance economic efficiency by limiting the nature and scope of bank conduct. Government has, for instance, an interest in ensuring that banks will provide loans in an equitable manner at fair rates of interest. Such banking services are vital to economic growth. Third, government regulation exists to ensure that the banking system can honor its deposits—that is, that the system is sufficiently liquid. As we shall see, the regulations imposed on the banking system sometimes work at cross-purposes to these three goals and actually exacerbate the problems they are designed to prevent. First, however, we will look at the regulatory agencies charged with enforcing these regulations.

Regulatory Bodies

In the United States, several regulatory bodies have overlapping responsibilities for the supervision of banking. In this section, we will look at the bodies themselves, and in the section following we will examine their responsibilities.

To gain a perspective on how regulatory responsibility has changed over time, we must examine the regulators in a historical context. The U.S. financial sector is regulated by several different entities, each with its own responsibilities and limitations, each created in response to different economic and political conditions. To fully understand their roles in today's economy, then, we must know *why* they were originally created. In the following sections, we will examine the origins of four regulatory bodies: state banking commissions, the Comptroller of the Currency, the Federal Reserve, and the FDIC.

State Banking Commissions

From the colonial era to modern times, state banking commissions have played an important role in our financial system. Before 1863, state commissions retained the sole power to charter banks. To this day, state banking commissions continue to charter state banks, and they retain some supervisory power over those institutions as well.

The Comptroller of the Currency

The National Banking Act of 1863 granted the **Comptroller of the Currency,** an office of the Department of the Treasury, the power to charter all national banks. Created in response to the excesses of wildcat banks, the national banking system was designed to hold the massive amounts of government debt issued during the Civil War. Today, the Comptroller of the Currency continues as the chartering body for national banks and retains a significant amount of regulatory responsibility.

The Federal Reserve System

Between 1863 and 1913, financial panics swept the nation, causing many solvent but illiquid banks to fail.[4] To protect themselves against panics, many banks banded together in groups called *clearinghouses* to establish a source of emergency funds in the event of a bank run. This system worked well for isolated bank panics but could not deal with shocks affecting the system as a whole. If all banks in a clearinghouse experienced large withdrawals simultaneously, there was no way for them to obtain additional funds. What the system needed was a "lender of last resort" to provide liquidity during such episodes. Following a particularly severe panic in 1907, lawmakers began seriously to consider the establishment of a central bank; their talks culminated in the Federal Reserve Act of 1913. The creation of the Federal Reserve System provided a potential source of emergency reserves for the banking system as a whole. The Fed was also given the sole responsibility for issuing a uniform currency, the Federal Reserve note, which would coexist with the gold certificates, silver certificates, and coins issued by the Treasury. Every national bank was (and still is) required to be a member of the Federal Reserve System. We will study the structure and functions of the Fed in greater detail throughout the rest of the text, especially in Chapter 12.

The Federal Deposit Insurance Corporation

Through 1934, the Federal Reserve carried much of the responsibility for the stability of the banking system. However, as we will see in Chapter 16, the Fed virtually abdicated that responsibility during the critical years of the Great Depression (1929–1933). When a rash of bank failures (one-third of all banks) rocked the nation, Congress responded with strong legislative reform of the banking system in 1933 and 1934. The Banking Act of 1933 created a system of deposit insurance, to be supervised by the newly created Federal Deposit Insurance Corporation (FDIC). Initially, deposits were insured to a limit

---

[4]Chapter 9 explained what happens when a bank faces massive withdrawals. If the withdrawals are enough to deplete its excess reserves, the bank will have to sell assets to replenish its liquidity. If the bank has to sell those assets in a hurry (as during a financial panic), it may be forced to accept fire sale prices, absorbing the losses through a declining capital account. If the withdrawals are great enough, a perfectly sound bank may fail.

of $2500 per depositor per account. The limit has been raised over the years and now stands at $100,000. By law, every national bank must purchase FDIC insurance, as must every state bank that is a member of the Federal Reserve System. Only state banks that are not members of the Federal Reserve System can elect to decline FDIC insurance. Today, FDIC insurance covers all but a few hundred small state banks.

Regulatory Responsibilities

The preceding section introduced the four regulatory authorities in the American banking system: the state banking commissions, the Comptroller of the Currency, the Federal Reserve, and the FDIC. The regulatory responsibilities of each of these entities is best understood by focusing on the banks themselves. National banks are chartered by the Comptroller of the Currency, and the Comptroller retains responsibility for their supervision and examination. State banks that are members of the Federal Reserve are chartered by state banking commissions but are supervised and examined by the Federal Reserve. State banks that are *not* Federal Reserve members but *do* carry FDIC insurance are supervised by the FDIC. State banks that are *not* Fed members and *do not* carry FDIC insurance are supervised and examined by state authorities. Finally, the Federal Reserve retains the right to supervise the activities of bank holding companies, firms which own a controlling interest in one or more banks but do not actually engage in the business of banking. This rather complicated division of responsibilities is summarized in Table 10-1.

Regulatory Reform

Given the rather complicated scheme illustrated in Table 10-1, it is not surprising that representatives of the public and the banking community, as well as regulators themselves, have called for a simplification of the system, pointing to the inefficiencies and confusion it creates. Though change has been slow, increasing attention is being given to the structure of bank regulation.

Table   10-1

Division of Regulatory Responsibilities in U.S. Banking

Bank	Chartering Body	Supervisor	Insurer
National banks	Comptroller of the Currency	Comptroller of the Currency	FDIC
State banks: Federal Reserve members	State authorities	Federal Reserve	FDIC
State banks: not Federal Reserve members, FDIC insured	State authorities	FDIC	FDIC
State banks: not Federal Reserve members, not FDIC insured	State authorities	State authorities	Private or state insurer

The Case for Regulatory Reform

Obviously, the chartering, insurance, and Fed membership options that are open to banks, coupled with the system of multiple regulators, creates some duplication of regulatory effort. Overlapping responsibility is common, particularly since the FDIC has a vested interest in scrutinizing the finances of every institution it insures. Critics of the current regulatory system point to the high cost of duplication and the lack of coordination among agencies. They assert that large gains in efficiency could be realized if the number of regulatory agencies were reduced. Information-gathering costs would decrease substantially, and overhead expenses for buildings, staff, computers, and travel could be reduced.

Another potential benefit of reducing the regulatory burden would be enhanced consistency and fairness in the treatment of banks. Currently, institutions governed by different agencies are subject to different rules and differing interpretations of laws that should apply uniformly. Many financial institutions find it profitable to play the regulatory agencies against one another. Thus, a merger denied by one regulator may be proposed to and approved by another. In the late 1970s, for instance, many national banks were rechartered as state banks to avoid the high reserve requirements imposed on Federal Reserve members.[5] This kind of shopping around involves substantial information-gathering costs for banks and tends to discriminate against smaller institutions with fewer resources. Eliminating such disparities would place all banks on the same playing field.

Finally, it has been argued that overlapping responsibility may reduce the effectiveness of the regulatory system in time of crisis. Critics point to the FDIC's inability in the 1980s to pay off depositors at failing institutions until the banks were declared insolvent by the chartering bodies. If regulators' efforts were consolidated and/or coordinated, their response speed and effectiveness could be improved.

The Case against Regulatory Reform

Despite the regulatory system's obvious problems, there are some advantages to overlapping supervision. First and most obvious is that it provides a natural system of checks and balances. If one regulator overlooks a problem, another may discover it. The problem, critics maintain, is a lack of communication among the agencies, not the agencies themselves.

Second, proponents of the system point to potential benefits in the form of financial innovations which would not be likely to occur under a single set of rules and a single regulator. They note that many financial instruments and institutions were developed in response to loopholes in one regulator's rule book. The growth of *nonbank banks* (institutions which accept deposits or make loans but do not engage in both activities) during the 1980s occurred primarily because of the liberal chartering policies of the Comptroller of the Currency. Interstate banking, which was disallowed by federal regulation, grew because of the increasing liberalization of state banking law. Other examples abound: NOW accounts, adjustable-rate mortgages, and multibank holding companies all stemmed from loopholes in federal or state laws. Without multiagency regulation, we might have fewer such innovations, many of which benefit depositors as well as borrowers.

Finally, proponents of the status quo argue that a single regulatory agency could turn out to be an unresponsive bureaucratic nightmare. With limited exceptions, the financial sector has thrived under the current system. There is no compelling reason to overhaul it.

---

[5]To improve control of the money supply and promote fairness, all banks were brought under the same set of reserve requirements in the 1980s. You will learn more about this issue in Chapter 18.

Admittedly, there is room for better communication and coordination, but a restructuring might create more problems than it solves. Critics of the one-regulator plan point out that the savings and loan debacle of the late 1980s, the most devastating financial episode since the Great Depression, occurred under the watch of a single regulator, the Federal Home Loan Bank Board.

Recent Proposals for Reform

Proposals for regulatory reform are still on the table. The most recent, initiated in the Department of the Treasury and backed by President Clinton in 1995, would form a **Federal Banking Commission** (FBC) to assume the regulatory authority for all federally insured banks, holding companies, and thrift institutions. The FBC would also charter all new national banks and thrifts. Under the proposal, the FDIC would continue to insure deposits and could conduct special examinations to protect the deposit insurance fund, while the Federal Reserve would continue to conduct monetary policy and would have limited power to examine institutions deemed vital to the nation's financial health. Both the FDIC and the Fed would have access to all records of the FBC relating to depository institutions and their holding companies.

Critics of the plan worry about loss of the political independence regulators currently enjoy. The Clinton plan calls for a five-member FBC board: three members appointed by the president and confirmed by the Senate (one of whom must be from an opposing political party); the secretary of the Treasury; and one member of the Board of Governors of the Federal Reserve. Under this plan, four or even all five members could be appointees of a sitting president, making the board sensitive to political pressures. Critics also claim that the proposal squanders the expertise that current regulators, particularly the Federal Reserve, have acquired over the years. That experience currently enables regulators to view macroeconomic crises from a microeconomic perspective, dealing with problems pragmatically and with close attention to the impact of Fed actions on the financial sector in general and the banking sector in particular. To avoid throwing such valuable experience away, the Federal Reserve has proposed an alternative reform that gives the Fed responsibility for state-chartered banks and consolidates the supervision of all national banks under the Federal Banking Commission. The two organizations would be jointly responsible for large banks that play an important role in the financial sector. As of mid-1996, no action had been taken on either proposal, but the issue is too important to remain buried for long.

THE ECONOMICS OF BRANCH BANKING

Our brief overview of U.S. banking has illustrated several ways in which the U.S. financial sector is different from that of virtually every other nation. Foremost among them is the fact that banking services in the United States are generally provided by a large number of small firms, each of which has only a few offices. In the following section we will examine the branch bank system and evaluate the economic consequences of its structure.

Table 10-2

Branch Banking by Decade

Decade	Number of Unit Banks	Number of Branches	Total
1990s	5,288	6,848	12,136
1980s	7,069	6,978	14,047
1970s	8,828	5,275	14,103
1960s	10,260	3,111	13,371
1950s	11,590	1,706	13,296
1940s	12,309	1,059	13,368
1930s	12,950	869	13,819

Source: Federal Deposit Insurance Corporation, *Historical Statistics on Banking, 1993*. The data by decade are averages of yearly figures.

Restrictions on Branching

Branching restrictions are as old as the banking system itself. During the national banking era, only the Bank of the United States was allowed to branch across state borders. But the perceived excesses of the Bank of the United States caused the states to lobby for restrictions on its ability to branch. The National Banking Act of 1863 granted states the power to limit branching within their borders, so as to limit competition in the financial sector and ensure banks a low-cost source of funds. An underlying motive was to stabilize the banking industry following the era of free banking. In 1927, the federal government went one step further in aiding state banks by passing the **McFadden Act.** This act prohibited national banks from operating outside the borders of their home states and compelled them to abide by state regulations governing intrastate branching.

State branching restrictions took a wide variety of forms. Many states allowed statewide branching, which permits a bank to open an unlimited number of offices within state borders. Other states adopted **limited branching** restrictions, which restricted banks to a certain number of offices. The most restrictive form of limited branching was unit banking, which allowed each bank only one office. Limited branching and unit banking were found primarily in sparsely populated agricultural states; they reflected a Jeffersonian mistrust of the concentration of wealth and financial power. Kansas, the last of the unit banking states, relaxed its restrictions in 1986.

Despite the initial strength of branching restrictions, bank branches have increased in number over time. Table 10-2 shows the growth of branch banking since the 1930s. It reflects both the relaxation of branching restrictions by the states and increased efforts on the part of banks to circumvent state restrictions. The response of banks to branching restrictions is the subject of the next section.

Responses to Restrictions on Branching

The banking industry has not viewed federal and state branching restrictions favorably. The history of American banking indicates that banks have left no alternative unexplored in attempting to circumvent such legislation. Their efforts culminated in several developments, including bank holding companies, the division of banking services, the growth of electronic banking, and intensive lobbying for reduced restrictions on branching.

Bank Holding Companies

The earliest response to branching restrictions was the advent of the bank holding company. Suppose a bank in Missouri wants to acquire a bank in Iowa, but interstate branching restrictions prevent a direct purchase. The Missouri bank can set up a shell corporation—a **bank holding company**—that is not itself a bank but that can become the Missouri Bank's legal owner. The bank holding company can then purchase the Iowa bank and operate it as a wholly owned subsidiary. The shell corporation then becomes a multibank holding company. You are probably familiar with bank holding companies; one example is Citicorp, which owns Citibank, one of America's largest banks.

This kind of legal maneuvering was very popular during the first half of the twentieth century, particularly in states where branching was heavily restricted. But in 1956, the **Bank Holding Company Act** prohibited such expansions unless state law permitted interstate acquisitions. The act "grandfathered" existing multibank holding companies, allowing them to continue operations.

The Division of Banking Services

Banks have also discovered other ways of circumventing branching restrictions. The Bank Holding Company Act defined a bank as an entity that "accepts demand deposits *and* makes commercial loans." The logical reaction of enterprising bankers was to split the two functions and conduct them separately. They set up "nonbank banks" that accepted deposits but did not make loans and "nonbank offices" that made loans but did not accept deposits. Funds were channeled from the nonbank banks to the nonbank offices through the parent corporation.

The growth of this type of activity was so rapid that pressure soon mounted to restrict nonbank activity. The Competitive Equality Banking Act of 1987 prohibited the establishment of new nonbank banks. Existing institutions were again grandfathered but were limited in their opportunities for future growth. Despite these restrictions, nonbank banking remains a big business. Citicorp, the largest of the nonbank bankers, operates more than a thousand nonbank facilities nationwide.

Electronic Banking

Another response to branching restrictions was the development of an electronic banking system. As a college student, you are probably intimately familiar with the automatic teller machine (ATM).[6] But the struggle for electronic banking was a difficult one. Several states resisted the installation of automatic tellers, claiming that if they were owned by a bank, they were legally considered branches of that bank. However, if an ATM was owned by another business or allowed access to a network of multiple institutions (such

---

[6]Originally, most ATMs were located on the grounds of banking facilities to provide nighttime access to deposits. Recently, most of the growth in electronic banking has occurred off premises. The most heavily used ATMs are on college campuses, averaging well over 300 transactions per machine per day.

as VIA or CIRRUS), it was deemed exempt from restriction. As a result, many large banks have used electronic networks to establish a presence in markets that were previously inaccessible to them. It is highly unlikely that electronic banking would have evolved to the extent that it has if the branching laws had not been so restrictive.

Reduced Restrictions on Branching

Since passage of the Bank Holding Company Act of 1956, the United States has witnessed slow but steady progress toward free interstate banking. The act granted the states the power to govern branch banking, virtually ensuring that interstate banking would eventually become a reality. After its passage, several states entered into reciprocal agreements whereby banks from one state could open branches in another only if banks from the other state were accorded the same privilege. In 1975, Maine became the first state to allow full interstate branching. In the early 1980s, several other New England states followed suit, spawning superregional banks that rivaled the established money center banks in size and scope.[7] By the end of the 1980s, most states had substantially relaxed their interstate and intrastate branching restrictions. Only Hawaii continues to prohibit any form of interstate banking.

In September 1994, President Clinton signed into law the **Riegle-Neal Interstate Banking and Branching Efficiency Act of 1994,** which eliminates most branching restrictions from interstate banking. This monumental act revoked the rights granted states by the National Banking Act of 1863 concerning branching within their borders. Beginning in September 1995, bank holding companies were allowed to acquire banks anywhere in the nation. After June 1, 1997, holding companies will be allowed to convert banks in various states into branches of a single interstate bank.

What do these developments imply for the banking industry? If we examine the period 1988–1993, when states were relaxing their branching restrictions, we may get a glimpse of what is to come. During that period, bank holding companies did take advantage of new opportunities to acquire banks in other states, but change was gradual because they proceeded with caution. However, as the laws became more liberal, holding companies were quick to consolidate multiple banks into branches of a single bank. If this experience holds true in the coming decade, we can expect to see a gradually increasing number of acquisitions, coupled with rapid movement toward the consolidation of semi-independent holding company institutions. Consolidation is the subject of the next section.

THE ECONOMICS OF CONSOLIDATION

After banks had managed to circumvent branching restrictions and the legal environment had been liberalized, pressure mounted on banks to merge, consolidate, and expand. To understand the reasons for the pressure, we must put the U.S. banking industry into a global perspective. Table 10-3 shows the largest banks in the world and the largest banks in the United States. Note that all of the 10 largest banks in the world are located in Japan. The largest bank in the United States, Chase Manhattan, barely ranks in the top 20.

---

[7]New York banks were so worried about competition from superregional banks that they challenged their constitutionality in federal court. But the laws allowing regional interstate banking were upheld in 1985, and today those banks rival the money center banks in size and scope of activity.

Table 10-3

The Largest Banks in the World and the United States

Largest Banks in the World

Rank	Bank	Assets
1	Sanwa Bank, Osaka	$588 billion
2	Dai-ichi Kangyo Bank, Tokyo	$588 billion
3	Fuji Bank, Tokyo	$577 billion
4	Sumitomo Bank, Osaka	$571 billion
5	Sakura Bank, Tokyo	$565 billion
6	Mitsubishi Bank, Tokyo	$553 billion
7	Norinchukin Bank, Tokyo	$500 billion
8	Industrial Bank of Japan, Tokyo	$437 billion
9	Mitsubishi Trust, Tokyo	$394 billion
10	Long Term Credit Bank of Japan, Tokyo	$376 billion

Largest Bank Holding Companies in the United States*

Rank	Bank	Assets	Approximate World Rank
1	Chemical Bank–Chase Manhattan	$305 billion	20
2	Citicorp	$257 billion	26
3	Bank of America	$227 billion	32
4	NationsBank Corp.	$184 billion	37
5	Morgan Guaranty Trust	$166 billion	44
6	First Union–First Fidelity	$124 billion	—†
7	First Chicago–NBD Corp.	$123 billion	—†
8	Fleet Financial	$114 billion	—†
9	Wells Fargo Bank–First Interstate	$108 billion	—†
10	Bankers Trust, New York	$103 billion	—†

*Pending mergers.
†Bank not ranked in top 50 world banks.

Source: *Standard & Poor's Industry Surveys, 1995*. Foreign bank assets as of December 31, 1994; rounded to the nearest billion dollars.

Furthermore, economic concentration in the U.S. banking industry is relatively low. In the United States, the market share of the five largest banks is only 18 percent, in sharp contrast to other industrialized nations such as Germany (62 percent), England (57 percent), and Canada (78 percent). But though the U.S. banking sector is composed mostly of small firms, the large number of small firms should *not* be interpreted as a sign of heavy competition. Rather, many small banks enjoy a local monopoly. Interstate and intrastate branching restrictions have so effectively insulated small banks from competition that even the most inefficient are often able to stay in business.

But U.S. banking is clearly catching up with banking in the rest of the world. Between 1981 and 1996, the total number of U.S. banks declined significantly, from about 14,400 to fewer than 10,000. The decline is due not to a slowdown in the establishment of new banks but to a dramatic rise in mergers and consolidations of existing banks. The market share of the top 300 bank holding companies is now greater than 70 percent, a phenomenal sum given the large number of banks in existence. Figure 10-1 illustrates the trend of bank mergers over the last 60 years. Notice the phenomenal growth in mergers following the relaxation of branching restrictions in the 1980s. Over the next few decades, we will see fewer and larger banks because of the continuing liberalization of banking law.

Will the relaxation of branching restrictions and the merging and consolidation of many banks produce a more efficient banking sector? Intuition suggests that the answer should be "yes," though the extent of the gains in efficiency may be difficult to measure. Observers note that other factors unrelated to efficiency may be driving the consolidation movement. In the following sections we will consider four factors that are driving the trend, only two of which are related to cost efficiency.

Economies of Scale

One area in which potential efficiency gains likely exist is in the area of overhead costs. If a holding company owns two banks that operate independently, each bank must invest separately in information gathering, electronic data processing equipment, and management staff. Much of that overhead might be reduced by sharing staff and equipment. Cost

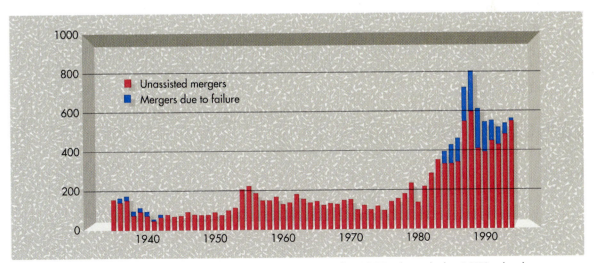

Figure 10-1   Number of Bank Mergers, 1935–1994. From the 1950s through the 1970s, bank mergers averaged just over 100 per year. Since 1980, the number of mergers has escalated dramatically. *Source:* Federal Deposit Insurance Corporation.

reductions which accrue from expansion are commonly referred to as **economies of scale;** they are illustrated diagrammatically in Figure 10-2.

Figure 10-2 relates the average cost of producing financial services to the quantity of services provided (that is, the size of the institution). Notice that as bank size increases from $0 to $100 million in deposits, the average cost per dollar of deposits declines. Cost advantages may accrue through higher utilization of existing capacity or through reduction of duplication. For example, a bank may require the same size management staff whether it has deposits of $10 million or $200 million. If two relatively small banks merge into one, they may be able to share data processing equipment and staff. Between $100 million and $400 million of deposits, there exists no distinct cost advantage to increasing size. In fact, the cost per deposit begins to slowly rise. After $400 million, banks are vulnerable to **diseconomies of scale,** which spring from the disorganization, duplication of effort, and confusion of a large bureaucracy.

To achieve the greatest profitability, then, a competitive bank should operate at the *minimum efficient scale,* the point of lowest average cost. Economists have estimated the minimum efficient scale for U.S. banks as being no more than $125 million in deposits. If significant economies of scale exist, a competitive bank should expand via branching until the minimum efficient scale is reached. However, most studies of the banking industry suggest that economies of scale are quickly exhausted. In a survey of 13 studies of bank cost curves, 11 found no significant economies of scale beyond $100 million in deposits. Additional studies report significant *diseconomies of scale* for banks with assets of $1 billion or more. This evidence suggests that the impetus for the current wave of consolidations is not cost savings but other factors unrelated to economic efficiency.

It must be emphasized, however, that these studies are based on historical data that may not reflect the current banking environment. The recent growth of electronic banking has decreased the need for personal account service and its associated costs, such as multiple offices, extended service hours, and a full staff of tellers and account represen-

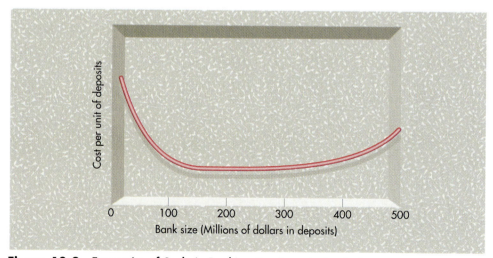

Figure 10-2   Economies of Scale in Banking Services. As bank size grows, the average cost per unit of banking services first declines, then remains stable, and finally begins to rise as a bank becomes very large.

tatives. Because electronic banking is relatively new, bankers argue, historical cost estimates may understate the point of minimum efficient scale. Though rough guesses suggest that the true minimum efficient scale may be in the tens of billions of deposit dollars, no sophisticated statistical analysis has yet been completed. Until such claims are verified, however, we must look for other factors besides efficiency that may be fueling the movement to consolidate and expand.[8] Exhibit 10-1 illustrates in greater detail this trend toward consolidation. Given the explosion of mergers and acquisitions, it is no surprise that economists are searching for explanations more convincing than economies of scale as the motivation behind such consolidations.

Risk Management and Portfolio Diversification

A second likely contributor to the trend toward consolidation is the enhanced potential for geographical diversification of assets. Banks with offices in more than one region can lend to a variety of customers, thus avoiding the trap of "putting all their eggs into one basket." Indeed, the disastrous experience of Texas banks following the dramatic decline in oil prices in the mid-1980s testifies to the benefits of diversification. Figure 10-3 illustrates how costly the Texas banks' lack of diversification of assets was. Between 1986 and 1990, Texas banks accounted for almost half of all bank failures in the United States.

[8]Evidence from Japan indicates that these estimates of bank cost structure are not unique to the United States. Japan's largest banks are not the most profitable—rather, the most profitable Japanese bank ranks only about thirtieth in size.

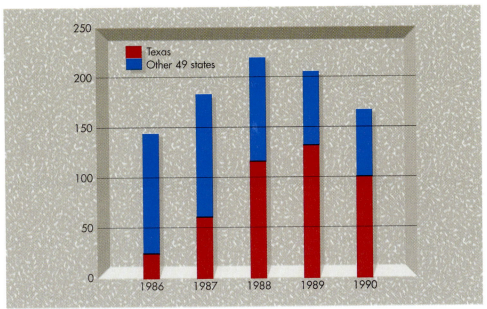

Figure 10-3   Number of U.S. Bank Failures, 1986–1990. From 1986–1990, Texas accounted for a disproportionate share of U.S. bank failures. This provides evidence of the benefits of portfolio diversification. *Source:* FDIC.

EXHIBIT 10-1

Merger Mania Hits Wall Street Banks

On August 28, 1995, two of the largest banks in the United States announced a $10 billion stock swap that would create the nation's biggest bank. Chemical Bank, with assets of $178 billion, and Chase Manhattan, with assets of $119 billion, proposed a merger that would create a financial giant larger than the $257 billion Citibank, then the nation's largest bank. The new bank, which took the Chase name, became the leading lender to large corporations, the largest securities processor, the third largest mortgage originator, and the fourth largest issuer of credit cards.

The spectacular merger followed a slew of similar combinations earlier in the year—196, to be exact—involving a total of more than $194 billion in net worth. These mergers and two that followed in 1995 account for eight of the largest U.S. bank mergers of all time. These mergers are shown in the table below. Chemical Bank had itself acquired Manufacturers Hanover Trust in 1991.

The Big Acquisitions of 1995*

Date	Banks	Equity Value
Feb. 21	Shawmut National/Fleet Financial	$3.8 billion
June 19	First Fidelity/First Union	$5.1 billion
July 10	Midlantic/PNC Bank	$2.9 billion
July 12	First Chicago/NBD Bancorp	$5.3 billion
Aug. 28	Integra Financial/National City	$2.1 billion
Aug. 28	Chemical/Chase Manhattan	$9.9 billion
Sept. 5	NationsBank/Bank South	$1.6 billion
Dec. 19	NatWest Bank/Fleet Financial	$3.3 billion

*This table does not include the highly publicized Wells Fargo–First Interstate merger, which was announced in January 1996. The hostile takeover of First Interstate for an estimated equity value of more than $11 billion was the biggest merger of all time in terms of net worth, but not in terms of assets. The combined assets of Wells Fargo and First Interstate are estimated to be $108 billion, substantially behind the $305 billion of Chase and Chemical.

Sources: *The New York Times,* various dates; *Standard & Poor's Industry Surveys,* Nov. 2, 1995; *Facts on File,* 1995–1996.

EXHIBIT 10-1 (CONTINUED)

In the midst of such a wave of consolidations, the natural question to ask is: Why? Officials of Chemical and Chase claim that their merger will eliminate unneeded duplication of effort and overhead. By closing 100 overlapping branches and eliminating 12,000 jobs at branches and at headquarters, they estimate a cost savings of $1.5 billion a year. The news hit the New York banking community hard—since 1988, New York has lost more than 40,000 banking jobs, approximately one-third of its total.

Critics claim that the banks' estimate of cost reductions is too high. The two banks' strengths are complementary: Chase is oriented toward consumer and mortgage lending, while Chemical focuses on commercial lending. A large portion of the Chase empire is based in Florida, while Chemical bases much of its mortgage lending in Cleveland. If the new bank hopes to retain the level of service it currently provides, these disparities in geography and services may preclude significant cost cutting.

Experts note that neither Chase nor Chemical will gain anything by simply growing bigger. Economies of scale do not exist in banks of this size, and both banks already provide such a wide array of services that the potential gains from economies of scope are likely to be small. William Silber and Roy Smith, professors of economics at New York University, put it this way: "After cost cutting, the new bank will have to be different to be better. They will have to redeploy resources better, retain top talent, and rethink their strategies to deal efficiently with both domestic and international competition. They cannot allow the bank to sink back into the businesses that both banks consider usual, in which all the emphasis is on cutting costs, then finding another bank to acquire to cut more costs. There has to be more, or the new Chase may end up looking much like the old one."

Despite such concerns, the stock market viewed the merger favorably. An index of 24 bank stocks jumped 3 percent on the announcement, and the share prices of Chase and Chemical both rose by more than 10 percent.

The benefits of diversification are often, however, partially offset by increased information and monitoring costs. For example, a rural Arkansas bank may have difficulty assessing risk in the Kansas aircraft industry. Do the benefits of diversification outweigh the costs? A 1991 study of intrastate branching found that the relaxation of branching restrictions had indeed produced greater portfolio diversification, providing at least a partial explanation for the movement toward consolidation. However, Table 10-4 suggests that large banks, which are presumably more diversified, may not be safer than small banks. In the 1970s and 1980s, large banks experienced higher fail-

Table 10-4		
Relationship Between Bank Size and Safety, 1971–1988		
	Failure Rates	
Asset Size	**1970s**	**1980s**
Small (<$1 billion)	0.49%	5.71%
Large (>$1 billion)	2.19	8.00

Source: Federal Deposit Insurance Corporation.

ure rates than small banks did. If the increased diversification that size allows does not improve safety, it should be discounted as a motive for consolidation.

Executive Compensation

If the benefits of consolidation are uncertain, why are so many banks consolidating? Most likely, factors unrelated to efficiency and profitability are contributing to the trend. A 1991 study by the Minneapolis Federal Reserve Bank attempted to pinpoint why bigger seems to be better in the banking industry. The authors were skeptical that economies of scale and portfolio diversification were the real motives for consolidation. In searching for a more plausible explanation, they examined managers' incentives to increase bank size. Their findings indicate that while managers' salaries are not significantly linked to profitability or growth, they do depend heavily on a bank's total assets. Because the regulatory environment virtually precludes hostile takeovers—one of the most effective mechanisms for ousting managers who pursue their own interests at the expense of the shareholders—managers have a personal financial incentive to expand their firms. This hypothesis, although somewhat cynical, may serve to promote further inquiry into the motives that are driving the consolidation movement.

Monopoly Power

Many of the recent bank mergers and consolidations have involved competitors in the same geographic market. If banks are able to reduce competition and gain a monopoly position by merging, depositors and borrowers will be at the bank's mercy with regard to loan rates and interest paid on deposits. That is exactly the type of power Jefferson and the Anti-Federalists feared. Was their concern justified? Several studies have shown a strong positive correlation between market concentration and the spread between the interest rates charged on loans and those paid on deposits. Thus, the benefits banks reap from increased market power may outweigh the costs of any diseconomies of scale they encounter in expanding.[9]

Conclusions

We have seen mixed evidence on the existence of economies of scale and the advantages of portfolio diversification in banking, and we have seen support for the theory that managerial compensation and the desire for monopoly power are fueling the consolidation of U.S. banks. What benefits might consumers expect from the recent wave of mergers? Certainly, we should expect to see increased convenience for consumers as branching continues. The ability to obtain personal account service across a city or across the nation should increase. Figures on the establishment of bank offices bear this out. After slow growth during the merger-happy 1980s, the number of bank offices is now growing at a 3 percent annual rate. For consumers in previously isolated local markets, the relaxation of branching restrictions is likely to increase competition, with greater personal service and more favorable loan and deposit rates as a result. But if the true motives behind bank consolidation are the maximization of managerial salaries and establishment of monopoly power, we should expect to pay for increased convenience in the form of increased costs passed on to the consumer.

Clearly, the structure of the banking industry is changing. Through mergers, through branching, and through natural growth, U.S. banks are getting bigger and market concentration is increasing. U.S. banks are also becoming more diverse in the activities they pursue. The next section discusses industry responses to the Glass-Steagall Act and the effects of Glass-Steagall restrictions on the banking community and the macroeconomy in general.

THE ECONOMICS OF ACTIVITY RESTRICTION

In the past, banks were restricted not only with respect to *where* they might operate but also with regard to *how* they might operate, particularly with respect to the types of assets they might hold. The most significant legislation affecting bank activity, passed in 1933, was the Glass-Steagall Act.

---

[9]One possible way of determining the motivation behind a merger is by examining the stock prices of the merging firms' competitors. If a merger is undertaken to enhance monopoly power, the price of banking services will be expected to rise, and the stock prices of competitors should follow. If, on the other hand, a merger is undertaken for cost considerations, the decline in costs should, at least in part, be passed on to the consumer, implying lower prices for banking services as a whole. Competitors' stock prices should then fall. The Chase-Chemical merger discussed in Exhibit 10-1 was ostensibly carried out to reduce costs. But bank stocks as a whole rose on the announcement, suggesting an increase in market power rather than efficiency considerations as motivation for the merger.

The Glass-Steagall Act drew a sharp line between commercial and investment banking. But over the past few decades, the dividing line between commercial and investment banks has grown fuzzy. The two types of banks are now competing more directly on a wide variety of fronts. By exploiting loopholes in existing laws and taking advantage of a relaxation of the Glass-Steagall restrictions, banks are becoming increasingly homogeneous.

First, commercial banks are making strong advances into what used to be investment bankers' turf by playing an increasing role in the underwriting of securities. Banks were once limited to the underwriting of securities backed by government taxing power, such as federal government bonds and general-obligation municipal bonds. But in 1988, the Supreme Court gave the Federal Reserve the power to authorize commercial bank underwritings of high-quality debt, such as industrial revenue bonds, commercial paper, and pass-through securities backed by consumer debt. Then, in 1989, some commercial bank subsidiaries were permitted to compete directly with investment banks in the underwriting of corporate bonds. Now commercial banks are permitted to offer brokerage services (discount brokerage services were first offered in 1983), and since 1987 banks and bank holding companies have been authorized to offer full brokerage services, including investment advice. Commercial banks have also begun to manage and market their own mutual funds. While their current market share is small, the closeness of the bank-customer relationship and the convenience of branch banking will make commercial banks a formidable competitor for investment banks in decades to come.

Furthermore, investment banks are increasingly acting like commercial banks. By establishing nonbank banks and nonbank offices, they can compete with commercial banks for customers' deposits and loans. Most investment banks offer money market mutual funds that function like checking accounts. Others have been permitted to acquire failed banks and thrifts and turn them into nonbank banks.[10]

Finally, the dividing line between banking and industry is eroding. You may be familiar with the highly publicized Sears Financial Network, which at one time offered brokerage services, credit cards, and a host of other financial services. And all of the American automobile manufacturers engage in financial intermediation on many fronts, from lending and credit services to selling insurance.

What is important, however, is not whether industrial firms can act as banks or commercial banks can operate as investment banks. Rather, we must ask whether they should be *permitted* to do so. The Glass-Steagall Act was passed in response to concerns about abuses of power on the part of commercial banks, such as overstating the quality of underwritten issues, securitizing and marketing nonperforming loans, placing poor-quality underwritings in commercial clients' trust accounts, and bearing undue risk in securities holdings. These concerns may be as justified today as they were in 1933. Exhibit 10-2 illustrates the damage that deception and excessive risk taking can do to an otherwise healthy institution.

Several recent studies have cast doubt on the validity of those concerns, however. One study shows that, during the Great Depression, the failure rate of national banks that were operating bond departments and securities affiliates was about 7 percent, while

---

[10]This privilege was permitted for a brief time during the 1980s and was revoked by 1987. Expect to see similar provisions resurface with the increasing liberalization of banking laws.

Banking on Derivatives

On February 23, 1995, a young man hurriedly packed his bags and fled the country of Singapore for Germany. Securities trader Nicholas Leeson had single-handedly driven his employer, Britain's Barings Bank, into insolvency. In just a few short weeks, Barings, a 232-year-old institution that held $1 million of the queen mother's deposits, had lost more than $1 billion of net worth at the hands of the 28-year-old man.

Leeson, an arbitrageur, was employed by the bank to buy futures contracts in Japan and sell them on a newly developed capital market in Singapore. By exploiting small differences in prices between the two exchanges, Leeson could easily turn small but steady profits for his bank. But small and steady wasn't enough for power-hungry Leeson. He began a series of aggressive one-sided purchases of Nikkei 225 Stock Index futures for his bank, channeling them into a secret account, No. 88888.

Derivatives are volatile securities that are based on the value of some financial asset. If the underlying asset's value changes, the value of the derivative changes more. Some derivatives, such as "swaptions" and "inverse floaters," are complex. But the futures contracts Leeson purchased for Barings were one of the simplest types of derivative, one that is used primarily to *reduce* risk. Leeson was betting that the Nikkei Index would rise and then stabilize at about 19,000. At the time, it seemed a safe bet—the Nikkei was rebounding following a 30-month recession. What trader Leeson didn't count on was the fury of Mother Nature. When a strong earthquake ravaged the industrial city of Kobe, the Nikkei plummeted to just over 18,000. Desperate to recoup his losses, Leeson increased his holdings of futures. But the index continued to fall, and eventually Leeson's losses exceeded the bank's net worth.

This episode raises questions not only about the advisability of banks holding derivatives as assets but also about the ability of commercial banks to function as investment banks, maintaining inventories of securities. Barings, an old and traditional bank, was exploring new territory with its expansion into Singapore's money market. But it did not have the experience and wisdom to put appropriate financial controls in place. Leeson was not only making the trades, he was also recording them, a security breach so wide that a child could have exploited it. Later, evidence revealed that a 1994 audit had exposed the breach to top brass, who had ignored it because Leeson was bringing in millions in profits.

Some observers believe that the experience of Barings provides a compelling argument for maintaining the separation of commercial from investment banking. Watch the papers closely for news about the progress of legislation to merge the two functions—and should the legislation pass, keep a wary eye on your bank's balance sheet.

Leeson was eventually apprehended in Germany and extradited to Singapore, where he is currently serving a 6-year sentence for fraud. Barings was quickly sold to the Dutch firm ING for $1.60, an amount objective observers believe dramatically overstated the bank's true value.

the failure rate of national banks as a whole was over 26 percent. The economies of scale and the potential for portfolio diversification that investment banking offers were probably responsible for the disparity. Keeping these figures in mind, let us examine several rationales for and against merging the activities of commercial and investment banks.

Economies of Scope

The basis of the economies-of-scope argument is similar in nature to that of economies of scale. **Economies of scope** exist when services may be produced more efficiently as a group than separately. Because information is a vital and expensive input in the production of financial services, the opportunity to exploit it fully in a number of services naturally increases efficiency. For instance, before granting loans, lenders collect extensive information about the creditworthiness of borrowers. Underwriters gather the same information before packaging and marketing securities. Merging commercial and investment banking would eliminate the duplication of information gathering involved in providing these services separately. Banks may also find that many financial products can share the same marketing and distribution network. Several studies have found economies of scope in the financial services sector; to the extent they can be exploited, they provide a compelling incentive for the merging of investment and commercial banking services.[11]

Misallocation of Capital

Some economists reason that merging commercial and investment bank activities would foster a more efficient and equitable allocation of funds. Evidence from the financial sector points to the systematic exclusion of small and medium-sized businesses from the underwriting process. Though investment banks actively pursue the business of large companies, the cost of an underwriting may be prohibitive to a small firm. As a result, small firms have limited financing alternatives and frequently end up borrowing from commercial banks.

Unfortunately, most business loans tend to be short term. By matching the maturity of their assets to the maturity of their liabilities, banks can avoid exposure to interest rate risk. They can also keep a tighter leash on a firm's business activity, an important factor in reducing risk. The danger is that banks' short-term focus may force entrepreneurs to bypass opportunities that they would willingly undertake if they had a source of long-term capital such as the bond market. When the structure of the financial system works against small businesses, entrepreneurial incentives are distorted and the economy suffers.

Allowing commercial banks to underwrite corporate securities would solve this problem. It would place long-term financing decision in the hands of banks that have large amounts of information about firms that has been obtained through their working relationship with them. Since commercial banks already have information about firms,

---

[11]Though many of these studies have failed to find "global" economies of scope, which encompass the entire range of financial services and products, a sizable portion of the literature reports the existence of economies of scope among smaller groups of financial products. These "cost complementarities" can provide an incentive for the merging of commercial and investment banking.

the cost savings to firms could be substantial. Increased competition in underwriting would also translate into a more efficient market for securities.

Conflicts of Interest

A strong rationale for the Glass-Steagall Act was the belief that commingling banking and investment functions produced significant conflicts of interest. Critics charged that commercial banks had taken advantage of unsophisticated investors and bank customers by misrepresenting the risk characteristics of the securities they underwrote. Banks had also exhibited a tendency to place low-quality securities that were difficult to market in their commercial customers' trust accounts, exposing them to undue risk. These claims were not unique to the period; the potential for conflict of interest exists in nearly all financial transactions. Even today, commercial banks may encourage businesses to borrow from them rather than finance a project through an underwriter. And securities firms have a vested interest in counseling clients to purchase securities they themselves have underwritten.

Potential conflicts of interest, then, may not constitute a valid reason for maintaining the distinction between commercial and investment banking. The problem is one that may be dealt with more effectively by regulating certain types of activity, rather than by prohibiting all activity. Furthermore, many problems could be better dealt with if banking and underwriting were both available at the same facility. For example, a bank is more likely to give sound advice to a potential business borrower if that bank can offer both commercial loans *and* underwriting services. And small savers are more likely to get sound investment advice if their bank can offer mutual funds, stocks, and bonds in addition to traditional savings and time deposit accounts.

A recent study actually noted a major *benefit* of potential conflicts of interest. After studying the risk characteristics of securities underwritten by commercial banks in the 1920s, researchers concluded that the securities underwritten by commercial banks were of higher quality and lower default risk than the securities underwritten by investment banks. Apparently, the commercial banks' desire to reduce potential conflicts of interest had caused them to underwrite safer grades of assets because depositors were monitoring their activities. Thus, the merging of commercial and investment banking may serve to reduce the risk of securities offerings.

SUMMARY

From the earliest days of the United States, popular sentiment has viewed the financial sector with suspicion and mistrust. To prevent the concentration of power, banks have been limited as to where and how they may operate. But in the past 15 years, we have seen innovation and legal evolution change the nature of the banking industry. The depth and scope of services offered to-

day are staggering compared to those of just a short time ago. New institutions, mergers, products, and legislation have affected not only the banks themselves but virtually every consumer and firm that partakes of banking services. Proposals have recently surfaced to change the manner in which the financial sector is regulated. Consolidating regulatory responsibilities would reduce overlapping supervision, substantially decreasing information-gathering and overhead costs. Furthermore, proponents argue, the current lack of coordination between agencies leads to oversights and the inequitable treatment of banks.

The last 15 years have seen a gradual evolution in the restrictions on branch banking. Relaxation of restrictions at the state level essentially superseded the McFadden Act. A wave of recent mergers has greatly increased size and concentration in the banking industry. Passage of the Riegle-Neal Act of 1994 has made free interstate banking a reality. But economists remain uncertain about the true motivation behind the recent wave of mergers and consolidations. The existing explanations for this trend—economies of scale, portfolio diversification, executive compensation, and

monopoly power—can only partly account for what we are observing.

Finally, the dividing line between commercial and investment banking put into place by the Glass-Steagall Act is eroding, and arguments for the act's repeal are becoming increasingly compelling. Repeal of the act would allow banks to take advantage of economies of scope and reduce discrimination against small and medium-sized firms. However, advocates of the status quo point to the potential for excessive risk taking on the part of bankers and the potential for conflicts of interest. Sweeping changes are expected in bank regulation, structure, and activity. With so much potential for gain, future changes are certain to be even more dramatic than those of the past 15 years.

KEY TERMS

Bank of the United States
Second Bank of the United States
unit banking
Free Banking Era
National Banking Act of 1863
dual banking system
investment bank
Banking Act of 1933 (Glass-Steagall Act)
Comptroller of the Currency
Federal Banking Commission

McFadden Act
limited branching
bank holding company
Bank Holding Company Act of 1956
Riegle-Neal Interstate Banking and Branching Efficiency Act of 1994
economies of scale
diseconomies of scale
economies of scope

STUDY QUESTIONS

1 Why were the founding fathers so firmly opposed to big banks? What legislation stemmed from their viewpoint? Are Americans today as opposed to big banking as their ancestors were?

2 What is the dual banking system? Why did it develop?

3 Describe the economic forces that triggered the passage of the Glass-Steagall Act. Was the act a natural reaction to circumstances? What provisions of the act deal directly with problems encountered during the 1920s and 1930s?

4 Why might the FDIC have more interest in maintaining its supervisory power over banks than the Comptroller of the Currency or the Federal Reserve does?

5 Discuss the advantages and disadvantages of the Treasury's "one regulator" plan, proposed in 1995.

6 Enumerate the forces that are driving the trend toward bank mergers and consolidations, and discuss each briefly. Is there a consensus on which forces are most important?

7 How do economies of scale differ from economies of scope? How are they similar? How might both pertain to the trend toward bank mergers and consolidations?

8 Explain how changes in the legal environment have contributed to the explosion of bank mergers. How might the banking crisis of the late 1980s have contributed?

9 Have there been any disadvantages to you, the consumer, in the liberalization of branch banking?

10 What reasons are given for repealing the Glass-Steagall Act? Is there any potential benefit to you, the consumer?

11 "Since the United States has so many more banks than other nations, U.S. banking must be more competitive." Analyze.

SUGGESTIONS FOR ADDITIONAL READING

A number of fine books detail the history of the U.S. banking system, including Benjamin Klebaner's *Commercial Banking in the United States: A History* (Hinsdale, Ill.: Dryden Press, 1974). For an opposing view on the free banking era, consult Arthur Rolnick and Warren Weber, "The Free Banking Era: New Evidence on Laissez-Faire Banking," *American Economic Review*, 1983, pp. 1080–1091. A concise description of Clinton's regulatory plan and its pros and cons is presented in Robert D. Hankins, "Treasury's Single Regulator Plan Could Create More Problems Than It Solves," Federal Reserve Bank of Dallas *Financial Industry Issues*, 1 (1994). Economies of scale and scope are both critically examined in Jeffrey A. Clark, "Economies of Scale and Scope at Depository Financial Institutions: A Review of the Literature," Federal Reserve Bank of Kansas City *Economic Review*, September–October 1988. Elizabeth Laderman examines portfolio diversification in "Location, Branching, and Bank Portfolio Diversification: The Case of Agricultural Lending," Federal Reserve Bank of San Francisco *Economic Review*, Winter 1991, pp. 24–38. An excellent review of the forces behind bank mergers is John Boyd and Stanley Graham, "Investigating the Banking Consolidation Trend," Federal Reserve Bank of Minneapolis *Quarterly Review*, Spring 1991, pp. 3–15. The recent history of the U.S. banking structure and the impact of changes on consumers and the macroeconomy is thoroughly discussed in Allen Berger, Anil Kashyap, and Joseph Scalise, "The Transformation of the U.S. Banking Industry: What a Long, Strange Trip It's Been," *Brookings Papers on Economic Activity,* 2 (1995), pp. 55–218. Historical rationales for Glass-Steagall are presented and debated in "The Underwriting of Commercial Bank Affiliates Prior to the Glass-Steagall Act: A Re-examination of Evidence for Passage of the Act," *Journal of Banking and Finance,* 1994, p. 351. Benjamin Stein examines the cons of merging commercial and investment banking in "You Can Bank on It: Without Glass-Steagall, History Will Repeat," *Barron's,* February 4, 1991. Sean Becketti discusses the derivatives question in "Are Derivatives Too Risky for Banks?," Federal Reserve Bank of Kansas City *Economic Review,* 3d quarter, 1993. Finally, James L. Pierce offers an overview of what our banking industry could potentially become in *The Future of Banking* (New Haven: Yale University Press, 1991).

■
The Savings and Loan Debacle, Commercial Bank Failures, and Deposit Insurance

I n Chapters 4, 9, and 10, we discussed the nature and structure of U.S. depository institutions ("banks"), with particular emphasis on commercial banks. We outlined the sources and uses of bank funds, the constraints that limit a bank's acquisition of earning assets, and the types of risk banks are exposed to. We discussed the nature and functions of the capital accounts and the trade-off between risk and the short-term returns earned by depository institutions. Such analyses apply not only to commercial banks but to thrift institutions such as savings and loan (S&L) associations as well.

In this chapter, we will discuss the events that impaired the financial condition of both the savings and loan industry and the commercial banking sector in the 1980s and early 1990s. We will emphasize the underlying economic causes of those bank failures and the role of the regulatory apparatus in general, and the deposit insurance system in particular, in contributing to the problem. We will argue that, given the regulatory mechanisms and deposit insurance system in place at the time, the depository institutions fiasco—especially the S&L disaster—was essentially an accident waiting to happen. In retrospect, it is surprising that the crisis did not happen sooner. Finally, in light of the S&L and commercial bank problems of the past 15 to 20 years, we will discuss the implications of the crisis for the design of regulatory policy and deposit insurance in the future.

One of the lessons of this chapter is that the financial system is not static. It is best viewed as a system in a state of continual evolution, driven by continuing financial innovation and economic events. Look at Table 11-1, which summarizes the key financial legislation enacted in the United States in this century, beginning with the Federal Reserve Act of 1913. An examination of this table indicates that a common pattern is that problems arise from time to time and result in the imposition of "solutions" in the form of legislation. Though these solutions typically take care of the initial problem, they also frequently produce other adverse consequences unforeseen by those who enact the legislation. A few examples may be illustrative.

One example is the creation of the Federal Reserve System, which helped to prevent the severe macroeconomic disruptions caused by widespread banking panics— with the glaring exception of the early 1930s. But together with the Employment Act

Table 11-1

Key Twentieth-Century Financial Legislation

Federal Reserve Act (1913)
Created the Federal Reserve System

Banking Acts of 1933 (Glass-Steagall) and 1935
Created the Federal Deposit Insurance Corporation (FDIC)
Restricted checkable deposits to commercial banks
Prohibited interest payments on checkable deposits
Placed interest rate ceilings on savings and time deposits
Separated commercial banking from the securities industry

Depository Institutions Deregulation and Monetary Control Act of 1980 (DIDMCA)
Phased out deposit rate ceilings
Authorized NOW and ATS accounts nationwide for commercial banks and thrifts
Broadened permissible activities of thrift institutions
Imposed uniform reserve requirements on all depository institutions
Increased FDIC deposit insurance from $40,000 to $100,000 per account

Depository Institutions Act of 1982 (Garn–St. Germain Act)
Further broadened the permissible range of activities of thrift institutions
Authorized depository institutions to issue money market deposit accounts
Granted FDIC and Federal Savings and Loan Insurance Corporation (FSLIC) emergency powers to
    merge troubled thrifts and banks

Competitive Equality in Banking Act of 1987 (CEBA)
Granted $10.8 billion to increase FSLIC insurance fund
Authorized regulatory forbearance in depressed areas

Financial Institutions Reform, Recovery, and Enforcement Act of 1989 (FIRREA)
Abolished the FSLIC and Federal Home Loan Bank Board
Created the Office of Thrift Supervision (OTS) to regulate thrifts
Created the Resolution Trust Corporation (RTC) to resolve insolvent thrifts
Provided funds to resolve failures of thrift institutions
Reimposed restrictions on S&L activities
Increased insurance premiums for depository institutions

Federal Deposit Insurance Corporation Improvement Act of 1991 (FDICIA)
Recapitalized the FDIC
Established provisions for prompt resolution of impaired depository institutions
Increased capital requirements for banks and thrifts
Limited brokered deposits
Moderated "too-big-to-fail" policy
Mandated that the FDIC establish risk-based deposit insurance premiums
Increased the Federal Reserve's authority to supervise foreign banks in the United States

of 1946, it tended to build an inflationary bias into the U.S. economy. Another example is the **Banking Act of 1933,** which sought to bolster the financial condition of banks impaired by the Great Depression by prohibiting the payment of interest on checking accounts and limiting the interest rates payable on savings and time deposits. Those restrictions contributed to instability in the housing sector in the 1970s and had to be removed in the 1980s to avoid bankrupting thousands of depository institutions. The same act also provided for federal insurance of bank deposits to reduce the occurrence of banking panics. While it succeeded in doing so, the deposit insurance it created also tended to encourage the excessive risk taking that depository institutions engaged in during the 1980s. Finally, the **Garn–St. Germain Act** of 1982, which partially deregulated the thrift industry to enable it to compete with money market mutual funds and other industries, also triggered a massive increase in risk taking in the industry. It thus contributed to the insolvencies of hundreds of S&Ls, costing taxpayers some $140 billion. Garn–St. Germain led, in turn, to the Financial Institutions Reform, Recovery, and Enforcement Act of 1989 (FIRREA). A good exercise would be to examine the provisions of the act (see Table 11-1) to see if it is likely to produce any adverse consequences in the future.

Several lessons may be drawn from the history of the legislation we have just examined. First, given the near certainty of continuing financial innovations and changing economic conditions, financial institutions must not be prevented from adapting to change by artificial constraints such as interest rate ceilings and unnecessary restrictions on the types of activity in which they are allowed to engage. (We will argue, however, that certain restrictions are necessary.) Second, regulations must be designed so as to minimize exposure to the *moral hazard* problem—that is, the incentive for institutions to take actions that are socially detrimental. This lesson implies that depository institutions must be required to maintain a substantial amount of their own equity at stake in order to minimize the incentive to take unnecessary risks. When such equity is perilously thin, these institutions must be closed or at least carefully monitored. Furthermore, deposit insurance should be designed to discourage excessive risk taking by depository institutions. The deposit insurance premiums that are levied on any one depository institution should reflect the degree of risk it engages in. Incentives can also be given to depositors to avoid institutions that take excessive risk, a tactic that requires that at least some depositors be subject to losses in the event an institution becomes insolvent.

Finally, history has shown that a stable macroeconomic environment is essential to a healthy financial system. Exposure to severe economic shocks triggers distress in depository institutions. It is therefore imperative that monetary and fiscal policies contribute to an environment of economic stability based on relatively low and stable inflation. That topic is the subject of Parts 4 and 5 of this book.

We will begin by analyzing the S&L crisis, which, by the time it was resolved at the end of 1995, had cost U.S. taxpayers approximately $140 billion. We will then turn to the problems experienced in the commercial banking sector in the late 1980s and early 1990s. Finally, we will outline general principles and specific proposals aimed at minimizing the likelihood of a recurrence of these costly episodes.

SAVINGS AND LOAN FAILURES

The Savings and Loan Disaster of the 1980s

In the latter half of the twentieth century, two separate crises struck the S&L industry. The first was caused by the macroeconomic forces of severe inflation and recession, which impaired S&L income statements and balance sheets in the late 1970s and early 1980s. The second and more damaging crisis was provoked by the response of Congress, the Reagan administration, and the regulatory authorities to the first crisis. We will argue that government policy decisions severely compounded the initial crisis and were largely responsible for the S&L fiasco.

Flaws in the Original S&L Structure

It must be emphasized at the outset that the S&L concept was fundamentally flawed from the beginning. Government fostered savings and loan associations in the 1930s as a way to encourage homeownership among middle-class Americans. The **Federal Home Loan Bank Board (FHLBB)** was established by Congress to regulate the S&Ls, and its subsidiary—the **Federal Savings and Loan Insurance Corporation (FSLIC)**—was created to insure S&L deposits. The S&Ls were to issue short-term savings deposits to the public and use the proceeds to grant 20- and 30-year mortgages to local homebuyers at interest rates guaranteed to remain constant over the life of the mortgage.

Clearly, if the interest rates paid to depositors were ever to rise above the average interest rate earned on an S&L's portfolio of mortgages, the institution would lose money. If the situation were to persist for a lengthy period, an S&L's capital could be wiped out, rendering the institution insolvent. In borrowing short and lending long, S&Ls were inherently vulnerable to rising interest rates and inverted yield curves—that is, periods in which short-term yields exceed long-term yields. Because government regulations prevented S&Ls from diversifying their assets, requiring them instead to confine themselves predominantly to fixed-rate mortgages, there was no way for them to get out of this trap.

For approximately four decades, the S&L industry was stable and prosperous. From the 1930s to the mid-1960s, interest rates were low and stable and the yield curve was almost always upward sloping. Life was simple in those stable, low-inflation times. Outsiders joked enviously about the "3-6-3" lifestyle enjoyed by S&L managers—borrow at 3 percent, lend at 6 percent, and head for the golf course at 3:00 P.M.! Unfortunately, in the mid-1970s, interest rates began to trend upward. At first the increase was mild and gradual, so S&Ls did not suffer major problems. But then, in the late 1970s, all hell broke loose!

The Effects of Rising Inflation and Interest Rates

In the late 1970s, rising inflation exerted upward pressure on interest rates (through the Fisher effect, analyzed in Chapter 5), moving them well above the ceiling rates thrifts were permitted to pay depositors. To avert a severe episode of *disintermediation,* the regulatory authorities authorized banks to issue money market certificates, a new instrument issued in $10,000 denominations that permitted banks and thrifts to match the yield on 6-month Treasury bills. In early 1980, banks and thrifts were authorized to issue 2½-year floating-rate certificates, which were intended to compete with 2½-year Treasury notes. Passage of the **Depository Institutions Deregulation and Monetary Control Act (DIDMCA)** in 1980 provided that interest rate ceilings would be phased out over a 6-year period ending in March 1986.

While these regulatory changes allowed S&Ls to stave off disintermediation, they did not address the fundamental problem, which was that the assets of S&Ls were composed predominantly of fixed-rate mortgages, the bulk of which had been issued several years in the past and still had many years to run. Contractual agreements specified that the S&Ls could not increase interest rates charged on fixed-rate mortgages already outstanding.[1] Now suppose thrift institutions require a 1 percent "spread"—the difference between the yield earned on assets and the cost of obtaining funds—to meet their operating expenses and remain profitable. Suppose also that the average return on the existing mortgage portfolio is 10 percent. Clearly, if S&Ls are forced to pay more than 9 percent to obtain funds, they will incur losses.

Because the S&Ls' asset structures were heavily weighted with old, relatively low-interest fixed-rate mortgages, it could take years to pull the average return on the mortgage portfolio up by a full percentage point. Any increase in the cost of funds, which is payable to *all* depositors, could be shifted only onto *new* homebuyers. This problem was compounded by the fact that new homebuyers are sensitive to mortgage rates. They postpone buying homes when mortgage rates are high, a phenomenon that prevented S&Ls from pulling up their average returns quickly by dramatically jacking up interest rates on new mortgages. Obviously, periods of sharply rising interest rates pose a serious problem for S&Ls, given the way they have historically been structured. Again, federal regulations *required* S&Ls to invest most of their funds in fixed-rate mortgages.

In sum, we see that the financial instability of thrift institutions prior to 1982 was caused not by interest rate ceilings on deposits but rather by the forces that exerted a strong upward pressure on interest rates, together with the legally mandated structure of thrift institutions.[2] The high interest rates of the 1970s and early 1980s had several causes. Most instrumental were stimulative macroeconomic policies, which contributed to rising inflation in the late 1960s, and two dramatic oil price hikes (in 1973 and 1979), which fueled inflation through the 1970s.

The Squeeze on S&Ls' Profits

Figure 11-1 illustrates the recent historical relationship between the interest rate earned by S&Ls on new mortgages and the yield on U.S. Treasury bills. The Treasury bill yield may be thought of as a proxy for the yield S&Ls need to pay depositors to remain competitive with money market mutual funds—and thus prevent them from fleeing to MMMFs.

---

[1] Federally chartered S&Ls were first authorized to issue adjustable-rate mortgages (ARMs) in spring 1981. In an ARM, the mortgage rate is adjusted periodically (typically once per year) in line with the changes in some benchmark interest rate, such as the yield on 1-year Treasury notes.

[2] If interest rate ceilings had been kept in place through the 1980s rather than being phased out by DIDMCA, massive outflows of funds from thrifts to money market mutual funds would likely have bankrupted hundreds or thousands of S&Ls. Thrifts would have been forced to liquidate mortgages at low prices in order to obtain funds to pay out to depositors. The losses on mortgages would have depleted their capital, rendering them insolvent.

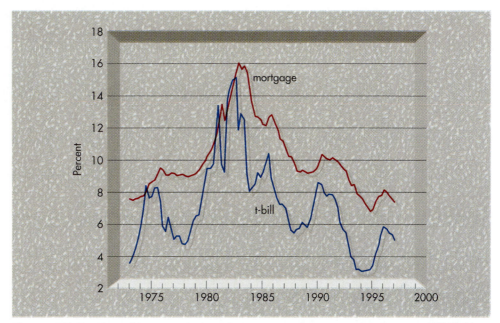

Figure 11-1   Home Mortgage Interest Rates versus the 1-Year U.S. Treasury Bill Yield, 1972–1996. In the period 1977–1981, short-term interest rates increased sharply relative to the interest rate on newly issued mortgages. This impaired the financial condition of S&Ls.   *Source: Citibank Economic Database.*

The figure illustrates the dramatic upsurge in short-term interest rates during 1977 to 1981. Note that although the rate on new mortgages also increased sharply, the *differential* between the new mortgage rate and the Treasury bill yield was virtually eliminated for about 2 years, beginning in late 1979. Furthermore, the figure significantly understates the severity of the problem faced by S&Ls, inasmuch as the average yield earned on the *entire* S&L mortgage portfolio lags behind the rate on *new* mortgages. In 1981, the spread between the yield earned on total assets and the cost of funds for the S&L industry was a *negative* 0.8 percent.[3]

This negative spread, together with the losses associated with loan defaults during the 1980 and 1981–1982 recessions, caused the S&L industry to experience huge operating losses in 1981 and 1982. The financial pressures on S&Ls in the early 1980s were severe. Industry operating losses were $6 billion in 1981 and $5 billion in 1982. Approximately 85 percent of all S&Ls lost money in 1981, and 68 percent lost money in 1982. Figure 11-2 illustrates the income performance of the S&L industry from 1970 to 1985 in terms of the annual rate of return earned on total assets (industry profits divided

---

[3]Note, however, that short-term yields decreased sharply after 1981, reinstating the positive spread between mortgage rates and Treasury bill rates. If S&Ls had retained their conservative posture during this period, limiting themselves to mortgage lending, they would likely have muddled through and regained their financial strength in the mid-1980s. Instead, a new element, big-time risk taking, came into play and became a decisive force in the S&L fiasco.

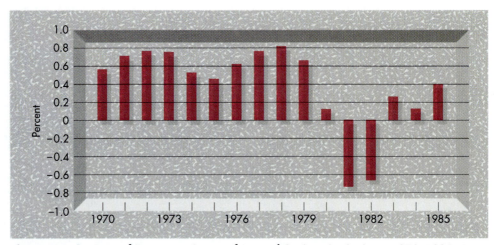

Figure 11-2 Rate of Return on Assets of Insured Savings Institutions, 1970–1985. During the 1970s, the return on assets earned by S&Ls averaged about 0.6 percent per year. In 1981 and 1982, this rate of return was sharply negative. *Source:* Federal Deposit Insurance Corporation.

by total assets). Note that while this return averaged approximately 0.6 percent per year in the 1970s, it swung strongly into negative territory in the early 1980s.

In addition to the short-term problems caused by the rapid escalation of interest rates during 1977–1981, the S&L industry faced long-term structural problems caused by financial innovations. In the late 1970s, increasing competition from newly emerged money market mutual funds meant that S&Ls had to pay more for their deposits than they would have had to otherwise. Financial innovations also squeezed S&Ls on the asset side of their balance sheets. The securitization of mortgages caused pension funds and life insurance companies to increase their demand for these mortgage instruments significantly, thereby reducing mortgage rates. While beneficial to the consumer, these forces produced a reduction in the S&L "spread." This phenomenon signaled a contraction of the S&L industry, independently of the short-term crisis caused by surging interest rates. By the end of 1982, about one-fourth of the S&Ls that had been operating in the 1970s—some 800 institutions—were gone.[4] Some had been closed down, others merged with stronger institutions. Estimates indicate that the net worth of the industry declined from approximately $32 billion in 1979 to only $4 billion by the end of 1982, before rebounding.[5]

---

[4]Today there are fewer than 1500 S&Ls in the United States, down from some 3900 in 1970.

[5]In December 1981, the low point of S&Ls' valuation, a widely quoted estimate put the net worth of the S&L industry at *minus* $100 billion. This estimate was derived by estimating the value of S&Ls' assets at the point when interest rates were at all-time peak levels (and bond and mortgage prices were at corresponding lows). The 1980–1981 spike in interest rates *temporarily* put the net worth of the S&L industry at an all-time low (negative) level. Two years later, after interest rates had come down sharply, the increase in bond and mortgage values returned the industry's net worth to a positive level.

The Government's Response to the Savings and Loans' Problems

The response of the U.S. government to the financial problems encountered by the S&Ls in the early 1980s consisted of three principal elements: deregulation, forbearance, and inadequate funding for the supervision of the financially impaired industry. Coupled with the existence (and expansion) of federal deposit insurance coverage, this response turned out to be very costly to the nation.

Deregulation   Because the first heavy losses S&Ls suffered in the early 1980s were essentially caused by government policies that had handcuffed the S&Ls from the very beginning and then caused inflation to escalate after the mid-1960s, strong sentiment prevailed to implement legislation allowing S&Ls to compete on a level playing field. In 1982, Congress implemented the Garn–St. Germain Depository Institutions Act, which accelerated the deregulation of the S&Ls (begun under the Depository Institutions Deregulation and Monetary Control Act of 1980) by authorizing them to issue money market deposit accounts without interest ceilings in order to compete with money market mutual funds. The act also broadened the powers of S&Ls by authorizing them to make loans to consumers, businesses, and the commercial real estate sector.

In order to make sure their institutions were not at a disadvantage relative to federally chartered S&Ls, several state legislatures went to extremes in deregulating their state-chartered thrifts. In Texas, California, and Florida, S&Ls were almost totally deregulated. These institutions were permitted to invest in junk bonds, windmill farms, and real estate ventures in the desert. Not surprisingly, a large portion of the losses incurred in the S&L industry involved state-chartered institutions in Texas, California, and Florida (see Exhibit 11-3 on page 268). While most economists had long advocated major deregulation of the financial sector, Garn–St. Germain could not have been implemented at a more inopportune time. It was enacted when most of the S&Ls in the United States were technically insolvent and therefore eager to engage in increased risk taking.

Had Congress deregulated the thrift institutions a decade earlier, the entire S&L fiasco might have been avoided. In 1971, the Hunt Commission (a bipartisan group appointed by President Nixon) had recommended a series of measures to deregulate the nation's depository institutions. It recommended eliminating interest rate ceilings, broadening the range of permissible lending activities, and approving adjustable-rate mortgages. But at that time the thrift industry was quite prosperous and did not support the deregulation of interest rates payable on deposits. Nor did the public embrace adjustable-rate mortgages. Unfortunately, Congress bowed to the political winds and ignored the Hunt Commission's recommendations until it was too late.

Forbearance   Instead of closing down or merging insolvent S&Ls, the regulatory authorities decided to keep these institutions operating in the hope that better times would restore them to health. This policy was given the pleasant name **forbearance.** Closing or merging all S&Ls that were technically insolvent in 1982 or 1983 would have exhausted the entire FSLIC insurance fund. This would have necessitated substantial taxpayer assistance, raising embarrassing questions about the competence of the regulatory authorities and their congressional overseers. So the government opted to let most of the insolvent S&Ls continue to operate. In each year of the critical period from 1983 through 1989, more than 400 insolvent S&Ls were open for business.

To practice the policy of forbearance, the regulatory authorities first liberalized the accounting standards in the S&L industry. Even with the more lenient accounting standards in place, as conditions in the industry deteriorated in the early 1980s, the authorities reduced **capital standards**—the minimum required ratio of capital to total assets—first from 5 percent to 4 percent in 1980, then to 3 percent in 1982. This reduction in capital standards increased the moral hazard problem. With less of their own equity at stake, S&Ls had an incentive to take more risks because they had less to lose if things went wrong.

Deposit insurance also contributed to the moral hazard problem. If potential losses are fully covered by insurance, the insured has little incentive to avoid the event insured against. For this reason, that event is more likely to occur. (For example, if an individual has theft insurance, he or she has less incentive to install an expensive alarm system in the home or car. Thus theft insurance increases the number of thefts that occur.) Once depositors are insured against the failure of their commercial bank or S&L, they have no incentive to keep an eye on the institution to see if it is behaving prudently. In raising federal deposit insurance from $40,000 to $100,000 per account in 1980, Congress inadvertently signaled thousands of additional depositors that they could safely ignore the activities of their S&L or bank. By increasing the deposit insurance level, Congress thus increased the number of bank failures.

Perhaps more important, the increase in deposit insurance coverage helped trigger a socially costly financial innovation known as **brokered deposits.** Brokerage firms such as Merrill Lynch took multimillion-dollar blocks of funds, broke them down into fully insured $100,000 lots, and sold them to depository institutions as CDs. By paying a slightly higher interest rate than other institutions, an insolvent S&L could attract a large amount of funds with which to grow (or gamble) itself out of insolvency. (On the role of brokered deposits in boosting risk taking, see Exhibit 11-1.)

As thousands of S&Ls became financially impaired in the early 1980s, they had powerful incentives to take additional risks to shoot for higher returns that would strengthen their financial position. The most impaired institutions had the most incentive to take long risks. If an S&L is on the brink of insolvency, it bears no downside risk. If owners have none of their own equity at stake, the situation becomes a "heads we win, tails the government loses" proposition. Because such an increase in risk taking is highly predictable in such circumstances, one must ask why the regulatory authorities permitted it to take place.

Inadequate Funding for S&L Supervisors and the FSLIC

In view of the moral hazard problem, it is unfortunate that the Reagan administration and the regulatory authorities (the FHLBB and FSLIC) did not move aggressively to close the insolvent S&Ls or at least to impose strong surveillance on the activities of the **zombie institutions,** insolvent S&Ls that were still in operation. Instead, the administration denied requests for increased funding for S&L examiners, delayed a request for funds to bolster the sagging FSLIC insurance fund, and generally swept the problem under the rug.

Finally, in 1986, as increasing losses threatened to bankrupt the FSLIC insurance fund, the Reagan administration requested $15 billion from Congress. Though the sum requested was only a fraction of what was needed to close down the insolvent S&Ls, Congress granted only $10.8 billion to the FSLIC in the Competitive Equality in Banking Act of 1987. The act perversely ordered the FHLBB to continue the policy of regu-

EXHIBIT 11-1

The Moral Hazard of Deposit Insurance and Brokered Deposits

An important problem with insurance of any kind is *moral hazard.* Once insured, one has less incentive to take measures to prevent the loss one is insured against. For example, if you purchase fire insurance on your home, you have less incentive to make costly improvements to make the house fireproof. The same principle holds for deposit insurance. Once my deposit is insured, I am no longer concerned about the financial condition of my bank, because even if it fails, I do not lose anything.

Suppose High-Tech Corporation has $100 million to invest in short-term interest-bearing financial assets. Safety is uppermost in the mind of management. To minimize risk, one normally has to accept a modest rate of return. However, in the 1980s, the combination of deposit insurance, insolvent and desperate S&Ls, and brokered deposits allowed lenders to circumvent the trade-off between risk and return. With deposit insurance, High-Tech could earn enormous returns on fully insured (riskless) CDs.

Suppose Merrill Lynch, the big brokerage house, takes High-Tech's $100 million and packages it into a thousand $100,000 parcels, which it sells off to depository institutions that are willing to pay very high interest rates to attract the funds to finance rapid growth. By spreading the $100 million among many banks, Merrill Lynch keeps the funds fully insured (the federal deposit insurance ceiling is $100,000 per account). Suppose that one of the parcels is bought by the financially troubled Smalltown Bank, which was formerly limited in its ability to attract funds by its small local economic base and its inability to issue large CDs. By bidding aggressively for brokered deposits, the insolvent but operating Smalltown Bank is able to attract an almost unlimited amount of funds with which to finance risky ventures. Smalltown seeks out High-Tech's funds to finance risky investments, hoping to earn high returns and pull itself out of insolvency. From High-Tech's vantage point, the risk Smalltown Bank is taking with its money is beside the point, because Smalltown's deposits are fully insured.

Many of the S&Ls that failed in the 1980s were a lot like Smalltown Bank. Whether such banks were in poor shape to begin with or just always aspired to be high rollers, brokered deposits facilitated an enormous increase in risk taking. At least one of three conditions must exist if depository institutions are to be prevented from taking excessive risks: they must have a large amount of their own capital at stake; depositors must have a vested interest in the financial condition of their bank; or the regulatory authorities must carefully regulate and monitor banks in order to keep risk taking in check. In the United States in the 1980s, all three conditions were frequently absent. That explains the S&L fiasco.

Where did all the S&L "bailout" money go? Part of it is represented by vacant (and perhaps now bulldozed) apartment buildings in Texas and defunct shopping centers in the desert. But a significant portion went to lenders like High-Tech Corporation, which collected untenably high returns on investments that were totally without risk to them because of the existence of brokered deposits and deposit insurance. While High-Tech and other lenders picked up the marbles, the taxpayers picked up the tab. Much of the bailout can be viewed as a redistribution of wealth from the taxpayers to the big lenders, who, together with Merrill Lynch and others who created brokered deposits, milked the system and bilked the taxpayers.

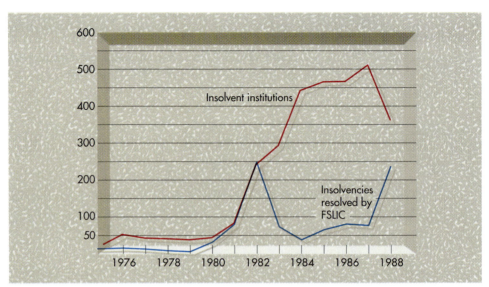

Figure 11-3 **Estimated Number of Insolvencies and Resolved Insolvencies at FSLIC-Insured Institutions, 1975–1988.** After 1981, the number of insolvent S&Ls that were still operating increased dramatically. The government was slow to resolve insolvencies by closing or merging failed S&Ls. *Source:* Federal Deposit Insurance Corporation.

latory forbearance, at least in certain depressed areas. Figure 11-3 illustrates the discrepancy between the total number of insolvent institutions and the number of insolvencies resolved by the FSLIC in the critical years from 1982–1988, when most of the damage was done. Hundreds of insolvent S&Ls were permitted to remain open for several years. Not until the Bush administration took office in early 1989 was the S&L problem brought out into the open. Legislation was then quickly enacted for the purpose of closing down insolvent S&Ls and reducing the chance of a recurrence of the problem.

Legislative Reform

In August 1989, the most comprehensive piece of legislation to affect the thrift industry since the 1930s was enacted. The **Financial Institutions Reform, Recovery, and Enforcement Act (FIRREA)** abolished both the FHLBB and the FSLIC, both of which had demonstrated ample justification to warrant their termination. A new bureau within the Treasury Department, the Office of Thrift Supervision (OTS), replaced the FHLBB, and the FDIC took over the regulatory functions of the FSLIC. Two new insurance funds were created: the Bank Insurance Fund (BIF) for commercial banks and the Savings Association Insurance Fund (SAIF) for thrift institutions. FIRREA also created the Resolution Trust Corporation (RTC) for the purpose of managing and resolving insolvent thrift institutions and liquidating the assets of failed institutions. By the time the RTC closed its doors for good at the end of 1995—a year ahead of schedule—it had disposed of 747 bankrupt or ailing S&Ls and recovered more than 85 percent of the thrift institution assets (valued at $450 billion) it had inherited from failed thrift institutions. Rather

EXHIBIT 11-2 (CONTINUED)

- *Regulatory authorities.* Because closing insolvent S&Ls after 1982 would have bankrupted the FSLIC and wrecked the careers of many government officials, regulatory authorities implemented their costly policy of forbearance—that is, of letting bankrupt S&Ls continue to operate in the hope that they might recover. In doing so, authorities engaged in the same act as the impaired S&Ls: they gambled that the industry would be bailed out by improving economic conditions. The FSLIC also disguised the deteriorating condition of its insurance fund from Congress and the public.

- *Big accounting firms.* By law, government must shut down insolvent depository institutions. But insolvency is a gray area; it depends on how various assets of an institution are valued. Accounting firms engaged in "creative accounting"—that is, they cooked the books, allowing insolvent S&Ls to keep operating.

- *The Reagan administration.* The administration's large income tax cuts, unaccompanied by expenditure cuts, ushered in an era of large budget deficits which in the early 1980s kept interest rates high. The administration was also overzealous in its pursuit of deregulation, confusing the general merits of deregulation with the propriety of permitting a deregulated and insolvent industry to go unsupervised. Finally, the administration acquiesced in a cover-up of the problem. Only in 1989, after President Bush was inaugurated, was the S&L problem brought out into the open.

- *The Federal Reserve.* The Fed's stimulative monetary policy, coupled with two dramatic oil price increases, contributed to escalating inflation in the late 1970s, which boosted interest rates and helped to create the initial S&L crisis. To fight inflation, the Fed tightened its policy dramatically, contributing to the severity of the 1981–1982 recession, when many borrowers defaulted on loans. The "double whammy" of high interest rates and severe recession crippled the S&L industry and set the stage for the mistakes that followed.

- *The deposit insurance system.* Depositors who were insured against losses had an incentive to place their funds in the riskiest, most financially impaired S&Ls, because those institutions paid the highest interest rates. In 1980, the increase in deposit insurance from $40,000 to $100,000 increased S&Ls' ability to attract "hot money" through brokered deposits. That in turn encouraged risk taking among S&Ls.

- *The S&L industry.* Even honest S&L executives share some blame. S&Ls made major campaign contributions in return for such favors as postponing needed increases in deposit insurance premiums, easing capital requirements, and delaying removal of the management of insolvent S&Ls. Also, many S&L managers were ill prepared to function effectively in the new, more wide-open financial environment of the 1980s.

- *The economics profession.* Because economists are acutely aware of the merits of competitive markets, most of them wholeheartedly supported the deregulation of the S&Ls. Few recognized the dangers of fraud and unhealthy risk taking in an industry that was in a weakened state and in which budgets of supervisory authorities were woefully inadequate. Most economists supported the removal of interest rate ceilings, neglecting to consider the possibility that high-rolling S&L managers might bid funds away from conservative, safe institutions.

COMMERCIAL BANK FAILURES

The Escalation of Bank Failures in the 1980s

In the 1980s and early 1990s, the financial condition of the U.S. banking system was adversely impacted by a series of financial innovations and macroeconomic shocks that impaired commercial banks' income statements and balance sheets. The number of banks on the regulatory authorities' "problem list" increased from around 200 in 1980 and 1981 to more than 1400 in 1986. The capital position of thousands of banks deteriorated as bank officers wrote off bad loans and increased their loan loss reserves. The strained financial conditions increased the moral hazard problem, prompting an increase in bank risk taking of the sort that contributed to the S&L disaster, although much less extreme. In the 1980s, bank failures reached the highest levels since the early 1930s. Let us look more closely at the causes of commercial bank distress.

The Effects of Financial Innovations and Regulatory Actions

Partly because of the protection afforded by regulations, commercial banks prospered in the period from the Great Depression of the 1930s to the mid-1970s. Thousands of local banks were protected from competition on their own turf by the restrictions on branch banking. In this period of economic stability, the prohibition of interest payments on demand deposits, coupled with interest rate ceilings on time deposits, assured banks of a healthy spread between the return earned on assets and the cost of funds. In fact, the cheapest source of bank funds—demand deposits—was the dominant source of commercial bank funds through the 1960s.

All these conditions gave way in the 1970s and 1980s, negatively impacting the ability of commercial banks to earn profits. Restrictions on branching were eased, stimulating competition. Financial innovations accelerated in the 1960s and 1970s, with negative implications for bank profits. On the liability side of the commercial bank balance sheet, the development of money market mutual funds forced banks to pay higher rates in order to retain the depositors' accounts. And the innovation of repurchase agreements meant essentially that banks would pay interest to corporate depositors, which had formerly been interest-free sources of funds. Over the years, the portion of total bank funds raised through the cheapest source—demand deposits—declined steadily from around 60 percent in the 1950s to around 20 percent today. Market interest rates ratcheted upward from the mid-1960s until the early 1980s. Finally, the interest rate ceilings, formerly a helpful regulation, started to trigger disintermediation. By 1986, they had been totally removed, a change that increased the cost of bank funds. Large foreign banks—particularly Japanese banks with access to the massive low-cost pool of Japanese savings—became formidable competitors for U.S. banks.

Financial innovations also hurt banks on the asset side of their balance sheets. The development of the commercial paper market was instrumental in reducing business demand for bank loans, traditionally a key source of bank profits. The burgeoning money market mutual fund industry stimulated the growth of the commercial paper market by providing a rapidly growing source of demand for these corporate IOUs. The increased demand reduced the cost of corporate borrowing via the commercial paper market, encouraging firms to tap that market in lieu of borrowing from banks. Even the development of the junk bond market hurt banks as low-quality business borrowers began to issue low-grade bonds instead of borrowing from banks.

The Effects of Economic Instability

In addition to the structural forces brought about by financial innovation, unstable economic conditions contributed powerfully to the banks' financial problems. As interest rates climbed in the 1970s and early 1980s, the cost of bank funds escalated. In order to maintain their "spread," banks had to earn higher interest rates on their assets. In the face of declining business loan demand, banks sought out riskier loans and investments.[7] Banks increased their *portfolio risk* by making large loans in the agriculture and energy sectors and by making massive loans to less developed countries (LDCs). All three of those areas—agriculture, energy, and LDCs—ran into severe problems in the 1980s.

Less developed countries have traditionally relied heavily on their earnings from the export of raw materials to meet their interest payments on loans from U.S. banks. The severe worldwide recession of 1981–1983 depressed both the volume of those exports and the price of raw materials, making it impossible for many LDCs to meet their loan payments. Several huge U.S. money center banks had outstanding loans to LDCs in amounts significantly larger than their capital accounts. Fearing that the failure of one of those banks could trigger a financial panic, the U.S. regulatory authorities apparently adopted a **"too-big-to-fail" policy.** This meant that the FDIC would see to it that no depositors or creditors lost money if the bank became insolvent. One example of the policy was the 1988 bailout of the First Republic Bank of Dallas, which cost taxpayers $3 billion. But the widespread perception that a "too-big-to-fail" policy was in place stimulated the moral hazard problem, signaling large banks to increase their risk taking.

At home in the United States, back-to-back recessions in the early 1980s produced an increase in loan defaults, further reducing banks' capital. Midwestern banks were hit hard by severely depressed agricultural land prices and the impairment of export- and import-competing industries, such as automobiles, due to the dramatic appreciation (and overvaluation) of the U.S. dollar in 1983 and 1984. When the price of oil fell sharply, banks in such states as Texas, Louisiana, and Oklahoma, which depend heavily on oil for their income, were severely impacted. Bank branching restrictions had prevented banks in those states from diversifying out of the energy sector. Eventually, 9 of the 10 largest banks in Texas had to be merged or closed because of financial distress attributable to the collapse of oil prices. Exhibit 11-3 discusses the geographic distribution of commercial bank and S&L failures.

General economic volatility also played a role in the upsurge of bank failures because many bankers had never experienced the fluctuations in interest rates and exchange rates that were common in the 1970s and early 1980s, and had not learned the hedging techniques that can reduce or eliminate such risks. The misfortune continued into the next decade. In the late 1980s and early 1990s, a decline in real estate prices in several U.S. cities bankrupted many real estate developers, leaving banks holding empty office build-

---

[7]Also, to maintain their rate of return on capital, many banks deliberately reduced their capital ratios. Such an action directly increases the likelihood of insolvency.

EXHIBIT 11-3

The Geographic Implications of Savings and Loan and Commercial Bank Failures

An interesting issue surrounding the S&L and bank failures of the 1980s is the geographic impact of the fiasco. We will argue that the depository institutions debacle, coupled with associated costs to the U.S. taxpayers, produced a redistribution of wealth from north to south.

The accompanying map shows the number of bank failures (first figure) and S&L failures (second figure) in each state in the period 1982–1994. Note the line that extends from San Francisco to Washington, D.C., splitting the nation into north and south. Of the 2573 institutions that failed in this period, more than 2000, or approximately 80 percent, were located in the 24 states constituting the southern half of the country. Texas alone accounted for 782 failures, or 30 percent of all the commercial bank and S&L failures in the country. The cost of the failures was borne by U.S. taxpayers, and the divisiveness of the issue is indicated by the title of one article, entitled "Looting the North for Texas' Benefit."

The point is that many of the bad loans made by banks and S&Ls went for the purpose of constructing shopping centers, office buildings, and apartment buildings across the Sunbelt, especially in Texas. When hard times hit the region, due in large part to the collapse of oil prices, many tenants of those properties were unable to pay their rent. Developers who could not make the payments on their loans defaulted, and the properties were resold at discounted prices. While the glut of properties depressed real estate values for a while, in the long run the Sunbelt benefitted at the expense of the rest of the country by the presence of the buildings. Houston, for example, mounted a marketing campaign to attract business to the city. A chief selling point: some of the lowest-cost office space in the United States. What the campaigns didn't mention, of course, was why rents were so low and who had paid for the buildings.

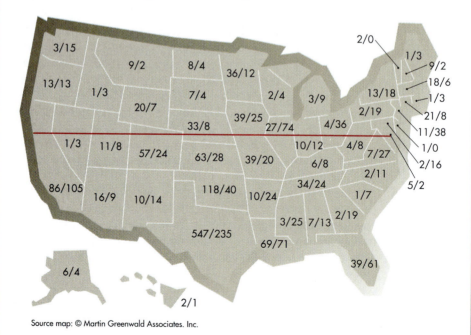

Source map: © Martin Greenwald Associates. Inc.

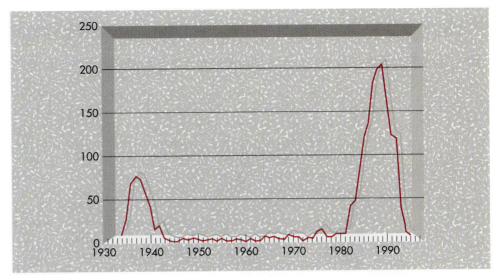

Figure 11-4   Number of U.S. Commercial Bank Failures, 1934–1995. From 1950–1981, U.S. commercial bank failures averaged only 5 per year. From 1982–1992, they averaged 130 per year. They then declined sharply in the mid-1990s.   *Source:* Federal Deposit Insurance Corporation, *Annual Report, 1995.*

ings and other real estate investments. In the same period, banks increased their exposure to risky loans. For example, they financed leveraged buyouts, many of which later ran into trouble. As a result of these forces, bank failures escalated to more than 20 times the rate experienced in the period 1945–1981. Figure 11-4 shows the number of banks failing in each year from 1934–1995.

After the mild U.S. recession of 1990–1991, improving economic conditions aided the financial condition of commercial banks. Interest rates remained quite low during 1992–1995, and rising output and income boosted the demand for bank loans. As a result, the number of banks on the "problem list" fell sharply, and bank failures plummeted from 158 in 1990 and 105 in 1991 to only 11 in 1994 and 6 in 1995. Nevertheless, given the role of regulation and deposit insurance in creating the banking crisis of the 1980s, economists called for reforms. We now turn to that subject.

Regulating Bank Capital Ratios

Bank capital serves a number of purposes. It provides a cushion that protects the FDIC and large depositors, as well as bank owners, from unexpected losses stemming from bad loans and other problems. A healthy capital position is essential to attracting large depositors with more than $100,000 (the FDIC insurance ceiling). By providing reassurance of a bank's financial condition, a strong capital position also lowers a bank's borrowing costs and attracts business customers. Because it is costly for firms to line up loan arrangements, they will avoid a bank that might not be in business in a couple of years.

Hence, additional capital provides benefits to a bank. However, once bank creditors, large depositors, and business borrowers are satisfied that a bank is in good condition, additional increments of capital provide sharply diminishing benefits to a bank. Any such gains must be balanced against the fact that a higher capital to total assets ratio implies a lower rate of return on equity. For example, a bank that earns 0.8 percent per year on total assets and has a capital to total assets ratio of 5 percent will earn a 16 percent return on equity (0.8 percent $\times$ 20). If the same bank operates with a 10 percent capital to total assets ratio, it will earn only 8 percent on equity.

This analysis suggests that each bank, in deciding its optimal capital ratio, must balance the additional benefits from the higher capital against the higher costs—that is, the reduced rate of return on equity for the owners. On the basis of such an analysis, each bank determines its optimal capital ratio. However, the optimal ratio from banks' vantage point is lower than the optimal ratio from society's viewpoint. This follows from the fact that **negative externalities** are associated with bank failures—that is, the costs of bank failures to society exceed the costs incurred by the banks' owners. When a bank fails, the owners lose only their equity in the bank. But because banks are seldom closed before their net worth becomes negative, the FDIC and therefore taxpayers incur additional costs. Large depositors with more than $100,000 in deposits (the insurance ceiling) may also incur losses. Finally, when a large bank fails, there may be a ripple effect. Customers of other marginal banks may withdraw their funds, causing them to fail also. Because rational bank managers ignore the *external costs* a bank failure would impose on society, they systematically elect to take more risk than is optimal from society's viewpoint.

For this reason, the regulatory authorities are justified in taking steps to limit risk taking by banks. Before 1981, banks were allowed in large part to set their own equity ratios. Since then, the capital standards have been tightened. Regulations restrict the types of assets banks are allowed to acquire: they cannot buy corporate stocks or bonds, and loans to any one customer cannot exceed 10 percent of the bank's capital. And the capital standards are now enforced by the regulatory authorities. Keep in mind, however, that because optimal risk taking from banks' viewpoint exceeds that from society's viewpoint, banks are likely to attempt to circumvent the effect of tougher capital standards by increasing other types of risk. For example, they may respond to higher capital standards by increasing their loans to total assets ratio, entering into more risky loans, or engaging in arcane and complex derivatives transactions in an effort to maintain their rate of return on equity. In 1994, many U.S. banks that were speculating in derivatives lost heavily when interest rates climbed. The cat-and-mouse game between banks and the regulatory authorities often leaves the regulators one step behind.

Because any nation that unilaterally imposes relatively strict capital standards will put its banks at a competitive disadvantage relative to foreign banks, the United States and 12 other nations, all members of the Bank for International Settlements (BIS), adopted uniform capital standards in November 1988. The BIS capital standards distinguish between two types of capital, Tier 1 and Tier 2. *Tier 1 capital* is stockholder equity in the bank;

Tier 2 capital includes subordinated debt (long-term bonds) issued by the bank and loan loss reserves. The required amount of each type of capital is based on *risk-adjusted assets* rather than total assets. Tier 1 capital and total capital requirements (Tier 1 plus Tier 2) are set at 4 percent and 8 percent of each bank's risk-adjusted assets, respectively.

A weighting scheme is employed to determine a bank's risk-adjusted assets. The weights reflect the risk inherent in each type of asset or off-balance-sheet activity. The lowest category, which carries a weight of zero, includes reserves (vault cash and deposits at the Fed) plus U.S. government securities. Because those assets have zero default risk, they are not counted as risk-adjusted assets, meaning that capital requirements do not apply to those assets. The second category, which carries a weight of 20 percent, includes fully backed mortgage bonds, U.S. government agency securities, and interbank deposits. The third, somewhat higher, risk category carries a weight of 50 percent and includes residential mortgages and municipal bonds. The fourth, and highest, risk category carries a weight of 100 percent. It includes loans, commercial paper, and the bank's fixed assets—buildings, equipment, and so forth. By placing capital standards on risk-adjusted assets rather than total assets, the BIS scheme provides incentives that inhibit banks' propensity to engage in excessive risk taking. The more risky a bank's asset portfolio, the higher will be its required capital to total assets ratio.

FEDERAL DEPOSIT INSURANCE

Federal deposit insurance was introduced in 1934 in response to the periodic banking panics that had culminated in the disaster of the early 1930s. Such panics had caused bank failures, cut off borrowers from essential credit, and destabilized economic activity. Legislators reasoned that if depositors could be protected against loss in the event of a bank failure, bank runs would be unlikely to occur. As we have seen, FDIC insurance has served its intended function. Gone are the old-fashioned banking panics in which hundreds of depositors who feared their banks would run out of money lined up at teller windows.

However, we have also seen that the existence of deposit insurance stimulates banks' propensity to take risks (the moral hazard problem) and encourages regulatory authorities to delay the closing of insolvent institutions (the principal-agent problem). To the extent that deposit insurance reduces the incentive of depositors to monitor the activities of their banks, its existence encourages banks to increase their risk taking—that is, to reduce their capital ratios and increase the riskiness of their assets. And by eliminating the prospect of incurring the wrath of depositors who have their money in failed institutions, deposit insurance also reduces regulators' incentive to shut down insolvent institutions quickly. In these ways, deposit insurance contributed to the moral hazard and principal-agent problems that came home to roost in the 1980s and early 1990s.

Clearly, the deposit insurance system was ripe for reform in the 1980s. Before turning to the actual and proposed changes in the system, a brief history of the system since

Table 11-2

Key Aspects of FDIC Insurance, 1934–1994

| End of Year | Insurance Coverage (per depositor) | Deposits in Insured Banks | | Insured (%) | Insurance Fund (in billions) | Insurance Fund/Insured Deposits (%) | Premium (cents per $100 of deposits) |
		Total Deposits (in billions)	Insured Deposits (in billions)				
1934	$ 5,000*	$ 40	$ 18	45%	$ 0.29	1.61%	N.A.
1940	5,000	65	27	41	0.50	1.86	8.3
1950	10,000	168	91	54	1.24	1.36	3.7
1960	10,000	260	150	58	2.22	1.48	3.7
1970	20,000	545	350	64	4.38	1.25	3.6
1975	40,000	876	569	65	6.72	1.18	3.6
1980	100,000	1,324	949	72	11.02	1.16	3.7
1985	100,000	1,974	1,503	76	17.96	1.19	8.3
1990	100,000	2,540	1,929	76	4.04	0.21	12.0
1994	100,000	2,464	1,896	77	21.85	1.15	23.6†

*Initial coverage of $2,500 was increased to $5,000 on July 1, 1934.
†Beginning in 1993, the premium is based on a risk-related premium system under which institutions pay assessments in the range of 23¢ to 31¢ per $100 of deposits. In 1996, the premium was abolished for certain high-capital banks.

Source: Federal Deposit Insurance Corporation, *Annual Report*, 1995.

its implementation in 1934 is in order. Table 11-2 summarizes some important aspects of FDIC insurance from 1934–1994. As shown in the table, insurance coverage was established at $2,500 per depositor at the beginning of 1934, raised 6 months later to $5,000, and increased over the years to its current level of $100,000.[8] Over the years, coverage has increased much faster than the nation's price level. If the initial $2,500 coverage limit had been indexed to the consumer price index, coverage today would be in the neighborhood of only $30,000 to $35,000. Because of the contribution of deposit insurance to the moral hazard problem, some economists advocate rolling back insurance coverage to $40,000 or perhaps even $20,000.

Table 11-2 also shows that the percentage of total deposits in the nation's insured banks covered by FDIC insurance has increased from 41 percent in 1940 to 77 percent

[8]Coverage was increased to $10,000 in 1950, $15,000 in 1966, $20,000 in 1969, $40,000 in 1974, and $100,000 in 1980. This coverage pertains to *each* depositor in *each* bank. A wealthy individual can insure millions of dollars of deposits by opening $100,000 accounts in numerous banks and by using different account names in a single bank (single name, joint name, trust account name, and so forth).

today. Some 99 percent of all depositors are covered (not shown).[9] The total value of the insurance fund increased persistently over the years before declining in the late 1980s. It dropped precipitously in 1990 and 1991 in response to the surging cost of resolving failed banks, becoming negative before it was recapitalized by congressional appropriations. Through the mid-1990s, the fund was bolstered by sharply reduced bank failures and higher deposit premiums. By 1995, improved financial conditions in the banking system had restored its strength. In fact, by 1996 the insurance fund was sufficiently robust that insurance premiums were reduced to zero for banks with strong capital positions.

Recent Legislative Reform

One of FIRREA's important provisions mandated that the U.S. Treasury conduct a comprehensive study of the federal deposit insurance system and submit proposals for reform. This study was completed in 1991 and led to the enactment of the 1991 **Federal Deposit Insurance Corporation Improvement Act (FDICIA).** The act had two primary purposes: to recapitalize the nearly insolvent FDIC and to redesign the federal deposit insurance system with the intent of minimizing future taxpayer losses. FDICIA restricted the access of certain banks to brokered deposits, limited the "too-big-to-fail" principle, and required the FDIC to step in quickly and vigorously when a bank's capital falls below a certain threshold.

The act also required the regulatory authorities to conduct on-site examinations of every bank each year; to monitor and restrict real estate lending by banks; and to modify existing risk-based standards to include interest rate risk (in addition to credit risk). The FDICIA resulted in banks being classified into five categories, based on the strength of their capital positions. A bank's classification now influences both the activities in which it is permitted to engage and the deposit insurance premium it is required to pay. For example, "well-capitalized" banks—those with capital significantly in excess of required capital standards—are classified in Group 1. Such banks are allowed to underwrite securities. The brokered deposits they purchase are covered by FDIC deposit insurance, and their deposit insurance premiums are relatively low (they were waived entirely in 1996). Group 2 includes "adequately capitalized" banks. Such banks are extended fewer benefits than Group 1 banks. Group 3 banks are classified as "undercapitalized," and are treated more stringently than the first two groups. Group 4 and Group 5 banks ("significantly undercapitalized" and "critically undercapitalized") are prohibited from paying higher-than-average interest rates to attract deposits. Their brokered deposits are not insured by the FDIC, and they are also charged higher insurance premiums than Group 1 and 2 banks are. In fact, Group 5 banks—those with equity ratios below 2 percent—must be closed down or sold off to new owners by the FDIC.

---

[9]The discrepancy between the *number of depositors* covered and the *portion of deposits* covered is due to the fact that a relatively small number of depositors (typically corporations) have huge, multimillion-dollar deposits. Only the first $100,000 of such deposits is covered.

The Effectiveness of Reform Measures

The FDICIA was the first fundamental change in the deposit insurance system since its inception in 1934. To what extent will it fix the moral hazard and adverse selection problems inherent in the bank regulatory system? We will argue that it does a great deal to cure the ills of the system but perhaps does not go quite far enough. First, the act increased the percentage of bank depositors who have an incentive to monitor their banks. It did so primarily by eliminating deposit insurance on brokered deposits (except for those purchased by well-capitalized banks) and by moderating the "too-big-to-fail" policy. In determining what risks to undertake, banks now have to consider the possibility of losing depositors. High-risk banks now have to pay more than safe banks pay for brokered deposits, to compensate depositors for the greater risk.

The FDICIA also created strong incentives for banks to reduce risk taking. If a bank's capital falls, it is granted fewer privileges and becomes subject to higher insurance premiums and more rigorous regulation. Forcing very poorly capitalized banks to close as soon as their net worth falls below 2 percent, rather than waiting until it is negative, should be especially effective in reducing taxpayer losses. Prompt corrective action should also reduce the principal-agent problem associated with regulators and politicians. The policy of regulatory forbearance, which dramatically increased the moral hazard incentive for banks in the 1980s, is no longer an option. Finally, the stipulation requiring annual on-site examinations should reduce the excessive risk and fraud that contributed to the S&L fiasco.

Banks that take on higher risk by reducing their capital ratios or purchasing riskier assets are now subject to higher insurance premiums. Unfortunately, though risk-based insurance premiums reduce the moral hazard problem, an important inherent shortcoming of this policy is that assessing the degree of risk a bank is engaging in is difficult. A bank can increase its capital ratio without reducing its overall risk level by simultaneously undertaking more risky loans or other activities. Such risks are not easy to measure. Furthermore, loans that appear safe when they are made often turn risky when economic conditions change.

Other Proposed Reforms of Deposit Insurance

While most economists believe that the FDICIA is a socially beneficial piece of legislation, some would prefer more radical efforts to address the problems of moral hazard and adverse selection. We will now discuss a few of their proposals.

Elimination of Deposit Insurance

A straightforward approach might be simply to eliminate deposit insurance. Depositors would then have a powerful incentive to monitor their banks and make sure their funds are deposited in strong, prudent institutions. Such a measure might impose discipline on banks as well, forcing them to forgo excessive risk. Unfortunately, it would also unleash the same types of problems that led to the implementation of deposit insurance in the Great Depression: banks in marginal financial condition would be subject to runs—long lines of frightened depositors trying to protect their wealth by withdrawing their money.

Most economists believe that deposit insurance has contributed to economic stability since the Great Depression. In addition, many economists are skeptical of the view that depositors are capable of evaluating the degree of risk their bank engages in. Certain key information, such as examiners' reports, is confidential and therefore unavailable to depositors. And clearly, to have tens of thousands of individual depositors spend significant amounts of time monitoring their banks would be a misallocation of society's resources. However, large depositors might be able to evaluate banks efficiently, particularly those larger banks whose operations are analyzed by Standard & Poor's and other advisory services.

Reduction of the Limits of Coverage

As we saw earlier, the amount of deposits per customer covered by FDIC insurance has outpaced inflation. Suppose we reduced the deposit insurance ceiling to $25,000 per customer. Depositors who currently have between $25,000 and $100,000 in their accounts would be given an incentive to monitor the risks their banks are taking. That might impose some measure of discipline on banks. But if depositors are risk averse and poorly informed, implementation of such a proposal could result in occasional runs on suspect banks, thereby destabilizing the system.

Coinsurance

Some reformers propose to make deposit insurance more like medical and hazard insurance, in which the insured often pays an up-front deductible or a certain percentage of the cost. Suppose that only 90 percent of each depositor's funds (up to $100,000) was insured. All depositors would then have an incentive to keep an eye on their banks. But this measure would suffer from the same potential drawbacks as a reduction in coverage limits or the elimination of insurance coverage.

Abolition of the "Too-Big-to-Fail" Policy

While the FDICIA limited the "too-big-to-fail" policy, many critics think it did not go far enough. The Treasury, Fed, and FDIC still have the authority to implement the policy when they deem it appropriate, bailing out uninsured depositors. Knowing this, big banks are not likely to be influenced by fear that large depositors will defect. On the other hand, allowing a large bank to fail could have extremely costly ripple effects. In spite of its unfairness, many observers believe there is no alternative to preventing the failure of huge money center banks.

Private Deposit Insurance

Advocates of private deposit insurance argue that, unlike the government, private insurance companies would have an incentive to monitor banks whose deposits they insure. Private insurers would also charge aggressively higher insurance premiums to banks that engage in high-risk activities.[10] But critics of this proposal ask who would bail out the private insurance company in the not unlikely event it failed. A private insurance company is unlikely to have the resources to repay depositors in the event of large losses. If the public perceived that to be the case, bank runs might become more prevalent, as the public would not be convinced that the insurance would be viable in the event their bank did fail. The runs on state-insured Ohio and Maryland S&Ls in 1985, at a time when there were no runs on federally insured institutions in the same states, seem to support this view.

---

[10]Critics of the FDICIA deposit insurance system point out that, while it is clearly superior to the previous system (which employed fixed premiums irrespective of risk), the differences between the insurance premiums—0.23 percent for the safest banks and 0.31 percent for the riskiest banks—do not fully reflect the differences in risk between these types of banks. Their charge is borne out by the fact that the spread between the large CD rates paid by the two types of banks is much larger (relatively) than the spread between the insurance premiums. A private insurance company would likely reduce or eliminate this discrepancy.

Deposit Insurance Systems

Today, most industrial nations have deposit insurance systems. The U.S. system, established in 1934, is the oldest in operation (Czechoslovakia established the first—which is no longer in operation—in 1924). Norway's system, established in 1961, is the second oldest. Though many nations did not establish deposit insurance systems until the 1970s or 1980s, by the early 1990s 32 nations had such systems.

The United States has one of the highest deposit insurance coverage levels (behind only Norway and Italy) and charges the highest premiums of any nation. Many nations charge no premiums and have no insurance fund; instead, they assess insured members as losses occur. Such a system provides incentives for banks to keep an eye on one another to see that regulations are complied with. Other nations (Argentina, Chile, Italy, Ireland, and the United Kingdom) have coinsurance. For example, in England depositors pay 25 percent of any loss up to the ceiling level, and insurance covers the remaining 75 percent. By increasing the incentive for depositors to monitor their banks, coinsurance schemes reduce the moral hazard problem.

Of the 32 national depository insurance systems in existence in 1990, membership was voluntary in 9 countries and mandatory in 23. Systems are administered in one of three ways: in 12 countries, they are sponsored and administered by the government; 13 nations use private insurance; and 7 employ a system administered jointly through public and private arrangements. The increasing worldwide integration of financial markets has stimulated a movement toward the standardization of regulations across countries. Accordingly, the European Union is currently moving in the direction of standardizing deposit insurance systems.

Aspects of Deposit Insurance in Various Countries

Country	Year Established	Maximum Amount Covered (in U.S. dollars)*	Membership (voluntary or compulsory)	Administered by
Canada	1967	$44,000	Compulsory	Government
France	1980	$81,000	Voluntary	Private insurance
Germany	1966	30% of bank's liable capital per customer	Voluntary	Private insurance
Italy	1987	$634,000 (coinsurance)	Voluntary	Private insurance
Japan	1971	$95,300	Compulsory	Private insurance
Norway	1961	Unlimited	Compulsory	Joint (private-government)
Spain	1977	$12,400	Voluntary	Government
United Kingdom	1982	$30,900 (coinsurance)	Compulsory	Government
United States	1934	$100,000	Compulsory	Government

*Calculated using exchange rates prevailing on January 15, 1996.

Source: *Reforming Federal Deposit Insurance* (Washington, D.C.: Congressional Budget Office, 1990).

SUMMARY

In the past 15 years, first the savings and loan industry and then the commercial banking industry were buffeted by severe financial problems, and a major shakeout occurred in both industries. Thousands of depository institutions failed. Because of financial innovations, deregulation, and a series of historical accidents, the problems of adverse selection and moral hazard increased dramatically in the 1980s, resulting in huge losses to the S&L industry and to U.S. taxpayers. These financial problems were triggered by unstable macroeconomic conditions in the United States—rising inflation and interest rates in the 1970s, followed in the early 1980s by the most severe recession since the Great Depression. Because savings and loan associations were set up to borrow short-term funds to fund long-term mortgages, they were inherently susceptible to periods of sharply rising interest rates. As interest rates increased dramatically in the late 1970s and early 1980s, S&Ls experienced huge losses. Both politicians and depository institution regulators are subject to the principal-agent problem. Because they were driven by incentives other than minimizing losses to taxpayers, they responded to the S&L crisis by removing restrictions on risky assets, relaxing capital standards, and implementing a policy of forbearance, thus allowing insolvent institutions to remain open. Because financially impaired S&Ls predictably responded by increasing their risk taking, these government actions sharply increased the ultimate cost to taxpayers. Important legislation was implemented in 1989 and 1991 to reduce the chances of a recurrence of losses to taxpayers. The Financial Institutions Reform, Recovery, and Enforcement Act (FIRREA) reinstated restrictions on S&Ls that had unwisely been relaxed in 1982 by the Garn–St. Germain Act, and increased capital requirements on thrift institutions. The Federal Deposit Insurance Corporation Improvement Act of 1991 reformed the regulatory system and deposit insurance system to reduce the incentive for banks to take risks. However, if history is a guide, implementation of financial legislation to solve a particular problem may trigger unforeseen problems in other areas.

KEY TERMS

Banking Act of 1933
Garn–St. Germain Act
Federal Home Loan Bank Board (FHLBB)
Federal Savings and Loan Insurance Corporation (FSLIC)
Depository Institutions Deregulation and Monetary Control Act (DIDMCA)
forbearance
capital standards

brokered deposits
zombie institutions
Financial Institutions Reform, Recovery, and Enforcement Act (FIRREA)
principal-agent problem
"too-big-to-fail" policy
negative externality
Federal Deposit Insurance Corporation Improvement Act (FDICIA)

STUDY QUESTIONS

1 Explain carefully the fundamental flaws in the original structuring of our savings and loan industry. What forces created the impairment of the industry during 1978–1981?

2 "If the counterproductive Regulation Q interest rate ceilings had not been in place, the S&L fiasco of the 1980s would never have occurred." Analyze carefully the validity of this statement.

3 "If Garn–St. Germain had been enacted in 1962 instead of 1982, taxpayers would have been spared the enormous cost of the $140 billion bailout that occurred in the late 1980s and 1990s." Do you agree or disagree? Explain.

4 If FDIC insurance exists to protect depositors, how could the comprehensive deposit insurance system have contributed to the S&L fiasco? Explain.

5 Assess the role of government and the Federal Reserve in the S&L crisis.

6 Explain the forces that led to the invention of adjustable-rate mortgages. Had ARMs been invented 30 years ago, could they have staved off

the problems encountered by the S&L industry in the 1980s?

7 Explain why, during periods of rising interest rates, S&Ls cannot pass on all of the increase in their cost of funds to new mortgage holders.

8 What forces were responsible for the rapid growth of brokered deposits? Did those deposits help get S&Ls out of trouble? Did they *cause* problems for the FSLIC and U.S. taxpayers? Explain.

9 Explain carefully how the following factors contributed to the moral hazard problem in the S&L industry:

a The disintermediation of the 1970s.

b The policy of regulatory forbearance.

c Deposit insurance changes implemented in the DIDMCA.

d Liberalization of S&L asset structures implemented in the Garn–St. Germain Act.

e The budget deficits of the early to mid-1980s.

10 "The provisions of FIRREA could place S&Ls in exactly the same situation they faced in the late 1970s. FIRREA, therefore, is not a step forward but rather a step backward." Explain why this statement is partly but not completely true.

11 Discuss the way in which financial innovations contributed to the problems of the commercial banking industry in the 1980s and early 1990s.

12 Discuss the "historical accidents," or macroeconomic shocks, that contributed to commercial bank problems in the 1980s.

13 Why were the losses in the commercial banking industry less severe than those experienced by S&Ls?

14 Explain the trade-offs involved in maintaining a strong capital accounts position, as viewed by depository institutions. Explain why different depository institutions might have different optimal capital ratios. Why might a bank's optimal capital accounts ratio be too low by society's standards?

15 Explain how the following proposals would reduce potential moral hazard problems in the banking industry:

a Reducing FDIC insurance limits to $20,000.

b Eliminating public deposit insurance altogether.

c Implementing a coinsurance scheme.

d Mandating private insurance for deposits.

SUGGESTIONS FOR ADDITIONAL READING

An excellent early article that views the thrift industry's problems from the perspective of the early 1980s is Andrew S. Carron, *The Plight of the Thrift Institutions* (Washington, D.C.: Brookings Institution, 1982). For a clear analysis of the ingredients that produced the S&L crisis, see George J. Benston and George G. Kaufman, "Understanding the Savings and Loan Debacle," *The Public Interest,* Spring 1990, pp. 70–95. An excellent analysis that foresaw the demise of the FSLIC is Edward J. Kane, *The Gathering Crisis in Federal Deposit Insurance* (Cambridge, Mass.: MIT Press, 1985). A pertinent series of articles by Lawrence J. White, David L. Mengle, Angelo R. Mascaro, and William G. Gale is published in *Contemporary Policy Issues,* April 1990, pp. 62–121. The structural flaws in our political system that created the incentives for the authorities to ignore the exploding S&L problem are analyzed in Edward J. Kane, *The S&L Insurance Mess: How Did It Happen?* (Washington, D.C.: Urban Institute Press, 1989). A very brief version of this view by the same author appeared in *Science,* October 27, 1989, pp. 451–456. A lucid article that lays bare the roots of the S&L problem is Robert E. Litan, "Remedy for S&Ls: Operation Clean Sweep," *Challenge,* November–December 1990, pp. 26–32. A symposium on deposit insurance reform is published in the Fall 1989 issue of *Journal of Economic Perspectives,* pp. 3–47. A series of more technical papers on the same issue is published in the Fall (September) 1991 issue of *Journal of Banking and Finance.* For a fascinating story of the politics involved in the government cover-up, see L. J. Davis, "Chronicle of a Debacle Foretold: How Deregulation Begat the S&L Scandal," *Harper's,* September 1990, pp. 50–66.

PART

4

P A R T

The Federal Reserve System and the Money Supply Process

4

The supply of money is believed to play a critical role in a nation's economy■ Too much money can lead to inflation, while too little can result in recession or worse, a *depression* like the 1930s■ Central banks around the world attempt to influence economic activity in large part by changing the supply of money■ In the United States, the Federal Reserve System is responsible for governing the nation's supply of money■ In this section, we explore the nature, structure, and functions of the Federal Reserve System■ We then examine in detail how the activities of the nation's banks, in conjunction with the behavior of the public and the Federal Reserve, determine the quantity of money in the United States■ We then explore the roles of these three parties in accounting for the collapse of the money supply during America's greatest economic catastrophe—the Great Depression of the 1930s■

■ **The Federal Reserve System:
Its Structure and Functions**

One of the most crucial institutions of any nation is its central bank. In the United States, the central bank is known as the Federal Reserve System, or simply the Fed. In this chapter we will discuss the origin, structure, and functions of the Federal Reserve System.

Central banks are different from private banks, such as the one in which you keep your money. Unlike private banks, central banks are not concerned about making a profit. And unlike private banks, most central banks neither make loans to the public nor issue checking or savings accounts. They are governmental or quasi-governmental institutions, charged with providing certain services and achieving certain goals perceived to be in the nation's broad economic interest. Historically, for example, a chief goal of central banks in industrial nations has been to foster price level stability.

A natural question to ask is: In which of the three branches of government is the Federal Reserve System located? The correct answer is none. The Fed's relationship with the government is rather complicated. Technically, the Federal Reserve is a private corporation owned by the private banks which are members of the Federal Reserve System. In reality, the Federal Reserve operates more like a government agency accountable to Congress. The Federal Reserve, then, is a complex organization which is essentially part of government yet maintains a certain detachment from it.

THE ORIGINS OF THE FEDERAL RESERVE SYSTEM

In some nations, such as England, the central bank evolved from a private commercial bank over a long period of time. In other nations, such as the United States, the central bank was originally established solely as a central bank. The Federal Reserve System, of course, is much younger than the central banks in most industrial nations. The central banks in England and France (the Bank of England and Bank of France), for example, were established in 1694 and 1800, respectively.

Two early experiments with establishing a central bank in the United States failed. These experiments included the First Bank of the United States (1791–1811) and the Second Bank of the United States (1816–1836). Each of these banks was initially granted a 20-year charter by Congress, but in each case Congress refused to renew the charter when it expired. The reasons can be found in the widespread public view that these banks were vested with excessive financial power. The United States has a history of populist sentiment that includes profound distrust of both the government in Washington and the big banks of the eastern establishment. A widespread fear existed, particularly in small towns and rural areas, that a central bank would be controlled by Wall Street and New York bankers. Chiefly for this reason, the United States was without a central bank between 1836 and 1913.

In the half century preceding the legislation that created the Federal Reserve System in 1913, nationally chartered banks were regulated by provisions of the National Banking Act of 1863. Under this regime, smaller commercial banks held deposits in other (larger) commercial banks as well as cash. The cash and the deposits in larger banks counted as **legal reserves,** or simply **reserves.** Banks were required to maintain a certain portion of their deposit liabilities in the form of reserves. Banks in New York, Chicago, and St. Louis were classified as Central Reserve City Banks. Banks in approximately fifty other cities were classified as Reserve City Banks. All other commercial banks were classified as Country Banks. Country Banks held reserves in the form of cash and deposits at Reserve City Banks; Reserve City Banks held reserves in the form of cash and deposits in Central Reserve City Banks. In order to earn interest on the funds deposited by smaller banks, the larger banks typically invested the funds in loans to stockbrokers, known as *call loans.*

There were several problems with this system. For one thing, it lacked flexibility. In a **fractional reserve banking system,** each bank maintains only a small percentage of its deposit liabilities in the form of reserves—that is, cash and deposits in other banks. If a seasonal or panic-induced withdrawal of currency from banks occurs, pressure converges on the larger banks as small banks draw down their deposits to obtain cash for their customers. As we will demonstrate in the next chapter, in the absence of a central bank, banks collectively—that is, the banking *system*—cannot recover their lost reserves when the public withdraws currency. Without help from a central bank, therefore, the banking system could recover from a reserve deficiency only through experiencing a painful and destructive multiple contraction of deposits. Historically, when larger banks were forced to call in their loans to brokers, a panic in the nation's financial markets often ensued. Farmers, businesses, and others who relied on bank loans to conduct their economic affairs often found themselves cut off from essential credit. As the nation underwent urbanization and industrialization in the late nineteenth and early twentieth centuries, and as the financial sector became relatively more important to overall economic development, these periodic financial breakdowns increased the cost to the nation of being without a central bank. Major banking and financial market panics occurred in 1857, 1873, 1884, 1893, and 1907. The panic of 1907 was so costly that it finally triggered the congressional action which culminated in the establishment of the Federal Reserve System. The Fed was created by the **Federal Reserve Act,** which was signed into law by President Woodrow Wilson in December 1913.

What was conspicuously missing before 1913 was an institution responsible for providing a flexible amount of reserves to the banking system to promote stability. The absence of a viable **lender of last resort** to provide temporary cash reserves to the banking system in time of crisis, when the psychological force of panic is capable of triggering a monetary and financial collapse, was particularly costly to the nation.[1] Other factors leading to the creation of the Federal Reserve System were the needs to provide more supervision of the nation's banks, to improve on the check collection system, to provide for the issue of currency, and to establish an agency to serve as banker for the U.S. Treasury. Today, the U.S. Treasury pays for its huge expenditures by writing checks on its account at the Federal Reserve.

The Federal Reserve Act, like the U.S. Constitution, represents an interesting compromise among diverse forces and interests. The act achieved a delicate balance and diffusion of power in three different areas: between the government and the private sector; among the various regions of the nation and between rural and urban interests; and among bankers, the nonbank business sector, and the rest of society. In the early years of this century, before the Federal Reserve Act, urban business leaders favored a highly centralized organization whose purpose would be to stabilize the nation's price level. Rural interests lobbied for a highly decentralized, government-managed central bank dedicated to making loans available on favorable terms. The Federal Reserve Act achieved decentralization by establishing 12 **Federal Reserve district banks** with significant individual autonomy. It fostered centralization through the creation of a Board of Governors in Washington, D.C., which was to share power with the 12 regional Federal Reserve Banks. Although the organization of the Fed was changed somewhat by legislation in the 1930s, many of its original features are intact today. The 12 regional Federal Reserve banks remain, as does the Board of Governors in Washington. However, a significant shift in power away from the 12 Federal Reserve district banks and to the Board of Governors occurred with legislation in the 1930s.

Today, we routinely attribute to the Federal Reserve broad responsibility for stabilizing the nation's economy through its influence on bank lending, the quantity of money, and the level of interest rates. It is important to note that the Fed was not originally conceived with such a broad and difficult mandate. In the early part of this century, deliberate efforts to manage economic activity were considered neither appropriate nor desirable. (As we will note in Chapter 26, some economists still hold this view.) The massive responsibility which is today accorded the Federal Reserve System evolved over time on the basis of experience, the development of macroeconomic analysis, and legislation. Today, the Employment Act of 1946 and the Full Employment and Balanced Growth Act of 1978 (the Humphrey-Hawkins Act) give the federal government responsibility for keeping the economy operating at a high level of output and employment. Thus, the Federal Reserve is essentially charged with maintaining prosperity as well as reasonable price level stability. Its original functions were serving as a lender of last resort to the banking system, issuing currency, improving on check collection, serving as bank or fiscal agent to the U.S. Treasury, and improving the supervision and examination of the nation's banks.

---

[1]Unfortunately, as we shall see in Chapter 16, the existence of a central bank such as the Federal Reserve does not guarantee that the "lender-of-last-resort" function will be provided. To the great detriment of the nation, the Federal Reserve failed to serve this function in the 1930s, when it was sorely needed.

THE FINANCIAL STATUS OF THE FEDERAL RESERVE SYSTEM

Key to understanding the nature and role of the Federal Reserve System are two important financial statements—the balance sheet and the income statement. We will begin by examining the Fed's balance sheet.

The Balance Sheet of the Federal Reserve System

Table 12-1 presents the consolidated balance sheet of the 12 Federal Reserve banks—a snapshot indicating the assets, liabilities, and capital accounts of the Fed at a given point in time. The Fed's assets are those things it owns and claims it has on outside entities; its liabilities are debts it owes, or claims that outside entities have on the Federal Reserve. The Federal Reserve's capital accounts are simply the difference between its total assets and total liabilities. We will begin with the Fed's assets.

Federal Reserve Assets

"U.S. government securities" refers to interest-bearing securities acquired by the Federal Reserve for the purpose of influencing the nation's financial and monetary conditions. Federal Reserve holdings of U.S. government securities amount to more than 85 percent of the Fed's total assets. As we shall emphasize later, the primary tool of Federal Reserve policy is **open market operations**—the buying and selling of government securities for

---

Table 12-1

Consolidated Balance Sheet of the 12 Federal Reserve Banks, March 31, 1996 (in billions of dollars)

Assets		Liabilities and Capital	
U.S. government securities	$384.48	Federal Reserve notes	$392.90
Loans to depository institutions	.04	Deposits held at Fed by:	
Coin	.58	Depository institutions	24.74
Cash items in process of collection	4.20	U.S. Treasury	7.02
Gold certificate account	11.05	Foreign and other	.54
Special Drawing Rights certificate account	10.17	Deferred-availability cash items	4.07
		Other liabilities	4.27
Denominated in foreign currencies	19.99	Total liabilities	$433.54
Other assets	11.48	Capital accounts	8.45
Total assets	$441.99	Total liabilities and capital	$441.99

Source: *Federal Reserve Bulletin,* June 1996.

the purpose of influencing bank lending, the level of interest rates, and the nation's money supply. The Fed's massive government security portfolio has been gradually accumulated over the years as the result of measures taken by the Fed to expand the nation's money supply to accommodate a growing economy.

Loans made by Federal Reserve banks to depository institutions are known as "discount loans," or **discounts and advances.** These very short-term loans are initiated by depository institutions (banks) in response to temporary reserve deficiencies. Such reserve deficiencies result from unexpected net check clearings against banks' reserve accounts at the Fed and from withdrawals of currency from banks by the public.

The relatively small item "coin" consists of coins issued by the Treasury that are currently held by the 12 Federal Reserve banks. The Fed holds coins to accommodate requests for coins by depository institutions, which respond to the public's demand for coins.

"Cash items in process of collection" refers to checks being processed by the Fed for which the Fed has not yet received payment. The Fed collects on such checks by debiting the reserve accounts of the depository institution on which they are written (right-hand side of the Fed's balance sheet). These cash items are an asset to the Fed because they are claims against the depository institutions, which the Fed will exercise within a few days by debiting the institutions' reserve accounts at the Fed.

The Fed's gold certificate account is more of historical interest than of current significance. For each dollar's worth of gold the U.S. Treasury acquires, it issues a one-dollar gold certificate and presents it to the Federal Reserve. The Fed compensates the Treasury by making a bookkeeping entry in which it credits the Treasury's deposit account at the Federal Reserve (on the liability side of the Fed's balance sheet). Years ago, a law required that the paper currency issued by the Fed (Federal Reserve notes) be backed by gold certificates. This requirement placed constraints on the amount of currency the Fed could issue.[2] As the volume of Federal Reserve notes needed to accommodate a growing economy increased over the years, and as the U.S. gold stock gradually diminished in response to persistent balance-of-payments deficits, the gold certificate requirement was reduced and then eliminated in 1968.[3] The final vestige of the gold standard was abandoned.

The Special Drawing Rights (SDR) certificate account is similar in nature to the gold certificate account. SDR certificates represent the Fed's claims against Special Drawing Rights, which are issued by the International Monetary Fund and held by the U.S. Treasury

---

[2]This aspect of a gold standard—its rigid constraint on the quantity of money—is at once the source of its appeal and the source of its shortcomings. Advocates of a gold standard emphasize the long-term stability of the price level that would exist under a gold standard, owing to the natural limits placed on the money stock. Critics charge that it handcuffs the central bank by preventing it from increasing the money supply to boost economic activity in times of recession.

[3]Until the U.S. "gold window" was closed in 1971, foreign governments which had accumulated dollars by running balance-of-trade surpluses vis-à-vis the United States were entitled at their discretion to convert them into gold at the U.S. Treasury at the official gold price. By 1971, the U.S. gold stock, which had stood at $25 billion (half the gold in the world) in 1949, had diminished to around $11 billion. In that year the United States terminated the right of foreign governments to convert dollars to gold. Since then, the U.S. gold stock has been relatively stable at around $11 billion (valued at the official price of $42.22 per ounce). Because the government's official price has been dramatically lower than the free market price for more than 20 years, little or no gold has been sold to the Treasury in recent times.

(and by other governments). Special Drawing Rights are issued by the IMF to help finance international trade. When the Treasury acquires additional SDRs from the IMF, it issues SDR certificates to the Federal Reserve, which compensates the Treasury by crediting its deposit account at the Fed.

The item "denominated in foreign currencies" consists chiefly of foreign government bonds—bonds denominated in such currencies as yen and deutsche marks. These foreign assets provide ammunition to the Federal Reserve for supporting the exchange value of the U.S. dollar at times when the Fed deems it essential. In times of excessive weakness of the dollar, the Fed can liquidate these interest-earning assets and use the foreign currencies they bring to purchase dollars in the foreign exchange market.

Other assets of the Federal Reserve include such items as the Fed's physical facilities—its buildings, furniture, equipment, computers, and fleet of automobiles.

Federal Reserve Liabilities

The dominant liability on the Fed's balance sheet is Federal Reserve notes, the paper money issued by the Fed. This item constitutes approximately 90 percent of total Federal Reserve liabilities. The Fed issues this currency in response to the public's demand for it, as manifested by the withdrawal of currency from depository institutions. When depository institutions run low, they contact the Fed, which issues the notes and sends them to the depository institutions in armored trucks. The Federal Reserve charges for this currency by debiting the depository institutions' deposit accounts at the Fed.

Deposits are maintained at the Federal Reserve by various organizations. Commercial banks and other depository institutions hold the major portion of their legal reserves in this form in order to meet the Fed's reserve requirements and to facilitate the clearing of checks through the Federal Reserve. When a check is deposited at a particular bank, the Fed processes it and credits that bank's reserve account at the Fed. A check written by a bank's customer results in a debit to that bank's account at the Fed.

The U.S. Treasury pays for the bulk of its expenditures through checks written on its account at the Federal Reserve, and regularly replenishes the account by transferring funds from its accounts in private banks, known as **tax and loan accounts.**[4] Foreign central banks also maintain checking accounts at the Federal Reserve, as do other international organizations such as the World Bank and the International Monetary Fund. Such organizations use their Federal Reserve account to make payments in the United States. The Fed processes checks written by these organizations by debiting the account of the international organization at the Fed and crediting the accounts at the Fed of the U.S. banks in which the checks are deposited.

"Deferred-availability cash items" corresponds to "cash items in process of collection" on the asset side of the Fed's balance sheet. This item represents the aggregate value of checks being processed by the Fed which will soon be credited to the accounts of the depository institutions which received the checks. These banks have a claim on the Fed, and in a day or two the Fed will be making a bookkeeping entry crediting their reserve accounts. The difference between "cash items in process of collection"

---

[4]Government deposits in private banks originate from the receipt of federal taxes and from the proceeds of the sale of government bonds to the public. These monies are initially deposited in commercial banks and are later transferred to the Treasury account at the Federal Reserve to be spent.

and "deferred-availability cash items" is known as Federal Reserve **float.**[5] Float is normally positive because the Fed typically credits the account of the bank in which a check is deposited a day or so before it debits the account of the bank on which it is written. (Float is discussed in more detail in Chapter 14.)

Federal Reserve Capital Accounts

The capital accounts of the Federal Reserve System consist of the difference between its total assets and total liabilities. A major portion of the Fed's capital accounts derives from capital paid in—that is, the equity the owners of the Federal Reserve have invested in the Fed. The remainder comes from funds that the Fed has transferred from its net income to "surplus," a component of the capital accounts.

Technically, the Federal Reserve is "owned" by the member banks of the Federal Reserve System. Each member bank is required to purchase shares of stock in the Federal Reserve in the amount of 6 percent of the bank's own capital accounts. In return, the Fed pays the bank a 6 percent dividend on its shares. The "ownership" of the Fed by private institutions (the member banks) is a manifestation of the distrust of government that influenced the writers of the Federal Reserve Act. It is, however, a highly unusual form of ownership, because the member banks do not exert significant influence over the Fed's operations or policies. Indeed, if they did, the Fed would be unable to carry out its chief functions in a satisfactory manner.

Federal Reserve Earnings and Expenses

Note, on the Federal Reserve's balance sheet for the end of March 1996, that the total value of interest-earning U.S. government securities held by the Fed was approximately $385 billion. This represents approximately 10 percent of the marketable national debt of the United States. While the Fed does not conduct its policies with the deliberate intention of earning a large profit, a natural by-product of its huge portfolio of Treasury securities is a handsome annual income. Table 12-2 indicates the sources and disposition of the income of the 12 Federal Reserve banks for 1995.

Table 12-2 indicates that the predominant source of Federal Reserve income, interest on U.S. government securities, was approximately $24 billion in 1995. Other sources of income (chiefly interest earned on foreign securities and fees collected for services provided) brought the Fed's gross income to $25.40 billion. After deducting operating expenses and making other accounting adjustments, the Fed's net income was approximately $24 billion.[6] The Fed allocated $230 million for payment of dividends to member banks and transferred

---

[5]This concept is analogous to another type of float that you may be familiar with. You have probably written a check a day or so before you had adequate funds in your account to cover it, knowing it would take at least a day for the check to be presented to your bank. If so, you have engaged in "playing the float."

[6]Because the Fed's portfolio is weighted heavily with *short-term* government securities, its income is sensitive to interest rates. The Fed's gross income averaged $22.8 billion a year during 1989–1991, primarily because of higher interest rates. Extremely low interest rates in 1992 and 1993 depressed the Fed's income to less than $20 billion per year. Short-term interest rates were higher again in 1994 and 1995, and the Fed's earnings rose from the depressed levels of 1992 and 1993.

Table 12-2	

Earnings and Expenses of All Federal Reserve Banks in 1995 (in billions of dollars)

Income from:	
Interest on government securities	$23.83
Loans to depository institutions	.01
Foreign securities	.78
Priced services	.74
Other	.04
Total	$25.40
Net expenses*	(2.35)
Additions to income†	0.86
Net income	$23.91
Disposition of income:	
Dividends paid to member banks	.23
Transferred to surplus account	.28
Payment to U.S. Treasury	$23.40

*Includes current expenses of the Federal Reserve banks and assessments by the Board of Governors for the Board's expenditures and the cost of currency.
†In 1995, the Federal Reserve earned profits of approximately $1.00 billion on foreign exchange market transactions. The Fed incurred small losses on U.S. Treasury and agency bond transactions. The result was a $0.86 billion addition to net income in 1995.

Source: Board of Governors of Federal Reserve System, *Annual Report*, 1995, pp. 294–301.

$280 million to its surplus account (part of its capital accounts) to match the capital paid in by member banks. It then turned over $23.40 billion to the U.S. Treasury. Because the bulk of the interest income paid by the Treasury to the Federal Reserve on the Fed's security portfolio is simply given back to the Treasury, the portion of the national debt the Treasury sells to the Federal Reserve is financed almost without cost to the Treasury.[7]

The unique financial status of the Federal Reserve—its possession of its own internal source of funds and its resulting lack of dependence on congressional appropriations—is a key source of its political independence. In recent decades, the Federal Reserve has come under attack from time to time by members of Congress who tend to regard the Federal Reserve as somewhat of a loose cannon, operating without appropriate constraints. Some legislators who frequently take issue with the Fed's policies seem to dislike the Fed's financial and political independence and would like to tighten its accountability to the democratic

---

[7]This raises a potential conflict of interest. To save money, the Treasury might be motivated to pressure the Federal Reserve into buying large blocks of the national debt. As we will learn later, this would result in a rapid expansion of the nation's money supply, provoking severe inflation. Such a potential conflict of interest is a major reason why the Fed was originally established with safeguards to prevent undue influence by the Treasury, the Congress, and the president.

process. Some have even suggested that the Fed be required to turn over *all* its revenues to the Treasury and submit annual budget requests to Congress as government agencies do. Needless to say, the Fed defends its financial status and political independence vigorously, pointing to the fact that its operating expenditures are typically only 10 percent of its gross income. We shall have more to say on this issue shortly, when we examine the case for an independent central bank.

THE STRUCTURE OF THE FEDERAL RESERVE SYSTEM

The key units of the Federal Reserve System are the Board of Governors; the Federal Open Market Committee; the 12 regional Federal Reserve banks, with a total of 25 branches; and some 3900 member banks. These units and their interrelationships are sketched in Figure 12-1. You will find it useful to refer to this organizational chart as we

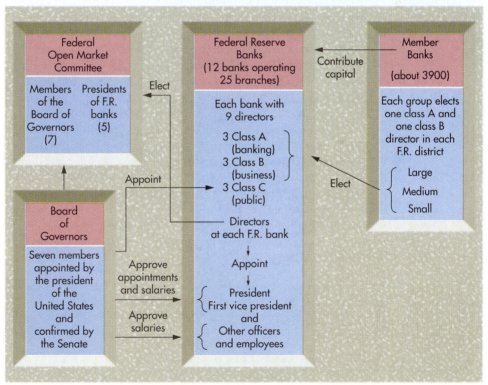

Figure 12-1   Organization of the Federal Reserve System. The complex structure of the Federal Reserve System reflects the Federal Reserve Act's framers' distrust of both government and the concentration of financial power.   *Source:* Adapted from Board of Governors of Federal Reserve System, *The Federal Reserve System: Purposes and Functions,* 6th ed. (Washington, D.C.: 1974), p. 18.

discuss the structure of authority within the Federal Reserve System and the historic rationale for its existing organization. We begin with one of the most important elements of the system, the Board of Governors.

The Board of Governors

The **Board of Governors of the Federal Reserve System** (originally known as the Federal Reserve Board) is the heart of the Fed. Its major responsibilities include setting the level of reserve requirements (within congressionally established limits); reviewing and "determining" the level of the discount rates set by the 12 Federal Reserve district banks; and serving as voting members on the important **Federal Open Market Committee (FOMC).** The FOMC is responsible for buying and selling securities with a view toward influencing credit availability and monetary conditions throughout the nation. Thus the Board of Governors dominates the monetary policy decision-making process.

In addition, the Board of Governors is charged with establishing bank supervision and examination procedures and with evaluating applications for bank mergers and acquisitions. The Board also sets **margin requirements** for the purchase of stocks and bonds by the public. (Margin requirements refer to the percentage of the value of the purchase of securities which must be paid for out of the buyer's own funds, as opposed to borrowed funds.) The Board of Governors even has considerable influence over the actions of the individual Federal Reserve banks. Its influence stems from the fact that the Board reviews the budgets of the individual Fed banks and also determines the salaries of their top officers.

Each member of the Board of Governors is appointed by the president of the United States for one 14-year term, subject to confirmation by the U.S. Senate. Not more than one Board member can come from any one of the 12 Federal Reserve districts. Board members may not be reappointed after serving a full term.[8] Once appointed, a Board member cannot be fired by the president over policy disagreements. Appointments are overlapping—that is, staggered so that one Board member's term expires every 2 years. The intent is to prevent the president from "stacking" the Board with individuals sympathetic to the president's political objectives. In fact, the rationale for both the staggered terms and the long, nonrenewable appointments of Board members is that the exposure of the conduct of monetary policy to political influence by the executive branch of government will thus be reduced and a "long view" into the management of the nation's money and credit machinery will be instilled.[9]

---

[8]A Board member may, however, serve a total of more than 14 years by serving as a replacement for someone who fails to fill out a full term, and then accepting a new 14-year term. Curiously, a technical loophole exists that allows a member of the Board to resign near the end of a full 14-year term and still be eligible for another full 14-year term. This loophole allowed William McChesney Martin to serve on the Board of Governors for 28 years, from 1942 until 1970. The loophole has not been used since then.

[9]In recent times, few members of the Board of Governors have served a full 14-year term. In fact, in the past 25 years, fewer than half the Board members have lasted as long as 7 years on the Board. Recently, Board members have been tempted to step down by lucrative offers from Wall Street firms involving salaries that are sometimes 10 times higher than those paid for service on the Board of Governors. Thus, President Carter appointed four governors during his first 3 years in office (1977–1979); President Reagan appointed seven governors by the end of his second term (1989); and President Clinton made his fourth appointment to the Board at the beginning of his fourth year in office (early 1996).

The president appoints a chairman of the Board of Governors to a 4-year term. This term is not synchronized with the president's term. The chairman of the Board of Governors may be reappointed to additional 4-year terms, within the limits of the 14-year overall term on the Board. For example, in early 1996 Alan Greenspan (see Exhibit 12-1) was appointed to a third term as chairman. The chairman of the Board of Governors is potentially an extremely powerful figure because of his or her influence over nominations to the Board, over the attitudes and voting behavior of other members of the Board and the Federal Open Market Committee, and over public opinion through testimony before congressional committees, speeches, and public statements.

The Federal Open Market Committee (FOMC)

This key committee meets eight times annually (approximately every 6 weeks) at the Board of Governors' headquarters in Washington, D.C., to chart the intended course of Federal Reserve policy in general and open market operations in particular. In attendance at these meetings are the seven members of the Board of Governors, the 12 presidents of the Federal Reserve banks, key advisors to the Federal Reserve bank presidents, and key staff of the Board and FOMC. At the meeting, members of the FOMC voice their opinions regarding current economic conditions and the appropriate course of monetary policy. Staff members give projections of the course of output, employment, and inflation that would hypothetically ensue, given various alternative growth rates of the monetary aggregates (M2, M3, etc.) and levels of short-term interest rates.

Further discussion takes place, and when a consensus appears to be at hand, a **directive** is drafted indicating the desired conduct of monetary policy until the next meeting of the FOMC. The directive typically specifies the approximate range within which certain key variables, such as M2 or short-term interest rates, are to be maintained. The directive is then put to a formal vote. Although the seven members of the Board of Governors and the 12 Federal Reserve bank presidents attend the FOMC meetings and participate in the discussion, only the Board members and *five* of the presidents are allowed to vote at a given meeting. The New York Federal Reserve bank president is a permanent voting member of the FOMC; the remaining 11 Fed bank presidents alternate as voting members, with four exercising voting privileges in any given year.

When the directive is approved by a formal vote, it is issued to the **manager of the System Open Market Account,** who is an officer of the Federal Reserve bank of New York. This individual is responsible for carrying out, through a network of government securities dealers, the open market transactions needed to meet the specifications outlined in the FOMC directive. (This process is examined in detail in Chapter 17.)

Because open market operations are generally considered the foremost instrument of Federal Reserve policy, the importance of the FOMC is obvious. The FOMC is also responsible for conducting occasional operations in the foreign exchange market for the purpose of stabilizing the exchange value of the U.S. dollar vis-à-vis other currencies.

EXHIBIT 12-1

Alan Greenspan, Chairman of the Board of Governors, 1987–Present

The view is commonly expressed that the chairman of the Board of Governors of the Federal Reserve System is the second most powerful individual in the United States. The chairman of the Board has great influence over the nation's powerful monetary machinery, helping to set the level of interest rates and ultimately influencing the rates of unemployment and inflation. This individual sets the agenda for meetings of the Board of Governors and presides over meetings of the Federal Open Market Committee, the group that meets eight times a year in Washington, D.C., to decide on the basic posture of monetary policy. The chairman of the Board of Governors also communicates and negotiates with key congressional committees, the secretary of the Treasury, and the president of the United States; supervises the huge staff of professional economists and advisors who work for the Board; and communicates current Federal Reserve policy through appearances before congressional committees and public statements.

In 1987, Alan Greenspan was appointed chairman of the Board of Governors of the Federal Reserve by President Ronald Reagan. He was reappointed to additional 4-year terms as chairman by President Bush (1992) and President Clinton (1996). He is only the seventh individual to occupy that crucial seat since 1934. Greenspan graduated summa cum laude from New York University in 1948. He received a Ph.D. from the same institution in 1977. In the interim, he compiled an impressive record in consulting and government service. From 1954 to 1977, he was CEO of Townsend Greenspan, an economic consulting firm in New York. In the early 1970s, he served as a consultant to both the U.S. Treasury and the Federal Reserve Board, and in the mid-1970s he was a member of the President's Council of Economic Advisors in the Nixon and Ford administrations, serving as chairman of the Council during the troubled years 1974–1977. Then during 1981–1983, he chaired the important National Committee on Social Security Reform. A keen student of business cycle statistics, Greenspan spends long hours poring over data to help formulate his position on the appropriate thrust of monetary policy.

The 12 Federal Reserve Banks

The decentralized organization of the Federal Reserve System, with 12 district banks instead of one central bank, is unique, as other nations have a single central bank. We have seen that, historically, Americans have been wary of the concentration of power and authority in a few hands. At the time the Federal Reserve Act was under discussion, many legislators from western and southern states insisted on a decentralized structure of central banking authority. Some members of Congress, representing the populist element, suggested that 50 or more autonomous, regional Federal Reserve banks would be appropriate. These legislators held that regional variations in financial conditions required different financial policies for different parts of the country. Other legislators, particularly those in the east, desired to follow the traditional model of a single central bank. The resulting compromise produced the network of 12 regional Federal Reserve banks that we know today.

Figure 12-2 shows the geographic boundaries of the 12 Federal Reserve districts, along with the cities in which each of the 12 Fed district banks is located. The figure also shows the location of the Board of Governors in Washington, D.C.

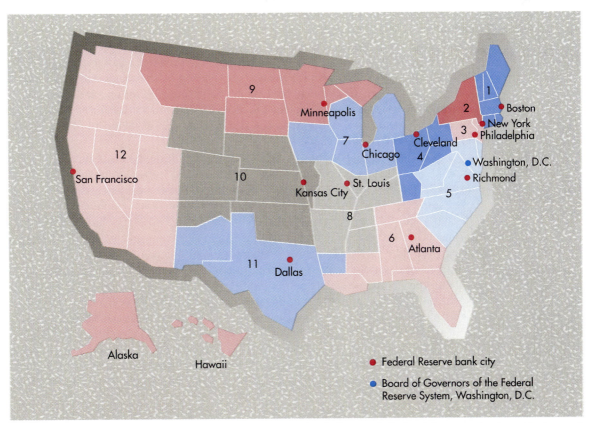

Figure 12-2 Federal Reserve Districts. The nation is divided into 12 Federal Reserve districts. Alaska and Hawaii are included in the twelfth district. The Board of Governors is located in Washington, D.C.

The 12 Federal Reserve district banks perform the following functions:

1 Issuing new currency and withdrawing old or damaged currency from circulation

2 Clearing checks

3 "Establishing" the discount rate for the district, administering the discount window operation (setting the criteria for bank borrowing), and making loans to banks in the district

4 Examining state-chartered banks in the district that belong to the Federal Reserve System

5 Conducting research on regional economic issues and national monetary policy and publishing the findings[10]

Technically, each Federal Reserve district bank is an incorporated institution, owned by the member banks of the district and governed by a nine-person board of directors. These directors select the Federal Reserve district bank president, thereby influencing the composition of the important Federal Open Market Committee. The nine directors are grouped into three classes. Class A directors are professional bankers elected by the member banks of the district. Class B directors are typically prominent business leaders (from industry, commerce, or agriculture) and are also elected by the member banks. Class C directors represent areas other than banking or the business sector and are appointed by the Board of Governors in Washington. The Board of Governors designates two of these Class C directors to serve as chairman and deputy chairman of the board of directors of the Federal Reserve district banks.

The historical rationale for the three-tier structure of the board of directors is that representation of the various constituencies influenced by the conduct of monetary policy will thus be ensured: Class A directors look out for the interests of bankers; Class B directors protect the interests of the nonbank business community; and Class C directors are supposed to represent the general public. Proposals have occasionally been made to increase the number of Class C directors. Sentiment has also been expressed from time to time in favor of reducing the influence of bankers in the formulation of monetary policy. Such influence presents a potential conflict of interest because monetary policies that are appropriate for the nation as a whole sometimes differ from the policies that are best for commercial banks' profits. As previously mentioned, bankers elect six of the nine directors, who in turn select the president of each Federal Reserve bank. These presidents participate in the crucial Federal Open Market Committee policy deliberations. The influence of bankers on the conduct of monetary policy could be reduced by declaring them ineligible to serve as directors of the Fed-

---

[10]Federal Reserve *Reviews,* published by each of the 12 district banks, are typically published four or six times annually and are written for the educated lay public. Subscriptions are available free of charge. For the address of each Federal Reserve bank, see the list at the end of this chapter.

eral Reserve district banks or by revoking the voting privileges of Federal Reserve bank presidents on the FOMC. The latter action, of course, would mean that the FOMC would be made up solely of the Board of Governors.[11]

Member Banks

In 1996, approximately 40 percent of the nation's 10,000 commercial banks were members of the Federal Reserve System. All national banks (approximately 3,000) chartered by the Comptroller of the Currency are required to belong to the System. Banks chartered by individual states may join the Federal Reserve System if they wish, provided they meet certain requirements. The conditions for membership are that the bank must abide by the Fed's regulations concerning mergers, establishment of branches, maintenance of capital standards, and numerous other matters. Less than 20 percent of the approximately 7,000 state-chartered banks currently belong to the Federal Reserve System.

The benefits of Federal Reserve membership include participation in the selection of six of the nine directors of the Fed district bank and perhaps some prestige. The most significant deterrent to membership over the years has been strict supervision and regulation by Federal Reserve authorities and, until the 1980s, the higher reserve requirements applicable to member banks. Reserve requirements may be considered a form of taxation levied on banks, because they require banks to hold more of their assets in non-interest-earning form (cash and deposits at the Fed) than they would maintain in the absence of reserve requirements. Because member banks were once subject to higher reserve requirements than nonmembers, member banks were placed at a disadvantage. During the late 1960s and 1970s, as inflation and interest rates ratcheted upward (thus raising the opportunity cost of holding reserves), the percentage of banks that chose to be members of the Federal Reserve System steadily declined. The Depository Institutions Deregulation and Monetary Control Act of 1980 (DIDMCA) leveled the playing field and stopped the erosion of Federal Reserve membership by requiring all depository institutions to abide by uniform reserve requirements set by the Federal Reserve, regardless of their membership status.[12]

Your Turn

> What features in the structure of the Federal Reserve System serve to spread power between the government and the private sector? Among the various geographic regions of the country?

---

[11]In reality, the directors of the district Fed banks are less influential than they appear to be. Typically, only one candidate is nominated to be a district Federal Reserve bank president, and that nominee is put forward by the Board of Governors in Washington or by the officers of the district Fed bank itself. Hence, the directors simply "rubber-stamp" a nominee they had no influence in nominating.

[12]DIDMCA reduced both the costs and benefits of membership in the Federal Reserve System, with the result that there has been no major change in the proportion of the nation's banks that belong to the Federal Reserve since the early 1980s. By equalizing reserve requirements for all depository institutions, it removed the chief cost of belonging to the Federal Reserve System. And by permitting nonmember depository institutions to borrow from the Federal Reserve and providing them access to other Fed services previously denied nonmembers, it reduced the benefits of membership.

The Allocation of Power within the Federal Reserve System

Since the early 1930s, power has resided more with the Board of Governors in Washington than with the Federal Reserve district banks. For example, while the Federal Reserve district bank presidents are formally appointed by the district's nine-person board of directors, the Board of Governors in Washington retains veto power over their choices. And while the discount rate is set by each district bank, it is subject to review and determination by the Board of Governors. In essence, the Board of Governors determines the discount rate. Finally, in the early days, each Federal Reserve bank was authorized to purchase government securities at its own discretion. Today, decisions concerning such transactions are made in Washington by the FOMC for the system as a whole, and the securities are apportioned among the Fed district banks on the basis of their total assets.

The Board of Governors sets the salaries of the Federal Reserve district bank officers and has the authority to remove a district bank president in the event of incompetence or willful obstruction of Federal Reserve policy. (Exhibit 12-2 discusses the salary structure of top Federal Reserve officials.) For practical purposes, we may regard the Board and the FOMC as the governing units of the Federal Reserve today; the Federal Reserve district banks are little more than branches.

Among the 12 Fed district banks, the Federal Reserve bank of New York has always held a position of preeminence. Not only does the New York Fed own 30 percent of the total assets of the Federal Reserve System, it physically carries out open market operations on behalf of the system. The New York Fed has its finger on the pulse of the major financial markets, which are located in New York. Also, as previously indicated, the New York Fed president is the only Fed district bank president with permanent voting privileges on the FOMC. Finally, the New York Fed handles the system's dealings with foreign central banks and international institutions.

Figure 12-3 gives a rough, subjective idea of the actual distribution of power within the Federal Reserve System, as estimated by a former member of the Board of Governors. Note that the chairman of the Board of Governors wields disproportionate power for the reasons we mentioned earlier. The staffs of the Board and the FOMC—highly trained professional economists—and the manager of the Open Market Account in New York also have considerable influence. According to this estimate, the 12 Federal Reserve district banks account for only about 10 percent of the power. Of course, this estimate is approximate and changes somewhat over time, depending on the personality of the chairman of the Board of Governors and other factors. For example, most students of the Federal Reserve believe Chairmen Paul Volcker (1979–1987) and Alan Greenspan (1987–present) were more powerful than Volcker's predecessor, William Miller (1977–1979).

THE QUESTION OF FEDERAL RESERVE INDEPENDENCE

Relative to central banks in most other nations and to agencies of the U.S. government, the Federal Reserve System exhibits considerable political independence. The Fed's independence was deliberately created by the authors of the Federal Reserve Act and was

EXHIBIT 12-2

Salaries of Top Federal Reserve Officials

The accompanying table shows the annual salaries of the members of the Board of Governors of the Federal Reserve System and the presidents of the Fed district banks as of December 31, 1995. Also indicated are the number of officers and average salaries of officers for each Federal Reserve district bank.

Several items are noteworthy. First, note the rather large range of salaries of the presidents of the Federal Reserve district banks. Such salaries range from a high of $253,200 for the San Francisco bank president to a low of $177,550 for the Boston bank president. To a limited extent, the large salary range reflects regional differences in the cost of living. But mostly, it reflects other factors. More important, note that the chairman of the Board of Governors, arguably one of the two most powerful individuals in the United States, earns far less than the lowest-paid Federal Reserve district bank president and only slightly more than half the salary earned by the president of the Federal Reserve Bank of San Francisco. The chairman of the Board of Governors is also known to earn less than the division heads of the Board's own staff. The relatively low pay of members of the Board of Governors helps to account for the fact that the typical Board member in the past 15 years has served only about 5 years of the 14-year term before departing for other activities. When Paul Volcker and Wayne Angell left the board in 1987 and 1994, respectively, each was reputed to have been offered a salary in the $1 million range with a Wall Street firm. Even Alan Blinder's salary increased when he left the Board (after serving less than 2 years) in 1996 to return to his position in academia as professor of economics at Princeton.

What accounts for the relatively parsimonious salaries of Board members vis-à-vis other high Federal Reserve officials? The answer lies in the fact that, while the salaries of other Federal Reserve officials are set by the Fed itself, salaries of members of the Board of Governors are established by federal statute.

Board of Governors:

Officer	Salary
Chairman	$133,600
Other Board members	$123,100
Division heads of Board staff	More than $160,000*

Presidents and other officers of 12 Federal Reserve district banks:

District	Federal Reserve Bank	President's Salary	Officers' Salary	Number of Officers
1	Boston	$177,550	$102,036	58
2	New York	228,500	122,777	204
3	Philadelphia	203,700	95,677	57
4	Cleveland	183,000	98,943	49
5	Richmond	178,500	90,828	76
6	Atlanta	235,900	93,987	75
7	Chicago	202,650	96,507	102
8	St. Louis	209,500	90,540	49
9	Minneapolis	192,300	96,945	49
10	Kansas City	178,700	91,583	58
11	Dallas	180,000	92,590	58
12	San Francisco	253,200	109,416	88
	Average	$201,960	$ 98,485	77

*Salaries of the staff of the Board of Governors are not public information. However, salaries of division heads (Research and Statistics, Monetary Affairs, International Finance, and Banking Supervision) are known to exceed the salary of the chairman of the Board of Governors.

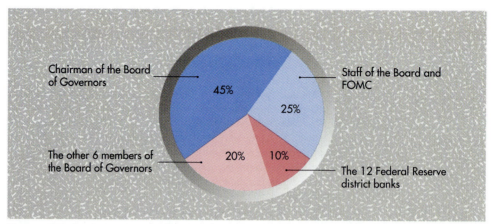

Figure 12-3   De Facto Distribution of Power within the Federal Reserve System. Actual power in the Fed is believed to be heavily concentrated in the chairman of the Board of Governors and the Board's staff. The Fed district banks have relatively little power. *Source:* Based on Sherman Maisel, *Managing the Dollar* (New York: Norton, 1972).

further strengthened by legislation in the 1930s. This independence derives partly from the lengthy, nonrenewable 14-year terms of the members of the Board of Governors, which prevent their intimidation by the executive branch of government. No member of the Board need curry favor with the president, since Board members may neither be reappointed to a second term nor dismissed by a president over disagreements about the appropriate conduct of monetary policy.

Perhaps even more significant is the fact that the Fed's operating revenues are derived from its portfolio of securities rather than from congressional appropriations. Other government agencies are required to submit annual budget requests to Congress. Such a procedure inevitably permits Congress to influence an agency's behavior. The Fed has not only remained financially independent of Congress but at one time even flaunted its independence by refusing to submit to an audit by the General Accounting Office.[13] Thus, in its day-to-day conduct of monetary policy, the Fed has traditionally occupied the enviable position of taking orders from no one. In numerous instances the Fed has implemented policy actions that were received with open irritation by the president and Congress.

The independence of the Federal Reserve tends to be overstated, however. In reality, both the president and Congress have influence over the Fed. Because the Fed is reluctant to oppose the views of the person selected by the whole nation, it would prefer to act in a manner consistent with the president's wishes. Also, because the Fed is actively involved in congressional legislation concerning regulation of banks and other matters, it needs the president's support and thus desires to remain in the president's good graces. The independence of the Fed vis-à-vis Congress is especially tenuous.

---

[13]Today, most of the Fed's operations are thoroughly audited by the General Accounting Office. However, the Fed has vigorously and successfully resisted any audit of its operations in the foreign exchange market and its other international dealings.

EXHIBIT 12-3

What Motivates the Fed—The Public Interest or Bureaucratic Empire Building?

We have described the Federal Reserve as a benevolent organization dedicated solely to the public interest. By smoothing the ups and downs of the business cycle, supervising and regulating banks, and serving as a lender of last resort, the Fed ostensibly contributes magnanimously to the national interest. Such is the traditional view of the Fed.

Public choice economists have suggested an alternative explanation of the forces that motivate the Federal Reserve and other bureaucracies. In their view, just as consumers seek to maximize utility and business firms act to maximize profit, the Federal Reserve is motivated to pursue actions which maximize its own welfare. The welfare of the Federal Reserve, like that of any bureaucracy, is directly related to its *power*—the size and strength of its empire. In this view, the Fed consistently acts to maximize its own welfare rather than the welfare of the public.

To test this rather cynical theory of Federal Reserve behavior, one would want to specify its predictions and compare them with the Fed's actual behavior. Such predictions include the following: The Fed will strive to maintain its financial autonomy, fight any proposals that would reduce its authority or responsibilities, and avoid or minimize conflict with those who have authority to change the nature of the Federal Reserve—that is, Congress.

One can easily cite examples of Fed behavior that are consistent with these predictions. The Federal Reserve has repeatedly and effectively fought congressional proposals to change its financial status and has even refused to submit to a government audit of its books. When the Clinton administration proposed collapsing the nation's four separate and overlapping banking supervisory agencies (the Federal Reserve, the FDIC, the Comptroller of the Currency, and individual state organizations) into a single new regulatory authority to save money, the Fed resisted with vigor. In 1995, the Fed supported a proposal to permit banks to expand into investment banking activities, which had been prohibited by the Glass-Steagall Act of 1933. Such an expansion would produce a corresponding expansion of Federal Reserve responsibility—an increase in the Fed's empire.

On numerous occasions over the years, the Fed has bowed to congressional pressure by keeping interest rates artificially low. The Fed chairman is an acknowledged expert at "obfuscation"—the art of making ambiguous statements that are virtually impossible to decipher or interpret. When Congress required the Fed to specify and justify in advance its targets for money growth rates, the Fed responded by specifying a multitude of targets (for M1, M2, M3, etc.) to minimize potential criticism—if the Fed missed one target it would likely hit another! The Federal Reserve is also notoriously secretive. It has long resisted congressional pressure to abandon its policy of delaying release of its FOMC directives until several weeks after FOMC meetings. Transcripts of the details of FOMC meetings are not released until 5 years after the meetings. Most economists believe that such tactics serve little useful function other than to protect the Fed from criticism.

Still, the view that the Fed is motivated predominantly by self-interest seems harsh. Clearly, the Fed is dedicated to providing a stable long-run economic climate. A more charitable interpretation of the Fed's behavior might be the following: When there is no serious conflict with the public interest, the Fed will act according to the theory of bureaucratic behavior. When there is serious conflict, the Fed is likely to act as it is supposed to act—in the public interest.

Central Bank Independence and Economic Performance

Those who advocate an independent central bank believe that such an arrangement is more conducive to favorable economic performance, as indicated by a relatively stable price level over a period of years. A recent study discovered a significant negative association across nations between the degree of independence of central banks and the average magnitude of inflation experienced over a period of years. Professor Alberto Alesina of Harvard University ranked the degree of independence of central banks of industrial nations on a scale of 1 to 4. Highly independent central banks were ranked 4, while the least independent central banks were ranked 1. The rankings were established on the basis of objective criteria: the extent of the presence of government officials on the board of directors of the central bank; the extent to which the central bank is required to help finance government budget deficits; the prevalence of informal contacts between officials in the executive branch and the central bank; and the formal relationship between the central bank and the government.

We have updated the Alesina study by computing the average inflation rate (CPI) experienced by each of the 17 countries during 1971–1994. The findings are illustrated in the accompanying figure. Countries whose central banks were judged to be highly independent exhibited relatively low inflation rates. The two nations with the most independent central banks, Germany and Switzerland, experienced the lowest rates of inflation. Countries with the least independent central banks (for example, Spain and Italy) consistently experienced relatively high rates of inflation.

Were the low inflation rates enjoyed by such nations as Germany and Switzerland purchased at the cost of relatively high unemployment rates? The answer is no. Germany, Switzerland, and Japan experienced lower unemployment rates on average over the 23-year period than such high-inflation nations as Italy and England. The implication: the United States will perhaps be best served if Congress doesn't challenge the Fed's independent status.

The ultimate authority to govern the money creation process rests with the legislative branch of government. Also, the U.S. Constitution does not mandate a central bank; Congress created the Fed in 1913, altered it significantly in the 1930s, and retains authority to further modify or even abolish it. In addition, the Fed is subject to all U.S. laws, including the Employment Act of 1946 and the Humphrey-Hawkins Act of 1978. Hence, it is clear that the Fed's independence from the legislative branch is conditional and fragile. In the end, the Federal Reserve is accountable to Congress and is acutely aware of being so. The factors motivating the Fed's behavior are discussed in Exhibit 12-3.

The Case for Federal Reserve Independence

The case for an independent central bank rests on the view that control of the central bank by the executive or legislative branch would result in favoritism based on party affiliation, patronage, and other political considerations. What is more significant, political control of

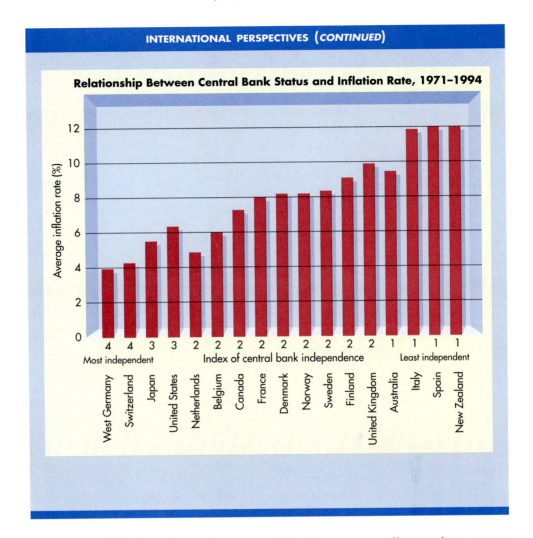

INTERNATIONAL PERSPECTIVES (*CONTINUED*)

Relationship Between Central Bank Status and Inflation Rate, 1971–1994

the Fed would likely introduce an "easy money" bias into monetary policy, creating a propensity toward inflation (on this, see the "International Perspectives" box on page 302). The argument is that politicians love to spend money but hate to levy taxes to pay for their expenditures. This propensity toward budget deficits means that the government must frequently borrow. A politically expedient—but highly inflationary—method of financing deficit spending would be to simply have the government sell bonds to a subservient Federal Reserve. This process is equivalent to printing money to finance government expenditures. The Fed has long been regarded as the guardian of price level stability, providing something of a check and balance against the excesses of government budgetary imprudence. Advocates of an independent central bank believe the tendency of the U.S. economy to experience inflation would be stimulated by any appreciable reduction in the Fed's independence.

The above considerations are made more acute by the short terms of the U.S. president and Congress. Those who support an independent central bank also emphasize the need for continuity in the conduct of monetary policy. Politicians tend to be myopic, looking only as far ahead as the next election. If the central bank were subservient to the executive or legislative branch of government, the conduct of monetary policy might at times be dictated by the short-term political needs of incumbent politicians rather than legitimate long-term objectives such as price level stability. Monetary policy influences output and employment more quickly than it affects the inflation rate, and politicians might therefore be motivated to boost economic activity as election time approaches, even though such measures might necessitate a post-election recession engineered to bring down the inflation resulting from the pre-election economic stimulus. Most economists believe that such a "stop-and-go" policy would be the worst prescription for the nation's economic health.

In sum, those who support an independent Federal Reserve emphasize that monetary policy is simply too complicated and important to entrust to politicians. In support of this view, one can point to the conduct of government budgetary policy in the past 15 years.

The Case against Federal Reserve Independence

Critics of the independent status of the Federal Reserve argue that, in a democracy, those responsible for monetary policy should be accountable to the electorate. If the Fed were made part of the executive branch, the argument goes, the administration in power could be held accountable for the overall conduct of macroeconomic policy, including monetary policy. Poor performance could be penalized, through the democratic process, by "throwing the rascals out."

Another consideration frequently voiced by critics of the Fed's independent status is that the various elements of national economic policy need to be coordinated rather than allowed to run at cross-purposes. Given that expenditure and tax policy—fiscal policy—is determined by the executive and legislative branches, while monetary policy is set by the Federal Reserve, lack of coordination is a distinct possibility. The Reagan administration clashed openly with the Fed in 1981 and 1982, when tax cuts aimed at stimulating production and employment were countered by high interest rates resulting from the Fed's restrictive policies.

Finally, critics of the Fed's independence tend to argue that the Federal Reserve has not used its independence effectively over the years. The Fed presided passively over the collapse of the financial system in the early 1930s, contributed to inflationary pressures in the 1940s, the late 1960s, and the late 1970s, and hit the monetary brakes too hard in the severe recession of the early 1980s. The rejoinder to this point, of course, is that the Fed has learned from its past mistakes and is a far more effective institution today.

Attacks on the Fed's independence seem to come in spurts and are particularly virulent in times when interest rates are extremely high. One example is the early 1980s, when the Fed pushed interest rates to extremely high levels in an effort to stem the severe inflation that had been building for 15 years. Various proposed reforms to reduce the Fed's autonomy were seriously discussed at that time. Today, any reforms affecting the Fed's independence seem likely to be modest. One proposal is to make the 4-year term of the chairman of the Board of Governors concurrent with that of the U.S. president so the president could appoint a new chairman upon taking office. The term of office of Board members might also be shortened, particularly in view of the propensity of appointees to serve only a portion of the term. More radical proposals include putting the secretary of the Treasury on the FOMC and requiring the Fed to turn all its revenues over to the Treasury and be financed by congressional appropriations.

In 1993, Henry Gonzalez, then chairman of the House Banking Committee, presented a bill that would have given the U.S. president the authority to appoint the Federal Reserve district bank presidents, reduce the input of private banks in overseeing the Fed district banks, and require the Fed to make more timely and detailed disclosures about its policy decisions. So far, only the last proposal has received serious consideration. The Fed has moved (albeit very gingerly) in the direction of reducing its propensity for secrecy. In 1995, the Fed began announcing major changes in Federal Open Market Committee decisions the day after the meeting rather than after the previous 6-week delay. Also, detailed transcripts of FOMC meetings are now made available to the public 5 years after meetings (previously, the details of the meetings were never made public). Most economists applaud these moves but argue that the Fed should move farther in the direction of openness.

Since 1978, the Federal Reserve has been required to confer with congressional committees twice a year regarding its intended monetary policy posture. The Fed's testimony is made available to the public. It seems reasonable to argue that such dialogues help to pave the way for intelligent discussion of monetary policy without encroaching on the Fed's independence. At this writing, the Federal Reserve remains one of the most independent central banks in the world (see International Perspectives).

SUMMARY

A central bank is an organization charged with many tasks, the most important and difficult of which is conducting monetary policy—that is, influencing the nation's credit conditions and interest rates and controlling its money supply. The U.S. central bank, established early in this century, is known as the Federal Reserve System (or the Fed). By determining key items on its own balance sheet, the Fed is able to influence credit, interest rates, and the money supply. The most important units in the Federal Reserve System are the Board of Governors and the Federal

Open Market Committee. These groups make the important decisions about the fundamental posture of monetary policy. Because Federal Reserve policies strongly influence the nation's economy, the founders of the Federal Reserve established numerous safeguards to reduce the influence of the executive and legislative branches of government on the short-term conduct of monetary policy. However, students of central banking disagree about the extent to which a central bank should be independent of the political process in a democracy.

Answers to Your Turn (p. 297)

Power is vested in the government because the president of the United States appoints the members of the Board of Governors (including the chairman), because the profits of the Fed revert to the Treasury, and because the Fed must report and defend its monetary policy targets twice annually before congressional committees. Power resides in the private sector because the presidents of the 12 Federal Reserve banks are selected by private citizens (directors of the individual Fed banks) and because the 12 Fed banks are "owned" by the private commercial banks which are members of the Federal Reserve System.

Geographic representation derives from the fact that there are 12 Federal Reserve banks spread throughout the nation and the fact that not more than one member of the Board of Governors can come from any one of the 12 districts.

KEY TERMS

legal reserves (reserves)

fractional reserve banking system

Federal Reserve Act

lender of last resort

Federal Reserve district banks

open market operations

discounts and advances

tax and loan accounts

float

Board of Governors of the Federal Reserve System

Federal Open Market Committee (FOMC)

margin requirements

directive

manager of the System Open Market Account

STUDY QUESTIONS

1 Discuss the problems that led to the creation of the Federal Reserve System.

2 Explain why the following items are listed on the asset side of the Federal Reserve's balance sheet:

a Loans to depository institutions

b Cash items in process of collection

3 Explain why the following items are listed on the liability side of the Federal Reserve's balance sheet:

a Depository institution deposits at the Fed

b Deferred availability cash items

4 Who owns the Federal Reserve? Explain the nature of the ownership.

5 Explain how the Federal Reserve is financed.

6 Discuss the composition of the Federal Open Market Committee. How do members obtain their positions, and what is the rationale for this method of selecting them? In your view, should any changes be made in those procedures? Explain.

7 "The Board of Governors is the heart of the Federal Reserve System." Evaluate this statement.

8 Carefully analyze the merits of the case for a central bank's independence from the legislative and executive branches of government.

9 Is there any reason for maintaining 12 separate Federal Reserve banks today? Why might this arrangement have made more sense in 1913 than it does today?

10 Go to the library and find out who the seven members of the Fed's Board of Governors are and what their backgrounds are.

11 Why do you suppose the president of the New York Fed has a permanent seat on the FOMC?

12 Can you think of any reason why the state of Missouri has two Federal Reserve district banks, yet the entire western third of the United States has only one (in San Francisco)?

13 Can you think of any measures that would increase the Fed's accountability without seriously infringing on its autonomy?

SUGGESTIONS FOR ADDITIONAL READING

For a discussion of the events leading up to the creation of the Federal Reserve, see James Parthemos, "The Federal Reserve Act of 1913 in the Stream of Monetary History," Federal Reserve Bank of Richmond, *Economic Review,* July–August 1988, pp. 19–28. On the structure of the Federal Reserve System, see Chap. 1 of *The Federal Reserve System: Purposes and Functions,* 8th ed. (Washington, D.C.: Board of Governors, 1994). For a discussion of the role of political considerations on the conduct of monetary policy, see Steven M. Roberts, "Congressional Oversight of Monetary Policy," *Journal of Monetary Economics,* August 1978, pp. 543–556. An evaluation of the power of the chairman of the Board of Governors is presented in Edward J.

Kane, "The Impact of a New Federal Reserve Chairman," *Contemporary Policy Issues,* January 1988, pp. 89–97. Good sources on the factors that motivate Fed behavior include John T. Wooley, *Monetary Politics: The Federal Reserve and the Politics of Monetary Policy* (Cambridge, England: Cambridge University Press, 1984), and Thomas Mayer (ed.), *Political Economy of American Monetary Policy* (New York: Cambridge University Press, 1990). Political pressures facing the Fed are discussed in Thomas Havrilesky, *The Pressures on American Monetary Policy* (Boston: Kluwer Academic Publishers, 1992). To get a flavor of the view of Alan Greenspan and the other six members of the Board of Governors on many of the issues discussed in this chapter, see "Statements," *Federal Reserve Bulletin,* December 1993, pp. 1100–1116. The minutes and directives of each FOMC meeting are collected each year in the Board of Governors of the Federal Reserve System *Annual Report.* For an interesting and somewhat muckraking account of the Federal Reserve, see William Greider, *Secrets of the Temple* (New York: Simon and Schuster, 1987). Finally, an interesting recent piece detailing why a recent member of the Board of Governors (Alan Blinder) stepped down after only 2 years of service to return to academia is John Cassidy, "Fleeing the Fed," *The New Yorker,* February 19, 1996, pp. 38–46.

Note: Each of the Federal Reserve district banks publishes regular *Review*s that present their research findings. You may subscribe to the *Review*s at the following addresses:

Bank and Public Information Center
Federal Reserve Bank of Boston
600 Atlantic Avenue
Boston, MA 02106

Public Information Department
Federal Reserve Bank of New York
33 Liberty Street
New York, NY 10045

Public Information Center
Federal Reserve Bank of Chicago
P.O. Box 834
Chicago, IL 60690

Publications Section
Research Department
Federal Reserve Bank of Cleveland
P.O. Box 6387
Cleveland, OH 44101

Bank and Public Relations Department
Federal Reserve Bank of Richmond
P.O. Box 27622
Richmond, VA 23261

Information Center
Federal Reserve Bank of Atlanta
104 Marietta Street, N.W.
Atlanta, GA 30303

Office of Public Information
Federal Reserve Bank of Minneapolis
250 Marquette Avenue
Minneapolis, MN 55480

Public Information Department
Federal Reserve Bank of St. Louis
P.O. Box 442
St. Louis, MO 63166

Public Services Department
Federal Reserve Bank of Philadelphia
P.O. Box 66
Philadelphia, PA 19105

Public Affairs Department
Federal Reserve Bank of Dallas
Station K
Dallas, TX 75222

Public Information Section
Federal Reserve Bank of San Francisco
P.O. Box 7702
San Francisco, CA 94120

Public Information
Federal Reserve Bank of Kansas City
925 Grand Avenue
Kansas City, MO 64198

■

13

The Deposit Expansion Process: A Simple Analysis

In Chapter 12, we outlined the structure of the Federal Reserve System, which is ultimately responsible for the behavior of the nation's money supply. In Chapter 9, we discussed several aspects of commercial banking, skipping over the role depository institutions play in the money supply process. In this chapter we will analyze the way in which depository institutions—commercial banks, savings and loan associations, mutual savings banks, and credit unions, hereafter called "banks"—influence the money supply through their lending and investing activities. And we will briefly study the mechanism through which the Federal Reserve influences credit conditions and the growth rate of the money supply. In Chapters 14 and 15, we will examine the money supply process in more depth.

BANKS AND THE CREATION OF BANK DEPOSITS

An important aspect of banking stems from the fact that banks' actions influence the availability of credit and the supply of money. These variables are believed to have an important effect on such crucial macroeconomic variables as output, employment, and the nation's price level.

We will begin by illustrating the effect of bank lending and investing activities on the money supply—that is, on such monetary aggregates as M1 and M2. To illustrate the process, we will use T-accounts. A T-account indicates the *change* in the balance sheet of the depository institution resulting from a given event. Suppose your hometown bank lends $10,000 to a local shoe store owner for the purpose of increasing her inventories. Hometown Bank's T-account for this event summarizes the changes in its balance sheet as follows:

Hometown Bank			
Loans	+10,000	Demand deposits	+10,000

By adding a new loan to its assets, Hometown Bank has created new money—an increase in its demand deposits. Because demand deposits are included in all measures of the money supply, the monetary aggregates (M1, M2, M3) all increase. As soon as the loan is granted, the nation's money supply expands by $10,000.

Of course, the shoe store merchant did not take out the $10,000 loan for the purpose of leaving the funds in a checking account. When she purchases a new shipment of shoes, a $10,000 check drawn on her account at Hometown Bank is sent to a shoe manufacturer in St. Louis. After the check is deposited in a St. Louis bank and has been cleared, demand deposits in the Hometown Bank return to their original, pre-loan level. However, demand deposits in the St. Louis bank have increased by $10,000. The T-accounts of the two banks then appear as follows:

Hometown Bank		St. Louis Bank	
1. Loans +10,000	Demand deposits +10,000		
2. Deposits at Federal Reserve −10,000	Demand deposits −10,000	2. Deposits at Federal Reserve +10,000	Demand deposits +10,000

Note that the $10,000 created by Hometown's loan is still in the banking system. As long as Hometown's loan is outstanding, the U.S. money supply will be elevated by $10,000. The Federal Reserve clears the check by making a bookkeeping transaction transferring $10,000 from Hometown Bank's Federal Reserve deposit account to the St. Louis bank's Fed deposit account (step 2 in the T-accounts).

In the unlikely event that the merchant requests the loan in the form of currency rather than as a bookkeeping entry (a demand deposit), the result is the same—that is, M1, M2, and other monetary aggregates expand by $10,000. Because the currency granted to the merchant comes from the bank's vault (vault cash is not included in the money supply while in the bank), the monetary aggregates increase as soon as the cash is handed over to the borrower.[1] The main point can be easily summarized: Whenever banks increase their loans—whether in the form of currency or in the form of a demand deposit entry on the banks' books—the money supply increases by the amount of the loan.

The same result occurs whenever a bank purchases securities from the public or from securities dealers. Suppose Hometown Bank purchases $200,000 of U.S. government securities from a dealer located in New York City. Hometown Bank sends a $200,000 check written on its account with the Federal Reserve. After the securities dealer deposits the

---

[1]The narrow measure of the money supply, M1, equals $DDO + C^p$. The latter variable, currency in the hands of the public, includes only currency and coins *outside* depository institutions, the Treasury, and the Federal Reserve. Currency and coins held in banks are *not* included in C^p. Hence, when Hometown Bank grants the loan to the merchant in the form of currency, C^p rises and the various money supply measures (M1, M2, etc.) also increase.

check in a New York bank and the check is processed and cleared by the Federal Reserve System, the balance sheet changes as follows:

Hometown Bank		New York Bank	
U.S. government securities +200,000		Deposit at Fed +200,000	Demand deposits +200,000
Deposit at Fed −200,000			

When the dealer deposits the check in its New York bank, the money supply rises by $200,000.[2] The Federal Reserve handles the transfer of funds between the two banks by making two bookkeeping entries: one crediting the Fed account of the New York bank by $200,000, another debiting the Fed account of the Hometown Bank by the same amount. The point is clear: any time a bank purchases securities from a member of the nonbank public—any entity other than the Treasury, the Federal Reserve, or another bank—the money supply is boosted by the amount of the transaction.

These two examples demonstrate that banks create demand deposits (and money) whenever they expand their earning assets in the form of loans and securities. Because bank loans and securities earn interest and are therefore profitable, one is naturally inclined to ask: Is there a limit on the amount of money that depository institutions can create in making loans and purchasing securities? The answer is found in the existence of legal reserve requirements, which limit the acquisition of earning assets by banks. Depository institutions are required by law to maintain *reserves*—cash and deposits at the Federal Reserve—in amounts not less than a specified percentage of their demand deposit liabilities.[3]

At this point, it is useful to review certain key concepts: reserves, reserve requirements, required reserves, and excess reserves. **Reserves** are defined as cash in banks plus deposits at the Federal Reserve. The **reserve requirement** is a percentage figure specified by the Federal Reserve. **Required reserves** are the dollar amount of reserves a bank is required to maintain or exceed. This number is calculated by multiplying the reserve requirement percentage by the amount of demand deposits outstanding in a bank. **Excess reserves** are the difference between reserves and required reserves. If reserves exceed required reserves, banks have positive excess reserves.

Recall that when Hometown Bank made a loan or purchased securities, it lost reserves in the amount of the transaction (review the previous T-accounts). Once a bank has no excess reserves, it cannot afford to lose any reserves. Hence, any bank is limited in the amount of loans it can make or securities it can purchase by the amount of excess reserves it has on hand. Yet, as we will demonstrate, the *banking system* can generate new loans

---

[2]The check written by Hometown Bank does not reduce the demand deposits in that bank because the check was drawn by the bank itself from its Federal Reserve account. Hometown Bank's Federal Reserve account (not included in the money supply) is reduced by $200,000, but the deposits in Hometown Bank are not reduced.

[3]Even in the absence of reserve requirements, banks would be motivated to maintain a reasonable quantity of reserves to avoid the risk of illiquidity. Depository institutions would likely maintain fairly sizable reserve-to-deposit ratios (though smaller than they currently maintain) even if no explicit reserve requirements existed.

or securities purchases by a *multiple* of the excess reserves in the system. The key to this puzzle resides in the fact that while an *individual bank* loses reserves when it grants a loan or purchases a security, the *banking system* does not lose reserves.

Multiple Expansion of Bank Deposits

Because a fractional reserve banking system requires that banks maintain only a small portion of their demand deposits outstanding in the form of reserves (cash and deposits at the Fed), any new reserves that find their way into the banking system can support deposits that are a *multiple* of these new reserves. Suppose, for purposes of illustration, that banks have run up against the reserve requirement constraint. That is, suppose they have no excess reserves—no more reserves than the amount they are required to hold to meet the Fed's reserve requirements. They are therefore incapable of making additional loans or buying additional securities; they cannot create any additional money. Now suppose explorers discover a sunken ship off the coast of Florida that contains $5 million in coins. If the coins are placed in a checking account in a Florida bank (Bank A), the T-account effect is as follows:

Bank A			
Currency and coins	+5m	Demand deposits	+5m

Now, to demonstrate the phenomenon of multiple deposit expansion, we will make the following assumptions:

1 Each bank in the nation desires to rid itself of all its excess reserves. That is, each bank continues to acquire earning assets (loans and securities) until it runs up against the reserve requirement constraint.

2 The public's demand for currency (C^p) is independent of the amount of demand deposits held. Therefore, changes in demand deposits will cause no change in the demand for currency by the public.

3 The legal reserve requirement for all demand deposits in all banks is 10 percent.

As a result of assumption 3, Bank A finds itself with excess reserves of $4.5 million.[4] Remember that, in making loans or buying securities, a bank will lose reserves in the amount of the transaction. Hence, each bank is limited in its ability to lend and to purchase securities by the amount of its excess reserves. Suppose Bank A uses these excess reserves to grant loans to real estate developers. Initially, the bank makes the funds available through bookkeeping entries in which the bank marks up the demand deposit accounts of

---

[4]Note the T-account above. Because demand deposits have increased by $5 million, and because the percentage reserve requirement is 10 percent, the dollar amount of required reserves has increased by 10% × $5 million, or $0.5 million. Because the bank has gained $5 million of reserves from the deposit of the coins, its excess reserves are initially up by $4.5 million.

the real estate developers. Of course, the developers do not leave the funds idle in their checking accounts. When they use the $4.5 million to purchase land from individuals who bank with Bank B, the T-account transactions of Banks A and B are as follows:

Bank A				Bank B			
1. Currency and coins	+5m	Demand deposits	+5m				
2. Loans	+4.5m	Demand deposits	+4.5m				
3. Deposit at Fed	−4.5m	Demand deposits	−4.5m	3. Deposit at Fed	+4.5m	Demand deposits	+4.5m

In step 1, Bank A receives the initial deposit of $5 million in coins from the sunken ship. In step 2, it grants loans of $4.5 million. In step 3, the checks written by the real estate developers against Bank A are cleared through the Federal Reserve. This is accomplished by two pairs of bookkeeping entries. In the first, the Fed transfers $4.5 million (bookkeeping account) from Bank A's account at the Fed to Bank B's account. In the second, Bank A debits the demand deposit accounts of the real estate developers by $4.5 million, and Bank B credits the land sellers' demand deposit account by the same amount.

When we net out the effects of these three steps on Bank A's balance sheet, we see that it ends up with reserves up by $0.5 million, loans up by $4.5 million, and demand deposits up by $5 million. In granting loans of $4.5 million, Bank A has used up its original $4.5 million in excess reserves and created $4.5 million of demand deposits, which now reside in Bank B. But the deposit expansion process has only begun! Bank B, in receiving both demand deposits and reserves in the amount of $4.5 million, now has $4.05 million of excess reserves.[5] Following assumption 1, suppose this bank rids itself of all excess reserves by purchasing U.S. government securities from a New York securities dealer. After the bank's check is deposited in a New York bank (Bank C) and processed, the T-accounts look like this:

Bank B				Bank C			
1. Deposit at Fed	+4.5m	Demand deposits	+4.5m				
2. U.S. government securities	+4.05m			2. Deposit at Fed	+4.05m	Demand deposits	+4.05m
Deposit at Fed	−4.05m						

Bank B pays for the securities with a check in the amount of $4.05 million written on its Federal Reserve account. As soon as the check is deposited in Bank C, the money supply rises by $4.05 million. The Fed completes the transfer of funds from Bank B to Bank C by marking down Bank B's account by $4.05 million and crediting Bank C's account by the same amount.

---

[5]Because demand deposits in Bank B increase by $4.5 million, required reserves increase by $0.45 million. Since actual reserves increase by $4.5 million, excess reserves are up by the difference, $4.05 million.

Note that Bank B still retains the demand deposit account ($4.5 million) of the people who sold the land to the developers. Bank B has also acquired U.S. securities in the amount of $4.05 million and paid for them with a deduction equal to the amount in its Federal Reserve deposit account. Thus, Bank B's final position is: Federal Reserve account up by $0.45 million; portfolio of government securities up by $4.05 million; and demand deposits up by $4.5 million. Bank B has participated in the money supply process by receiving a new demand deposit of $4.5 million and by purchasing securities in the amount of $4.05 million, thereby creating the same amount of demand deposits in another bank (Bank C). Keep in mind that total reserves in the banking system are *not* increasing. They are simply being shuffled from banks that are lending and buying securities to other banks in the system.

You should now be able to grasp the pattern that is emerging. Bank C is now in a position similar to that which Banks A and B were previously in. Bank C has received new reserves in the full amount of its new deposits but is required to maintain only 10 percent of those funds in the form of reserves. Bank C can now grant loans and/or purchase securities in the amount of its excess reserves, $3.645 million. In doing so, it will contribute to the creation of demand deposits in the amount of $3.645 million in yet another bank (Bank D).

Given our three assumptions, the resulting pattern of multiple deposit creation and rearrangement of reserves in the chain of banks is shown in Table 13-1. The initial deposit of $5 million in coins directly increases deposits by $5 million. More significantly, after considering bank lending and investing, it produces an additional $45 million in demand deposits. The total expansion in deposits is thus 10 times the initial $5 million injection of reserves into the banking system resulting from the deposit of the coins. Stated another way, the *induced* expansion of deposits *beyond* the direct deposit of $5 million is 10 times the initial amount of excess reserves ($4.5 million), or a total of $45 million. Note that the $5 million of reserves initially placed in Bank A ends up being scattered

Table 13-1

Creation of Deposits and Disposition of Reserves

Bank	Change in Deposits	Disposition of Reserves
A	+5,000,000 (original deposit of coins)	+500,000
B	+4,500,000	+450,000
C	+4,050,000	+405,000
D	+3,645,000	+364,500
E	+3,280,500	+328,050
·	·	·
·	·	·
·	·	·
Total	$50,000,000	$5,000,000

throughout the banking system. Because each bank along the line rids itself of all its excess reserves, it ends up with an increase in actual reserves equal to 10 percent of the increase in its deposits.

If we lump all banks together and look at the T-account for the banking system as a whole, the effects of the entire operation are easily summarized:

All Depository Institutions			
Currency and coins	+5m	Demand deposits	+50m
Loans and investments	+45m		

The initial injection of $5 million in cash reserves remains in the banking system and is capable of supporting $50 million in new demand deposits. Of this, $5 million is *directly* attributable to the deposit of the coins. The remaining $45 million comes about as the result of an aggregate expansion in bank loans and security holdings. The formula for the maximum expansion of deposits is as follows:

$$\text{Induced expansion of deposits} = \text{Initial excess reserves} \times \frac{1}{\% \text{ reserve requirement}}$$

In this example, the expansion of deposits = $4,500,000 \times \frac{1}{10\%} = \$45,000,000$.

Keep in mind, however, that the assumptions we have made are rather *unrealistic*. In the real world, banks deliberately hold some excess reserves as a precautionary measure. And because the public's demand for currency tends to increase as demand deposits increase, the real-world deposit expansion multiplier is smaller than the simple

Your Turn

Suppose the reserve requirement for all banks is 20 percent and the nation's banks initially have no excess reserves. Suppose you find $1 million of old currency in your grandmother's attic and deposit it into her bank checking account. Calculate

a. The change in reserves in your grandmother's bank

b. The change in required reserves in your grandmother's bank

c. The change in excess reserves in your grandmother's bank

d. The maximum amount by which your grandmother's bank can expand its loans

e. The maximum amount by which the entire banking system can expand its loans

f. The potential expansion in the nation's deposits resulting from the initial deposit in your grandmother's bank

g. The potential expansion in M1

one developed here. Thus, the true deposit expansion multiplier effect is normally considerably less than 10 to 1. (A more sophisticated and realistic expression of the money supply multiplier is developed in Chapter 15.)

Multiple Contraction of Bank Deposits

Just as an injection of new reserves into the banking system touches off a multiple expansion of deposits (and hence money), a withdrawal of reserves from the banking system precipitates a multiple *contraction* of deposits. This process was painfully experienced in the United States in the early 1930s and played a major role in the Great Depression. (That episode is examined in depth in Chapter 16.)

Let us retain the three assumptions we made earlier and suppose that the banking system is just meeting the reserve requirement—that is, assume it has no excess reserves. Now suppose customers of Bank Q obtain $7 million in currency by drawing down their demand deposits. The impact of their cash withdrawal on Bank Q is

Bank Q			
Cash	−7 million	Demand deposits	−7 million

Given the 10 percent reserve requirement, Bank Q's required reserves decline by $0.7 million, but actual reserves decline by the full $7 million. Bank Q's reserves are therefore deficient (required reserves exceed reserves) by $6.3 million. Bank Q (and the aggregate banking system) initially exhibits excess reserves of *negative* $6.3 million.

Any individual bank can gain reserves, and thereby alleviate its reserve deficiency, by selling securities or reducing its loans in the amount of its reserve deficiency. Thus, Bank Q can alleviate its reserve deficiency by selling $6.3 million in securities, by demanding repayment of $6.3 million worth of loans, or by some combination of those two actions. But, in doing so, Bank Q simply shifts its reserve deficiency to another bank, Bank R. The individuals or firms that purchased Bank Q's securities or repaid Bank Q's loans wrote their checks on their accounts in Bank R. Bank R therefore becomes deficient in reserves and must liquidate loans or securities, thereby shifting the hot potato to another bank, Bank S. Ultimately, the T-account of the whole banking system appears as follows:

All Banks			
Currency and coins	−7m	Demand deposits	−70m
Loans and investments	−63m		

Note that the initial withdrawal of $7 million in currency ends up producing a contraction in demand deposits of $70 million. The withdrawal of currency causes a direct reduction in deposits of $7 million. In addition, it touches off a contraction of loans and security holdings by depository institutions totaling $63 million, which produces a matching drop in demand deposits.[6]

The key to understanding this process lies in the fact that each bank, in recovering its lost reserves by liquidating securities or loans, does nothing to increase the reserves of the *entire banking system.* The selling of securities and the reduction of loans merely transfer reserves from one bank to another. The only way *the banking system* can remedy a reserve deficiency is by reducing the amount of *required reserves* by the amount of the reserve shortage, and that can be done only by triggering a much larger contraction of deposits. To achieve a $1 reduction of required reserves in a fractional reserve banking system with a 10 percent reserve requirement, demand deposits must decline by $10.

In short, the banking system cannot control its own reserves; it is at the mercy of the public and the Federal Reserve. The public influences reserves by depositing or withdrawing currency from banks. The Federal Reserve System influences reserves by buying and selling securities and by lending to banks. Thus the Fed is in a position to dominate the amount of reserves in the banking system. We now turn to a brief discussion of the Fed's role in determining the amount of aggregate reserves in the banking system.

HOW THE FEDERAL RESERVE GETS A GRIP ON THE MONEY SUPPLY

At the beginning of this chapter, we looked at an example in which additional reserves came into the banking system as a result of the deposit of coins found in a sunken ship. That example was atypical, to say the least! In reality, the Federal Reserve controls the aggregate amount of reserves at any given time, as well as the growth in reserves over time. It is true that many factors outside Federal Reserve control can induce fluctuations in bank reserves. One of those factors is fluctuations in the demand for currency by the public. However, with its unlimited authority to purchase or sell government securities on the open market, the Fed can easily swamp the influence of outside forces and control the supply of reserves in the banking system.

Recall that bank reserves consist of vault cash plus deposits maintained by banks at the Federal Reserve. Whenever the Fed purchases securities in the open market, it pays for those securities by writing a check on itself to the seller. The recipient of the check deposits it in a depository institution, which makes a bookkeeping entry showing that the seller's demand deposit account has increased by the amount of the check. The Federal Reserve pays off the depository institution by marking up its Federal Reserve account (a bookkeeping entry). In this way, Federal Reserve security purchases inject an equivalent amount of reserves into the

---

[6]Let R, r, and D represent reserves, the percentage reserve requirement, and deposits, respectively. Then $R = r(D)$ and $\Delta R = r(\Delta D)$. Solving for the change in deposits, we get $\Delta D = \Delta R/r$. This means that the final change in deposits will equal the change in reserves times the reciprocal of the reserve requirement (that is, $1/r$). In this example, $\Delta D = -\$7$ million $\times 10 = -\$70$ million.

nation's banking system.[7] If the Fed purchases $900 million of securities from the public, the T-accounts of the Federal Reserve and the banking system will appear as follows:

Federal Reserve		Banking System	
U.S. government securities +900m	Deposits of banks +900m	Deposits at Fed +900m	Demand deposits +900m

The Fed writes checks to private individuals totaling $900 million. These checks are deposited into private banks, which credit the checking accounts of the individuals involved. The banks then send the checks to the Fed, which pays off the banks by crediting their reserve accounts with the Fed by $900 million. Note that the nation's bank reserves have expanded by $900 million. The Fed has paid for its securities acquisition by creating new reserves in the banking system.

When the Fed *sells* securities to individuals, firms, or banks, aggregate reserves are withdrawn from the banking system. The buyers of these securities write checks on their accounts in depository institutions. The checks are presented to the Fed, which collects on them by debiting the deposit accounts (reserve accounts) of the banks on which the checks are written. Reserves are reduced on a dollar-for-dollar basis.

Given the Fed's ability to control the aggregate amount of both reserves and required reserves (by setting the percentage reserve requirement), the Fed can trigger changes in the amount of excess reserves in banks—reserves above and beyond the amount banks are required to hold. When the Fed injects excess reserves into the banks, this gives rise to a multiple expansion of deposits. By the same token, deficient reserves trigger a multiple contraction of deposits.

This sketch of the Federal Reserve's monetary control is superficial; in reality, many complications must be taken into account. Nevertheless, it captures the essence of the Federal Reserve's monetary control mechanism. Chapters 14 to 18 provide a thorough treatment of the role of the Federal Reserve System in the money supply process.

Your Turn

Suppose the percentage reserve requirement set by the Federal Reserve is 15 percent. Now suppose the Fed purchases $1000 million worth of U.S. Treasury securities through government securities dealers in New York. Calculate the impact of the Fed's action on

a. Reserves

b. Required reserves

c. Excess reserves

d. The initial change in the money supply

e. The eventual change in the money supply, after all banks have rid themselves of all their excess reserves

---

[7]This holds true unless the Fed buys securities directly from the U.S. Treasury, in which case bank reserves are unaltered. Such activity is restricted by regulations governing the Federal Reserve. When the Fed buys securities from individuals, firms, or depository institutions, reserves are increased on a dollar-for-dollar basis.

SUMMARY

Modern monetary systems are based on a system of fractional reserve banking. This means that banks maintain only a relatively small percentage of their customers' deposits in the form of reserves—that is, as vault cash and deposits at the Federal Reserve. Because banks earn income by lending or investing their deposit customers' funds rather than holding such funds as reserves, they find it undesirable to hold substantially more reserves than are required. Whenever a bank increases its loans or purchases securities, it creates new deposits in the banking system. Because all measures of the money supply include these deposits, these actions by banks increase the money supply. Be-

cause each dollar of bank reserves supports several dollars of deposits, new reserves received by the banking system result in the creation of new *deposits* that are a *multiple* of the new *reserves*. Conversely, a contraction of reserves in the banking system leads to a multiple contraction of deposits. The public influences bank reserves by depositing cash in or withdrawing cash from banks. However, the Federal Reserve can easily counteract the effects of such actions by the public. By controlling the amount of reserves existing in the banking system, it can strongly influence bank lending and investing and therefore the amount of deposits and the quantity of money in the nation.

Answers to Your Turn *(p. 314)*

a. *$1,000,000*

b. *$1,000,000 × 20% = $200,000*

c. *$1,000,000 − $200,000 = $800,000*

d. *The amount of its excess reserves, or $800,000*

e. *Excess reserves × 1/%RR, or $800,000 × 5 = $4,000,000*

f. *$4,000,000 plus the initial $1,000,000 = $5,000,000*

g. *Recall that M1 = DDO + C^p. DDO increases by $5,000,000, but C^p declines by $1,000,000 because your grandmother's old currency was counted as C^p while in the attic but not after it is deposited in the bank. Hence, the potential net change in the money supply is $4,000,000.*

Answers to Your Turn *(p. 317)*

a. *$1000 million*

b. *15% × $1000 million, or $150 million*

c. *$1000 million − $150 million, or $850 million*

d. *$1000 million*

e. *$1000 million × 1/.15, or $6667 million*

KEY TERMS

reserves
reserve requirement
required reserves
excess reserves

STUDY QUESTIONS

1 Suppose you deposit $100 cash into your checking account. Assume the reserve requirement is 12 percent.

   a What is the effect on your bank's reserves?

   b What is the effect on your bank's required reserves?

   c What is the effect on your bank's excess reserves?

   d By how much is your bank now able to expand its loans?

2 Illustrate the multiple deposit expansion process in the first problem using T-accounts and assuming banks use all their excess reserves to grant loans. Carry the example through Banks A, B, C, and D. At each step of the process, calculate what happens to

   a The individual bank's total, required, and excess reserves

   b The total amount of demand deposits in the banking system

   c Total reserves in the banking system

   d Required reserves in the banking system

   e Excess reserves in the banking system

3 While climbing in the Yukon, you find $1000 worth of old paper currency, which you promptly deposit in your checking account. If the reserve requirement is 10 percent, how much money creation will you ultimately be responsible for?

4 Suppose the Federal Reserve buys government securities worth $1000. Assume the reserve requirement is 10 percent.

   a Illustrate this transaction with T-accounts for the Fed and all banks.

   b The money supply expands immediately by how much?

   c Banks will begin to make loans and purchase securities. When the multiple deposit expansion process is complete, by how much will the money supply have grown?

   d Does your answer to part c differ from your answer to question 3? Why or why not?

5 Because you fear nuclear war is imminent, you decide to liquidate your $20,000 checking account and bury the currency in a coffee can in your backyard. (Assume 10% res. requirement.)

   a Draw the T-account for this transaction.

   b Does your transaction, by itself, immediately change the money supply?

   c Draw T-accounts illustrating the multiple deposit contraction your action touches off. Show three rounds of contraction.

   d Calculate the ultimate effect your action has on the money supply.

6 Suppose the Fed buys $1 million of securities from dealers; the reserve requirement is 10 percent. If the Fed's action results in an $8 million expansion of deposits, is the banking system in equilibrium? Why or why not?

7 Suppose there are $1000 million worth of checkable deposits in the banking system. The reserve requirement is 10 percent.

   a What will ultimately happen to the money supply if the Fed cuts the reserve requirement to 5 percent?

   b What will ultimately happen to the money supply if the Fed increases the reserve requirement to 15 percent?

8 Suppose the reserve requirement is 10 percent. The Fed buys $1000 million worth of securities from a New York dealer.

    a What will be the ultimate effect on the money supply?

    b If banks choose to maintain 5 percent of their deposits as reserves over and above the Fed's reserve requirements, what will be the ultimate effect? (Hint: Draw a few rounds of T-accounts.)

SUGGESTIONS FOR ADDITIONAL READING

For alternative explanations of the simple deposit expansion process, see any principles of economics textbook. For example, see Chap. 14 of Campbell McConnell and Stanley Brue, *Economics,* 13th ed. (New York: McGraw-Hill, 1996). Also, see Federal Reserve Bank of Chicago, *Modern Money Mechanics: A Workbook on Bank Reserves and Deposit Expansion,* 1992.

14

Money Supply Determination: The Monetary Base

A s we pointed out in Chapter 1, the money supply is regarded as an important variable influencing economic activity. Changes in the monetary aggregates (M1, M2, etc.) are believed to portend changes in the nation's output, employment, and price level. For this reason, financial market analysts keep a close eye on the monetary statistics the Fed makes public each week. A sharp, unexpected change in the money supply can send shock waves through the financial markets.

In this chapter and the next, we will develop the tools you need to understand the *money supply process*—the factors that bring about changes in the quantity of money. Because banks' lending and purchasing of securities creates money, banks are clearly involved in the money supply process. The public also participates in the process through its role in allocating its financial wealth among currency, checking accounts, and other financial assets, as well as through its actions in requesting loans from banks. But the most important player in the money supply process is the Federal Reserve, which is capable of dominating the growth rate of the money supply. In this chapter and the one to follow, we will provide a comprehensive explanation of the elements that govern the money supply.

THE BASE AND MULTIPLIER FRAMEWORK

The framework we employ to analyze the determination of the money supply is outlined in a simple equation which expresses the money supply as the product of two fundamental variables. These variables are the **monetary base** and a **money supply multiplier,** which encompasses the multiple deposit expansion process inherent in a fractional reserve banking system. We may express the relationship as follows:

(14-1)
$$M = B \cdot m$$

where

M = the money supply

B = the monetary base, and

m = the money supply multiplier

The money supply multiplier may be expressed as follows:

(14-2)
$$m = \frac{M}{B}$$

Recall from Chapter 1 that there are several alternative measures of the U.S. money supply, including M1, M2, M3, and L. M1 is defined to include demand deposits and other checkable deposits in depository institutions (hereafter called "banks"), plus currency and coins held by the public outside banks. M2, M3, and L broaden this measure of money by progressively adding to it the public's holdings of such liquid financial assets as savings deposits, money market mutual fund shares, overnight repurchase agreements, and so forth.

The monetary base (B) consists of bank reserves (cash in banks and deposits at the Fed) and currency held by the nonbank public. The money supply multiplier (m) is the ratio of the money supply to the monetary base. For each measure of the money supply, there is a corresponding money supply multiplier. For example, we may write $m_1 = $ M1$/B$ and $m_2 = $ M2$/B$. This link that connects the monetary base and the money supply reflects portfolio decisions by banks and the public and is also partially influenced by Federal Reserve actions.

The procedure of expressing the money supply as the product of the monetary base and a money supply multiplier is useful in understanding the sources of change in the money supply. Clearly, any change in the money supply must be the result of a change in B, a change in m, or some combination of the two. This simple framework permits us to analyze some important issues of monetary policy. For example, what sort of roadblocks make it difficult for the Federal Reserve to control the money supply accurately? In the absence of aggressive efforts by the Fed to hit specific targets for the money supply, what factors might cause the money supply to change? What are the mechanisms through which the Federal Reserve's instruments of policy influence the money supply?

We will have a much better handle on these questions after we have analyzed the factors underlying the monetary base and the money supply multiplier. Accordingly, this chapter provides an in-depth discussion of the monetary base. Chapter 15 is devoted to an analysis of the money supply multiplier. Chapter 16 will use the monetary base–money supply multiplier framework to analyze the behavior of the money supply and the role of the Federal Reserve in the Great Depression of the 1930s. Finally, Chapters 17 and 18 cover the tools of Fed policy—the instruments the Fed employs to initiate changes in the money supply, credit conditions, and interest rates.

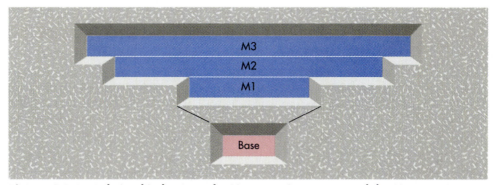

Figure 14-1   Relationship between the Monetary Aggregates and the Monetary Base.
The monetary base is the foundation of the measures of the money supply, or the monetary aggregates.

REASONS FOR STUDYING THE MONETARY BASE

There are two important reasons for singling out the monetary base for special attention. First, a significant body of theory supports the view that monetary aggregates such as M1, M2, and M3 exert an important influence on economic activity. That is, they affect output, employment, and the nation's price level. Second, there is good reason to believe the Federal Reserve is capable of controlling the monetary base and, by doing so, strongly influencing the levels and growth rates of the monetary aggregates—M1, M2, and M3. Hence, a major chain of influence runs from Federal Reserve policy actions to the monetary base to the monetary aggregates to the nation's GDP, income, and price level.

The monetary base forms the foundation on which the superstructure of bank credit and money is built. Figure 14-1 shows the relationship of the monetary base to the monetary aggregates. The monetary base supports the various measures of the U.S. money supply—that is, the monetary aggregates. Because each dollar of monetary base supports several dollars of money, the base is sometimes known as "high-powered money."

The monetary base may be viewed as an important type of monetary asset supplied by the monetary authorities. Depository institutions are required to hold specified quantities of the items included in the base in the form of reserves in support of their deposit liabilities. As we noted in earlier chapters, banks are in the business of making a profit by acquiring such earning assets as securities and loans. Their acquisition of those earning assets creates demand deposits. Demand deposits are the bookkeeping entries that make up the major portion of M1, the narrow measure of the U.S. money supply. Although there are some slips 'twixt the cup and lip, the Fed can exert considerable influence over the money supply through its ability to control the monetary base accurately.[1] We will shortly see how.

---

[1] We focus on the monetary base and its associated multiplier rather than on reserves and their associated multiplier because the Federal Reserve has greater control over the base than over reserves: reserves are influenced by changes in the public's demand for currency (C^p); the monetary base is not.

THE MONETARY BASE: FUNDAMENTAL CONCEPTS

The monetary base consists of *those liabilities of the monetary authorities—the Fed and the Treasury—which could potentially be used by depository institutions as reserves.*[2] These monetary liabilities include deposits held by depository institutions in the Federal Reserve banks, as well as currency and coins issued by, and residing outside, the Treasury and the Fed. This includes currency and coins held by depository institutions and the general public. This definition of the monetary base is expressed in Equations 14-3 and 14-4.

(14-3) $$B = R + C^p$$

where

B = the monetary base

R = bank reserves, which may be subdivided into bank deposits at the Fed (F_b) and currency and coin held by banks (C_b), and

C^p = currency and coins held by the nonbank public, which is equivalent to all the currency and coins issued by the Treasury and the Fed minus the currency and coins held by Federal Reserve banks, the Treasury, and banks

And, because $R = F_b + C_b$,

(14-4) $$B = F_b + C_b + C^p$$

Derivation of the Monetary Base

The monetary base, as defined in Equation 14-4, consists of the net monetary liabilities of a consolidated balance sheet of the *monetary authorities*—the Treasury and the Federal Reserve. The Treasury's net monetary liabilities are the outstanding currency and coin it has issued, exclusive of that held in the Treasury and the Fed. Today, this consists chiefly of coins.[3] The Federal Reserve's net monetary liabilities consist of all Federal Reserve notes outstanding (our paper money) that are not held in the Fed or Treasury, plus the reserve deposits of banks at the Federal Reserve (F_b). As we have indicated and will

---

[2]Remember that bank reserves consist of bank deposits at the Federal Reserve and cash residing in banks. The base is the pool of items that can be used as reserves. Today, reserves make up only about 15 percent of the base. The remainder of the base is held by the public as currency (C^p).

[3]In the past, much of the paper currency (including all dollar bills) was issued by the Treasury. Today, all paper money is issued by the Federal Reserve in the form of Federal Reserve notes. Some of the paper money issued by the Treasury in the past, though recalled by the government, is still in private collections and thus technically constitutes a portion (though less than 0.1 percent) of the monetary base.

Table 14-1

The Sources of and Uses for the Monetary Base, March 31, 1996 (in millions of dollars)

Sources of the Monetary Base			Uses for the Monetary Base		
Positive Influences:					
(P)	Federal Reserve security portfolio	$384,478	$(C_b + C^p)$	Currency in circulation	$416,204
(A)	Discounts and advances	43	(F_b)	Depository institution balances at	
(Fl)	Float	29		the Federal Reserve	$24,740
(G)	Gold certificate + SDR account	21,221	(B)	Total uses for the monetary base	$440,944
(OA)	Other assets	31,447			
(TC_u)	Treasury currency outstanding	24,193			
		+$461,411			
Negative Influences:					
(F_t)	Treasury deposits at the Federal Reserve	$7,021			
(F_f)	Foreign and other deposits at the				
	Federal Reserve	539			
(TC_a)	Treasury cash holdings	314			
(OLC)	Other liabilities and capital	12,593			
		−$20,467			
(B)	Total sources of the monetary base	$440,944			

Source: *Federal Reserve Bulletin,* June 1996.

explain shortly, the Federal Reserve can accurately control the magnitude of these net monetary liabilities by controlling its own balance sheet.

The best way of understanding the monetary base is by beginning with the factors that determine the base, called the **sources of the base,** and the ways in which the base is allocated or used, called the **uses for the base.** Table 14-1 summarizes the sources of and uses for the monetary base on March 31, 1996. The individual sources of the base and their magnitudes are listed in the left-hand column, and the individual uses and their magnitudes are shown in the right-hand column. We will discuss both the sources of and uses for the monetary base in the following sections.

Sources of the Monetary Base

As indicated in Equation 14-4, a key component of the monetary base is deposits held at the Federal Reserve by banks (F_b). We may derive an expression for the sources of the monetary base by using an accounting identity to solve for F_b and substituting this expression for F_b into Equation 14-4 to solve for the monetary base, *B*.

Table 14-2	

Federal Reserve Balance Sheet

Assets	Liabilities
U.S. government securities (*P*)	Federal Reserve notes (*FRN*)
Loans to banks (*A*)	Deposits at Fed, held by
Coin (*FCa*)	a. Depository institutions (*F_b*)
Cash items in process of collection (*CIPC*)	b. U.S. Treasury (*F_t*)
Gold certificate account and SDR account (*G*)	c. Foreign and other (*F_f*)
Denominated in foreign currencies and other	Deferred-availability cash items (*DACI*)
assets (*OA*)	Other liabilities and capital accounts (*OLC*)
Total assets	Total liabilities and capital

Let us begin by returning to the Federal Reserve's balance sheet (see Table 14-2).[4] The accompanying simplified Fed balance sheet indicates the various assets and liabilities of the Fed, together with a symbol to designate each variable. Keeping in mind the simple accounting identity that the total assets of the Fed must equal its total liabilities plus its capital accounts, it follows that the magnitude of F_b (a major component of the base, located on the liability side of the Fed balance sheet) is equal to the total assets of the Fed minus all other liabilities and capital accounts of the Fed. We may therefore write the expression for bank deposits at the Federal Reserve (F_b) as follows:

$$(14\text{-}5) \quad F_b = P + A + FCa + CIPC + G + OA - FRN - F_t - F_f - DACI - OLC$$

where

P = the Fed's portfolio of securities, including U.S. government securities, agency securities, and banker's acceptances

A = discounts and advances (loans by the Fed to depository institutions)

FCa = the Fed's cash holdings (coins)

$CIPC$ = cash items in the process of collection by the Fed

G = the Fed's gold certificate and SDR accounts

OA = other assets of the Federal Reserve, including foreign assets

FRN = Federal Reserve notes outstanding

F_t = Treasury deposits at the Federal Reserve

F_f = foreign and other deposits at the Federal Reserve

---

[4]To review the *magnitudes* of the various Federal Reserve assets and liabilities, review Table 12-1 on page 286.

DACI = deferred-availability cash items of the Federal Reserve, and

OLC = other Federal Reserve liabilities and capital accounts

If we define **float** (*Fl*) to be the difference between cash items in the process of collection (*CIPC*) and deferred-availability cash items (*DACI*), and substitute float (*Fl*) for *CIPC* and *DACI* in Equation 14-5, we obtain

$$(14\text{-}6) \qquad F_b = P + A + FCa + Fl + G + OA - FRN - F_t - F_f - OLC$$

This is an expression for the sources of the bank's *reserve accounts* at the Federal Reserve (F_b). To get the monetary base (*B*), we simply add to F_b the currency and coins held by banks (C_b) and the currency and coins held by the public (C^p), as indicated in Equation 14-4. This yields

$$(14\text{-}7) \qquad B = P + A + FCa + Fl + G + OA + C_b + C^p - FRN - F_t - F_f - OLC$$

Now let *TCu* represent Treasury currency outstanding and let *TCa* represent the Treasury's cash holdings. We can simplify Equation 14-7 somewhat by recognizing that all paper money (*FRN*) and coins (*TCu*) in existence must be held in one of four places: at the Fed (*FCa*), at the Treasury (*TCa*), in depository institutions (C_b), or in the hands of the public (C^p). There is literally nowhere else the currency and coins could be, given that C^p includes all currency and coins that do not reside at the Fed, the Treasury, or depository institutions. We convey this idea as follows:

$$(14\text{-}8) \qquad FRN + TCu = FCa + TCa + C_b + C^p$$

If we rearrange this equation by moving *FRN* to the right-hand side of the equation and *TCa* to the left-hand side, we obtain

$$(14\text{-}9) \qquad TCu - TCa = FCa + C_b + C^p - FRN$$

This expression states that if we subtract the currency issued by the Federal Reserve (*FRN*) from the total currency and coins held by the Fed, the banks, and the public, we obtain the total amount of currency and coins issued by the Treasury (*TCu*) that is not residing in the Treasury itself (*TCa*).

When we substitute into Equation 14-7 the two terms on the left-hand side of Equation 14-9 (in place of the four terms on the right side), we arrive at our final expression for the sources of the monetary base:

$$(14\text{-}10) \qquad B = P + A + Fl + G + OA + TCu - F_t - F_f - TCa - OLC$$

This equation indicates that there are 10 factors that determine the monetary base. These 10 sources of the base include factors which supply base money (positive influences, preceded by a plus sign) and factors which absorb base money (negative influences, preceded

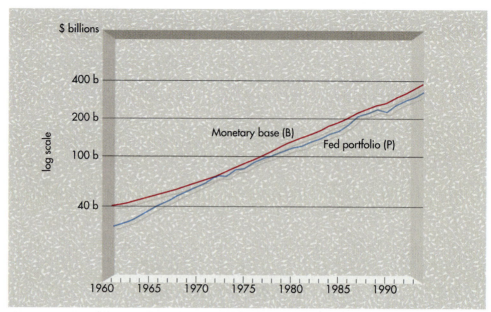

Figure 14-2 The Federal Reserve's Securities Portfolio versus the Monetary Base, 1960–Present. The behavior of the monetary base is dominated by the Federal Reserve's securities portfolio (*P*). *Source:* Federal Reserve System.

by a minus sign). We now have the sources of the monetary base in order, as listed in Table 14-1.

We will analyze each of these 10 factors later in this chapter. For the time being, it is sufficient to emphasize the fact that the Federal Reserve's portfolio of securities (*P*)—a variable totally under the control of the Fed—has dominated the behavior of the monetary base in recent decades. By judiciously changing its portfolio of securities (*P*), the Fed can also dominate the short-term behavior of the monetary base. Figure 14-2 shows the close link between the Federal Reserve's security portfolio (*P*) and the monetary base (*B*) over the past 35 years.

Note the high degree of statistical association between the Fed's portfolio and the monetary base. The connection between the two may be described as follows: the Federal Reserve security portfolio, which is determined totally by Fed policy, is the independent variable; the monetary base is the dependent variable that moves in response to Fed portfolio decisions.

Uses for the Monetary Base

The right-hand portion of Table 14-1 shows the allocation of the monetary base, or the uses to which the base is put, together with the magnitude of each use as of the end of March 1996. "Currency in circulation" is defined by the Federal Reserve as all Treasury currency and coins and Federal Reserve notes outstanding, except those held in the Treasury or the

Weekly Federal Reserve Data

On most Thursdays, the Federal Reserve releases detailed monetary data. The next day, *The Wall Street Journal* publishes these data on the monetary base, aggregate bank reserves, and all their sources. They can be found in a column titled "Federal Reserve Data." The portion of the table titled "Member Bank Reserve Changes" lists the most recent weekly averages of each of the sources of the monetary base, together with the change in each source over recent weeks and in the past year. (See the facsimile below.) The table also shows currency in circulation, which is not a *source of* but rather a *use for* the monetary base.

Note that in the week ending March 13, 1996, the Federal Reserve purchased more than $2300 million (net) worth of U.S. government and federal agency securities (refer to the middle column and take the net change in the four items). The two other sources of the base that showed the largest weekly fluctuations were float (up $685 million) and Treasury deposits at the Federal Reserve (up $1196 million).

The portion of the table titled "Reserve Aggregates" shows the daily averages over a 2-week period of various measures of reserves and the monetary base. Note that while the average monetary base was up more than $1 billion from 2 weeks earlier, total reserves were up by only approximately $500 million. What accounts for the difference between the changes in B and R? (*Hint:* Review Equation 14-3.)

FEDERAL RESERVE DATA

MEMBER BANK RESERVE CHANGES

Changes in weekly averages of reserves and related items
during the week and year ended March 13, 1996 were as follows
(in millions of dollars)

	Mar. 13, 1996	Chg fm Mar. 6, 1996	Wk end Mar. 15, 1995
Reserve bank credit:			
U.S. Gov't securities:			
Bought outright	377,113	− 462	+ 12,698
Held under repurch agreemt	2,591	+ 2,591	+ 488
Federal agency issues:			
Bought outright	2,568	− 60	− 923
Held under repurch agreemt	314	+ 314	+ 254
Acceptances			
Borrowings from Fed:			
Adjustment credit	5	− 5	− 10
Seasonal borrowings	7	− 1	− 42
Extended credit	....	....	....
Float	1,271	+ 685	+ 851
Other Federal Reserve Assets	30,812	+ 389	− 3,018
Total Reserve Bank Credit	414,681	+ 3,451	+ 10,298
Gold Stock	11,053		+ 2
SDR certificates	10,168		+ 2,150
Treasury currency outstanding	24,151	+ 14	+ 975
Total	460,053	+ 3,465	+ 13,426
Currency in circulation	415,723	+ 1,381	+ 14,434
Treasury cash holdings	282	+ 3	− 67
Treasury dpts with F.R. Bnks	5,507	+ 1,196	+ 333
Foreign dpts with F.R. Bnks	181	− 17	+ 8
Other dpts with F.R. Bnks	392	− 5	+ 8
Service related balances, adj	6,432	+ 667	+ 2,061
Other F.R. liabilities & capital	13,309	+ 162	+ 459
Total	441,826	+ 3,386	+ 17,235

RESERVE AGGREGATES
(daily average in millions)

	Two weeks ended:	
	Mar. 13	Feb. 28
Total Reserves (sa)	55,573	55,058
Nonborrowed Reserves (sa)	55,558	55,011
Required Reserves (sa)	54,472	54,066
Excess Reserves (nsa)	1,101	992
Borrowings from Fed (nsa)-a	15	47
Free Reserves (nsa)	1,086	945
Monetary Base (sa)	435,401	434,282

a-Excluding extended credit. nsa-Not seasonally adjusted.
sa-Seasonally adjusted.

Federal Reserve banks. In other words, currency in circulation equals the sum of cash in depository institutions (C_b) and currency and coins held by the public (C^p). Don't confuse it with currency held by the public (C^p)!

By adding the figure for currency in circulation ($416,204 million) to the depository institutions' balances at the Fed ($24,740 million), we obtain the magnitude of the monetary base on March 31, 1996: $440,944 million, or $440.944 billion. To get a feel for the U.S. monetary base, see "From the Financial Pages," which shows an important table normally released by the Federal Reserve each Thursday and published in *The Wall Street Journal* on Friday.

Your Turn

Suppose you observe in the column "Federal Reserve Data" in this Friday's *Wall Street Journal* that the following changes occurred in the most recent week in the sources of the monetary base: float increased $800 million, discounts and advances fell by $300 million, Treasury deposits at the Fed increased by $1300 million, and Treasury cash declined $200 million.

a. Assuming all other factors influencing the monetary base remained unchanged, calculate the change in the monetary base.

b. If the Fed desires to keep the base constant, what will it have to do with its security portfolio?

Figure 14-3 shows the behavior of the monetary base and its two components, depository institutions' reserves (R) and currency held by the nonbank public (C^p), since 1960. The magnitudes are plotted using a ratio, or log, scale, so growth rates are indicated by the *slope* of the curve. Note that, over the period as a whole, currency held by the nonbank public has expanded at a significantly faster rate than bank reserves. Its rate of growth has also been more stable.

TEN FACTORS THAT CAN PRODUCE CHANGES IN THE MONETARY BASE

By definition, any event that produces a change in either bank reserves (R) or currency held by the public (C^p) without causing an offsetting change in the other item must change the monetary base.[5] As we saw in Table 14-1 and Equation 14-10, there are 10 sources of the monetary base. We will now analyze the effect of changes in each of those

---

[5] An example of an offsetting change is an increase in currency held by the public (C^p), which drains cash from banks and therefore reduces reserves in a dollar-for-dollar fashion. An increase in currency demanded by the public leaves the monetary base unchanged.

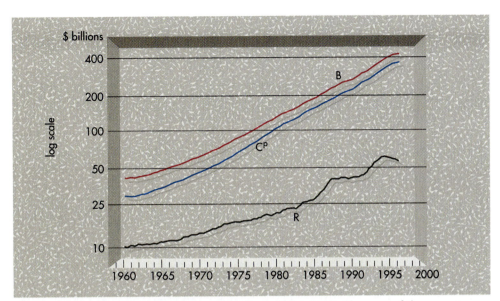

Figure 14-3   The Monetary Base and Its Uses, 1960–1996. The uses of the monetary base include reserves of depository institutions (*R*) and currency held by the public (*C^p*). *Source: Citibank Economic Database.*

10 sources on the monetary base. This analysis will demonstrate how and why the base changes over both the short and long run. It will also prove that the Federal Reserve can easily control the growth rate of the monetary base. We will begin with the most important source, the Fed's portfolio of U.S. government securities.

The Federal Reserve's Securities Portfolio

This item, the dominant element in the monetary base, is totally determined by the Fed. Today, it constitutes more than 85 percent of the monetary base (review Figure 14-2 or Table 14-1). Such has not always been the case. Before the 1930s, the Fed's securities portfolio made up less than 10 percent of the monetary base. Gold, Treasury currency outstanding, and Federal Reserve loans to banks were all larger than the Fed securities portfolio. This portfolio climbed from 10 percent to 50 percent of the base in the 1940s, and in the late 1950s began to escalate from 50 percent to its current figure of 85 to 90 percent.

How does the Fed's portfolio of securities affect the monetary base? When the Fed purchases securities in the open market, it pays by a check *written on itself.* The seller of the securities (normally a securities dealer) deposits the check in a depository institution (bank). The bank then sends the check to the Federal Reserve district bank, which credits the bank's balance at the Fed. When this bookkeeping entry is made, bank reserves (and thus the monetary base) increase by the amount of the transaction. If the Fed purchases $175 million of U.S. government securities in the open market, the T-account mechanics are as follows:

Federal Reserve System		All Banks	
U.S. government securities +175m	Deposits by banks +175m	Deposits at Fed +175m	Demand deposits +175m

To recap: The Fed gives the dealer a check in exchange for securities. The dealer deposits the check in a bank. The bank sends the check to the Federal Reserve district bank, which credits the dealer's bank's account at the Fed (F_b) in the amount of $175 million. At this moment, both reserves and the monetary base increase by $175 million. Thus, bank reserves and the monetary base can easily be manipulated by the Federal Reserve!

The Federal Reserve currently holds a portfolio of government securities that amounts to about 10 percent of the net U.S. national debt, or approximately $400 billion in early 1997. The Fed has complete authority to increase or decrease the portfolio as it sees fit. The only criterion that governs the Fed's decision to buy or sell government securities is the current magnitude of bank reserves and the monetary base in relation to their *desired* magnitudes. If the monetary base is smaller than the Fed deems appropriate, the Fed purchases securities, adding to its portfolio and boosting the base. If the Fed desires to reduce the monetary base, it sells securities from its portfolio.[6]

Federal Reserve Discounts and Advances

Discounts and advances refer to the borrowing of reserves from the Federal Reserve by depository institutions. Banks borrow either by having the Fed send currency or, more commonly, by receiving a bookkeeping entry in which the Fed credits the bank's account at the Fed. Suppose a large bank borrows $10 million from the Fed by requesting an increase in its Federal Reserve deposit account. The balance sheet mechanics are as follows:

Federal Reserve		All Banks	
Discounts and advances +10m	Deposits by banks +10m	Deposits at Fed +10m	Borrowings (discounts and advances) +10m

Because bank deposits at the Federal Reserve (F_b) are included in the definition of both reserves and the monetary base, both variables increase by $10 million. The lesson is clear: When the volume of discounts and advances increases, bank reserves and the

---

[6]When the Fed sells securities, dealers write checks to the Federal Reserve. The Fed collects on the checks by debiting the deposit accounts of the banks on which the checks were written. (Hence, the T-accounts above would exhibit minus signs rather than plus signs.) Bank reserves and the monetary base decline dollar for dollar with Federal Reserve sales of securities.

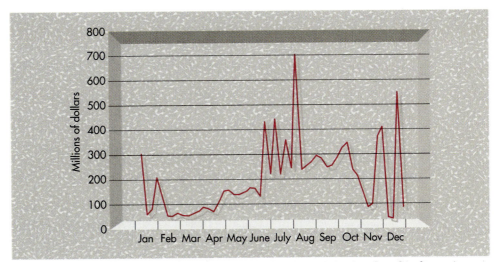

Figure 14-4   Federal Reserve Discounts and Advances, 1995 (Wednesday figures).
Bank borrowing at the Fed fluctuates over time. An increase in discounts and advances
increases bank reserves and the monetary base on a dollar-for-dollar basis.   *Source: Federal Reserve Bulletin*, 1995 and 1996.

monetary base rise by an identical amount; when discounts and advances decline, reserves
and the base decline by a like amount.

The phenomenon of bank borrowing at the Fed will be examined in detail in Chapter 18. For the time being, we may regard the volume of borrowing to be largely determined at the initiative of the banks. The Federal Reserve influences the decision of banks
to borrow at the Fed by setting the *discount rate*—the interest rate charged banks by the
Fed—and by establishing and enforcing the rules and procedures under which banks are
permitted to borrow.

Figure 14-4 shows the pattern of discounts and advances for 1995. The magnitude
of bank borrowing at the Fed during 1995 ranged from a weekly low of less than $50 million to a high of approximately $700 million.

Federal Reserve Float

Float is a phenomenon which arises out of the Fed's procedure for processing checks.
One of the services the Fed provides to banks is the clearing of checks involving banks
in other cities. Suppose you are a student from Los Angeles who is attending school at
the University of Colorado at Boulder. Halfway through the term, you write a check on
your L.A. bank to pay a merchant in Boulder. The merchant deposits the check in her local Boulder bank, which sends the check to the Federal Reserve district bank in Kansas
City for collection.

All checks received by the Fed for processing are classified as items for immediate
credit, credit deferred for 1 day, or credit deferred for 2 days. The classification depends

on the distance and transportation time between the bank on which the check was issued and the Federal Reserve district bank. The Fed maintains a prearranged schedule which estimates the length of time needed to send your check to the Federal Reserve district bank in San Francisco and on to your local bank in Los Angeles. This schedule assumes nearly ideal conditions.

When the allowed time has elapsed, the Fed credits the reserve account of the Boulder bank.[7] However, unless the check has been received by your bank in Los Angeles, its account at the Fed has not yet been debited. Thus, two banks simultaneously have credit at the Fed, when theoretically only one should. The resulting float may be regarded as an interest-free loan from the Federal Reserve to your bank in Los Angeles.[8]

When the Los Angeles bank finally receives your check, its reserve account at the Fed is debited and your check no longer contributes to float. However, because millions of checks are processed by the Fed on any given day, float is a continuing phenomenon.

A simple way of calculating float is by subtracting the Federal Reserve liability "deferred-availability cash items" from the asset "cash items in process of collection." A T-account for the Federal Reserve System will help to illustrate.

Federal Reserve System

Assets	Liabilities
Step A: Cash items in process of collection +	Deferred-availability cash items +
Step B:	Deferred-availability cash items − Member bank deposit (Boulder bank) +
Step C: Cash items in process of collection −	Member bank deposits (L.A. bank) −

When the Boulder bank sends your check written on the L.A. bank to the Kansas City Federal Reserve bank, the Fed makes two bookkeeping entries (step A). The increase in "cash items in process of collection," an asset, indicates that the Fed will be receiving payment (later) from your L.A. bank. The increase in the corresponding liability item "deferred-availability cash items" indicates that the Fed must soon pay the Boulder bank. Of course, on any given day the Fed will have thousands of entries such as these on its books.

According to the time schedule used by the Fed, credit for the Boulder bank is deferred for 2 days. When the two days elapse, step B takes place. The Fed simultaneously removes the initial liability, "deferred-availability cash items," and replaces it with a new

---

[7]The classification and processing of checks are handled by electronic data processing equipment. Look at the coded numbers on the bottom left-hand corner of your personal checks. The first two digits refer to the Federal Reserve district in which your commercial bank is located. The third digit designates the Fed office (main or branch) to which the check will be sent for processing. The fourth digit designates the number of days (0, 1, or 2) that credit is to be deferred—that is, the number of days that must pass before credit is given to the recipient bank's reserve account. This prearranged time period depends on the distance between your bank and the district Fed bank. The last five numbers at the bottom of your check identify your bank to the Fed.

[8]Because of improvements in check collection procedures, float has occasionally been *negative* in recent years. The Fed could reduce the average magnitude of float to zero by basing its schedules on *average* rather than *ideal* collection times.

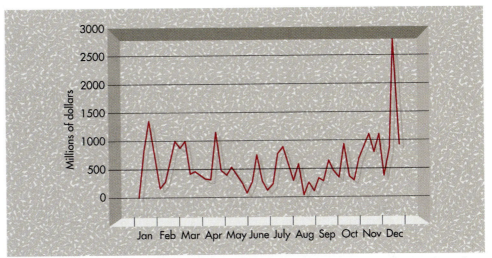

Figure 14-5   Federal Reserve Float in 1995 (Wednesday figures). Float arises from the Federal Reserve's check-processing mechanism. Its magnitude fluctuates because of changes in the volume of checks in the process of collection.   *Source: Federal Reserve Bulletin,* 1995 and 1996.

liability entry, "member bank deposits," that is, F_b. The Boulder bank has now received reserve credit in the amount of the check. Float increases as soon as the Boulder bank's reserve account is credited by the Fed.

Suppose that one day later your L.A. bank receives the check. At this point, step C occurs. The Fed simultaneously cancels the previous entry, "cash items in process of collection" and debits the L.A. bank's Federal Reserve account. The check has now been collected and the float it created is nullified. Thus, float occurs in the time interval between steps B and C. Because the time schedule used by the Fed for crediting the Federal Reserve account of the bank in which the check is deposited is based on nearly ideal collection times, the value of checks in the process of collection by the Fed normally exceeds the amount of deferred-availability cash items.

Figure 14-5 shows the pattern of float in 1995. Note that the float can easily fluctuate by $1000 million or more from week to week. This variation is due largely to the seasonal fluctuation in the volume of checks processed by the Fed. The pattern of float is influenced by such institutional factors as pay schedules, bill due dates, and holiday shopping. In addition to the seasonal pattern, events that impede the transportation of checks—snowstorms, airline strikes, and the like—can delay the collection of checks, increasing the magnitude of float. The "blizzard of '96," for example, which closed down East Coast airports in early January 1996, triggered a huge, temporary increase in float.

Whenever float rises, bank reserves and the monetary base increase in a dollar-for-dollar fashion. In the 1980s, the Fed implemented a series of measures that sharply reduced the average magnitude and absolute variability of float. The move helped to reduce undesired volatility in the monetary base.

The U.S. Gold Stock and the Federal Reserve's Special Drawing Rights Account

The U.S. Treasury stands willing to purchase, at the official government price, any and all gold offered. If the Treasury were to purchase gold, either domestically or from foreign governments, the monetary base would rise dollar for dollar with the transaction.

Suppose the Treasury were to purchase $66 million worth of gold from domestic miners, paying via checks drawn on its account with the Federal Reserve. The recipients of the checks then deposit them in private banks. After the banks send the checks to the Federal Reserve district banks for collection, their reserve accounts at the Fed are marked up by $66 million. The Fed handles the transaction via a simple bookkeeping entry on the liability side of its balance sheet. It marks up the banks' accounts by a total of $66 million and simultaneously marks down the U.S. Treasury's account. Bank reserves and the monetary base have both increased by the amount of transaction—that is, $66 million.

At this point, the U.S. Treasury prints up gold certificates in the amount of $66 million and presents them to the Federal Reserve. The Fed then replenishes the Treasury's Federal Reserve deposit account. The final effect of the entire transaction on the Fed's balance sheet is as follows:

Federal Reserve System			
Gold certificates	+66m	Deposits by banks	+66m

Thus, reserves and the base both expand by $66 million. The same result would occur if the U.S. government were to purchase gold from foreign governments. The foreign governments would deposit the Fed's checks in U.S. banks, initiating the same series of effects. The upshot is that both reserves and the monetary base move dollar for dollar with the magnitude of gold certificates held by the Federal Reserve.

In practice, gold certificates have been of almost no importance since 1971, when the United States closed its "gold window," ending its agreement to sell gold to foreign governments at the official gold price. On the domestic scene, the large premium by which the free market gold price exceeds the official government price has removed any incentive domestic gold producers might have to sell their gold to the U.S. Treasury.

Special Drawing Rights (SDRs) are issued by the International Monetary Fund to national governments, which use them to settle international debts. When the U.S. Treasury receives SDRs from the IMF, it issues SDR certificates to the Federal Reserve. The Fed compensates the Treasury by crediting its account at the Fed. As we will see shortly, when the Treasury writes checks to spend the funds, both bank reserves and the monetary base expand. Given the other nine factors which determine the monetary base (including F_t), an increase in the SDR account (included in G in Equation 14-10) produces an equivalent increase in the base.

Other Federal Reserve Assets

This item includes other items owned by the Federal Reserve, such as buildings, furniture, and equipment. It also includes the Fed's holdings of foreign assets, which are typically held as government bonds and deposits denominated in foreign currencies.

EXHIBIT 14-1

Federal Reserve Foreign Exchange Operations

The U.S. dollar's foreign exchange rate with the United States' major trading partners is considered to be of strategic national importance. Because the U.S. government believes that exchange rate movements are sometimes driven by speculative activity rather than by underlying fundamentals, the Fed occasionally intervenes in the foreign exchange market for the purpose of stabilizing the exchange rate. To prevent the value of the dollar from falling excessively, the Fed purchases dollars with foreign currencies, such as yen and deutsche marks. To prevent an undesired appreciation of the dollar, the Fed buys foreign currencies with dollars.

Typically, more than two-thirds of the $30 billion balance sheet item "other assets" consists of Fed holdings of bonds and savings accounts denominated in foreign currencies. These currency holdings serve as the Fed's ammunition for defending the dollar against undesired speculative attacks.

In March 1995, the dollar descended to record lows against the Japanese yen and the German mark. By that time, the depreciation of the dollar against each currency had amounted to more than 10 percent in the most recent year, and more than 60 percent since the dollar had reached its high-water mark some 10 years earlier. Experts at the Fed believed the depreciation was not justified by fundamentals and was likely to have undesired consequences for the United States. For example, a falling dollar tends to stimulate inflation in the United States by boosting the cost of imported goods and by stimulating foreign demand for U.S. products.

In March 1995, the Fed aggressively deployed its yen and deutsche mark holdings to purchase dollars. The monetary effects of the transaction were the same as those of an open market sale of securities by the Fed. In exchange for the yen and marks, foreign exchange dealers wrote checks denominated in dollars. The Fed collected on the checks by debiting the Fed accounts of the foreign exchange dealers' banks in New York. Thus, bank reserves and the monetary base declined as the Fed sold off its holdings of yen and deutsche marks.

To prevent this operation from producing an undesired contraction of reserves and the monetary base, the Fed then had to purchase U.S. government securities in the open market. Such operations are said to "sterilize" the Fed's foreign exchange market transactions, preventing them from disturbing the monetary base and the monetary aggregates.

The Fed holds such assets for the purpose of intervening to stabilize the U.S. dollar through direct foreign exchange transactions (see Exhibit 14-1). For example, if the Fed buys Mexican pesos to support the peso vis-à-vis the dollar, it writes checks on itself, which are then deposited in U.S. banks by foreign exchange dealers. When the checks are cleared, the banks' Federal Reserve accounts are boosted, thus increasing the monetary base.

Alternatively, suppose the Fed decides to purchase a posh new table for Federal Open Market Committee meetings. The Fed writes a check for $80,000, and when the furniture dealer deposits the check, the bank in which it is deposited receives an $80,000 increase in its reserve account (F_b). The monetary base increases by $80,000. Thus, changes in "other assets" cause equivalent changes in the monetary base.

Treasury Currency Outstanding

The U.S. Treasury mints all the coins in the United States. Unless it is accompanied by an offsetting transaction, an increase in this item causes an identical increase in the monetary base. The increased Treasury currency ends up either as cash in depository institutions (in which case it is classified as reserves, R) or as currency held by the nonbank public (in which case it contributes to C^p).

The amount of Treasury currency outstanding adapts itself to the public's need for it. Suppose the public withdraws an additional \$60 million in coins from banks by drawing down checking accounts. The balance sheet impact is

All Banks		
Cash −60m	DDO −60m

Because the banks are being drained of coins, they wire the Fed and request the delivery of more. The Fed handles the transaction by deducting the banks' reserve accounts (F_b). The balance sheet mechanics of this transaction are

All Banks			Federal Reserve System	
Cash	+60m		Cash −60m	Deposits
Deposits at				by banks −60m
Fed	−60m			

Now the Fed itself is beginning to run low on coins. The Fed contacts the U.S. Treasury and requests \$60 million worth of coins. The Treasury obliges by minting \$60 million worth of new coins and shipping them to the 12 Federal Reserve district banks. The Fed pays for the currency by crediting the Treasury's account at the Fed. The T-accounts appear as follows:

Federal Reserve System			U.S. Treasury	
Cash	+60m	Deposits by U.S.	Deposits at	Treasury currency
		Treasury +60m	Fed +60m	outstanding +60m

Thus we see that the public determines the amount of Treasury currency outstanding. When the public wants more coins, the message is transferred first to the banks, then to the Fed, and finally to the U.S. Treasury. In essence, the Treasury mints or withdraws coins at the request of the public. The commercial banks and the Federal Reserve banks act only as agents in the process. If we net out the impact of the process on the balance sheets of all banks and the Fed, we get the following:

All Banks			Federal Reserve System	
Deposits at		DDO −60m		Deposits
Fed −60m				by banks −60m
				Deposits by U.S.
				Treasury +60m

Note carefully the impact on the monetary base, $R + C^p$. In this example, the base is *unchanged.* Currency held by the public (C^p) has increased, but bank reserves (R) have fallen by an equal amount. Though the banks have restored their cash reserves, they have done so by reducing their deposits at the Federal Reserve. Looking at the net effect from the point of view of the sources of the monetary base, the impact on the base of the increase in Treasury currency outstanding has been exactly neutralized by a simultaneous change in another determinant—the Treasury's deposits at the Fed (F_t). As we will demonstrate shortly, the Treasury normally attempts to keep its balance at the Federal Reserve stable over time. When the Treasury returns its Federal Reserve balance to its original amount, the monetary base will indeed rise by the $60 million increase in Treasury currency outstanding.

Treasury Deposits at the Federal Reserve

Expenditures made by the U.S. government are paid for by checks written on the U.S. Treasury's account at the Federal Reserve. The accounts are distributed among the Fed's 12 district banks. When the recipient of a Treasury check deposits it in a bank account, the Fed clears the check by crediting the bank's account at the Fed and debiting the Treasury's account (F_t).

Suppose an employee of the U.S. Postal Service receives a paycheck from the U.S. government in the amount of $950. The worker deposits the check in a bank account. The bank sends the check to the Federal Reserve, which makes a bookkeeping entry shifting $950 from the Treasury's account to the account of the postal worker's bank. The result of these transactions is that the monetary base and bank reserves both increase by $950. The relevant T-accounts appear as follows:

Federal Reserve System		All Banks		
	Deposits by banks +950m	Deposits at Fed +950m	DDO	+950m
	Deposits by Treasury −950m			

Thus, when Treasury deposits at the Fed decline, reserves and the monetary base increase because checks written by the Treasury end up as deposits in banks. (In the event the postal worker cashes the paycheck rather than depositing it, bank reserves do not increase. However, currency held by the public [C^p] does increase, and with it the monetary base.)

Besides its account at the Fed, the U.S. Treasury maintains deposit accounts in approximately 85 percent of the banks in the United States.[9] These accounts are periodically replenished by federal tax receipts and by the proceeds from the sale of new

---

[9]Practically any bank can qualify as a "depository bank." The only requirements are that the bank pledge collateral in the form of U.S. government securities and that the bank be endorsed or recommended by the Federal Reserve district bank.

Treasury securities to the public; hence the name *tax and loan accounts* is given to these accounts.[10]

Expenditures by the U.S. Treasury are not paid for out of these tax and loan accounts but rather from the Treasury's account at the Federal Reserve. However, when large payments are scheduled to be made by the Treasury from its Fed account, funds are transferred from the tax and loan accounts to the Treasury's account at the Fed.[11] The net effect is to neutralize the potential expansionary impact of Treasury expenditures on bank reserves and the monetary base.

In the preceding example, when the government paid the postal worker $950, bank reserves and the monetary base increased by the same amount. But the Treasury can neutralize the effect of the transaction by transferring $950 from its tax and loan accounts to its account at the Fed. The balance sheet impact of such a transfer is as follows:

Federal Reserve		All Banks	
	Deposits by U.S. Treasury +950m	Deposits at Fed −950m	Deposits by U.S. Treasury −950m
	Deposits by member banks −950m		

This transaction, coupled with the one in which the postal worker deposited a government paycheck, leaves both bank reserves and the monetary base unchanged.

The idea behind the transfer of funds is to minimize potentially disruptive swings in the monetary base. Suppose, as a result of underwithholding of income taxes, that in the week of April 15, American taxpayers present checks totaling $18 billion to the IRS. If the funds are deposited and left in the Treasury's tax and loan accounts, reserves and the monetary base will be unaffected. The $18 billion is simply cleared out of the reserve accounts of taxpayers' banks and redeposited by the Treasury into banks, which therefore collectively lose no reserves. The monetary base remains constant.

Now, suppose that the Treasury's tax and loan accounts did not exist and all Treasury funds were kept at the Federal Reserve. In that event, when the Treasury received the $18 billion in tax receipts, bank reserves and the monetary base would fall by $18 billion. After the Treasury had spent the funds, R and B would return to their original levels, as Treasury checks were deposited in banks. Given the lack of synchronization between Treasury disbursements and receipts, monetary variables such as reserves and the base would be subject to large and disruptive fluctuations. This would complicate the Federal Reserve's efforts to stabilize the economy.

---

[10]The Treasury typically recycles the funds back to the banks on which the public wrote the checks. Before 1978, tax and loan accounts were a free source of funds for banks. Since 1978, the Treasury has required banks to pay interest on such deposits, at a rate 0.25 percent below the average federal funds rate for the week.

[11]Transfers are accomplished following a "call," whereby the Treasury notifies banks that on a given day (usually within a day or two), a specified portion of its deposits will be withdrawn and transferred to the Treasury account at the Fed. On the specified date, the Fed handles the transfer by crediting the Treasury's account and debiting the banks' accounts at the Fed. At that time, the monetary base decreases by the amount of the transaction. Of course, as soon as the Treasury spends the funds, bank reserves and the monetary base return to their original levels.

Thus, the two-tier Treasury deposit system (tax and loan accounts and deposits at the Fed) was developed to minimize the infringement of government fiscal affairs on monetary management. This implies that the Treasury's tax and loan accounts should be treated as a residual—that is, allowed to fluctuate in order to stabilize the Treasury deposits at the Fed. In a period in which government spending is considerably less than its receipts from taxes and bond sales, the Treasury should build up its tax and loan accounts in private banks rapidly. Otherwise, the payment of taxes and the purchase of bonds by the public will not be fully countered by the replenishing effect of government spending. Bank reserves, the monetary base, and ultimately the money supply will decrease. If government expenditures are running ahead of receipts, the Treasury should decrease its tax and loan accounts by transferring such funds to its account at the Federal Reserve. Otherwise, the operation will have a net expansionary impact on reserves, the base, and the monetary aggregates.

The Fed uses its securities holdings to counteract undesired changes. To neutralize the monetary effects of an increase in the Treasury's Federal Reserve account, the Fed purchases securities. To offset the effect of a decline in Treasury deposits at the Fed, the Fed sells securities.

The U.S. government spends more than $1500 billion per year ($6 billion per business *day*). In spite of the Treasury's efforts to stabilize its account at the Fed (F_t) by manipulating its tax and loan accounts at private banks, its Fed account does fluctuate considerably. Figure 14-6 illustrates the magnitude of F_t on each Wednesday throughout 1995.

Note the volatility in the magnitude of the Treasury's deposits. The *average* magnitude of F_t in 1995 was approximately $6 billion, but the *changes* in its amount often exceeded $2 billion in a given week. Because fluctuations in the Treasury's Federal Reserve account have a potentially destabilizing influence on the monetary base, the Fed must keep a close watch on this item. Toward that end, the Fed and the Treasury are in daily communication.

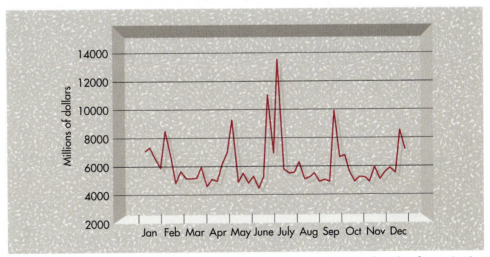

Figure 14-6   Treasury Deposits at the Federal Reserve, 1995 (Wednesday figures). The Treasury maintains large deposits at the Federal Reserve in order to finance its huge expenditures. *Source: Federal Reserve Bulletin,* 1995 and 1996.

The effect of an increase in F_t is to reduce bank reserves and the monetary base by an identical amount. Hence, the Fed must purchase securities in the open market to neutralize the monetary effects of an increase in the Treasury's Federal Reserve account, other things being equal. When Treasury deposits at the Fed decline, R and B expand. The Fed must sell securities (reduce P) by an identical amount to maintain R and B in *status quo*.

Foreign and Other Deposits at the Federal Reserve

Foreign central banks and governments maintain deposits at the Federal Reserve, chiefly for the purpose of financing purchases of U.S. goods and services. Some government agencies, such as the Federal Home Loan Bank, and certain international organizations, such as the World Bank, also keep deposits at the Federal Reserve. We lump these foreign and other deposits at the Fed together and designate them F_f.

Changes in these deposits (F_f) exert the same effect on the monetary base as changes in the Treasury deposit at the Fed. Suppose the government of France purchases $88 million worth of mainframe computers from IBM. The French government writes a check on its account at the Fed for $88 million. Upon receipt of the check, IBM's bank sends it on to the Fed for collection. In a bookkeeping entry, the Fed transfers the funds from the French government's account at the Fed to the bank's account. Bank reserves and the monetary base increase by $88 million, and foreign deposits at the Fed decline by the same amount.

Treasury Cash Holdings

Treasury cash (TCa) consists primarily of paper money and coins accumulated by the Treasury in connection with fiscal operations. As the Treasury dispenses this till money, the monetary base rises because it must end up either as currency held by the public (C^p) or as cash in depository institutions (C_b). By the same reasoning, when Treasury cash holdings increase, the monetary base declines.

Other Liabilities and Capital

This item (OLC) is the counterpart of "other Federal Reserve assets" (OA). An increase in this item exerts a contractionary effect on the monetary base and bank reserves. Suppose, for instance, that the Federal Reserve issues additional stock to its owners, the nation's member banks.[12] The Fed would collect from the banks by deducting their reserve accounts. Hence, both R and B would decline. Quantitatively, changes in this item are typically of minor importance.

---

[12]During 1991–1996, in response to pressure from regulatory authorities and favorable economic circumstances, depository institutions experienced a dramatic improvement in their equity (capital accounts) positions. Because member banks are required to purchase stock in the Federal Reserve in proportion to their capital accounts, "other liabilities and capital" of the Fed experienced significant growth in that period.

FEDERAL RESERVE OPERATIONS AND THE MONETARY BASE

We may summarize our discussion of the monetary base by referring back to Equation 14-10, which expresses the magnitude of the monetary base in terms of its 10 individual sources. Basically, the Federal Reserve controls only 2 of the 10 items—its portfolio of securities (*P*) and "other Federal Reserve assets" (*OA*). The other 8 items are outside its direct control. However, the Fed's total control over its huge portfolio of securities (*P*) enables it to achieve firm control over the monetary base.[13] To a significant extent, the Fed can predict or concurrently observe the changes in the other 9 items (besides *P*) that influence the monetary base. The Fed then manipulates its portfolio (*P*) accordingly, to achieve the desired monetary base. On any given day, the Fed's estimation of float, Treasury deposits at the Fed, and the other sources of the base may be somewhat inaccurate. If so, the daily figures for the monetary base and bank reserves will deviate somewhat from the Fed's desired levels. But if we look at a weekly average of the daily figures, we will find the Fed has more control. The Fed's ability to control the monetary base accurately increases significantly as we lengthen the time horizon. As we will demonstrate in the next chapter, any problems the Federal Reserve may encounter in controlling the money supply result mainly from unpredictable changes in the money supply multiplier.

SUMMARY

The money supply may be viewed as the product of a monetary base and a money supply multiplier. Changes in the money supply can thus be caused either by changes in the base or by changes in the multiplier. The Federal Reserve's ability to control the money supply rests on its ability to determine the monetary base and forecast the money supply multiplier. Because each dollar of monetary base supports several dollars of money, the base is sometimes known as "high-powered money." The monetary base may be analyzed from the viewpoint of its uses or its sources.

The base is used as reserves of depository institutions (*R*, consisting of vault cash and banks' deposits at the Federal Reserve) and currency in the hands of the public (C^p). There are 10 sources of the base, or 10 factors that determine the base. The Fed controls only 2 of those 10 factors directly. By far the most important factor is the Federal Reserve's portfolio of U.S. government and agency securities. By controlling its security portfolio, the Fed can counteract the influence of changes in the other sources of the base, thus accurately controlling the monetary base.

---

[13]One might compare the Fed's control of the monetary base to engineers' control of the water level in a reservoir. Engineers cannot control rainfall, evaporation, and other exogenous factors which influence the water level in a reservoir. However, by controlling the rate of outflow at the dam, they can accurately control the reservoir's water level.

KEY TERMS

monetary base
money supply multiplier
sources of the base
uses for the base

STUDY QUESTIONS

1 Define the monetary base. Why have we selected this particular variable for intensive study?

2 Write an equation indicating the 10 sources of the monetary base. Define each of the 10 variables.

3 "Several of the sources of the monetary base are clearly outside Federal Reserve control. Therefore, the Fed is not responsible for the monetary base." Evaluate this statement.

4 Explain the impact of the following two events on aggregate bank reserves and the monetary base:

  a The Fed sells $3 billion of securities to dealers.

  b A commercial bank sells $3 billion of securities to dealers.

5 Suppose that, in a given week, float rises by $1400 million, Treasury deposits at the Fed increase by $900 million, discounts and advances decline by $300 million, and foreign deposits at the Fed increase by $400 million. What is the net effect of these changes on the base? If the Fed desires to keep the base constant, what must it do?

6 While reading *The Wall Street Journal,* you notice that the Fed purchased an abnormally large quantity of securities last week. Does this purchase signal a change in policy stance toward an increased monetary base, increased money supply, and lower interest rates? Why or why not?

7 Explain the meaning of Federal Reserve float. Explain how float would change with the following events:

  a A tornado closes down the Atlanta airport for a week.

  b People write fewer checks in a given week.

  c The Fed increases deferral time on all checks by one day.

8 Suppose the public reduces its demand for coins by $400 million. Trace the effects on the T-accounts of banks, the Federal Reserve, and the Treasury.

9 Explain carefully how the Treasury uses its two-tier deposit system (in private banks and the Federal Reserve) to minimize the effect of its operations on reserves and the monetary base.

10 Calculate the effect of the following events on the monetary base:

  a The public withdraws $600 million of currency from banks.

b   The Treasury writes checks to Social Security recipients for $700 million.

c   The Fed sells $1200 million of securities in the open market.

d   The Fed buys a new fleet of cars for $22 million.

e   The Treasury transfers $600 million from tax and loan accounts to its Federal Reserve account.

f   The Federal Reserve sells $1.5 billion of its German government bonds.

11   Using T-accounts to facilitate your explanation, demonstrate how Federal Reserve purchases of $400 million of U.S. government securities from dealers would affect the monetary base.

12   Recently, a financially troubled bank borrowed $600 million from the Federal Reserve. What impact did this have on the monetary base? Explain.

13   In the late 1980s, Japan was accused of keeping the yen artificially weak vis-à-vis the dollar to stimulate exports to the United States. What kind of action would be required for Japan to accomplish this? What would be the effect on its holdings of U.S. dollars? What would be the effect on the monetary base in Japan?

14   Why does a large change in the volume of discounts and advances usually signal only a temporary change in the monetary base?

SUGGESTIONS FOR ADDITIONAL READING

The seminal work employing the monetary base–money supply multiplier framework was conducted by Karl Brunner and Allan Meltzer. An early but excellent reference is Brunner and Meltzer, "An Alternative Approach to the Monetary Mechanism," House of Representatives, Committee on Banking and Currency, Subcommittee on Domestic Finance, 88th Congress (Washington, D.C.: U.S. Government Printing Office, 1964). There are two separate series of data for the monetary base, one published by the Board of Governors of the Federal Reserve System and the other by the Federal Reserve Bank of St. Louis. The St. Louis Fed has published numerous articles on the monetary base over the years in its *Review*. See, for example, Anatol Balbach and Albert Burger, "Derivation of the Monetary Base," in the November 1976 *Review*. The entire December 1980 issue of the *Review* is devoted to issues of measuring and revising the monetary base. On the Treasury's two-tier deposit system, see Richard Lang, "Treasury Tax and Loan Accounts and the Money Supply Process," Federal Reserve Bank of St. Louis *Review*, October 1979. The *Treasury Bulletin*, published quarterly by the U.S. Treasury, contains detailed data on Treasury deposits at the Fed as well as tax and loan accounts. Finally, the monthly *Federal Reserve Bulletin* provides detailed data on the monetary base and its sources in the statistical tables at the back of each issue.

C H A P T E R

15

Money Supply Determination: The Money Supply Multiplier

At the beginning of the last chapter, we expressed the money supply as the product of the monetary base and a money supply multiplier which summarizes the multiple deposit expansion mechanism in a fractional reserve banking system. Expressed algebraically, the relationship is

(15-1)
$$M = B \cdot m$$

(15-2)
$$m = \frac{M}{B}$$

In these equations, M represents the money supply, while B and m represent the monetary base and the money supply multiplier, respectively. According to the first equation, any change in the supply of money must be attributable to a change in the base, a change in the multiplier, or some combination of both. The second equation defines the money supply multiplier as the ratio of the money supply to the monetary base.

We established in Chapter 14 that the Federal Reserve is capable of exerting a very high degree of control over B. Equation 15-1 therefore implies that if m is a stable, predictable variable which is largely independent of B, the Fed is capable of exerting accurate control over the nation's money supply, M. That is, changes in B engineered by the Federal Reserve should dominate any changes in the money supply multiplier, allowing the Fed to control the money supply.

On the other hand, if m fluctuates erratically and unpredictably or is induced to change in an unpredictable manner by changes in the monetary base engineered by the Federal Reserve, it may be difficult for the Fed to gain firm control over the money supply. In that event, changes in B that are produced by the Fed may be dominated by relatively large changes in m. If so, the true sources of change in the money supply may be the factors that underlie the money supply multiplier. Such factors are largely outside Federal Reserve influence. Indeed, some economists regard the money supply to be a largely endogenous variable—a variable that is determined by economic activity—in the short run, say over a week or a month. They believe that short-run changes in the money supply are caused primarily by changes in the money supply multiplier, which in turn moves in response to such economic variables as interest rates, income, and wealth.[1]

In this chapter, we will develop an understanding of the meaning of the money supply multiplier and analyze the factors that determine its magnitude. Essentially, the money supply multiplier summarizes all forces other than the monetary base that influence the money supply. Specifically, the money supply multiplier reflects portfolio decisions made by the public regarding the distribution of financial wealth among currency, demand deposits, and other financial assets. It also reflects the portfolio decisions of depository institutions (banks) regarding the distribution of assets between reserves (cash and deposits at the Fed) and earning assets such as loans and securities. As such, the money supply multiplier is an important behavioral variable in macroeconomics.

The money supply multiplier expresses the "productivity," or "magnification," factor by which the banking system transforms base money into actual money, much of which consists of demand deposits. For each measure of money, there is a corresponding money supply multiplier. Hence, $m_1 = M1/B$, $m_2 = M2/B$, and $m_3 = M3/B$. We will focus chiefly on m_1, the ratio of the narrow measure of money to the monetary base. In the next section, we will derive m_1.

THE MONEY SUPPLY MULTIPLIER: DERIVATION AND APPLICATIONS

We begin by deriving an expression which specifies the variables that determine the magnitude of the money supply multiplier. Recall the narrow definition of the money supply in the United States:

$$(15\text{-}3) \qquad\qquad \mathbf{M1 \; = \; DDO + C^p}$$

This equation states that the narrow money supply (M1) consists of demand deposits and other checkable deposits in depository institutions plus currency in the hands of the public. Because it incorporates only items that are actually used to make transactions, this measure of money is sometimes called the *transactions measure* of the money supply.

---

[1]Even if this hypothesis is valid, the Fed could still control the money supply in the short run if the changes in the multiplier are predictable in advance and are independent of the monetary base. If the Fed knows what the multiplier will be next week, it can set the monetary base at the approximate level required to produce the desired money stock. For example, if the multiplier will be 2.50 and the desired money stock is $1250 billion, the Fed would want to target a monetary base of $500 billion.

Let us derive the multiplier for M1, that is, M1/B. In Chapter 14, we defined the monetary base in terms of its uses, or the way in which it is allocated:

(15-4) $$B = R + C^p$$

This expression states that the monetary base (B) is equal to the sum of bank reserves (R) and the currency held by the nonbank public (C^p). Recall that *reserves (R)* include depository institutions' cash and their deposits at the Federal Reserve. C^p includes all currency and coins except that which resides in banks, the Treasury, and the Federal Reserve. If we substitute the expression for M1 given in Equation 15-3 and the expression for B given in Equation 15-4 into Equation 15-2, which defines the money supply multiplier, we obtain

(15-5) $$m_1 = \frac{DDO + C^p}{R + C^p}$$

Bank reserves (R) can be broken into two components, required reserves (R_r) and excess reserves (R_e). Recall from Chapter 13 that *required reserves* are those reserves which banks must hold in order to abide by the reserve requirements stipulated by the Federal Reserve. *Excess reserves* are those reserves which, in view of current and expected future economic conditions, banks elect to hold above and beyond the required amount.[2] Therefore:

(15-6) $$R = R_r + R_e$$

We may define the variables in Equation 15-6 as follows:

(15-7) $$R_r = r_r(DDO) \qquad \textbf{where } r_r = \frac{R_r}{DDO}$$

(15-8) $$R_e = r_e(DDO) \qquad \textbf{where } r_e = \frac{R_e}{DDO}$$

Equation 15-7 states that the dollar amount of required reserves (R_r) is some fraction (r_r) of the amount of demand deposits and other checkable accounts. This fraction is known as the **required reserve ratio (r_r).** Equation 15-8 states that the dollar magnitude of desired excess reserves (R_e) is some fraction (r_e) of such deposits. This fraction is known as the **desired excess reserve ratio (r_e).** If we substitute these expressions of r_r and r_e into Equation 15-6, we see that R may be expressed as the product of

---

[2]We use the term "banks" generically to include all depository institutions subject to reserve requirements. We assume that banks adjust their actual holdings of excess reserves to the desired amounts instantaneously. While this assumption is obviously an exaggeration, the adjustment process is likely to be quite rapid in our age of highly developed money markets, computers, and instant communication.

the sum of the required and excess reserve ratios (r_r and r_e) and the magnitude of checkable deposits (DDO):

$$(15\text{-}9) \qquad R \ = \ r_r(DDO) + r_e(DDO) \ = \ (r_r + r_e)(DDO)$$

Let us now substitute the expression for R given in the right-hand side of Equation 15-9 into our formula for the money supply multiplier (Equation 15-5):

$$(15\text{-}10) \qquad m_1 \ = \ \frac{DDO + C^p}{(r_r + r_e)(DDO) + C^p}$$

If we divide both the numerator and the denominator by DDO, we obtain

$$(15\text{-}11) \qquad m_1 \ = \ \frac{1 + C^p/DDO}{(r_r + r_e)(1) + C^p/DDO}$$

To simplify the notation, we will define C^p/DDO as k, the **currency ratio**—the ratio of currency held by the public to demand deposits. If we insert this notation into Equation 15-11, we get our final expression for the money supply multiplier, m_1:

$$(15\text{-}12) \qquad m_1 \ = \ \frac{1 + k}{r_r + r_e + k}$$

Equation 15-12 indicates that the money supply multiplier is determined by three variables: the currency ratio (k), the weighted average required reserve ratio (r_r), and the banks' desired excess reserve ratio (r_e). Later in this chapter, we will carefully examine the factors that underlie each of these three variables. For the time being, we simply note that k is determined by the public, r_e is determined by the banks, and r_r is determined predominantly by the Federal Reserve. Therefore, we see that the money supply is influenced not just by the Fed but also by the public and the banks.

Comparison with the Simple or Naive Deposit Expansion Multiplier

It is useful to compare the formula we have just derived with the simplified deposit expansion multiplier presented in Chapter 13.[3] That naive multiplier, which is simply the reciprocal of the percentage reserve requirement applicable to demand deposits, was derived on the basis of the following assumptions:

1   A change in demand deposits will not induce a change in the demand for currency by the public. The demand for currency (C^p) is independent of DDO.

---

[3] Review Table 13-1 on page 313 and the assumptions and discussion surrounding it.

2 A change in demand deposits will not induce a change in banks' demand for excess reserves. The demand for excess reserves is assumed to always be zero.

3 The percentage reserve requirement applicable to demand deposits is the same for all demand deposits in all banks. Also, there are no reserve requirements on other bank liabilities.

Let us interpret these assumptions in the context of our money supply multiplier expression (Equation 15-12). The first assumption implies that $k = 0$. That is, the marginal propensity to convert demand deposits into currency as *DDO* increases is zero. The second assumption implies that r_e is zero. That is, bankers do not want to hold any excess reserves. The third assumption implies that r_r is constant; it is simply the percentage reserve requirement set by the Federal Reserve for demand deposits and other checkable deposits. (In reality, r_r is a bit more complicated, as we will see later in this chapter.)

Given these three restrictive assumptions, if we insert $k = 0$ and $r_e = 0$ into Equation 15-12, our multiplier expression reduces to $1/r_r$—the naive or simple deposit expansion multiplier of Chapter 13. Thus the simple deposit expansion multiplier is logically valid given the assumptions which underlie it. Because those assumptions are unrealistic, however, the resulting multiplier expression, $1/r_r$, is of little use in analyzing real-world monetary phenomena.

The beauty of our money supply multiplier expressed in Equation 15-12 is that it moves much closer to reality. It takes account of banks' behavior concerning excess reserves and of the public's behavior concerning currency holdings. It is of necessity more complicated than the naive deposit expansion multiplier, because it does take these factors into account. In the naive deposit expansion multiplier, the multiplier remains constant as long as the reserve requirement is unchanged. In this more realistic formulation, the money supply multiplier changes continuously in response to forces exerted by the public and the banks.

The Role of the Federal Reserve in Influencing the Money Supply Multiplier

Because we are interested in the degree to which the Federal Reserve can control the money supply, we will now sketch the Fed's influence on each of the three variables that determine the money supply multiplier—that is, k, r_r, and r_e. We will provide a more complete analysis of the determinants of these variables later in this chapter.

The Fed and *k*

The Federal Reserve has no direct influence over the currency ratio (k). This variable responds directly to the public's demand for currency and demand deposits. The public obtains currency by withdrawing funds from checking and savings accounts. If the banks run short, they obtain currency from the Federal Reserve, paying for it with a debit to their reserve deposit accounts at the Fed. The Fed obtains the currency by printing Federal Reserve notes as they are needed and by requesting coins from the

U.S. Treasury. Because these responses of banks, the Fed, and the Treasury are all triggered by actions of the public, the public is properly viewed as determining the currency ratio.

The Fed and r_r

The ratio of required reserves to *DDO*—that is, (r_r), is dominated by the reserve requirement percentages set by the Fed. Currently, each bank is subject to a 3 percent reserve requirement on all demand deposits up to a certain level—$52.0 million in 1996—and a 10 percent reserve requirement on all demand deposits in excess of this amount. Changes in the distribution of deposits among banks of different sizes therefore induce changes in r_r.[4] Occasionally, the Fed changes the percentage reserve requirements, triggering significant changes in r_r. For example, in 1992 the Fed reduced the reserve requirement for all demand deposits above the threshold level from 12 percent to 10 percent.

The Fed and r_e

The desired excess reserve ratio (r_e) is chiefly determined by banks' decisions and is subject only to marginal Federal Reserve influence. This variable responds to the costs and benefits of holding excess reserves, as perceived by bank management. It is sensitive to interest rate levels, expectations about future Federal Reserve policy, and other economic phenomena.

The Fed and the Multiplier: Recap

In sum, the public essentially determines k, the banks determine r_e, and the Fed largely determines r_r and the monetary base. We can therefore assert that at a given point in time the money supply is determined jointly by the public, the banks, and the Federal Reserve. The critical topics of debate among professional economists are the following: Is it feasible for the Federal Reserve to accurately control short-term movements in the money supply, and is it important for it to do so? Some economists believe that, in a given month, the Federal Reserve is capable of dominating the effects that banks and the general public have on the money supply multiplier and can therefore come very close to hitting a desired target level for the money supply in the short run. Others have expressed rather strong doubts about this proposition. This latter group believes that short-run instability in k, r_r, and r_e produces volatility in the money supply multiplier, making it difficult or impractical for the Fed to hit monthly money supply targets.

Let us now breathe life into these concepts by employing some hypothetical, though not grossly unrealistic, data.

Some Arithmetic Examples

Suppose we make the following assumptions concerning aggregate banking variables and reserve requirements:

1 Demand deposits and other checkable accounts (DDO) = $1000 billion

2 Currency held by the public (C^p) = $400 billion

---

[4] A check cleared from a large bank to a bank with less than the threshold magnitude of *DDO* would therefore reduce r_r. The threshold magnitude ($52 million in 1996) is indexed to total transactions accounts (*DDO*); thus, it changes each year by 80 percent of the percentage change in aggregate *DDO* in the nation's banks.

3   Reserve requirements for all DDO = 10 percent

4   Reserves = $101 billion

We begin by computing R_r and R_e in Equation 15-6. We know that reserves (R) = $101 billion (this is given). To compute the dollar amount of R_r, we multiply the reserve requirement applicable to DDO by the amount of DDO. We get R_r = 10%($1000 billion) = $100 billion. Since we know that actual (and desired) excess reserves (R_e) = $R - R_r$, we know that R_e = $1 billion.

We can now calculate r_r and r_e. Using Equation 15-7, we compute r_r = $100b/$1000b = .10. The volume of required reserves is 10 percent of total checkable deposits. Once we know R and R_r, we can compute r_e. Using Equation 15-8, we get r_e = $1b/$1000b = .001. The desired (and actual) excess reserve ratio is 0.1 percent. To calculate the money supply multiplier, we still need to calculate k, the ratio of currency held by the public to demand deposits. With the data given above, this is simple:

$$k = \$400b/\$1000b = .40$$

We are now in a position to calculate the size of the money supply multiplier, as expressed in Equation 15-12:

$$m_1 = \frac{1 + .40}{.10 + .001 + .40} = 2.79$$

We have thus calculated the money supply multiplier to be 2.79. The meaning of this is as follows: given the propensities of the public to maintain a ratio of C^p to DDO of 40 percent and of banks to maintain a ratio of excess reserves to DDO of 0.1 percent, and given the ratio of required reserves to DDO to be held fixed at 10 percent, a $1 increase in the monetary base will lead to a $2.79 increase in M1, the narrow measure of the money supply.[5]

Thus the multiplier signifies the productivity of the monetary base in creating money. It measures the collective magnifying power of the monetary system in money creation. An increase in m_1 indicates that each dollar of base has become more powerful in producing money (M1).

THE IMPACT OF CHANGES IN k, r_r, AND r_e ON THE MULTIPLIER

We will now present the arithmetic analyses, as well as the more interesting and important economic behavioral analyses, of how changes in k, r_r, and r_e influence the money supply multiplier and the stock of money (M1).

---

[5]Regarding k and r_e, it is important to note that we are assuming the *average* and *marginal* propensities to be equal. For example, the public *holds* 40 percent of total DDO in C^p and *changes* its holdings of C^p by 40 percent of any change in DDO. Similarly, banks *hold* excess reserves in the amount of 0.1 percent of DDO and *change* their excess reserves by 0.1 percent of any change in DDO. These *marginal* propensities are what counts in the money supply multiplier.

The Impact of a Change in *k*

Suppose the currency ratio (k) increases from .40 to .45. Assuming *all other factors remain unchanged,* including r_r (.10) and r_e (.001), we can calculate the multiplier as follows:

$$m_1 = \frac{1 + .45}{.10 + .001 + .45} = 2.63$$

Note that the increase in the currency ratio reduces the multiplier from 2.79 to 2.63. Given such an event, if the Federal Reserve holds the monetary base constant, both m_1 and M1 would fall by about 6 percent.

So much for the arithmetic showing an inverse relationship between the currency ratio and the money supply multiplier. Now we examine the more important economic intuition. Given the size of the monetary base, the increase in currency demanded by the public (C^p) has to come from bank reserves (R) as the public withdraws currency from banks. Given that the monetary base equals $R + C^p$, the increase in C^p implies an equivalent reduction in bank reserves, R. As people withdraw currency from banks, a larger portion of the (unchanged) monetary base becomes immobilized and unavailable to banks for lending and purchasing securities. The portion of the base consisting of R decreases.

To maintain desired excess reserve levels and abide by the Fed's reserve requirements in the face of the reduction in actual reserves triggered by the public's withdrawal of cash, banks are forced to liquidate some earning assets (loans and securities). As explained in Chapter 13, such actions by banks produce a contraction in the nation's demand deposits and monetary aggregates. Buyers of the assets sold by the banks pay via checks drawn on their accounts in banks, thereby extinguishing demand deposits, and causing M1 to decline. When k rises, *DDO*, m_1, and M1 must fall.[6]

The Impact of a Change in r_r

To illustrate the impact of a change in r_r, let us go back to our original assumptions. When we let $k = .40$, $r_r = .10$, and $r_e = .001$, we found m_1 to be 2.79. Now suppose r_r increases from .10 to .11 as the result of a policy decision by the Fed to raise the percentage reserve requirements applicable to demand deposits. The new multiplier is

$$m_1 = \frac{1 + .40}{.11 + .001 + .40} = 2.74$$

---

[6]Another way of making this point is by noting that one additional dollar of B in the form of C^p supports only one dollar of additional money (in the form of currency), while one additional dollar of B in the form of reserves supports several additional dollars of money (in the form of *DDO*). Therefore, an increase in k, by reducing R and increasing C^p, means that the existing base will support less money ($DDO + C^p$).

If other factors remain constant, an increase in r_r of 1 percentage point reduces the money supply multiplier from 2.79 to 2.74—a contraction of about 2 percent.[7]

The economic interpretation of this phenomenon is straightforward. The increase in required reserves triggered by the hike in the reserve requirement does not change actual reserves (R). However, it does increase the dollar amount of required reserves, thereby reducing actual excess reserves to a level below the desired excess reserves level. In fact, actual excess reserves initially become negative as banks fall short of the reserve requirement. To satisfy the new reserve requirement and restore their excess reserves to the desired level, banks are forced to liquidate earning assets (reduce loans and sell securities).[8] This activity produces a contraction in the money stock as government securities dealers and the general public write checks to banks, thus extinguishing demand deposits.

Impact of a Change in r_e

The effect on the money supply multiplier of a change in banks' desired excess reserve ratio (r_e) is quite similar to that of a change in the required reserve ratio (r_r). Suppose that, as the result of anticipation of imminent restrictive monetary actions by the Federal Reserve, banks sharply increase their desired excess reserve ratio from .001 to .005. Returning to our original assumptions for k and r_r, we compute the money supply multiplier as follows:

$$m_1 = \frac{1 + .40}{.10 + .005 + .40} = 2.77$$

The result of the scramble by banks to obtain excess reserves is a reduction in the money supply multiplier from 2.79 to 2.77, a contraction of a little less than 1 percent. Given a constant monetary base, this precautionary action by banks implies a reduction in their lending and investing; banks reduce loans and sell off securities in order to build up excess reserves. As the public writes checks to banks, the multiplier (and the money supply) falls. However, r_e is currently so small that even a dramatic change in its magnitude will exert a relatively modest effect on the money multiplier. Today, this variable (r_e) is quantitatively the least important player in the money supply process.[9]

---

[7]Note that the impact is considerably smaller than that indicated by the simple, or naive, deposit expansion multiplier formulation. In the latter formulation, an increase in the reserve requirement from 10 percent to 11 percent reduces the deposit multiplier from 10 to 9.1, a contraction of about 9 percent. Can you explain why the impact of a change in the reserve requirement is smaller in our more sophisticated multiplier framework?

[8]Remember that when banks collectively liquidate loans and securities, they gain no additional reserves. However, by reducing aggregate demand deposits, such activity does reduce required reserves. In this way, banks are collectively able to meet reserve requirements and restore their desired r_e position without gaining additional reserves.

[9]As we show in the next chapter, however, the behavior of r_e was a crucial factor in the great contraction of the money supply in the 1930s. The magnitude of r_e increased dramatically from 1932–1935, reaching 8 percent at the end of 1935. It averaged approximately 6 percent from 1934–1938. Today, it is approximately 0.1 percent.

Your Turn

Suppose you are given the following data: *DDO* = $1500 billion, C^p = $500 billion, reserves = $122 billion, and the reserve requirement = 8 percent for all *DDO*. Compute the currency ratio (k), the desired excess reserve ratio (r_e), and the money supply multiplier. Also compute the monetary base (B) and the money supply (M1).

Historical Behavior of the Money Supply Multiplier

Figure 15-1 illustrates the money supply multiplier (m_1) in the period since 1960. This multiplier may be calculated in one of two ways—by dividing M1 by the monetary base (B) or by calculating k, r_r, and r_e and substituting these values into the expression for the money supply multiplier (Equation 15-12). As we examine the behavior of these important variables, you will be able to understand the causes of the major movements in the multiplier shown in this figure. (For a discussion of the m_2 multiplier—that is, M2/B, see Exhibit 15-1.)

THE VARIABLES UNDERLYING THE MONEY SUPPLY MULTIPLIER (k, r_r, AND r_e)

Because the currency ratio (k), the required reserve ratio (r_r), and the desired excess reserve ratio (r_e) significantly influence the U.S. money supply, we will look at each variable in some detail, paying particular attention to the determinants of each.

Figure 15-1   The Money Supply Multiplier (m_1), 1960–Present. The money supply multiplier fluctuates over time in response to changes in k, r_r, and r_e.   *Source:* Board of Governors of the Federal Reserve System.

EXHIBIT 15-1

The M2 Multiplier (m_2)

Our discussion of the money supply multiplier has been couched in terms of the link between the base (B) and the *narrow* measure of money (M1). Beginning in the early 1980s, the link between M1 and the nation's GDP (known as the velocity of M1) loosened dramatically. Changes in the nation's GDP resulting from changes in M1 became much more uncertain. This meant that M1 was no longer a reliable variable for the Federal Reserve to employ as an intermediate monetary policy target. Beginning in 1987, the Fed stopped specifying target ranges for M1 growth.

For its new target, the Fed chose M2. M2 includes M1 plus savings and small time deposits held by the public, money market mutual fund shares, overnight repurchase agreements, and Eurodollars. If we designate all the non-M1 components of M2 as "other monetary assets held by the public" (*OMA*), we can write the money supply multiplier for M2 as follows:

$$m_2 = \frac{DDO + C^p + OMA}{R + C^p}$$

or

$$m_2 = \frac{1 + k + o}{r_r + r_e + k}$$

Note that the only difference between the narrow money supply multiplier (m_1) and the broad money supply multiplier (m_2) is the term *OMA*, or *o*, in the numerator, *o* being the marginal propensity of the public to acquire "other monetary assets" relative to *DDO*.

The accompanying graph shows the behavior of the m_2 money supply multiplier over the past 35 years. As the figure shows, the m_2 multiplier is unstable. Controlling M2 may be as difficult a task as controlling M1.

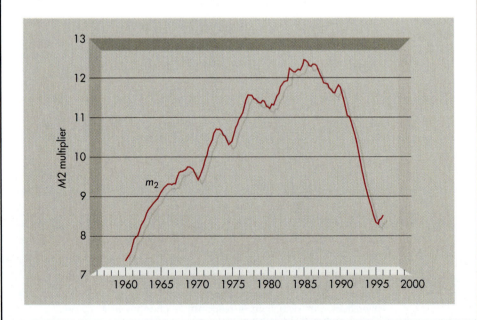

Determinants of the Currency Ratio (*k*)

Because the currency ratio is determined strictly by the preferences of the public, the ratio of C^p to DDO is largely a function of the costs and benefits of using currency relative to the costs and benefits of using demand deposits and other checkable accounts (DDO). Certain considerations favor the use of currency over DDO. In small transactions, currency is more convenient and saves time. And personal checks are not always acceptable, especially in less familiar surroundings. Thus the use of currency escalates during travel and in times of war. Currency is used heavily to purchase nondurable goods (candy bars, tennis balls) and inexpensive services (taxi rides, restaurant tips). On the other hand, purchases of durable goods (refrigerators, stereo sets) and financial assets (stocks, bonds) are almost always financed through the transfer of demand deposits. As the relative magnitude of these various types of transactions changes over time, we would expect to observe changes in the nation's currency ratio. Also, before the existence of federal deposit insurance, fear of bank failures had an important influence on the currency ratio (see Chapter 16).

For shady characters who are strongly motivated to leave no paper trail, currency provides an obvious advantage over checks and credit cards. Included in this category are merchants and others who intend to underreport their income for tax purposes, participants in illegal drug transactions and other vices, and participants in illegal political slush funds. The magnitude of the United States' "underground economy"—economic activities that go unreported in the nation's GDP accounts—has been estimated at approximately 10 percent of reported GDP, or more than $700 billion.

On the other hand, several considerations favor the use of checks and credit cards over currency. Canceled checks and credit card receipts provide evidence of payment in the event of claims to the contrary. They also serve as a record of tax-deductible expenses for those who itemize their income tax deductions. Safety is another factor—checks and credit cards are safer to carry than large amounts of currency.

Figure 15-2 shows the behavior of the U.S. currency ratio over the past century. In analyzing the currency ratio, it is important to recognize that shifts in the demand for DDO and shifts in the demand for currency (C^p) will both precipitate changes in k. With this in mind, let us examine some of the specific factors that influence the currency ratio, k.

Development of Substitutes for *DDO*

Factors that reduce the public's demand for DDO will increase the currency ratio. The long-term trend of k was one of decline before 1930 and of increase thereafter. One simple hypothesis is that before 1930, the spread of checking account facilities throughout the country pulled k down, while after 1930 the spread of *substitutes* for bank checking accounts increased k. The period after World War II witnessed a tremendous growth in nonbank thrift institutions offering savings accounts, as well as the development of the corporate and municipal bond markets, the stock market, and the U.S. government securities market. More recently, the advent of money market mutual funds, bank repurchase agreements, sweep accounts, and numerous other instruments has induced the public to economize on DDO holdings relative to other financial assets. As the new alternatives came on line, the opportunity cost of holding DDO increased, contributing to the general upward trend of the currency ratio in the past 35 years.

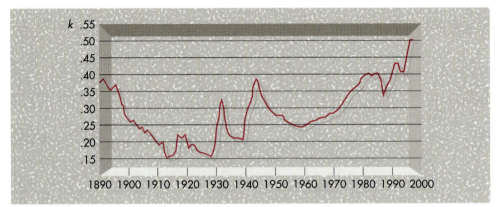

Figure 15-2 **The U.S. Currency Ratio (k), 1890–Present.** The U.S. currency ratio exhibited a downward trend from 1890 until about 1930. Since then, its trend has been upward. Note the dramatic increases during wartime (1917–1918 and 1941–1945).
Source: Citibank Economic Database.

Income Tax Rates and the Underground Economy

The incentive to hide income depends on the level of income tax rates. When income tax rates are raised, as they were during World War II, the incentive to underreport income rises. Underreporting of income is facilitated by the use of currency in place of checks or credit cards. Thus, part of the increase in k during past wars was due to the public's desire to hide income to avoid confiscatory levels of income taxes. Another likely cause of the post-1960 uptrend of k was the rapid growth of illegal activities such as drug peddling, prostitution, and gambling. Today, average currency holdings (C^p) come to about $1500 per person. Since very few people hold currency in such large amounts, some individuals must be holding enormous amounts of cash![10] A partial explanation for the tremendous increase in currency in circulation is provided in Exhibit 15-2.[11]

Interest Rate Levels

An obvious opportunity cost of holding currency is the interest banks pay on *DDO*. Given other factors, an increase in the interest rate payable on *DDO* induces people to hold more deposits, thus reducing the currency ratio. Before 1980, banks were prohibited from paying interest on checking accounts, so an increase in interest rates reduced the demand for *both* currency and *DDO* as people switched into interest-bearing assets. Because interest-bearing money market securities and money market mutual fund shares are closer substitutes for *DDO* than for currency, an increase in interest rates tended to increase the currency ratio. Today, to the extent that higher market interest rates are reflected in higher rates paid by banks on *DDO,* an increase in interest rates will reduce the currency ratio.

---

[10]Peter Gutmann argues that the rise in k over the past 30 years is attributable primarily to the growth of the underground economy. However, many economists believe that such activity accounts for only a portion of the increase in the currency ratio. See the reference to Gutmann in the "Suggestions for Additional Reading" at the end of this chapter. See also the article on currency in the October 1996 issue of *The Federal Reserve Bulletin.*

[11]Also, review Exhibit 2-2 on page 30 and note the enormous number of $100 bills in circulation. The table in the exhibit indicates that there are more $100 bills in circulation than either $5 or $10 bills. Most of these $100 bills are outside the confines of the United States.

However, banks are slow to change the rate they pay on *DDO*. Therefore, an increase in interest rates on government securities and money market mutual fund shares may reduce the demand for *DDO,* thereby increasing the currency ratio.

Income and Wealth Levels

We have seen that expenditures on inexpensive consumer services and nondurable goods tend to be financed with currency, while purchases of more expensive durable goods and financial assets are almost always paid for with checks. To understand the effect of income growth on *k,* then, one would need to ascertain the income elasticity of demand for various types of goods and services. We know that the growth of income and wealth boosts the demand for durable goods and stocks, bonds, and mutual funds relative to nondurable goods such as candy bars and soda pop. This fact suggests that, other things being equal, income growth is likely to increase the demand for *DDO* more than the demand for currency, thereby reducing the currency ratio, k.[12]

Other Factors

Age distribution and other demographic considerations also influence the currency ratio. For example, younger people exhibit a much higher currency ratio than older people do. As these demographic factors change over time, k changes accordingly. And historically, urban dwellers have been more accustomed to using banks than have rural people, who rely more heavily on currency. Thus, the urbanization movement partially accounts for the long decline in k from the late nineteenth century to the 1930s. Confidence in banks can also play a role in the currency ratio, as shown by the dramatic increase in k during the early 1930s (see Figure 15-2). Finally, a significant part of the increase in currency in recent years is attributable to an expansion in the use of dollars abroad. Because of the political stability of the United States, the dollar is increasingly favored as a medium of exchange in other nations, including those undergoing the transition to capitalism (see Exhibit 15-2).

The Importance of *k* in the Money Supply Multiplier

Figure 15-3 (on p. 362) shows the behavior of the currency ratio after 1960 together with that of m_1, the narrow money supply multiplier. Note that for the past 35 years, m_1 has been almost a mirror image of k. Clearly, k has been the most important determinant of the money supply multiplier.

Determinants of the Required Reserve Ratio (r_r)

Recall that the required reserve ratio (r_r) is the ratio of the dollar amount of required reserves (R_r) to total checkable deposits (*DDO*). The Fed has the authority to levy reserve requirements on other bank liabilities besides *DDO*—time deposits, negotiable CDs,

---

[12]However, this issue is clouded by the fact that currency may be a luxury good, in the sense that the income elasticity of demand for currency may exceed 1. Consider the convenience (time saved) of using currency rather than paying by check or credit card. Because the value of time rises with income, the demand for currency may increase more than proportionately with income. Such a hypothesis is consistent with the recent rapid growth of C^p (8.5 percent per year on average during 1970–1995 versus 6.6 percent per year for *DDO*). However, the rapid growth of C^p may be attributable to other factors.

EXHIBIT 15-2

Where Is All That Currency?

How large is the currency component (C^p) of the U.S. money supply? Look it up in the *Federal Reserve Bulletin.* In the past 20 years, currency has increased at an average annual rate of approximately 9 percent, far exceeding the growth rates of M1 and M2. In mid-1996, currency in the hands of the public stood at approximately $390 billion, or more than $1400 for every man, woman, and child in the United States. If this strikes you as way too high, you are on the right track. The Federal Reserve estimates that more than 60 percent of U.S. currency is held outside the borders of the United States.

The U.S. dollar is the only currency that enjoys instant recognition around the globe. Demand for dollars abroad stems from a search for stability. From Latin American nations exhibiting a historic propensity toward hyperinflation, to war-ravaged nations such as Vietnam and the former Yugoslav republics, to former Soviet states now in transition to capitalism, dollars are coveted. They are viewed as a "hard currency," acceptable almost anywhere because they are trusted to retain their value over time.

In spite of the fact that the U.S. dollar has depreciated by more than 50 percent against the German mark and Japanese yen in the past decade, dollars are often favored over deutsche marks and yen. In part, this reflects the reluctance of Japan's central bank to push the yen as an international currency. It also reflects a historic animosity that makes it impossible for residents of the former Soviet Union to embrace the German currency. Some estimates have placed the amount of U.S. currency now residing in the former Soviet Union as high as $20 billion.

How does all this U.S. currency find its way abroad? Some is spent by American tourists abroad, some by U.S. firms that buy foreign products. Much of the estimated $600 million now residing in Vietnam was accumulated during the American military involvement that ended in 1974. (A portion has been sent back to Vietnam by relatives now residing in the United States.) Because U.S. banks are required to report to the government only those cash withdrawals that exceed $10,000, it is easy to take cash out of the United States in large quantities.

While some economists have jumped to the conclusion that the dramatic increase in U.S. currency mirrors a rapid expansion of the "underground economy," such an inference

---

Eurodollar borrowings, and so forth. During much of the past 30 years, the Fed has in fact imposed reserve requirements on such non-*DDO* bank liabilities. At the present time, however, reserve requirements are levied only on *DDO*. Hence, r_r currently depends only on the two *DDO* reserve requirement percentages (3 percent and 10 percent), the threshold level at which the reserve requirement jumps from 3 to 10 percent ($52 million in 1996), and the distribution of deposits among banks above and below the threshold.

Consider the following formulation:

$$R_r = (\%RR_L)(DDO_L) + (\%RR_H)(DDO_H)$$

This equation states that the dollar amount of required reserves (R_r) is equal to the reserve requirement percentage for all *DDO* below the threshold ($\%RR_L$) times the amount of such deposits (DDO_L) plus the reserve requirement percentage for all *DDO* above the

EXHIBIT 15-2 (CONTINUED)

seems unwarranted. A more plausible explanation is the tremendous growth in foreign demand for the U.S. dollar. One implication of this phenomenon: To the extent that U.S. currency increasingly resides outside the United States, the link between the reported U.S. money supply and domestic economic activity is likely to have weakened. This hypothesis is consistent with the evidence of the past 15 years.

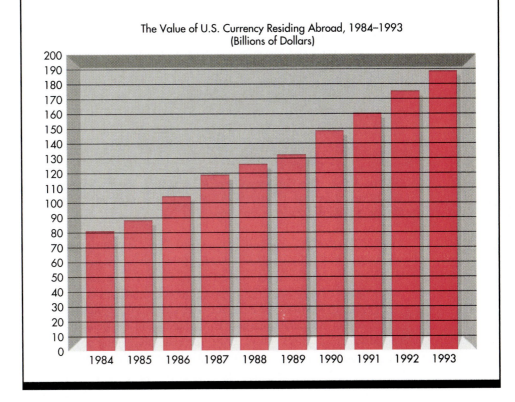

The Value of U.S. Currency Residing Abroad, 1984–1993
(Billions of Dollars)

threshold ($\%RR_H$) times the amount of such deposits (DDO_H). Because r_r is defined as the ratio of R_r to DDO, and because $DDO = DDO_L + DDO_H$, we may write

$$r_r = \frac{(\%RR_L)(DDO_L) + (\%RR_H)(DDO_H)}{DDO_L + DDO_H}$$

Dividing both the top and the bottom of this expression by DDO_L, we obtain

$$r_r = \frac{\%RR_L + (\%RR_H)(Z)}{1 + Z}$$

In this formulation, Z is DDO_H/DDO_L, the ratio of deposits in the banking system above the threshold to deposits below the threshold. The variable Z represents the weights to be accorded the two classifications of deposits in computing r_r. The Fed sets $\%RR_L$ (currently

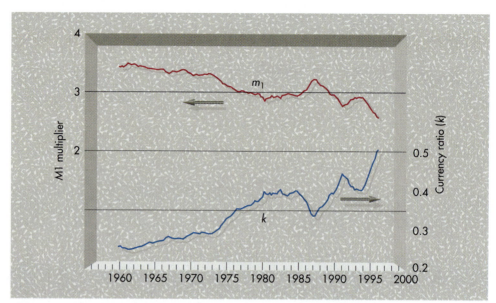

Figure 15-3   The Currency Ratio (k) versus the Money Supply Multiplier (m₁),
1960–Present. In recent years, fluctuations in m_1 have been dominated by fluctuations in k.
Source: Citibank Economic Database.

3 percent) and $\%RR_H$ (currently 10 percent). But Z is determined by the division of deposits among banks of different sizes. Because Z fluctuates over time, r_r also fluctuates even if the two reserve requirements set by the Fed are fixed. The Fed occasionally changes the reserve requirements ($\%RR_L$ and $\%RR_H$), precipitating significant changes in r_r.

Figure 15-4 shows the behavior of r_r since 1960. Note the strong downward trend in r_r after 1960, attributable largely to reductions in the percentage reserve requirement.[13] The Monetary Control Act of 1980, for example, which required all banks (both members and nonmembers) to meet the Fed's reserve requirements, was accompanied by a series of scheduled reductions in reserve requirements phased in during the early 1980s.

Determinants of the Desired Excess Reserve Ratio (r_e)

The impression is sometimes conveyed that, from a bank's point of view, the optimal amount of excess reserves is zero. Because banks earn no interest income on reserves, one might tend to assume that sensible bankers would use every dollar of excess reserves

---

[13]As is explained in more depth in Chapter 18, reserve requirements are essentially a tax levied on banks. The bank behavior induced by this tax has caused problems for the Federal Reserve over the years. In the 1960s and 1970s, a large number of banks were induced to leave the Federal Reserve System in order to enjoy the lower reserve requirements set by states for nonmember banks. Furthermore, financial innovations made by banks in response to the reserve requirement tax have made it more difficult for the Fed to control the nation's aggregate expenditures. For both of these reasons, the Fed has acted to reduce reserve requirements over the years.

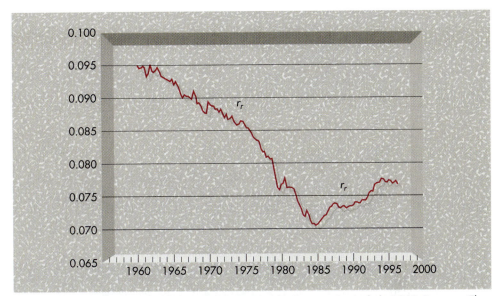

Figure 15-4   The Weighted-Average Reserve Requirement Ratio (*rr*), 1960–Present. The weighted-average reserve requirement ratio (r_r) has trended downward over much of the past 35 years.   *Source: Federal Reserve Bulletin.*

to purchase earning assets. Banks can maximize profits, it might be assumed, only if they rid themselves of *all* excess reserves, so as to hold no more reserves than required.

Such a viewpoint represents a naive oversimplification. More sophisticated analysis reveals that what are excess reserves from a definitional point of view (i.e., reserves minus required reserves) are not necessarily "surplus" or "excessive" reserves from a managerial or rational economic point of view. Bankers operate in a world of uncertainty. Because checks are continually being deposited into and cleared against the bank's reserve account at the Federal Reserve during the day, bankers do not know their reserve position until after the close of business, when the figures become available. Also, currency is continually being deposited into and withdrawn from banks during banking hours. Such transactions have a dollar-for-dollar effect on bank reserves. For the purpose of meeting the Fed's reserve requirements, the bank's reserve position at the end of the day is what counts.

Though the manager of the bank's reserve position is likely to have a "feel" for this position from past experience, he or she is not clairvoyant. If the bank comes up short of reserves as a result of larger-than-expected adverse check clearings or currency withdrawals, costs are involved. To meet reserve requirements, the bank will find it necessary to sell off securities, to "buy" federal funds (that is, borrow excess reserve deposits of other banks at the Fed, which it must pay interest on), or to borrow from the Federal Reserve discount window. Such operations involve transactions costs and other costs.

In deciding on the optimal r_e level, bank managers must strike a reasonable balance among the opposing costs. The cost of holding excess reserves—an opportunity cost—is the interest income forgone. The cost of attempting to get by with inadequate reserves includes the transactions costs and other costs associated with adjusting to frequent reserve

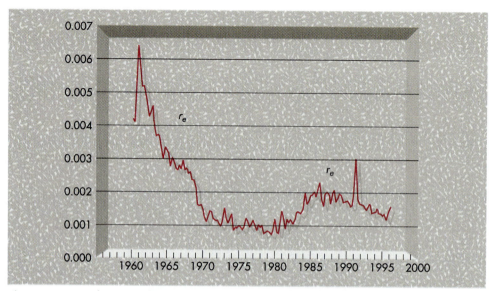

Figure 15-5   The Desired Excess Reserve Ratio, 1960–Present. Because of uncertainty, banks deliberately hold a small amount of excess reserves—typically less than 0.25 percent of *DDO.*   *Source: Federal Reserve Bulletin.*

deficiencies. Within this general framework, changes in some specific factors can influence r_e. We will briefly consider four of them. But first, note the post-1960 pattern of r_e, illustrated in Figure 15-5.

Treasury Bill Yield

Treasury bills provide an efficient, sensitive mechanism for adjusting a bank's reserve position. Because these securities are highly liquid and have very low transactions costs, banks often adjust their reserve positions by buying or selling Treasury bills. Thus the yield on Treasury bills is a good indicator of the opportunity cost of holding excess reserves. Given other factors, we would expect an increase in Treasury bill yields and other short-term interest rates to reduce r_e. When yields are high, the cost of holding excess reserves is high, and bank demand for excess reserves is therefore low. When yields decline, the demand for excess reserves increases. Note in Figure 15-5 that the magnitude of r_e was lower in the 1970s and early 1980s, when interest rates were relatively high, than in the periods before and after, when interest rates were lower.[14]

Discount Rate Levels

The *discount rate* is the rate charged by the Federal Reserve for loans of reserves to banks that are experiencing reserve deficiencies. It may be viewed as a proxy that indicates the cost of reserve deficiencies to banks that have attempted to manage their reserve positions too aggressively. Holding other interest rates constant, an increase in the discount rate boosts r_e as banks seek to reduce their exposure to reserve deficiencies.

---

[14]The long-term decline in r_e illustrated in the figure may be attributed to financial market developments that have reduced the transactions costs of adjusting a bank's reserve position. The development of the federal funds market in the 1960s, for example, reduced r_e because it provided access to a reliable, inexpensive source of funds for banks when needed.

Variability in Deposit and Currency Flows

Variability in check clearings and in currency withdrawals and deposits can influence a bank's prospects of incurring reserve deficiencies. If the variability increases, the likelihood of a bank becoming deficient in reserves increases, and its managers must increase the excess reserves they keep on hand as a precautionary measure to avoid reserve deficiencies. Thus, one might expect r_e levels to be higher for banks that experience sharp fluctuations in deposits and withdrawals than for banks with more stable reserve positions.[15]

Expected Federal Reserve Policy

Bankers react not only to current financial conditions but also to expected financial and monetary phenomena. If they perceive that the economy is moving into a period of increasing inflationary pressures, they are likely to expect the Federal Reserve to implement restrictive monetary policy actions to increase interest rates and cool off the economy. A prudent bank, anticipating such measures (including a possible boost in the discount rate), will move its asset structure into a more liquid position. This implies that it will increase its desired excess reserve ratio, r_e.

The Federal Reserve's Control of the Money Supply: The Debate

We have seen how the money supply multiplier is influenced by fluctuations in the currency ratio (k), the weighted-average reserve requirement ratio (r_r), and the banks' desired excess reserve ratio (r_e). Because k and r_e are in turn affected by such fundamental economic variables as interest rates, income, and wealth, those latter variables also have an influence on the money supply multiplier and the monetary aggregates (M1, M2, M3). In this sense, the money supply is to some extent an *endogenous variable,* influenced in the short run by economic forces apart from Federal Reserve actions.[16]

A key issue in monetary economics is the stability and predictability of the money supply multiplier. The relative importance of changes in B, k, r_r, and r_e in explaining *actual* historical changes in the money supply has been documented.[17] When viewed from a long-run perspective, it is clear that changes in the money supply have been caused predominantly by changes in the monetary base. From a short-range perspective, however, changes in the multiplier have been at least as important as changes in the monetary base in producing weekly, monthly, and quarterly movements in the money supply. Over the past 100 years, changes in the currency ratio have been the most important cause of fluctuations in the multiplier. These findings are *factual* and not subject to serious dispute.

---

[15]Banks in regions ravaged by floods, earthquakes, and tornadoes are likely to increase their excess reserve holdings following a natural disaster, in anticipation of losing funds as local customers write checks to finance repairs and reconstruction.

[16]For this reason, the money supply is sometimes shown as an upward-sloping (positive) function of the interest rate: an increase in interest rates induces the money supply to increase.

[17]Phillip Cagan, who employed a slightly different framework than the one developed here, reported the causes of changes in the money stock during the period 1877–1953. Peter Frost has reported the role of various factors in explaining fluctuations in both M and m from 1961–1974. See the reference to these works, as well as the more recent book by Ralph Bryant, cited in "Suggestions for Additional Reading" at the end of this chapter.

However, evidence from the past does little to settle the issue of the Fed's *potential* capacity to accurately control the money supply on a monthly, quarterly, or annual basis. Before the 1970s, there is little evidence that the Fed made any effort to hit money supply targets. It was preoccupied with controlling other variables, such as short-term interest rates. Economists disagree about the extent to which the Fed could have manipulated the monetary base to offset the concurrent effects on the money supply of changes in k, r_r, and r_e to achieve a given money supply target.

As a general proposition, monetarist economists believe the Fed is quite capable of exerting accurate control over the short-term path of the money supply. And they believe it is important to do so. Monetarists attribute past failures to produce stable money growth either to the Fed's preoccupation with other considerations or to obstacles of the Fed's own making.[18] Keynesians and other nonmonetarists tend to be skeptical of the proposition that the Fed can or should fine-tune short-term money supply growth. They also believe that the *trend* of money supply growth is what is important and view short-term gyrations in the money supply as harmless and irrelevant.

SUMMARY

The money supply multiplier is an important macroeconomic variable that links the monetary base to the nation's money supply. Changes in the money supply can be produced by changes either in the monetary base or in the money supply multiplier. The size of the money supply multiplier is determined by three key variables: the currency ratio (k), the required reserve ratio (r_r), and the desired excess reserves ratio (r_e). Because people can convert deposits to currency at will, the currency ratio is determined by the public. The required reserve ratio is determined primarily by the reserve requirement percentages set by the Federal Reserve but fluctuates as checks clear among banks of different size. The desired excess reserve ratio is determined by banks on the basis of the current and expected monetary environment. While long-run changes in the money supply are dominated by changes in the monetary base, short-run changes are often triggered by changes in the money supply multiplier. To attempt to hit targets for the money supply, the Fed would need to forecast the money supply multiplier and set the monetary base accordingly.

Answer to Your Turn (p. 355)

The currency ratio (k) = \$500b/\$1500b = .333. The desired excess reserve ratio (r_e) = \$2b/\$1500b = .001333. The money supply multiplier can be computed in two ways: by using Equation 15-12 or by simply taking M1/B. In either case, the answer is 3.215. The monetary base (B) = \$122b + \$500b = \$622b. The money supply (M1) = \$1500b + \$500b = \$2000b.

---

[18]For example, until fairly recently, the Fed had a very complicated reserve requirement structure in place. Banks were required to hold reserves for time deposits and other liabilities besides *DDO*. The reserve requirement scheme for *DDO* was quite complex and was structured so that significant unpredictable changes in r_r, the multiplier, and the money supply occurred. The Monetary Control Act of 1980, together with the Fed's elimination of reserve requirements for non-*DDO* bank liabilities, put into place a system of reserve requirements that has increased the stability of r_r.

KEY TERMS

required reserve ratio (r_r)
desired excess reserve ratio (r_e)
currency ratio (k)

STUDY QUESTIONS

1 Write an equation which expresses the money supply multiplier for M1 in terms of its three determinants. Define each of the three variables and explain carefully why a *decrease* in each variable produces an *increase* in the money supply multiplier.

2 Suppose you are given the following data:

a DDO = $900 billion

b C^p = $360 billion

c Reserve requirements for all DDO = 8 percent

d Actual reserves = $73 billion

Compute k, r_r, r_e, and m_1. Now suppose k falls to 0.35; compute the new multiplier. Compute the new multiplier if r_r falls to 7 percent (use k = 0.40).

3 Compare the simple deposit expansion multiplier presented in Chapter 13 with the more sophisticated multiplier developed in this chapter. Explain *intuitively* why the naive multiplier is larger than the sophisticated one developed in this chapter. Begin by assuming that the Fed injects $1 billion of new reserves into the banks through open market purchases.

4 Suppose the Fed's reserve requirements for DDO_L and DDO_H are 3 percent and 10 percent, respectively, and that the amount of DDO above the threshold is twice as large as the amount below. Compute r_r.

5 What could the Federal Reserve do if it desired to reduce the magnitude of the money supply multiplier?

6 Suppose the U.S. government enacts legislation to legalize the sale and purchase of marijuana, cocaine, and heroin. What would happen to k? What would happen to m_1? What would the Federal Reserve need to do in order to keep the money supply from changing in response to this legislation?

7 Analyze the factors that influence the currency ratio, k.

8 Analyze the factors that influence banks' desired excess reserve ratio, r_e.

9 Suppose the Fed announces a sharp increase in its discount rate, surprising the financial community and triggering expectations of a more restrictive financial climate in the months ahead. Analyze the impact of this announcement on

a r_e

b The money supply multiplier

c M1

d M2

10 Suppose the U.S. Treasury writes checks totaling $30 billion this week to purchase military equipment. Assuming these checks are deposited into large banks, analyze the impact on

a r_r

b The money supply multiplier

11 Suppose the Fed aggressively increases the monetary base (B). Is there any reason to suppose that this action might induce a change in the magnitude of the money supply multiplier (m_1)? Explain.

12 What factors could produce a sustained decline in the currency ratio in the next decade? Explain.

SUGGESTIONS FOR ADDITIONAL READING

The acknowledged pioneer of the monetary base–money supply multiplier framework was Karl Brunner. For a highly sophisticated analysis, see Karl Brunner and Allan Meltzer, "Liquidity Traps for Money, Bank Credit, and Interest Rates," *Journal of Political Economy,* January–February 1968. Entire books devoted to the money supply process include Albert Burger, *The Money Supply Process* (Belmont, Calif.: Wadsworth, 1971); Ralph Bryant, *Controlling Money* (Washington, D.C.: Brookings Institution, 1983); and Laurence H. Meyer (ed.), *Improving Money Stock Control* (Boston: Kluwer-Nijhoff, 1983). Pertinent empirical articles include Peter Frost, "Short-Run Fluctuations in the Money Multiplier and Monetary Control," *Journal of Money, Credit, and Banking,* February 1977, pp. 165–181, and Robert H. Rasche, "Predicting the Money Supply Multiplier,"

Journal of Monetary Economics, July 1979, pp. 301–325. Also see Anatol Balbach, "How Controllable Is Money Growth?," Federal Reserve Bank of St. Louis *Review,* April 1981, pp. 3–12, and M. Garfinkel and D. L. Thornton, "The Multiplier Approach to the Money Supply Process: A Precautionary Note," Federal Reserve Bank of St. Louis *Review,* July–August 1991, pp. 47–64. On the currency ratio, an important early historical work is Phillip Cagan, *Determinants and Effects of Changes in the Money Stock, 1875–1960* (New York: Columbia University Press, 1965), especially Chap. 4. On the role of the underground economy, see Peter Gutmann, "The Subterranean Economy," *Financial Analysts Journal,* November–December 1977, pp. 26–34. An important recent article on currency in circulation is published in the October 1996 issue of *Federal Reserve Bulletin.*

16

The Role of the Federal Reserve in the Great Depression of the 1930s

The Great Depression of the 1930s was the worst economic catastrophe in the history of the United States. While the sheer terror visited upon families by the disaster cannot be expressed in numbers, the general dimensions of the Depression may be sketched with a few pertinent facts. In the period extending from fall 1929 to spring 1933, the nation's output (gross domestic product) fell by approximately 50 percent in nominal terms and 30 percent in real terms. Industrial production fell by half, and the unemployment rate rose from 3 percent to 25 percent. Stock prices lost more than 80 percent of their value. Approximately 9000 banks failed, impairing the savings of millions of families. The nation's money supply fell by approximately 30 percent. The price level (consumer price index) fell by approximately 25 percent. Business failures and farm and home foreclosures soared, and the great majority of Americans experienced a substantial decline in their standard of living. Over the entire decade of the 1930s, the nation's unemployment rate averaged 18 percent; it did not fall below 10 percent until 1941. Table 16-1 lists some of the major indicators of general macroeconomic conditions in the United States in the 1930s.

What was the role of the Federal Reserve in this catastrophe? Should the Fed be held accountable for the fiasco, or was it largely an innocent bystander lacking the power to stop the cascade of events that brought the country down? Economists strongly disagree on this issue. In this chapter we will examine their viewpoints on the Federal Reserve's role in America's greatest depression. The debate centers on the accountability of the Federal Reserve for the actual behavior of the money supply, as well as the importance of the money supply in determining economic conditions. Some economists claim that the experience of the 1930s illustrates the lack of importance of monetary forces; others insist that the episode demonstrates the crucial importance of money to the economy.

THE DEBATE ON THE CAUSES OF THE DEPRESSION

In explaining the causes of the Great Depression, Keynesian economists emphasize the role of negative shocks to the nation's aggregate demand curve originating from nonmonetary sources. For example, they point to the stock market crash and the blow to consumer con-

Table 16-1

Key Macroeconomic Indicators, 1928–1938

	Nominal GNP (in billions)	Real GNP (in billions)	Unemployment Rate (percent)	Stock Prices*	Bank Failures	Consumer Price Index
1928	$ 98.2	$ 98.5	4.2%	153	498	100.0
1929	104.4	104.4	3.2	201	659	100.0
1930	91.1	95.1	8.7	161	1350	97.4
1931	76.3	89.5	15.9	100	2293	88.7
1932	58.5	76.4	23.6	36	1453	79.7
1933	56.0	74.2	24.9	79	4000	75.4
1934	65.0	80.8	21.7	78	57	78.0
1935	72.5	91.4	20.1	80	34	80.1
1936	82.7	100.9	16.9	112	44	80.9
1937	90.8	109.1	14.3	120	59	83.8
1938	85.2	103.2	19.0	80	54	82.3

*Index of common stock prices for June of each year; 1935–1939 = 100.

Sources: U.S. Department of Commerce, *Historical Statistics of the United States;* Board of Governors of the Federal Reserve System, *Banking and Monetary Statistics* (Washington, D.C.: National Capital Press, 1943).

fidence caused by the attendant destruction of financial wealth, a major force in pushing the nation's consumption expenditures down. And they argue that the boom in building activity the nation experienced in the 1920s meant that a significant decline in construction would follow.[1] Indeed, in 1933, expenditures on residential structures amounted to only 15 percent of such expenditures in 1929. Gross investment expenditures declined from more than $14 billion in 1929 to less than $3 billion in 1933. Furthermore, fiscal policy in the 1930s was contractionary: the Revenue Act of 1932 actually raised taxes. Also, a major contraction in exports occurred, partially as a result of the worldwide movement toward economic nationalism triggered by the infamous Smoot-Hawley Tariff Act of 1930. Keynesians emphasize that all these factors were largely unrelated to the Federal Reserve's monetary policy.

Monetarists disagree, laying the blame squarely on monetary factors and the Federal Reserve System. In their view, a normal business cycle contraction was converted into the catastrophe of the Great Depression by the collapse of the money supply and the banking system, which was triggered by banking panics coupled with and exacerbated by a series of blunders by the Fed. The Federal Reserve, by failing to perform its traditional function of "lender of last resort" and by committing other key mistakes, was responsible for the precipitous contraction in the money supply. This, in turn, accounted for the severe **deflation**—that is, the declining general price level—which set into motion the

---

[1]Think about the buildings on your campus, for example. Unless yours is a new campus, chances are that a disproportionate number of the buildings were erected in the 1920s and that very few buildings date from the 1930s.

wave of bank failures, the denial of credit to legitimate customers, and the widespread defaults on debt that impaired business and economic activity in general.

Before we can weigh these two opposing points of view, we will need to study the facts more carefully. In the next section, we will take a close look at what actually happened to banks and key monetary variables in the Great Depression.

BANK FAILURES AND MONETARY PHENOMENA: THE FACTS

Certain facts about bank failures and money supply behavior are indisputable. In this section, we examine these facts. In the following section, we examine the differing interpretations that economists give to these facts.

Bank Failures and the Run on Banks

To understand the Great Depression of the 1930s, it is important to look at the experience of U.S. banks in the 1920s. In those days, agriculture was more important to the economy than it is today. And while the period from the 1880s to World War I was a "golden age" for agriculture, the 1920s were a time of considerable distress for farmers. In 1920 to 1921, a severe decline in farm prices took place: on average, prices fell by more than 50 percent. Although agricultural prices recovered somewhat from their lows of 1921, the 1920s were a decade of worldwide deflation of agricultural prices. Profits fell, pulling down farm values. Thousands of farmers who had purchased land with borrowed money in the decade before 1920 became victims of the deflation and were foreclosed on by their banks in the 1920s.

The deflation in agricultural prices in the 1920s that caused the farm foreclosures also weakened the balance sheets of thousands of rural banks which had extended credit to farmers. In the 1920s, bank failures were surprisingly frequent, considering the general prosperity of the nation: they averaged nearly 600 per year. The failed banks were located predominantly in the nation's agricultural regions. Almost half of the bank failures occurred in the seven-state north-central region extending from Kansas and Missouri northward through the Dakotas and Minnesota. Figure 16-1 shows the number of bank failures in the United States each year during the period 1915–1929.

But though more than 5800 banks failed in the 1920s, their failure did not lead to panics or general bank runs, in which rumors of a bank's problems touch off a mad dash to withdraw cash from the bank. The bank failures of the 1930s were a different story. These failures came in three waves. The first began in October 1930. In the midwest and south, a series of bank failures touched off panic. As fear about the condition of the nation's banking system spread across the country, people began converting their bank deposits into currency. This phenomenon continued into December, when the Bank of the United States failed. That bank failure carried special significance for two reasons. First, it was the largest bank ever to fail in the United States. Second, its name caused some

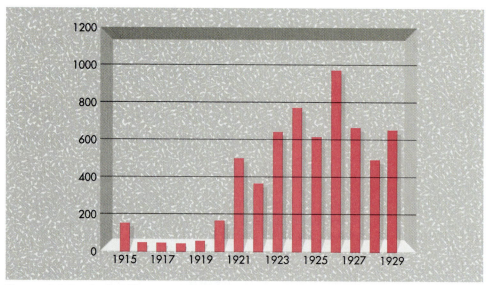

Figure 16-1 Bank Failures, 1915–1929. Nearly 6000 banks failed in the prosperous decade of the 1920s. This set the stage for the banking panics of the early 1930s.
Source: Board of Governors of the Federal Reserve System, *Banking and Monetary Statistics* (Washington, D.C.: National Capital Press, 1943).

people to conclude (incorrectly) that a huge bank associated with the U.S. government had failed. This added to the atmosphere of pandemonium.

In early 1931, the crisis subsided, only to resume again in the spring. In May, a major Austrian bank, the Kreditanstalt, failed. This shocked depositors around the world. Shortly thereafter, in September 1931, England abandoned the gold standard. The resulting scramble to convert dollars into gold at the U.S. Treasury caused the Federal Reserve to raise its discount rate by two full percentage points, a dramatic increase. These events contributed to the atmosphere of crisis in which the second run on American banks took place.

The final panic occurred in early 1933. The weakened condition of the banks after years of deflation, the uncertainty associated with the incoming and untested administration of President Franklin D. Roosevelt, and the general atmosphere of fear produced this final destructive crisis. In the 4 years encompassing 1930–1933, more than 9000 banks were suspended. In 1933 alone, 4000 banks failed. On March 6, FDR's third day in office, a "banking holiday" was declared and all banks were closed for 1 week. The public was informed that all banks would be inspected and only the sound ones allowed to reopen. More fundamentally, Congress soon established the Federal Deposit Insurance Corporation to provide nationwide insurance of bank deposits. For the remainder of the decade (1934–1939), bank failures numbered fewer than 60 each year (see Table 16-1).

As we will see, the banking panics of the early 1930s played a key role in the severe contraction in the U.S. money supply.

Table 16-2

Monetary Variables during the Great Depression

	M1 (in billions)	B (in billions)	m_1	k	r_r	r_e
Dec. 1928	$26.7	$ 7.08	3.77	.155	.105	−.002
June 1929	26.2	6.82	3.84	.161	.104	.001
Dec. 1929	26.4	6.94	3.80	.156	.107	−.003
June 1930	25.1	6.62	3.79	.155	.110	.000
Dec. 1930	24.6	7.07	3.48	.172	.113	.005
June 1931	23.5	6.92	3.40	.184	.116	.004
Dec. 1931	21.9	7.32	2.99	.257	.114	−.002
June 1932	20.2	7.39	2.73	.296	.116	.010
Dec. 1932	20.4	7.90	2.58	.297	.123	.037
June 1933	19.2	7.72	2.49	.330	.126	.033
Dec. 1933	19.8	8.25	2.40	.318	.124	.057
June 1934	21.4	9.21	2.32	.279	.126	.104
Dec. 1934	23.1	9.64	2.40	.252	.124	.098
June 1935	25.2	10.55	2.39	.234	.126	.118
Dec. 1935	27.0	11.47	2.35	.222	.124	.128
June 1936	29.0	11.87	2.44	.220	.122	.114
Dec. 1936	31.0	13.15	2.36	.217	.182	.078
June 1937	30.7	13.35	2.30	.218	.239	.035
Dec. 1937	29.6	13.58	2.18	.235	.243	.051
June 1938	29.7	14.48	2.05	.223	.211	.118
Dec. 1938	31.8	15.58	2.04	.222	.212	.123

Source: Computed from data in Board of Governors of the Federal Reserve System, *Banking and Monetary Statistics* (Washington, D.C.: National Capital Press, 1943).

Causes of the Contraction of the Money Supply

To understand the role of monetary factors in the Great Depression, we must look at some key monetary data. Table 16-2 shows the behavior of the money supply, the monetary base, and the money supply multiplier and its components (k, r_r, and r_e) during the period extending from the end of 1928 to the end of 1938.[2]

Note that the immediate cause of the contraction in the money supply was the collapse of the money supply multiplier (m_1). Between the end of 1929 and the end of 1933, it fell by more than 35 percent. In the same period, the transactions measure of money (M1) fell from $26.4 billion to $19.8 billion, a decline of 25 percent, while the

---

[2]Here we focus on the narrow (M1) measure of the money supply to keep the analysis simple. During the 1930s, the broader (M2) measure of money behaved in roughly the same way as M1. In fact, M2 fell by a relatively larger amount than M1 during 1929–1933 (see Table 16-4 on page 380). It contracted by 37 percent from October 1929 to March 1933, while M1 fell 32 percent in the same period.

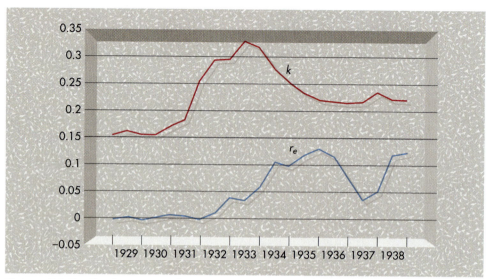

Figure 16-2   The Currency and Excess Reserve Ratios, 1929–1938. First the currency ratio (k) and then the excess reserve ratio (r_e) increased sharply in the early 1930s, triggering a sharp contraction of the money supply multiplier and the money supply.
Source: Board of Governors of the Federal Reserve System, *Banking and Monetary Statistics* (Washington, D.C.: National Capital Press, 1943).

monetary base increased by approximately 19 percent. The collapse of the money supply multiplier was triggered by the dramatic increase in the currency ratio (k), which resulted from banking panics in which the public withdrew large amounts of cash from their bank. (Remember that federal deposit insurance did not yet exist.) Then, in the latter half of 1933, as the banking panic subsided and the currency ratio declined, bank holdings of excess reserves (and r_e) climbed sharply. For a period in 1935, excess reserves even exceeded required reserves. In other words, banks were holding more than twice as many reserves as were required! The sharp increases in both k and r_e conspired to produce the precipitous contraction in the money supply multiplier in the 1930s.[3] Figure 16-2 illustrates the behavior of the two crucial variables that account for the money supply collapse.

These are the facts, but the interpretation of these facts, and the extent of the Fed's responsibility for the contraction in the money supply, differ considerably among economists.

---

[3]Actually, an increase in the weighted-average required reserve ratio (r_r) also contributed to the collapse of the money supply multiplier (see Table 16-2), although it clearly played a less important role than the increase in the currency and excess reserve ratios (k and r_e) did. From the end of 1929 to the middle of 1933, r_r increased from 10.7 percent to 12.6 percent. The increase was caused by a shift in deposits from smaller banks to larger banks (which were subject to higher percentage reserve requirements) in response to the public's perception that larger banks were safer than smaller banks.

INTERPRETING THE FACTS: KEYNESIANS VERSUS MONETARISTS

One of the interesting things about economics is that it is seldom difficult to find eminent economists on either side of almost any economic issue. Sorting out the true explanation of the role of the Federal Reserve in the debacle of the 1930s is particularly difficult because extremely cogent arguments have been presented on both sides of the issue. One can find Nobel laureates who vehemently disagree about the role of the Federal Reserve in the Great Depression. Here, we will examine the Keynesian and monetarist interpretations.

The Keynesian View: You Can't Push on a String

The conventional interpretation of the Great Depression—the one advanced by the Federal Reserve itself and supported by the great British economist John Maynard Keynes—was generally accepted before the publication of a provocative work by Milton Friedman and Anna Schwartz.[4] In the Keynesian view, though the Federal Reserve instituted an easy money policy, it could not prevent the collapse of the money supply and the economic catastrophe that followed because of powerful events beyond its control. Keynesians point out that yields on short-term government securities fell from 4 percent in October 1929 to less than 1 percent by mid-1932, and remained below 1 percent for the remainder of the decade. The Federal Reserve Bank of New York reduced its discount rate eight times, dropping it from 6 percent in October 1929 to 1.5 percent in mid-1931 (before raising it sharply in late 1931 in response to international economic considerations).[5] Figure 16-3 shows the pattern of the discount rate, along with short-term and long-term government security yields during this period.

In addition, between the end of 1929 and the middle of 1938, the monetary base doubled (see Table 16-2). After mid-1932, excess reserves began to pile up in banks, reaching massive levels by 1934, when they equaled approximately 10 percent of checking accounts. In the conventional (Keynesian) view, these data indicate that the Fed's policy actions were not overly restrictive.

Keynesians tend to absolve the Fed from responsibility for the Great Depression, arguing that "you can't push on a string." Once short-term interest rates have been pushed to very low levels and banks are flush with excess reserves, they argue, there is little more the Federal Reserve can do. If the public is unwilling to borrow from banks, and if yields

---

[4]*A Monetary History of the United States, 1867–1960* (see "Suggestions for Additional Reading" at the end of this chapter).

[5]In the 1930s, it was typical for the different Federal Reserve banks to have different discount rates. The New York Fed was somewhat more aggressive in lowering its discount rate during 1929–1931 than the other Federal Reserve banks. In the period from May to September 1931, while the New York Fed posted a 1.5 percent discount rate, the only other Federal Reserve bank with a discount rate below 2.5 percent was the Boston Fed.

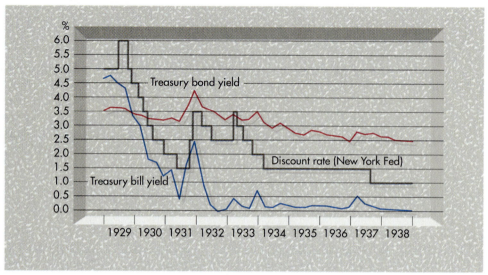

Figure 16-3   Government Securities Yields and the Discount Rate, 1929–1938. Short-term yields reached very low levels in the early 1930s. The Fed reduced its discount rate eight times between fall 1929 and summer 1931.   *Source:* Board of Governors of the Federal Reserve System, *Banking and Monetary Statistics* (Washington, D.C.: National Capital Press, 1943).

on short-term securities are so low that banks aren't interested in purchasing securities (note, in Figure 16-3, the extremely low level of the Treasury bill yield after 1932), there is no way the Fed can force banks to use their excess reserves.[6] Because short-term interest rates had reached extraordinarily low levels by 1932, the demand for excess reserves by banks was thought to be perfectly elastic with respect to the interest rate. This hypothesis, known as a **bank liquidity trap,** is a key element in the dispute between Keynesians and monetarists over the accountability of the Federal Reserve for the Great Depression. It is illustrated in Figure 16-4.

Keynesians argue that, in this situation, the link between the monetary base and the money supply had been severed. The Fed had allegedly lost control over the money supply because banks were unwilling to use the additional reserves supplied to them by the Fed to expand loans or invest in securities. Banks didn't lend because loan demand on the part of legitimate borrowers was depressed; they didn't buy securities because yields were extremely low. In this extreme case, the money multiplier moves in inverse proportion to changes in the base engineered by the Fed. Had the Federal Reserve aggressively purchased securities on the open market in 1932 and 1933 and quickly doubled the monetary base, the money supply multiplier would have fallen in half as even more excess re-

---

[6]Note also that the long-term Treasury bond yield was dramatically higher than the Treasury bill yield. One may wonder why, if banks weren't attracted to low-yielding Treasury bills, they didn't load up on long-term government bonds. The answer is that long-term bonds are risky, in the sense that their prices fluctuate significantly over time. Once such bonds are purchased, an increase in market interest rates can mean substantial capital losses. Banks are therefore reluctant to hold large quantities of long-term government bonds.

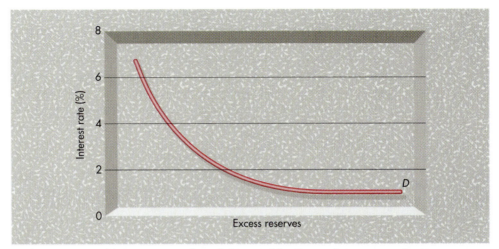

Figure 16-4   Keynesian View of Bank Demand for Excess Reserves. In the Keynesian view, bank demand for excess reserves becomes infinitely elastic at some low interest rate. Thus, banks willingly hold whatever quantity of excess reserves the Fed might supply, rather than lending out the funds or purchasing securities.

serves would have piled up in the banks. Thus, the situation was alleged to be beyond the Federal Reserve's control. Though the Fed did what it could, only a fiscal stimulus (such as increased government spending) could have saved the nation. Monetary policy, say the Keynesians, was therefore impotent: "You can't push on a string."[7]

The Monetarist View: The Fed Didn't Push

Monetarists dispute the Keynesian explanation for the Depression at almost every turn. They believe the Fed's monetary policy in the 1930s was not stimulative, as Keynesians assert, but rather highly contractionary.[8] In this view, a typical business cycle contraction was converted into the Great Depression by a series of policy errors on the part of the

---

[7]We focus here on the alleged existence of a bank liquidity trap, which would make it impossible for the Federal Reserve to induce banks to expand loans and purchase securities. This is only one of several hypotheses advanced by Keynesians in support of the proposition that Federal Reserve policy in the 1930s was inherently impotent. Other factors that allegedly emasculated monetary policy include the proposition that any increase in the money stock engineered by the Fed would have failed to push down interest rates and the proposition that investment expenditures were not responsive to interest rates in the early 1930s—that is, the marginal efficiency of investment schedule was nearly vertical. Since Keynesians have traditionally held that monetary policy works by changing the money supply, interest rates, and investment expenditures, these propositions suggest that, in a depression situation such as the 1930s, monetary policy is inherently ineffective.

[8]In the words of Friedman and Schwartz, "The monetary collapse from 1929 to 1933 was not an inevitable consequence of what had gone before. It was a result of the policies followed during those years. As already noted, alternative policies that could have halted the monetary debacle were available throughout those years. Though the Federal Reserve proclaimed that it was following an easy-money policy, in fact, it followed an exceedingly tight policy" (*A Monetary History of the United States, 1867–1960,* p. 699).

Federal Reserve. For example, the Fed implemented a restrictive policy in 1928 and 1929 in response to escalating stock market speculation; permitted bank reserves to fall sharply during the banking panic; raised its discount rate dramatically in 1931 and maintained it at a very high level relative to the Treasury bill yield throughout the 1930s; sterilized gold inflows to the U.S. which would otherwise have strongly expanded the monetary base; and doubled reserve requirements in three quick steps in 1936 and 1937. Monetarists are convinced that if the Fed had implemented truly stimulative policy actions in 1930 and 1931, the U.S. economy would have experienced only a normal recession rather than the catastrophe that occurred.

What evidence can monetarists marshal to refute the view that Federal Reserve policy during the Depression was "easy"? Several arguments seem compelling. First, it is true that the monetary base increased during the Depression. However, the monetary base consists of two components, reserves and currency held by the public (R and C^p). In the face of the dramatic increase in C^p triggered by the banking panic, the Fed allowed bank reserves to decline by 18 percent between October 1929 and April 1933. Thus, the behavior of the monetary base was misleading because an increasing portion of it was unavailable to banks for the purpose of extending credit. The Fed should have recognized that fact. To compensate for the increased demand for currency by the public and the resulting decline in bank reserves, the Fed should have aggressively boosted the monetary base through open market purchases of securities.

Keynesians also contend that the low short-term interest rates indicated a stimulative posture by the Fed. But monetarists consider this inference invalid. First, because the price level was changing significantly, it is essential to focus on *real,* not *nominal,* interest rates. Recall that, in the 1930s, the U.S. experienced severe *deflation*—that is, negative inflation or falling prices. Table 16-3 shows various measures of the rate at which prices fell in the years 1930–1933.

During 1929–1933, the consumer price index declined at an average rate of more than 6 percent per year. Therefore, the *real,* or *inflation-adjusted,* interest rate during this

Table 16-3

Measures of Inflation Rates, 1930–1933

Price Index	Changes in Price Indexes (percent)			
	1930	1931	1932	1933
Consumer price index	−2.6%	−9.0%	−10.1%	−5.4%
Producer price index	−9.1	−15.7	−10.7	+1.3
GNP deflator	−2.6	−9.1	−10.2	−2.2
Personal consumption expenditures deflator	−3.1	−10.6	−11.7	−4.0

Sources: *Economic Report of the President* and *Historical Statistics of the United States.*

period was extremely high.[9] In addition, after 1931 a "flight to quality" on the part of lenders created an abnormally high level of demand for safe, short-term Treasury securities. This contributed to the remarkably low level of Treasury bill yields shown in Figure 16-3. For these reasons, the low short-term security yields cannot be taken as an indicator that the posture of monetary policy was stimulative.[10] Even though there was very little scope for the Fed to push down short-term yields, it could have prevented the disastrously high real interest rates of 1931 and 1932 by aggressively implementing measures to arrest the ongoing deflation of prices.

Monetarists also point out that the Fed sharply tightened its discount window policy in the early 1930s. The incentive for banks to borrow from the Fed is a function not of the level of the discount rate per se but rather of the difference between the discount rate and short-term money market yields. A banker who is short on reserves will not find the discount window an attractive source of funds if the discount rate is 1.5 percent while the yield on Treasury bills the bank holds is 0.3 percent. In that event, the bank will likely sell off Treasury bills rather than borrow from the Fed. Note, in Figure 16-3, the huge gap by which the discount rate exceeded the Treasury bill yield throughout the 1930s. To monetarists, this suggests that Federal Reserve discount policy during the 1930s was highly restrictive.

The Fed raised the discount rate from 1.5 percent to 3.5 percent in two steps in 1931 in response to international crises, at a time when the U.S. unemployment rate exceeded 15 percent. The Fed also took a tightfisted attitude about lending to banks. A letter was sent to the banks by the Fed in 1931, admonishing them about the impropriety of excessive borrowing from the discount window. In the face of the national panic caused by increasing bank failures, the Federal Reserve apparently forgot its historic function to act as a "lender of last resort." The Fed seems to have forgotten that there is no other way that banks collectively can obtain reserves except from the Federal Reserve. The Fed should have reduced the discount rate to zero, opened the discount window full throttle, and encouraged banks to borrow until the panic subsided. Instead, the Fed's defensive actions only aggravated the panic.[11]

---

[9]Recall from Chapter 6 that the expected real rate of interest is given by the equation $r = i - P^e$, where r represents the real interest rate, i represents the nominal interest rate, and P^e represents the expected rate of inflation. Although we do not know the *expected* real rate, we can calculate the *realized* or *ex post* real rate by subtracting the *actual* inflation rate from the nominal interest rate. Using the 1931 consumer price index inflation rate of -9 percent, and assuming the interest rate charged on bank loans was 3 percent, we compute a real rate of 12 percent for 1931—a very high rate indeed.

[10]An indication of the "flight-to-quality" phenomenon is the fact that the spread between the corporate Baa bond yield and the U.S. government bond yield (that is, the risk premium on corporate bond yields) increased from 2.3 percentage points in mid-1929 to 7.9 percentage points in mid-1932. By 1932, people were avoiding risky securities like the plague. The associated increased demand for safe securities artificially depressed the yields on government securities, helping create the illusion that the Fed was pursuing "easy money" policies.

[11]Friedman and Schwartz believe that a good part of the ineptitude of the Federal Reserve in the 1930s may be attributed to the untimely death in 1928 of Benjamin Strong, longtime president of the Federal Reserve Bank of New York. His death resulted in an absence of intellectual leadership and a struggle for power within the Federal Reserve System in the 1930s. For a fascinating discussion, see *A Monetary History of the United States, 1867–1960*, pp. 411–419. (In fact, it would be well worth your while to read Chap. 7, "The Great Contraction," in its entirety.)

Table 16-4

Evidence of a Restrictive Monetary Policy in the 1930s

	M1 (in billions)*	M2 (in billions)*	Bank Reserves (in billions)*	Inflation Rate (percent)	Real T-bill Yield† (percent)	Discount Rate Minus T-bill Yield‡ (percent)
1929	$26.3	$46.0	$3.20	0%	+4.5%	+0.2%
1930	25.3	45.3	3.22	−2.5	+4.7	+0.6
1931	23.8	42.6	3.26	−8.8	+10.0	+0.9
1932	20.3	34.5	2.87	−10.3	+11.1	+2.1
1933	19.2	30.1	2.96	−5.1	+5.4	+2.2
1934	21.2	33.1	4.69	+3.4	−3.1	+1.4
1935	25.1	38.0	5.92	+2.5	−2.4	+1.4
1936	29.5	43.2	6.76	+1.0	−0.9	+1.3
1937	30.6	45.2	7.93	+3.6	−3.1	+0.9
1938	29.2	44.1	9.11	−1.9	+2.0	+1.0

*Averages of monthly figures for May, June, and July.
†Average monthly T-bill yield minus CPI inflation rate.
‡New York Fed discount rate minus T-bill yield in June.

Source: Milton Friedman and Anna J. Schwartz, *A Monetary History of the United States, 1867–1960* (Princeton, N.J.: Princeton University Press, 1963), Appendix Tables A-1 and A-2.

Table 16-4 summarizes the evidence that monetarists might present to support their view that Federal Reserve policy during the early 1930s was highly restrictive. Note first the contraction in M1 and M2 during 1929 to 1933. Because monetarists always maintain that the central bank is accountable for the behavior of the money stock, they view the sharp contraction of M1 and M2 as evidence of the Fed's ineptitude. The Fed also acquiesced in the contraction of bank reserves in the early 1930s, a crucial phenomenon which was triggered by the public's increased demand for currency. Note also the extremely high level of real interest rates in the early 1930s (look at the "real Treasury bill yield" column), which induced a massive increase in bankruptcies and foreclosures among debtors in general—particularly among farmers and businesses. In addition, note the unusually large differential by which the Fed's discount rate exceeded U.S. Treasury bill yields. To monetarists, all this evidence suggests a highly restrictive monetary posture on the part of the Federal Reserve.

Finally, monetarists dispute the Keynesian view that the buildup of excess reserves in banks reflected a lack of loan demand by the public, together with security yields so low that bankers preferred holding cash to purchasing securities. Instead, monetarists claim that the buildup of excess reserves was the predictable defensive reaction of banks to the earlier banking panics, coupled with a lack of confidence in the central bank's willingness to serve its traditional function as lender of last resort. The buildup of excess reserves, in this view, reflected an upward shift in banks' demand for excess reserves, as shown in Figure 16-5.

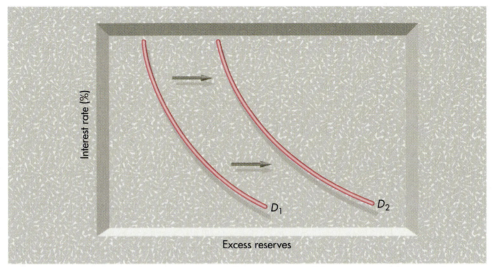

Figure 16-5   Monetarist Interpretation of Bank Demand for Excess Reserves in the 1930s. In the monetarist interpretation, a relatively steep demand curve for excess re-serves shifted rightward in the 1930s, as banks took precautions to protect themselves against further bank runs and inept Federal Reserve policy.

In other words, banks failed to make loans and purchase securities in the early 1930s not because of a lack of viable opportunities but because they felt it prudent to hold more excess reserves to protect themselves. Had the Fed recognized that banks' demand curve for excess reserves was relatively steep (rather than horizontal, as claimed by the Keyne-sians), it would have acted to satisfy the increased demand by providing new reserves or by reducing the reserve requirement. Banks would have proceeded to use the additional funds supplied by the Fed to expand loans and purchase securities, putting a halt to the contraction in the money supply. But the Fed misinterpreted the cause of the buildup of excess reserves in the banks and therefore failed to act.

This view of the Fed's interpretation of the buildup of excess reserves in the banks after the middle of 1932 is supported by the Fed's decision in 1936 and 1937 to sop up the excess reserves by doubling the percentage reserve requirement. The Fed viewed these excess reserves as superfluous and potentially inflationary and decided to eliminate them quickly via the severe reserve requirement hikes. This incredible restrictive action by the Fed helped to trigger a second severe contraction, the recession of 1937–1938. Note in Table 16-2 the behavior of r_r and the money supply multiplier, as well as the money sup-ply, in the period from mid-1936 to the end of 1937.

Hence, in the monetarist view, the link between the monetary base and the money stock—that is, the money supply multiplier—was not broken but only bent. During the Great Depression, control over the money supply was never out of the Fed's hands; there had merely been a discrete downward shift in the magnitude of the money supply mul-tiplier. The Fed should have recognized this and should have pursued more stimulative actions to increase the monetary base and cut short the monetary contraction, thereby

---

EXHIBIT 16-1

Explanations of the Fed's Behavior in the 1930s

Today, an objective student of the Federal Reserve's actions during the Great Depression would conclude either that the Fed pursued a restrictive monetary policy in the face of a downward economic spiral or that it sat back and passively watched the U.S. financial and economic system collapse. At a minimum, one can accuse the Fed of failing to take aggressive actions that might have cut short the deflation of prices and the tragic contraction of economic activity. How can one account for the Federal Reserve's failure to act? There are several possible explanations.

In one view, the Federal Reserve was fooled by its own flawed strategy—its propensity to focus on the wrong indicators of its monetary posture. In looking at the low level of its discount rate and money market yields and the burgeoning quantity of excess reserves after mid-1932, the Fed incorrectly inferred that its policies were stimulative. A related view emphasizes the role of discount window activity as an indicator of monetary policy. Beginning in the 1920s, the Fed came to view a large amount of bank borrowing at the Fed as an indicator that money was "tight." Hence, the Fed interpreted the contraction in discount window borrowing that followed the 1929 stock market crash as a sign that its posture was stimulative, rather than an indication that banks had become more conservative. This theory helps explain why the Fed did not aggressively purchase securities in the 1930s—it wrongly believed that it was already in a stimulative policy mode. Rather than keeping its eye on bank reserves and the declining monetary aggregates, the Fed was focusing on nominal interest rates, excess reserves, and borrowing at the discount window. Some would argue that the Fed was wrongheaded or incompetent, its intellectual capital diminished by the death of Benjamin Strong.

Another view emphasizes the inherent conflict between the Fed's dual roles of stabilizing the nation's economy and ensuring the safety and profitability of commercial banks. In the early 1930s, either because of increased caution on the part of banks or because of a decline in viable loan customers, banks engaged in a massive reallocation of their earning assets from loans to short-term government securities. In early 1932, the Fed finally embarked on a program of aggressive purchases of government securities. As yields on these government securities plunged to extraordinarily low levels by mid-1932, the Fed abandoned its short-lived stimulative program out of fear of impairing (the already depressed) bank profits. The Fed became concerned that interest rates were too low for banks to earn a decent profit. As weird as it may sound, some members of the Fed also believed that occasional depressions, by weeding out inefficient firms and holding down wages, play a beneficial, "cleansing" role in capitalistic societies.

A third interpretation rests on the fact that, until 1932, each Federal Reserve bank was required to hold gold as "backing" for the paper money it issued (Federal Reserve notes). In the early 1930s, the level of "free gold," or gold held in excess of the Fed's collateral requirements, was precariously low at several Federal Reserve banks. When foreign nations began converting their dollar holdings into gold in September and October 1931 in response to England's abandonment of the gold standard and the ensuing atmosphere of uncertainty, the Federal Reserve banks dramatically increased their discount rates. This classic central bank response to international crisis is one indication that the Fed may have been heavily constrained by international economic considerations and thus limited in its ability or willingness to react to domestic economic events.

preventing the Great Depression. (Exhibit 16-1 discusses alternative explanations of the Fed's failure to implement aggressive, stimulative policies in the early 1930s.)

In sum, the monetarists assert that the hypothesis "you can't push on a string" was never tested in the 1930s. Instead, they believe the Fed was not pushing at all and in fact was conducting highly restrictive monetary policies. Friedman, Schwartz, and other monetarists have established convincing evidence that Federal Reserve policy was in fact tragically misguided in the 1930s. Many Keynesians and other nonmonetarists now accept the argument that the Fed made a series of mistakes—though many regard the Fed's sins chiefly as errors of *omission* rather than of *commission*. However, many other economists are still convinced that aggressive actions by the Fed in 1931 and 1932 would have led to a further buildup of excess reserves in the banks—that the link between Fed actions and bank lending and investing had in fact been broken. Thus the issue is joined! It may never be resolved to the satisfaction of both groups.

SUMMARY

The role of the Federal Reserve in the Great Depression of the early 1930s is a matter of disagreement among economists. The money supply fell sharply from 1929–1933, even though the monetary base increased. The money supply multiplier collapsed because of dramatic increases in the currency ratio (k) and, somewhat later, the excess reserve ratio (r_e). While the immediate cause of the multiplier collapse was the rush to convert deposits into currency, economists disagree about whether the Fed had the power to turn around the contraction of deposits and the deflation of prices in 1931, 1932, or 1933. The traditional (Keynesian) interpretation holds that a series of nonmonetary shocks reduced aggregate expenditures and that, by 1931, the Fed was powerless to stop the downward spiral of events. In this view, low short-term interest rates and ample excess reserves in the banks suggest that the Fed was in a stimulative mode. Because loan demand was depressed and short-term yields were extremely low, banks would have willingly held whatever amount of excess reserves the

Fed might have provided through more stimulative actions. In such circumstances, monetary policy is impotent. In the monetarist view, this interpretation of events is incorrect. A series of mistakes by the Fed accounted for the contraction of money and economic activity. Though nominal interest rates were low, severe price level deflation caused by monetary contraction implied that real rates were extremely high. Banks' demand for excess reserves increased as a predictable response to the banking panics and indications that the Fed could not be counted on to counter any additional bank runs through stimulative measures. Had the Fed aggressively expanded bank reserves to satisfy the increased demand, banks would have increased their lending and securities purchases, thereby increasing the money supply and ending the economic downturn. In other words, monetarists believe the Fed never lost its capacity to increase the money supply and that its failure to implement stimulative policies is largely responsible for the severity and duration of the Great Depression.

KEY TERMS

deflation
bank liquidity trap

STUDY QUESTIONS

1 Suppose you are to defend the position that Federal Reserve policy was stimulative in the 1930s. What facts would you marshal in support of your position?

2 Suppose you are to defend the position that Federal Reserve policy was highly restrictive in the 1930s. What facts would you marshal in support of your position?

3 Examine Figure 16-2, which illustrates the currency and excess reserve ratios. Explain in historical context why movements in the excess reserve ratio might duplicate but lag behind movements in the currency ratio.

4 Suppose you know someone who was an officer of a major bank during the 1930s. What questions might you pose to this individual to gain insight into the debate over the causes of the buildup of excess reserves in the banks in the 1930s?

5 "Because the monetary base increased significantly in the 1930s, it is quite clear that the Federal Reserve cannot be considered a guilty party in the Great Depression." Evaluate this statement.

6 "While it is true that the Federal Reserve made some mistakes in the 1930s, those mistakes were not a major contributor to the Great Depression." Evaluate this statement.

7 In the early 1930s the Fed regarded a high level of discount window borrowing (bank borrowing from the Fed) as a sign of tight monetary policy; monetarists now view it as a sign of stimulative policy. Evaluate the disagreement and explain how the Fed's perception may have produced a policy error on its part.

8 "The experience of the 1930s confirms the existence of an asymmetry in the power of monetary policy. You can 'pull on a string' but you cannot 'push on a string.'" What does this statement mean? Does the experience of the 1930s confirm it?

9 Examine Figure 16-3, which illustrates the Fed's discount rate in the 1930s. In your view, did the Fed's discount policy become more restrictive or more stimulative after 1929? Defend your position.

10 After beginning to recover in mid-1933, the U.S. economy suffered a major relapse in the recession of 1937–1938. Examine the pertinent tables in this chapter, and evaluate the role of the money supply and the Federal Reserve in this second contraction.

11 It seems clear that the Federal Reserve *did* make major policy mistakes in the early 1930s. List some of those mistakes, and discuss possible reasons why the Fed committed these mistakes.

SUGGESTIONS FOR ADDITIONAL READING

The past 20 years have witnessed a renaissance of interest in the economics of the Great Depression of the 1930s, and there is an abundance of recent literature. An important catalyst and point of reference is the monumental work by Milton Friedman and Anna J. Schwartz, *A Monetary History of the United States, 1867–1960* (Princeton, N.J.: Princeton University Press, 1963). An early and brilliant review of this classic book is James Tobin, "The Monetary Interpretation of History," *American Economic Review,* June 1965, pp. 646–695. Recent reviews of the Friedman-Schwartz work include articles by Robert Lucas, Jeffrey Miron, and Bruce Smith in the 1994 issue of *Journal of Monetary Economics,* pp. 5–45. An excellent recent overview of monetary factors and Federal Reserve policy in the 1930s is David C. Wheelock, "Monetary Policy in the Great Depression: What the Fed Did, and Why," Federal Reserve Bank of St. Louis *Review,* March–April 1992, pp. 3–23. See also Wheelock's excellent study of the Fed's misguided discount policy, "Member Bank Borrowing and the Fed's Contractionary Monetary Policy during the Great Depression," *Journal of Money, Credit, and Banking,* November 1990, pp. 409–426. An indispensable source is Karl Brunner (ed.), *The Great Depression Revisited* (Boston: Nijhoff Publishing, 1981). This book contains articles and comments by such economists as Anna Schwartz, Robert Gordon and James Wilcox, Peter Temin, William Poole, James Pierce, Karl Brunner, and several others. Journal articles supporting the monetarist interpretation of the Great Depression include James D. Hamilton, "Monetary Factors in the Great Depression," *Journal of Monetary Economics,* 19 (1987), pp. 145–169; B. L. Anderson and J. L. Butkiewicz, "Money, Spending, and the Great Depression," *Southern Economic Journal,* 1980, pp. 388–403; and Bennett T. McCallum, "Could a Monetary Base Rule Have Prevented the Great Depression?" *Journal of Monetary Economics,* 26 (1990), pp. 3–26. An interesting article that probes into the forces driving the Federal Reserve's behavior in the 1930s is Gerald Epstein and Thomas Ferguson, "Monetary Policy, Loan Liquidation, and Industrial Conflict: The Federal Reserve and the Great Contraction," *Journal of Economic History,* December 1984, pp. 957–983. Those critical of the hypothesis that the Depression was caused chiefly by monetary factors include Peter Temin, *Did Monetary Forces Cause the Great Depression?* (New York: Norton, 1976); Charles Kindleberger, *The World in Depression* (Berkeley, Calif.: University of California Press, 1973); and the Tobin piece cited above. Recent work placing the U.S. depression in the larger context of the world economy and its institutional framework include Ben Bernanke, "The Macroeconomics of the Great Depression: A Comparative Approach," *Journal of Money, Credit, and Banking,* February 1995, pp. 1–28, and Barry Eichengreen, *Golden Fetters: The Gold Standard and the Great Depression, 1919–1939* (New York: Oxford University Press, 1992). Finally, the Spring 1993 issue of *Journal of Economic Perspectives* contains a symposium on the Great Depression. See especially Charles Calamoris, "Financial Factors in the Great Depression."

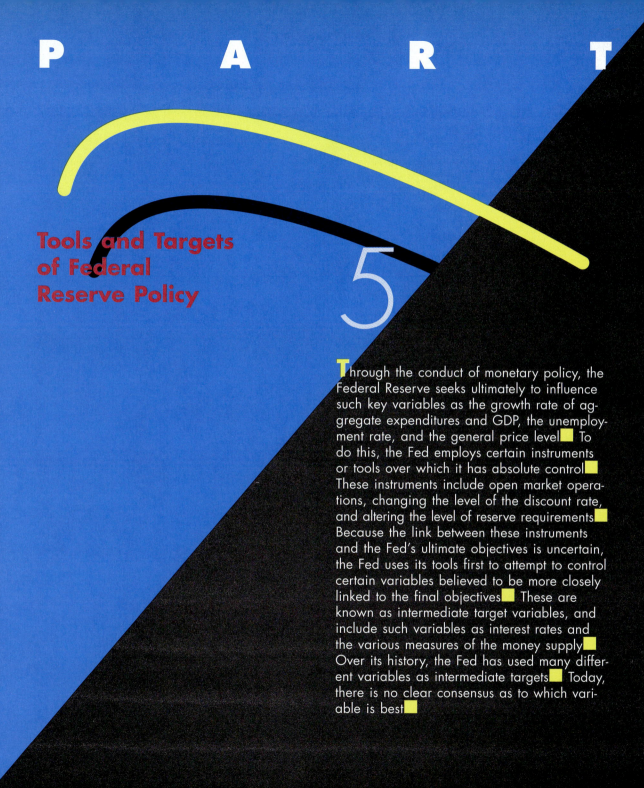

P A R T

Tools and Targets of Federal Reserve Policy

5

Through the conduct of monetary policy, the Federal Reserve seeks ultimately to influence such key variables as the growth rate of aggregate expenditures and GDP, the unemployment rate, and the general price level■ To do this, the Fed employs certain instruments or tools over which it has absolute control■ These instruments include open market operations, changing the level of the discount rate, and altering the level of reserve requirements■ Because the link between these instruments and the Fed's ultimate objectives is uncertain, the Fed uses its tools first to attempt to control certain variables believed to be more closely linked to the final objectives■ These are known as intermediate target variables, and include such variables as interest rates and the various measures of the money supply■ Over its history, the Fed has used many different variables as intermediate targets■ Today, there is no clear consensus as to which variable is best■

Open Market Operations: The Primary Tool of Federal Reserve Policy

In order to influence such ultimate macroeconomic objectives as the level of output, the unemployment rate, and price level behavior, the Federal Reserve tries to control certain variables it believes are closely linked to the objectives. These intermediate variables include the monetary aggregates (M1, M2, M3) and short-term interest rates. For example, if the economy is in recession and the Fed wishes to stimulate economic activity, it is likely to implement measures to increase the growth rate of M1, M2, and M3 and reduce short-term interest rates. To bring about these changes, the Fed uses certain instruments, or tools, of monetary policy.

An **instrument,** or **tool, of monetary policy** is a variable which the Fed is capable of controlling completely and which is strongly linked to such intermediate variables as reserves, the monetary base, M1, M2, and short-term interest rates. There are three general instruments or tools of monetary policy at the Fed's disposal: open market operations, discount window policy, and reserve requirement policy. In this chapter and the next, we will provide an in-depth analysis of these instruments of monetary policy, beginning in this chapter with open market operations. Chapter 18 is devoted to the Federal Reserve's discount window policy—the procedures and conditions concerning Federal Reserve lending to depository institutions—and to an analysis of the reserve requirement instrument.

OPEN MARKET OPERATIONS: FUNDAMENTAL CONSIDERATIONS

Open market operations are the bread-and-butter instrument of Federal Reserve policy. The Fed is empowered with the authority to buy and sell U.S. Treasury securities, federal agency securities, bankers' acceptances, and certain other securities on the open market. The magnitude and timing of these transactions are entirely up to the discretion of the Fed, which implements open market purchases and sales on the basis of their desired impact on bank reserves, the monetary base, the monetary aggregates, interest rates, and credit conditions.

Because the Federal Reserve earns interest income from its securities portfolio, the total revenues earned by the Fed vary in direct proportion to the magnitude of its portfolio. However, this consideration plays no role in the Fed's decision to acquire or sell securities. Indeed, if it did, the Federal Reserve could not perform the chief function of a central bank—conducting monetary policy in a way that contributes to the stability of aggregate expenditures and economic activity.

Suppose the U.S. economy is encountering excessive aggregate demand and escalating inflation. The Fed is therefore intent on implementing a policy of monetary restraint. In that event, the Fed would sell securities on the open market. Assume that the Fed sells $225 million in U.S. Treasury bills to a government securities dealer, receiving payment via a check written against the dealer's bank checking account. When the Fed receives the check, it "collects" by debiting the reserve account of (making a bookkeeping entry against) the dealer's commercial bank and returns the check to that bank. Upon receipt of the check, the commercial bank debits the dealer's demand deposit account. The relevant balance sheets exhibit the following changes:

Federal Reserve System		All Commercial Banks	
U.S. securities −225m	Deposits by member banks −225m	Deposits at the Fed −225m	Demand deposits −225m

The important thing to note is that both bank reserves and the monetary base have moved dollar for dollar with the Federal Reserve's securities holdings.[1] When the Fed sells $225 million of securities, both reserves (R) and the monetary base (B) decrease by $225 million, because aggregate bank deposits at the Fed decrease by $225 million. If the Fed *buys* $660 million of securities, R and B *increase* by $660 million, because the sellers of those securities receive checks from the Federal Reserve totaling $660 million. The Federal Reserve pays for these securities by creating new reserves—that is, by crediting the reserve accounts of the dealers' banks at the Fed. Clearly, the open market operations tool allows the Fed to dominate the behavior of both bank reserves and the monetary base.

Recall from our discussion of the money supply multiplier in Chapter 15 that

$$M = B \cdot m$$

In a fractional reserve banking system, each dollar change in the monetary base results in a *multiple* change (totaling approximately $2.50) in the narrow measure of money (M1).

---

[1]Because this transaction increases the dealer's inventory of government securities by $225 million, the dealer is likely to reestablish its desired inventory level by selling about $225 million of government securities to the public. In the highly competitive government securities market, a dealer can normally accomplish this by lowering its ask price somewhat. This reduction in price (increase in yield) induces purchases of securities by the public (individuals, firms, pension funds, etc.). Note that the dealer essentially serves as a middleman between the Federal Reserve and the public. In other words, the Fed sells to the public via dealers. The final balance sheet changes are exactly as shown above. When the public purchases government securities from dealers, their demand deposits are reduced by $225 million, and the dealers' demand deposits return to the levels that existed before the Federal Reserve transaction as reserve deposits are transferred from the public's banks to the dealers' banks. Therefore, aggregate reserves (and the monetary base) remain down by $225 million. Because dealers are simple middlemen in this process, one can capture the essence of the process by skipping the dealers and thinking in terms of the Fed selling securities directly to the general public.

In other words, by purchasing (or selling) securities, the Fed triggers a multiple expansion (or contraction) of deposits and the monetary aggregates. For this reason, open market operations are a powerful and highly important instrument of Federal Reserve policy. In the next few sections, we will discuss the historical accident that elevated open market operations to its role as the premier tool of policy and look at some institutional details of open market operations.

The Banking Act of 1935

Early in the history of the Federal Reserve System, open market operations were unimportant. The operation of the discount window was essentially the Fed's only policy tool. In fact, the Fed stumbled onto the use of open market operations by accident in the early 1920s. Since the creation of the Federal Reserve, the primary source of the Fed's operating revenues had been the interest received on the Fed's loans to commercial banks, known as **discounts and advances.** But in a severe recession in the early 1920s, the volume of those loans to banks dropped off sharply, impairing the Fed's revenues. To supplement their dwindling revenues and achieve a steady flow of interest income, the individual Federal Reserve district banks purchased U.S. government securities. The Fed noticed that when it purchased securities, interest rates immediately fell and credit conditions eased. Thus a new policy tool was born!

In the early years, there was little coordination among the 12 Federal Reserve district banks and no coherent national monetary policy. In 1923, the Federal Reserve Board in Washington authorized a committee of five Federal Reserve bank "governors"—that is, heads of Federal Reserve district banks (now known as presidents)—to coordinate purchases and sales for the Federal Reserve System as a whole. The committee, named the Open Market Investment Committee, was expanded in 1928 to include all 12 Federal Reserve bank "governors." Still, individual Federal Reserve banks retained the right to engage in open market operations on their own account and could elect not to participate in the system's purchases and sales.

The Banking Act of 1935 ended this unsatisfactory state of affairs. Essentially a major amendment to the original Federal Reserve Act, the Banking Act shifted a significant amount of power from the individual Federal Reserve banks to the Board of Governors in Washington, D.C. The act created the Federal Open Market Committee (FOMC) to replace the Open Market Investment Committee for the purpose of buying and selling government securities for the Federal Reserve System as a whole. The committee's composition was dramatically altered by revocation of the voting privileges of 7 of the 12 Federal Reserve bank presidents and by the addition of the 7 members of the Board of Governors in Washington. The act also implemented numerous other provisions that remain in effect today.[2]

---

[2]The Banking Act of 1935 also authorized the Board of Governors to change reserve requirements (within congressionally established ranges); granted the Board the final say in setting the discount rates of each of the Federal Reserve banks; and authorized the Board to determine the budgets of the individual Fed banks and the salaries of their top officers. In addition, the act made the Federal Reserve more independent of the U.S. president by removing both the Secretary of the Treasury and the Comptroller of the Currency (presidential appointees) from the Board of Governors; by lengthening the terms of Board members from 10 to 14 years; and by providing for overlapping appointments to the Board, so that one new Board member is appointed by the president every 2 years.

The Domain of the Federal Reserve's Open Market Activity

From a technical point of view, the Federal Reserve's open market operations could be carried out in corporate bonds, common stocks, municipal bonds, or pork belly futures rather than in U.S. government securities and federal agency securities. No matter what items the Fed purchases, it pays via a check written on itself. When the recipient of the check deposits it in a bank, the Fed reimburses the bank by crediting the bank's reserve account at the Fed. Because the Fed pays for its purchase by creating new bank reserves in the form of deposits at the Fed, the balance sheet impact will always be the same regardless of the type of asset purchased.

When the Fed buys assets from the *public,* bank reserves and the monetary base increase on a dollar-for-dollar basis. If the Fed's check is deposited in a checking account, M1 and the broader monetary aggregates will directly increase by the amount of the transaction. When the Fed buys financial assets (bonds and bills) from *banks,* reserves and the monetary base expand dollar for dollar, but the money supply is *not directly or immediately* affected. The T-accounts associated with a $400 million Fed purchase of U.S. government securities from banks are as follows:

Federal Reserve System		All Commercial Banks	
U.S. government securities +400m	Deposits by member banks +400m	Deposits at the Fed +400m U.S. government securities −400m	

Because no demand deposits are created initially, this transaction does not *directly* increase the money supply. However, bank reserves and the monetary base increase dollar for dollar with the Fed transaction. The money supply then increases as banks trigger the multiple deposit expansion process by acquiring earning assets—that is, loans and securities.

To minimize the Fed's direct influence on the markets for privately issued securities, federal law requires that the Fed's transactions be carried out in U.S. government and agency securities and bankers' acceptances. This prevents charges of conflict of interest, favoritism, or "politics" which might occur if the Fed conducted transactions in common stocks, corporate bonds, municipal bonds, or mortgages. Another reason to conduct most open market operations in government securities is the fact that no other domestic financial market is so highly developed—no other market possesses as much depth, breadth, and stability as the U.S. government securities market. Such a highly developed market is required to absorb the huge daily volume of Federal Reserve transactions. On a typical day, the Fed conducts billions of dollars' worth of open market transactions. Only the U.S. government securities market has the capacity to absorb transactions of that magnitude without experiencing major price fluctuations. In 1995, more than 98 percent of the Fed's securities holdings were in the form of U.S. government securities; the remainder were issued by federal agencies. During 1995, the Fed made gross purchases of about $2,500 billion ($2.5 trillion) worth of U.S. government securities and approximately $35 billion worth of federal agency securities.

During the 1950s, the Fed restricted its open market operations almost exclusively to U.S. government securities of less than 15 months' maturity. This stemmed from the desire of the Federal Reserve to accomplish its reserves and monetary base objectives with minimum impact on security prices and yields. Because the short end of the government securities market is the most highly developed, active, and liquid, Fed transactions in short-term securities have less impact on prices and yields than do comparable transactions in long-term securities. The Fed's policy of confining itself almost entirely to the short-term portion of the market became known as *bills only.*

Since the 1950s, the Fed has broadened the range of maturities in which it conducts open market operations. For a period in the 1960s, the Fed even attempted to influence the term structure of interest rates by buying and selling different maturities of government securities simultaneously.[3] In recent years, although the majority of Federal Reserve open market operations has been conducted in maturities of less than 1 year, a considerable volume of activity has been conducted in maturities of 1 to 5 years. Open market operations in long-term instruments are considerably less common.[4]

The number of countries in which effective central bank open market operations is feasible is surprisingly small. What is required is a government securities market that is sufficiently well developed that central bank buying and selling of securities does not cause large, potentially disruptive changes in the prices (and yields) of securities. Such markets exist in the United States, Canada, and the United Kingdom. Japan is in the process of developing such a market. Most other nations do not have highly developed government securities markets. The central banks of some of those nations do, however, conduct open market operations in the foreign exchange market, by buying and selling foreign currencies.

The Federal Reserve's Operations in the Foreign Exchange Market

The Federal Reserve also conducts occasional operations in the foreign exchange market, buying or selling foreign currencies as do foreign central banks. The object of these actions is to influence foreign exchange rates directly. For example, in 1995 the Federal Reserve

---

[3]Many economists are skeptical of the view that the Federal Reserve is capable of significantly influencing the term structure of interest rates by purchasing and selling different maturities of government securities simultaneously. In the pure expectations theory (see Chapter 7), the term structure is determined by expectations about future interest rates relative to current interest rates. Buying and selling of different maturities of securities by the Fed is likely to have little impact on such expectations. On the other hand, the segmented markets hypothesis asserts that institutional factors governing the relative supplies and demands for various maturities determine the term structure. Since the Fed can influence the relative demand for various maturities via its open market operations, this theory considers the Fed capable of altering the term structure of interest rates.

[4]In 1996, approximately 60 percent of U.S. government securities held by the Federal Reserve were of 1 year's maturity or less; approximately 25 percent had maturities in the 1–5 year range; and only 15 percent had maturities in excess of 5 years. The average maturity of the Fed's government securities portfolio was 38 months.

EXHIBIT 17-1

Federal Reserve Intervention in the Foreign Exchange Market

Occasionally, the Federal Reserve intervenes directly in the foreign exchange market for the purpose of altering the exchange rate. For example, the Fed can support the dollar by buying dollars with foreign currency (that is, by selling foreign currencies for dollars). For this purpose, the Fed maintains a stock of financial assets denominated in foreign currencies such as yen and deutsche marks.

In the early spring of 1995, the U.S. dollar was hitting record lows against the Japanese yen almost daily (see figure). Depreciation of the U.S. dollar tends to boost the aggregate demand for goods and services in the United States and decrease the trade deficit. For example, if the dollar depreciates from 100 yen to 80 yen, an American-made sport coat selling for $100 in the U.S. declines in price in Japan from 10,000 yen to 8000 yen (neglecting transportation costs, tariffs, and taxes). That means that U.S. exports to Japan are likely to increase. On the other hand, when a dollar fetches only 80 yen rather than 100 yen, 20 percent more dollars are needed to purchase sufficient yen to buy a Japanese product. As the prices of items imported from Japan rise, imports are likely to fall.

While the U.S. government may have been happy to see a gradual depreciation of the U.S. dollar reduce the nation's trade deficit and stimulate economic activity, in early 1995 the Federal Reserve became concerned about the *speed* and *extent* of the depreciation. By raising the cost of imported items, boosting the demand for U.S. products, and reducing the need for U.S. firms to hold the line on wages and other production costs to remain competitive with foreign products, rapid depreciation of the dollar can also boost inflationary pressures in the United States. In March 1995, Fed Chairman Alan Greenspan remarked before the House Budget Committee, "The weakness of the dollar against other major currencies is both unwelcome and troublesome. Dollar weakness . . . adds to potential inflation pressures in our economy." Purchases of dollars against the yen and deutsche mark by the Federal Reserve and the Treasury's Exchange Stabilization Fund totaled $1.42 billion in the first quarter of 1995. Even more dollars were purchased in April. As you may note from the accompanying figure, these efforts to bolster the dollar did not arrest its decline against the yen during March and April 1995 (other interventions have sometimes been more successful).

Critics of central bank intervention in foreign exchange markets believe those markets are more competent at establishing the "correct" exchange rate than governments are.

intervened on several occasions to support the dollar against the Japanese yen and German mark (see Exhibit 17-1).

But such transactions also influence U.S. bank reserves, the monetary base, and other monetary variables, just as the Fed's transactions in U.S. government securities do. If the Fed purchases yen with dollars in order to strengthen the yen (hold down the dollar), it writes checks denominated in dollars to foreign exchange dealers located in New York. Because the checks are deposited in New York banks, that action would expand reserves and the monetary base in the same manner as an open market securities purchase by the Fed. If the Fed purchases dollars with Japanese yen (sells yen for dollars),

EXHIBIT 17-1 (*CONTINUED*)

They point out that, in the past, the Federal Reserve has sustained substantial losses when it intervened in foreign exchange markets. But governments, which are charged with maintaining economic prosperity and minimizing inflation, believe that exchange rates "overshoot"—that is, overreact—to changes in fundamental determinants. In their opinion, the exchange rate is too important a variable to be allowed to be determined entirely by free market forces.

U.S.-Japanese Exchange Rate
(March–April 1995)

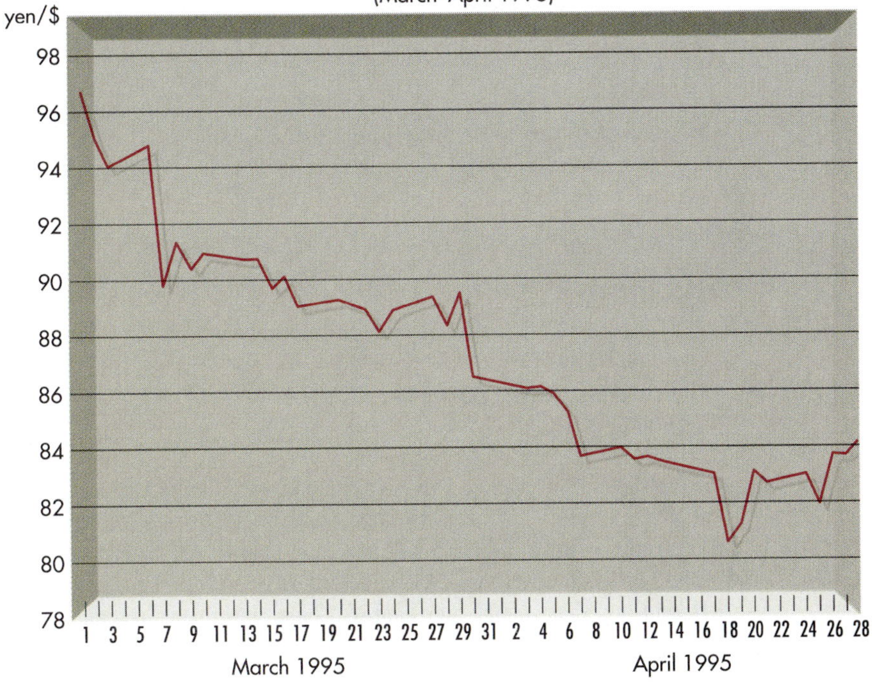

foreign exchange dealers write checks on their accounts at New York banks to the Federal Reserve. The Fed collects on these checks, which are written in dollars, by debiting the reserve accounts of the foreign exchange dealers' banks. Bank reserves and the monetary base are reduced dollar for dollar by the transaction.

The Fed can easily neutralize the influence of its foreign exchange transactions on bank reserves and the monetary base via appropriate open market transactions in government securities. In doing so, the Fed "sterilizes" the effect of its foreign exchange transactions on monetary variables. For example, the Fed could offset the contractionary monetary effects of purchases of dollars in the foreign exchange market by purchasing a comparable amount of U.S. government securities on the open market.

Your Turn

Suppose the U.S. dollar rises sharply against the Japanese yen and the Federal Reserve desires to limit the appreciation to prevent a further increase in the United States' trade deficit with Japan.

a. What foreign exchange operations could the Fed implement in an effort to hold down the dollar?

b. If the Fed wishes to "sterilize" its foreign exchange operations, what must it do?

THE EFFECTIVENESS OF OPEN MARKET OPERATIONS

Open market operations are a powerful, efficient instrument of monetary policy, and influence economic activity through several channels. We will note that they have clear advantages over the other policy instruments.

The Impact of Open Market Operations

Open market operations can influence the economy through three channels: the monetary aggregates, securities prices and yields, and the public's expectations. We will begin with the monetary aggregates.

Bank Reserves, the Monetary Base, and the Monetary Aggregates

As we have emphasized, the Fed can exert relatively accurate control over bank reserves and the monetary base by manipulating its securities portfolio. If the factors governing the money supply multiplier (k, r_r, and r_e) are relatively stable and independent of the monetary base, open market operations will exert a strong and fairly predictable effect on M1 and other monetary aggregates. These variables, in turn, will influence aggregate expenditures on goods and services, thereby influencing economic activity in general.

Securities Prices and Interest Rates (Yields)

When the Fed buys securities on the open market, it bids up their prices and therefore reduces their yields. The initial expansion in bank reserves (and excess reserves) which is produced by the Fed's securities purchases also tends to induce banks to purchase securities, causing further price increases and downward pressure on the yields of government securities. Given the fact that securities are substitutes for one another, the downward pressure on government securities yields tends to spill over into the market for corporate and municipal bonds, as well as into the mortgage market, thus reducing interest rates in general. This encourages expenditures by corporations and municipalities, as well as by individuals, who may be induced to buy homes. The reduction in lending rates also tends to stimulate borrowing and spending by bank customers. Also, there is evidence that the stock market responds favorably to lower interest rates. By increasing the wealth or net worth of the public, the resulting capital appreciation in stocks and bonds is likely to exert a positive impact on consumption and investment expenditures.

The Public's Expectations

Suppose the public has not anticipated the increase in bank reserves and the monetary aggregates induced by Federal Reserve open market purchases. For example, suppose that the Fed's weekly release discloses unexpected outright net purchases of $2 billion of U.S. government securities. It is possible that this stimulative action will be interpreted as a signal of a shift in the Fed's basic policy stance. If so, the public may expect further measures in the same direction. In this case, the change in expectations is likely to produce a positive effect on expenditures and economic activity. In other words, the aggregate demand for goods and services is likely to be stronger if the public expects Fed policy to be stimulative than if a restrictive monetary policy is expected.

Alternatively, the public may perceive a policy-induced change in reserves or monetary aggregates as being an atypical departure from normal. If so, the public might anticipate compensatory measures to return those variables to their normal or expected levels. For example, an announcement that restrictive open market operations have resulted in a slowdown in the growth of the monetary aggregates to rates below the Fed's specified "tolerance ranges" for those variables may produce expectations of easier credit conditions as the Fed seeks to raise the rate of monetary growth to get back on target. Such expectations can in and of themselves lead to an easing of credit conditions and a boost in stock prices.

Although the expectations effect of open market operations is hard to quantify, at times it can be an important channel through which Fed policy influences the U.S. economy.

Advantages of Open Market Operations

The open market operations instrument possesses certain advantages over the other instruments of Federal Reserve policy—that is, changes in the discount rate and reserve requirements. Those advantages include the *precision* with which reserves and the base may be influenced, the *flexibility* of open market operations, and the fact that the *initiative for change* is totally in the hands of the Fed.

Precision

Open market operations enable the Fed to exert firm, accurate control over aggregate bank reserves and the monetary base, especially when these are calculated as weekly or monthly averages of daily figures. If the Fed wishes to inject $115 million of reserves into the banking system, it simply purchases $115 million of U.S. government securities. This high degree of accuracy cannot be achieved through the use of the discount rate or reserve requirements. If the Fed wanted to reduce reserves via discount policy for example, all it could do would be to raise the discount rate and perhaps even issue a statement admonishing banks not to borrow so heavily at the Fed. The extent to which these actions would produce a decline in discounts and advances, reserves, and the monetary base would be impossible to predict.

A similar argument can be made with respect to changes in the reserve requirement. First of all, a change in the reserve requirement influences the money supply through the money supply multiplier rather than through reserves and the monetary base. In addition, even a fairly small change in the percentage reserve requirement produces a relatively large change in required reserves and excess reserves. In principle, the Fed could implement frequent and tiny changes in the reserve requirement—for example, increasing it from 10 to 10.02 percent in a given week. However, both banks and the Fed are averse to such measures. Frequent reserve requirement changes would be inconvenient for banks. In short, this instrument is relatively blunt and not well suited to frequent use as a tool of Fed policy.

Flexibility

The Federal Reserve is in the open market each day, buying and selling large quantities of U.S. government securities through its network of dealers. For this reason, it is easy for the Fed to alter the tone of monetary policy, and even reverse its direction, through open market operations—at a moment's notice, if desirable. Only the most perceptive of observers would detect such a change.

The same does not hold for changes in the discount rate and reserve requirements, which are highly visible to the general public. For example, if the Fed raises the discount rate or reserve requirements, this is hailed in the media as a restrictive action that is likely indicative of further monetary restraint to follow. The Fed has thus gone on record as indicating a need for monetary restraint. Reversing direction and lowering the discount rate or reserve requirement the following week would embarrass the Fed. By doing so, it would be publicly admitting to a mistake. Consequently, it is unlikely to reverse the direction of these policy tools until overwhelming evidence indicates that a change in policy is essential. For this reason, the discount rate and reserve requirement instruments are not very flexible in the short run. On average, reserve requirements are changed only a few times each decade. The discount rate is adjusted somewhat more frequently, typically several times each year. By contrast, the Fed conducts enormous transactions in U.S. government securities every day.

Initiative

If the Federal Reserve is to influence economic activity through such variables as reserves, the monetary base, or excess reserves, changes in those variables must result from Fed policy decisions rather than being imposed by outside forces. That is, the initiative for changes in reserves and/or excess reserves should reside with the Fed. Such is the case with open market operations: by initiating such operations, the Fed is able to dominate the behavior of aggregate bank reserves and the monetary base. A similar case can be made for the reserve requirement instrument, which potentially gives the Fed control over required reserves and thus over excess reserves in the banking system. However, such is not the case with the discount window instrument. Fluctuations in the volume of bank borrowing (discounts and advances) and therefore in reserves and the monetary base produced thereby are not the result of conscious Federal Reserve actions. Banks initiate requests for loans at the Fed, and the Fed tends to accommodate such requests passively. In other words, fluctuations in the volume of discounts and advances result from changes in banks' demand for discounts and advances, not from deliberate Federal Reserve actions.

Disadvantages of Open Market Operations

Some 30 or 40 years ago, open market operations exhibited one important drawback relative to changes in the discount rate and reserve requirements. Because the U.S. financial markets—particularly the federal funds market and the market for negotiable CDs—were not highly developed, open market operations had an uneven regional impact. Their effects were not dispersed as quickly across the nation as were those of reserve requirement and discount rate changes.

Let us examine the reason for this regional effect. When the Federal Reserve enters into government securities transactions with securities dealers, the only banks *directly* affected are those of the dealers. There are only about 40 dealers in government securities, and most of them are located in New York. Therefore, only a handful of banks initially gain or lose reserves when the Fed buys or sells securities, and these banks are concentrated in New York. Decades ago, bankers in Tucumcari, New Mexico and Tupelo, Mississippi were not likely to be aware of, much less influenced by, a change in the direction of Federal Reserve open market operations. Changes in reserve requirements, on the other hand, immediately affect every bank in the United States. And changing the Fed's discount rate immediately affects every bank that is borrowing at the Fed, as well as providing an immediate signal or announcement effect about the general thrust of Federal Reserve policy. This signal is likely to influence the lending decisions of thousands of banks. Thus the concentration of the early effects of open market operations in the select urban areas in which government securities dealers are located was a disadvantage of that instrument relative to the Fed's other policy instruments.

Today, however, the Fed's open market operations quickly influence the federal funds market and the market for negotiable CDs, both of which are national in scope. Remember that the federal funds market is the market in which banks with more reserves than they need lend those reserve deposits at the Fed to banks that have less reserves than desired. This lending and borrowing of reserves is known as "selling" and "buying" fed funds. The interest rate at which fed funds are bought and sold is the *federal funds rate.* Figure 17-1 depicts the federal funds market and the effect that open market operations have on this market.

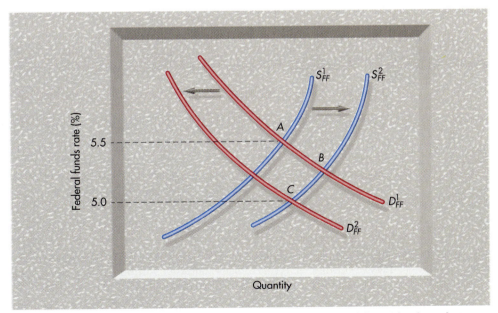

Figure 17-1 The Federal Reserve's Open Market Purchases and the Federal Funds Rate.
When the Federal Reserve purchases securities on the open market, the supply of federal funds increases and the demand decreases. The fed funds rate thus falls.

When the Fed purchases securities on the open market, bank reserves are boosted in a dollar-for-dollar fashion. Because required reserves increase only fractionally, most of these newly created reserves are excess reserves. This means that more banks find themselves with more reserves than they wish to keep, while fewer banks find themselves short on reserves; the supply of federal funds increases and the demand for them falls. In the figure, the supply curve shifts rightward while the demand curve shifts leftward. The equilibrium moves from A to C, and the fed funds rate quickly falls from 5.5 percent to 5 percent. Banks all over the country immediately experience access to funds (via the fed funds market) at a reduced interest rate. This reduction in the cost of funds permits banks to lower their interest rates on loans.

When the Fed sells securities, bank reserves decline. Because required reserves fall by only a small portion of the decline in reserves, excess reserves fall. Fewer banks find themselves with excess reserves, and more banks come up short on reserves. The supply of fed funds thus decreases (shifts left), the demand increases (shifts right), and the fed funds rate increases.

Likewise, the market for negotiable CDs is now national in scope. An open market securities purchase by the Fed increases the funds available to banks by boosting reserves and excess reserves. Fewer banks find it necessary to issue negotiable CDs to obtain funds, and the supply of CDs issued by banks (the demand for funds) declines. The rate on negotiable CDs quickly falls, and banks nationwide have access to funds at a lower cost. As the cost of funds declines, banks reduce their lending rates. In today's economy, the effect of the Fed's open market operations is quickly transmitted across the nation.

TECHNICAL ASPECTS OF OPEN MARKET OPERATIONS

Defensive Operations versus Dynamic Operations

Conceptually, Federal Reserve open market operations may be divided into two categories: defensive operations and dynamic operations. As the name implies, **defensive operations** refer to the Fed's open market operations made for the purpose of "defending" bank reserves and the monetary base against the influence of outside forces over which the Fed has no control. As we saw in Chapter 14, many factors can directly influence both bank reserves and the monetary base. In the absence of defensive open market operations, those factors would cause reserves and the monetary base to fluctuate somewhat erratically. On average, changes in such factors as float, Treasury deposits at the Fed, and so forth would cause aggregate reserves to fluctuate by about 4 percent each week. In its defensive operations, the Fed manipulates its portfolio of securities to prevent such outside forces from causing unwanted fluctuations in R, B, M1, and M2.

In its **dynamic operations,** the Federal Reserve makes a deliberate effort to change the course of economic activity in line with its policy objectives. If the unemployment rate is high, for example, the Fed's aim is likely to be to push down short-term interest rates and increase the growth rates of *R, B,* and the monetary aggregates in order to stimulate economic activity. If the inflation rate is intolerably high, the Fed is likely to aim to restrict the growth rate of those monetary variables and work to push up short-term yields.

The modern image of the Fed is that of conducting dynamic operations. One pictures the Fed at the front of a machine, pushing and pulling levers to try to control unemployment, inflation, and other economic evils. Contrary to this image, the Fed was actually created with the defensive aim foremost in the minds of its founders. These founders viewed the proposed central bank primarily as an institution charged with the objective of preventing the banking system from exerting a disruptive impact on the economy.

Recall from Chapter 12 that before the establishment of the Fed in 1913, seasonal credit demands and currency withdrawals caused periodic episodes of credit stringency and occasional panics in which customers withdrew their money from banks. The withdrawals forced banks to liquidate their assets in order to meet depositors' demands for currency, thus precipitating an undesirable contraction of deposits, credit availability, and the money supply. In times of acute stress, banks were sometimes forced to close. The Federal Reserve was established in part to provide a "lender of last resort" in times of financial stress, to prevent the fractional reserve banking system from doing positive damage to the economy. The Fed's founders did not conceive of the institution in its modern, dynamic role of implementing measures to moderate the ups and downs of the business cycle.

In practice, it is difficult to distinguish the Fed's defensive and dynamic open market operations. The Fed never states publicly whether a given transaction, or the total of transactions for a given day or week, is intended to move monetary variables in a given direction or merely to defend these variables from outside forces and thereby maintain the status quo. The Fed does release a statement each Thursday afternoon which lists the most recent money supply figures and the changes for the week in the various factors that influence bank reserves, including the Fed's open market transactions. This statistical release (H.4.1) is published on Fridays in *The Wall Street Journal* and certain other newspapers. It is an important source of information for those who follow Federal Reserve policy.

As we have indicated, in terms of volume, the Fed's defensive operations dominate its dynamic operations. In 1995, for example, the net increase in the Fed's aggregate securities portfolio for the year was less than 0.5 percent of total Federal Reserve open market transactions during the year. This indicates that the major portion of the Fed's open market operations was defensive in nature.

Outright Transactions versus Repurchase Agreements

Federal Reserve open market transactions may be classified into two types: outright transactions and repurchase agreements. In general, the Fed uses outright transactions to bring about a long-run or permanent change in reserves and the monetary aggregates; it uses repurchase agreements to neutralize the potential impact on reserves and the monetary base of *transitory* changes in *R* and *B* caused by factors outside the Fed's direct control, such as float, Treasury deposits at the Fed, and discounts and advances. (These factors were discussed in some detail in Chapter 14.) In other words, many of the Fed's defensive open market operations are conducted through repurchase agreements.

A **repurchase agreement** (sometimes called a **repo**, or **RP**) is a money market instrument through which government securities dealers mobilize temporarily idle funds. The dealers sell these securities with an explicit agreement to buy them back at a specified future date and price. The buyback date is normally between 1 and 15 days in the future. The buyback price is established at a sufficient premium over the initial price so that the lender's (buyer's) return is equivalent to the yield on collaterized short-term money market loans. Such lenders—the initial buyers of the securities from dealers—typically include banks, nonfinancial corporations, and the Federal Reserve System.[5]

From the viewpoint of a lender—say, a nonfinancial corporation such as IBM—an RP is a convenient, attractive substitute for demand deposits. Firms' expenditures and receipts are not perfectly synchronized over time. Thus, IBM's need for cash balances (money) tends to be uneven, increasing sharply at dividend dates, paydays, and quarterly income tax dates. Pending the arrival of such dates, the firm may conveniently use its demand deposits to purchase RPs, in effect loaning its excess funds to dealers. To obtain the funds, the dealer sells U.S. government securities to the firm, agreeing to buy them back on the date at which the firm needs the funds to pay its dividends, meet its payroll, or pay taxes.

Because dividend dates, paydays, and income tax deadlines tend to cluster on specific dates, U.S. government securities dealers are placed in a position of stress on dates when they are scheduled to repurchase large amounts of securities. In the absence of Federal Reserve assistance, credit markets would be strained at such times, and yields would increase as dealers scrambled for funds to buy back the securities. To minimize seasonal pressures and contribute to the stability of the financial markets, the Fed frequently enters the market to purchase these RPs.

The Fed also engages in RP transactions for other reasons. For example, as Christmas approaches each year, the public increases its holdings of currency. This drains bank reserves. After Christmas, much of this cash finds its way back into banks, replenishing their reserves. To provide temporary relief in December, the Fed purchases securities under repurchase agreements. This temporarily pumps reserves into banks and offsets the currency drain. After Christmas, the dealers repurchase the securities from the Fed. This reduces bank reserves, neutralizing the expansionary effect of the cash that is redeposited into banks.

RPs are also useful to the Fed when the Treasury is conducting heavy financing operations, exerting upward pressure on yields. To help spread the upward pressure over time, the Fed times its purchases for days when the Treasury is borrowing heavily. The Fed's purchases of securities under RPs inject reserves into the banking system, boosting excess reserves and bank demand for securities and thereby moderating the upward pressure on yields. The Fed schedules the dates on which dealers are to repurchase the securities to coincide with periods of light financing by the Treasury.

The Fed's use of repurchase agreements may be regarded as a provision of bank reserves "with strings attached." Because the transactions are classified as repurchase agreements, the financial community is aware that they provide reserves on a purely tem-

---

[5]One might view an RP as a loan to the government securities dealer to help it finance the dealer's large inventory of securities. The dealer would view an RP as an alternative to a regular bank loan. Because rates on RPs are lower than bank loan rates, dealers frequently make use of this financial instrument.

Table 17-1

Federal Reserve Operations in U.S. Government Securities, 1994 and 1995 (billions of dollars)

	1994	1995
Outright purchases and sales:		
Gross purchases	$ 35.3	$ 20.6
Gross sales	2.3	2.4
Repurchase agreements:		
Gross purchases	309.3	331.7
Gross sales	311.9	328.5
Matched sale-purchase transactions:		
Gross sales	1,701.3	2,202.0
Gross purchases	1,700.8	2,197.7
Net change in U.S. government securities holdings	+29.9	+17.1

Source: *Federal Reserve Bulletin*, April 1996, Table 1.17.

porary basis. As soon as the dealer buys back the securities from the Fed, the additional reserves vanish. Thus, an outright Fed purchase of securities would signal a more expansionary monetary policy than a similar Fed purchase under a repurchase agreement.

The Federal Reserve can also conduct repurchase agreements in reverse. Temporary events frequently produce an undesired increase in bank reserves and the monetary base. For example, an increase in float or a reduction in Treasury deposits at the Fed will increase R and B on a dollar-for-dollar basis. To neutralize these effects, the Fed engages in a **matched sale-purchase transaction,** also known as a **reverse repurchase agreement,** or **reverse RP.** In such a transaction, the Fed sells securities to dealers, agreeing to buy them back on a specific date for a specific price. The reverse repurchase agreement, or matched sale-purchase agreement, is analogous to the RP but has precisely the opposite effect.[6]

Table 17-1 shows the relative magnitudes of the Federal Reserve's outright transactions, repurchase agreements, and matched sale-purchase transactions in 1994 and 1995. Note that the amount spent on outright purchases and sales of U.S. government securities was trivial compared to that spent on repurchase agreements and matched sale-purchase transactions. In 1995, gross purchases and sales of U.S. government securities in all forms amounted to approximately $2,550 billion and $2,533 billion, respectively. Therefore, the

---

[6]By engaging in repurchase agreements and matched sale-purchase transactions rather than outright transactions, the Fed saves on transactions costs: an outright purchase followed by an outright sale involves two transactions costs, while a repurchase agreement transaction involves essentially only one transactions cost, thereby reducing the Fed's expenses and benefitting the U.S. Treasury.

net change in the Fed's portfolio of U.S. government securities for 1995 was approximately +$17 billion, or approximately one-third of 1 percent of total Federal Reserve open market transactions. *Other things being equal,* this implies that the Fed's open market operations in U.S. government securities increased the U.S. monetary base by approximately $17 billion in 1995.[7]

POLICY DIRECTIVES

A key Fed document is a written statement that the Federal Open Market Committee (FOMC) produces at each meeting. This document, the **policy directive,** indicates the intended posture of Federal Reserve policy. In the next two sections, we will discuss how the Fed produces and implements such directives.

Production of a Policy Directive

Approximately every 6 weeks, the FOMC meets in Washington for the purpose of formulating the direction and thrust of open market operations. The voting members of the FOMC include the 7 members of the Board of Governors and 5 of the 12 presidents of the Federal Reserve district banks. The president of the New York Federal Reserve bank is a permanent voting member. The presidents of the other Federal Reserve banks serve as voting members of the FOMC on an alternating basis, four at a time. However, all 12 Fed bank presidents or their representatives attend the FOMC meetings and participate in the discussions leading up to the formulation of a policy directive—a written statement indicating the desired thrust of monetary policy.

Discussion at each FOMC meeting covers several areas. First, members give their interpretations of current economic conditions and the likely near-term trend of such key economic variables as national output, unemployment, price level behavior, the exchange rate, and the U.S. trade deficit. Second, each member of the FOMC outlines his or her view concerning what the Fed's dynamic aim should be, both for the near term and for a longer-term horizon.

In an effort to arrive at a consensus on a relatively specific policy directive, an informal give-and-take ensues. The directive is to be issued to the **manager of the System Open Market Account.** The manager, an officer of the Federal Reserve Bank of New York, is charged with carrying out the directive issued by the FOMC. The directive needs to be sufficiently specific so that the manager can interpret the FOMC's objective without ambiguity. Originally, these directives were kept secret. For many years, they have been released to the public with a delay of 45 days. Recently, as a result of congressional prodding, the Fed has begun to announce significant policy changes the day after each FOMC

---

[7]Critics believe that the Fed's open market transactions are excessive and they refer to such activity as "churning." Excessive transactions are costly because they reduce the Fed's net income and consequent payment to the U.S. Treasury. In the critics' view, the Fed conducts excessive numbers of transactions to obscure the thrust of its policy, thereby minimizing its exposure to criticism.

meeting. But the specific directive is still not made public until approximately 45 days after the meeting. Since the 1970s, when "tolerance ranges" of several key variables were added, the directive has specified the target growth rates for various monetary aggregates.

An excerpt from a typical directive, from the FOMC meeting of Jan. 31 to Feb. 1, 1995, is given here:

> The Federal Open Market Committee seeks monetary and financial conditions that will foster price stability and promote sustainable growth in output. In furtherance of these objectives, the Committee at this meeting established ranges of growth of M2 and M3 of 1 to 5 percent and 0 to 4 percent, respectively, measured from the fourth quarter of 1994 to the fourth quarter of 1995. The Committee anticipated that money growth within these ranges would be consistent with its broad policy objectives. The monitoring range for growth of total domestic nonfinancial debt was lowered to 3 to 7 percent for the year. The behavior of the monetary aggregates will continue to be evaluated in the light of progress toward price level stability, movements in their velocities, and developments in the economy and financial markets.
>
> In the implementation of policy for the immediate future, the Committee seeks to increase somewhat the existing degree of pressure on reserve positions, taking account of a possible increase in the discount rate. In the context of the Committee's long-run objectives for price stability and sustainable economic growth, and giving careful consideration to economic, financial, and monetary developments, somewhat greater reserve restraint or somewhat lesser reserve restraint would be acceptable in the intermeeting period. The contemplated reserve conditions are expected to be consistent with moderate growth in M2 and M3 over coming months.[8]

When a near consensus appears to exist among members of the FOMC on the wording of the directive, including the appropriate "tolerance ranges" for key variables, a vote of the 12-person committee is taken. It is not unusual for one or more members to vote against the directive.[9] Given that different individuals have different viewpoints concerning the relative priorities to be placed on objectives such as price level stability and a low unemployment level, the lack of unanimity is not surprising. Furthermore, disagreement will always exist over the appropriate variables to focus on to achieve a given objective. This subject—the appropriate intermediate targets of monetary policy—will be examined in Chapter 19.

At any rate, the Fed's policy actions often provoke controversy in Congress, among economists, and among other groups whose interests are intimately affected by Fed policy. Exhibit 17-2 discusses the *Shadow Open Market Committee,* an informal committee of monetary economists that "shadows," or critiques, the FOMC and its policy decisions.

Implementation of the Directive

The manager of the System Open Market Account oversees the traders who carry out the Fed's purchases and sales of securities. Early in the morning, before the markets open, the manager reads a report indicating the amount of reserves in the banking system at the close

---

[8]*Federal Reserve Bulletin,* May 1995, p. 446.

[9]For example, of the 32 directives drawn up for the 32 meetings of the FOMC from 1992–1995, 20 directives were approved unanimously. In 12 cases one or more members of the FOMC voted against the directive.

EXHIBIT 17-2

The Shadow Open Market Committee

In August 1971, frustrated by years of persistent and intransigent inflation, the Nixon administration imposed rigid wage-price controls. Almost immediately, Karl Brunner and Allan Meltzer, two eminent monetarists, enlisted about a dozen economists to sign a statement opposing controls. The group felt that, by disguising inflationary pressures, the controls would actually exacerbate inflation, because controls would reduce the resolve of the Federal Reserve to hold down the growth of the money supply. Their intuition proved correct. In 1973 and 1974, after the wage-price controls were lifted, inflation averaged more than 10 percent per year.

This early effort by Brunner and Meltzer turned out to be the genesis of the Shadow Open Market Committee (SOMC), formed in 1973. The SOMC is a group of about eight monetarists (the number fluctuates) who meet twice a year in Washington, D.C. The group's purpose is to "shadow," or critique, the Federal Open Market Committee (FOMC) in particular and the Fed's monetary policy in general. The SOMC consistently offers alternatives to the policies implemented by the FOMC.

The SOMC's principal view is that because inflation is always caused by excessive money growth, the Federal Reserve's chief goal should be to maintain price level stability by limiting money growth. Funded by foundation grants, the group is often critical of the Fed for not being sufficiently aggressive in the battle against inflation. Members believe that, historically, the Fed has paid too much attention to interest rates and not enough attention to the money supply. The SOMC advocates relatively low and stable rates of money growth. Noting, for example, that the money growth (M2) rate had fallen from an annual rate of 10 percent to 8 percent, the September 1994 SOMC meeting produced a consensus recommendation that this rate be further reduced to 7 percent.

Every March and September, the group meets in Washington for a 2-day conference. On the first day (Sunday), papers are presented on fiscal and trade policy as well as monetary policy. Economists, business reporters, and other non–SOMC members may attend these meetings, which are characterized by lively debate. As the session moves into the evening, the SOMC prepares a statement of proposed monetary policy. The day after the working session, the SOMC releases its policy statement at a press conference.

Over the years, media attention to the SOMC has been strongest in periods of high inflation. In recent years, because inflation has been relatively subdued, interest in the group's views has diminished. However, it is a measure of the committee's status that a Counter–Shadow Open Market Committee is rumored to have been formed to "shadow" the SOMC. The group's aim? To promote the view that price level stability should not be the sole objective of an enlightened monetary policy.

---

of the previous day's business. He also reviews the level of and recent movements in the federal funds rate. A declining federal funds rate suggests that excess reserves are plentiful and pressure on bank reserve positions is easing; a rising federal funds rate suggests the opposite. Together, the information on reserves and the federal funds rate gives the manager a feel for what money market conditions are likely to be when the financial markets open.

A 9:00 A.M., the manager contacts several dealers in government securities to get their expectations of conditions during the day. At approximately 10:00 A.M., the manager

EXHIBIT 17-2 (CONTINUED)

Some Members of the Shadow Open Market Committee

Allan Meltzer
Carnegie Mellon University
Chair of SOMC

Charles Plosser
University of Rochester

William Poole
Brown University

Anna Schwartz
National Bureau of Economic Research

receives a report from the Federal Reserve staff, indicating the expected movement of several important factors that influence bank reserves and the monetary base—float, currency held by the public, and so forth. If, for example, float is expected to rise because of fog at several major airports, the manager knows he will have to sell securities to offset an undesired expansion in reserves and the monetary base.

EXHIBIT 17-3

Open Market Operations: How the Fed Carries Them Out

A hypothetical Federal Reserve open market transaction, as described by a key New York Federal Reserve Bank official:

The time is just before noon on the Tuesday before Thanksgiving Day. The place is the eighth floor trading room of the Federal Reserve Bank of New York. The manager of the Federal Reserve System's Open Market Account has made his decision. He tells his second in command to buy about $500 million in United States Treasury bills for immediate delivery.

The decision made, the officer in charge turns to the ten officers and securities traders who sit before telephone consoles linking them to . . . primary dealers in U.S. government securities. "We're going in to ask for offerings of [U.S. Treasury] bills for cash," he says. Each person is quickly assigned two to four dealers to call.

Joan, a New York Federal Reserve trader, presses a button on her telephone console, sounding a buzzer at the corresponding console of a government securities dealer.

"Jack," Joan says, "we are looking for offerings of all bills for cash delivery."

Jack replies, "I'll be back in a minute." The salesmen of his firm quickly contact customers to see if they wish to make offerings. Jack consults the partner in charge about how aggressive he should be in offering the firm's own holdings.

Ten minutes later Jack calls back. "Joan, I can offer you for cash $5 million of January 5 bills to yield 5.85 percent, $10 million of January 26 bills at 5.90, $20 million of March 23 bills at 6.05, and $30 million of May 30 bills at 6.14."

Joan says, "Can I have those offerings for a few minutes?"

"Sure."

Around 10:30, the manager phones the U.S. Treasury to gain information that will enable him to fine-tune the Fed staff's preliminary forecast of the change in Treasury deposits at the Fed for the day. A Treasury official indicates the government's transactions that are to be made that day through the Treasury's account at the Fed. The conversation is likely to get around to the Treasury's debt-financing plans for the next few days. If the Treasury is to auction an atypically large amount of new debt that day, the Fed is likely to inject reserves into the banking system by engaging in repurchase agreements with dealers.

Armed with this information, the manager then reviews the formal directive issued by the FOMC. The directive typically indicates the intended growth rates for such monetary aggregates as M2 and M3, sometimes supplemented with a suggested range for the federal funds rate. The manager then arrives at the dynamic policy actions needed to stay within the target ranges. Coupled with the anticipated open market operations that would achieve

---

EXHIBIT 17-3 *(CONTINUED)*

Within minutes the "go-around" is completed. The traders have recorded the offerings obtained from their calls on special preprinted strips. The officer-in-charge arrays the individual dealer offerings on an inclined board atop a stand-up counter. A tally shows that dealers have offered $1.8 billion of bills for cash sale—that is, with delivery and payment that very day.

The officer then begins circling with a red pencil the offerings that provide the best—that is, the highest—rate of return for each issue. The large quotation board facing the open end of the U-shaped trading desk tells him the yields on Treasury bills as they were in the market just before the "go-around" began. An associate keeps a running total of the amounts being bought. When the desired amount has been circled, the individual strips are returned to the traders, who quickly telephone the dealer firms.

"Jack, we'll take the $5 million of January 5 bills at 5.85 and the $30 million of May 30 bills at 6.14, both for cash; no, thanks, on the others," Joan says.

Forty-five minutes after the initial decision, the calls have been completed, and $523 million in Treasury bills purchased. Only the paper work remains. The traders write up tickets, which provide the basic authority for the Bank's government bond department to receive and pay for the specific Treasury bills bought. The banks that handle the dealers' deliveries—the clearing banks—will authorize deductions of the securities from the book entry list of their holdings at the Federal Reserve. In return, they will receive credit to their reserve accounts the banks maintain at the New York Reserve Bank.

The Federal Reserve credits to the dealers' banks immediately add over $500 million to the reserves of the U.S. banking system.

Source: Paul Meek, *Open Market Operations* (New York: Federal Reserve Bank of New York, 1978), pp. 1–2.

---

the defensive aim of neutralizing the potential effects of the non–Federal Reserve factors that influence monetary conditions, the manager formulates his plan of action for the day.

Shortly after 11:00 A.M., the manager contacts several members of the FOMC to outline his intended actions for the day. As soon as he gets their approval, the manager's traders phone the approximately 40 firms that serve as dealers in U.S. government securities to obtain current quotations on prices and yields. The Fed attempts to purchase securities at the lowest possible price and sell them at the highest possible price. If it intends, for example, to purchase $1.8 billion of Treasury bills, it obtains the "ask" prices of each of the 40 dealers for various issues of Treasury bills, together with the quantities each dealer is willing to sell. Prices are ranked in ascending order (low to high), and the manager simply goes down the list and purchases securities until the quota of $1.8 billion is reached. The process is typically completed around noon. On most days this ends the Fed's trading, although occasionally special developments require Fed action in the afternoon. Exhibit 17-3 provides a flavor of the discussions that go on between the Fed and government securities dealers as the Fed conducts its open market operations.

SUMMARY

The most important instrument, or tool, of Federal Reserve policy is open market operations—the buying and selling of U.S. government securities by the Fed through a network of dealers. With this tool, the Fed is capable of accurately controlling aggregate bank reserves and the monetary base. This in turn enables the Fed to influence economic activity, chiefly by influencing the monetary aggregates (M1, M2, M3) and the level of interest rates. The precision and flexibility of open market operations are clear advantages of this instrument over the Fed's other policy tools. Today, the effects of open market operations are dispersed rapidly across the nation. The Fed can accurately control the federal funds rate through its open market operations and, by doing so, strongly influence other short-term money market yields and bank lending rates. Most of the Fed's transactions in any week are *defensive* in nature—that is, they are designed to offset the effects of the many transitory factors that influence bank reserves. This obscures the *dynamic* thrust of Federal Reserve policy, making it difficult for outside observers to pinpoint changes in the direction of Fed policy. The committee that decides on the posture of monetary policy is the Federal Open Market Committee. To implement its open market operations, the FOMC hammers out and approves a policy directive at each FOMC meeting. This directive indicates the intended thrust of monetary policy and is used by the manager of the System Open Market Account at the New York Fed as the basis of the Fed's open market operations.

Answers to Your Turn (p. 396)

a. *The Fed must buy Japanese yen with dollars. This action will strengthen the yen and hold down the dollar.*

b. *In buying yen with dollars, the Fed is writing checks to foreign exchange dealers. When these checks are cleared, the foreign exchange dealers' banks have their accounts at the Fed credited, thus boosting both aggregate bank reserves and the monetary base. To prevent this monetary expansion, the Fed must sell securities in the same magnitude as its purchases of dollars.*

KEY TERMS

instrument, or tool, of monetary policy
open market operations
discounts and advances
defensive operations
dynamic operations

repurchase agreement (repo, or RP)
matched sale-purchase transaction (reverse repurchase agreement, or reverse RP)
policy directive
manager of the System Open Market Account

STUDY QUESTIONS

1 Define the term "instrument, or tool, of Federal Reserve policy." How does an instrument differ from an intermediate target variable?

2 Using T-accounts, explain how Federal Reserve purchases of $340 million of U.S. government securities from dealers affect bank reserves and the monetary base.

3 What difference does it make for bank reserves and the monetary base whether the Federal Reserve purchases government securities from dealers or automobiles from General Motors? Explain.

4 Suppose the Federal Reserve becomes concerned that the dollar is becoming too strong and enters the foreign exchange market to purchase German marks with dollars. Other things being equal, what will be the effect of this transaction on bank reserves and the monetary base in the United States? Explain.

5 Suppose the Federal Reserve is supporting the dollar by purchasing dollars with Japanese yen (selling yen for dollars). What will be the impact on bank reserves, and what could the Fed do to counteract the effect of the transaction on reserves and the monetary base? Explain.

6 Explain the difference between the Treasury financing a budget deficit by selling bonds to private citizens and by selling bonds to the Federal Reserve.

7 Suppose, in a given week, the Federal Reserve purchases $3.2 billion (net) of U.S. Treasury securities on the open market. What can we conclude

from this information about the dynamic aim of the Federal Reserve? Explain.

8 Suppose that the Federal Reserve is intent on restraining aggregate expenditures through restrictive open market operations. Explain how restrictive open market operations would affect the economy via

  a Bank reserves, the monetary base, and the monetary aggregates

  b Security prices and yields

9 Discuss the nature of repurchase agreements, or "repos." Explain the circumstances under which the Fed might purchase securities in this way. Do the same with "reverse repos," or matched sale-purchase transactions.

10 What are the advantages of open market operations relative to the other instruments of monetary policy? Explain.

11 Explain how the following markets help transmit the impact of restrictive open market operations across the nation:

  a federal funds market

  b negotiable CD market

12 Look at the table that indicates the factors that change bank reserves, published in Friday's *Wall Street Journal*. Compute the change in the monetary base in the most recent week. Explain why this change differs from the change in the Fed's securities portfolio in the same week.

SUGGESTIONS FOR ADDITIONAL READING

An excellent general reference on open market operations is Paul Meek, *Open Market Operations* (New York: Federal Reserve Bank of New York, 1985). On institutional aspects of open market operations, see Chapter 3 of *The Federal Reserve System: Purposes and Functions,* 8th ed. (Washington: Board of Governors of Federal Reserve System, 1994). For a review of the Fed's open market operations with special emphasis on the repurchase agreement technique, see Howard Roth, "Federal Reserve Open Market Techniques," Federal Reserve Bank of Kansas City *Economic Review,* March 1986, pp. 3–15. Each year in February or March, the Federal Reserve Bank of St. Louis publishes an article on the previous year's Federal Open Market Committee meetings and decisions.

The June issue of the *Federal Reserve Bulletin* also discusses the previous year's open market operations. To examine the most recent FOMC policy discussion and directive, consult the most recent issue of the *Federal Reserve Bulletin,* published monthly by the Board of Governors. A quarterly report describing Federal Reserve and Treasury foreign exchange operations is published in the March, June, September, and December issues of the *Bulletin.* Finally, all the directives and discussions of the FOMC in a given year are collected in Board of Governors of the Federal Reserve System, *Annual Report,* published each year in April or May. This publication also contains a wealth of statistical information on open market operations and other Federal Reserve data.

Tools of Federal Reserve Policy: Discount Window Policy and Reserve Requirement Policy

In Chapter 17, we saw that an instrument, or tool, of monetary policy is an economic variable that can be manipulated by a central bank in order to influence such intermediate variables as the money supply or short-term interest rates with a view toward achieving an ultimate policy goal. The goals of monetary policy include high levels of output and employment and price level stability. Unlike its intermediate targets and final goals, the Federal Reserve controls its policy tools, or instruments, with precision. The three general instruments or tools of monetary policy are open market operations, discount window policy, and reserve requirement policy. We treated open market operations in some depth in Chapter 17. In this chapter we turn to an analysis of discount window and reserve requirement policy.

THE DISCOUNT WINDOW: POLICY AND PROCEDURES

In financial market terminology, the **discount window** is a facility through which the Federal Reserve lends reserves to depository institutions. Bank borrowing from the Federal Reserve System is known as discount window borrowing, or **discounts and advances.** The term *discount window policy* refers to the set of conditions under which banks are permitted to borrow reserves from the Fed's discount window, including the interest rate charged by the Fed, known as the *discount rate.*[1]

During the first 2 decades of the Federal Reserve's history, discount window policy was the Fed's primary policy tool. The Federal Reserve Act of 1913 established reserve requirements, but the Fed did not gain the authority to *change* those reserve requirements until 1933. And though the Federal Reserve Act did empower the individual Federal Reserve banks to

---

[1]In reality, there is no discount "window" today. When a bank seeks a loan from the Federal Reserve, it calls the Federal Reserve district bank and asks the Fed to grant a short-term loan to the bank by crediting the bank's account with the Fed by the desired amount. The transaction is accomplished by a bookkeeping entry.

purchase U.S. government securities, that tool was initially viewed as only a means of earning interest income in periods when Fed loans to banks were depressed. Its use as a monetary policy tool did not develop until much later. Thus, by default, discount window policy was the principal instrument of Federal Reserve policy from its inception until the 1930s.

Beginning in the early 1930s, the relative importance of discount window policy declined dramatically. Partly, this was due to the Fed's increasing use of the other instruments. Mostly, however, it was attributable to a sharp decrease in the demand by banks for discounts and advances.[2] A massive influx of gold into the United States expanded bank reserves in the 1930s. Also, the weak state of the U.S. economy during the 1930s, together with a discount rate that was high relative to money market yields, served to limit banks' demand for credit at the discount window. In the decade beginning in 1934, bank borrowing at the Fed averaged only $12 million. The Federal Reserve bond support program of 1942–1951 assured banks of ample credit, so there was little activity at the discount window during this period. In 1951, the Federal Reserve–U.S. Treasury "Accord" terminated the bond support program.

For these reasons, discount window policy was largely ineffectual or nonexistent from the early 1930s to the early 1950s. Beginning in the 1950s, however, discount window policy increased in importance, though it never again approached its early role as the most important tool of Federal Reserve policy.

Four classes of credit are extended by the Federal Reserve at its discount window: adjustment credit, seasonal credit, extended credit, and emergency credit. **Adjustment credit** is routinely available to depository institutions to meet an unexpected temporary need for reserves or to cushion against more persistent needs while fundamental balance sheet adjustments are being made. **Seasonal credit** is available to small depository institutions that are subject to strong seasonal fluctuations in loan demand; for example, small banks in farming communities and resort areas are sometimes granted seasonal credit by the Fed. **Extended credit** is occasionally provided on a longer-term basis (sometimes for months or years) to depository institutions with serious liquidity problems. Finally, in rare and exceptional circumstances, the Fed may extend **emergency credit** to individuals or firms other than depository institutions. This authority has not been used since the 1930s.

By far the most prevalent and significant activity at the discount window involves adjustment credit. This type of credit also has the most important implications for Federal Reserve monetary policy. Our analysis will therefore focus chiefly on adjustment credit—short-term loans to banks that find themselves temporarily deficient in reserves.

Criteria for Bank Borrowing at the Federal Reserve

In general, adjustment loans from the Fed to banks are intended to be of very short duration. They are designed to cover short-term reserve deficiencies stemming from *unanticipated* events. Such events might include unexpectedly large currency withdrawals by

---

[2]The term *discounts and advances* is today somewhat of an anachronism. In its early days, the Fed charged interest up front by "discounting" its loans. In other words, a bank seeking a million-dollar loan from the Fed would have its account at the Fed credited, but perhaps by only $990,000. The interest on the loan—in this case $10,000—was deducted by the Fed when the loan was granted. Today, however, interest is collected when the loan comes due. Such loans are "advances" rather than "discounts."

bank customers or unexpectedly large net check clearings against the bank. An unanticipated increase in loan demand would also be considered a legitimate reason to borrow at the Fed. However, borrowing to finance lending in the federal funds market or to purchase Treasury bills to secure a profit on yield differentials is not legitimate. Also illegitimate would be bank borrowing in order to make routine loans to bank customers or to reduce loan rates to established customers. In general, the broad criterion employed by the Fed is that banks should borrow only for "need," not for "profit." As we will see, this is a highly ambiguous distinction.

In judging whether a particular bank is abusing the intent of discount window policy, the discount officer of a Federal Reserve district bank considers the frequency and duration of the bank's loan requests from the Fed, the magnitude of the requests relative to the bank's required reserves, and any special circumstances surrounding the bank and region. Also considered is the appropriateness of the loan request, as judged by looking at the bank's balance sheet. Continued requests for credit at the discount window will bring increased Federal Reserve scrutiny of the bank's operations and perhaps even eventual harassment of the bank's officers. Often, the mere specter of a thorough examination of the bank's books by the Federal Reserve is sufficient to prevent banks from abusing the discount window privilege. For those not easily intimidated, the Fed reserves the authority to refuse loan requests.

Adjustment to Reserve Deficiencies

If a bank is deficient in reserves, it will naturally seek the least costly method of obtaining reserves. The alternatives available to a typical bank include selling short-term securities such as Treasury bills, borrowing in the federal funds market, and borrowing at the Fed's discount window.[3] Typically, the decision will hinge on the level of the discount rate relative to other short-term yields or interest rates. If the Treasury bill yield and federal funds rate are both 5 percent while the Federal Reserve discount rate is 3 percent, the most profitable choice would be to borrow at the discount window. Why sell a security yielding 5 percent or borrow fed funds at 5 percent, when you can borrow from the Federal Reserve at 3 percent? Conversely, when the discount rate exceeds the other interest rates or yields, one would expect the opposite. Why borrow at the Fed at 6 percent if Treasury bills are yielding 4 percent and the federal funds rate is 5 percent?

This suggests that one would expect the volume of discounts and advances to be greater in periods in which short-term market yields exceed the Fed's discount rate than in periods in which the relationship is reversed. Figure 18-1 shows the extent to which the aggregate amount of bank borrowing at the Fed is related to this market incentive—that is, the yield differential. The right-hand vertical axis measures the incentive to borrow—the differential, or spread, between the federal funds rate and the discount rate. The left-hand vertical axis shows the amount of bank borrowing at the Fed—that is, discounts and advances.

Figure 18-1 indicates that the volume of bank borrowing from the Federal Reserve is tightly linked to the incentive to borrow. Banks typically borrow heavily from the Fed

---

[3]Larger banks located in metropolitan areas often use additional methods of obtaining funds, such as issuing large negotiable CDs or borrowing in the Eurodollar market.

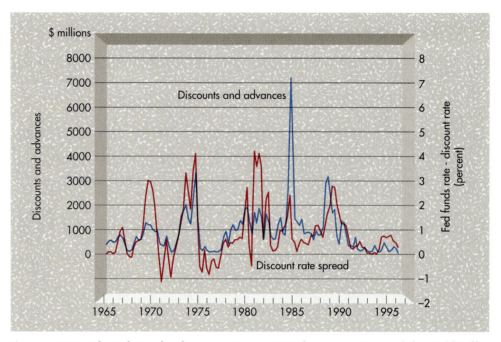

Figure 18-1 The Relationship between Discount Window Borrowing and the Yield Differential, 1965–1996. The amount of bank borrowing from the Federal Reserve is closely related to the yield differential—the spread between the federal funds rate and the discount rate. The greater the differential, the greater the incentive to borrow. *Source:* Data from *Citibank Economic Database.*

in periods in which the federal funds rate is considerably higher than the Fed's discount rate (e.g., 1973–1974, 1988). They borrow much less in periods in which the federal funds rate is lower than or not significantly above the discount rate (e.g., 1975–1976, 1992–1994).[4] The same basic pattern would emerge if we used the Treasury bill yield in place of the federal funds rate as our measure of the incentive for banks to borrow at the Federal Reserve.

However, the fact that the federal funds rate and the yields on short-term securities often rise significantly above the Fed's discount rate indicates that factors other than financial incentives (yield differentials) also influence the volume of discounts and advances. Otherwise, there would be absolutely no demand for federal funds when the federal funds rate exceeds the discount rate. Anytime the federal funds rate nudged above the discount rate, banks would borrow from the Fed discount window and use the funds to make a risk-free profit by lending in the federal funds market. The same arbitrage principle would apply to U.S. Treasury bills when their yields moved above the discount rate. Such arbitrage activity would ensure that the federal funds rate and Treasury bill yield never exceeded the discount rate by more than the associated administrative and transactions costs.

---

[4]Two large surges in the volume of discounts and advances, in 1974 and 1984, were attributable chiefly to the extended credit the Fed advanced to the severely impaired Franklin National Bank (1974) and the Continental Illinois Bank (1984). The blip in 1988 was attributable to extended loans made to several troubled southwestern banks impaired by a collapse of oil and real estate prices.

Factors That Inhibit Bank Borrowing at the Fed

There are two major considerations that limit bank borrowing from the Federal Reserve in periods in which the yield incentive is positive. One is a tradition or preference of some banks not to be indebted to the Fed. The other is the set of procedures employed by the Fed to practice nonprice rationing, that is, to inhibit bank borrowing at the discount window.

Banks' Reluctance to Borrow at the Fed

In any given year, the great majority of banks do not borrow at the Fed. Students of banking history believe that there is a tradition among many banks of being reluctant to borrow at the Fed. This tradition developed in response to the experiences of financial instability in the nineteenth century and was strongly reinforced by the banking collapse of the 1930s.[5]

Indeed, many bankers whose banks are indebted to the Federal Reserve would prefer not to have that fact known. Such a disclosure could be interpreted as reflecting weakness or imprudent management and could result in a loss of confidence in the bank by the public. This attitude is probably more prevalent among small-town banks than among performance-minded big-city banks. Nevertheless, when the huge, troubled Continental Illinois Bank took out massive loans from the Fed in 1984, other large banks avoided going to the discount window for appearance's sake. And during the 1990–1991 recession, which followed the surge of bank failures in the late 1980s, banks' reluctance to borrow at the Fed became extreme. (Some economists question this explanation because it does not appear to conform to the norm of profit maximization.) See Exhibit 18-1 for a statistical investigation of whether banks borrow for "need" or for "profit."

Administration of the Discount Window

The Federal Reserve is fond of pointing out that borrowing at the Fed is a *privilege* rather than a *right*. Unlike the federal funds market, the discount window does not permit a bank to borrow continuously. The Fed automatically grants the first loan request by any bank. Such loans are generally for a very brief time period, often a single day for larger banks and commonly 1 week or less for smaller banks. But if a bank seeks to extend the loan or frequently requests access to reserves through the discount window, accommodation is *not* passively granted. The discount officer of the Federal Reserve district bank will study each loan request and establish surveillance of the bank's operations in order to judge whether the request is consistent with the Fed's borrowing criteria.

In the next section, we examine the channels through which a change in the discount rate influences the nation's economy.

ECONOMIC EFFECTS OF A CHANGE IN THE DISCOUNT RATE

Let us now paint a broad picture of the way in which the Fed's discount window policy influences the economy. When the economy suffers from excess demand for goods and services and escalating inflationary pressures, the Fed typically responds with restrictive

[5]More recently, the fiasco in the savings and loan industry, together with the financial problems encountered by many commercial banks in the late 1980s and early 1990s, have tended to reinforce this tradition as banks sought to avoid the appearance of financial weakness.

EXHIBIT 18-1

Borrowing at the Fed: For "Need" or for "Profit"?

To establish whether borrowing from the Federal Reserve meets the Fed's criterion of borrowing for "need" rather than for "profit," it is best to look at the facts. The figure below shows the relationship between the volume of discounts and advances and the "spread," or the amount by which the federal funds rate exceeds the Fed discount rate. The observations plotted are 4-month averages of daily figures for the spread and the volume of discounts and advances during 1964–1995. Note that, on average, bank borrowing at the Fed is higher when the spread is larger.

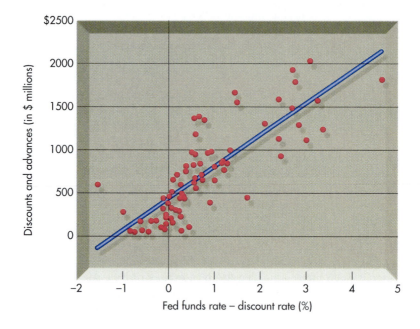

If we fit a regression line to the points shown in the figure and estimate its equation, we get

$$A = \$442\text{m} + \$370\text{m} \cdot \text{spread}, \qquad R^2 = .66$$

In the equation, A represents the volume of discounts and advances and "spread" is the difference between the federal funds rate and the Federal Reserve discount rate. The coefficient on the "spread" term, $370 million, indicates that, for each percentage point the federal funds rate exceeds the discount rate, banks step up their borrowing at the discount window by $370 million. This means that bank borrowing from the Fed is positively and strongly linked to the profitability of doing so.

Note, however, that the intercept of the equation (sometimes known as the "constant" term) is +$442 million. This indicates that on average during 1964–1995, even when there was no incentive to borrow (that is, when the spread was zero), banks borrowed $442 million. This suggests a significant element of "need" in bank borrowing at the Fed. Even when money market yields are not above the discount rate, banks borrow at the Fed.

Finally, note the relatively high explanatory power of the model, as indicated by the high R^2. This indicates that, during 1964–1995, variation in the spread accounted for 66 percent of the variation in bank borrowing at the Federal Reserve.

open market operations—sales of U.S. government securities. As reserves are drained by the Fed's open market securities sales, many banks find themselves deficient in reserves. In the short term, banks are forced into the Fed's discount window to obtain reserves in order to meet their reserve requirements.[6]

However, accommodation at the discount window is purely temporary; banks are placed under pressure individually to repay the Federal Reserve. Unless the reserve pressure is transitory, banks will be forced to make fundamental balance sheet adjustments. That, of course, is the Fed's intention. The banks' first line of reaction is typically to sell off short-term securities. Their willingness to sell their securities, and the speed with which they react, will depend on the level of the discount rate relative to short-term yields. If the discount rate exceeds yields on short-term securities, banks will not hesitate to liquidate their short-term securities. Their balance sheet adjustments and repayment of the Fed will be quite rapid. However, if the discount rate is substantially below short-term yields, the banks' reluctance to borrow and the Fed's pressure for banks to repay will be counteracted by financial incentives—that is, the profitability of borrowing at the Fed. Bank adjustments will therefore be more deliberate, and the average duration of bank indebtedness to the Fed will increase. In such circumstances, the aggregate volume of discounts and advances tends to be relatively high.

If the Fed is pursuing stimulative open market operations in response to a business recession, banks will find their reserve positions easing. Individual banks will pay off their debts at the discount window, purchase U.S. Treasury securities, and expand their loans. Again, the actual mix of these options will be influenced by the level of the discount rate relative to other yields. If the discount rate is higher than other yields, banks will pay off the Fed immediately. If the discount rate is significantly below other yields, banks will take their time paying off the Fed.[7] Thus the level of the discount rate relative to other yields is an important factor influencing the speed with which balance sheet adjustments are made by banks.

A change in the Fed's discount rate influences the economy through three channels: bank reserves, the monetary base, and the monetary aggregates; the level of interest rates and security prices; and the expectations of bankers and the public.

---

[6]The federal funds market facilitates the transfer of reserves from banks with excess reserves to banks that are deficient in reserves. However, this market does *not* provide for any increase in reserves to the banking system *as a whole*. It merely reallocates reserves within the system. The discount window, on the other hand, provides access to additional reserves for the aggregate banking system.

[7]This suggests that the optimal Federal Reserve procedure might be to establish the discount rate *below* other yields during periods of depressed economic activity and *above* other yields when aggregate demand is excessive. By keeping the discount rate relatively low during a recession, the Fed would be providing incentives to banks to use any new funds to purchase securities or make loans rather than repay the discount window. That would tend to expand the monetary aggregates and reduce interest rates. Conversely, in setting the discount rate relatively high when the economy is overheated, the Fed would provide a strong incentive for banks to liquidate assets to repay the Fed. At the margin, this would tend to restrict credit, reduce the monetary aggregates, and raise interest rates. Historically, the Fed's discount policy has been perverse in this sense: relative to money market yields, the discount rate has been low during booms and high during recessions.

Impact on Reserves, the Monetary Base, and the Money Supply

Figure 18-1 showed the positive relationship between the volume of bank borrowing at the discount window and the incentive to borrow, as indicated by the spread between the federal funds rate and the discount rate. When the Fed raises the discount rate, this spread is reduced, possibly becoming negative. At the margin, some banks will find it expedient to pay off their debt at the discount window quickly. Suppose banks contact the Federal Reserve and collectively request that the Fed accept repayment of $125 million of discounts and advances. The Fed accommodates their request by debiting their reserve accounts. T-accounts would show the following changes:

Federal Reserve System		All Commercial Banks	
Discounts and advances −125m	Deposits by member banks −125m	Deposits at the Fed −125m	Discounts and advances −125m

Note, in this event, that bank reserves and the monetary base each decrease by $125 million. This contraction in bank reserves and the monetary base will produce a reduction in M1, M2, and the other monetary aggregates. Given other factors, then, a hike in the Federal Reserve discount rate reduces reserves, the monetary aggregates, aggregate expenditures, and the nation's output of goods and services.

Conversely, a reduction in the Fed's discount rate triggers an increase in bank borrowing at the Fed, thus expanding R, B, M1, and M2. Eventually, a cut in the discount rate boosts aggregate expenditures and economic activity.

Impact on Yields, Loan Rates, and Security Prices

Suppose the Fed raises the discount rate. Some of the banks currently indebted at the Fed will be induced to sell securities on the open market, borrow in the federal funds market, or encourage some customers to repay their loans. The funds they obtain through these actions can then be used to pay off their debts at the Fed's discount window. These actions by banks in response to the discount rate hike are consistent with the Fed's aims— to push up yields in the money market and trigger an increase in bank lending rates. Many banks not currently borrowing from the Fed will also be influenced by the increase in the discount rate. Because the cost of having to borrow at the Fed has increased, banks in general will want to reduce their exposure to reserve deficiencies. That is, they will deliberately build up their holdings of excess reserves in order to reduce the probability of coming up short on reserves and having to borrow at the Fed.

Such actions by banks place upward pressure on interest rates throughout the economy. As banks sell off securities to meet their increased demand for reserves, security prices fall and yields rise. Demand also increases in the federal funds market as an alternative to the discount window, putting upward pressure on the sensitive federal funds rate. To preserve the normal relationship between money market yields and loan rates and to encourage some borrowers to repay their loans, banks are likely to increase their loan

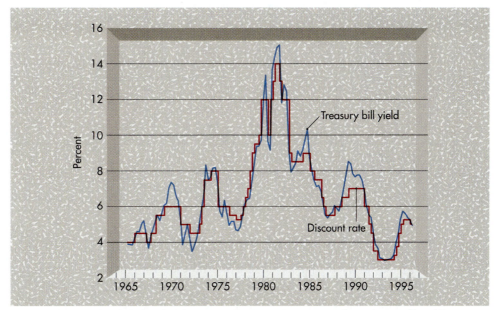

Figure 18-2   The Relationship between the Discount Rate and Treasury Bill Yields, 1995–1996. A strong positive correlation exists between the discount rate and other short-term yields. In part, this stems from the influence of the discount rate on other yields. Mostly, it reflects the Fed's propensity to keep its discount rate aligned with other yields. *Source:* Data from *Citibank Economic Database.*

rates. This upward pressure on yields is likely to be transmitted through market forces to corporate, municipal, and government bonds. The general increase in interest rates is likely to exert a restraining effect on expenditures and therefore on economic activity in general. And because higher bond yields go hand in hand with lower bond prices, the resulting decline in private-sector wealth exerts a contractionary effect on aggregate expenditures and economic activity.

Figure 18-2 shows the historical relationship between the Federal Reserve discount rate and other short-term interest rates. Note that the relationship is quite strong. At first glance, it may appear that by setting the discount rate, the Fed exerts tremendous influence over other yields. In that sense the illustration is misleading, tending to overstate the influence of the discount rate on money market yields. Quite often the Fed moves its discount rate *in response to* the movement of other yields or interest rates, which in turn are triggered largely by forces other than the Fed's actions. In fact, a close look at the figure indicates that changes in the discount rate typically lag behind changes in short-term yields.

Notwithstanding this point, if the Fed moves the discount rate for any reason, yields at the margin tend to move sympathetically, for the reasons sketched earlier. It is perhaps valid to characterize the discount rate as having a significant, but certainly not dominant, effect on the general level of interest rates.

The measures the Fed takes to limit the volume of discounts and advances, together with banks' tradition against borrowing at the discount window, make it possible for the discount rate to remain well below money market yields for extended periods. Note in Figure 18-2 that this has tended to occur during latter stages of economic expansions (e.g., in 1967–1969 and 1987–1989), when yields are high and rising. There have also been periods when the discount rate has remained significantly *above* short-term yields for months, even years. This phenomenon tends to occur in periods of depressed economic activity, when loan demand is down and banks have already paid off their debts at the discount window. If banks are no longer indebted at the Fed and the discount rate is above money market yields, there are no forces tending to push yields toward the discount rate. On this point, the Fed has frequently been chastised for not reducing the discount rate adequately during recessions.

The Announcement Effect

Sometimes a change in the Fed's discount rate signals a change in the general posture of monetary policy. Suppose that in the most recent year, a period of recession, the Fed has reduced its discount rate four times, each time by 0.25 percentage point. Now, suppose the Fed unexpectedly announces an *increase* of a full percentage point. The public is likely to expect the Fed to follow with restrictive open market operations in the weeks ahead. Expectations of interest rates will therefore be revised upward. Now, an increase in interest rates inevitably implies a reduction in the prices of fixed-income securities such as bonds. For this reason, speculators and many other bondholders will seek to unload in a hurry. Note that the mere *announcement* of the discount rate hike will cause bond prices to decline and yields to increase. The stock market, fearing a more restrictive monetary environment down the road, is likely to fall sharply immediately after the announcement.

Sensing that interest rates have seen their lows for a while, bankers may quickly sell off some municipal and U.S. government bonds. Bank investment committees are also likely to move their portfolios in the direction of increased liquidity. As holdings of excess reserves (and r_e) increase, banks will seek to pay off their debts (if any) at the discount window. Depository institutions may announce an increase in their loan rates and begin to scrutinize loan applications more carefully. In terms of the money supply framework introduced in Chapters 14 and 15, both the monetary base and the money supply multiplier will tend to decline, thereby reducing the money supply. The monetary base will decline to the extent that banks collectively reduce their indebtedness at the discount window. The money supply multiplier will be reduced to the extent that r_e is boosted as banks elect to hold more excess reserves in anticipation of restrictive Fed policies.

Assuming that the hike in the discount rate is announced in response to valid evidence that the economy needs restrictive medicine, these adjustments are socially desirable. The announcement helps to promote the desired objectives of slowing the extension of credit by banks, slowing the growth of the monetary aggregates, and pushing up interest rates to inhibit aggregate expenditures on goods and services.

In the real world, however, the case is rarely so clear cut. In the first place, as is evident in Figure 18-2, the Fed commonly moves the discount rate passively, *in response to* other yields, rather than actively, in order to *influence* yields. One can frequently anticipate changes in the discount rate by observing the current level and recent movements of the Treasury bill yield and the federal funds rate. Indeed, in recent years, the majority of the changes in the discount rate have been predictable and have therefore had little or no announcement effect.

Unfortunately, when the Fed announces a change in its discount rate, it rarely makes its intentions clear. Is the change in the discount rate merely a technical adjustment designed to keep it in alignment with other yields, or is it intended to signal a basic shift in the posture of Federal Reserve policy? The public is typically left guessing. Because the discount rate typically does not change in any given week or month, when a change does occur it is likely to receive widespread media coverage. And because the change is highly visible, there is a tendency for it to be blown out of proportion to its real significance.

In the next few sections, we will look at some criticisms of the way in which the Fed conducts its discount policy, together with some proposals for changing the policy.

CRITICISMS AND PROPOSED REFORMS OF DISCOUNT WINDOW POLICY

Critics of Federal Reserve procedures point to some apparent shortcomings in discount window policy. These critics charge that the Fed allows banks to circumvent the intended Federal Reserve policy and that the way in which the Fed operates its discount window causes a *procyclical* pattern of discounts and advances, which tends to destabilize both the money supply and the economy. Some also charge that changes in the discount rate are a very unreliable way of communicating changes in the Fed's policy to the public. We will analyze these alleged shortcomings and then briefly examine some proposed reforms.

Alleged Shortcomings of Discount Window Policy

Critics charge that the Fed's discount window procedures allow banks to circumvent the Fed's intentions, produce a procyclical pattern of discounts and advances, and result in ambiguous announcement effects. Let's look at each charge.

Circumvention   How can banks use the discount window to circumvent or avoid the intent of Federal Reserve policy? When the Fed sells securities on the open market in a period of inflationary pressure, it drains reserves from the banking system. The Fed's intention is to force depository institutions to curtail their lending, thus restricting credit availability, driving up interest rates, and slowing the growth of M1 and M2. However, if banks react by sharply increasing their borrowing at the discount window, they may collectively postpone or avoid liquidating their earning assets, thereby frustrating the

Fed's intentions.[8] As Figure 18-2 shows, the Fed has historically encouraged this state of affairs by setting a relatively low discount rate in boom periods (e.g., in 1973 and 1988–1989).

During recessions, the Fed pumps reserves into banks through open market purchases. To the extent that banks use those funds simply to repay their loans at the discount window, they again thwart the Fed's intention—that is, to stimulate bank lending, boost the growth rate of the monetary aggregates, and bring down interest rates. And by setting its discount rate high relative to money market yields during periods of economic weakness, the Fed has encouraged this result (e.g., in 1975–1976 and 1991–1992).

The Procyclical Behavior of Discounts and Advances

A second criticism of the Fed's discount window policy involves the procyclical behavior of bank borrowing at the Fed. Note the pattern in Figure 18-3, which indicates a systematic tendency for discounts and advances to expand during the latter phases of cyclical expansions and decline during recessions (shaded areas). To contribute to economic stability, one would want the Federal Reserve to accelerate the growth of such variables as $R, B,$ M1, and M2 during periods of economic weakness and restrain them in periods of excessive economic activity. The Fed would then be conducting a **countercyclical monetary policy,** one that reduces swings in economic activity. However, U.S. business cycle history indicates that R and B have more often moved *procyclically* than countercyclically. And the volume of discounts and advances continues to exhibit a procyclical pattern, thus contributing to the procyclical tendencies of the monetary aggregates (see Figure 18-3).

What accounts for the procyclical movement of bank borrowing at the Fed? The answer lies in the procyclical behavior of market interest rates, coupled with the Fed's failure to change its discount rate enough to prevent important changes in the incentive for banks to borrow at the Fed. In the latter stages of the cyclical upswing, the demand for bank loans and security yields both rise in response to increased demands for credit. These forces reduce banks' desired excess reserve positions (that is, r_e declines). As more banks experience reserve deficiencies, bank activity at the discount window increases. During recessions, the demand for loans and security yields both decline, so banks' demand for excess reserves (r_e) increases. Fewer banks find themselves coming up short on reserves, and discount window borrowing declines.

This tendency for discounts and advances to move procyclically is exacerbated by the Fed's relatively timid moving of its discount rate. During cyclical expansions, as interest rates rise, the Fed is slow to raise the discount rate. The incentive to borrow at the Fed increases, as does the volume of discounts and advances. An 8 percent discount rate may appear high, but it is no deterrent to bank borrowing if money market yields are 10 or 11 percent. On the other hand, a 4 percent discount rate may seem very high to bankers if Treasury bills and the federal funds rate are in the 2 to 3 percent range. Because the

---

[8]Because banks that borrow from the Fed are under pressure to repay their loans quickly, "temporary avoidance" might more accurately describe the situation than "circumvention." Through the "hot-potato" effect, however, the banking system as a whole manages to sharply increase discounts and advances *throughout* periods of credit restraint. Thus, such variables as $R, B,$ M1, and M2 remain higher than they would in the absence of bank activity at the discount window.

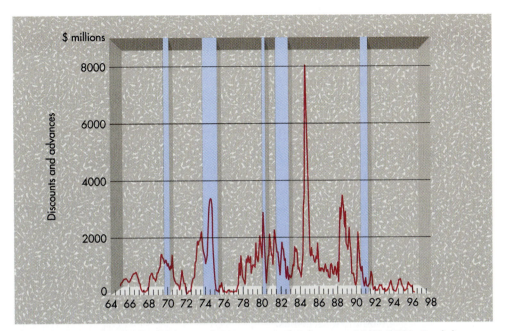

Figure 18-3   The Cyclical Pattern of Discounts and Advances, 1965–1996. Bank borrowing at the Fed exhibits a strong procyclical pattern, rising during economic expansions and declining during recessions. (Shaded areas depict periods of recession.)   *Source:* Data from *Federal Reserve Bulletin,* various issues.

Fed tends to be slow to reduce its discount rate during cyclical downturns when money market yields are falling, the incentive to borrow at the Fed declines during recessions. In short, by moving its discount rate too little and too late over the course of the business cycle, the Fed promotes a procyclical pattern in the incentive to borrow at the discount window.[9]

Ambiguous Announcement Effects

The third shortcoming of Federal Reserve discount window policy involves the ambiguous nature of the announcement effect. The Fed may change the discount rate for two reasons: to align it with other short-term interest rates or to implement a basic shift in policy. The problem lies in the fact that it is generally difficult to know which reason has motivated a given change in the discount rate. When changing the discount rate, the Fed seldom clarifies its motive. Hence, a significant possibility exists that the market will mistake the Fed's intent.

---

[9]The obvious question arises: Why does the Fed allow this to happen? Political considerations, along with the basically cautious and conservative nature of the Federal Reserve, are probably to blame. When economic activity is strong and cyclical forces have pushed interest rates to high levels, politicians seeking reelection often accuse the Fed of being too restrictive, and discussion of possible measures to reduce the Fed's independence sometimes arises. The Fed is sensitive to the charge that it is fostering high interest rates; by holding down its discount rate, the Fed is in a better position to withstand the politicians' wrath.

Given this ambiguity, some students of Federal Reserve policy believe that the announcement effect is as likely to operate perversely as it is to promote economic stability. The conclusion seems clear: the use of the discount rate to bring about monetary change is, in an age of advanced communication technology, an unreliable and outmoded type of sign language.

Proposed Reforms of Discount Window Policy

Several proposals have been advanced for changing the way discount window policy is conducted in the United States. Here, we examine two proposals: abolishing the discount window and bank borrowing from the Fed, and setting the discount rate at a "penalty" level.

Abolition of the Discount Window

Advocates of this radical proposal point out that the original purpose of the discount window—to provide a source of funds to the banking system in the event of a general panic by depositors—is now largely obsolete. The FDIC now insures most bank deposits, making a general banking panic unlikely. And such a function is redundant because the Fed can provide needed reserves to the banking system through its open market purchases of government securities.[10]

Advocates of this proposal point out that all three of the shortcomings of the Fed's discount policy would be alleviated by abolishing the discount window. Clearly, their point is indisputable! Without the opportunity to borrow at the Fed, banks could not use the discount window to circumvent Fed policy. And without bank borrowing at the Fed, discounts and advances could not behave in a procyclical fashion. Nor could discount rate changes be misinterpreted; there would be no discount rate![11]

Opponents of the proposal to abolish the discount window disagree with the premise that the discount window weakens Fed policy. On the contrary, they argue, the window serves as a "shock absorber" or "safety valve," actually *increasing* the overall effectiveness of Federal Reserve policy. Consider the conduct of monetary policy in the absence of the discount window facility. In a period of intended monetary restraint, the Fed would have to be very careful not to create a severe shortage of bank reserves. Because the discount window would be unavailable, banks caught short on reserves would be forced to dump securities or call in loans from customers. The potentially

---

[10]Before 1934, there was no national system of deposit insurance, and open market operations had not yet been developed as an effective policy instrument. Hence, the discount window provided an essential mechanism through which the banking system could obtain reserves during banking panics.

[11]Anna Schwartz presents the case for abolishing the discount window—see her 1992 article cited in "Suggestions for Additional Reading" at the end of this chapter. In addition to the points made here, Schwartz emphasizes that the Fed's discount window policy has evolved from one of lending to healthy banks with short-term reserve deficiencies to a policy of making extended loans to hundreds of banks rated as having a high probability of failure. Further, she points out that abolishing the discount window would eliminate the political pressure placed on the Fed, in this era of large budget deficits, to lend off budget to nonbanks and government agencies that are in trouble.

disruptive effect on securities markets and bank borrowers would force the Fed to be relatively timid in pursuing restrictive action, perhaps so timid as to be ineffectual. The discount window allows the Fed to use its open market tool aggressively, knowing that banks can temporarily obtain reserves through the window and adjust their balance sheets more deliberately. Thus, if the discount window is available, the Fed can act more decisively.[12]

The Penalty Discount Rate Proposal

This proposal calls for maintaining the Fed's discount window but altering the way the discount rate is set. Specifically, it calls for setting the discount rate at a fixed margin above the rate of return on banks' earning assets, such as Treasury bills and bank loans, and for borrowing at the discount window to be made a "right" rather than a "privilege." In this scheme, all adequately collateralized bank requests for credit at the discount window would be granted automatically, without question. But a discount rate set at 4 percentage points above the Treasury bill yield, or 2 percentage points above the banks' prime loan rate, would be sufficiently unattractive to eliminate the incentive to borrow from the Fed for "profit." By making borrowing at the Fed a right, yet discouraging it by making it unprofitable, banks would clearly borrow only for "need" and not for "profit."[13] Furthermore, the administrative costs of operating the discount window would be significantly reduced, with benefits accruing to the U.S. Treasury.

While maintaining the discount window's "lender-of-last-resort" function, the penalty discount rate scheme would sharply reduce any tendency for bank borrowing at the Fed to circumvent the Fed's restrictive open market operations. When the Fed sells securities and drains bank reserves during a period of rising inflation, banks would quickly liquidate Treasury bills rather than borrow at the Fed. Thus the procyclical behavior of discount window activity would be reduced or eliminated because the incentive to borrow would be stabilized over time as the discount rate would be tied to other rates. Furthermore, all announcement effects would be eliminated. Because the discount rate would be set by formula, the public would not read anything into a change in the discount rate. The Fed would then be forced to communicate policy changes in words rather than sign language.

---

[12]Those who defend the current operation of discount window policy also argue that the procyclical behavior of discounts and advances is not a serious problem. To the extent that the Fed is aware of this tendency, it can use its open market operations tool to ensure that bank reserves and the monetary base do not move procyclically, even if discounts and advances do.

[13]As indicated earlier, the Fed's rule of thumb in administering the discount window is that banks may borrow for "need" but not for "profit." Thus it has been considered improper to borrow at the Fed to buy Treasury bills or lend federal funds to secure a profit. Yet it *has* been considered legitimate to borrow at the Fed if a reserve deficiency arises while, at the same time, the bank is holding Treasury bills with yields above the discount rate. There seems to be an element of hypocrisy in the interpretation of "need" here. Clearly, in such a case, a bank could sell some Treasury bills rather than borrow at the Fed. In this sense, banks very seldom borrow for "need." They borrow because borrowing is the most profitable method of adjusting to reserve deficiencies. Setting the discount rate at a penalty level and opening up the discount window could eliminate this hypocrisy.

THE RESERVE REQUIREMENT INSTRUMENT

So far, we have analyzed two of the Fed's general tools or instruments, open market operations (Chapter 17) and discount window policy. The third major instrument of Federal Reserve policy is the authority to change the percentage reserve requirement (within limits set by Congress) applicable to demand deposits, other checkable accounts, and certain other liabilities of commercial banks and thrift institutions. Remember that reserves consist of depository institutions' holdings of vault cash plus deposits at the Federal Reserve.

Since 1935, the Federal Reserve has had the authority to set and change the reserve requirements, or required reserve ratios, which banks that are members of the Federal Reserve System must maintain. Such reserve requirements may be considered a "tax" on depository institutions, in the sense that they force those institutions to hold a larger portion of their assets in non-interest-earning form (reserves) than they would voluntarily maintain. (The reserve requirements for nonmember banks were traditionally much lower than those for member banks.[14]) When interest rates began to trend upward in the 1960s and 1970s, the magnitude of this "tax" on member banks increased and membership in the Federal Reserve System declined significantly. (Estimates of the magnitude of the reserve requirement tax during the period 1965–1995 are presented in Exhibit 18-2.) The chairman of the Board of Governors, concerned about the implications of this declining membership for the Fed's ability to control credit conditions, pleaded with Congress to force all banks to join the Federal Reserve System.

In 1980, Congress responded, though not by forcing banks to join the system. The Depository Institutions Deregulation and Monetary Control Act (DIDMCA) extended the Fed's authority to set and change reserve requirements to nonmember banks and thrift institutions—that is, savings and loan associations, mutual savings banks, and credit unions. Not just the 6000 member commercial banks but all 35,000 depository institutions in the United States were forced to abide by the reserve requirements set by the Federal Reserve.

Institutional Aspects of Reserve Requirements

DIDMCA established a new structure of reserve requirements for all banks and thrift institutions. The structure in place in 1996 is shown in Table 18-1. This scheme considerably simplified the system of reserve requirements that had been in place before 1980. The new system was designed to address the issue of equity or fairness among depository institutions, as well as the issue of monetary control. All depository institutions were made subject to a reserve requirement of 3 percent on all transactions accounts (*DDO*) up to a specified break point ($52.0 million in 1996) and 10 percent on such accounts in excess of the break point. The break point itself is indexed to the yearly increase in aggregate transactions accounts (*DDO*).

---

[14]Before federal legislation enacted in 1980, banks that were not members of the Federal Reserve System were governed by reserve requirements set by the state in which they were located. Such state reserve requirements were typically lower than those set by the Fed for the member banks. Furthermore, many states allowed banks to count certain interest-bearing assets, such as U.S. Treasury bills, as reserves for purposes of meeting the reserve requirement.

Table 18-1

Reserve Requirements Established by the Federal Reserve

Component	Current Reserve Requirement (%)	Federal Reserve Range (%)*
I. Normal reserves		
A. Transactions Accounts†		
1. First $52 million	3%	—
2. Above $52 million‡	10	8–14%
B. Nonpersonal time deposits	0	0–9
C. Eurocurrency liabilities	0	0–9
II. Supplementary reserves	0	0–4

*The Federal Reserve is authorized by Congress to change reserve requirements within these limits.
†Includes demand deposits, NOW accounts, ATS accounts, telephone transfer accounts, and share drafts.
‡This is the 1996 break point. The break point increases in December of each year by 80 percent of the percentage increase in total U.S. transactions accounts in the previous fiscal year (June 30–June 30).

Within the congressionally set ranges indicated in Table 18-1, the Federal Reserve has the authority to set reserve requirements for other bank liabilities, such as nonpersonal time deposits (large negotiable CDs) and Eurocurrency liabilities. In December 1990, the Fed eliminated its 3 percent reserve requirement on short-term nonpersonal time deposits and Eurocurrency liabilities. At the present time, the Fed levies reserve requirements only on *DDO*. The Federal Reserve is also authorized under certain conditions to invoke a supplementary reserve requirement of up to 4 percent on transactions accounts. If it does so, the Fed will pay interest on supplementary reserves at a rate that is linked to the rate the Fed earns on its portfolio of securities.

DIDMCA improved the Fed's capacity for short-run control of the money supply.[15] It did so by implementing measures to decrease the instability of r_r and the money supply

---

[15] Today there are only two categories of reserve requirements for transactions accounts. In the old system, banks were subject to a progressive structure of five levels of reserve requirements, ranging from 7 percent on the first $2 million of transactions accounts to a top rate of 16¼ percent on deposits in excess of $400 million. Also, nonmember banks were subject to a wide range of reserve requirements set by the individual states. Under the pre-1980 regime, therefore, the transfer of funds among banks of different size and membership status introduced instability into r_r, the money supply multiplier, and the money supply itself. By reducing these instabilities, the Monetary Control Act strengthened the Fed's grip over the nation's money supply (hence the name of the legislation). However, economists of monetarist persuasion are not satisfied. They point out that even the current two-tier system (3 percent and 10 percent) leaves unnecessary and undesirable variability in the money supply multiplier. They would propose going to one flat rate (perhaps 9 percent) for all transactions deposits in all depository institutions. (See Table 18-1.)

EXHIBIT 18-2

The Reserve Requirement Tax

Banks do not earn interest on bank reserves, which include cash on hand plus deposits at the Federal Reserve. Cash obviously pays no interest, and the Federal Reserve has never been authorized by Congress to pay interest on deposits banks keep at the Fed. Therefore, in forcing banks to maintain more reserves than they would voluntarily keep, the government is essentially imposing a tax on banks. The magnitude of the tax depends on the level of interest rates and the amount of reserves banks must maintain over and above what they would voluntarily keep.

When a tax is levied on any entity—an individual, a nonfinancial company, or a financial firm such as a bank—that entity will alter its behavior in an effort to avoid the tax. Before 1980, one way banks reacted to the reserve requirement tax was to opt for nonmembership in the Federal Reserve System, so as to enjoy lower reserve requirements. Another important reaction of banks has been to develop new financial instruments that are substitutes for demand deposits but are not subject to reserve requirements. Examples of such financial innovations include repurchase agreements and negotiable CDs. In an overnight repurchase agreement, a large bank trades securities for its biggest customers' (typically large firms) demand deposits at the end of the day, with an agreement to reverse the transaction the next morning. The transaction reduces the bank's reported *DDO,* lowering the amount of reserves it is required to maintain. The depositor also earns a respectable return by engaging in the transaction. At the opening of business the next day, the bank "repurchases" the securities from the depositor, replenishing the depositor's account and making the funds available for the customer's use.

Such behavior by banks reduces the Fed's effectiveness in conducting monetary policy, because it tends to destabilize the velocity of money—the multiplier that links the nation's money supply to its gross domestic product. One way of reducing the banks' incentive to circumvent reserve requirements would be by paying them interest on their reserves. In fact, the Fed has made that proposal to Congress numerous times, but to no avail. Paying interest on reserves would cost the Fed (and hence taxpayers) billions of dollars each year.

---

multiplier. By forcing all depository institutions to abide by a uniform set of reserve requirements and by replacing the complicated, progressive structure of reserve requirements in place before 1980 with a simpler scheme, the Fed reduced instability in r_r and the money supply multiplier.

Banks' Management of the Reserve Position

Before 1984, the dollar volume of required reserves to be held in a given settlement period was based on average deposits held *2 weeks earlier.* This system of *lagged reserve accounting* allowed each bank to know with certainty its precise amount of required re-

EXHIBIT 18-2 (CONTINUED)

The accompanying figure shows the magnitude of the reserve requirement tax, which ratcheted upward after 1965, reaching more than $2 billion in 1981, when interest rates skyrocketed to record levels. By 1996, the reserve requirement tax had been reduced by approximately 50 percent, following sharp declines in interest rates and the percentage reserve requirement.

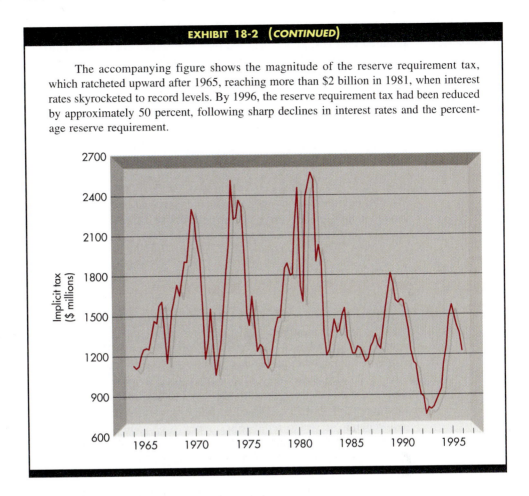

serves for a given week even before the week began. Because this lagged reserve system posed problems for the Federal Reserve in exerting monetary control, however, it was abandoned in 1984 in favor of the current system of *contemporaneous reserve accounting*. The Federal Reserve facilitates the management of depository institutions' reserve positions through reserve averaging and the use of a carryover allowance.

Reserve Averaging

Banks and thrift institutions are not asked to meet the required reserve ratio each day but must average it over the settlement period, a 2-week period that ends on a Wednesday. Thus, if a depository institution comes up short of the reserve requirement each day until the last day of the settlement period, it can still abide by the reserve requirement by exhibiting a substantial amount of excess reserves on Wednesday. For this reason, Wednesdays tend to be characterized by considerable activity in the financial markets.

Carryover Allowance Reserve deficiencies or excesses, up to a maximum of 2 percent of the dollar amount of required reserves, may be carried over one settlement period. This feature eliminates the need for many depository institutions to scramble at the end of a settlement period either to obtain reserves or to rid themselves of them.

ECONOMIC EFFECTS OF CHANGES IN THE RESERVE REQUIREMENT

We will now look at the way in which changes in the reserve requirement influence the money supply. Along the way, we will also examine the strengths and weaknesses of changes in reserve requirements as a tool of Federal Reserve policy.

Influence on the Money Supply

In Chapter 15, we pointed out that a change in reserve requirements impinges on the money supply in a different way than open market operations or changes in discount window policy do. Whereas the latter instruments derive their influence predominantly by changing the monetary base, changes in reserve requirements leave the base unaltered but directly change the money supply multiplier. A reduction in reserve requirements increases the money supply multiplier—that is, it increases the total amount of bank credit and money supply that can be supported by a given monetary base. An increase in reserve requirements serves to reduce the money supply multiplier by reducing the amount of bank credit, deposits, and money supply consistent with a given monetary base.

It is instructive to review two basic expressions from Chapter 15 here:

$$(18\text{-}1) \qquad m_1 = \frac{1 + k}{r_r + r_e + k}$$

$$(18\text{-}2) \qquad r_r = \frac{\text{Required reserves}}{\text{Total } DDO}$$

Equation 18-1 expresses the money supply multiplier (for M1) in terms of its three fundamental determinants: the currency ratio (k), the weighted-average required reserve ratio (r_r), and the desired excess reserve ratio (r_e). Equation 18-2 defines the weighted-average required reserve ratio, r_r, as the ratio of the dollar amount of required reserves to the total amount of transactions accounts—demand deposits and other checkable deposits (DDO).

Note that r_r will be affected by the clearing of checks between depository institutions which have different marginal reserve requirements. For example, when a check written on a $200 million bank is deposited in a $30 million bank and clears, r_r declines. Thus, clearing of checks among banks of different sizes introduces short-run variation into r_r and the money supply multiplier. This is one reason why the Federal Reserve is able to exert considerably more accurate control over the average money supply on a quarterly basis than on a daily or weekly basis.

In Chapter 15, we sketched the impact of an increase in r_r on the money supply multiplier. Let us now analyze both the arithmetic and the economics of a reduction in the required reserve ratio, with a view toward understanding the behavioral phenomena that cause the change in the money supply multiplier and the money stock.

Suppose initially that $r_r = 0.10$, $k = 0.40$, and $r_e = .005$. Using the expression for the money supply multiplier (Equation 18-1), we compute

$$m_1 = \frac{1 + .40}{0.10 + .005 + .40} = \frac{1.40}{.505} = 2.77$$

We see that each dollar of monetary base supports \$2.77 worth of money supply (M1). Now suppose that as a result of an across-the-board reduction of reserve requirements on demand deposits, r_r is reduced from .10 to .09—that is, from 10 percent to 9 percent. We calculate the new money supply multiplier as follows:

$$m_1 = \frac{1 + .40}{.09 + .005 + .40} = \frac{1.40}{.495} = 2.83$$

Assuming that the currency ratio (k) and the desired excess reserve ratio (r_e) are not induced to change by the reduction in r_r, the money supply multiplier (m_1) rises from 2.77 to 2.83. This represents an approximately 2 percent increase in both the money supply multiplier and M1.

In this example, when the Fed reduces the reserve requirement, the monetary base is unaltered. Bank reserves are also unaltered. However, a smaller portion of the existing base and reserves is impounded, or "frozen," in the form of required reserves. And a greater portion of the base and reserves now qualifies as excess reserves, available for the purpose of extending bank credit—that is, acquiring earning assets in the form of loans and securities. Because existing excess reserves are boosted above desired excess reserves by the reduction in r_r, banks expand their loans and security holdings. Demand deposits are created for those who take out loans and for those who sell securities to banks. Thus, the money supply increases.

As banks make loans and purchase securities, thereby expanding *DDO* in the system, the dollar magnitude of required reserves rises. In this way, the volume of excess reserves is gradually reduced until it comes into equilibrium with the desired amount, as indicated by r_e. At this point, the acquisition of banks' earning assets ceases and the money supply reaches a new equilibrium. Given a multiplier of 2.83, this new equilibrium occurs at a level of M1 about 2 percent above the initial level.

The increased supply of bank loans to the public that was induced by the reduction in r_r tends to trigger a reduction in bank loan rates. Also, the increased demand for Treasury securities by banks tends to drive up the prices of securities, thus reducing their yields. One would therefore normally expect a reduction in reserve requirements to be followed by a general reduction in interest rates. Indeed, this is quite consistent with the

---

EXHIBIT 18-3

Reserve Requirement Changes in the 1990s

While changes in reserve requirements are capable of influencing the nation's credit conditions, interest rates, and money supply, they have other important implications as well. In the 1990s, changes in reserve requirements have been implemented with those other factors foremost in mind.

Reserve requirements have been reduced twice in the 1990s. Neither measure was implemented principally to boost economic activity. How do we know? Because in each case the potentially stimulative effects of the reserve requirement cuts were neutralized by open market sales of securities by the Federal Reserve System. In December 1990, the Fed eliminated its 3 percent reserve requirement on nonpersonal savings and time deposits (large negotiable CDs) and on banks' Eurocurrency liabilities. In December 1992, the Fed reduced the reserve requirement for *DDO* in each bank above the break-point magnitude ($52.0 million in 1996) from 12 percent to 10 percent. Each of these measures created more than $10 billion of excess reserves, which the Fed immediately mopped up through open market sales of government securities.

The level of reserve requirements has important implications for the way in which the profits associated with money creation are distributed between banks and the government. If reserve requirements are high, bank profits will be relatively low. A larger portion of each bank's assets must be held in non-interest-bearing form (reserves). By the same token, higher reserve requirements imply a smaller money supply multiplier. This, in turn, implies that the monetary base must be larger in order to achieve the Fed's desired money supply target. To provide a larger monetary base, the Fed must hold a larger portfolio of securities. A side effect of a larger Fed security portfolio is more revenues for the Fed and hence for the U.S. Treasury. Higher reserve requirements imply lower profits for banks and larger revenues for the Fed and the U.S. Treasury.

In the 1980s, the balance sheets and earnings of U.S. banks were ravaged by widespread problem loans in the agricultural and oil sectors, as well as by bad loans by many of the nation's largest banks to such less developed countries as Brazil, Mexico, and Argentina. Some observers felt the nation's banks were destined to suffer the same debacle as the savings and loan industry had gone through. Largely out of concern for the weakened condition of many of the nation's banks, in 1990 and 1992 the Fed made the decision to cut its reserve requirements. This decision effectively transferred some of the revenues normally earned by the Federal Reserve (and routinely turned over to the U.S. Treasury) to American banks. This subtle measure, which went almost unnoticed by the American press, was politically easier to implement than more overt and direct subsidies from taxpayers to the nation's ailing depository institutions would have been.

---

objective of the monetary authorities: to increase the willingness of individuals and firms to borrow and spend on goods and services, thus stimulating economic activity. Exhibit 18-3 discusses reserve requirement changes implemented in the 1990s.

In the remainder of this chapter, we will discuss the advantages and disadvantages of the reserve requirement instrument.

Advantages of the Reserve Requirement Tool

We will now outline some of the advantages of using the reserve requirement tool relative to the use of open market operations and discount window policy.

Speed of Impact

Changes in the reserve requirement induce banks to make balance sheet adjustments quite rapidly. When the Fed changes r_r, thousands of banks and thrift institutions experience an immediate change in their excess reserve positions. Therefore, changes in interest rates, credit conditions, and the monetary aggregates occur relatively quickly. This contrasts with open market operations, which impinge immediately only on those banks in which government securities dealers maintain accounts. Some time may elapse before the impact of open market operations extends to the majority of banks. Likewise, a change in the Fed's discount rate may not exert any immediate impact on those institutions not currently borrowing or contemplating borrowing at the discount window. Therefore, if economic conditions require *immediate* action, use of the reserve requirement tool may be preferable to the Fed's other instruments.

Neutrality

A related argument is that the reserve requirement instrument is less discriminatory across depository institutions than are the other instruments of Federal Reserve policy. The impact of reserve requirement changes is spread across all banks and thrift institutions uniformly. One may therefore prefer the use of this instrument on the basis that many more institutions are influenced in a similar way than is the case with the other instruments.

More Straightforward Announcement Effect

Because this instrument is not employed frequently, and because changes in the reserve requirement are typically not made for purely technical reasons (unlike the use of open market operations for defensive purposes and changes in the discount rate to align it with other yields), changes in the reserve requirement are usually easy to interpret. A cut in the reserve requirement can usually be interpreted to signal an easing in the basic posture of monetary policy. Hence, if the Fed strongly desires to communicate a policy change to the public, this tool may be superior to the other tools. However, it is difficult to see how this instrument would be as effective as a public statement of policy intent. The use of any type of sign language in place of verbal language is difficult to rationalize.

Potential Use in an Emergency

At times when other tools cannot do the job, changes in the reserve requirement may be needed to neutralize major changes in the monetary base. In time of war, for instance, the government generally finances an increased level of expenditures by issuing short-term and long-term securities. To assist the Treasury in financing the effort without incurring exorbitant interest expense, the Fed may help by purchasing significantly larger than normal quantities of securities on the open market. But although this helps the Treasury, it also paves the way for an inflationary expansion of credit and money, because it directly expands bank reserves and the monetary base. In this case, the open market securities purchase could be combined with an increase in reserve requirements to avoid triggering a multiple expansion of deposits in the banking system. That is, as the monetary base is expanded by the Fed's security purchases, the money supply multiplier would be reduced by the increase in required reserves and r_r. In this way, money supply growth could be limited to a rate consistent with the Fed's overall objectives.

Disadvantages of the Reserve Requirement Tool

Many bankers would like to see the Fed abandon the use of the reserve requirement instrument as a regular tool of monetary policy. And many economists would agree, primarily on the basis that in most instances, the Fed's objectives can be achieved more easily and smoothly via other policy instruments. A couple of points have been raised in support of the view that the level of reserve requirements should remain fixed over time and that the Fed should accomplish its aims through its other policy tools. We will now examine the disadvantages of the reserve requirement tool.

Bluntness

Given that today aggregate *DDO* is in the vicinity of $1 trillion, a 1 percentage point reduction (increase) in the reserve requirement would release (absorb) $10 billion of excess reserves. Such a magnitude is simply too large to warrant regular manipulation of the reserve requirement. In fact, use of the reserve requirement tool has been likened to the use of an ax by a surgeon. By contrast, open market operations may be calibrated to bring about small, continuous changes in reserves and the monetary aggregates. Open market operations are thus a much more sensitive mechanism for bringing about monetary change.

Of course, this argument depends on the assumption that changes in the reserve requirement must come in full percentage point doses. In principle, reserve requirements could be changed by 0.1 percentage point, 0.002 percentage point, or any other magnitude needed to produce a more moderate change in the money supply and credit conditions. The standard rebuttal to this point is that it would be administratively costly to depository institutions to implement frequent, tiny changes in their reserve requirements.

Lack of Flexibility

Suppose the Fed raises the reserve requirement with the intent of restricting aggregate expenditures to combat inflationary pressures. Suppose that, a couple of weeks later, it becomes clear to most observers that unemployment and underutilization of capacity are emerging as more serious problems than inflation. Then a *reduction* of reserve requirements would be called for. However, given that the Fed had recently *raised* reserve requirements, a reversal of direction would constitute an admission of error. Some observers believe the Fed would be unwilling to admit the error and would be likely to maintain the status quo until the evidence of a need for monetary stimulus became overwhelming.

Open market operations have a decided advantage in this regard, both because it is very difficult for the public to pinpoint the changes in the dynamic thrust of open market operations and because such actions have little overt announcement effect. If the Fed switches direction in its open market operations, only the most astute observers will detect the switch. In a sense, the vanity of human beings (and Federal Reserve officials) is responsible for the inflexibility, which would likely impede the regular use of reserve requirement changes as an effective instrument of Federal Reserve policy.

Moreover, frequent changes in reserve requirements create uncertainty for banks and make bank liquidity management more difficult. Raising the level of reserve requirements can also trigger liquidity problems for banks. For this reason, the Federal Reserve has displayed a much stronger propensity to implement reductions in reserve requirements than increases. In the past 40 years, there have been approximately twice as many reserve requirement reductions as increases, and the top reserve requirement rate for *DDO* has declined from 26 percent in the early 1950s to 10 percent today. The reserve requirement tool is actually redundant in the sense that the Fed's objectives can be amply met through open market operations coupled with discount window policy. In sum, a strong case can be made for choosing an optimal level of reserve requirements and simply leaving them at that level indefinitely.

SUMMARY

Although the Fed's chief tool of monetary policy is open market operations, the Fed has two other general policy tools at its disposal: discount window policy and reserve requirement policy. Together, these tools give the Fed strong ammunition to influence bank lending, the monetary aggregates, and credit conditions. Changes in the Fed's discount rate influence interest rates, the monetary aggregates, and the monetary outlook. When the Fed increases its discount rate, other interest rates move in sympathy and the money supply tends to fall. When the Fed cuts its discount rate, interest rates generally decline and the monetary aggregates increase. Changing the reserve requirement is potentially a very powerful tool of policy. An increase in reserve requirements reduces the money supply multiplier and the monetary aggregates and boosts interest rates. A reduction in reserve requirements increases the money supply multiplier and the monetary aggregates and reduces interest rates. Reserve requirements may be regarded as a tax on banks, increasing the portion of a bank's total assets that must be held in the non-interest-bearing form of cash and deposits at the Fed. Because a high level of reserve requirements tends to increase banks' incentives to develop new demand deposit substitutes not subject to the requirements, the Fed's ability to control aggregate expenditures may be weakened by high reserve requirements. In part because of this reason, central banks around the world have been moving to reduce or eliminate reserve requirements.

KEY TERMS

discount window
discounts and advances
adjustment credit
seasonal credit

extended credit
emergency credit
countercyclical monetary policy

STUDY QUESTIONS

1   Present a step-by-step explanation of the mechanism through which an unexpected cut in the Federal Reserve discount rate might affect

   a   The level of short-term interest rates

   b   M1

2   Analyze the argument that the existence of the Federal Reserve discount window creates a loophole through which the banking system is able to circumvent the Federal Reserve's efforts to exert monetary control.

3 "Far from creating a loophole in Federal Reserve monetary control, the existence of the discount window significantly strengthens overall Fed policy." Do you agree or disagree? Explain.

4 Explain why, historically, the volume of discounts and advances has exhibited a *procyclical* pattern. What change in the *modus operandi* of the Federal Reserve would reduce or eliminate this tendency? Explain.

5 Analyze the proposal to abolish the discount window—that is, to abolish all bank borrowing at the Federal Reserve.

6 Analyze the proposal to set the discount rate at a penalty level and, at the same time, to make depository institution borrowing at the Fed a right rather than a privilege.

7 In what sense are reserve requirements a "tax" on depository institutions? What problems does this "tax" create? Explain. How could this "tax" be eliminated?

8 Explain why the reserve requirement changes enacted in DIDMCA enhanced the ability of the Federal Reserve to accurately control the behavior of the money supply.

9 Explain on a step-by-step basis the mechanism through which an increase in reserve requirements applicable to *DDO* influences interest rates and the supply of money.

10 Analyze the advantages and disadvantages of the use of the reserve requirement as a tool of policy relative to the use of open market operations.

11 Explain how the level of reserve requirements influences

   a The profitability of depository institutions

   b Revenues generated for the Treasury by the Fed

12 Suppose the Fed engages in major open market sales of U.S. Treasury securities to prop up a falling dollar.

   a What happens to security prices and yields?

   b What happens to the spread between the T-bill yield and the discount rate?

   c What is likely to happen to the volume of discounts and advances?

   d What are the implications of part *c* for the Fed's effectiveness?

13 In the spring of 1995, the FOMC voted to increase *both* the discount rate and the federal funds rate by 0.5 percentage point. This followed six previous hikes in the federal funds rate. What might this action signal to you? Was there any ambiguity in the Fed's motive for hiking the discount rate? Explain.

14 Suppose the Fed decides to float the discount rate, linking it to the federal funds rate exactly 1 percentage point *below* that rate. What problems of discount policy would be solved by this procedure? What problems would not be solved?

15 Is the discount window an obsolete concept? Why or why not? Why might the Fed be reluctant to eliminate the discount window?

16 Discuss *two* ways in which the Depository Institutions Deregulation and Monetary Control Act (DIDMCA) enhanced monetary control in the United States.

17 Evaluate the Fed's current structure of reserve requirements. Is there room for improvement? In what sense?

18 After a period of remarkable economic stability, the Fed reduces the discount rate by 1 percentage point.

   a What happens to the federal funds rate-discount rate spread and discounts and advances?

   b What happens to bank lending and security holdings?

   c What happens to market yields?

SUGGESTIONS FOR ADDITIONAL READING

A straightforward discussion of discount window policy is provided in David L. Mengle, "The Discount Window," in Timothy Cook and Robert LaRoche, *Instruments of the Money Market,* 7th ed. (Richmond: Federal Reserve Bank of Richmond, 1993). Detailed information on matters of discount window administration is provided in *The Federal Reserve Discount Window* (Washington, D.C.: Federal Reserve System, 1990). For an update on the discount window, see "Recent Developments in Discount Window Policy," *Federal Reserve Bulletin,* November 1994, pp. 965–977. A good empirical study of the determinants of discount window borrowing is Kausar Hamdani and Stavros Peristiani, "A Disaggregate Analysis of Discount Window Borrowing," Federal Reserve Bank of New York *Quarterly Review,* Summer 1991, pp. 52–62. On the effects of discount rate changes on money market yields, see Michael Dueker, "The Response of Market Interest Rates to Discount Rate Changes," Federal Reserve Bank of St. Louis *Review,* July–August 1992, pp. 78–91. A critical view of the Fed's discount window procedures is presented in Anna J. Schwartz, "The Mis-

use of the Fed's Discount Window," Federal Reserve Bank of St. Louis, *Review,* September–October 1992, pp. 58–69. On the reserve requirement instrument, excellent general references include Marvin Goodfriend and Monica Hargraves, "A Historical Assessment of the Rationales and Functions of Reserve Requirements," Federal Reserve Bank of Richmond *Economic Review,* March–April 1983, pp. 3–21, and Ann-Marie Muelendyke, "Reserve Requirements and the Discount Window in Recent Decades," Federal Reserve Bank of New York *Quarterly Review,* Autumn 1992, pp. 25–43. Also see Stuart Weiner, "The Changing Role of Reserve Requirements in Monetary Policy," Federal Reserve Bank of Kansas City *Economic Review,* 4 (1992), pp. 45–63. to exert monetary control, see Michael Klein, "Monetary Control Implications of the Monetary Control Act," Federal Reserve Bank of San Francisco *Review,* Winter 1981. Finally, on the role of reserve requirements, see E. J. Stevens, "Is There Any Rationale for Reserve Requirements?," Federal Reserve Bank of Cleveland *Economic Review,* 1991, 3d quarter, pp. 2–17.

■ **Conducting Monetary Policy:
Ultimate Goals
and Intermediate Targets**

I n the last two chapters, we analyzed the tools of monetary policy. In this chapter, we sketch the ultimate goals or objectives of monetary policy, such as maintaining price level stability. The link between the Fed's policy tools, which it controls precisely, and its goals or objectives, is highly uncertain and variable. Changes in the Federal Reserve's discount rate or securities portfolio may take a year or longer to impact aggregate output, employment, and the nation's price level. For this reason, the Federal Reserve aims instead for certain *intermediate targets* that are thought to be strongly linked to aggregate expenditures and the Fed's ultimate policy goals. In this chapter, after briefly sketching the goals of Federal Reserve policy, we will discuss the procedure of using intermediate targets in the conduct of monetary policy. In Chapter 24, we will return to the subject of intermediate targets of Fed policy and treat the issue more analytically.

THE ULTIMATE GOALS OF MONETARY POLICY

The ultimate objectives of the Federal Reserve are achievement of a relatively stable price level, maintenance of a high employment level (a low unemployment rate), fostering of a stable dollar exchange rate vis-à-vis the currencies of other major industrial nations, and encouragement of long-term economic growth.[1] We will briefly discuss each of these objectives.

---

[1]Other goals of monetary policy, such as maintaining stable interest rates and stable financial markets, are sometimes mentioned. Such goals may be considered important to the extent that they contribute to the four chief goals mentioned here or enhance economic efficiency.

Price Level Stability

A traditional goal of central banks is maintenance of price level stability. In the United States, the Federal Reserve has long been considered a guardian of the nation's price level, providing something of an antidote to the fiscal imprudence of Congress.

Maintenance of price stability is a major policy goal because of inflation's negative consequences. Inflation capriciously redistributes the nation's income, simultaneously helping some families and impairing others' buying power. In the process, it inevitably creates tension among various groups in society. Inflation also creates uncertainty, thereby reducing investment expenditures on plant, equipment, and technology. The reduction in investment slows the long-term growth of the nation's capital stock, thereby slowing the growth of living standards. And inflation misallocates resources by creating a discrepancy between the type of behavior that is rational for an individual and that which is optimal for society as a whole. For example, in a period of inflation it pays a business firm or individual to spend more time on financial affairs, including learning about hedging and other ways of protecting against inflation. From society's vantage point, such behavior is inefficient because it constitutes a waste of resources. Finally, by obscuring the behavior of the *relative* prices of goods and services, inflation also impairs the efficiency of the price mechanism in allocating resources, thereby reducing economic efficiency.

In the 1970s, severe inflation (an average of 7 percent a year) doubled the U.S. price level within a decade. Since then, inflation has been relatively subdued, averaging less than 4 percent per year after 1982. Because the nation's chief price indexes (the consumer price index and producer price index) tend to overstate the true inflation rate, most economists believe that a 1 percent reported inflation rate implies essential price level stability. During most of the past 15 years, the inflation rate has been stuck in the 2.5 to 4 percent range. The desirability of implementing measures to reduce the inflation rate to zero has been the subject of debate within the Federal Reserve System and among economists in general. In recent years, the central banks of several countries have formally adopted a zero-inflation goal. In New Zealand, the officers of the central bank set a low-inflation goal and have to resign if inflation exceeds that goal.

Full Employment

For many reasons, a high employment level is one of the paramount goals of monetary policy. Unemployment deprives families of their chief source of income, triggers a host of social problems such as increased incidence of crime and mental illness, and impacts most heavily on the disadvantaged and those at the lower end of the income scale. Collectively, increased unemployment reduces the nation's level of output and income as well as tax revenues at all levels of government, thereby impairing such public services as roads, police protection, and education. For these reasons, both the Employment Act of 1946 and the Full Employment and Balanced Growth Act of 1978 (commonly known as the Humphrey-Hawkins Act) commit the U.S. government to maintain a high level of employment, consistent with price level stability.

Monetary policy affects the unemployment rate by influencing aggregate expenditures on goods and services and the level of the nation's gross domestic product (GDP). As monetary policy becomes more stimulative, aggregate expenditures and GDP increase and the unemployment rate falls, sometimes below the natural rate. The **natural unemployment rate** is defined as the lowest level at which the nation's unemployment rate can be maintained without triggering an increase in the existing inflation rate. If monetary policy becomes too stimulative and the nation's unemployment rate falls below the natural rate, inflation accelerates. Hence, a goal of Federal Reserve policy is maintenance of the nation's unemployment rate as close as possible to the natural unemployment rate without going below it. Unfortunately, the natural unemployment rate changes over time and is uncertain at any point in time. Most economists believe it is currently somewhere in the 5 to 6 percent range.

Stable Exchange Rate

When the dollar fluctuates dramatically in foreign exchange markets, costs are involved. Volatile exchange rates may impair international economic activity, reducing international trade and worldwide economic efficiency. As discussed in Chapter 8, a sharply falling dollar stimulates U.S. inflation because the cost of imported goods rises while pressure on domestic firms to hold down their prices is reduced. Indeed, a chronically depreciating currency is often interpreted as reflecting underlying structural problems in a nation's economy. In the mid-1990s, the Federal Reserve became concerned about the persistent depreciation of the dollar vis-à-vis the Japanese yen and the German mark.

On the other hand, an excessively strong currency can also be detrimental to a nation. Domestic products can be priced out of world markets by an overvalued currency. For example, during 1983 and 1984, the dollar appreciated strongly against the Japanese yen and other currencies. A flood of inexpensive imported autos and other products caused heavy unemployment in the American automobile industry and other sectors subject to foreign competition. For these reasons, a stable exchange rate, at an appropriate level, is one of the goals of Federal Reserve policy.

Long-Term Economic Growth

The long-term growth of a nation's real GDP is crucial because it determines the fate of living standards over the long haul. Societies that do not increase the average output produced per person over time simply cannot experience rising living standards. The chief determinants of long-term economic growth are the growth rate of the stocks of physical and human capital (the skills and education embodied in the workforce), as well as the rate of technological change. Investment in plant, equipment, technology, and human capital is the key to long-term economic growth.

The Fed's role in this process is relatively simple. It must foster a stable financial climate with low inflation in order to facilitate low levels of long-term interest rates and high levels of investment expenditures. Because inflation creates uncertainty and impairs investment spending, it is essential that the Fed remain vigilant against inflation if satisfactory long-term growth is to be experienced.[2] To contribute to long-term growth, the Fed must also try to prevent or reduce the severity and duration of recessions.

In times of recession, investment spending declines. This means the nation's capital stock will be permanently lower than would have been the case if the recession had been prevented or moderated. Thus, by contributing to economic stability and preventing severe economic downturns, the Fed contributes positively to long-term economic growth.

Having sketched the ultimate goals of Fed policy, we are now prepared to examine the intermediate targets the Fed employs in its effort to achieve those goals.

INTERMEDIATE MONETARY POLICY TARGETS

In order to monitor its week-to-week progress in attaining policy goals, the Fed needs to employ a variable that both responds sensitively to the Fed's policy tools and strongly influences aggregate expenditures, thereby helping to achieve the Fed's policy goals. Assume the Fed desires the nation's nominal GDP to rise at a 6 percent rate over the next year. The Fed can influence GDP growth only indirectly. Suppose the Fed's research staff believes that 4 percent growth in M2 would lead to 6 percent growth in nominal GDP. Then the Fed will target M2 to expand at a 4 percent rate in the next year. In this case, M2 would be selected as an **intermediate target of monetary policy**—that is, a variable whose magnitude the Fed attempts to control in order to achieve its policy goals.

Considerable disagreement exists among professional economists (and among individual members of the Federal Open Market Committee) concerning the appropriate variables to select as intermediate targets of monetary policy. There is no consensus as to which variable or variables the Fed should attempt to control during a given week or month in order to achieve, for example, a boost in aggregate expenditures and a reduction in the nation's unemployment rate.

It might seem more reasonable to specify targets in terms of the Federal Reserve's policy tools. Suppose the economy is in a severe recession and the Fed desires to implement a stimulative monetary policy. What would be wrong with using as the Fed's policy target, say, a 10 percent growth rate of the Fed's portfolio of government securities? Or, alternatively, a 0.1 percent reduction each month in the percentage reserve

---

[2]The *mix* of monetary and fiscal policy is important to long-term growth because it helps to determine long-term interest rates. Investment expenditures depend on long-term interest rates, especially long-term *real* interest rates. A stimulative fiscal policy (large budget deficits) coupled with restrictive monetary policy (slow or negative money growth) is a bad mix for long-term economic growth because it produces relatively high long-term real interest rates. The reverse mix—restrictive fiscal policy (low budget deficits or budget surpluses) coupled with stimulative monetary policy—is likely to lead to low real long-term interest rates, greater investment expenditures, and more rapid long-term growth. In this sense, measures to reduce the federal structural budget deficit and thereby allow room for more stimulative Federal Reserve policy are conducive to improved long-term economic growth.

requirement applicable to *DDO*? Since the Fed has total control over its own securities portfolio and reserve requirements, it should be feasible to achieve those desired magnitudes with precision. At first blush, therefore, it might seem desirable to employ these variables as targets, rather than variables over which the Fed exerts less-than-total influence.

The problem with this approach is that the impact of a given change in the Fed's policy tools on aggregate expenditures and its ultimate policy goals is highly uncertain. The rigid change in the policy instruments may be either reinforced or counteracted by other factors. During a given week or month, a 10 percent rate of increase in the Fed's securities portfolio might very well be consistent with a zero or even negative growth rate of bank reserves, the monetary base, M1, and M2. On the other hand, a 10 percent growth rate might also result in a 20 percent or higher growth rate of reserves, the monetary base, M1, and M2. As emphasized in Chapters 14 and 15, many factors besides Federal Reserve policy influence the monetary base, bank reserves, and the nation's money supply. The same point holds regarding interest rates, which are heavily influenced by business cycle developments, inflationary expectations, and other factors besides Federal Reserve policy. Because the Fed is only one of many players that influence such crucial variables as bank reserves, the monetary base, the money supply, and interest rates, it must retain flexibility in the use of its policy tools to achieve maximum influence over those variables.

Criteria for an Effective Intermediate Target

In order for a particular variable to be a good intermediate target of Federal Reserve policy, it must be measurable. That is, accurate data on the variable must be available on a timely basis. In addition, the Fed must be capable of accurately controlling or at least strongly influencing the intermediate target variable. Finally, the variable must be strongly linked in a causal way to such variables as aggregate expenditures, nominal GDP, unemployment, and price level behavior. In other words, the variable should be an important determinant of aggregate expenditures and the final goals of monetary policy. We will discuss these characteristics in turn.

Measurability

Accurate, timely measurement is essential for a suitable intermediate target variable. The Fed cannot shoot for a 4 percent growth rate for M2 if there is no way to get an accurate reading on M2. Nor can the Fed hit a daily interest rate target if data are not available on the interest rate in question. On the measurability criterion, interest rates score exceptionally high, because continuous, accurate readings are available on the federal funds rate, Treasury bill yields, government bond yields, and other interest rates. Furthermore, interest rate data are seldom subject to revision. *Real* interest rates do not fare as well (particularly real *long-term* yields) because of the difficulty in accurately measuring inflation expectations. The monetary aggregates (M1, M2, M3) score somewhat lower than interest rates on this criterion because they are available only with a 2-week delay and are subject to significant revision even later.

Controllability

If a particular variable is to be a useful intermediate target, the Fed must be capable of exerting predominant influence over it in the short run. In the parlance of economists, an intermediate target variable should not be *endogenous,* or strongly influenced by such forces as the business cycle and inflation expectations. Interest rates are said to be endogenous because they are heavily influenced by business cycle forces and the outlook for inflation. Because the Fed exerts only marginal influence over long-term interest rates, they are not a satisfactory intermediate target of monetary policy.

A variable that is not significantly influenced by the business cycle and other economic forces, called an *exogenous* variable, is a more appropriate intermediate target. The Fed may face little difficulty in dictating the magnitude of such variables, which are "sitting ducks" rather than moving targets. Ideally, an intermediate target variable would be entirely exogenous and controllable by the Federal Reserve. In the real world, however, the variables proposed as intermediate targets are neither totally exogenous nor totally endogenous. Part of the disagreement among economists over the appropriate variable to be chosen as an intermediate target stems from disagreements concerning the Fed's ability to exert short-run control over various variables.[3] (Shortly, we will discuss an example of the Fed's employment of an endogenous intermediate target variable.)

Importance   That the behavior of the intermediate target should contribute significantly to the policy goals is obvious. If the Fed is capable of exerting complete control over a particular variable but the variable is found to have no influence on the ultimate objectives of Fed policy, the variable is irrelevant. (The Fed can, for example, exert absolute control over the number of cars in its fleet, but no one proposes the Fed automobile fleet as an intermediate target of monetary policy.) If the Fed selects an unimportant variable as its intermediate target, at best it is misallocating time and effort in controlling the variable. At worst, it may be doing considerable damage to the economy because efforts to control the *irrelevant* variable may be incompatible with the appropriate movement of the *relevant* variables. In focusing on the irrelevant variable, the Fed may inadvertently cause the important variables to move in the wrong direction. The Fed has frequently been attacked in the past for making precisely this mistake.

Net Free Reserves: A Flawed Intermediate Target

An example of the problems caused by the choice of a highly endogenous variable as a target was the use in the 1950s and 1960s of **net free reserves (NFR)** as an intermediate target. NFR is defined as aggregate excess reserves held by depository institutions minus the volume of discounts and advances—that is, the volume of bank borrowing at the Fed. Economists believed that by focusing on a variable constructed from *excess* reserves rather than *total* reserves, they had selected a superior target. (A major and fluctuating portion of total reserves is required to be held and is therefore not available for purposes of extending bank credit, while excess reserves are potentially available to create new credit.) Net free reserves were thought to be a better target than excess reserves because the latter variable includes a relatively large and volatile portion of *borrowed reserves*—that is, discounts and advances—and banks are believed to be reluctant to extend

---

[3]An even greater source of dispute concerns the relative *importance* of different variables in exerting influence over economic activity and achieving policy goals.

credit on the basis of borrowed reserves. Thus, by subtracting borrowed reserves from excess reserves, economists believed that they had derived the ideal intermediate target.

If the Fed desired to implement a more stimulative policy, it would raise its target for NFR, perhaps from $1.2 billion to $1.5 billion. To hit this target, the Fed would purchase securities in the open market. Bank reserves and excess reserves would rise, and banks would tend to pay off some of their debt at the discount window. NFR would therefore increase. Banks, having more NFR, would tend to expand their earning assets: loans and securities. In buying securities and expanding loans, banks would boost the money supply and cause interest rates to fall. Economic activity would therefore be stimulated when the Fed increased its target for NFR.

However, historical evidence as well as more sophisticated economic analysis indicates that NFR is likely to be an unsatisfactory intermediate target. The description above presupposes that NFR is exogenous—that is, that economic activity does not feed back to influence NFR strongly. In other words, the assumption is that fluctuations in NFR reflect not changes in bank *demand* for NFR but rather changes in NFR *supplied* by the Federal Reserve. Such an assumption is suspect. Recall our analysis of banks' demand for excess reserves in Chapter 15, as well as our analysis of discount window borrowing in Chapter 18. Both banks' demand for excess reserves and discount window borrowing fluctuate with changes in interest rates, economic uncertainty, and other factors.

Because NFR is an endogenous variable, its magnitude fluctuates even when the Fed is "standing still"—that is, not pursuing any policy of buying or selling securities or changing the discount rate. Suppose the Fed desires to pursue a restrictive policy of zero money growth in the next 3 months and attempts to achieve this objective by maintaining a target level of $1.2 billion for NFR. Suppose also that initially the Fed is on target at $1.2 billion and the economy is in the expansion phase of the business cycle: demand for credit and interest rates are rising. As rates rise, banks reduce their excess reserves (r_e declines). Also, both because banks are facing rising loan demand from their customers and because the Fed's discount rate tends to lag behind money market yields in a cyclical upswing, the volume of discounts and advances increases. Hence, NFR declines because of endogenous forces.

As NFR drops below the Fed's target level of $1.2 billion, the Fed must purchase government securities on the open market to push NFR back to the target level. In purchasing securities, the Fed expands reserves, the monetary base, and the money supply at a time when economic activity is already expanding strongly. If one uses the money supply as a criterion, the Fed policy is perverse: a policy which was intended to produce *no growth* in the money supply has turned out to be highly expansionary because of the use of NFR as an intermediate target. Not only did the money supply increase as a result of an increase in the money supply multiplier induced by the reduction in bank demand for excess reserves, but the Fed aggravated the situation by purchasing securities and thus expanding the monetary base.

NFR, then, is a moving target. A constant magnitude of NFR does not imply a constant money supply or a constant level of GDP expenditures. A given change in reported NFR may be due to Fed action, to endogenous forces, or to a combination of the two. In order to construct a legitimate target out of NFR, the Fed would have to sort out the changes which result from endogenous forces and the changes which result from Fed policy. Barring the feasibility of doing so, NFR is a poor choice for an intermediate target. In the 1960s, after persistent criticism from economists, the Fed abandoned NFR as an intermediate target.

LINKS AMONG POLICY, TARGETS, AND GOALS

Figure 19-1 shows the linkage through which the Federal Reserve's monetary policy tools exert an effect on its goals. The variables connecting the Fed's policy tools with its goals are divided into two categories: short-range objectives or operating targets and intermediate-range objectives or targets. The basis of the two-tier classification is the order and speed with which these variables respond to Fed policy tools.

The short-range variables respond very quickly to changes in the Fed's policy tools, while the intermediate-range variables generally do not respond until after the short-range variables have moved. To a considerable extent, the intermediate-range variables respond *because of* movements in the short-range variables. Because the variables in both groups are believed to be significant links in the transmission of monetary policy, they are all potential targets of Federal Reserve policy. We now discuss the merits of these variables as targets of monetary policy.

Short-Range Variables

In Figure 19-1, this group of variables is positioned in close proximity to the Fed's policy tools. The Fed is capable of exerting a quick, strong influence over the short-range variables. Certainly within 1 week, and in many cases on a daily or hourly basis, the Fed has the capacity to push the short-range variables in any desired direction. On the basis of the criterion of controllability, the short-range variables make better policy targets than do the intermediate variables, which generally cannot be influenced as quickly or accurately.

On the other hand, the short-range variables are less tightly linked to aggregate expenditures and the ultimate goals of monetary policy than are the intermediate-range variables. On that criterion, the intermediate-range variables are superior monetary policy targets. In practice, the Fed has often used a two-tier targeting strategy, shooting at short-range targets (sometimes known as *operating targets*) thought to be consistent with more important intermediate-range objectives, such as M1 or M2. For example, the Fed may employ a short-range federal funds rate or nonborrowed reserves target to hit an intermediate M1 or M2 target. The short-range objectives may be divided into two categories: (1) measures of bank reserves and the monetary base and (2) nominal and real money market yields—that is, yields on short-term debt instruments.

Measures of Bank Reserves and the Monetary Base

The various measures of bank reserves and the monetary base are a critical group of variables within the transmission linkage. When the Fed implements open market operations, the reserve and base variables move quite rapidly. Variables in this category include bank reserves, the monetary base, nonborrowed reserves, the nonborrowed base, discounts and advances (borrowed reserves), and net free reserves.

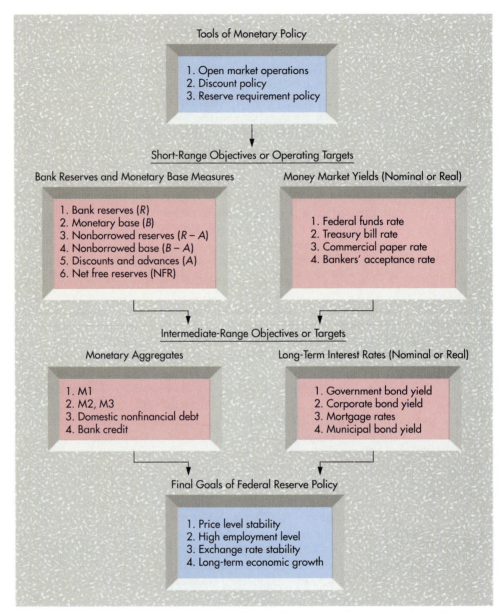

Figure 19-1   Links in the Transmission of Federal Reserve Policy. The Fed employs its tools of monetary policy in an effort to hit certain short- and intermediate-range targets in order to achieve its long-range goals such as price level stability.

Bank Reserves (R) and the Monetary Base (B)

The Fed exerts great influence over reserves and the monetary base, and these variables constitute an important link in the Fed's influence over economic activity. Suppose the Fed wishes to promote a policy of economic stimulus, so it purchases securities on the open market. As explained in Chapter 17, Fed securities purchases produce a dollar-for-dollar expansion in R and B. This boosts purchasing of securities and lending by banks, which triggers the deposit expansion process. The money supply rises, short-term yields fall, and economic activity increases.

In one aspect, bank reserves are probably superior to the monetary base as a policy target: reserves provide a more reliable indication of the ability of banks to extend credit and create money.[4] Recall that the monetary base consists of reserves plus currency held by the public. Because the amount of currency held by the public fluctuates considerably, however, a given monetary base of $400 billion might include currency of $320 billion and reserves of $80 billion or currency of $350 billion and reserves of $50 billion. The former combination is capable of generating a considerably larger volume of bank credit and money than the latter. In another aspect, however, the monetary base is superior to bank reserves. Because changes in demand for currency by the public affect reserves but not the base, the Fed can more accurately control the base than reserves.

Nonborrowed Reserves ($R - A$) and Nonborrowed Base ($B - A$)

The monetary base and bank reserves contain a significant element of endogeneity because of discount window borrowing and other factors. Recall that each dollar of bank borrowing at the Fed creates one dollar of R and B. As explained in Chapter 18, the volume of discounts and advances exhibits a marked *procyclical* pattern, rising during business cycle expansions and declining during recessions. As the economy experiences a strong economic expansion, banks become strapped for funds and increasingly use the discount window to obtain funds. Because discounts and advances tend to be granted passively by the Fed, the monetary base and bank reserves fluctuate endogenously—unless the Fed systematically neutralizes the effects of changes in discounts and advances with aggressive open market operations. That is, total reserves and the monetary base sometimes fluctuate because of cyclical swings in credit demands, not because of deliberately exercised Fed policy.

To eliminate this endogenous characteristic, some economists have suggested subtracting discounts and advances (A) from the total base and from total bank reserves to obtain the variables known as the **nonborrowed base ($B - A$)** and **nonborrowed reserves ($R - A$).** Among all the short-range and intermediate-range variables listed in Figure 19-1, these come closest to being 100 percent exogenous. The Fed is capable of exerting very accurate control over nonborrowed reserves and the nonborrowed base.

Discounts and Advances (A)

The Fed has continuous information on depository institutions' borrowing from the Fed (A); hence, this variable scores very high on the measurability criterion. However, because it is highly endogenous, it ranks poorly on controllability. Nor is it tightly linked to the ultimate objectives of Fed policy. Nevertheless, the Fed employed discounts and

---

[4]Another way of making this point is by stating that the multiplier that links reserves to the money stock is more stable than the multiplier that links the base to the money stock. Thus the Fed can achieve greater control over the money supply by hitting R targets rather than B targets.

advances throughout much of the 1980s (as well as in the 1920s and 1930s) as a short-range operating target. (Because discounts and advances is a poor short-range operating target, one must conclude that the Fed adopted it not because of its merits but rather for political reasons.[5])

Net Free Reserves (NFR)

We discussed this variable in some depth earlier, noting its strong endogenous quality. The link between net free reserves and aggregate expenditures is likely to be highly unstable. Today, NFR is not considered an effective monetary policy target.

Money Market Yields and Interest Rates

Like prices in other competitive markets, money market yields are determined by supply and demand. The Federal Reserve influences securities prices and yields via the demand side of the market. Suppose the Fed desires to bring down short-term yields in order to stimulate economic activity; it would then purchase U.S. Treasury securities on the open market, pushing up the prices of the securities and lowering their yields.

The Fed's open market purchases also trigger an increase in bank reserves and the monetary base. Because bank excess reserves have increased above desired levels, the supply of funds available in the federal funds market expands, while demand decreases as fewer banks come up short on reserves. As a result, the federal funds rate falls quickly. To the extent that depository institutions use their excess reserves to purchase Treasury bills and commercial paper, downward pressure is brought to bear on the yields on those instruments. Even if all Federal Reserve and bank securities purchases were concentrated entirely in Treasury bills, investors' behavior would spread the downward yield pressure throughout the money market.[6]

The decline in short-term money market yields may itself exert some positive impact on aggregate spending. For example, if the commercial paper rate declines sharply owing to expansionary Fed policy measures, business firms may be encouraged to float more of these IOUs and use the proceeds to finance expenditures on inventory, materials, or other goods and services. To a large extent, however, the economic impact of the Fed's policy of driving down money market yields will depend on the extent to which the downward pressure is transmitted to long-term interest rates. If the Fed sustains its policy, government and corporate bond yields and mortgage rates will move downward, stimulating borrowing and spending and exerting an expansionary effect on the economy.

---

[5]In putting short-term interest rate targets at extremely high levels in the early 1980s to combat entrenched double-digit inflation, the Fed inevitably became the victim of congressional criticism. Utilizing a discounts and advances operating target is essentially the same as using a short-term interest rate operating target. The Fed probably employed the discounts and advances target in an effort to minimize its exposure to attack by politicians and other critics.

[6]The various money market instruments are a good example of substitute goods. When the price of good X (say U.S. Treasury bills) rises, investors will switch to substitute goods Y and Z (commercial paper, bankers' acceptances, etc.). This ensures that part of the price increase on U.S. Treasury bills (that is, yield *decrease*) will be transmitted to the substitute goods (commercial paper, acceptances, etc.). This phenomenon is, of course, an important cause of the strong propensity for the various money market yields to move in tandem.

Intermediate-Range Variables

As we have seen, intermediate-range variables have a more predictable effect on aggregate expenditures than do the Fed's short-range operating variables. On the other hand, these variables are more difficult for the Federal Reserve to control. We will discuss the merits of the monetary aggregates and long-term interest rates as intermediate targets.

Monetary Aggregates

In the 1970s and early 1980s, the money supply measures gained increased acceptance as appropriate targets for monetary policy—although their luster has dimmed in the past 15 years. In the late 1960s, the Fed began conducting open market operations with an eye on the money supply as well as on money market yields and reserve measures. And beginning in the 1970s, the FOMC specified to the open market account manager certain "tolerance ranges" within which the growth rates of the various money supply measures were to be maintained until the next FOMC meeting.

A significant problem confronting the use of monetary aggregates as intermediate targets is the relatively poor quality and availability of the data. Weekly data for M1, M2, and so forth are available with a 2-week lag, but even then tend to be subject to substantial revision. Intraweekly monitoring and control are therefore not feasible. Furthermore, even if good weekly data were available, short-run volatility in the money supply multiplier would make accurate weekly control of the money supply quite difficult. It thus seems likely that the shortest time horizon over which the Fed can be expected to control the money supply measures accurately is one month, using averages of the weekly data; some economists believe that a quarter is a more feasible time frame. For these reasons, the Fed is forced to consider other operating guides in planning its day-to-day open market operations. (This would be true even if the Fed believed that the monetary aggregates were the only variables influencing economic activity.)

Long-Term Interest Rates

Long-term interest rates are believed to have a greater impact on spending decisions than short-term interest rates do. Investment in plant and equipment, housing, and other structures depends on long-term rates. Thus, the long-term interest rate—particularly the corporate bond yield, the mortgage rate, and the municipal bond yield—is a potential candidate for selection as a monetary policy target.

Suppose the Fed wishes to bring down long-term yields as part of an anti-recession program. It would purchase securities, preferably bonds, in the open market. As the Fed buys bonds, their prices are bid up somewhat, reducing their yields. And since Fed securities purchases boost bank reserves, banks will begin buying securities, including some bonds. Other things held constant, the Fed's move will tend to increase bond prices, lowering their yields.

However, long-term interest rates depend heavily on such endogenous factors as inflation expectations, private credit demands, government borrowing, and the flow of private saving. For this reason, the Fed cannot exert accurate near-term control over long-term interest rates. Frequently when mortgage rates are relatively high, Congress and others bring pressure on the Fed to lower rates by pursuing more stimulative policies.

Unfortunately, because more stimulative policies are likely to increase the nation's inflation rate, such policies run the risk of actually *boosting* long-term interest rates through the Fisher effect.[7]

Real versus Nominal Interest Rates

The real interest rate is the actual (nominal) rate minus the average inflation rate expected to prevail over the life of the instrument. If the 30-year mortgage rate is 8 percent and inflation is expected to average 3 percent annually over the next 30 years, the real mortgage rate is 5 percent. Economists believe that real long-term interest rates are more important in influencing expenditure decisions than are nominal rates. For this reason, some economists advocate that real interest rates be employed in place of nominal rates as intermediate targets of monetary policy. What would be wrong, for example, with the Fed targeting a real interest rate of 4 percent? The problem is that while real long-term interest rates are important for determining expenditures, long-term inflation expectations are almost impossible to ascertain. Because of inertia in the inflation process, we have a fairly high degree of confidence in our estimate of expected inflation for the next 6 months or year. There are also numerous surveys of the outlook for short-term inflation. Hence, our estimates of real *short-term* interest rates are likely to be fairly reliable. However, the inflation rate expected to prevail over the next 30 years is impossible to ascertain with any confidence. Too many uncertain political and economic forces influence long-term inflation trends. Therefore, while short-term real interest rates might be employed as monetary policy targets, the use of long-term real yields is simply not practical. Long-term real interest rates fail the first criterion for an effective monetary policy target—that is, measurability.

Exhibit 19-1 evaluates the various candidates for intermediate targets on the basis of our three criteria. In the next section, we look at the differences of opinion among economists about the merits of the various potential intermediate targets of monetary policy.

Monetarists versus Keynesians on Appropriate Targets

The disagreements between Keynesians and monetarists regarding appropriate monetary policy targets follow logically from their disagreements over the factors that influence economic activity. Keynesians view shifts in particular types of expenditures, such as housing, plant and equipment, consumer durables, and state and local government expenditures as the channels through which monetary policy affects the economy. Because these types of expenditures are likely to be sensitive to interest rates, Keynesians argue that the Fed should attempt to influence economic activity by triggering changes in interest rates. Some even argue that the Fed should ignore the monetary aggregates.

---

[7]The populist appeal to the Fed for "easy money" is essentially a request that the Fed run on a treadmill. The harder the Fed tries to bring down long-term interest rates in the short run via stimulative policies, the greater will be the inflationary pressures and the induced *upward* pull of market forces on interest rates. Ironically, we arrive at the conclusion that the most effective way for the Fed to foster low long-term interest rates is to pursue a protracted policy of moderation in the growth of reserves, the monetary base, and the monetary aggregates.

EXHIBIT 19-1

The Usefulness of Various Intermediate Targets

The three criteria on which to judge the merits of an intermediate target are *measurability, controllability,* and *importance.* If we were to grade the various short- and intermediate-range target variables on each of those criteria, we might obtain the following results.

Variable	Measurability	Controllability	Importance
Bank reserves and the monetary base	B+	A	B
Nonborrowed reserves and nonborrowed base	B+	A+	B
Discounts and advances	A	C	D
Net free reserves	A−	C	C
Short-term interest rates:			
Nominal	A+	B+	B−
Real	B	B−	B+
Long-term interest rates:			
Nominal	A+	C	B
Real	D	D	A or A−
Monetary aggregates	B	B	A or B

Source: "Educated guesses" of the author.

Like all grades, these contain an element of subjectivity and are subject to dispute; economists of different persuasions will assign slightly different grades. On the criterion of "measurability," short-term and long-term nominal or actual yields get the top grade. On the criterion of "controllability," the nonborrowed base and nonborrowed reserves score highest. But the crucial criterion is "importance." Note that we have hedged in this category by specifying two grades for both long-term real interest rates and the monetary aggregates. These grades are hotly disputed: monetarists assign a higher grade to the monetary aggregates, Keynesians give a higher grade to long-term real interest rates.

Monetarists tend to view monetary policy as influencing aggregate demand more broadly, rather than through particular sectors such as housing or plant and equipment. An increase in the money supply upsets the equilibrium between actual and desired money holdings. Some of the excess money is spent directly on goods and services. Therefore, much of the impact of an increase in the money supply occurs independently of its effect on interest rates. Thus, monetarists believe that the quantity of money, not the interest rate, is the crucial variable. Monetarists would like to see the Fed drop interest rates as a target of monetary policy and focus exclusively on the various monetary aggregates, such as M1 and M2. They commonly argue that the Federal Reserve, by attempting to stabilize such variables as net free reserves and interest rates, has historically *destabilized* both the money supply and economic activity. Instead of conducting a *countercyclical* monetary policy, monetarists charge, the Fed has inadvertently conducted *procyclical* policies, amplifying rather than dampening the severity of business cycles.

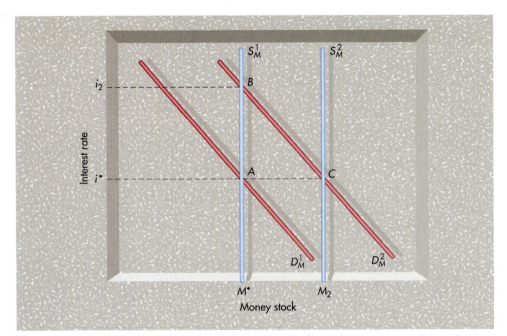

Figure 19-2 The Market for Money Balances. In the face of an uncertain demand curve for money, the Fed can hit either an interest rate target or a money supply target, but not both; it must make a choice.

Money Supply Targets versus Interest Rate Targets

One thing is clear. The Fed cannot successfully target both the money supply and interest rates simultaneously. Figure 19-2 demonstrates this fact. The figure shows the supply and demand curves for money, which jointly determine the interest rate. The supply curve, shown here as a vertical line, is determined by the Federal Reserve.[8] The Fed can shift it rightward by purchasing securities, lowering the discount rate, or reducing reserve requirements. The demand curve for money is downward sloping because a decrease in interest rates reduces the opportunity cost of holding money, thereby increasing the amount of wealth people choose to hold in the form of currency and demand deposits. The demand curve for money shifts in response to such factors as changing income and a changing economic outlook. An increase in income shifts the demand curve for money rightward as people choose to hold more money in order to finance a higher level of expenditures. An increase in uncertainty also increases the demand for money because money is the safest and most conservative of all assets.

---

[8]A case can be made for drawing the money supply curve as an upward-sloping function of the interest rate. Because both the money multiplier (via bank excess reserve behavior, r_e) and the monetary base (through discount window activity) are likely to be positively related to the interest rate, the money supply is likely to respond positively to interest rates. Here, for simplicity, we assume that the supply curve is vertical and shifts in response to Federal Reserve policy actions.

Suppose initially the S_M^1 curve and the D_M^1 curve intersect at A, at an interest rate of i^* and a money supply of M^*. Suppose that both this interest rate and this money supply are exactly those targeted by the Federal Reserve. Initially, then, the Fed is hitting both its targets. Now assume that the nation's income expands significantly during an economic recovery or that economic uncertainty increases because of an announcement of a sharp cutback in oil production or an unexpected drop in the stock market. In either case, the demand for money shifts rightward to D_M^2. If the Fed concentrates on its money supply target, we move from A to B in the figure, with the interest rate rising from i^* to i_2. In this case, the Fed hits its money supply target (M^*) but misses its interest rate target, i^*.

On the other hand, suppose the Fed is determined to maintain the interest rate at i^*. To do so in the face of the increased demand for money, the Fed must pursue stimulative monetary actions to boost the supply curve of money from S_M^1 to S_M^2. We are now at C in the figure; the money supply is now M_2. Note that the Fed has successfully maintained the interest rate at i^* but has missed its money supply target. The money supply (M_2) now exceeds the desired level of M^*.

In principle, if the Fed were omniscient, the interest rate target could be changed rapidly enough over the course of the business cycle to prevent a destabilizing money supply pattern. As the economy gained strength in a recovery, the Fed could aggressively boost the interest rate target to a position consistent with stable growth of the monetary aggregates. In recessions, the Fed could quickly lower the interest rate target to prevent a contraction in the money supply. In theory, a *highly flexible* interest rate target is not inconsistent with hitting established money supply growth targets. In practice, however, it is too much to expect the Fed to be able to know at any point in time the precise interest rate that is consistent with the desired growth rate of the monetary aggregates. The uncertainty is exacerbated by the fact that, in order to change its targets, the FOMC must vote to do so. Remember that the FOMC meets only approximately eight times annually.

Occasionally, Fed policy mistakes have stemmed from this conflict between money growth targets and interest rate targets. For example, the Fed sometimes exceeded its money growth targets in the 1970s, as it adhered to its interest rate targets. As a result, inflation was stimulated.

EFFECTS OF FEDERAL RESERVE TARGETING PROCEDURES

We will now review past targeting policies and examine the charge that the Fed has actually destabilized the U.S. economy during much of the period since the 1920s.

Pegging Treasury Bond Yields, 1942–1951

To finance World War II, the U.S. Treasury had to float a huge volume of securities during the early 1940s. Given normal market behavior, a major increase in yields would have been required in order to induce private firms and individuals to absorb the abnormally large supply of Treasury bills, notes, and bonds.[9] And the rise in yields would have substantially increased interest expense to the U.S. Treasury and U.S. taxpayers.[10]

In order to prevent a dramatic increase in yields, the government appealed to patriotic U.S. citizens to buy government bonds. But more important, the Treasury coerced the Federal Reserve into agreeing to prevent interest rates from rising during the financing effort. The agreement stipulated that the Fed would not allow yields on various classifications of government securities to rise above specific levels. Yields were not to rise above 0.375 percent on Treasury bills, 0.875 percent on 1-year Treasury notes, and 2.5 percent on long-term government bonds.

To prevent market interest rates from breaking through these artificially low ceilings, the Fed had to make sure that securities prices did not decline below corresponding, specific levels. When the Treasury (or public) was selling securities, the Fed was obliged to purchase them to keep their prices from falling. Because Fed purchases of securities increase bank reserves, the monetary base, and the monetary aggregates, the Fed essentially sacrificed its control over the money supply in order to carry out its agreement with the Treasury. The money supply was determined by the amount of securities issued by the Treasury and the public's propensity to hold them. Because the low yields were not attractive to the public, the Fed was forced to purchase an abnormally large quantity of government securities during the war. The resulting increases in the Fed's security portfolio, the monetary base, and the monetary aggregates are shown in Table 19-1. Note the highly inflationary growth rates of the monetary aggregates. And this occurred at a time when government fiscal stimulus in the form of increased wartime expenditures was strongly boosting output!

During this period, the Fed was remarkably successful in maintaining government security yields at the target levels. But the cost of doing so was an undesirable and powerful monetary stimulus. The program of wage-price controls in place during the war temporarily disguised and postponed the inflationary consequences of the Fed's bond support program. When the controls were lifted at the end of the war, prices increased dramatically. By 1948, the wholesale price index stood at twice the 1940 level.

At the end of the war, the Treasury insisted that the Fed continue the bond support program. What if the Fed had withdrawn its support after the removal of wage-price controls led to sharp increases in the reported price indices? A major increase in yields and a collapse of security prices would have occurred—a highly unfair result for those Americans who had purchased government bonds in wartime. A collapse of securities prices would also have raised the prospect of massive losses and financial distress for banks, life insurance companies, and other institutions that had accumulated large blocks of government bonds.

---

[9]The national debt increased by approximately 400 percent during 1941–1945. That is, the U.S. Treasury borrowed approximately four times more during this 4-year period than it had borrowed in the previous 165 years of U.S. history.

[10]Financing the $250 billion national debt in 1945 at 8 percent interest would have meant spending $20 billion per year just to meet the interest on the debt. Given the level of GDP at that time, about 10 percent of GDP would have been required to pay the annual interest on the debt. While such payments would not have involved any direct loss of economic resources, they would have necessitated substantially higher income tax rates for many years. By keeping interest rates artificially low, the U.S. government essentially made a decision to shift much of the financial burden of World War II from taxpayers to those citizens who purchased government bonds.

Table 19-1

Annual Growth Rates of the Federal Reserve Securities Portfolio, Monetary Base, and Money Supply Measures, 1942–1945

Year	Change in the Fed's Portfolio (%)	Change in the Monetary Base (%)	Change in M1 (%)	Change in M2 (%)
1942	+164.5%	+19.6%	+30.0%	+23.1%
1943	+98.8	+16.1	+27.6	+25.5
1944	+16.0	+17.8	+13.6	+16.1
1945	+25.9	+12.2	+12.9	+15.4

Sources: Calculated from data in *Federal Reserve Bulletin*, various issues, and Milton Friedman and Anna J. Schwartz, *A Monetary History of the United States, 1867–1960* (Princeton, N.J.: Princeton University Press), Appendix Table A-1.

The Fed continued its bond support program for several years. As time passed, the emergency rationale behind the bond support program diminished, and the fundamental absurdity of the policy became more widely understood. Finally, the Fed pressed for the freedom to pursue a discretionary monetary policy. In 1951, in a Treasury–Federal Reserve "Accord," the Fed was absolved of the responsibility for supporting government securities prices.

Has the Federal Reserve Been a Destabilizing Influence?

Critics of the Federal Reserve charge that the bond support program of the 1940s represents only an extreme example of the Fed's general policy approach. Specifically, they have charged that by attempting to stabilize such variables as net free reserves and short-term money market yields, the Fed has systematically (though inadvertently) contributed to the instability of the monetary base, the monetary aggregates, and economic activity in general. Consider the evidence in Table 19-2, which illustrates the variation in the monetary base over 8 decades. Because the Federal Reserve is capable of exerting predominant influence over the monetary base, we can take the behavior of the base as an indication of the Fed's monetary posture. In years in which the growth rate of the base was quite high, we can assume that monetary policy was quite stimulative unless the money multiplier was falling sharply (for example, during 1930–1934).

To examine the historical variability of the monetary base, annual growth rates were calculated for each 12-month period ending each month from January 1920 to April 1996 (more than 900 calculations). The 76-year period was then divided into decades. Table 19-2 shows the maximum and minimum growth rates of the base for any 12-month period ending in each decade. Several observations may be made. First, in each decade, the difference between the maximum and minimum 12-month growth rates of the base is

Table 19-2

Historical Behavior of the Monetary Base, 1920–1996*

Period	Maximum 12-Month Growth of Base (%)*	Minimum 12-Month Growth of Base (%)*	Average over 10-Year Period (%)
1920s	+11.3% (Year ending 6/1920)	−15.5% (Year ending 10/1921)	+0.8%
1930s	+26.6 (Year ending 9/1939)	−5.7 (Year ending 11/1930)	+10.0
1940s	+25.7 (Year ending 3/1940)	−9.4 (Year ending 11/1941)	+10.4
1950s	+9.8 (Year ending 10/1951)	−8.5 (Year ending 1/1950)	+1.1
1960s	+6.9 (Year ending 12/1968)	+0.4 (Year ending 5/1961)	+4.2
1970s	+9.7 (Year ending 6/1978)	+5.5 (Year ending 11/1970)	+7.9
1980s	+10.4 (Year ending 1/1987)	+3.8 (Year ending 11/1989)	+7.4
1990s†	+11.4 (Year ending 7/1993)	+2.1 (Year ending 3/1996)	+8.0

*These figures represent the maximum and minimum growth rates of the monetary base for any 12-month period *ending* within the interval specified in the column on left.
†Through April 1996.

Source: Based on data from *Citibank Economic Database*.

large. It ranges from more than 35 percent in the 1940s to less than 5 percent in the 1970s. The mean of these differences, taken over the 8 decades, is approximately 17 percent.

Even the average growth rates of the base, taken over entire decades, vary considerably from decade to decade. Compare the inflationary 1940s and 1970s with the deflationary 1920s and the stable price period of the 1950s.[11] This variability in base growth may be taken as an indication that the Fed has historically ignored the behavior of the monetary base in favor of other target variables. Note, however, that the variability of the base declined significantly after the 1950s, indicating that the Fed has become more conscious of the behavior of the base and the monetary aggregates in recent decades.

---

[11]A glance at the right-hand column for the past 5 decades gives a thumbnail sketch of the rise and fall of monetarist doctrine. Monetarism, which argues that the necessary and sufficient cause of inflation is money growth in excess of the trend growth of potential output, gained ascendancy in the U.S. and around the world as monetary base growth (and money growth) accelerated from the 1950s through the 1970s. (Note the acceleration of base growth from 1.1 percent in the 1950s to 4.2 percent in the 1960s and 7.9 percent in the 1970s.) However, the period after the 1970s, when inflation has remained subdued, has witnessed approximately the same money growth rate as the inflationary 1970s. The coexistence of rapid money growth and low inflation can be explained by a sharp change in the behavior of the velocity of money, the multiplier that links the money stock to GDP. We will analyze velocity in Part 6.

According to critics of the Fed, the instability of the monetary base is attributable to the Fed's historical propensity to target endogenous variables such as net free reserves and short-term interest rates. As we saw earlier, in the expansion phase of the business cycle, short-term yields rise and NFR fall. To stay on its yield or NFR target, the Fed must buy securities, thereby injecting reserves into the banking system. This causes both the monetary base and monetary aggregates to rise. The more powerful the upward thrust of the economy, the more aggressive the Fed must be in its open market purchases to achieve its yield and NFR targets. Hence, the stronger the economy, the more rapid is the growth of *R, B,* M1 and M2.

In recession, yields fall and NFR rise. To stay on target, the Fed must sell securities, reducing *R, B,* and the monetary aggregates. Again, the stronger the downward momentum of the economy, the more aggressively must the Fed pursue its contractionary money supply policies to keep short-term interest rates and NFR on target. Those who view the monetary aggregates as more crucial to economic activity than NFR and money market yields accuse the Fed of being myopic. By attempting to stabilize the *wrong* variables, they say, the Fed causes the *important* variables to move perversely!

To see whether this interpretation is consistent with U.S. business cycle history, let us examine the behavior of the monetary base after World War II. Table 19-3 shows the annual growth rates of the monetary base for each expansion (trough to peak) and each contraction (peak to trough) in the nine full business cycles that were experienced in the

Table 19-3

Annual Growth Rate of Monetary Base during Recession and Expansion Phases of Business Cycles (Post–World War II)

Expansion Phase		Recession Phase	
Trough to Peak	**Change in *B* per Year (%)**	**Peak to Trough**	**Change in *B* per Year (%)**
10/1945–11/1948	+2.9%	11/1948–10/1949	−10.3%
10/1949–7/1953	+3.6	7/1953–8/1954	−2.7
8/1954–7/1957	+1.3	7/1957–4/1958	−3.2
4/1958–5/1960	+0.6	5/1960–2/1961	−3.5
2/1961–11/1969	+5.2	11/1969–11/1970	+5.0
11/1970–11/1973	+5.5	11/1973–4/1975	+6.5
4/1975–1/1980	+7.9	1/1980–7/1980	+6.2
7/1980–7/1981	+5.0	7/1981–11/1982	+6.6
11/1982–9/1990	+7.7	7/1990–3/1991	+10.5
3/1991–6/1996	+7.0*		

*The most recent business cycle peak has not yet been determined by the National Bureau of Economic Research.

Source: Based on data from *Citibank Economic Database*. Business cycle turning points are National Bureau of Economic Research classifications.

EXHIBIT 19-2

The 1979–1982 Experience: A Monetarist Experiment?

Monetarists have long argued that slow, steady money growth would yield results superior to those delivered by discretionary monetary policies. Keynesians have asserted that Fed discretion will outperform the monetarist prescription. Because the Fed has never adhered religiously to money supply targets, there has been no way to test the two competing views. For this reason, when the Fed announced in October 1979 that it was de-emphasizing the federal funds rate target, ostensibly to place higher priority on hitting money growth rate targets, economists eagerly anticipated the results of the new procedure, which they dubbed the "monetarist experiment."

But was the episode really a "monetarist experiment"? Though the Fed greatly widened the permissible band of fluctuation of the federal funds rate, the following data raise doubts about this episode qualifying as a monetarist experiment.

M1 Target Ranges and Actual Growth Rates

Year	M1 Target Range (%)	Actual M1 Growth Rate (%)
1980	4.0–6.5%	6.8%
1981	3.5–6.0	5.3
1982	2.5–5.5	7.8

Monetarism prescribes slow, steady money supply growth. Note that while the Fed did de-emphasize the federal funds rate, in two of the 3 years it failed to stay within its prescribed money growth range. Money (M1) growth was variable; furthermore, the accompanying figure indicates that its average rate of growth was approximately the same in the period 1979–1982 as in the previous 3-year period. (Annual M2 growth did decelerate, from 12 percent during 1976–1978 to 9 percent during 1979–1982.)

In retrospect, Chairman Paul Volcker and the Federal Reserve may never actually have been committed to a "monetarist experiment." Indeed, they never claimed to be. Many economists believe Volcker wanted instead the latitude to squeeze inflation out of the U.S. economy by driving interest rates dramatically higher (note the federal funds rate during 1979–1982 in the upper portion of the figure)—and he knew that to make that goal politically feasible, the federal funds rate would have to be de-emphasized. In other words, the so-called monetarist experiment was a smokescreen that allowed the

1945–1996 period. For the early postwar business cycles, the findings are strongly consistent with the monetarist hypothesis. In the first four postwar business cycles, the monetary base increased during each expansion and fell in each recession. Beginning in the 1960s, however, the results are not so clear. In the three of the five full business cycles after 1960, the Fed managed to boost the base faster during recession than during expansion (including the two most recent episodes). A learning process appears to be at work!

EXHIBIT 19-2 (CONTINUED)

Fed to administer the harsh medicine required to cool off aggregate expenditures quickly and bring down inflation. The Fed was successful in that venture—the annual inflation rate declined from more than 12 percent per year in October 1979 to less than 4 percent 3 years later. But the nation paid a high price for this victory in the form of the most severe economic downturn since the Great Depression.

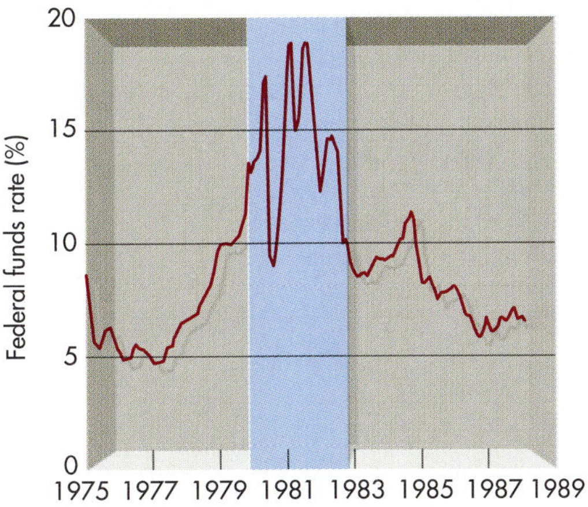

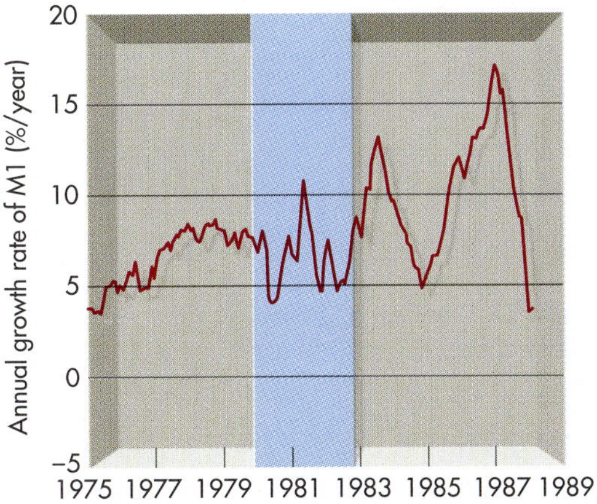

Exhibit 19-2 discusses a 3-year episode in the early 1980s, when the Fed explicitly emphasized money growth targets over interest rate targets. This episode became known as the "monetarist experiment."

We will return to the issue of monetary policy targets in Chapter 24, and discuss the conditions that determine whether interest rates or monetary aggregates make better targets.

SUMMARY

The ultimate goals of Federal Reserve policy are reasonable price level stability, full employment, a stable exchange rate at a level that allows U.S. products to be competitive with foreign goods, and long-term growth in real GDP and living standards. The general tools of Fed policy include open market operations, discount window policy, and reserve requirement policy. Because the link between the Fed's tools and its goals is so loose and uncertain, the Fed employs certain variables as intermediate targets in order to better achieve its long-term goals. A good intermediate target of monetary policy has three characteristics: it can be measured readily and accurately; it is relatively free from cyclical and other endogenous forces, so that the Fed can control it accurately; and it has an important effect on aggregate expenditures and hence on the

ability of the Fed to achieve its goals. The targets that the Fed can influence most quickly and accurately are various measures of bank reserves and short-term interest rates. However, these variables are less important in influencing aggregate expenditures than are the monetary aggregates and long-term interest rates, variables over which the Fed has less control. While the Fed is capable of hitting either a money supply or an interest rate target, it is typically unable to hit both targets simultaneously. Generally, therefore, it will have to make a choice. Economists differ as to the variables they believe to be the most appropriate intermediate targets. While Keynesians prefer various nominal and real interest rate targets, monetarists believe the Fed is best advised to concentrate its attention on the monetary aggregates.

KEY TERMS

natural unemployment rate
intermediate target of monetary policy
net free reserves (NFR)

nonborrowed base $(B - A)$
nonborrowed reserves $(R - A)$

STUDY QUESTIONS

1 Discuss the four main goals of monetary policy. Explain why each is worthy of being considered an important goal.

2 Explain the meaning of an intermediate monetary policy target variable. Explain why the Fed uses a procedure of setting intermediate targets.

3 Explain the three criteria that are used to determine whether a particular variable is a worthy candidate to be an intermediate target of monetary policy. Now, on the basis of these criteria, evaluate the following variables as intermediate targets:

  a   90-day Treasury bill yield

  b   The real federal funds rate

  c   The real 30-year U.S. government bond yield

  d   The nonborrowed monetary base

  e   M2

  f   Excess reserves

4 Draw a diagram with the interest rate on the vertical axis and the quantity of money on the horizontal axis. Draw the supply and demand curves for money under the following conditions and indicate the equilibrium.

  a   Assume the Fed is targeting interest rates and a severe recession occurs, due to declining consumer confidence. What will happen to the money supply?

  b   What would have happened had the Fed been targeting the money supply?

  c   Which target is preferred in this case, the money supply or interest rates?

5 Why did the Fed decide to peg government securities yields in the 1940s? What were the consequences? Do you believe it was a wise policy? Explain.

6 Explain why, in targeting such variables as the federal funds rate and net free reserves, the Fed may inadvertently destabilize economic activity.

7 Evaluate the merits of discounts and advances as an intermediate monetary policy target variable.

8 Explain why strict adherence to a money supply target is likely to require the Fed to relinquish its control over short-term interest rates.

9 Since 1987, the Fed has been unwilling to use M1 as an intermediate monetary policy target. Evaluate this decision in the context of the three criteria for a good intermediate target.

10 We know that decisions about capital expenditures are heavily influenced by the real long-term interest rate. Why, then, doesn't the Fed employ this variable as an intermediate target?

SUGGESTIONS FOR ADDITIONAL READING

A good general reference is Richard G. Davis, et al., *Intermediate Targets and Indicators for Monetary Policy: A Critical Survey,* Federal Reserve Bank of New York, 1990. For an analysis by a Federal Reserve insider, see Donald Kohn, "Policy Targets and Operating Procedures in the 1990s," *Federal Reserve Bulletin,* January 1990. On targeting interest rates, see William Roberds, "What Has the Fed Wrought? Interest Rate Smoothing in Theory and Practice," Federal Reserve Bank of Atlanta *Economic Review,* January/February 1992, pp. 25–36, and Thomas Humphrey, "Can the Central Bank Peg Real Interest Rates," Federal Reserve Bank of Richmond *Economic Review,* September/October 1984, pp. 12–21. Two excellent sources are the symposia published by the Federal Reserve Bank of Kansas City, *Monetary Policy Issues in the 1990s,* and *Changing Capital Markets: Implications for Monetary Policy,* published in 1990 and 1994, respectively. On the use of intermediate targets in other countries, see Bruce Kasman, "A Comparison of Monetary Policy Operating Procedures in Six Industrial Countries," *Quarterly Review,* Federal Reserve Bank of New York, Summer 1992, pp. 5–24. For a discussion of the current monetary environment and the most recent money growth targets, see *Monetary Policy Objectives,* a summary report of the Federal Reserve Board, published semiannually by the Board of Governors of the Federal Reserve System. This is available at no charge from your district Federal Reserve Bank.

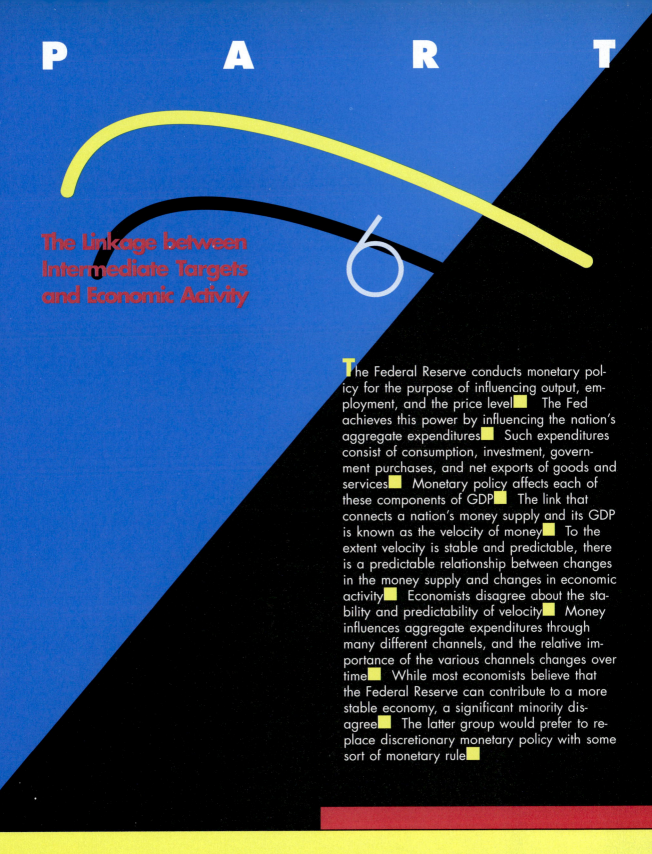

P A R T

The Linkage between Intermediate Targets and Economic Activity

6

The Federal Reserve conducts monetary policy for the purpose of influencing output, employment, and the price level■ The Fed achieves this power by influencing the nation's aggregate expenditures■ Such expenditures consist of consumption, investment, government purchases, and net exports of goods and services■ Monetary policy affects each of these components of GDP■ The link that connects a nation's money supply and its GDP is known as the velocity of money■ To the extent velocity is stable and predictable, there is a predictable relationship between changes in the money supply and changes in economic activity■ Economists disagree about the stability and predictability of velocity■ Money influences aggregate expenditures through many different channels, and the relative importance of the various channels changes over time■ While most economists believe that the Federal Reserve can contribute to a more stable economy, a significant minority disagree■ The latter group would prefer to replace discretionary monetary policy with some sort of monetary rule■

■ **The Aggregate Demand–Aggregate Supply Model**

I n Part 4 of this text, we saw how the money supply is determined and studied the Federal Reserve's role in the money supply process. In Part 5, we discussed how the Fed uses its policy tools to aim for specific intermediate targets in an effort to achieve such ultimate goals as price level stability and high output and employment. In Part 6, we will see how changes in the money supply and interest rates actually influence economic activity. We will examine the link between the nation's money stock and its gross domestic product. The analysis of the relationship between the nation's money supply and economic activity is known as **monetary theory.**

Before we turn to monetary theory, however, we will devote one chapter to a simple framework of macroeconomic analysis known as the *aggregate demand–aggregate supply model.* For some students, this chapter will constitute a review of material that was covered in their introductory macroeconomics course. Nevertheless, a thorough reading of this chapter will pay dividends. The aggregate demand–aggregate supply framework is important and useful because the changes in the money supply and interest rates the Fed engineers influence economic activity chiefly by shifting the nation's aggregate demand curve. After developing the aggregate demand–aggregate supply model, we will use it to explain key developments in the U.S. economy over the past 70 years.

THE AGGREGATE DEMAND–AGGREGATE SUPPLY FRAMEWORK

Figure 20-1 shows the basic model of aggregate demand and aggregate supply. The figure shows the nation's price level on the vertical axis and its real output level on the horizontal axis. The nation's equilibrium price and real output levels are determined by the intersection of the aggregate demand (*AD)* and aggregate supply (*AS*) curves. A rightward shift of the *AD* curve, for example, increases both the equilibrium price level and the level

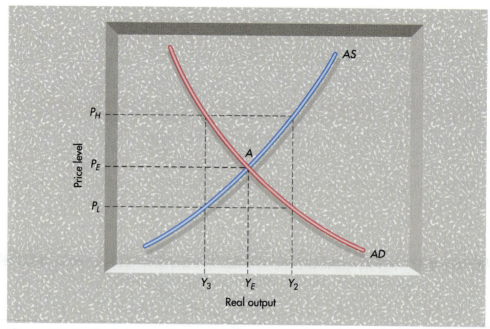

Figure 20-1   The Aggregate Demand–Aggregate Supply Model. In the aggregate de-mand–aggregate supply model, the nation's price level and real output are jointly deter-mined by the aggregate demand for and aggregate supply of goods and services.

of real output. A rightward shift of the *AS* curve increases the equilibrium level of real output and reduces the nation's price level.

Note that the supply and demand curves shown in Figure 20-1 look quite similar to the familiar supply and demand curves for a particular good, such as wheat. It is impor-tant to note, however, that *AS* and *AD* curves are fundamentally different from the supply and demand curves for individual goods.

The Aggregate Demand Curve

The nation's **aggregate demand curve** (*AD* curve) is defined as the relationship between the nation's price level and the amount of real output demanded, *other factors remaining constant.* In this relationship, the price level is the independent variable, while real out-put demanded is the dependent variable that responds to changes in the price level.

Recall the reasons why the demand curve for an individual good such as wheat is downward sloping: A reduction in the price of wheat triggers a substitution effect and an income effect, both of which increase the quantity of wheat demanded. As the price of wheat falls, consumers substitute wheat for corn and rice. Also, as the price of wheat de-clines, the *real* income of consumers increases, causing them to purchase more wheat (as-suming that wheat is not an inferior good), as well as more of other normal goods. The existence of substitution and income effects accounts for the downward slope of the demand curve for any particular good.

In the case of the *aggregate* demand curve, however, there is no substitution effect because the *AD* curve involves the demand for *all* goods and services. Also, there is no income effect involved in the *AD* curve. As the nation's price level declines, so do its nominal output and income, leaving real income unaffected.[1] Given the absence of the substitution and income effects, we must look elsewhere for the explanation for the downward-sloping *AD* curve.

The downward slope of the *AD* curve is actually attributable to the fact that several of the components of aggregate demand are influenced by the nation's price level. The nation's aggregate demand for goods and services consists of four components: consumer demand (*C*), investment demand (*I*), government purchases of goods and services (*G*), and net U.S. exports of goods and services (*X* − *M*), where *X* and *M* represent exports and imports, respectively. Consumer demand, investment demand, and net exports of goods and services are all affected by the U.S. price level.

Let us see why this is true. First, as the price level falls, the *real value* of such assets as the nation's money supply ($DDO + C^p$) and government bonds increases. In other words, the real wealth of the private sector of the economy increases. This **wealth effect** of a lower price level increases consumers' demand for goods and services (*C*). A decrease in the price level also increases the *real money supply,* lowering interest rates and stimulating housing and other forms of investment expenditures (*I*). In addition, if other factors are held constant, a decline in the U.S. price level makes U.S. goods and services relatively more attractive in foreign markets. This stimulates U.S. exports. Lower U.S. prices also tend to cause U.S. buyers to redirect demand from imported goods toward U.S. products. Both these forces boost the net foreign demand for U.S. goods (*X* − *M*).[2] While economists disagree about the *magnitude* of these price level–induced effects on expenditures, there is little dispute that they add up to a downward-sloping *AD* curve.

The Aggregate Supply Curve

The **aggregate supply curve** (*AS* curve) is defined as the relationship between the nation's price level and the amount of output firms collectively desire to produce, *other factors remaining constant.* In this relationship, the price level is the independent variable, while the quantity of real output supplied is the dependent variable.

Note that the *AS* curve in Figure 20-1 is upward sloping. A higher national price level stimulates the aggregate production of goods and services. Again, the explanation for this

---

[1]A fundamental national income identity states that the nominal value of output produced equals the nominal value of income generated. If the prices of all goods and services were cut in half, the nation's nominal income would also be cut in half. Real income would therefore remain constant. Hence, there is no income effect associated with a changing national price level.

[2]This analysis is contingent on the assumption that the exchange rate does not move sufficiently to offset the advantages gained for U.S. goods by a lower U.S. price level. If a 10 percent decline in the U.S. price level is accompanied by a 10 percent appreciation of the dollar in the foreign exchange market, the competitive edge of U.S. products will be negated and the net foreign demand for U.S. goods (*X* − *M*) will be unaffected.

phenomenon differs from that for the supply curve of an individual product, such as wheat. As the price of wheat rises, farmers are signaled to take land out of corn and soybean production and plant more wheat. But because the aggregate supply curve is for the *aggregate* of the nation's goods and services, no such substitution is possible.

The upward slope of the *AS* curve hinges on the fact that certain costs of production are fixed in the short run. Wage rates, equipment costs, raw material prices—all tend to be sticky, changing only infrequently. Firms often contract to purchase inputs at prices that are fixed for a year or longer. Because certain costs remain fixed in the short run, profit margins increase as the nation's price level increases, inducing firms to step up production.

As the time period under consideration lengthens, more and more input prices are able to adjust to the higher general price level. Hence, the impetus given to profit margins by higher output prices diminishes. This means that the longer the time period under consideration, the weaker is the supply response to higher prices and the steeper is the AS curve. In the *long run*—a period long enough for all input prices to adjust fully to the general price level—the nation's *AS* curve is vertical. That is, in the long run the aggregate quantity of output produced is independent of the nation's price level.

Equilibrium Output and the Equilibrium Price Level

In Figure 20-1, the *AS* and *AD* curves intersect at *A,* yielding an equilibrium price level of P_E and an equilibrium real output of Y_E. Any other level of prices and real output will produce *disequilibrium,* generating forces that will tend to push the economy back to *A.* For example, if the price level were at P_H (above P_E), aggregate production (Y_2) would exceed aggregate expenditures or sales (Y_3), resulting in an increase in the nation's inventories. The increase in inventories would signal firms to cut prices and reduce output in order to get back to optimal inventory levels. As the price level declined, production would be scaled back and sales would expand until the economy reached *A.* On the other hand, if the price level were initially at P_L (below P_E), aggregate sales would exceed aggregate production. Inventories would decline each period, resulting in shortages and a loss of sales and profits to firms. The shortage of goods and services would signal firms to step up production and raise prices. The increase in prices would cause buyers to reduce their purchases. Thus the economy would return again to *A.*

In this elementary but useful model, any changes in the nation's equilibrium price and output levels are attributable to shifts in the *AD* and *AS* curves. Any increase in the nation's output level must be caused by a rightward shift in the *AS* or *AD* curve. And any increase in the price level must be due either to a rightward shift of the *AD* curve or a leftward shift of the *AS* curve. Another term for a persistent increase in the nation's price level, of course, is **inflation.** It follows that inflation is caused by either a persistently *rightward*-shifting *AD* curve or a persistently *leftward*-shifting *AS* curve (or both). Historically, the predominant cause of inflation in all nations has been rising government expenditures financed by an increasing supply of money—forces that produce a persistent rightward shift of the *AD* curve.

Factors That Shift the Aggregate Demand Curve

Other than a decrease in the nation's price level, any factor that increases any of the four components of AD ($C, I, G,$ or $X - M$) will shift the AD curve rightward (an *increase* in aggregate demand). Non–price level factors that reduce $C, I, G,$ or $(X - M)$ will shift the AD curve leftward (a *reduction* in aggregate demand).

Consump-
tion (C)

Determinants of consumer expenditures (C) include disposable income, wealth, interest rates, and consumer confidence. A reduction in income taxes, by increasing disposable income, would increase consumption expenditures, shifting the AD curve rightward. An increase in stock and bond prices, by directly increasing wealth in the private sector, would stimulate consumption, shifting the AD curve to the right. Lower interest rates engineered by the Federal Reserve would boost consumer expenditures on big-ticket items typically bought on credit, such as cars, furniture, and major appliances, shifting the AD curve to the right. And an increase in consumer confidence owing perhaps to increased job stability or reduced consumer indebtedness would stimulate consumption, again shifting the AD curve to the right.

Investment
(I)

Key determinants of investment include interest rates, business confidence, the expected growth of aggregate expenditures or sales, the current rate of capacity utilization of existing plant and equipment, and federal tax policy. Lower interest rates stimulate investment in plant, equipment, inventories, housing, and other structures, shifting the AD curve rightward. Similarly, by boosting investment expenditures associated with any given interest rate, an improvement in business confidence shifts AD rightward. A fundamental rationale for investment expenditures is to provide capacity to meet future market demand. If sales are expected to expand sharply and the current utilization rate of plant and equipment is relatively high, firms will increase their investment spending in order to provide needed capacity for the future. Hence, an increase in expected sales and/or an increase in the capacity utilization rate will stimulate investment, shifting the AD curve rightward. On the other hand, if expected sales growth is meager and/or the current capacity utilization rate is low, firms will anticipate no need for additional capacity and investment spending will be depressed. Finally, tax policy toward business in general, and investment spending in particular, influences investment spending. Implementation of more rapid depreciation allowances, enactment of an investment tax credit, or a reduction in the corporate income tax will stimulate investment, shifting the AD curve rightward.

Government
Purchases
of Goods
and Services
(G)

Government expenditures hinge on political decisions made by federal, state, and local units of government. State and local government expenditures (and, to a lesser extent, federal expenditures) also depend on tax revenues and therefore on the general level of economic activity. Changes in government purchases will shift the AD curve. When government purchases increase, the AD curve shifts rightward. When government purchases decrease, the AD curve shifts leftward.

Net Exports of Goods and Services ($X - M$)

Net U.S. exports ($X - M$) are influenced by the foreign exchange rate, income in foreign nations, U.S. income, and other factors. Suppose the U.S. dollar depreciates against other major currencies and U.S. products become cheaper abroad. Given other factors, foreign demand for U.S. exports (X) will increase. Because foreign-made products become more expensive in the United States when the dollar depreciates, some of the U.S. demand for imported goods (M) will be redirected toward U.S. goods and services. Hence, a lower U.S. dollar stimulates net exports ($X - M$) and aggregate demand for U.S. goods and services.

Because exchange rates have become increasingly sensitive to relative interest rates among countries, an increasingly important channel of Federal Reserve policy runs from Fed policy actions to interest rates to the exchange rate to ($X - M$) to the aggregate demand for U.S. goods and services. Other factors that would stimulate ($X - M$) include higher income abroad, trade negotiations that reduce unfair trade practices by foreign nations, and marketing campaigns by U.S. companies designed to promote U.S. products.

Your Turn

In June 1995, the Clinton administration persuaded Japan to agree to open its markets more fully to U.S. automobiles and auto parts. Given other factors, analyze the implications of this development for the *AD* curve in the United States, the U.S. output level, and the U.S. price level.

Factors That Shift the Aggregate Supply Curve

Other than the nation's price level, factors that influence production decisions include the quantity of inputs available (labor, capital, materials), the prices of inputs, and technological change. Increases in the quantity of inputs and improvements in technology increase aggregate supply—that is, they shift the *AS* curve rightward. Increases in input prices reduce aggregate supply, shifting the *AS* curve leftward.

Quantity of Inputs

Inputs into the production process include labor, capital, land, and raw materials. As the population grows, more labor becomes available and the nation's capacity to produce increases, shifting the *AS* curve rightward. Similarly, as the capital stock grows over time, the labor force can produce more output, and the AS curve shifts rightward. Because *capital deepening*—increasing the amount of capital per worker—stimulates productivity and shifts the *AS* curve rightward, policies that seek to promote long-term economic growth typically focus on stimulating investment expenditures. A war or natural disaster that reduces a nation's capital stock and/or labor force will shift the *AS* curve leftward.

Prices of Inputs

Other things equal, an increase in input prices makes production less profitable at each possible general price level, shifting the *AS* curve leftward. For example, if Congress boosts the minimum wage, the *AS* curve shifts leftward. And an increase in raw material prices, by reducing the profit margins associated with any given price level, shifts the *AS* curve leftward. When oil prices increased dramatically in the 1970s, the *AS* curve shifted sharply to the left. When oil prices collapsed in early 1986, the *AS* curve shifted rightward.

Technologi-cal Change Improvements in technology increase the amount of output the workforce can produce, shifting the *AS* curve rightward. Economists believe that, historically, technological innovation has been the most important single factor other than population growth in shifting the *AS* curve rightward. Hence, technology growth is a key factor in raising workers' productivity and living standards.

Table 20-1 on pp. 474–475 summarizes the factors that produce shifts in the *AD* and *AS* curves. It also indicates the direction of their influence on the nation's output and price level.

APPLICATIONS OF THE AGGREGATE DEMAND–AGGREGATE SUPPLY FRAMEWORK

The aggregate demand–aggregate supply model, though quite simple, is useful for understanding how Federal Reserve policy influences the nation's output, employment, and price level. In the next few sections, we use the aggregate demand–aggregate supply model to illustrate the challenges that confront the Federal Reserve when conducting monetary policy.

Equilibrium Output versus the Full Employment Output Level

Corresponding to each level of output is a certain level of employment and a certain unemployment rate. The economy's *natural unemployment rate* is defined as the lowest rate of unemployment that could be sustained without producing an acceleration of the nation's inflation rate. The level of output corresponding to this natural unemployment rate is known as the **natural output level,** also called the **full employment output level.** In Figure 20-2 on p. 476 the full employment output level is Y_F. The natural, or full employment, output level must be distinguished from the equilibrium output level, which is determined jointly by the nation's *AD* and *AS* curves. If the equilibrium output level is lower than Y_F, the unemployment rate exceeds the natural unemployment rate. In the left-hand panel of Figure 20-2, the equilibrium output (Y_{E1}) falls short of the full employment output level (Y_F). The magnitude by which the equilibrium output level falls short of full employment output is known as a **recessionary gap.**[3] This situation, which involves a loss of national output and income (and jobs), may call for stimulative measures by the Federal Reserve to shift the *AD* curve rightward, increase output, and reduce unemployment.

---

[3]Be sure you are clear on the distinction between a *recession* and a *recessionary gap*. A recession is a period of falling real output. A recessionary gap is the much more common phenomenon in which real output (whether rising or falling) lies below natural output. Output may be rising, but a recessionary gap may still exist because output lies below the natural output level.

Table 20-1

Some Factors that Shift the *AD* and *AS* Curves

Event	Impact on *AD* Curve	Impact on Real Output	Impact on Price Level
Congress cuts income taxes ($C\uparrow$)		+	+
Stock, bond, or house prices increase ($C\uparrow$)		+	+
Consumer confidence improves ($C\uparrow$)		+	+
Federal Reserve increases M and lowers interest rates ($C\uparrow, I\uparrow, [X-M\uparrow]$)		+	+
Expected sales increase or capacity utilization rate increases ($I\uparrow$)		+	+
Business confidence improves ($I\uparrow$)		+	+
Congress enacts 10% investment tax credit ($I\uparrow$)		+	+
Government expands interstate highway expenditures ($G\uparrow$)		+	+
U.S. dollar depreciates ($X-M)\uparrow$		+	+

Table 20-1

Some Factors that Shift the AD and AS Curves (continued)

Event	Impact on AS Curve	Impact on Real Output	Impact on Price Level
Income rises in Canada and Europe $(X - M)\uparrow$		+	+
Population increases		+	−
Capital stock increases		+	−
Wage and/or energy price increase		−	+
Technological innovation occurs		+	−

If the equilibrium output level exceeds the full employment output level (as in the right-hand panel of Figure 20-2), the economy is overstimulated. Aggregate demand is too strong, and the inflation rate is rising; an inflationary gap exists. The **inflationary gap** is the magnitude by which equilibrium output exceeds the full employment output level. Such a situation may call for restrictive action on the part of the Federal Reserve, to shift the AD curve leftward and bring down inflation. Whether or not the Fed should take actions to combat recessionary and inflationary gaps is a subject of debate among economists, as we shall see in the next section.

Stabilization Policies

Monetary and fiscal policies work their magic predominantly by altering the position of the nation's AD curve. On the one hand, the Federal Reserve strives to avoid an inflationary gap by preventing excessive aggregate demand. On the other hand, the Fed desires to

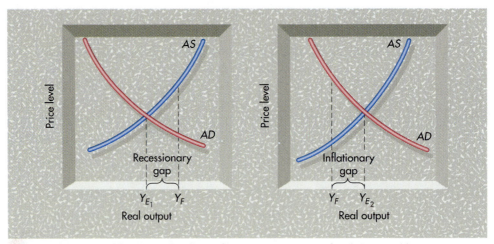

Figure 20-2   Equilibrium and Full Employment Output Levels. If the equilibrium output level (Y_E) falls short of the full employment output level (Y_F), a recessionary gap exists (left-hand panel). If equilibrium output exceeds the full employment output level, an inflationary gap exists (right-hand panel).

avoid large recessionary gaps and the associated losses of output, income, and jobs. It wants output to approach the full employment output level as closely as possible.

Given that the positions and slopes of the *AS* and *AD* curves are uncertain; given that there are significant time lags between the implementation of Fed policy actions and their impact on the nation's *AD* curve, output, and price level; and given that the natural unemployment rate (and Y_F) changes over time and is uncertain at any point in time, conducting effective monetary policy is a difficult task! In fact, some economists believe that the task is so formidable and fraught with technical and political obstacles that the Federal Reserve should not even make the attempt. In Chapter 26, we will discuss the "rules-versus-discretion" debate—the debate over whether the Federal Reserve should abandon discretionary monetary policy in favor of some sort of automatic rule governing the conduct of monetary policy. The best-known proposal calls for the Fed simply to increase M1 or M2 at some low and constant rate, regardless of economic conditions. That proposal is supported by only a minority of economists, however. Most economists believe that the Fed should continue to conduct monetary policy on a discretionary basis. They believe that, on balance, the Fed has contributed to economic stability (albeit with some glaring exceptions), especially in the past 15 years.

The Dilemma Posed by Adverse Aggregate Supply Shocks

In the 1970s, dramatic increases in world oil prices produced major leftward shifts in the *AS* curve in the United States and other industrial nations. The supply shocks created a dilemma for the Federal Reserve and central banks in other nations. Figure 20-3 illustrates the dilemma.

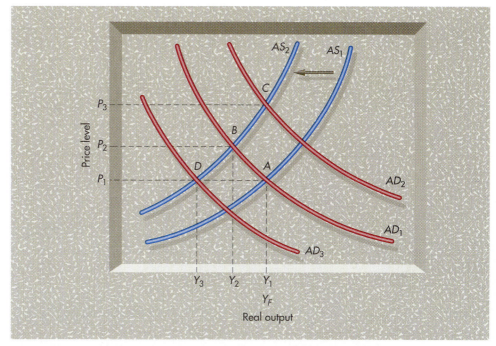

Figure 20-3   Adverse Aggregate Supply Shocks and Monetary Policy Alternatives. When oil prices increased sharply in the 1970s, the *AS* curve shifted leftward. This meant that the Federal Reserve would have to accept higher inflation, higher unemployment, or both.

Suppose that, before the oil price hike, the U.S. economy was at *A*, the intersection of AS_1 and AD_1. Equilibrium output (Y_1) coincided with the full employment level (Y_F), and the price level was P_1. Then, in early 1973, the OPEC oil cartel reached an agreement to curtail oil production sharply, and the price of oil soared. The *AS* curve shifted leftward, to AS_2. If the Federal Reserve had elected *not* to respond to this supply shock (leaving the *AD* curve unchanged), the economy would have moved to point *B* in the figure. The price level would have increased to P_2, and real output would have fallen to Y_2. A supply shock produces the worst of all worlds, a recession combined with higher inflation. This phenomenon has been dubbed **stagflation**—the combination of stagnant or falling output and severe inflation.

Suppose the Federal Reserve were committed to maintaining full employment. In that case, the Fed would implement stimulative measures to shift the nation's *AD* curve rightward, to AD_2. The economy would move to point *C* in the figure, with output returning to Y_F. Unfortunately, the price level would soar to P_3, and the nation would experience extremely severe inflation.

On the other hand, suppose the Fed were committed to maintaining price level stability—that is, maintaining the nation's price level at P_1. In that event, the Fed would have to counter the supply shock with restrictive monetary actions, shifting the *AD* curve down to AD_3. The economy would move to point *D*, preventing the oil shock from increasing the price level. Note, however, that output would decline to Y_3, a severely depressed level, causing the unemployment rate to soar.

As you can see, this is a no-win situation for the Federal Reserve. The Fed can choose between extremely high inflation coupled with full employment, extremely high unemployment accompanied by stable inflation, or some increase in both inflation and unemployment. As it turned out, the Fed attempted to steer a middle course. Inflation increased sharply in the 1970s, and the nation suffered two severe recessions in the decade beginning in 1973. During the 10-year period from 1963–1972, the U.S. unemployment rate had averaged 4.6 percent, while inflation had averaged 3.4 percent. The corresponding figures for the decade from 1973 to 1982 (the decade of the supply shocks) were 7.0 percent and 8.7 percent, respectively. A new term appeared in the jargon of popular economics as the nation's **misery index**—the sum of the unemployment and inflation rates—jumped from 8.0 percent to 15.7 percent. The decade went down in the annals of U.S. economic history as an unmitigated disaster. Exhibit 20-1 discusses the U.S. misery index and its relationship to stock prices.

In the remainder of this chapter, we will make the basic aggregate demand–aggregate supply model come alive by utilizing it to explain the major developments in U.S. macroeconomic history over the past 70 years.

THE AGGREGATE DEMAND–AGGREGATE SUPPLY MODEL AND MODERN U.S. MACROECONOMIC HISTORY

In the period since the 1920s, the U.S. economy has experienced periods of prosperity as well as periods of severe and widespread hardship. It has experienced episodes of inflation as well as times of relatively stable prices. It even experienced a rare episode of severe recession accompanied by rising inflation. Our aggregate demand–aggregate supply framework can help us understand the major macroeconomic phenomena of the past several decades.

The Great Depression of the 1930s

In Chapter 16, we analyzed the Great Depression and the role of the Federal Reserve in that episode. In terms of our aggregate demand–aggregate supply model, a series of events triggered a collapse of the nation's *AD* curve. In the late 1920s, the Fed tightened its monetary posture. The stock market crash, by reducing wealth and impairing consumer and business confidence, contributed to severe reductions in consumption and investment expenditures. From 1929–1933, the *AD* curve shifted persistently leftward, reducing both real output and the nation's price level. (This was the last significant episode of general **deflation**—a persistent decline in the price level—experienced in the United States.)

This deflation of prices sharply raised real interest rates, triggering widespread defaults by businesses, farmers, and households. That, in turn, impaired the health of the nation's banks, which were major lenders. The ensuing bank failures led to banking panics.

EXHIBIT 20-1

The Misery Index and Stock Market Performance

Unemployment is bad: it shrinks the nation's output and income, visits psychological harm on its victims, and triggers a host of societal problems, including increased incidences of alcoholism and crime. Inflation is also bad: it unfairly redistributes the nation's income, taking from some and giving to others. It also impairs economic efficiency and retards long-term economic growth. In seeking a simple index of the nation's economic health, politicians sometimes speak of a *misery index,* or *discomfort index*—the sum of the nation's inflation and unemployment rates.

The figure below shows the U.S. misery index for each month since 1959. Also shown is the S&P 500 Index, a good indicator of stock market performance. The association between the nation's economic health and stock prices is striking. Major stock market sell-offs in 1966, 1970, 1973–1974, and 1981–1982 were closely synchronized with spikes in the misery index associated with sharp escalations in inflation and/or unemployment. And the great bull markets of 1957 to 1965 and 1982 to 1996 were associated with significant, sustained declines in the misery index. Clearly, if major turns in the misery index could be foreseen, one could make a killing in the stock market.

Since 1959, the misery index has ranged from a low of 5.7 percent (November 1965) to a high of 21.9 percent (May 1980). In the 1990s, a period of relative economic stability, it has been confined to a range of approximately 8 to 12 percent.

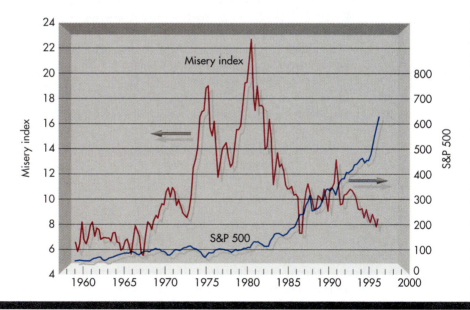

Together with inept Federal Reserve policy, these panics nearly destroyed the nation's banking system. As thousands of banks failed, the life savings of millions of families disappeared, feeding the pervasive atmosphere of gloom and further depressing stock prices, consumption, investment, and aggregate demand for goods and services.

On the international scene, a wave of economic isolationism caused a collapse of international trade, wrecking the export industries of the major industrial nations. U.S. authorities stood by passively during the downward-spiraling cascade of events, employing neither monetary nor fiscal actions to combat the massive leftward shift of the nation's *AD* curve. The result was the greatest economic catastrophe in U.S. history.[4]

World War II and Postwar Inflation

Beginning in the late 1930s, it became increasingly clear that the United States would ultimately become involved in the war being waged by Hitler. A military buildup begun in preparation for that involvement escalated dramatically after Japan bombed Pearl Harbor in December 1941. The resulting increase in government expenditures (*G*) stimulated aggregate demand. This fiscal stimulus was reinforced by the Federal Reserve, which maintained interest rates at abnormally low levels through heavy open market securities purchases, which rapidly expanded the monetary base and the monetary aggregates. From 1938 onward, the nation's *AD* curve shifted strongly rightward, sharply expanding real output.

By 1942 or 1943, an inflationary gap had developed (review Figure 20-2, right-hand panel). Because rigid wage-price controls were in place, however, the reported price indexes failed to reflect the inflationary pressures that were building up. When wage-price controls were removed at the end of the war, prices surged. By 1948, the price level had approximately doubled relative to the 1940 level.

In the 1950s, after 2 decades of bedlam, the U.S. economy finally returned to normal. Inflation was subdued, averaging about 2 percent per year throughout the decade, while the unemployment rate averaged 4.5 percent. The stock market appreciated strongly. Between 1952 and 1961, however, the nation experienced three recessions.

The Post-1960 Era

Figure 20-4 shows the 1960–1996 behavior of actual GDP and **potential,** or **natural, GDP**—the hypothetical GDP level that would be produced if the unemployment rate were always maintained at the economy's natural rate of unemployment. *Actual GDP* fluctuates over time because of shifts in the nation's *AD* and *AS* curves. *Potential GDP* trends upward over time because of growth in the population (and labor force) and productivity (output per worker). Its rate of growth fluctuates with changes in the growth rates of the labor force and productivity.

Figure 20-5 shows the nation's inflation rate over the last 35 years. The annual rates of change of both the consumer price index (CPI) and the more sensitive producer price

---

[4]See Table 16-1 in Chapter 16 for a review of the key U.S. macroeconomic indicators in the 1930s.

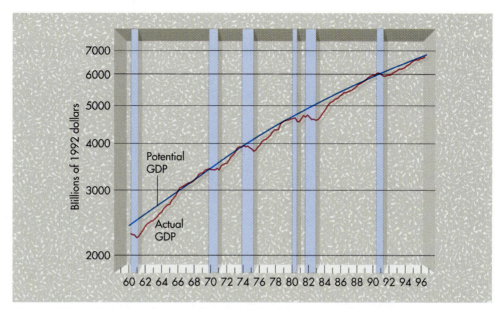

Figure 20-4   Actual and Potential GDP, 1960–1996. *Potential GDP* rises over time because of growth in the labor force and rising productivity. *Actual GDP* fluctuates as aggregate supply and aggregate demand shift. The United States experienced six recessions between 1960 and 1996; note how actual GDP dropped below potential GDP each time. (*Note:* Shaded areas depict periods of recession, as determined by the National Bureau of Economic Research.)   *Source:* Data from *Citibank Economic Database.*

index (PPI) are shown. Together with Figure 20-4, this graph provides a wealth of information about the macroeconomic history of the United States after 1960. You will want to refer back to both of these figures as we analyze recent events in U.S. economic history in the sections that follow.

The Early 1960s

In November 1960, John F. Kennedy was elected president. In his presidential campaign, Kennedy and his advisors had been critical of the sluggish performance of the U.S. economy in the 1950s. The Soviet Union had recently launched the satellite *Sputnik,* and some feared the Soviets might be on the threshold of surpassing the United States scientifically and perhaps even economically. Note in Figure 20-4 that the output gap was relatively large in the early 1960s. That is, actual GDP was far below potential GDP. Kennedy and his Keynesian advisors pressed for income tax cuts to stimulate the economy. An investment tax credit was also proposed for the purpose of fostering capital formation and boosting long-term economic growth.

Following President Kennedy's assassination in 1963, President Lyndon B. Johnson guided a major tax reduction bill through Congress. As a result, the nation's *AD* curve shifted rightward. This stimulated output in 1964 and 1965. By the summer of 1965, the nation's unemployment rate had declined to 4.4 percent, a level that most economists believed was very close to the nation's natural unemployment rate. Inflation remained low.

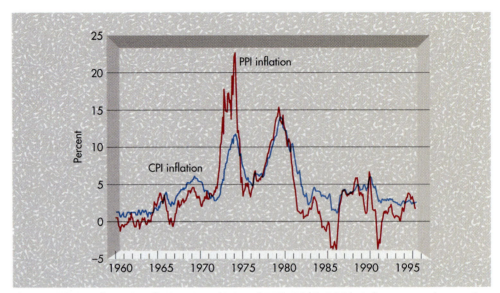

Figure 20-5   The U.S. Inflation Rate (CPI and PPI), 1960–1996. Inflation was low in the early 1960s but ratcheted upward from the mid-1960s to 1980. It came down dramatically in 1980–1982 and has remained relatively low and stable since then.   *Source: Data from Citibank Economic Database.*

The Keynesian-inspired tax cuts were hailed in the media as being highly successful. A picture of the great English economist John Maynard Keynes (who had died nearly 20 years earlier) appeared on the cover of *Time* magazine. The stock market hit an all-time high in 1965. Things looked good. Then all hell broke loose!

The Vietnam Era: 1965–1972

In the summer of 1965, the U.S. made a momentous decision to escalate its involvement in the Vietnam War. A major buildup of U.S. forces in Southeast Asia ensued, along with a large increase in military expenditures. Government purchases increased sharply, shifting the *AD* curve rightward. Given that the economy was already near full employment, the government's failure to cut back nonmilitary expenditures or raise taxes meant that an inflationary gap was sure to develop.[5] The excessive stimulus to aggregate demand during 1967–1969 reduced the unemployment rate to approximately 3.5 percent—well below the natural unemployment rate—and aggravated inflationary pressures. The U.S. inflation rate steadily escalated from 1.3 percent in 1964 to 5.9 percent in 1969.

After the 1968 presidential election, in which Richard Nixon narrowly defeated Hubert Humphrey, a serious effort was made to bring down inflation. Restrictive monetary policy actions, coupled with a modest income tax hike, shifted the *AD* curve leftward. In November 1969, the U.S. economy plunged into recession. Within a year the

---

[5]President Johnson's economic advisors warned him in the fall of 1965 that inflation would escalate significantly unless nonmilitary government expenditures were cut or taxes were increased. Because Johnson was seeking political support to prosecute the war, he did not request either a tax hike or a cut in expenditures. His policy mistake was thus attributable to political considerations, not faulty economic advice.

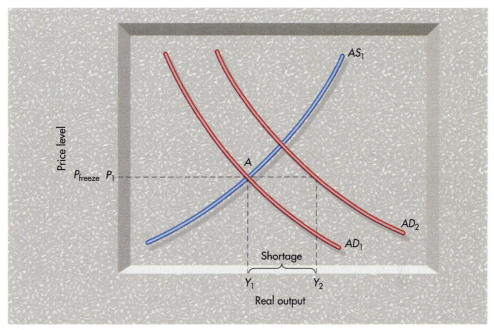

Figure 20-6   Wage-Price Controls and Economic Policy in the Early 1970s. If aggregate demand is stimulated when price controls are in place, shortages of goods and services develop. In such circumstances, the controls become counterproductive.

unemployment rate had increased from 3.5 percent to 6 percent. Inflation, though somewhat reduced, continued to exceed 5 percent throughout 1970, a level that seemed intolerable at the time.

Frustrated by the tenacity of inflation in the face of a fairly severe national recession, President Nixon abandoned his free market principles and, in August 1971, opted for a comprehensive set of wage-price controls. The economic rationale for the controls was to brake inflation expectations in an effort to slow wage hikes and combat the leftward shift of the nation's *AS* curve.[6] Then, with the 1972 presidential election approaching, the Nixon administration made a political decision to stimulate economic activity by shifting the *AD* curve rightward. The growth rate of the money supply accelerated in 1972. As Figure 20-6 shows, when combined with rigid price controls, such an event creates shortages and bottlenecks, aggravating the eventual increase in the nation's price level.

---

[6]Note that a leftward shift of the *AS* curve pushes up prices and reduces output (raising unemployment). Once inflation becomes heavily entrenched, wages and other input prices begin to anticipate future inflation. This phenomenon shifts the *AS* curve further to the left, exacerbating the problem of inflation and increasing the cost of fighting it. If the announcement of wage-price controls could significantly reduce the public's expectation of inflation, it would also moderate wage demands and slow the inflation rate of other input prices, such as those for raw materials. These actions, in turn, would slow or halt the leftward shift of the *AS* curve, permitting greater output with less inflation. This was the economic rationale for the wage-price controls. The *political* rationale for the controls, however, may have been quite different. Read on.

Initially, suppose the economy is at A in Figure 20-6, the intersection of AD_1 and AS_1. The price level is P_1, and output is Y_1. The price freeze is implemented, preventing the price level from rising above P_1. Then the government implements stimulative fiscal and monetary actions, shifting the AD curve rightward to AD_2. Note that while the quantity of goods and services demanded is now Y_2, producers are willing to produce only Y_1 units of output at the frozen price level. A general shortage of goods and services develops, in the amount of $Y_2 - Y_1$, as frustrated customers are unable to obtain products. A multitude of problems is unleashed, including a scarcity of certain raw materials and the development of black markets and other schemes to circumvent the controls. Given the excess demand for goods and services, the controls are clearly counterproductive—as they were in the early 1970s.

The Economic Nightmare of 1973–1983

In early 1973, Nixon's wage-price controls were terminated. As predicted by the analysis in Figure 20-6, a sharp burst of inflation occurred when controls were removed in the face of significant excess demand for goods and services. During 1973 and 1974, the inflation rate averaged 11.5 percent. By mid-1973, the unemployment rate had fallen below 5 percent, and the U.S. economy was becoming overheated. On top of this, the 1973 oil price shock shifted the AS curve sharply leftward. The United States experienced its first episode of severe *stagflation,* the simultaneous occurrence of severe inflation and falling output. By most measures, the 1973–1975 recession was the most severe downturn since the Great Depression. In spite of this, the U.S. inflation rate (CPI) averaged more than 10 percent during the 16-month economic contraction.

During 1975 and 1976, inflation slowed to approximately 5 percent. Jimmy Carter was elected president in November 1976, during a period of economic recovery. During the next 2 years, the economic expansion proceeded and the economy moved toward the peak of the business cycle. At the beginning of 1979, the unemployment rate stood at 6 percent, a level many economists believed matched the nation's natural unemployment rate. The U.S. economy was poised on the brink of another episode of inflation.

Then, in 1979, a second major oil price shock occurred, and oil prices zoomed to $40 per barrel. The shock shifted the AS curve leftward, triggering an escalation in inflation and a contraction in output. In 1980, the inflation rate shot above 12 percent and the nation endured the first of two back-to-back recessions. The first, a brief and mild downturn, lasted for only the first half of 1980. The second recession, which occurred early on President Reagan's watch, lasted from July 1981 to November 1982 and was a blockbuster. In fact, it exceeded the 1973–1975 downturn in severity; today it remains the most severe recession since the Great Depression.

The Federal Reserve played a role in the downturn by applying severe monetary restraint in 1981 and 1982, pushing short-term interest rates to the highest levels since the Civil War. The Fed cracked down in order to attack inflation, which had been running at double-digit levels since late 1978. The resulting downward shift in the AD curve, coupled with the oil price shock–induced leftward shift in the AS curve, produced the severe contraction of output of 1981–1982.

Supply-Side Economics of the Early 1980s

In the early 1980s, under the Reagan administration, the government instituted a series of measures intended to shift the nation's AS curve to the right. Figure 20-7 shows the rationale for the program, known as **supply-side economics.** Note that a rightward shift of the AS curve is materially beneficial to the nation. Not only does the level of real output

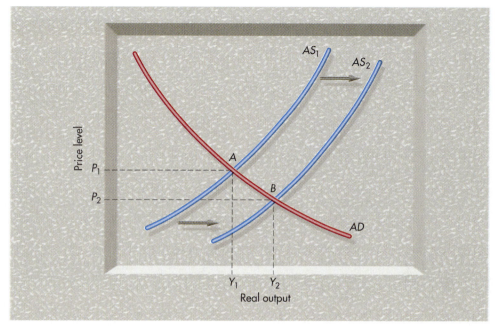

Figure 20-7   The Rationale for Supply-Side Economics. If government policies could produce a rightward-shifting *AS* curve, benefits would accrue to society in the form of greater output (and higher living standards) and a lower price level.

(and income) increase, but the price level declines. The latter phenomenon may make it possible to implement stimulative monetary and fiscal policies that boost aggregate demand and output without raising inflation. As long as the rightward shift of the *AS* curve is attributable to factors other than population growth, average living standards in the nation should rise.[7]

No economist would quarrel with the *goal* of supply-side economics: producing a persistently rightward-shifting *AS* curve. The disputes among economists involve the most desirable or appropriate methods of bringing about a rightward-shifting *AS* curve, as well as the potential *scope* of such measures. To organize your thinking about effective supply-side policies, reconsider the factors that would shift the *AS* curve rightward—that is, increases in the quantity of inputs, decreases in input prices, and increases in technology. Hence, an enlightened supply-side program should seek to expand the existing population's participation in the labor force, stimulate saving, investment, and capital formation, reduce the prices of inputs such as raw materials and capital goods, and promote the search for new technologies.

The Reagan supply-side program included major reductions in individual and corporate income tax rates that were aimed at stimulating saving, investment, and labor force participation; a series of deregulatory initiatives; and a commitment to eradicate the severe

---

[7]If the only cause of the rightward shift of the *AS* curve were population and labor force growth, living standards would likely fail to increase. Even though the *AS* curve were to shift rightward, output would likely increase no faster than the rate of increase in the labor force. Only if output increases faster than population will the nation enjoy a higher living standard.

EXHIBIT 20-2

The Reagan Supply-Side Program: Did It Work?

The purpose of any respectable supply-side economic program is to increase the incentive to work and produce, shift the mix of national output from consumption and government purchases toward investment spending, spur technological innovation, and boost the rate of productivity growth. Did the Reagan experiment of the 1980s do the job? That issue is debatable. But it may be instructive to look at some key macroeconomic indicators to see whether there was a discernible improvement in U.S. economic performance in the 1980s vis-à-vis the dismal 1970s.

In the accompanying table, certain positive aspects of economic performance in the 1980s are conspicuous. First, inflation came down dramatically, averaging slightly more than half the rate experienced in the 1970s. Second, on the heels of the bear market of the 1970s, the stock market turned in a magnificent performance. Stock prices appreciated by more than 10 percent per year, even after adjusting for inflation. And that figure understates the total returns from stocks, because it does not include dividends. The job creation figures are also impressive in view of the decline in the number of new workers coming into the labor force in the 1980s (because of a decline in the birth rate after the early 1960s).

On the other hand, the consumption share of the nation's output increased sharply—a fact that should not be surprising in view of the large personal income tax cuts enacted in the early 1980s. The investment share of output remained almost unchanged, in spite of tax incentives aimed at spurring investment. The increased consumption share of output came partially at the expense of government purchases but mainly at the expense of net exports of goods and services. The U.S. trade deficit hit record levels in the 1980s as the nation borrowed heavily from abroad to finance its domestic investment and federal budget deficits.

The bottom line in evaluating a supply-side program is its effect on the rate of productivity growth, the source of rising living standards. The results are shown in the final column of the table. Much of the motivation for implementing supply-side policies in the

---

inflation inherited from the 1970s. The cornerstone of the Reagan program was the large personal income tax cuts implemented in 1982, 1983, and 1984. The three consecutive annual tax cuts lowered the average American's income tax rate by approximately 25 percent. The supply-side rationale for the tax cuts was not simply to bolster expenditures but to increase the incentive to work and earn income. Rather than stimulating aggregate demand, the tax cuts were intended to shift the *AS* curve rightward. The Reagan administration believed that, by the early 1980s, marginal income tax rates had become so high as to significantly impair the incentive to work and achieve a high income.[8] To the extent that lower income tax rates strengthen the propensity to work, the supply and productivity of labor should increase, shifting the *AS* curve rightward. The Reagan program also included the following measures aimed at stimulating investment expenditures: tax incentives for

---

[8]During the 1970s, severe inflation coupled with an unindexed income tax system steadily pushed most Americans into higher marginal income tax brackets. By 1980, a surprisingly large number of families found that their combined federal and state marginal income tax rates exceeded 50 percent.

EXHIBIT 20-2 (CONTINUED)

1980s came from the dramatic slowdown in productivity growth that preceded the decade—from 2.9 percent per year during 1947–1969 to 1.4 percent annually in the 1970s. Unfortunately, the rate of productivity growth slowed even further in the 1980s, to 1.1 percent annually. Although productivity may have grown even more slowly in the absence of the Reagan initiatives, its performance after the early 1980s makes it difficult to give an unqualified endorsement to the Reagan supply-side program.

U.S. Macroeconomic Performance: 1980s versus 1970s

| | Inflation Rate (%)[1] | Unem-ploy-ment Rate (%) | Stock Market Performance (%)[2] | Annual Job Creation[3] | \multicolumn{4}{c}{Output Shares} | Produc-tivity Growth[4] (%) |
					C/GDP (%)	I/GDP (%)	G/GDP (%)	$\frac{(X - M)}{GDP}$ (%)	
1970s	7.4	6.2	−4.4	2,000,000	64.0	16.4	20.2	−0.6	+1.4
1980s	4.0	7.3	+10.6	1,900,000	66.7	16.3	19.0	−2.0	+1.1

[1]Average annual rate of change of consumer price index.
[2]Average annual rate of change of S&P 500, adjusted for CPI inflation.
[3]Average annual increase in total U.S. employment.
[4]Average annual rate of growth of productivity in the all-business sector.

Note: Starting and ending months were selected so that data for each decade run from cyclical peak to cyclical peak. Hence, the 1970s decade actually employs data from November 1969 through December 1979, while the data for the 1980s encompass July 1981 through June 1990.

Source: *Citibank Economic Database.*

---

saving, a reduction in the corporate income tax rate, investment tax credits, accelerated depreciation allowances, and a reduction in the capital gains tax rate.

Supporters of the Reagan supply-side policies point to several positive features of economic performance in the 1980s. First, the supply-side measures implemented in the early 1980s were followed by an economic expansion that lasted nearly 8 years. Nearly 17 million jobs were created during Reagan's two terms in office, and inflation declined after 1981 and remained quite low relative to the 1970s. Interest rates came down significantly relative to 1978–1982 levels, and the stock market soared to all-time highs.

Critics of the Reagan program charge that the program was poorly designed for purposes of shifting the AS curve rightward. Because the tax cuts were not accompanied by reductions in federal expenditures, large budget deficits ensued. The national saving rate (private saving plus government saving) plunged during the 1980s. Real interest rates were very high for several years. The investment share of national output failed to increase in the 1980s in spite of the tax breaks targeted toward investment. The rate of productivity growth in the United States remained stagnant through the remainder of the decade. Income inequality actually increased after enactment of the Reagan program: while the affluent did remarkably well, tens of millions of blue-collar and other middle-class workers suffered decreases in their real wages.[9]

In the opinion of these critics, the strong and lengthy economic recovery from the severe 1981–1982 recession was attributable to a rightward-shifting *AD* curve, not to a rightward shifting *AS* curve. In support of this view, they point out that productivity growth in the 1980s was even lower than it had been in the 1970s (see Exhibit 20-2). Many of the jobs created in the 1980s paid relatively low wages. In short, the critics claim that the Reagan episode of supply-side economics worsened the nation's distribution of income and failed to produce the desired macroeconomic effects. These critics derisively termed the Reagan policy "trickle-down economics."

Economic Stability and Low Inflation: 1983–1996

In its battle to conquer inflation, the Federal Reserve pushed interest rates to extreme levels in the early 1980s, and the results were dramatic. The prime loan rate hit 22 percent, and Treasury bill yields soared above 15 percent. Real interest rates remained at high levels for several years, causing considerable economic distress. Bankruptcies and foreclosures escalated. Unknown to the public, the savings and loan crisis was rapidly developing, as interest rates payable to depositors soared above the long-term rates earned by S&Ls on their mortgage holdings. The unemployment rate rose above 10 percent in 1982 and 1983 and did not fall below 7 percent until early 1986.

Nevertheless, one can perhaps find merit in the Fed's anti-inflation campaign because it laid the foundation for an era of low unemployment and relatively stable prices that persisted through the mid-1990s. Inflation came down sharply from 1980–1983. Aided by a strongly appreciating dollar during 1982–1985 and a collapse of oil prices in early 1986, which shifted the *AS* curve rightward, the U.S. economy embarked on an expansion that lasted from November 1982 until July 1990. Partly because of the strong dollar and weak oil prices, inflation remained surprisingly subdued for several years into the expansion. However, as the unemployment rate fell below 6 percent during 1987–1989, inflation began to escalate. At the beginning of 1990, the unemployment rate stood at 5.3 percent, while inflation was 5 percent.

In early 1990, Iraqi strongman Saddam Hussein invaded Kuwait and massed his troops on the Saudi Arabian border. Visions of massive oil price hikes and a repeat of the 1970s nightmare raced through the minds of President George Bush and his economic advisors. The initial uncertainty created by this crisis, together with high levels of consumer debt, resulted in a plunge in consumer confidence. The *AD* curve shifted downward (leftward), tilting the U.S. economy into recession.

The Federal Reserve quickly implemented stimulative measures, and the recession proved to be one of the mildest and briefest on record. It lasted only 9 months and involved a contraction of real output of less than 2 percent. The unemployment rate peaked at 7.7 percent, considerably lower than the peaks in the 1973–1975 and 1981–1982 recessions.

---

[9]How much of the increased income inequality in the 1980s resulted from the supply-side policies and how much was due to structural market forces which would have occurred in any event is the subject of some disagreement. Clearly, the demand for highly skilled workers has increased relative to the demand for unskilled workers. That phenomenon would have boosted the wage differentials between high- and low-income workers even if the supply-side measures had not been implemented.

But the early portion of the recovery from the recession was also unusually sluggish, with real output rising more slowly than the long-term trend of output growth until late 1993. By summer 1996, however, things looked bullish. The unemployment rate stood around 5.5 percent, inflation poked along in the 2 to 4 percent range, and the stock market barreled vigorously into record territory.

SUMMARY

The aggregate demand–aggregate supply model is a useful framework for analyzing the causes of fluctuations in economic activity. The aggregate demand (*AD*) curve summarizes the expenditures side of the economy, while the aggregate supply (*AS*) curve captures the production side. Shifts in the *AD* and *AS* curves produce changes in output, unemployment, and the price level. Changes in aggregate demand result both from forces unrelated to monetary and fiscal policies and from changes in such policies. The *AS* curve shifts as labor force, capital stock, technology, and input prices change. Increases in output and employment stem from rightward shifts in the *AD* and/or *AS* curve. Economic contractions result from leftward shifts in the *AD* and/or *AS* curve. Monetary policy works chiefly by shifting the *AD* curve. If the economy is weak and a recessionary gap exists, stim-ulative monetary policies can boost the *AD* curve and strengthen the economy. If the economy is overheated and suffers from an inflationary gap, restrictive monetary policies can shift the *AD* curve leftward, reducing output and slowing the inflationary pressures. Historically, most episodes of inflation have been caused by a rightward-shifting *AD* curve, while recessions have typically been triggered by downward shifts in the *AD* curve. In the 1970s, however, the nation experienced two episodes of stagflation—periods of declining output accompanied by accelerating inflation—caused by major leftward shifts in the *AS* curve. Supply-side economics refers to government measures designed to produce persistent rightward shifts in the *AS* curve. Such measures, if effective, result in higher living standards and lower inflation.

Answer to Your Turn (p. 472)

By reducing the barriers to the sale of U.S. automobiles and auto parts within Japan, the agreement should cause U.S. exports to Japan to increase. The U.S. AD curve should thus increase (shift rightward). As a result, U.S. output and the general price level should increase.

KEY TERMS

monetary theory
aggregate demand (*AD*) curve
wealth effect
aggregate supply (*AS*) curve
inflation
natural unemployment rate
natural, or full employment, output level

recessionary gap
inflationary gap
stagflation
misery index
deflation
potential, or natural, GDP
supply-side economics

STUDY QUESTIONS

1   Give *two* reasons why the nation's aggregate demand (*AD*) curve is a downward-sloping function of the price level.

2   Explain what happens to the position of the nation's *AD* curve, the level of output, and the price level if

   a   The Federal Reserve increases interest rates sharply.

   b   Congress enacts an income tax hike.

   c   A balanced budget amendment results in major cutbacks in government purchases of goods and services.

   d   The U.S. dollar appreciates strongly against the yen and other currencies.

   e   Consumer confidence increases.

   f   Congress enacts a 25 percent investment tax credit.

   g   Congress implements a major tax incentive for saving (e.g., tax-deductible IRA accounts).

3   Explain what happens to the nation's *AS* curve if

   a   Congress increases the statutory minimum wage.

   b   Oil prices drop to $12 per barrel.

   c   A new virus kills 25 percent of the population.

   d   New solar technologies cause energy prices to plummet.

   e   Crop restriction payments to farmers are eliminated.

   f   The U.S. dollar falls sharply (assume the U.S. imports raw materials).

4   Name and explain all the mechanisms you can think of through which monetary policy actions might shift the nation's *AD* curve. (*Hint:* Think in terms of *C, I, G,* and $X - M$.)

5   "Both the 1973–1975 recession and the 1981–1982 recession were deliberately engineered by the Federal Reserve to reduce inflation to acceptable levels." Assuming low inflation is a high priority of the Fed, is this statement logical? Explain, using aggregate demand–aggregate supply analysis to back up your reasoning.

6   If you were to design a supply-side economic program for the late 1990s, what aspects of Reagan's program would you implement? What features would you reject—that is, what would you do differently? Justify your position.

7   Credibility is considered essential if the Federal Reserve is to reduce inflation while minimizing loss of output and the associated increase in unemployment. Explain, using the aggregate demand–aggregate supply model, why a *credible, announced* anti-inflation policy may be more effective than one which is not credible or is not made public.

8   Explain the dilemma that confronts the Federal Reserve when a major negative aggregate supply shock occurs.

9   A wave of corporate downsizing occurred in the 1990s. What possible effects might the movement have on the economic decisions of those currently employed? What are the possible effects on the nation's *AS* curve? Explain.

10   In fall 1993, Congress passed the North American Free Trade Agreement (NAFTA), which removed barriers to trade among the United States, Canada, and Mexico. Using the aggregate demand–aggregate supply framework, discuss the short-run implications of NAFTA for the U.S. economy.

11   A significant portion of Germany's capital stock was demolished during World War II. Since that time, the *growth rate* of Germany's economy has been higher than that of the United States, while German inflation has remained low. Explain these phenomena in the context of the aggregate demand–aggregate supply model.

SUGGESTIONS FOR ADDITIONAL READING

On the basics of the aggregate demand–aggregate supply model, consult a principles of economics textbook and review the aggregate demand–aggregate supply chapter. More in-depth analyses can be found in any intermediate macroeconomics text. On the oil price shocks of the 1970s and the resulting stagflation and policy options, see Alan Blinder, *Economic Policy and the Great Stagflation* (New York: Academic Press, 1979). For sympathetic analyses of the Reagan supply-side program, see Lawrence Lindsey, *The Growth Experiment* (New York: Basic Books, 1990), or Michael Boskin, "Tax Policy and Economic Growth: Lessons from the 1980s," *Journal of Economic Perspectives,* Fall 1988, pp. 71–97. For critical

views on the same issue, see Benjamin Friedman, *Day of Reckoning: The Consequences of American Economic Policy under Reagan and After* (New York: Random House, 1988), or Barry Bosworth, *Tax Incentives and Economic Growth* (Washington, D.C.: Brookings Institution, 1984). An excellent and balanced presentation by one of the chief architects of the Reagan program is Martin Feldstein, "Supply-Side Economics: Old Truths and New Claims," *American Economic Review,* May 1986, pp. 26–30. For a discussion of the recent economic environment, read the most recent *Economic Report of the President,* published in February each year by the U.S. Government Printing Office.

■ ## The Demand for Money
and Velocity of Money

In Chapter 20, we developed the aggregate demand–aggregate supply model of macro-economic analysis. In that model, changes in the nation's real output and price level are initiated by changes in aggregate demand and aggregate supply. A rightward shift in the *AD* curve, for example, increases nominal GDP, pushing up both real output and the price level.

Figure 21-1 illustrates the actual behavior of nominal and real GDP over the last 35 years. Note that while output and income trend persistently upward (panel *A*), this progress occurs at a far from steady pace (panel *B*). Note, for example, the sharp contractions of real output that occurred in the 1973–1975 and 1981–1982 recessions (panel *B*).

Though the aggregate demand–aggregate supply model demonstrates that such cyclical fluctuations in nominal and real output may be caused by shifts in either the *AS* or *AD* curve, most economists believe that they are driven predominantly by shifts in the *AD* curve. Changes in the money supply are believed to be one important cause of shifts in the *AD* curve: an increase in the money supply shifts the *AD* curve rightward; a decrease in the money supply shifts the *AD* curve leftward. But a multitude of other forces examined in Chapter 20 is also capable of initiating shifts in the nation's *AD* curve. For example, changes in consumer confidence or business sentiment can initiate changes in consumption and investment expenditures, shifting the *AD* curve. Economists disagree about the relative importance of monetary and nonmonetary forces in causing aggregate demand and GDP to fluctuate.

In this chapter, we examine the relationship between the nation's money supply and its nominal GDP. We will explore the link through which changes in the money supply and other forces influence nominal GDP, real output, and the nation's price level. As we will see, the debate over the role of money in the economy boils down to a debate over the nature of the *velocity of money* and its close relative, the *demand for money*. The **velocity of money** (hereafter referred to simply as "velocity") is a multiplier that links the nation's money stock to its nominal GDP. As a general proposition, Monetarists believe that velocity is stable and predictable, while Keynesians and other nonmonetarists view it as unstable and unpredictable. Hence, monetarists believe that Federal Reserve–engineered changes in the money supply have a predictable effect on GDP, while nonmonetarists are skeptical of that proposition.

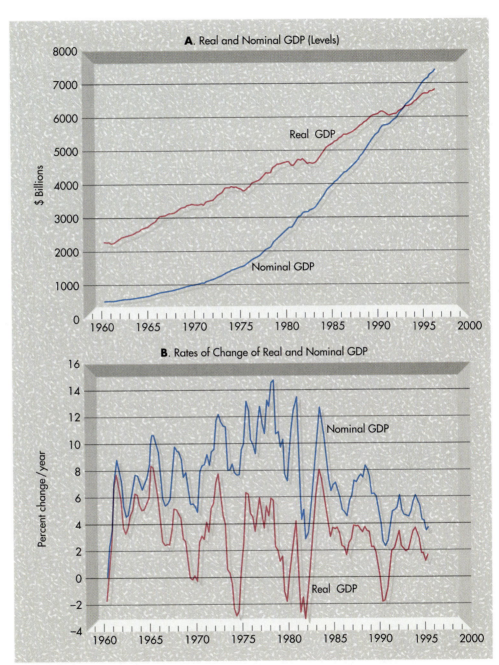

Figure 21-1   Real and Nominal GDP and Their Annual Growth Rates, 1960–1996.
While both nominal and real GDP trend strongly upward over time (panel *A*), their growth rates exhibit considerable variability (part *B*).   *Source:* Data from *Citibank Economic Database.*

THE VELOCITY OF MONEY

A useful way of illustrating the connection between money and economic activity is the **equation of exchange.** Originally developed by Professor Irving Fisher, perhaps the most eminent American economist of the first half of the twentieth century (see Exhibit 21-1), the equation is stated as

(21-1) $$MV_T \equiv PT$$

where

M = the average money supply in existence in a given year

V_T = the **transactions velocity of money**—that is, the number of times the average dollar is spent per year ($V_T \equiv PT/M$)

P = the average price of the transactions that take place during the year, and

T = the number of transactions occurring during the year

Note that the right-hand side of the equation (PT) is simply the total dollar value of annual transactions (the average price per transaction times the number of transactions). The left-hand side of the equation also expresses the value of annual transactions but does so in terms of the money stock and the transactions velocity of money. This equation is an identity or tautology—it is true by definition. It simply states that annual expenditures (MV_T) equal annual expenditures (PT).[1] Because V_T is defined as annual expenditures (PT) divided by the money stock (M), it is correctly viewed as the number of times the average dollar is spent per year.

It is important to emphasize that $V_T = PT/M$ by definition. To measure transactions velocity, one simply divides the total value of transactions (PT) in a given period by the average stock of money (M) held during the period. By definition, Equation 21-1 is an identity that holds at all times, as opposed to an equation that holds only under equilibrium conditions.

To give an example, suppose that in a given year your total expenditures are $8000. Suppose also that during the year you maintain an average money balance (demand deposits plus currency) of $400. If an average money balance of $400 is to accommodate total transactions of $8000 per year, your average dollar must be spent, or turned over, 20 times annually. Your transactions velocity is thus 20 per year:

$$V_T = \frac{\text{Annual expenditures}}{\text{Average money holdings}} = \frac{\$8000/\text{yr}}{\$400} = 20/\text{yr}$$

---

[1]Fisher referred to the left-hand side of the equation as the "money side" and the right-hand side as the "goods side." Thus, MV_T represents the value of money expenditures in a given period, while PT indicates the value of the items purchased and sold in the period. The two sides of the equation are equivalent because each side indicates annual expenditures.

EXHIBIT 21-1

Irving Fisher (1867–1947)

Considered the foremost American economist of the pre–World War II era (and arguably the greatest of all time), Irving Fisher spent his entire academic career at Yale University.

He received his B.S. from Yale in 1888 and earned his Ph.D. there 3 years later, at the age of 24. Fisher taught mathematics at Yale from 1892 until 1895. When a position in economics opened in 1895, he switched departments and remained in economics until his retirement in 1935. He loved the discipline because of its clear applicability to crucial real-world issues.

Among Fisher's numerous contributions to economics, those in the areas of monetary, capital, and utility theory stand out. Fisher clarified the role of money in the economy through his famous equation of exchange, $MV = PY$. In his book *The Purchasing Power of Money* (1911), he detailed the factors that influence the velocity of money (V) and real output (Y). Because Fisher believed that velocity and real output change slowly, he argued that the principal cause of inflation and deflation is changes in the quantity of money.

Perhaps because Fisher lived through an era of price level instability (including the long and slow 1873–1896 deflation, the severe World War I inflation, and the big deflations of 1920–21 and 1929–33), he stressed the evils of unstable prices. To prevent severe price level instability, he advocated a "compensated dollar" plan, in which the dollar would be tied to a fixed *value* of gold (determined by an index of prices) rather than a fixed *quantity* of gold. If the price level increased 5 percent, the amount of gold required to back one dollar would rise by 5 percent. Given the nation's gold stock and the existence of a gold standard regime, the plan would automatically produce a 5 percent contraction in the money supply, thereby nipping inflation. Fisher compiled more than three hundred documents (books, articles, letters to editors) supporting his "compensated dollar" proposal during the period 1912–1935.

Brilliant, versatile, and a passionate crusader, Fisher was actively involved in proposed reforms of the times, particularly in the areas of temperance, world peace, eugenics, conservation, and public health (while ill with tuberculosis, he invented a tent for its treatment). He made himself wealthy by devising and marketing an index-card file system in 1910. An indicator of the fortune he was able to amass is the fact that he lost an estimated $8 million to $10 million during the Great Depression of the 1930s.

Through the application of mathematical and statistical techniques to economics, Fisher contributed to the development of economics as a science. Not one but *two* important concepts are named after him: the "Fisher Equation" ($MV = PY$) and the "Fisher effect," the tendency for a change in expected inflation to produce a corresponding, similar change in nominal interest rates (see Chapter 5).

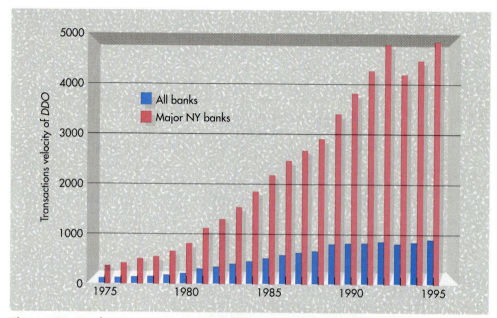

Figure 21-2 The Transactions Velocity of Demand Deposits, 1975–1995. The demand deposit turnover rate has increased dramatically over the years, particularly for major New York banks.   *Source:* Federal Reserve System.

The nation's aggregate *PT* includes expenditures on goods in the early and intermediate stages of production as well as spending on *final* goods and services (GDP). *PT* also includes transactions in common stocks, bonds, used cars, garage-sale items, and many other items which are not included in GDP. Because we do not have reliable data on total expenditures, *PT,* we cannot accurately measure the transactions velocity of money, *PT/M.* There is also no way to measure the transactions velocity of currency and coins, an important component of the money supply. However, the Federal Reserve does collect data on demand deposit turnover, or what could be called the transactions velocity of demand deposits. The data cover a large sample of banks. The demand deposit turnover rate is calculated by dividing total clearings through checking accounts in a given year by the average magnitude of demand deposits in that year. Because demand deposits constitute the bulk of the narrow money supply (M1), the rate of turnover of demand deposits is a proxy for the transactions velocity of narrow money, V_T.[2]

Figure 21-2 shows the behavior of the transactions velocity of demand deposits in recent years for all banks and for major New York banks. Note that the demand deposit turnover rates for commercial banks have increased sharply. The reasons for this phenomenon will become clear to you as we explore the determinants of velocity in this chapter and the next.

---

[2]The rate of turnover of demand deposits (*DDO*) is considerably greater than the rate of turnover of currency (C^p). Therefore, the transactions velocity of *demand deposits* is greater than the transactions velocity of *money* ($DDO + C^p$).

The Income Velocity of Money

For purposes of conducting monetary policy, we are more interested in the volume of expenditures on *final goods and services* (GDP) than in the volume of transactions in everything including stocks, bonds, raw materials, used cars, and garage-sale items. Therefore it is useful to reformulate the equation of exchange in terms of expenditures on final goods and services only. The formula is

(21-2) $$MV_Y \equiv PY$$

where

M = the average money supply in existence in a given year

V_Y = the **income velocity of money,** or the number of times the average dollar is spent on *final goods and services* per year ($V_Y \equiv PY/M$ or GDP/M)

P = the average price of all final goods and services purchased during the year—that is, the average price of all goods and services constituting GDP, or an index of such prices relative to some base year, and

Y = the number of final goods and services produced in the year, or an index of real GDP relative to the base year

In this formulation, PY is the dollar value of GDP expenditures in a given year (nominal GDP). MV_Y, or the average money supply (M) times the annual rate of turnover of money (V_Y), also stands for aggregate spending on these final goods and services. Again, V_Y is defined in such a way as to make the expression an identity ($V_Y \equiv PY/M$). Suppose Y is $4 trillion and P is 2.0 (which means that the current GDP price index is 200 in relation to some base year = 100). Aggregate spending for GDP is therefore $8 trillion per year. If the money supply is $1.6 trillion, the income velocity of money must be 5.0. That is, to finance annual GDP expenditures of $8 trillion, an average money stock of $1.6 trillion must exhibit an income velocity, or annual turnover rate, of five times per year. We see that V_Y is easily computed: one merely divides the annual rate of nominal GDP or (PY) by the average money supply (M).

Note that the money supply variables in Equations 21-1 and 21-2 are exactly the same. However, the dollar value of total annual expenditures (PT) in Equation 21-1 is several times larger than the dollar value of annual expenditures on final goods and services (PY) in Equation 21-2. It follows that the transactions velocity of money (V_T) is much larger than the income velocity of money (V_Y). However, the basic principles governing V_Y and V_T are the same, and their long-term trends and cyclical patterns are similar.

By itself, Equation 21-2 tells us nothing about real-world behavior. It makes no assertions about the causal relationships among its four variables. For example, the equation of exchange does *not* assert that an increase in M causes P, Y, or PY (nominal GDP) to rise. Nor does it imply that an increase in GDP expenditures or nominal GDP (MV_Y and PY) causes the price level to rise. Why, then, should you concern yourself with this equation? The answer is that it provides a useful framework for thinking about the role of money in macroeconomic analysis.

Equation 21-2 *does* indicate that if the money supply (*M*) changes, one of two things *must* happen:

1 Velocity (V_Y) must change proportionally in the opposite direction, so that aggregate GDP expenditures (MV_Y and PY) remain unchanged; or

2 GDP expenditures must move in the same direction as the money supply.

In other words, if the money supply increases 10 percent, GDP expenditures must also increase unless velocity declines 10 percent or more, negating the effect of the increase in *M*. Equation 21-2 also indicates that if GDP expenditures are to increase, either *M* or V_Y (or both) must increase.

At one hypothetical extreme, if V_Y is constant, the money supply is the sole determinant of the level of nominal GDP expenditures and economic activity. In that case, no tool other than control of the money supply is needed in order to control GDP expenditures accurately. If velocity (V_Y) is not constant but is independent of the money supply and is subject to reasonably good prediction, monetary policy can still be a highly effective method of influencing economic activity. At the other extreme, if *V* fluctuates in a totally unpredictable manner, changes in *M* engineered by the Federal Reserve will have no *predictable* effect on GDP. In that event, monetary policy would be totally ineffective. To the extent that velocity is random or unpredictable, the power of monetary policy and the influence of the Fed on GDP expenditures and general economic activity are compromised.

Concerning the effectiveness of fiscal policy in influencing the economy, we can state that if a tax cut or an increase in government expenditures is to successfully stimulate GDP expenditures in the face of a constant money supply, the fiscal stimulus must increase V_Y. If velocity is constant or is not influenced by fiscal policy initiatives, fiscal policy will be ineffective in influencing macroeconomic activity. On the other hand, if V_Y systematically increases with stimulative fiscal measures and decreases with fiscal restraint, fiscal policy may be powerful. Clearly, the nature and behavior of velocity are important. The determinants of velocity, and especially its responsiveness to monetary and fiscal actions, are key issues in macroeconomics.

Each measure of the money supply (M1, M2, M3) has a corresponding measure of income velocity. These are V_1 (GDP/M1), V_2 (GDP/M2), and V_3 (GDP/M3). Figure 21-3 shows the behavior of these three measures of V_Y since 1960. V_1 (GDP/M1) is the income velocity of the narrow measure of money. V_1 trended strongly upward until the early 1980s, when it became unstable and began to trend downward. We will explain some of the reasons for this change in behavior of V_1 later in this chapter and in Chapter 22. Note also the behavior of the velocity of the broader measures of money (M2 and M3). Because the growth rates of M2 and M3 exceeded the growth rate of M1 after 1960, it follows that the velocities of M2 and M3 increased less rapidly than the velocity of M1. In fact, their long-term trends have been relatively flat, although both V_2 and V_3 have increased significantly in the past 10 years.

Because the velocity of money is intimately connected to the motives for holding money, in the next few sections we will look at the reasons why people hold money, as well as the connection between these motives and velocity. The amount of money (M1 or M2) that people desire to maintain is known as the **demand for money.**

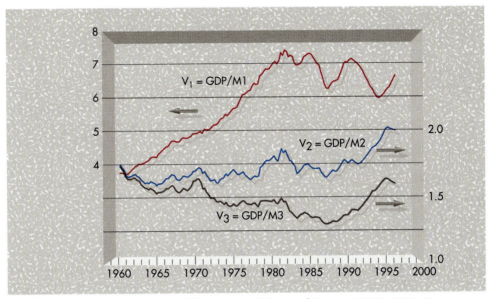

Figure 21-3   Three Measures of the Income Velocity of Money, 1960–1996. Since 1960, the velocity of M1 has trended upward, while the velocities of M2 and M3 have remained flat.   *Source:* Federal Reserve System.

Velocity and the Demand for Money

Let us return to Equation 21-1. If an individual spends $8000 per year and holds an average M1 money balance (currency plus demand deposits) of $400 throughout the year, her transactions velocity (V_T) must be 20 times per year. That is, if her average money balance of $400 is to accommodate transactions of $8000 per year, her average dollar must "turn over," or be spent, a total of 20 times per year. This is precisely equivalent to the statement that the individual holds an average money balance equal to one-twentieth of her annual transactions. That is, the ratio of her money balance to annual transactions is simply the reciprocal of the transactions velocity of her money. By the same token, if V_T in the U.S. economy is 40, the public holds, on the average, money balances equivalent to one-fortieth of aggregate annual U.S. transactions.

The same principle holds if we view the problem in terms of the income velocity of money, V_Y. If a U.S. money supply of $1.2 trillion accommodates annual GDP expenditures (PY) of $7.2 trillion (so that V_Y is 6.0), we know that, on average, the public holds one-sixth of the dollar value of annual GDP in the form of money. The magnitude of money balances held relative to annual GDP is the reciprocal of V_Y, the income velocity of money. Since $V_Y = GDP/M$, $1/V_Y = M/GDP$.

Note carefully the units associated with V_Y and its reciprocal. In the first case, V_Y is the ratio of an annual dollar *flow* (GDP) to an average dollar *stock* (M). Arithmetically, the dollar signs cancel out, and we are left with a pure number per year. If GDP is $7.2 trillion per year and M is $1.2 trillion, then V_Y is six *per year.* Now, if we look at the reciprocal of V_Y, we have the ratio of a stock of dollars of money (M) to an annual flow (GDP). Again, the dollar signs cancel out and we have a number expressed as a fraction of a year. If M is $1.2 trillion and GDP is $7.2 trillion per year, then the reciprocal of V_Y is one-sixth of 1 year, or 61 days. If the income velocity of money (V_Y) is 6, this means that the average individual or firm retains money balances sufficient to finance expenditures on final goods and services (GDP) for 61 days.

In the next section we will look at the demand for money, including the motives that cause individuals and firms to desire to hold money.

THE DEMAND FOR MONEY

Early in the twentieth century, an influential group of economists at Cambridge University in England began to analyze the economic role of money by focusing on the demand to hold money balances.[3] Their approach was a natural result of the widespread familiarity of the concept of demand in economics. Just as economists examine the demand for automobiles and the demand for housing, it seemed natural to devote attention to the factors underlying the demand for money balances. Their investigations produced important insights and advances in monetary theory.

Rather than using the equation, $MV_Y \equiv PY$, the Cambridge group and modern economists have typically used an expression such as

(21-3)
$$M_d = kPY, \qquad \text{where } k = \frac{M_d}{PY}$$

In this formulation, M_d is the *demand* for money rather than the supply of money; k is the fraction of GDP (or PY) that the public *desires* to hold in money balances. If the economy is in equilibrium, so that the demand for money (M_d) equals the supply of money (M), k will be the reciprocal of the actual income velocity of money, V_Y. In equilibrium, $V_Y = 1/k$ and $k = 1/V_Y$.

If the demand for money rises relative to GDP (that is, if k rises), income velocity (V_Y) will fall. If people desire to reduce their fraction of annual expenditures held in money (that is, if k falls), the income velocity of money will increase. Any theory which explains the behavior of k also explains the behavior of V_Y and vice versa. Given the important role of the variables k and V_Y, one can understand why professional economists have invested many more hours in researching the demand for money than the demand for automobiles or the demand for housing. In the next section, we discuss the reasons people hold money.

---

[3]The most influential of this group were Alfred Marshall and his colleague (and former student), A. C. Pigou. See the reference to Pigou's work in the "Suggestions for Additional Reading" at the end of this chapter.

Motives for Holding Money

Because money (currency and demand deposits) typically earns little or no interest, we might conclude that the average person would be foolish to maintain a money balance of $10,000 throughout the year.[4] Why hold wealth in the form of money if other financial assets yield a much higher rate of return? Economists have identified three different motives for holding money, which, together with the existence of credit cards, charge accounts, the frequency of paydays, and many other factors, determine the public's demand for money. The first and most essential motive is to finance expected transactions.

Transactions Demand

People hold money in part because they need to finance forthcoming expenditures for goods and services, but the timing of their income payments does not coincide with their expected pattern of expenditures. This demand for money to finance ordinary expenditures is called the **transactions demand for money.** The principle is easy to illustrate. Suppose a student receives a monthly income of $600 from part-time employment supplemented by parental assistance. Assume that her monthly expenditures are also $600. Suppose that on the first day of each month the student deposits $500 into a checking account and retains $100 in currency. She uses these money balances ($600) at a constant rate throughout the month, until they are depleted on the last day of the month. She then replenishes the balances at the beginning of the new month.

The heavy line in Figure 21-4 shows the student's spending pattern and money balances. She holds a balance of $600 on the first of the month, gradually depletes it, and ends the month with no money. If we average her balances on each day of the month, we obtain an average balance of $300. Because the student spends $7200 during the year and holds $300 on average, her (transactions) velocity of money is 24 times per year. That is, on an average day, she holds a balance equal to $\frac{1}{24}$ of her annual expenditures, a balance sufficient to finance 15.2 days of expenditures.

Now suppose the student begins to receive her paycheck and her parents' check on a weekly rather than a monthly basis. To simplify the calculation, assume there are exactly 4 weeks in each month. On the first day of each week, the student has a balance of $150 in the form of demand deposits and currency. By the end of each week, the funds have been depleted. The resulting pattern of the student's expenditures is shown by the lighter line in Figure 21-4. Though the student continues to spend $7200 per year, she now holds an average balance of only $75. Thus her transactions velocity is $7200/yr ÷ $75, or 96 times per year. She keeps only $\frac{1}{96}$ of her annual expenditures in the form of money—enough to finance slightly less than 4 days of expenditures.

The lesson of this example is clear: An increase in the frequency with which income payments are received produces a greater synchronization between receipts and expenditures,

---

[4]From 1933 until the early 1980s, U.S. law prohibited banks from paying interest on demand deposits. Though the Depository Institutions Deregulation and Monetary Control Act of 1980 ended that prohibition, interest rates payable by banks on *DDO* are still significantly lower than yields on Treasury bills and other short-term securities.

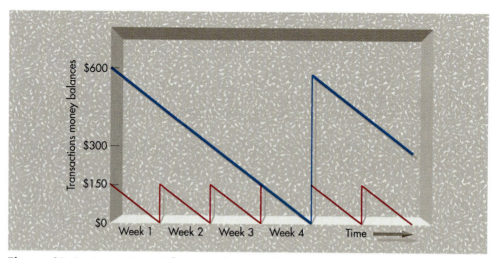

Figure 21-4   Transactions Balances with Expenditures Spread Evenly over Time. If a student spends her entire income at a constant rate and receives funds monthly (heavy line), her average money holdings are one-half of her monthly income, or $300. If she receives funds weekly (fine line), her average holdings are $75.

reducing the demand for money relative to annual expenditures. When the frequency of paydays increases, the velocity of money rises.[5]

   The time pattern of expenditures also has an effect on the demand for money balances. Let us return to the example of the monthly receipt of $600 and a transactions velocity of 24 per year. Suppose, however, that rather than spending her money balances at a constant rate, the student depletes them by the middle of each month. Figure 21-5 shows the student's spending pattern. During the first half of the month, she maintains an average balance of $300. In the second half of the month, her average money holdings are zero. For the month as a whole, therefore, the student keeps an average balance of $150. Given her annual expenditures of $7200, her transactions velocity is 48 (contrast that with a transactions velocity of 24 when she drew down her balances gradually over the entire month). Because the student's expenditures are now more closely timed to coincide with her receipt of income, her average demand for money is reduced and the velocity of her money increases. In general, *any factor that increases the degree of synchronization between the receipt and disbursement of funds reduces the demand for money and increases its velocity.*

   Let us look at a final example, which illustrates the impact of financial innovations on the demand for and velocity of money. Return to the assumptions illustrated in Figure 21-4, in which the student's transactions velocity was 24 times per year. Now suppose that the student obtains a credit card and runs up a bill of $300 each month (paying for half of her expenditures with the credit card). On the first day of each month, she spends $300 to

---

[5]Think for a minute about this phenomenon and its implications for money demand and velocity. If income were received just as frequently as it is spent, the demand for money would approach zero and velocity would approach infinity. People hold transactions balances only because their expenditures do not coincide with their receipts of funds.

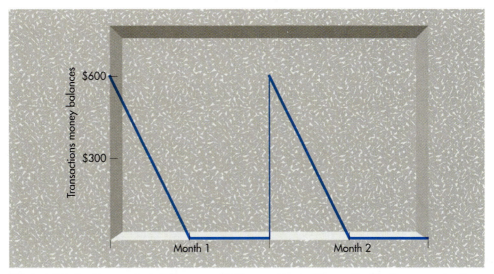

Figure 21-5 Transactions Balances with Uneven Expenditures. If a student spends all her funds in the first half of the month, her average money holdings are halved and the velocity of her money balances doubles.

pay off the credit card bill from the previous month. After the first day of each month, therefore, her balance is only $300. That suffices to cover her needs, because she uses her credit card to meet half of her transactions. Suppose the remaining $300 is used up at a constant rate throughout the remainder of the month. Figure 21-6 illustrates the student's spending and money balance pattern. A quick look at the figure shows that the use of a credit card reduces the average balance she holds during the month to approximately $150. Assuming that the student's annual expenditures remain at $7200, the transactions velocity of her money becomes $7200/yr ÷ $150 = 48/yr.

Note that the introduction of a credit card has allowed the student to reduce her average money balance by 50 percent, from $300 to $150. This doubles the velocity of her money. Credit cards raise the velocity of money by reducing the demand for money relative to annual expenditures. The same principle applies to other forms of credit, such as charge accounts, business credit lines, and bank overdraft protection. The proliferation of credit cards and other credit arrangements was an important contributing factor in the persistent uptrend in the velocity of M1 from World War II through 1980 (review Figure 21-3). In a sense, these arrangements have increased the *efficiency* of money by reducing the average amount of money required to finance a given amount of transactions.

Given payday schedules, the public's banking habits, and institutional arrangements governing the use of credit, the income level exerts a major impact on the transactions demand for money. As income rises, people step up their expenditures, and their average transactions demand for money rises accordingly. For example, if the student's monthly income rises from $600 to $1200, she begins the month with a cash balance of $1200 instead of $600. Assuming that she spends the entire $1200 evenly throughout the month,

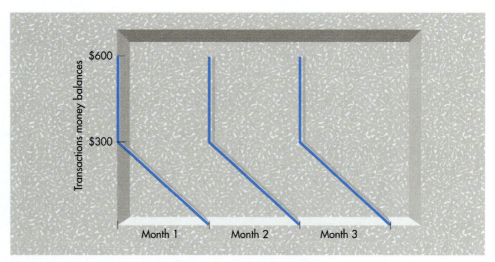

Figure 21-6 Transactions Balances of a Credit Card User. The use of credit cards improves the synchronization of receipts and disbursements. This reduces the demand for money and increases its velocity.

her average demand for money will be $600 rather than $300. The transactions velocity of her money remains unchanged, however, because her annual expenditures and her average money balance have both increased by 100 percent.

Your Turn

Assume that your monthly income and expenditures are $800. You spend your income at a steady rate, and you hold money only for transactions purposes.

a. Suppose you use your credit card to finance one-fourth of your purchases each month, while using cash and your checking account to pay for the rest of your transactions. The check you write to pay off your credit card bill clears on the first of each month (at the same time as your monthly $800 paycheck is deposited). Calculate your transactions demand for money and transactions velocity of money (V_T).

b. Suppose you throw away your credit card but maintain your expenditure habits. Calculate your new transactions demand and transactions velocity.

Precaution-ary Demand

If the discussion of personal money management in the preceding section struck you as being unrealistic, you are right! In the United States today, money balances (M1) are approximately twice as large as monthly income. M2 balances are more than six times larger than monthly income, or more than half of *annual* income—a figure too high to be explained by the need to hold money until the next payday.

One explanation of this phenomenon is the environment of uncertainty in which we live. To provide a margin of error, most of us keep funds above and beyond the amount we actually expect to use in a given period. Keynes labeled such funds "precautionary balances" and attributed their existence to the possibility of unforeseen events requiring additional expenditures. Unexpected medical or auto repair bills, the unanticipated markdown of a desired item to a bargain price (prompting its purchase)—these and a thousand other events may prompt expenditures not originally anticipated. Injury, illness, or an economic downturn could also disrupt the flow of family income. The maintenance of money balances to meet unforeseen circumstances is called the **precautionary demand for money.**[6] The magnitude of such a cushion is likely to depend on the level of income. An individual with an income of $60,000 per year is likely to maintain a higher precautionary balance than a person who earns $20,000 annually.

Speculative Demand

Keynes argued that, in the nation as a whole, a significant amount of money is held for the purpose of capitalizing on a good investment opportunity should one arise. In the words of Keynes, the **speculative demand for money** includes money balances held with the intent of "securing profit from knowing better than the market what the future will bring forth."[7]

Imagine a situation in which the Standard & Poor's 500 Index is 30 percent below its previous high. The economic outlook for the next 3 or 4 years is becoming increasingly favorable: interest rates and inflation are trending downward, and the outlook for sales and corporate profits is one of healthy and sustained growth. The time may be at hand to commit funds to the stock market and perhaps also to the corporate bond market. However, if an investor is already fully invested in stocks, bonds, and real estate and is holding no money balances in excess of those needed for transactions and precautionary purposes, it may be difficult or impossible to take advantage of the opportunity. The investor may be able to finance new purchases of stocks and bonds only by liquidating other securities or by selling real property.

The problem is that neither of those options is desirable. Since the securities market is depressed, selling some securities to purchase others is not a desirable choice. And real property is relatively illiquid; it is difficult to sell on short notice for its full value. The net result might well be that the investor is forced to pass up the opportunity to purchase securities at a most favorable time. Keynes hypothesized that, in order to avoid forgone opportunities, alert and perceptive individuals and firms maintain money holdings in excess of those needed to satisfy transactions and precautionary motives.

Keynes emphasized that the speculative demand for money is highly volatile, because it depends heavily on the changing nature of the public's expectations. If the outlook for the stock and bond markets turns increasingly bleak, the speculative demand for money will *increase* as people unload securities. As the outlook clears up and becomes more favorable, the speculative demand for money will *decline* as people "take the plunge" and use their money to purchase stocks and bonds. The speculative demand for *money* moves in the opposite direction from the speculative demand for *securities* or other nonmonetary assets.

The nature of the speculative demand for money is an important consideration in determining the relative stability of the velocity of money, the link between money and GDP

---

[6]The development of overdraft protection and a variety of "near monies" that are virtually free of market risk (such as money market mutual fund shares) may have substantially reduced the relative importance of precautionary M1 balances since Keynes' day. The precautionary demand for broader measures of money, such as M2 and M3, is likely to be much greater than the precautionary demand for M1, which includes only *DDO* and *C^p*.

[7]John Maynard Keynes, *op. cit.,* p. 170. The same qualification noted in footnote 6 would also apply to speculative money balances. That is, today the speculative demand for money applies more effectively to the broader money measures (M2 and M3) than to the narrow money measure (M1).

expenditures. If the speculative demand for money is highly volatile, velocity will be quite variable and difficult to predict. This issue therefore has a bearing on the issue of the effectiveness of monetary and fiscal policy. The nature and indeed the very *existence* of a speculative demand for money are therefore controversial.

In the next section, we will examine the relationship between interest rates and the demand for and velocity of money.

The Role of Interest Rates in the Demand for Money

The "price" one pays for holding money—in economic terms, the *opportunity cost*—is the interest rate one could have earned from nonmoney assets. (Or, in the event that banks pay interest on *DDO,* the cost is the difference between the yield on nonmoney assets and the yield on money.) One might expect the quantity of money demanded to be a function of its price or cost—that is, the market rate of interest. That would place money on the same ground as other goods or services, whose quantity demanded is inversely related to their price. Figure 21-7 shows how the demand for money might look in that case.

The nature of the demand curve shown in Figure 21-7 is one of the important issues in macroeconomics. It is an important consideration in determining whether monetary policy or fiscal policy more strongly and predictably influences the nation's *AD* curve and

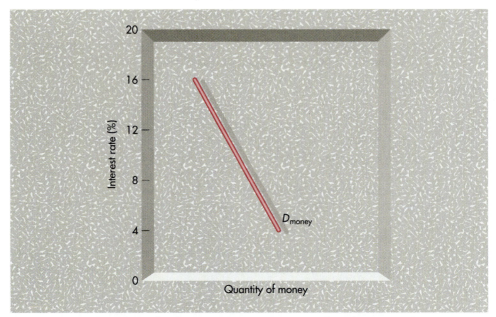

Figure 21-7   The Relationship between the Interest Rate and Total Money Balances Demanded. The opportunity cost of holding money is the interest rate one can earn on nonmoney assets. As interest rates rise, people prefer to hold less money (and more nonmoney assets).

the level of economic activity. Keynesians believe that the quantity of money demanded is quite sensitive to the interest rate. They view the curve in Figure 21-7 as being relatively flat. They also believe that the *position* of the curve is volatile, shifting back and forth in response to various events that trigger changes in outlook and therefore in the demand for money. Monetarists believe that the curve is very steep, close to vertical, and that its position is relatively stable, shifting chiefly in response to changes in income. Thus they assert that the demand for money is relatively unresponsive to the interest rate.[8] Further, they believe the curve shifts only slowly and predictably over time. (Exhibit 21-2 explains how economists study the demand for money.)

Let us examine the theoretical basis for the contention that the demand for money is inversely related to the interest rate. We will begin with the first of the three motives for holding money, the transactions demand for money.

Interest Rates and the Transactions Demand

As we have seen, transactions balances are those monies which must be held in order to bridge the inevitable time gap between the receipt of funds and their later disbursement. If these funds must be held to finance expenditures later in the month, how can their magnitude be related to the interest rate? The answer is that for the majority of individuals, the interest rate is probably *not* a relevant consideration. However, for wealthy individuals, large business firms, and other organizations that have large receipts and disbursements, the transactions demand for money is likely to be significantly influenced by interest rates.

Let us illustrate the principle with an example. Suppose a wealthy individual earns and spends $100,000 each month. Rather than deposit the full $100,000 in a checking account on the first of the month, this individual initially deposits $50,000 and uses the rest of the money to purchase U.S. Treasury bills with 15 days to maturity. At midmonth, as his checking account approaches depletion, he deposits the proceeds from the matured Treasury bills ($50,000 plus interest) into the account. Figure 21-8 illustrates this money management plan.

Note that by investing half his paycheck in Treasury bills, the wealthy person earns interest on $50,000 for half a month. Does his behavior make sense? Is it rational? That depends on the interest rate and the transactions costs associated with the purchase of the securities, including the inconvenience associated with making the extra transactions.[9] If the interest rate on the Treasury bills in this example is 8 percent and the securities are held for half of each month, the individual will gross $2000 per year, or $166.67 a month, for his trouble. From this must be deducted the out-of-pocket transactions costs—primarily the commission or brokerage fee charged by the agent who buys the securities. The net return, then, must be weighed against the inconvenience of engaging in the transactions

---

[8]Elasticity of demand is the crucial concept in this debate. Keynesians believe that the interest elasticity of the demand for money is fairly high (although not greater than 1.0) in absolute value. Monetarists believe it is quite low, though by no means zero. Milton Friedman once estimated the interest elasticity of the demand for money to be -0.1, which implies that a 10 percent increase in the interest rate (e.g., from 6 percent to 6.6 percent) will bring about a 1 percent reduction in the demand for money (e.g., from $1400 billion to $1386 billion). Keynesians have estimated the elasticity to be much higher, generally in the -0.5 to -1.0 range. See the references in the "Suggestions for Additional Reading" at the end of this chapter, particularly the book by David Laidler.

[9]Rather than buying securities each month, many individuals find it more convenient to transfer funds between a money market mutual fund and a bank checking account or to use an ATM to transfer funds from a savings to a checking account.

EXHIBIT 21-2

Estimating Money Demand Functions

Because it is of crucial significance to monetary policy, economists have invested literally hundreds of thousands of hours empirically investigating the demand function for money. Following our discussion of the motives for holding money, a general formulation for the money demand function is as follows:

$$M/P = f(Y, r, Z)$$

In this formulation, M stands for nominal money holdings and P represents the price level (so M/P stands for *real* money balances). The dependent variable to be explained in the model is the amount of real money balances people collectively choose to hold.

The independent variables include the income level (Y) and the level of interest rates (r). Also included is a third variable, Z, which represents the state of financial technology and other institutional factors—the availability of substitutes for money and their transactions costs, the use of credit cards, the frequency of paydays, and so forth. Z also encompasses "tastes," which determine one's willingness to spend time engaging in securities transactions, thinking about personal financial matters, and so on.

Mathematically, economists may write the function as follows, before estimating it via regression analysis:

$$M/P = (Z)(Y^a)(r^b)$$

Economists are particularly interested in the size of the income and interest rate elasticities of demand for money (a and b, respectively), the explanatory power of the overall model, and its stability over time. If variations in income and interest rates account statistically for a predominant portion of the variation in real money balances, and if the equation is relatively stable from year to year, money demand and velocity are predictable—one can predict them by knowing income and interest rates. This means that the Fed could set money supply targets that would come very close to achieving desired GDP goals. On the other hand, if the model does not account well for real money balances, or if it is highly unstable over time, then money demand and velocity are unstable. This means that the Fed has little confidence in the GDP levels that will result from any given money supply.

From the 1950s into the mid-1970s, a consensus existed among students of the money demand function that the function was stable and that income and interest rates did a good job in accounting for real money balances. Beginning in the mid-1970s, when the pace of financial technology accelerated in response to high inflation and high interest rates, the function became highly unstable and has remained so through the 1980s and 1990s. This means that the demand for and velocity of money have been hard to predict. The link between M1 and economic activity became so unreliable that in 1987 the Fed stopped specifying target ranges for M1. In 1993, it also de-emphasized M2 targets.

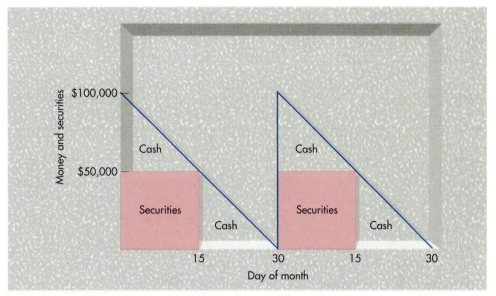

Figure 21-8   The Transactions Demand of a Wealthy Individual. By making transactions in interest-bearing assets and reducing money holdings, a wealthy person can earn a higher income. This behavior increases money velocity.

and making extra trips to the bank. In this case, it would appear to be sensible to make the transactions. In fact, one might even step up the number of transactions, purchasing $75,000 worth of Treasury bills on the first of the month and retiring $25,000 each on the first day of weeks 2, 3, and 4 (of a 4-week month). The gross return on such a scheme would be $250 per month, or $3000 per year.[10]

Suppose, on the other hand, that the current yield on Treasury bills is only 3 percent. In that case, the gross return earned by purchasing $50,000 worth of Treasury bills on the first of the month and liquidating them at midmonth would be only $750 per year, or $62.50 per month. After deducting transactions fees, some wealthy individuals might find the net return insufficient to compensate them for the inconvenience. We can conclude that for wealthy individuals and for many business firms, the interest rate is likely to be a significant influence on the transactions demand for money and therefore on the velocity of money.[11]

The higher the interest rate, the lower the quantity of money demanded (the more wealth is kept in bonds and other interest-bearing assets), and therefore the higher the velocity of money. Since a major portion of the money in the United States is held by business firms,

---

[10]Professors James Tobin and William Baumol independently demonstrated that a rational individual or firm will increase the number of such transactions as the interest rate rises. This means that average money balances demanded fall (and V_Y rises) as interest rates rise. See the references to Tobin and Baumol in the "Suggestions for Additional Reading" at the end of this chapter.

[11]These considerations clearly do not apply to the typical worker in the United States. Suppose a breadwinner earns $1600 take-home pay per month. On the first of each month, he deposits $800 in a checking and $800 in a savings account; on the fifteenth, he transfers $800 from savings to checking. Assuming 5 percent interest on savings accounts, the worker earns a piddling $20 per year for his trouble. And it is a good bet that the $20 gain will be washed out by the service charges levied on his checking account as a result of the lower average balance kept there.

wealthy individuals, and units of government (whose balances tend to be relatively large), it is plausible that the interest rate may significantly influence the transactions demand and the velocity of money.

Interest Rates and the Precautionary Demand

Precautionary money holdings—contingency balances against unforeseen circumstances—may also be somewhat sensitive to interest rates. When interest rates are very high, one may be tempted to pare down precautionary money balances and keep as much wealth invested in interest-earning assets as possible. Thus the treatment of these balances is similar to that of transactions balances.

Interest Rates and the Speculative Demand

One of the most significant (and disputed) aspects of Keynesian theory is the hypothesis that people and firms hold a significant amount of money for speculative purposes. For Keynes, the interest rate and the economic outlook or the public's expectations were the key variables influencing the quantity of money that is held for speculative purposes. Keynes concluded that the demand for speculative money balances is inversely related to the interest rate. That is, the lower the interest rate, the greater the desire to hold wealth in the form of money with which to speculate.

Keynes analyzed the problem in the context of an individual confronted with a choice between investing in government bonds or holding wealth in the form of non-interest-earning money balances. For Keynes, the crucial consideration was the current rate of interest on bonds relative to the rate regarded by the individual as "normal," or the level toward which the actual interest rate is expected to gravitate. According to Keynes, each individual forms a perception of the "normal" interest rate, largely on the basis of past experience. Further, the level of this "normal" rate was said to be not heavily influenced by the *current* interest rate. If the current interest rate is quite low relative to the "normal" rate, people will expect the interest rate to rise in the near future. If the current interest rate is above "normal," people will expect a decline in interest rates.

Consider an individual with $20,000 of financial wealth above and beyond other personal assets (automobile, house, clothing, etc.) and above and beyond transactions and precautionary money holdings. Suppose she is confronted with a choice of investing the wealth in long-term bonds or holding it in the form of money. Keynes illustrated the case with a perpetual bond issued by the British government, the *consol.* Exactly the same principle applies to any government, corporate, or municipal bond; the consol is simply easier to work with because the relationship between its yield and price is so straightforward. The following equation states this relationship.

(21-4) $$P = \frac{R}{i}$$

where

P = the current market price of the bond

R = the constant annual return in dollars (the coupon payment), and

i = the current yield on other assets of comparable risk (and therefore also the market-determined yield on this bond)

Table 21-1

The Relationship between Market Yield and Price on a Perpetual Bond Paying $50 a Year

i (%)	P ($)	i (%)	P ($)
10%	$ 500	4%	$1250
8	625	3	1667
6	833	2	2500
5	1000		

For any bond, R is fixed and guaranteed by the issuer (in the case of the consol, the British government). Barring insolvency of the issuer, it will be paid. Suppose that in this case R is fixed at $50 per year, in perpetuity. We can relate the consol's price to the market yield via Equation 21-4. Table 21-1 shows the prices for a range of yields. The table shows that if yields are currently running at 5 percent on securities of comparable risk, the market will dictate a price of $1000. If yields on comparable securities plunge to 2 percent, the price will be bid up sharply, to $2500. But if interest rates escalate to 10 percent, the right to the $50 annual payment will be worth only $500.

Suppose that, during an individual's lifetime, the observed range of yields on such bonds has been 2 to 10 percent. Keynes postulated that if the market interest rate reached 2 percent, the individual would feel strongly that in the future the rate could only rise. But, as Table 21-1 indicates, a rise in interest rates implies a decline in bond prices. The meager annual return (2 percent) would not be sufficient to compensate for the risk of incurring a future capital loss on the bond. Thus, when interest rates are unusually low, the prudent individual would avoid these bonds like the plague, holding on to cash (speculative money balances) until a better opportunity arose. In such circumstances, the demand for money would be high. An individual with $20,000 to speculate with would prefer to maintain the entire $20,000 in the form of money.

On the other hand, when yields are high, bond prices are at bargain levels. At a 10 percent yield, the consol is available for only $500 (see Table 21-1). According to Keynes, there are two reasons for an individual to invest the $20,000 in bonds and reduce his or her speculative money holdings to zero. First, the return is 10 percent annually—about as high as the individual has ever seen. Thus, the opportunity cost of holding idle money is 10 percent per year, a stiff penalty. Second, the individual is confident that the odds favoring a decline in yields are overwhelming. When yields decline, the individual who purchased the bonds at $500 will reap a capital gain as bond prices rise. There is every reason, then, for the individual to invest the full $20,000 in bonds.

To go from individual analysis to aggregate analysis, we must allow for the fact that different individuals have different perceptions regarding the "normal" level of interest rates. Keynes argued that the lower the current interest rate, the larger the number of people who will think that the current interest rate is below normal and likely to rise. Therefore, according to Keynes, the lower the current interest rate, the *lower* will be the demand for *bonds* and the *greater* the demand for *money*. This relationship between the interest rate and the demand for speculative money balances is known as the **liquidity preference schedule;** it is illustrated in Figure 21-9.

Note that at some high interest rate, i_H, the entire financial community would be convinced that yields were near their peak and could only decline in the future. Thus, the outlook for bond prices would be universally bullish, and the public would fully invest, reducing its speculative money holdings to zero. At the other extreme, the low yield of i_L, the public would be fully convinced that yields could only rise in the future. Should such a low yield occur, the public would seek to unload all bonds and sit tight, holding wealth in the form of money only. At yields between i_H and i_L, some difference of opinion among individuals would exist about which direction interest rates were likely to move in the future. At some median rate of interest, i_M, opinion would be about equally divided. Half the pool of potential investors might expect yields to rise, and many of these would thus prefer to be on the sidelines holding cash.[12] The other half might expect a decline in yields and would therefore prefer to be fully invested now, thus holding no speculative money balances. This difference of opinion among individual investors regarding the future trend of interest rates accounts for the smooth, continuous downward-sloping curve in Figure 21-9.[13]

The Role of Interest Rates in the Demand for Money: Conclusion

We have demonstrated that the demand to hold money may be responsive to the opportunity cost of holding money—that is, the market rate of interest. Each of the three motives for holding money may depend in part on the interest rate. An increase in interest rates makes holding money more costly, because money pays a relatively noncompetitive rate of interest, if any. To the extent that the demand for money and therefore its velocity vary with interest rates, the link between the money supply and GDP expenditures becomes more uncertain, because interest rates fluctuate significantly over time. If, for example, an increase in the money supply engineered by the Federal Reserve reduces interest rates and therefore reduces velocity, the impact on GDP will be partially negated. Figure 21-10 il-

---

[12]If one believes that the current interest rate is only slightly below "normal" and will move up only moderately and slowly, it may still be desirable to hold bonds rather than idle money. The annual interest return may more than compensate for the expected decline in the price of the bond, leaving a positive net return from holding the bond. Any positive return, of course, beats a zero return on money.

[13]Keynes' theory has been criticized for its unrealistic implication that each individual would logically hold her wealth entirely in bonds or entirely in money, depending on whether the current interest rate is above or below the critical interest rate, respectively. This implication is clearly at odds with the observed propensity of individuals to *diversify* their financial assets, holding money and bonds simultaneously. James Tobin has provided another theoretical framework that is capable of producing a speculative demand for money function which exhibits a smooth, downward-sloping relationship to the interest rate *for any given individual.* Tobin used a two-asset model (bonds and money), as Keynes did. Contrary to Keynes, however, Tobin assumed that the expected future change in the interest rate is zero, regardless of the current level of interest rates. That is, he assumed the public always regards the *current* interest rate as the "normal" rate. Given an individual's financial wealth, both the *risk* (of capital loss) and the *expected return* vary directly with the proportion of the wealth invested in bonds. An increase in interest rates, by increasing the return associated with bond holdings, may induce an individual to increase the proportion of wealth held in bonds in spite of the increase in risk. This implies that demand for money would be reduced. A likely but not necessary outcome of Tobin's model is a smooth, continuous speculative demand for money function for a given *individual.* See the reference to Tobin's famous 1958 article in the "Suggestions for Additional Reading" at the end of this chapter.

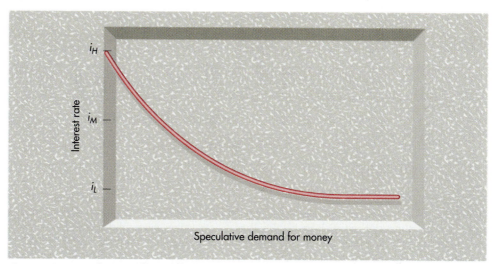

Figure 21-9   The Liquidity Preference Schedule, or the Speculative Demand for Money Function. A reduction in interest rates (increase in bond prices) induces speculators to hold more money for speculative purposes.

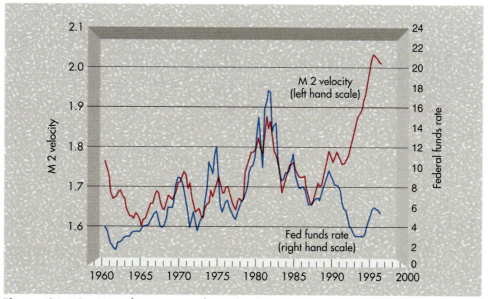

Figure 21-10   M2 Velocity versus the Federal Funds Rate, 1960–1996. Historically, M2 velocity has been positively associated with short-term yields. In the 1990s, however, the relationship broke down.   *Source:* Data from *Citibank Economic Database.*

lustrates the relationship between the velocity of M2, the money measure the Fed has paid most attention to in recent years, and the federal funds rate, a measure of short-term market interest rates. As the figure shows, velocity and the interest rate were highly correlated from 1965 to 1990, but the relationship between the two broke down in the 1990s. In the next chapter we will look carefully at the historical behavior of the velocity of money in the United States.

SUMMARY

The velocity of money—the variable that links a nation's money supply to its gross domestic product—is a key variable in the economy. Velocity is closely related to the demand for money. People are motivated to hold money—that is, they demand money—primarily to finance expenditures that are not perfectly synchronized with their receipt of funds. Money is also demanded for precautionary reasons and for speculative purposes. Except for changes in income, any factor that results in a change in the demand for money also produces a change in velocity. Factors that increase the demand for money reduce velocity, while factors that reduce the demand for money increase velocity. For example, the increasing use of credit cards, more frequent paydays, and higher interest rates, by reducing money demand, boost velocity. Economists disagree about the interest rate sensitivity and the general stability of the demand for money. If the demand for money is stable and relatively inelastic with respect to the interest rate, a change in the money supply will translate to a predictable change in GDP expenditures. If the demand for money is highly unstable and interest elastic, a change in the money supply will have a weak and uncertain effect on GDP expenditures. While monetarists believe that money growth dominates GDP expenditures because they believe the demand for money is stable and predictable, Keynesians are generally skeptical of this proposition.

Answers to Your Turn (p. 504)

a. *Because you begin the month with $600 (since your $200 check to the credit card company clears on the first) and spend it at a constant rate, your average money balance (transactions demand) is $300. Given your total transactions of $9600 per year, the transactions velocity of your money is $9600/yr ÷ $300, or 32 times per year.*

b. *If you stop using the credit card, your average transactions demand is now $400 (you begin the month with $800 and gradually draw down the balance to zero at the end of the month). The transactions velocity of your money is now $9600/yr ÷ $400, or 24 times per year. When you stop using the credit card, your transactions demand for money rises and the velocity of your money falls.*

KEY TERMS

velocity of money
equation of exchange
transaction velocity of money
income velocity of money
demand for money

transaction demand for money
precautionary demand for money
speculative demand for money
liquidity preference schedule

STUDY QUESTIONS

1 Write down the transactions version of the equation of exchange. Define the four variables involved, and explain what the equation tells us. Why is the equation of exchange a "tautology" or "identity"?

2 Explain the difference between the income velocity of money (V_Y) and the transactions velocity of money (V_T). Which measure is larger? Why?

3 Explain how the degree of synchronization between receipts and disbursements of money balances influences the transactions demand for money and the velocity of money.

4 In the late 1970s, extremely high interest rates triggered the substitution of money market mutual fund (MMMF) balances for traditional checking accounts. Given that personal MMMF balances are included in M2 and that institutional MMMF balances are included in M3 (neither is included in M1), what were the implications of the asset reallocation for the velocities of M1, M2, and M3?

5 Analyze the rationale for the view that the transactions demand for money is likely to depend on the level of interest rates.

6 Estimate your own average demand for money. Given that information, together with the amount of your annual expenditures (transactions), calculate the transactions velocity of your money. How many days' worth of expenditures do you hold in the form of M1, on average?

7 Explain why the stability of the demand for money is an important issue underlying the debate over the general effectiveness of monetary policy. Use the equation of exchange to facilitate your explanation.

8 Why might the concepts of the speculative and precautionary demands for money be more applicable to M2 and M3 than to M1, the narrow measure of money?

9 a Assume that you are paid $1000 monthly. Assuming you spend your entire income at a constant rate throughout the month, calculate your transactions demand for money and the transactions velocity of your money.

b Because of your exemplary job performance, your salary is boosted to $1500. Assuming you continue to spend your entire income at a constant rate, calculate your transactions demand for money and the transactions velocity of your money.

c A new company policy prompts a move to twice-monthly pay periods. If your spending patterns are unchanged, calculate your new transactions demand for money and the new transactions velocity of your money.

10 What would be the impact of the following events on the demand for and velocity of M1?

a Use of credit cards is restricted by law to people over age 40.

b   Banks begin paying interest equal to the Treasury bill yield on all checking accounts.

c   All employers move to a system in which workers are paid only six times annually.

d   Interest rates plunge as the United States sinks into a severe recession.

e   Fees for purchasing U.S. government securities double.

f   A proliferation of ATMs makes it more convenient to withdraw cash directly from savings accounts.

11   Suppose you have $10,000 available to you, above and beyond your near-term needs. You have the option of holding this wealth in the form of cash (speculative money balances) or investing it in perpetual bonds with an annual payment of $800. Assume that your perception of the "normal" rate on such a bond is 6 percent.

a   If the market rate is currently 8 percent and you expect rates to return to normal in the next year, how much wealth would you expect to gain or lose in the next year if you invested the $10,000 now?

b   If the market rate is currently 4 percent and you expect rates to return to normal in one year, how much wealth would you expect to gain or lose if you invested the $10,000 now?

c   In which case, *a* or *b,* would you be more likely to hold the $10,000 in the form of money? In the form of bonds? What does your answer imply about the slope of your speculative money demand curve (positive or negative)?

12   In the early 1990s, the Fed decided to de-emphasize M2 as an intermediate target. Examine Figure 21-10 carefully, and, with the benefit of hindsight, explain whether you think the Fed acted appropriately.

SUGGESTIONS FOR ADDITIONAL READING

The classic discussion of the equation of exchange is provided in Chapters 2 and 4 of Irving Fisher, *The Purchasing Power of Money* (New York: Macmillan, 1911). The book was reprinted in 1963 by Augustus M. Kelley, Bookseller, in its Reprints of Economic Classics series. On the demand for money, a seminal article is A. C. Pigou, "The Value of Money," *Quarterly Journal of Economics,* November 1917, pp. 38–65. The classic three-tier motive for holding money is presented in Chapters 13 and 15 of Keynes' work cited in this chapter but is more clearly presented in Chapter 8 of Dudley Dillard, *The Economics of John Maynard Keynes* (Englewood Cliffs, N.J.: Prentice-Hall, 1948). On the interest elasticity of the transactions demand for money, classic articles are James Tobin, "The Interest Elasticity of Transactions Demand for Cash," *Review of Economics and Statistics,* August 1956, pp. 241–247, and William J. Baumol, "The Transactions Demand for Cash: An Inventory Theoretic Approach," *Quarterly Journal of Economics,* November 1952, pp. 545–556. On the speculative demand for money, see James Tobin, "Liquidity Preference as Behavior toward Risk," *Review of Economic Studies,* February 1958, pp. 65–86. A terrific reference on all aspects of the demand for money is David Laidler, *The Demand for Money,* 4th ed. (New York, HarperCollins, 1993). This work presents all the theories of the demand for money, analyzes the problems involved in estimating such demand functions econometrically, and surveys the empirical studies on the demand for money. It also contains a comprehensive list of references on the subject. A massive volume of literature on the demand for money has developed over the past 30 years. The best place to start is with the review of the empirical literature provided in the aforementioned book by Laidler. On the stability of the demand for money, see John Judd and John Scadding, "The Search for a Stable Money Demand Function," *Journal of Economic Literature,* September 1982, pp. 993–1023.

22

The Behavior
of Velocity of Money
in the United States

I n Chapter 21, we provided a fairly thorough analysis of the factors underlying the demand for money and its close relative, the velocity of money. We demonstrated that any factor that reduces the amount of money people hold relative to their annual expenditures increases the velocity of money, while any factor that increases the demand for money relative to expenditures reduces velocity. We saw too that the nature of the demand for and velocity of money has important implications for the stability of economic activity, as well as for the relative power and importance of monetary and fiscal policy. For example, the propriety of using such intermediate monetary policy targets as M1 and M2 depends on the stability and predictability of velocity.

In this chapter, we will reinforce our understanding of the demand for and velocity of money by analyzing the historical behavior of velocity in the United States. Our discussion will include analyses of the long-run trends as well as of cyclical and short-term movements in velocity. We will begin with an analysis of the determinants of velocity.

DETERMINANTS OF VELOCITY

The determinants of velocity may be grouped into six categories: the institutional factors that underlie the synchronization between receipts and expenditures, the state of "financial technology," interest rate levels, the prevailing degree of economic uncertainty or state of economic confidence, inflation expectations, and income level.

Institutional Factors

In Chapter 21, we demonstrated that the demand for and velocity of money are related to institutional considerations such as the frequency of paydays, payment habits, the use of credit cards, and other institutional factors that govern the degree of synchronization between the receipt and disbursement of funds. Improvements in the synchronization of

517

receipts and disbursements—for example, more frequent paydays and increased use of credit cards—reduce the demand for money and increase its velocity. Institutional factors tend to evolve slowly and steadily over time.

Financial Technology

Encompassed within the category of financial technology are the availability of substitutes for money and the costs involved in using those money substitutes, as well as technical mechanisms developed by banks that allow individuals and firms to hold less money.

Financial innovations increase the opportunity cost of holding money, thereby reducing the demand for money. When money market mutual funds (MMMFs) became widely available in the 1970s, this increased the opportunity cost of holding bank checking accounts. Because yields on MMMF shares were highly attractive, millions of individuals used the funds in their checking accounts to purchase MMMF shares. Their actions reduced the demand for M1 and increased its velocity.[1] The advent of the *sweep account*—a device through which the bank's computer transfers the remaining funds (most commonly of business firms) out of customers' checking accounts and into interest-bearing financial assets at the end of the day—also pulled up velocity. So did the development of the overnight repurchase agreement (RP), an instrument through which the bank "purchases" a customer's checking account at the end of business each day, selling the customer government securities in return.[2] Another example is the proliferation of automatic teller machines (ATMs), which reduced the cost of switching funds from savings to checking accounts, thereby reducing the demand for M1. Anything that reduces the propensity to hold checking accounts increases the velocity of money. Other instruments that provide attractive alternatives to holding money have also become available during the past 40 years. Some of the more important of these instruments include negotiable CDs, commercial paper, and Eurodollars. Financial innovations, then, increase the velocity of money.

Interest Rates

We examined the role interest rates play in the demand for money in the last chapter. An increase in interest rates reduces the demand for money, that is, induces people to hold less of their wealth in the form of transactions, precautionary, and speculative money balances. Because the demand for and velocity of money are inversely related, an increase in interest rates raises velocity. Furthermore, because interest rates exhibit a distinct procyclical pattern (rising during economic expansions and falling during recessions), velocity also tends to move procyclically. (We will analyze this phenomenon later in this chapter.)

---

[1]Money market mutual fund shares are included in M2 but not in M1. When people reduce their bank checking account balances to purchase MMMF shares, the velocity of M1 increases while velocity of M2 is unaltered. (Why? Because M1 declines while M2 does not.)

[2]Because the Federal Reserve tabulates its figures on the money supply from deposit data after the close of business and because both overnight RPs and sweep accounts pull funds from *DDO* at the end of banking hours and redeposit them into *DDO* at the opening of business the next day, reported *DDO* is reduced by expanding the use of these instruments. Reported velocity (GDP/*M*) is therefore boosted by these instruments.

Economic Uncertainty

Money is the safest of all assets in the sense that its nominal value remains constant no matter what happens in the stock, bond, or real estate markets or in the economy itself. If the stock or real estate market collapses, $10,000 in a checking account is still $10,000. For this reason, any time an announcement or event raises the prospect or possibility of trouble in the economy, the demand for money increases. People become more conservative and sell their stocks and bonds, preferring instead to hold money. The day President John F. Kennedy was assassinated, the stock market fell dramatically as tens of thousands of people rushed to convert their stocks into cash. As the demand for money increased, its velocity was reduced. Thus, when the economic, political, or military outlook darkens, velocity falls. When public confidence improves, people become more aggressive about holding assets other than money. This means that the demand for money falls and its velocity rises.

Expected Inflation

Inflation imposes a tax on money, reducing its real value at a rate equal to the difference between the annual inflation rate and the interest rate (if any) paid on money. If inflation is running at 10 percent per year and money pays no interest, the real value of money depreciates at a rate of 10 percent per year.

Inflation of this magnitude is likely to influence the use of money appreciably. People will reduce their demand for money in an effort to escape the inflation tax. And because the value of money depreciates rapidly when inflation is high, people tend to spend it quickly, before it depreciates. Historically, during *hyperinflation,* when the implicit tax on money becomes extreme, velocity escalates dramatically as people desperately try to rid themselves of money before its value plunges again. At present, with inflation running at less than 4 percent annually, inflation expectations are not likely to exert much effect on velocity.[3]

Income

In general, an increase in income results in an increase in expenditures by individuals and firms. If a doubling of income were to result in a doubling of expenditures, and if people were induced to hold twice as much money to finance the doubled level of expenditures, money velocity would be unaffected by the increase in income. In that case the **income elasticity of demand for money**—the ratio of the percentage change in the demand for money to the percentage change in income—would be exactly 1.0 and changes in income would have no effect on velocity.

That is not necessarily the case in the real world, however. Some economists view money as a luxury good, meaning that the income elasticity of demand for money is greater

---

[3]If the Fisher effect were working full force, so that a 1 percent increase in expected inflation pulled up nominal interest rates by 1 percentage point, and if money paid interest equal to the market interest rate, then inflation expectations would have no effect on money demand and velocity. However, neither of those conditions is typical. Econometric studies typically estimate the Fisher coefficient to be less than 1.0, and interest paid on currency is zero. Interest paid on demand deposits is significantly below the market interest rate and adjusts sluggishly to changes in market rates.

than 1.0.[4] Remember that the more securities and less money one holds, the more time one must spend managing one's money balances. But an increase in income is likely to increase the value one places on leisure time. Thus an increase in income may boost the demand for money not only to accommodate higher expenditures but also to reduce valuable time spent on managing one's financial affairs. If an increase in income induces a greater-than-proportional increase in money demand, higher income leads to lower velocity.

On the other hand, there are "economies of scale" in cash management, so that a doubling of income may require less than a doubling of average money balances to finance the doubled level of expenditures. Individuals with higher incomes and expenditures are more likely to use credit cards; as income rises, firms are more likely to develop lines of credit with their banks. Both these phenomena reduce the demand for money and boost its velocity. Higher incomes and expenditures also tend to encourage the sort of intramonthly securities transactions analyzed in the latter part of Chapter 21. In that event, an increase in income and expenditures could lead to a less-than-proportional increase in the demand for money and an increase in its velocity.[5] The great majority of empirical studies of the demand for money have found an income elasticity of demand for money of less than 1.0, implying that the effect of long-run income growth is to increase the velocity of money.

Your Turn

Suppose your statistical research reveals that the income elasticity of demand for money is 1.20. Assuming that financial innovations continue at a steady pace and that income rises significantly in the next 5 years, while all other factors influencing velocity remain constant, in which direction will velocity move?

LONG-RUN BEHAVIOR OF MONEY VELOCITY

We are now in a position to discuss the historical behavior of money velocity in the United States over the last 125 years. Figures 21-2 and 21-3 in the last chapter illustrated the behavior of several measures of velocity during the last 35 years. Figure 22-1 shows the income velocity of M1 and M2 over a much longer time span.

---

[4]The income elasticity of demand for any good or service is defined as the percentage change in the quantity of the good demanded divided by the percentage change in the income that produced the change in demand for the good. If a 10 percent increase in income results in a 15 percent increase in the demand for steak or entertainment, the income elasticity of demand is 1.5 and those two goods are luxury goods. If a 10 percent increase in income results in a 2 percent increase in demand for food and clothing, those goods are classified as normal goods, because their income elasticities of demand are less than 1.0.

[5]An implication of both the Tobin and the Baumol models of transactions demand for money is that the income elasticity of demand for money is less than 1.0 because an increase in income increases the optimal number of securities transactions an individual conducts each month. Hence, in these models, an increase in income raises velocity. (See the references to Tobin and Baumol in the "Suggestions for Additional Reading" in Chapter 21.)

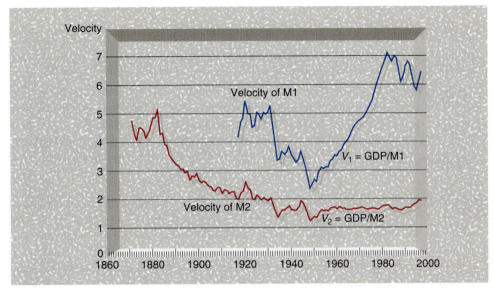

Figure 22-1   Income Velocity of Money in the United States, 1869–1996. The income velocities of M1 and M2 exhibit long-term trends as well as short-term cyclical fluctuations. *Source:* Drawn from data provided in Milton Friedman and Anna Jacobson Schwartz, *A Monetary History of the United States* (copyright © 1963 by National Bureau of Economic Research; Princeton, N.J.: Princeton University Press), p. 774, Table A-5, adjusted and updated to conform to data furnished by the Federal Reserve System for the period after 1959.

In the figure, V_1 represents the income velocity of M1, which includes demand deposits and currency held by the public. V_2 represents the income velocity of M2, which includes M1 and time and savings deposits. Note that V_2 runs from 1869 until the present, while V_1 extends from 1915 to the present.[6] The two measures exhibit the same turning points and move very much in parallel from 1915–1960. After 1960, V_1 and V_2 diverge.

Over the period 1869–1946, the velocity of money exhibited a long-term decline.[7] This secular downtrend was interrupted from 1915–1929, before resuming during 1929–1946. The secular decline in velocity of M1 was followed by a steady, persistent increase, beginning in 1946 and continuing until 1980. V_1 increased at an average annual rate of approximately 3 percent during that period. Since 1980, V_1 has been less stable, exhibiting a modest downward trend. M2 velocity increased persistently from 1946–1960 and fluctuated with no significant trend until the mid-1980s, when it began increasing.

Economists disagree about the relative importance of the various forces underlying the velocity of money (and hence the demand for money relative to income). We will examine the theories of two eminent American economists, Nobel Laureates Milton Friedman and James Tobin, on the behavior of velocity in the century following the end of the Civil War.

[6]V_1 cannot be extended back to 1869 because until 1915 recorded data from the period did not distinguish between time deposits and demand deposits. Before 1915, then, one can compute M2 but not M1.

[7]The velocity of M2 declined from 4.57 in 1869 to a low of 1.16 in 1946—an average compounded negative growth rate of 1.8 percent per year over the 77-year period.

Friedman's Luxury Good Explanation

Milton Friedman treats the demand for money within the same general framework that economists employ to analyze the demand for other goods and services. This suggests that the demand for money is a function of the utility or satisfaction derived from holding money, the cost of holding money, and the level of income or wealth. Concerning the relationship between the demand for money and income or wealth, Friedman believes that money should be classified as a "luxury" good, as opposed to a "normal" good. He notes that the long-term trend of per capita income in the United States has been strongly upward. It follows that if the income elasticity of the demand for money exceeds 1.0, the demand for money should increase at a faster rate than income and the long-term trend of velocity should be downward. Friedman asserts that money is a luxury good and one would therefore expect a long-run pattern of declining velocity over the broad sweep of history. Any sustained period in which velocity increased significantly in the face of growth in real income would therefore require special explanation.

When confronted with the "facts" shown in Figure 22-1, Friedman's theory works quite well up until the end of World War II. Between 1880 and 1946, the only significant interruptions to the downward trend of V_2 were World War I and the period 1932–1942. However, the period after 1946 presents problems for Friedman's theory. V_1 has exhibited a major increase since 1946, as the United States has experienced a substantial growth in per capita income. V_2 has been without a significant trend in the overall period since 1960 (although it has increased in the past decade). Friedman's model would have predicted a decline in money velocity during that period.

Writing in the early 1960s, Friedman rationalized the early post–World War II rise in money velocity. He contended that two factors had contributed to the "temporary" post-1946 reversal of the long-term downward trend. Friedman believed that once these temporary causes had spent themselves, the downtrend in velocity would resume. According to Friedman, velocity had become artificially depressed by the abnormal events associated with the Great Depression of the 1930s and World War II.[8] It seemed reasonable to expect a certain "catch-up" factor to increase velocity (that is, reduce demand for money relative to income) in the early postwar years.

Specifically, Friedman asserted that, after the dislocations of the 1929–1946 period, a gradual restoration of confidence in the economic future would reduce the demand for money and other highly liquid near monies (such as savings accounts) relative to common stocks, long-term bonds, and other more risky assets. The adjustment would produce a temporary increase in the velocities of M1 and M2. In the words of Friedman and Anna Schwartz, "Other things being the same, it is highly plausible that the fraction of their assets individuals and business enterprises wish to hold in the form of money, and also in the form of close substitutes for money, will be smaller when they look forward

---

[8]In chaotic and disorganized times such as depressions and wars, one expects people to seek to hold an abnormally large portion of their wealth in money. Also, U.S. interest rates were extremely low during the 1930s and 1940s. Together, greater economic uncertainty and extremely low interest rates depressed velocity.

to a period of stable economic conditions than when they anticipate disturbed and uncertain conditions."[9]

It is clear that Friedman and Schwartz did *not* believe that the economic dislocation of the 1930s and 1940s could explain the continuing rise in velocity (V_1) which would occur from the 1960s into the 1980s. To quote Friedman and Schwartz,

> The mildness and brevity of the 1953–54 recession must have strongly reinforced the lesson of the 1948–49 recession and reduced still further the fears of great economic instability. . . . The brevity of the 1957–58 recession presumably further reinforced confidence in stability, but, clearly, each such episode in the same direction must have less and less effect, so one might suppose that by 1960 expectations were approaching a plateau. If this be so . . . one might expect the rise in velocity to end and the long-term downward trend to emerge once more.[10]

Because the velocity of narrow money drifted steadily upward for 2 decades after Friedman and Schwartz made these remarks, their rationalization of the change in trend after 1946 seems weak. (Note, however, that V_1 has trended downward since 1980.) Indeed, the whole hypothesis that money is a luxury good now appears dubious. Modern econometric studies have established fairly clearly that the income elasticity of the demand for money is now less than 1.0, though it may have been higher in the nineteenth century.[11] That makes money a "normal" rather than a "luxury" good and implies that the influence of income growth on velocity is to gradually *increase* V_Y over time. If other factors remained constant, so that income was the only factor influencing velocity, velocity would rise persistently over time with rising income.

Tobin's Institutional Explanation

An alternative explanation of the long-term behavior of velocity, by James Tobin, places primary emphasis on the dramatic changes that have occurred in financial institutions, instruments, and markets in the past century.[12] Tobin sees no intuitive reason to suppose that money is a luxury good in the sense that, as income rises, individuals and firms desire to

---

[9]Milton Friedman and Anna J. Schwartz, *A Monetary History of the United States, 1867–1960* (Princeton, N.J.: Princeton University Press, 1963), p. 673.

[10]Friedman and Schwartz, *A Monetary History,* pp. 674–675. In fairness to the authors, it should be mentioned that their hypothesis was put forward very cautiously. Thus, "The conclusions in this section are highly tentative. Full confidence in them must await further evidence. Nevertheless, changing expectations about economic stability seem at the moment a more plausible explanation of postwar movements in the velocity of money than any of the other factors we have examined" (*Ibid.,* p. 675.)

[11]See pp. 169–170 of David Laidler's 1993 book on the demand for money, cited in the "Suggestions for Additional Reading" at the end of this chapter. See also the famous 1973 paper by Stephen Goldfeld cited there.

[12]Tobin's critique of Friedman and Schwartz is cited in the "Suggestions for Additional Reading." Important recent empirical work by Michael Bordo and Lars Jonung and by Pierre Siklos provides support for the institutional explanation of the long-run behavior of velocity. See the "Suggestions for Additional Reading" at the end of this chapter.

accumulate money holdings at a faster rate than other assets such as stocks, bonds, and real estate. Indeed, as we mentioned before, there is evidence of "economies of scale" in the management of cash positions, particularly in the case of business firms. Thus firms (and perhaps some individuals) would *not* find it advantageous to double their average money holdings when income and expenditures double. To them, money is a normal good rather than a luxury good. If this is so, the demand for money will not keep pace with the growth of GDP, and velocity will increase over time as income rises. While Tobin does not explicitly align himself with the "economies-of-scale" theory, he does reject Friedman's luxury good hypothesis. Instead, he relies primarily on institutional changes to explain the long-run behavior of money velocity.

Tobin notes that the 60-year era preceding World War II was a period in which money increasingly replaced barter and payments in kind. The availability and use of commercial bank checking accounts became widespread. The trend is especially true for the period 1880–1915, when the decline in velocity was most steady and distinct. In 1880, mutual savings banks (whose deposits were not included in M1 or M2) were approximately as important a repository of funds as were commercial banks. Practically all the mutual savings banks have been located in the northeast. As the U.S. economy expanded westward in the last part of the nineteenth and early part of the twentieth centuries, commercial banking facilities spread rapidly west, while mutual savings banks remained primarily in New York and New England; savings and loan associations and other financial intermediaries were relatively undeveloped. Tobin contends that the increasing use of money and the growing availability and acceptance of commercial banks in the 60 years before World War II produced a natural increase in the public's M1 and M2 holdings relative to claims on other financial institutions and also relative to GDP. In Tobin's view, this increase in "monetization" accounts for the long decline in velocity from 1880–1946.

In contrast, the 30-year period following World War II was marked by the growth of nonbank thrift institutions, especially savings and loan associations. Spurred by an upward ratcheting of interest rates, along with tremendous growth in home construction between the 1940s and 1980s, thrift institutions competed with commercial banks for the public's deposits. Thus, while the period up to World War II was the golden age of commercial banking growth, the period after 1946 witnessed the successful penetration of the banking market by thrifts and other nonbank institutions such as money market mutual funds (whose deposits are not included in M1). These developments would imply a decline in the demand for M1 and an increase in its velocity after 1946.

Many additional institutional changes can be cited to support the institutional hypothesis of long-term velocity behavior. The post–World War II growth of financial technology and the increasing availability of highly liquid, interest-bearing "near monies" have gradually reduced the relative propensity of individuals, firms, and governments to hold wealth in the form of money. During this period, access to liquid substitutes for money has become feasible for millions of individuals. The supply of short-term government securities, especially Treasury bills, has expanded dramatically, and the network of dealers in U.S. government securities has increased the efficiency of and reduced transactions costs in that market. Savings deposits and CDs have increased in variety and been made more attractive, and government insurance of such accounts has expanded substantially. The advent of bank overdraft protection reduced the need to hold precautionary balances in checking accounts. The widespread use of credit cards and other credit arrangements has gradually improved the synchronization of receipts and expenditures. In the mid-1970s, millions of Americans began to transfer funds from their checking and savings accounts to high-yielding money market mutual funds and money market deposit accounts (MMDAs). All these innovations helped to raise the velocity of the narrow measure of money.

Firms and state and local governments have benefited from countless improvements in cash management made possible by a variety of new financial instruments, including finance company paper, negotiable CDs, and short-term U.S. government agency obligations. Coupled with higher interest rates, the use of these instruments has exerted a powerful impact on corporate and governmental liquidity management since the late 1950s. Increased use of trade credit and the development of sweep accounts and repurchase agreements (RPs) have also reduced the demand for bank deposits by corporations and state and local governments and government agencies.[13] All these techniques reduce demand for money and increase its velocity.

Among the most important innovations of recent decades have been the development of the commercial paper market and the introduction in 1961 of negotiable CDs, along with the creation of a secondary market in them. Those changes have influenced cash management not only by corporations and other firms but also by municipal and state governments, pension funds, and nonprofit institutions. They have affected the demand for and velocity of money in two ways. First, the development of new markets and instruments has increased the range of available interest-bearing liquid assets, thereby raising the opportunity cost of holding money. Second, the availability of new instruments may have caused firms to maintain a less liquid asset structure—including a smaller cash position—than would otherwise have been feasible. Firms feel more secure in the knowledge that instruments such as commercial paper may be issued to attract funds if necessary. Banks know they can issue negotiable CDs to attract funds and make loans available to creditworthy firms even when the Fed is applying the monetary brakes. Bank borrowers, knowing that such loans are available if needed, are induced to hold less money as precautionary balances. Clearly, such financial innovations have contributed strongly to the uptrend in M1 velocity in the post–World War II era. (The International Perspectives box discusses long-run money velocity patterns in other nations.)

Having looked at the long-run behavior of money velocity, we now turn to an examination of its short-term, or cyclical, pattern.

SHORT-RUN BEHAVIOR OF MONEY VELOCITY

Suppose a major corporation wishes to step up its purchases of raw materials in order to build up its inventory of finished product in expectation of an increase in sales. Suppose the firm decides that the most efficient method of financing the inventory buildup is

---

[13]In the case of trade credit, interfirm credits and debits are allowed to accumulate over time, sharply reducing the need for frequent money transfers. This reduces the demand for money and increases its velocity.

International Comparisons of the Long-Run Behavior of Money Velocity

In important recent studies, Michael Bordo of Rutgers University and Lars Jonung of the Stockholm School of Economics examined the behavior of money velocity in a large number of nations over a period of more than 100 years. Their conclusion was that almost all nations have exhibited a U-shaped pattern of velocity over the years and that institutional factors have played an important role in that common pattern. Most nations have exhibited a pattern of velocity quite similar to the U.S. pattern shown in Figure 22-1.

Bordo and Jonung hypothesize that evolution of the financial sector introduces two competing forces on the long-run trend of money velocity. Each dominates a different stage in the process of industrialization. In the first phase, metallic money, barter, and payment in kind are increasingly replaced by money. In this "monetization" phase, velocity declines as commercial banking proliferates and the public holds more money relative to income or GDP. In the second phase, the introduction of such substitutes for money as bonds, stocks, and money market instruments reduces the demand for money and increases its velocity. Financial innovations such as credit cards, repurchase agreements, and overdraft facilities also boost velocity, as does increasing economic stability.

In almost all nations, velocity first declines with increasing monetization and then increases with financial innovation and increased economic stability. The *timing* of the reversal of the trend differs across countries, however. The United States, Canada, Italy, Japan, and the United Kingdom reached the low point in velocity around 1946, 2 decades after Sweden, Denmark, Norway, and Germany.

Bordo and Jonung employed proxies to measure the influence of certain institutional phenomena. For example, they used the ratio of the nonagricultural labor force to the nation's total labor force as a proxy for monetization, since the agricultural sector uses barter and payment in kind extensively in place of money. And they used currency/M2 as a proxy for banking. (The greater the proliferation and use of banks, the lower the ratio.) A moving average of the standard deviation of real GDP served as the proxy for economic stability. In the great majority of instances, the proxy variables were found to be significant determinants of velocity across a sample of 12 industrial nations.

Bordo and Jonung concluded that institutional developments affect the demand for and velocity of money across a very large number of countries. Thus a model that includes institutional variables improves appreciably on traditional models that consider only the effect of economic variables such as interest rates and income. Velocity is best understood through a full understanding of the long-run evolution of institutional forces.

through an issue of commercial paper (short-term business IOUs). These instruments have the advantage to the firm that their magnitude and maturity can be tailored to meet the needs of the firm. By issuing such obligations, the firm attracts idle funds from lenders, primarily other corporations, in return for a competitive rate of return. Because the firm that issues commercial paper immediately transfers the lenders' money balances to firms that supply raw materials, the money supply does not change. However, aggregate demand

and GDP rise as the borrowing firm steps up its production. Thus, when firms issue commercial paper and use the proceeds to finance expenditures, velocity increases.

A similar analysis may be applied to the issuance of negotiable CDs by large commercial banks. Suppose banks are strapped for funds to meet heavy loan demand during an economic boom. Historically, banks have liquidated their holdings of short-term U.S. government securities in order to make more money available to business borrowers. Such a move increases velocity, because the velocity of the money made available to businesses tends to be considerably greater than the velocity of the largely idle money that is extinguished when individuals and firms write checks to purchase the securities sold by banks.

Suppose, however, that banks have already depleted their short-term securities portfolios. An alternative employed by large banks in recent decades has been to issue large-denomination IOUs ($100,000 or more) in the form of negotiable CDs. The CDs are "negotiable" in the sense that they can be bought and sold on a secondary market after they are first issued. The principal buyers are corporations that have extra cash and are seeking a high-yielding liquid asset in which to invest their funds until they are needed to meet payrolls, quarterly tax payments, or other future scheduled expenditures. Through the instrument of negotiable CDs, the banks essentially facilitate the transfer of money from firms that do not immediately need the funds to businesses that wish to make immediate use of them. In so doing, they raise the velocity of money.

In the next few sections, we will see how short-term fluctuations in velocity may pose challenges for the successful conduct of monetary policy.

Induced Changes in Velocity and the Effectiveness of Monetary Policy

Such financial instruments as commercial paper and negotiable CDs pose potential problems for monetary policy. Suppose the Federal Reserve desires to restrain the economy during a sharp cyclical upswing. If the Fed holds the money supply constant over a 6-month period in an effort to cool off aggregate expenditures, firms and banks that issue commercial paper and negotiable CDs will activate idle money balances. The resulting increase in velocity will at least partially circumvent the intent of Fed policy. In terms of the $MV_Y \equiv PY$ framework, the increase in V_Y allows aggregate demand for goods and services (MV_Y) to increase in spite of a constant money supply. The more aggressively the Fed implements its policy of restraint, the greater will be the propensity of banks and nonbank firms to issue such instruments in order to finance desired expenditures. Instruments such as commercial paper and negotiable CDs weaken the Fed's grip on bank lending and aggregate expenditures.

The "Ratchet Effect" of Financial Innovations

Over a period of time, financial innovations seem to operate on money velocity with a "ratchet effect." In a period of tight money, when the demand for credit is high relative to its supply and interest rates reach peak levels, the environment is conducive to financial innovations which raise the velocity of money. The use of commercial paper, Eurodollar borrowing, negotiable CDs, repurchase agreements, and sweep accounts is stimulated in periods of Federal Reserve restraint. Once such devices become familiar to the financial community, their use tends to be maintained at a substantial level, even after the return of normal financial conditions. The net result is that as new financial innovations come into use, they gradually raise the normal level of the velocity of narrow money. One might conclude that the post-1946 long-term rise in velocity is likely to continue as long as financial innovations continue to be introduced.

The Cyclical Behavior of Velocity

The income velocity of money displays a fairly systematic procyclical pattern, rising during business cycle expansions and falling (or at least rising at a below-trend rate) during recessions and depressions. This tendency is illustrated in Figure 22-2, which shows the quarterly behavior of the velocity of M1 and M2 (V_1 and V_2, respectively) since 1960. In the figure, periods of recession are shaded; unshaded areas represent periods of expansion. In five of the six recessions shown, V_1 and V_2 either declined or experienced a slowdown in their rate of growth. The 1973–1975 recession marked the first time in 100 years

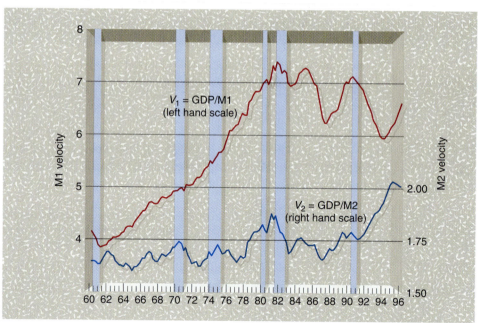

Figure 22-2 Cyclical Behavior of the Income Velocity of Money, 1960–1996. The income velocity of money exhibits a procyclical pattern, increasing during periods of expansion and declining (or growing more slowly than the trend) during economic downturns. *Source:* Federal Reserve data from *Citibank Economic Database.* Cyclical turning points are those of the National Bureau of Economic Research.

that velocity in the United States had increased significantly during a cyclical downturn.[14] Nevertheless, if one removes the upward trend from the velocity series, a uniformly clear pattern of procyclical variation in velocity remains. The velocity of both M1 and M2 dropped sharply in the severe 1981–1982 recession.

Economists have proposed three different theories to account for the procyclical behavior of the velocity of M1 and M2. Their hypotheses should not necessarily be viewed as mutually exclusive. It is likely that a combination of factors has contributed to the pattern illustrated in Figure 22-2. We will look at all three theories, beginning with the one based on interest rates.

Velocity and the Procyclical Pattern of Interest Rates

As we have seen, interest rates typically rise during cyclical expansions and fall during cyclical contractions. If the demand for money balances relative to income and expenditures is significantly related to the level of interest rates, we have an easy explanation for the results illustrated in Figure 22-2. As the economy expands in a cyclical upswing, interest rates rise. This reduces the demand for money relative to expenditures, thereby raising income velocity. During a recession, yields decline, raising the demand for money relative to expenditures and depressing velocity.

The validity of this explanation hinges on the interest elasticity of the demand for money. Keynesians, who believe that the demand for money is quite sensitive to interest rates, find this hypothesis highly plausible. Monetarists, because they believe that money demand is relatively insensitive to interest rates, tend to de-emphasize this hypothesis.

Velocity and the Keynesian Theory of the Business Cycle

In the Keynesian view, business cycles are driven by changes in consumption, investment, net exports, and the fiscal posture of the government. And they believe these changes to be typically unrelated to monetary phenomena. The supply of money is viewed as responding passively to economic activity rather than actively determining the behavior of output and employment. In such a framework, the velocity of money would naturally exhibit a procyclical pattern.

Suppose that, near the trough of a recession, a government economic stimulus coincides with an improvement in consumer confidence. The net result would be a sharp rise in the aggregate demand for goods and services. The *AD* curve would shift rightward, and GDP would rise. Such cyclical forces would be likely to induce a positive response in the money supply.[15] However, the money supply responds to business conditions somewhat

---

[14]If we use the Friedman and Schwartz V_2 measure (income/M_2), we find that V_2 declined during 13 consecutive recessions dating back before 1900. See Friedman and Schwartz, *A Monetary History,* p. 678, Chart 62.

[15]In terms of the money supply framework introduced in Chapters 14 and 15, business cycle developments are likely to influence both the monetary base and the money supply multiplier in a procyclical manner. As the economy expands and the demand for credit escalates, the volume of discounts and advances is likely to increase. This increases the monetary base. Also, as yields rise during the cyclical upswing, the banks' desired excess reserve ratio (r_e) declines. This increases the money supply multiplier. In this way, the supply of money is pulled up by the expansion of economic activity. Also, the Fed may step in and purchase securities to hold down interest rates and accommodate credit demands. This further increases both the base and the money supply. In sum, money is influenced endogenously by cyclical factors rather than by deliberate Federal Reserve policy actions. This view does not deny that the Fed *could* aggressively manage the money supply if it so desired; it asserts instead that in the past the Fed has *not* aggressively managed the money supply but rather has allowed it to be determined endogenously.

sluggishly. The short-term result is that velocity (GDP/*M*) rises. In this Keynesian framework, cyclical downturns are also induced by shifts in consumer expenditures, business investment, net exports, and the fiscal policy of government. If the net effect of such shifts is to produce a downturn in aggregate demand and GDP, the money supply shrinks, but only sluggishly. Again, simple arithmetic shows that money velocity must decline in such circumstances.

This simple explanation seems reasonable to many Keynesians. However, monetarists do not accept it because it attributes changes in GDP to autonomous shifts in consumption, investment, net exports, and government expenditures, rather than to changes in the supply of money.

Velocity and Friedman's Permanent Income Hypothesis

Milton Friedman developed an ingenious hypothesis to explain the procyclical pattern of velocity. In Friedman's theory, both consumer expenditures and the demand for money depend not on current income but on **permanent income,** or long-run average income. Thus, in the second half of a cyclical upswing, when current income or GDP exceeds permanent income or GDP, the demand for money does not keep pace with current GDP; thus velocity (GDP/*M*) rises. During a recession, actual GDP or income falls below permanent or "normal" levels. Again, because the demand for money depends on permanent income, the quantity of money demanded does not decline in proportion to the decline in actual GDP; velocity (GDP/*M*) falls.

Monetarists tend to align themselves with this hypothesis. The other two explanations presented here are inconsistent with the monetarist hypothesis that velocity is stable and predictable and that changes in the money supply are the predominant cause of short-run changes in aggregate expenditures and GDP.

RECENT HISTORICAL BEHAVIOR OF MONEY VELOCITY

Figure 22-2 showed a marked acceleration in velocity, particularly V_1, from around 1973 to the early 1980s. It also showed a significant decline in M1 velocity in the period after 1981. On average, M1 velocity declined at an annual rate of approximately 1 percent between the beginning of 1981 and the beginning of 1996. That pattern contrasts sharply with a positive trend of about 3 percent annually in the previous 35 years. The velocity of M2 changed only modestly over the 1981–1996 period as a whole, although it did increase significantly in the latter portion of the period.

It is not difficult to rationalize these phenomena after the fact. The acceleration of M1 velocity in 1973–1980 was likely due to a greater use of financial innovations such as MMMFs, repurchase agreements, and sweep accounts. Those innovations were stimulated by the severe inflation of the late 1960s and 1970s, and the associated high level of interest rates. The sharp decline in M1 and M2 velocity in 1982–1983 was probably the result of the very severe 1981–1982 recession, the accompanying increase in uncertainty, and the dramatic decline in inflation and interest rates. Also, when the U.S. financial system was deregulated in the early 1980s, banks began paying interest on checking accounts, a move that increased the demand for M1 and therefore reduced its velocity.

However, economists did not foresee these major departures from the 1946–1980 trend of velocity. More important, economic models that tracked the demand for money and velocity fairly impressively before 1973 had great difficulty explaining their behavior after 1973, even with the benefit of hindsight information regarding income, inflation, and interest rates. As a result, economists' confidence in the concept of a highly stable money demand function has significantly weakened since the early 1970s. An increasing skepticism about the stability of the link between money and economic activity has prevailed in recent years. For this reason, the Federal Reserve has de-emphasized money supply targets.

VELOCITY BEHAVIOR AND MONETARY POLICY

Velocity behavior has crucial and obvious implications for the conduct of monetary policy. If the velocities of the monetary aggregates (M1, M2, and M3) are stable and predictable, and if the Fed is capable of hitting its targets for M1, M2, and M3, targeting these aggregates is a wise, effective method of conducting monetary policy.

Recall that the income version of the equation of exchange is

$$(22\text{-}1) \qquad\qquad MV_Y \equiv PY$$

This relationship, which literally states that GDP expenditures viewed from the "money side" are identical to GDP expenditures viewed from the "goods side," holds at any point in time. To analyze the role of money *over time,* we can convert this equation into a dynamic version, as follows:

$$(22\text{-}2) \qquad\qquad \%\Delta M + \%\Delta V_y = \%\Delta P + \%\Delta Y$$

This dynamic version of the equation indicates that the percentage change in GDP expenditures viewed from the "money side" ($\%\Delta M + \%\Delta V_Y$) is equal to the percentage change in GDP expenditures viewed from the "goods side" ($\%\Delta P + \%\Delta Y$). Put another way, the growth rate of the money supply plus the growth rate of velocity equals the sum of the inflation rate and the growth rate of real output.

In conducting monetary policy, the Federal Reserve implicitly aims for a specific growth rate for GDP expenditures ($\%\Delta M + \%\Delta V_Y$ or $\%\Delta P + \%\Delta Y$). For example, suppose the Federal Reserve is seeking to achieve 4 percent real output growth ($\%\Delta Y$) and roughly 2 percent inflation ($\%\Delta P$), which it believes is consistent with 4 percent output growth. The Fed will then seek to promote growth of GDP expenditures of approximately

---

EXHIBIT 22-1

P-Star Analysis: The Search for an Indicator of Future Prices

The achievement of a reasonably stable price level has traditionally been considered the foremost goal of a central bank. Because monitoring progress toward achieving price level stability is important, the research staff of the Board of Governors of the Federal Reserve searches for reliable indicators of the future price level. Some variables that analysts have investigated as indicators of prospective inflation are the current behavior of commodity prices (especially gold and silver), the slope of the yield curve, and the behavior of the dollar on foreign exchange markets.

A few years ago, the Fed's research staff thought it had uncovered a superior indicator of the future price level. This was known as the P-star model. P-star is an estimate of the eventual price level implied by the current level of the M2 money supply. M2 was preferred over M1 because, for many years, M2 velocity was more stable and devoid of trends than M1 velocity. To derive P-star, the Fed's staff began with Fisher's equation of exchange in its two forms:

$$M2 \times V_2 = P \times Y \quad \text{and} \quad \%\Delta M2 + \%\Delta V_2 = \%\Delta P + \%\Delta Y$$

Solving for the price level (P) in the two versions, they got

$$P^* = (M2 \times V_2) \div Y \quad \text{and} \quad \%\Delta P = \%\Delta M2 + \%\Delta V_2 - \%\Delta Y$$

So far, we are looking at simple identities which tell us *nothing* about the future price level. Until we specify assumptions about the behavior of V_2 and Y, we can relate neither the money stock to the price level nor money supply growth to inflation. The key assumptions underlying the development of the P-star framework are that potential real output ($\%\Delta Y$) grows at 2.5 percent per year and is independent of money supply behavior, and that M2 velocity always reverts to its long-term mean (1.69 during 1955–1990). To use the model to forecast the price level consistent with any given money supply (M2), one simply plugs into the second set of equations the magnitude of M2, along with the (assumed) eventual velocity of 1.69; takes the product of the two; and divides by the potential output (Y) on the specified future date (calculated by assuming 2.5 percent annual output growth).

---

6 percent per year. In order to arrive at the appropriate growth rate for the money supply, the Fed must forecast or estimate the expected rate of change in velocity during the next year. The whole discussion of the efficacy and desirability of targeting the monetary aggregates boils down to the debate as to whether the Fed (or anyone else) is capable of accurately forecasting velocity. That, in turn, hinges on the stability of velocity.

We conclude this chapter with some food for thought in the form of a graph illustrating the historical pattern of the rate of change in velocity (see Figure 22-3). One can see from the figure that from the early 1950s through the end of the 1970s, the

EXHIBIT 22-1 (CONTINUED)

The crucial assumption (and potential flaw) underlying the P-star model is that M2 velocity will always revert to its long-term mean. The accompanying figure suggests that this was the case through most of the period of 1960–1995. Because M2 velocity has risen sharply since the early 1990s, however, use of the model is likely to lead to an underestimate of the future price level. That is, use of this indicator could lead to higher inflation. Recently, V_2 has been in the neighborhood of 1.95, with little sign of reverting toward its long-term average. By late 1996, it differed by nearly 15 percent from its 1955–1990 average. The potential errors from taking this indicator seriously are enormous. Since 1993, the Fed has discarded P-star analysis and downplayed the use of M2 as an intermediate target of monetary policy.

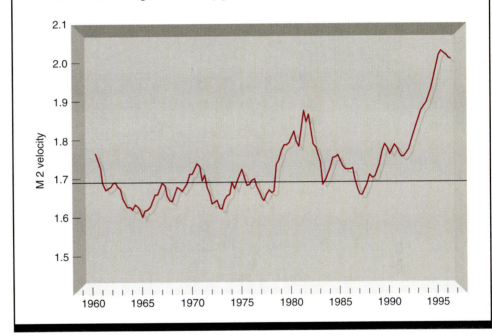

rate of change in V_1 and V_2 was relatively small. These velocities were significantly more volatile in the periods both before and after that interval. One would suspect that the more variable velocity is, the more difficult it would be to predict or forecast. That suggests that adherence by the Federal Reserve to rigid money growth targets would have been less successful in the period after 1980 than in the previous quarter century. It is no coincidence that sentiment for targeting monetary aggregates reached a high-water mark in the 1970s and decreased in the 1980s and 1990s. (Exhibit 22-1 evaluates a proposal for targeting M2 grounded on the premise that M2 velocity is constant in the long run.)

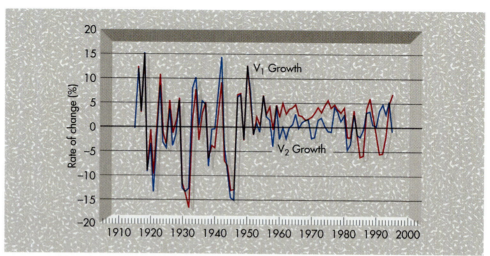

Figure 22-3   Annual Rate of Change in the Velocity of M1 and M2, 1915–1996.
Changes in velocity were relatively small and perhaps predictable from the 1960s to the
early 1970s. Before and after that period, velocity was unstable. (Calculated from the
data presented in Figure 22-1.)   *Source:* Drawn from data provided in Milton Friedman
and Anna Jacobson Schwartz, *A Monetary History of the United States* (copyright © 1963
by National Bureau of Economic Research; Princeton, N.J.: Princeton University Press),
p. 774, Table A-5, adjusted and updated to conform to data furnished by the Federal Reserve System for the period after 1959.

SUMMARY

The velocity of money is influenced by institutional
factors, the state of financial technology, interest rate
levels, the degree of economic uncertainty, inflation
expectations, and the income level. In the United
States and many other countries, velocity trended
downward in the century prior to World War II and has
increased substantially since then. The early downtrend
in velocity is attributable to the gradual movement
away from barter and payment in kind to the use of
money as the relative importance of agriculture declined and urbanization took place. The uptrend in velocity after World War II is largely attributable to improving financial technology, although rising income,
higher interest rates, and declining economic uncer-

tainty may also have contributed. Over the course of
the business cycle, velocity exhibits a procyclical pattern, rising during economic expansions and declining
during recessions. This pattern may be attributable to
the procyclical pattern of interest rates, to the tendency
for money to adapt to GDP in a lagged and sluggish
fashion, or to the fact that the demand for money depends on long-run average income rather than current
income. The case for using monetary aggregates as intermediate monetary policy targets hinges on the stability of velocity. Because velocity became more unstable
after the early 1980s, in recent years the Fed has become more reluctant to set and adhere to money
growth targets.

Answer to Your Turn *(p. 520)*

The direction in which velocity will move is uncertain because the two forces will pull velocity in opposite directions. Financial innovations will work to boost velocity, while income growth will tend to reduce it. The net effect will depend on which of the two forces has a stronger impact.

KEY TERMS

income elasticity of demand for money
permanent income

STUDY QUESTIONS

1 Discuss the basic long-term movements in the income velocity of money (V_1 and V_2) over the past 100 years, and outline the Friedman and Tobin explanations of such trends.

2 Explain how the use of financial instruments such as commercial paper and negotiable CDs loosens the Federal Reserve's grip on aggregate spending.

3 Discuss the improvements in financial technology which have contributed to the uptrend in the income velocity of money (V_1) since 1946.

4 Make assumptions about the trend of interest rates and income over the next 5 years. Based on those assumptions and your understanding of the factors underlying velocity (V_1), present a forecast of the behavior of the velocity of M1 over the next 5 years.

5 Outline Friedman's explanation for the procyclical behavior of velocity.

6 Outline the two explanations for the procyclical behavior of velocity that are basically incompatible with the tenets of monetarism.

7 Following a long uptrend during 1946–1980, V_1 declined significantly over the next 15 years. Based on your knowledge of the determinants of velocity, name and explain three factors that could have caused or contributed to the post-1980 decline in velocity.

8 Suppose you know that the income elasticity of demand for M1 is 0.5, and you expect interest rates and the level of financial technology to remain constant over the next 5 years. What would you expect to happen to V_1 during the next 5 years? Explain.

9 Suppose the income elasticity of demand for money is known to be 1.50 and income velocity is initially 6.0. Assuming the nation's nominal income, or *PY*, increases 100 percent in the next decade and all other factors influencing velocity remain constant, calculate the new level of velocity.

10 Suppose it were proven that money is a luxury good and that the demand for money depends only on *current* income, not *permanent* income. What would be the implications of cyclical changes in GDP for the cyclical behavior of velocity? Explain.

11 DIDMCA of 1980 authorized the nationwide issuance of NOW and ATS accounts (both of which are included in M1). What were the initial implications of DIDMCA for the behavior of M1 velocity?

12 During 1981–1983, inflation and interest rates fell sharply, and banks were authorized by DIDMCA to pay interest on DDO. What were the implications of each of those events for the velocity of M1? What was the net implication of all three events for the velocity of M1?

13 Examine Figure 22-2. Can you think of a reasonable explanation of the behavior of the velocity of M2 since 1987?

14 Suppose the world is stunned by the declaration of war by Egypt against Saudi Arabia. What would you expect to happen to the velocity of M2 in the United States? Explain.

15 Why does velocity often increase as inflation accelerates? Analyze the phenomenon in the context of a third-world nation's financing huge military expenditures by printing money. Discuss the implications in the context of the $MV_Y \equiv PY$ framework.

SUGGESTIONS FOR ADDITIONAL READING

The most comprehensive discussion of all aspects of the demand for money is to be found in David Laidler, *The Demand for Money,* 4th ed. (New York, Harper-Collins, 1993). Milton Friedman and Anna Schwartz's views on velocity are contained in *A Monetary History of the United States, 1876–1960* (Princeton, N.J.: Princeton University Press, 1963), Chap. 12. James Tobin's differing views are set forth in "The Monetary Interpretation of History," *American Economic Review,* June 1965, pp. 646–685. At a very high level of sophistication, Stephen Goldfeld's "The Demand for Money Revisited," *Brookings Papers on Economic Activity,* 3 (1973) is also pertinent. Contrast the conclusion of this article with Goldfeld's follow-up article, "The Case of the Missing Money," *Brookings Papers on Economic Activity,* 3 (1976), pp. 683–730. A major, important work that lends support to the institutional theory of long-term velocity behavior is Michael Bordo and Lars Jonung, *The Long-Run Behavior of Velocity of Circulation: The International Evidence* (New York: Cambridge University Press, 1987). An update by the same authors, together with related discussions and critiques by Laidler and John Huizinga, appeared in the *Journal of Policy Modeling,* 2 (1990), pp. 141–203. A critique and extension of Bordo and Jonung's work is James D.

Hamilton, "The Long-Run Behavior of Velocity of Circulation, A Review Essay," *Journal of Monetary Economics,* 1989, pp. 335–344. Friedman and Schwartz's response to the institutional approach to velocity is contained in "Alternative Approaches to Analyzing Economic Data," *American Economic Review,* March 1991, pp. 39–49. Recent support for the institutional hypothesis is provided by Pierre Siklos, "Income Velocity and Institutional Change: Some New Time Series Evidence, 1870–1986," *Journal of Money, Credit, and Banking,* August 1993, pp. 377–392. An authoritative study of the issue of the stability of the demand for money is the 1982 Judd and Scadding article cited in the "Suggestions for Additional Reading" at the end of the previous chapter. An informal discussion of the post-1980 instability of money velocity is "Recent Behavior of Velocity of Money," *Contemporary Policy Issues,* January 1987, pp. 1–33, with comments by Michael Darby, William Poole, David Lindsey, Milton Friedman, and Michael J. Bazdarich. An interesting use of the application of regional data to test velocity hypotheses is Peter Ireland, "Financial Evolution and the Long-Run Behavior of Velocity: New Evidence from U.S. Regional Data," Federal Reserve Bank of Richmond *Economic Review,* December 1991, pp. 16–26.

■

The *IS-LM* Model
of the Macroeconomy

Following the publication of Keynes' *General Theory* in 1936, a major portion of macroeconomic research for the next quarter century involved efforts to test, refine, and extend the general framework introduced by Keynes. During this era, monetary policy was subordinated to fiscal policy, which was believed to be more powerful. Few eminent economists questioned the case for *policy activism*—that is, it was widely believed that both fiscal and monetary policies could be *actively* and *effectively* implemented to contribute to economic stability. The high tide of Keynesian economics was probably around 1964 to 1965. This was *after* the Keynesian-inspired tax cuts in the early 1960s sparked a vigorous expansion of GDP, employment, and profits but *before* the Vietnam War produced serious economic problems. In the decade after 1965, monetarists made major inroads into the Keynesian constituency. However, beginning in the mid-1970s, increasing skepticism was voiced concerning the central proposition of monetarism, that the demand for money is highly stable. In the past 25 years, economists have moved toward a consensus that rejects the extreme positions of both monetarists and Keynesians. Today, few respected economists take the position that money is *all* that matters. On the other hand, few would argue that money doesn't matter. The truth is that *both* monetary and fiscal measures influence aggregate demand and GDP in a significant way.

In this chapter, we will develop a theoretical framework that integrates monetary and fiscal measures. This framework, known as the **IS-LM model,** is widely used in macroeconomic analysis. We will use the model to explain how various real and monetary forces influence the nation's output, income, and interest rates. In Chapter 24, we will employ the *IS-LM* model to analyze several important issues, including the crowding-out controversy and the problem of conducting monetary policy in a world in which policymakers are uncertain about the positions and slopes of the *IS* and *LM* curves.

We will begin by noting the interdependence of interest rates, the demand for money, and income or GDP. Figure 23-1 illustrates the principle.

In panel *A,* the initial money supply and demand functions are given as S_{M_0} and D_{M_0}, respectively. The resulting interest rate is i_0, the intersection of the two curves. In panel *B,* the interest rate of i_0 determines the magnitude of investment plus government spending, $(I + G)_0$. And in panel *C,* the magnitude of $I + G$ spending, together with the consumption

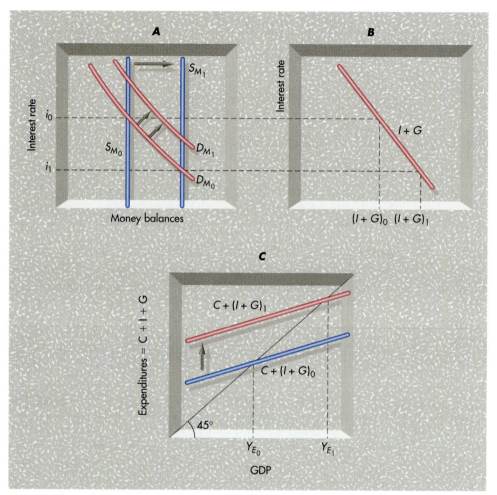

Figure 23-1   Interaction of Interest Rates, Income, and the Demand for Money. An increase in the money supply reduces interest rates, stimulating expenditures and GDP. The increase in GDP then feeds back to boost the demand for money.

function, determines the aggregate expenditures line, $C + (I + G)_0$, and the equilibrium level of GDP, Y_{E_0}. Given an interest rate of i_0 and investment plus government expenditures of $(I + G)_0$, equilibrium output must be Y_{E_0}.

Now suppose that the money supply increases to S_{M_1}. Given the demand for money, the interest rate falls to i_1, increasing $I + G$ expenditures to $(I + G)_1$ (panel B). In panel C, the increase in investment and government spending raises aggregate expenditures and the equilibrium level of GDP to Y_{E_1}. However, Y_{E_1} is not really a sustainable equilibrium level of output. The increase in GDP, or income, feeds back to panel A of the figure, increasing the demand for money from D_{M_0} to D_{M_1}. In doing so, it raises the interest rate above i_1, which in turn reduces the $I + G$ spending and hence

GDP. This reduction in GDP reverberates back to the demand for money, producing a downward shift in that schedule. Interest rates fall, stimulating $I + G$ spending and GDP. Further reverberations ensue until D_M, interest rates, $I + G$, and GDP settle into equilibrium.

You can now see the inadequacy of the model shown in Figure 23-1: we cannot determine the equilibrium level of GDP until we know the interest rate, but it is impossible to specify the interest rate without first knowing the level of GDP and the corresponding demand for money. The model is indeterminate.

The same conclusion applies if we assume that the initial disturbance to equilibrium originates in the "real" sector rather than the monetary sector.[1] Suppose government expenditures rise, while the money supply remains constant. The increase in government expenditures shifts the aggregate expenditures function (panel C of Figure 23-1) upward, raising the equilibrium level of GDP. This increase in GDP produces an increase in the demand for money (panel A of Figure 23-1), raising the interest rate. The higher interest rate reduces investment spending, an effect known as "crowding out," counteracting in part the expansionary effects of the increase in government expenditures. Once again, after an infinite number of reverberations among interest rates, investment expenditures, income, and the demand for money, the final equilibrium level of output cannot be determined in the framework of Figure 23-1. We need a model which integrates the role of monetary and real influences, allowing for interaction among them. That is the purpose of the *IS-LM* model, which we will now develop.

THE *IS-LM* MODEL: FUNDAMENTAL ELEMENTS

The *IS* curve summarizes the forces underlying equilibrium in the product market, while the *LM* curve illustrates equilibrium in the market for money. Together, equilibrium interest rates and output levels are shown to be influenced by both real and monetary forces. We begin our analysis with the *LM* curve, then turn to the *IS* curve, and finally discuss how monetary and real forces influence economic activity.

Equilibrium in the Money Market: The *LM* Curve

In order for equilibrium to exist in the market for money (which consists of demand deposits and currency), the quantity of money demanded must exactly equal the quantity of money supplied. We have established the fact that the demand for money depends on both the interest rate and the level of income. Specifically, the quantity of

---

[1] By a "real" disturbance, we mean a shift in C, I, or G caused by factors unrelated to changes in the supply of or demand for money. Examples include a change in G due to a government decision, a change in C due to a change in taxes or consumer confidence, and a change in I due to a change in the business outlook or in federal tax policy toward business.

money demanded varies *directly* with the level of income and *inversely* with the level of interest rates. Given a fixed money supply, this suggests that if the money market is to be in equilibrium, a higher level of income (which increases money demand) must be accompanied by a higher level of interest rates (which reduces money demand). Alternatively stated, lower interest rates, which increase the demand for interest-sensitive or speculative money holdings, must be accompanied by lower income, which reduces the quantity of money demanded for transactions purposes. These notions are expressed formally in Figure 23-2.

The speculative demand for money function (or interest-sensitive portion of money demand function) is shown in quadrant 1, the lower-right-hand portion of the

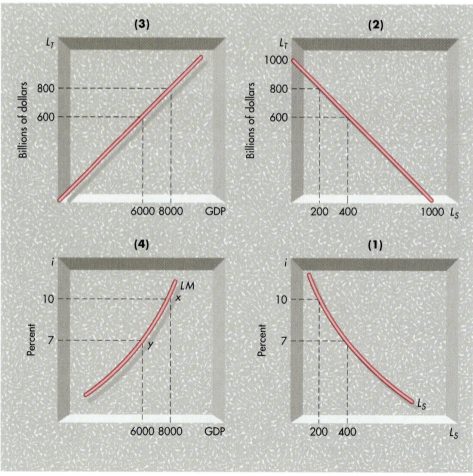

Figure 23-2   Derivation of the *LM* Curve. The *LM* curve (quadrant 4) shows all of the combinations of interest rates and income levels (GDP) that are consistent with equilibrium in the market for money.

figure.[2] The transactions and precautionary demands are lumped together as L_T in quadrant 3, which shows that they are a positive function of the nation's level of income, or GDP. (Recall that because an increase in income leads to an increase in expenditures, it also leads to an increase in average money balances held.) Quadrant 2 indicates all of the possible ways in which a given money supply can be divided up between speculative holdings (L_S) and transactions and precautionary balances (L_T). A change in the money supply produces a parallel shift of the function in quadrant 2, that is, the $L_T - L_S$ line. Quadrant 4 illustrates the *LM* curve, which is derived on the basis of the relationships expressed in the other three quadrants.

The **LM curve** is defined as the locus of all combinations of interest rates and income levels that equate the total demand for money with the existing supply of money. It is not a demand curve or a supply curve but a schedule showing an infinite number of potential money market *equilibrium* positions. If the market for money balances is to be in equilibrium, the interest rate and GDP level must be related to each other in such a way as to equate the supply of money with the demand for it. That is, they must fall on the *LM* curve.

Beginning in quadrant 1, suppose the interest rate is 10 percent. At that rate, the quantity of money needed to satisfy the speculative demand is $200 billion. Given the existing money supply of $1000 billion (quadrant 2), $800 billion remains to satisfy the transactions and precautionary motives (L_T). Quadrant 3 indicates that if the public is to willingly hold exactly $800 billion in transactions and precautionary balances, the level of GDP will need to be $8000 billion. One possible point of equilibrium, therefore, is a 10 percent interest rate in combination with a GDP level of $8000 billion. That combination is indicated as point *x* on the *LM* curve (quadrant 4).

If the interest rate should fall to 7 percent, the quantity of money demanded for speculative balances would increase to $400 billion (quadrant 1). Given the fixed money supply of $1000 billion, this would leave $600 billion for L_T holdings (quadrant 2). To produce transactions and precautionary demand (L_T) of exactly $600 billion, GDP would need to be $6000 billion per year (quadrant 3). Point *y* in quadrant 4 indicates this second potential point of equilibrium in the market for money. If the interest rate were to drop below 7 percent, the speculative demand for money would increase further. In order to release more money from transactions and precautionary balances, GDP would have to drop below $6000 billion per year. We see that the *LM* schedule is an upward-sloping curve.

Because the *LM* curve is constructed from the three relationships illustrated in quadrants 1, 2, and 3 of Figure 23-2, its shape and position depend on the supply of money (quadrant 2) and the shapes and positions of the money demand curves in quadrants 1 and 3. A change in the money supply or a movement (shift) in the demand for money relationship (quadrants 1 and 3) will shift the *position* of the *LM* curve. A change in the *slope*

---

[2]We refer here to the interest-sensitive portion of the demand for money as "speculative holdings" for convenience. The essential point is that the demand for money depends on both income and interest rates. Whether the interest-sensitive portion of the demand for money is actually related to speculative or transactions holdings (or to both) is not important in this analysis.

of the speculative and/or transactions demand for money curves will change the *slope* of the *LM* curve. In the following sections, we will examine some of the factors that can cause a shift in the position of the *LM* curve.

Factors That Cause a Shift in the *LM* Curve

Three types of factors can initiate shifts in the *LM* curve: changes in the money supply, shifts in the speculative demand function (L_S), and shifts or rotations in the transactions demand function (L_T).

A Change in the Money Supply

An increase in the supply of money produces a rightward shift in the money supply line in quadrant 2. To maintain equilibrium, the enlarged money supply must be absorbed into transactions and/or speculative holdings. For any given interest rate and corresponding L_S magnitude, the additional money must be absorbed into transactions balances, which requires a higher level of GDP. Alternatively stated, for any given income level and corresponding L_T holdings, the additional money must be absorbed into interest-sensitive speculative holdings, which requires a lower interest rate. Both of these statements imply that the *LM* curve will shift rightward. Similarly, a decrease in the money supply will shift the *LM* curve leftward.

A Shift in the Speculative Demand

Suppose a declaration of war by the United States boosts inflationary expectations. Because interest rates are now expected to rise, people will want to dump their securities and increase their speculative money holdings; the L_S curve in quadrant 1 immediately shifts rightward. Given the existing money supply, the increase in speculative demand at each and every interest rate implies that less money remains to finance transactions. To achieve equilibrium in the money market, the income level required to equate the total demand for money with the existing money supply must be lower at each and every interest rate; the *LM* curve shifts leftward. Similarly, any event that sets off expectations of lower inflation and interest rates will shift the L_S curve leftward and the *LM* curve rightward. A *decrease* in money *demand* exerts the same effect on the *LM* curve as an *increase* in the money *supply*. An *increase* in money *demand* has the same effect on the *LM* curve as a *decrease* in the money *supply*.

A Change in the Transactions Demand

Several factors may operate to change the magnitude of transactions holdings associated with each GDP level (quadrant 3). Some of them are institutional factors, such as the frequency of paydays and the use of money market mutual funds, repurchase agreements, overdraft facilities, credit cards, and so forth. In some instances, expectations of inflation may also change the relationship between transactions holdings and the income level. These phenomena may be treated as rotating the position of the L_T curve in quadrant 3 of Figure 23-2. For example, the increased use of credit cards would rotate the L_T curve rightward, or clockwise. So would the elimination of minimum balance requirements for demand deposits, more frequent paydays, or a dramatic increase in inflationary expectations; all these events would shift the *LM* curve rightward.

Given a constant money supply and a constant L_S curve (quadrant 1), a decrease in the L_T curve (clockwise rotation) implies that, at any interest rate, income must rise to offset the decrease in transactions holdings. Alternatively stated, given the income level, the interest rate must decline in order to induce an expansion of speculative money balances in order to compensate for the reduction in transactions demand. These statements imply a rightward shift in the *LM* curve.

Using similar reasoning, it can be shown that a decrease in credit card usage, a decrease in the frequency of paydays, or an increase in penalties levied for overdrafts would tend to rotate the L_T function counterclockwise, shifting the *LM* curve to the left.

Equilibrium in the Product Market: The *IS* Curve

In the simplified Keynesian model of the market for goods and services, there are two equivalent conditions that must be met in order to achieve equilibrium. They are:

(23-1) $$\textbf{GDP or } Y = C + I + G$$

(23-2) $$S + T = I + G$$

Equation 23-1 indicates that in equilibrium, aggregate expenditures in the form of consumption, investment, and government purchases $(C + I + G)$ equal output (GDP).[3] Equation 23-2 states that the equilibrium output level is the level at which leakages from the income stream in the form of savings and taxes $(S + T)$ are exactly balanced by investment and government purchases, $I + G$. Both of these equivalent conditions must be satisfied if equilibrium is to prevail in the market for goods and services (hereafter called the *product market*).

It should be intuitively clear that $I + G$ spending is a downward-sloping function of the level of interest rates. The lower the interest rate, the greater the magnitude of investment spending, and perhaps also local government spending (because issuing bonds becomes more attractive when interest rates are low). It follows that the lower the interest rate, the greater must be the magnitude of $S + T$ leakages in order to match the increased $I + G$ expenditures. Because both saving and tax revenues increase with income, we conclude that the lower the interest rate, the greater must be the level of income, or GDP, to produce product market equilibrium. These notions are set forth in Figure 23-3, which shows the derivation of the *IS* curve.

The ***IS* curve** is defined as the locus of all combinations of interest rates and income (GDP) levels which satisfy the equilibrium conditions for the product market. Like the *LM* curve, it is an *equilibrium locus*, not a demand or supply curve. If the product market is to be in equilibrium, the prevailing interest rate and income levels must lie somewhere on the *IS* curve.

---

[3]For purposes of simplicity, we have omitted exports and imports from the model. A more complete model would include net exports (exports minus imports) on the right-hand side of Equation 23-1 and imports and exports on the left- and right-hand sides, respectively, of Equation 23-2.

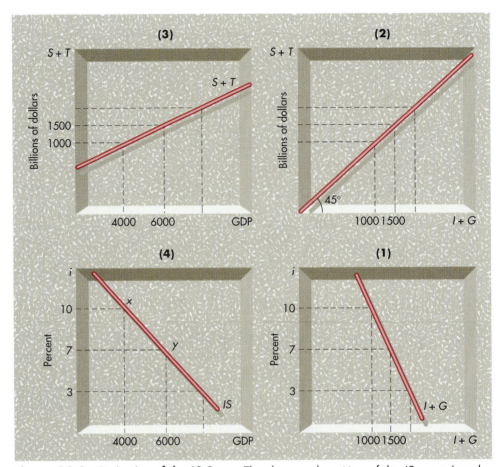

Figure 23-3 **Derivation of the *IS* Curve.** The slope and position of the *IS* curve (quadrant 4) depend on the slope and position of the interest rate–($I + G$) relationship (quadrant 1) and the slope and position of the ($S + T$)–income relationship (quadrant 3).

To derive the *IS* curve, we again begin in the lower-right-hand quadrant, this time with the interest rate–($I + G$) relationship. Suppose the interest rate is 10 percent. That implies $I + G$ expenditures of $1000 billion per year. Quadrant 2 is simply a 45-degree line which delineates points of equality between $I + G$ and $S + T$. Quadrant 3 indicates the functional relationship between $S + T$ and the level of aggregate income, or GDP. An increase in GDP induces an expansion of $S + T$; with higher incomes, people save more and pay more taxes. Given the 10 percent interest rate and the $1000 billion annual flow of $I + G$, $S + T$ must also amount to $1000 billion per year if the product market is to be in equilibrium. Quadrant 3 shows that a GDP level of $4000 billion would result in saving and taxes of exactly $1000 billion. Hence, one possible product market equilibrium occurs at an interest rate of 10 percent and a GDP level of $4000 billion—point *x* on the *IS* curve (quadrant 4).

If the interest rate is 7 percent, $I + G$ spending will flow at the rate of $1500 billion per year (quadrant 1). For $S + T$ to match that amount, GDP needs to be $6000 billion (quadrant 3). Point y on the *IS* curve indicates that this combination of interest rate and GDP level also satisfies the condition for product market equilibrium. We conclude that the lower the interest rate, the higher must be the level of GDP in order for the product market to be in equilibrium. Hence, the *IS* curve is downward sloping.

Factors That Shift the *IS* Curve

You may have noticed that the derivation of the *IS* curve is slightly less complicated than that of the *LM* curve. While three elements contribute to the *LM* curve—the money supply, the transactions and precautionary demands for money, and the speculative, or interest-sensitive, demand for money—only two elements contribute to the *IS* curve. The curve in quadrant 2 is merely a 45-degree guideline that delineates points of equality between $S + T$ and $I + G$. The only behavioral relationships that determine the position and slope of the *IS* curve are the interest rate–($I + G$) relationship (quadrant 1) and the ($S + T$)–income relationship (quadrant 3). Shifts in these two relationships shift the *IS* curve.

Shifts in the Interest Rate–($I + G$) Relationship

Suppose government expenditures are reduced due to congressional action. If I remains constant, the $I + G$ curve (quadrant 1) must shift leftward. To induce a reduction in $S + T$ sufficient to match the reduction in $I + G$, the level of GDP corresponding to each and every interest rate would have to fall. Hence, the *IS* curve shifts leftward. Each interest rate would be associated with a lower level of GDP.

Suppose an improvement in the business outlook increases the rate of return expected from investment. This shifts the interest rate–investment relationship and hence the $I + G$ curve (quadrant 1) to the right. The improved outlook shifts the *IS* curve rightward. At each and every interest rate, equilibrium GDP is higher.

Shifts in the ($S + T$)–Income Relationship

Suppose the government enacts a substantial tax increase. The $S + T$ schedule in quadrant 3 would shift upward and to the left because each and every GDP level would be associated with higher taxes (hence more $S + T$). Because higher taxes reduce consumer demand, equilibrium GDP corresponding to each and every interest rate is reduced; the *IS* curve shifts leftward. Stated another way, since consumer demand is depressed because of the tax hike, $I + G$ spending would have to increase in order to maintain the existing GDP level. An increase in $I + G$ requires lower interest rates. Again, this implies that the *IS* curve shifts leftward or downward. A tax hike is a contractionary event that depresses both output and interest rates.

To give another example, suppose an increase in consumer confidence reduces the propensity to save. The $S + T$ schedule shifts downward or to the right. In this case, the *IS* curve shifts upward or rightward, a fact that can be demonstrated easily. Because of increased consumption, each and every interest rate is associated with greater $C + I + G$ spending and thus greater equilibrium GDP. Alternatively, to maintain the original equilibrium GDP, interest rates would have to rise in order to choke back sufficient $I + G$ expenditures to compensate for the increase in consumption. Either way you view it, the *IS* curve moves upward or rightward; a reduction in the propensity to save is an expansionary phenomenon.

To summarize, any event that shifts $I + G$ or $S + T$ rightward shifts the IS curve rightward, thus exerting an expansionary effect on GDP. Any event that shifts $I + G$ or $S + T$ leftward shifts the IS schedule leftward, exerting a contractionary influence on GDP.

General Equilibrium and the Adjustment to Disequilibrium

We have shown that there exist an infinite number of possible combinations of interest rate and GDP levels that are consistent with equilibrium in the product market. The locus of all those combinations, the IS curve, is negatively sloped. We have also demonstrated that there are an infinite number of combinations of interest rate and GDP levels that are consistent with money market equilibrium. This collection of points, the LM curve, is positively sloped. If the IS and LM curves appear with slopes as illustrated in Figure 23-4, there can exist only one *general equilibrium*—that is, simultaneous equilibrium in the money market *and* the product market. It is the intersection of the IS and LM curves, shown in Figure 23-4. At point E in the figure, the money market and the product market are both in equilibrium. Given the relationships underlying both the LM curve and the IS curve, interest rates and aggregate demand or GDP will be stable. Any departures from E will produce forces that return the economy to E.

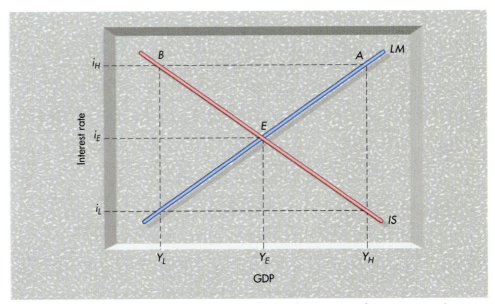

Figure 23-4 General Equilibrium in the Product and Money Markets. Because the LM curve (the locus of money market equilibria) slopes upward and the IS curve (the locus of product market equilibria) slopes downward, there can be only one point of *general* equilibrium—the simultaneous equilibrium in both markets, point E.

Suppose that the economy is initially at point *A,* with an interest rate of i_H and an output level of Y_H. Because point *A* falls on the *LM* curve, the total demand for money is equal to the supply of money. The market for money is in equilibrium. However, point *A* is not on the *IS* curve, which implies disequilibrium in the product market. The aggregate demand for goods and services is out of equilibrium with the aggregate supply. At the output level currently being produced (Y_H), the interest rate would have to be i_L to equate $I + G$ with $S + T$ or to equate $C + I + G$ with aggregate output (GDP).

Because the interest rate is actually much higher (i_H), we infer that $I + G$ is less than $S + T$ and aggregate expenditures are lower than output. This means that inventories are rising and firms will cut their production below Y_H. As GDP and income decline, the transactions demand for money will drop off. Given the existing money supply, the interest rate will begin to decline. Eventually, the decline in interest rates and the reduction in GDP will resolve the imbalance between aggregate expenditures and output. The reduction in output (GDP) and income will reduce saving and taxes, and the reduction in interest rates will stimulate investment and government spending. When the interest rate has fallen to i_E in Figure 23-4, actual output will have been reduced and expenditures will have been stimulated sufficiently to eliminate the excess supply in the product market. Equilibrium output will be achieved at Y_E, with an interest rate of i_E. At this point, $I + G$ will have caught up with $S + T$, and aggregate expenditures will just absorb GDP.

To give a second example, suppose the economy is initially at point *B* in Figure 23-4, with an interest rate of i_H and an output level of Y_L. Point *B* lies on the *IS* curve but not on the *LM* curve. The product market is in equilibrium, but the money market is not. The *LM* curve indicates that with an interest rate of i_H, income would have to be at Y_H in order to equate the demand for money with the existing money supply. Because income is actually only Y_L, the demand for money is lower than the level consistent with equilibrium in the money market. We infer that the supply of money exceeds the demand.

Beginning at point *B,* some of the excess money balances will spill over into the securities markets, driving up bond prices and driving down interest rates. The decline in interest rates stimulates investment spending and hence aggregate expenditures. GDP rises, and interest rates decline. Disequilibrium in the money market is finally alleviated via two channels: the declining yields induce an increase in speculative money balances, and the rising GDP pulls up the demand for transactions balances. The demand for money catches up with the existing supply of money at point *E*. (Note that disequilibrium in the money market has important implications for both output and employment.)

APPLICATIONS OF THE *IS-LM* MODEL

The beauty of the *IS-LM* model relative to the simple Keynesian framework shown in Figure 23-1 is that it is much more versatile. It is more effective in handling the analysis of changes originating in the monetary sector—that is, changes in the supply of or demand for money. It also comes to grips more effectively with the interaction between real and monetary forces—a feature conspicuously absent from the simple Keynesian model.

In the next two sections, we will use the *IS-LM* model to trace the implications of various changes in both the monetary and real sectors. In each case, you should take care to focus on the behavioral phenomena associated with these changes rather than simply memorizing the shifts in the *LM* and/or *IS* curves and their implications.

Disturbances Originating in the Monetary Sector

Monetary disturbances may result from changes in either the supply of money or the demand for money. We will look at each type of disturbance.

An Increase in the Money Supply

Figure 23-5 illustrates the impact of an increase in the money supply (a rightward and parallel shift of the money supply schedule in quadrant 2). At each and every interest rate, a larger GDP level is required to absorb the additional money supply into transactions balances and thus provide equilibrium in the money market. Alternatively stated, at each and every income level, a lower interest rate is required to absorb the additional money into desired holdings. The *LM* curve shifts rightward to LM_2 (quadrant 4). We see from its intersection with the *IS* curve that the interest rate falls to i_2 and the level of income or GDP rises to Y_2.

But what is the chain of reactions that produces this result? Initially, both the product and money markets are in equilibrium at point *A,* with the interest rate and output level at i_1 and Y_1, respectively. When the Fed boosts the money supply, an excess supply of money initially exists. The excess money is worked off through the purchase of securities by the public, which boosts security prices and lowers yields. Lower interest rates stimulate investment expenditures, increasing GDP. In this way the disequilibrium in the money market spills over to influence the product market. The result is that interest rates decline and investment, consumption, and GDP increase. In the new equilibrium, point *B,* the level of interest rates has been reduced to i_2 and the level of output has been increased to Y_2.[4] Both of these phenomena work to pull the quantity of money demanded up to parity with the increased supply of money. At point *B,* equilibrium is restored in both the money and product markets.

An Announcement of an Increase in Reserve Requirements

Suppose an announcement of an increase in reserve requirements catches the public totally by surprise, resulting in an expectation of a more restrictive monetary environment in the months ahead. Clearly, expectations for interest rates will be revised upward. The implications of such an announcement are shown in Figure 23-6.

Because visions of higher interest rates produce fears of lower stock and bond prices in the future, many individuals and firms will immediately seek to get out of securities into cash. In quadrant 1 of the figure, the speculative demand for money increases from

---

[4]It must be pointed out that this is a *Keynesian* view of the adjustment mechanism. A monetarist would assert that some of the excess money balances would be spent *directly* on goods and services. In this way, monetarists view changes in the money supply as impinging on GDP independently of the interest rate channel. Thus monetarists believe that an increase in the money supply shifts *both* the *IS* and *LM* curves rightward. The *IS* curve shifts because consumption is dependent on money balances as well as on income. An increase in the supply of money shifts consumption, aggregate demand, and the *IS* curve upward. If an increase in the supply of money produces a rightward shift in both the *LM* and *IS* curves, GDP increases, but the direction in which interest rates will move is uncertain.

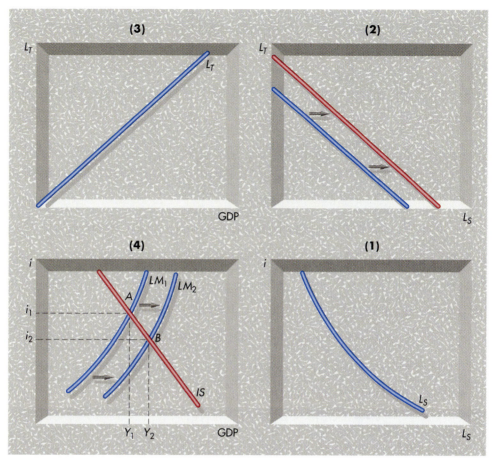

Figure 23-5   The Impact of an Increase in the Money Supply. An increase in the money supply (quadrant 2) shifts the *LM* curve rightward, reducing interest rates and increasing the equilibrium level of GDP (quadrant 4).

L_{S_1} to L_{S_2}. Given the supply of money (quadrant 2), and given the transactions demand curve (quadrant 3), the increased desire to hold money for speculative purposes at every interest rate can be accommodated only by releasing funds from transactions balances. This requires a reduction in the GDP level. Hence, the *LM* curve shifts leftward, raising the interest rate and reducing GDP. Note that any *increase* in the *demand* for money has the same impact on the *LM* curve as a *decrease* in the *supply* of money.

What is the behavioral explanation for this result? When the Fed announces a decision to increase reserve requirements, the demand for money immediately jumps above the supply, throwing the money market out of equilibrium. In an effort to increase money balances, people rush to sell securities, quickly depressing securities prices and exerting upward pressure on interest rates. The higher interest rates reduce investment spending, depressing GDP. The cycle of rising yields and declining output will cease only when the contraction of transactions and speculative money holdings has been sufficient to compensate for the initial

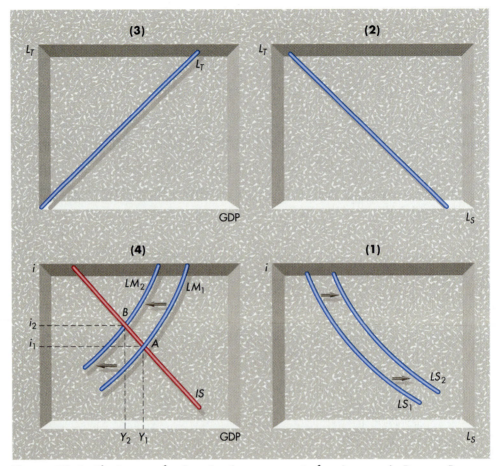

Figure 23-6   The Impact of a Surprise Announcement of an Increase in Reserve Requirements. Any announcement that produces expectations of tighter Federal Reserve policy boosts the speculative demand for money, increasing interest rates and reducing equilibrium GDP.

expansion in speculative demand. Note that the disequilibrium in the money market has a significant effect on the real sector—that is on output, income, and employment.

In terms of our $MV_Y \equiv PY$ framework, GDP (PY) falls because the increased speculative demand for money reduces velocity. In spite of a constant money supply, GDP falls.

Your Turn

Suppose the Federal Reserve surprises the financial markets by announcing a sharp reduction in the discount rate. Using the *IS-LM* model, analyze the impact of this announcement on interest rates and the level of GDP.

Initiation of Overdraft Protection

Suppose banks announce an extension of overdraft protection to all customers, together with the elimination of all associated fees. Except for the interest payable on the amounts overdrawn, the costs of overdrawing a checking account are eliminated by the banks' extension of automatic loans. With little or no penalty for overdrawing checking accounts, millions of bank customers will reduce the average balances they maintain and the demand for money will decline.

Figure 23-7 shows the implications of this institutional change. The reduction in the need to hold transactions balances at all income levels produces a clockwise rotation of the L_T schedule in quadrant 3. This reduction in the transactions demand for money means that, at each and every interest rate, income must increase in order to maintain a demand

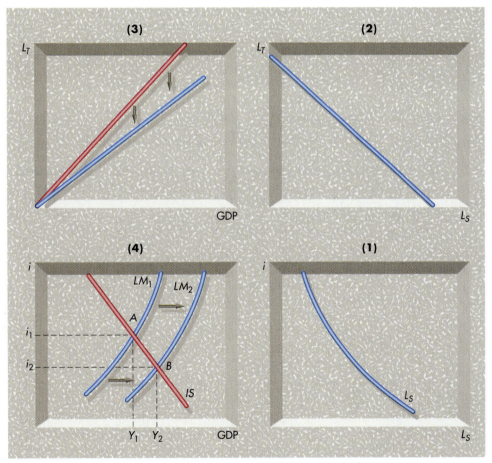

Figure 23-7   The Impact of the Implementation of Free Overdraft Services. Any event that reduces the transactions demand for money (rotates L_T clockwise) shifts the *LM* curve rightward, reducing interest rates and increasing GDP.

for money equal to the existing supply. Stated alternatively, at each and every income level, interest rates must decline in order to absorb the excess money into speculative holdings. The *LM* curve shifts rightward, and the general equilibrium point moves from *A* to *B*. The increase in "financial technology" has reduced the level of interest rates and increased the level of GDP.

How does this happen? With the transactions demand reduced but the money supply unchanged, an excess supply of money initially exists. This excess money is used to purchase securities, pushing down yields and stimulating the demand for goods and services. Again, note that the decrease in the demand for money has the same impact as an increase in the supply of money. In terms of the $MV_Y \equiv PY$ framework, the level of GDP expenditures (PY) increases because V_Y has been boosted by this change in financial technology.

Monetary Disturbances: Summary

We may now summarize our findings regarding monetary disturbances as follows:

1 Any event that *increases* the speculative or transactions demand for money (that is, shifts L_S rightward or rotates L_T leftward) has an effect on interest rates and GDP similar to a *decrease* in the money supply.

2 Any event that *decreases* the speculative or transactions demand for money (that is, shifts L_S leftward or rotates L_T rightward) has an effect on interest rates and GDP similar to an *increase* in the money supply.

3 Disturbances in the monetary sector spill over to the real sector, influencing the level of aggregate expenditures, GDP, and employment.

Disturbances Originating in the Real Sector

Analytically, we may specify two basic sources of real disturbances—that is, disturbances that directly affect the product market. They are the relationship between the interest rate and $I + G$ spending (quadrant 1) and the relationship between $S + T$ leakages and GDP (quadrant 3). Many different phenomena are capable of initiating shifts in these two relationships. A shift in either relationship shifts the *IS* curve, triggering a change in the equilibrium levels of interest rates and GDP. Those changes in turn spill over into the money market, inducing adjustments in that market. Let us look at two examples, both involving taxes.

A Reduction in the Corporate Income Tax Rate

Suppose a cut in the corporate income tax rate raises the stream of (aftertax) returns expected from investment in capital assets. Figure 23-8 illustrates the implications of such a change. In quadrant 1, the improvement in expected returns causes a rightward shift of the $I + G$ curve. Because $I + G$ expenditures increase at each and every interest rate, the equilibrium GDP corresponding to each and every interest rate also increases, by some

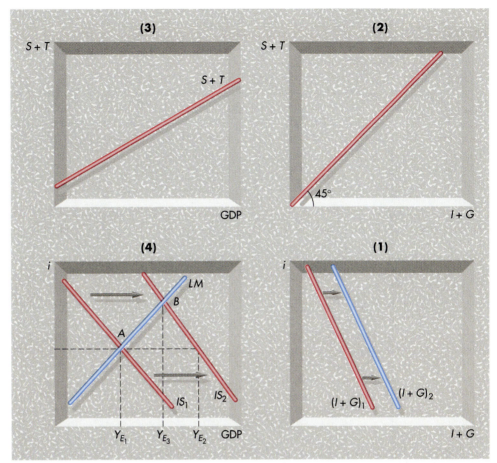

Figure 23-8   The Impact of Upward Revision of Returns Expected from Investment. An event that increases the returns expected from investment in plant and equipment shifts the *IS* curve rightward. This increases the equilibrium level of interest rates and GDP.

multiple of the shift in $I + G$.[5] In quadrant 4, the *IS* curve shifts rightward. Given the existing monetary conditions embodied in the *LM* curve, the result of the improved investment outlook is a movement of the general equilibrium from point *A* to point *B*—that is, an increase in the level of both GDP and interest rates.

---

[5]The magnitude of the horizontal shift of the *IS* curve will be equal to the magnitude of the horizontal shift of the $I + G$ schedule times the Keynesian multiplier. The multiplier varies inversely with the slope of the $S + T$ schedule in quadrant 3. The flatter the $S + T$ schedule, the larger is the multiplier and hence the greater is the magnitude of the shift in the *IS* curve relative to that of the $I + G$ schedule. In Figure 23-8, the slope of the $S + T$ schedule is constructed to be one-third, implying that the simple Keynesian multiplier is 3 and the magnitude of the horizontal shift of the *IS* curve is three times the magnitude of the horizontal shift of the $I + G$ schedule. Note, however, that equilibrium output does not actually rise by the full magnitude of the horizontal shift in the *IS* curve. Can you explain why?

EXHIBIT 23-1

The 1990–1991 Recession and the *IS-LM* Model

As of this writing, the United States had experienced only one recession in the past 15 years, from mid-1990 through the first quarter of 1991. According to the National Bureau of Economic Research, a recession occurs when real GDP declines for two or more consecutive quarters. From the peak of the business cycle (second quarter of 1990) to the trough (first quarter of 1991), real GDP declined 1.6 percent. The nation's unemployment rate also increased, from 5.1 percent in June 1990 to 6.8 percent in March 1991 and 7.7 percent in June 1992. Relative to past recessions, this one was brief and mild.

The *IS-LM* model indicates that falling output is attributable either to a leftward-shifting *IS* curve or to a leftward-shifting *LM* curve (or both). In other words, a recession may be triggered by either real or monetary forces. What caused the 1990–1991 recession? Let's look at some evidence.

It is clear that a decline in consumer confidence contributed to the recession. First, widely circulated reports that standard measures of consumer debt were exceptionally high may have caused consumers to become more conservative in their spending habits. Second, in the summer of 1990, Iraq invaded Kuwait and appeared poised to take over the oil fields in Saudi Arabia. Instability in the Middle East raised the specter of another round of oil price shocks, like the ones that hammered the U.S. economy in the 1970s. Consumer confidence plunged, shifting the *IS* curve leftward. In addition, weak balance sheets and fresh memories of the savings and loan disaster of the late 1980s prompted U.S. banks to tighten their lending standards sharply. A "credit crunch" ensued, and many reputable firms were cut off from bank credit. Potentially profitable investment projects had to be put on hold. The investment function shifted down, contributing to the leftward shift in the *IS* curve.

On the monetary front, both demand and supply factors may have contributed to a mildly leftward-shifting *LM* curve. First, one would expect the demand for money to increase in view of the uncertainty created by the Iraqi action. An increase in the speculative demand for money would have shifted the *LM* curve leftward, boosting interest rates. Second, the Fed may have contributed to the recession via earlier restrictive monetary actions. During the second half of 1988, the unemployment rate declined below 5.5 percent—a level that many economists regard as the natural unemployment rate. The Fed became increasingly concerned about the prospect of accelerating inflation. In the period extending from spring 1988 through the end of 1989, the Fed curtailed the growth of total reserves, the monetary base, and M1. Short-term interest rates increased from less than 6 percent in April 1988 to more than 8.5 percent a year later. Given the lag involved between monetary actions and their impact on output, the Fed's actions may have contributed to the onset of recession in 1990.

However, because interest rates began to decline after April 1989 and fell sharply during the recession, we conclude that the principal causes of the recession are to be found in the real sector. The Fed may have mistakenly interpreted the low interest rates of the early 1990s as indicating an "easy money" policy on its part, rather than a leftward shift in the *IS* curve. That may explain the Fed's failure to boost the growth rate of the monetary aggregates more aggressively during the recession and the anemic early portion of the economic recovery that followed.

In behavioral terms, as firms begin to increase their investment expenditures, the levels of GDP and income rise and the transactions demand for money begins to increase. Given a fixed money supply, this puts upward pressure on interest rates, reducing the quantity of money held for speculative purposes. Some of those balances are transferred to transactions balances to finance the higher level of expenditures, thus increasing the velocity of money. In the $MV_Y = PY$ framework, the increase in velocity accounts for the increase in aggregate expenditures (PY).

The upward movement of interest rates partially attenuates the impact of the shift in investment expenditures on the equilibrium level of output. If interest rates remained constant, equilibrium output would increase from Y_{E_1} to Y_{E_2}. Given a constant money supply and rising demand for money, however, the interest rate must increase. In quadrant 4 of Figure 23-8, the new equilibrium output level is established at Y_{E_3}, an output level between Y_{E_1} and Y_{E_2}.

Exhibit 23-1 uses the *IS-LM* model to show how a decline in consumer confidence can trigger an economic downturn.

An Increase in Individual Income Taxes

Suppose an increase in personal income taxes shifts the $S + T$ schedule upward or leftward (quadrant 3 in Figure 23-9). At each and every level of GDP, $S + T$ is higher because of the tax hike, and consumer demand is lower. At each and every interest rate, aggregate expenditures and equilibrium GDP are reduced—a phenomenon shown in quadrant 4 as a leftward shift of the *IS* curve. Given a constant money supply, the economy moves from point *A* to point *B* in the figure.

In terms of human behavior, what actually happens? Consumer demand drops off because of the reduction in take-home pay, so GDP begins to fall. With GDP and income reduced, the transactions demand for money declines, creating disequilibrium in the money market. Because the supply of money now exceeds the demand, interest rates decline. As interest rates decline, the demand for speculative money balances increases, absorbing the excess transactions balances. The decline in interest rates also bolsters investment spending, partially attenuating the contractionary effect on GDP of reduced consumer demand. Note that if the interest rate had remained firm, the tax hike would have reduced equilibrium output from Y_{E_1} to Y_{E_2}. Because of the decrease in interest rates and the resulting stimulus to investment, however, the new equilibrium occurs at Y_{E_3}, about midway between Y_{E_1} and Y_{E_2}. In the $MV_Y = PY$ framework, a decline in velocity attributable to lower interest rates accounts for the contraction in PY or GDP.

Real Disturbances: Summary

We may summarize our findings regarding disturbances originating in the real sector of the economy as follows:

1   Any event that shifts the $I + G$ curve (quadrant 1) or the $S + T$ curve (quadrant 3) to the right will shift the *IS* curve to the right, increasing the equilibrium level of GDP and interest rates.

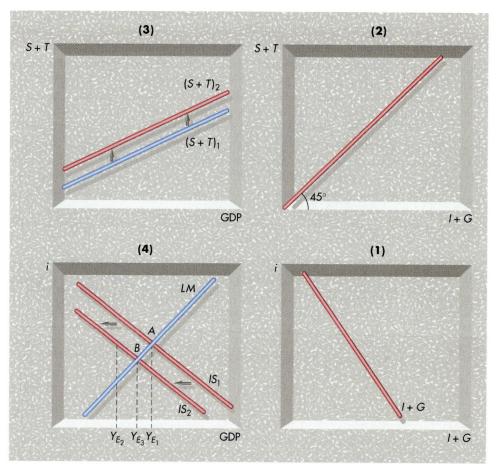

Figure 23-9   The Impact of an Increase in Income Taxes. An increase in income taxes (quadrant 3) exerts a contractionary effect on output. It shifts the *IS* curve leftward, reducing both GDP and interest rates (quadrant 4).

2   Any event that shifts the *I + G* curve or the *S + T* curve to the left will shift the *IS* curve to the left, reducing the equilibrium level of GDP and interest rates.

3   Disturbances in the real sector feed back to the monetary sector to influence the demand for money and interest rates. This partially attenuates the effect of the initial disturbance on the equilibrium levels of output and income.

Exhibit 23-2 analyzes the effects of aggregate supply shocks in the context of the *IS-LM* model.

EXHIBIT 23-2

Adverse Supply Shocks: An *IS-LM* Analysis

Twice during the 1970s, the United States and other industrial nations were hit by dramatic increases in the price of crude oil. The price of crude jumped from around $2.50 per barrel in late 1972 to $12 in 1974. Then, in 1979, a second boost took oil to $40 per barrel. In less than a decade, the price of oil had increased more than 15-fold.

The dramatic oil price hikes likely exerted direct effects on both the real and monetary sectors of the U.S. economy. Arguably, the oil price shocks themselves and perhaps also the ensuing monetary response shifted the *IS* and *LM* curves leftward. In the real sector, the oil price shocks created all kinds of uncertainties about the future economic environment. The *I + G* curve shifted leftward as business confidence plunged and firms revised their expected returns from investment downward due to sharply higher expected energy prices. To the extent that consumer confidence was damaged, the *S + T* curve likely shifted left as the shock reduced consumption spending and boosted saving. Hence, by impairing business and consumer confidence, the oil price shocks shifted the *IS* curve leftward. Other things held equal, such a shift reduces both output and interest rates.

But other things were not held equal. The uncertainty created by the announcement of the oil price hikes, together with the general decline in consumer and business confidence, boosted the demand for money, especially after 1979. Stock and bond prices declined through the 1970s and early 1980s as people unloaded financial assets and stashed the funds in checking accounts, money market mutual funds, and other safe, liquid instruments. This increase in the demand for money shifted the *LM* curve left after the second oil price shock, boosting interest rates and reducing output. The 1970s were characterized by both stagnant economic activity *and* rising inflation and interest rates.

How should the Federal Reserve respond to an oil price shock? Because an adverse supply shock reduces output and simultaneously increases inflation, the central bank faces a dilemma. If it tightens policy to head off incipient inflation, it will exacerbate the recession. If it takes stimulative actions to combat a recession, it will fan the fires of already accelerating inflation.

In October 1979, in a dramatic effort to defeat inflation, the Fed abandoned its long-held policy of targeting interest rates and moved to a policy of slowing the growth rate of money. For the next 2½ years, while the growth rate of the monetary aggregates declined, short-term Treasury bill yields averaged more than 12 percent. In 1981, the United States plunged into a severe recession, which many believe was the inevitable price of quashing an inflation that had been ratcheting upward for at least 15 years.

SUMMARY

The *LM* curve—the locus of all combinations of interest rates and GDP levels that are consistent with equilibrium in the market for money—summarizes a nation's monetary phenomena. The *IS* curve—the locus of all combinations of interest rate and GDP levels that are consistent with equilibrium in the market for goods and services—encompasses product market phenomena. The *IS-LM* model integrates monetary and real-sector phenomena and shows the impact of disturbances originating in the monetary and real sector on output and interest rates. Any event that reduces the demand for money or increases the money supply will shift the *LM* curve rightward, reducing interest

rates and increasing GDP. Any real-sector stimulus—that is, any nonmonetary force that increases expenditures—shifts the *IS* curve rightward, increasing the level of interest rates and GDP. A change in the supply or demand for money, by influencing interest rates, spills over to influence conditions in the product market. A nonmonetary source of change in expenditures, by influencing interest rates and income, spills over to influence the money market. Numerous types of phenomena can trigger these sorts of shifts in the *IS* and *LM* curves. Monetary policy operates chiefly by shifting the *LM* curve, while fiscal policy shifts the *IS* curve.

Answer to Your Turn (p. 550)

The announcement immediately changes the outlook for the course of interest rates over the next several months. Because financial market agents are likely to regard the cut in the discount rate as a signal of lower interest rates (higher bond prices), they will immediately use their money balances to purchase bonds and stocks. In other words, the speculative demand for money curve (quadrant 1 underlying the LM *curve) shifts leftward. This change shifts the* LM *curve rightward, reducing interest rates and boosting GDP. The reduction in the demand for speculative money balances means that velocity increases. Hence, in terms of the* MV_Y *framework, the economic stimulus is provided by the increase in velocity associated with the reduction in the demand for money.*

KEY TERMS

IS-LM **model**
LM **curve**
IS **curve**

STUDY QUESTIONS

1 Define the *LM* curve. Illustrate its derivation via the four-quadrant framework, and explain intuitively why the *LM* curve slopes upward.

2 Define the *IS* curve. Illustrate its derivation via the four-quadrant framework, and explain intuitively why the curve slopes downward.

3 Suppose the existing combination of interest rate and income level is such that the product market is in equilibrium but the interest rate is below

the level that would produce equilibrium in the money market. Draw *IS* and *LM* curves, and indicate the point described. Discuss the process by which the economy will return to general equilibrium.

4 Suppose banks sharply boost their service charges on all demand deposit accounts in which minimum monthly balances fall below $2000. Using the *IS-LM* model, analyze the effect on interest rates and the level of GDP.

5 In 1981, Congress approved major tax deductions for contributions to individual retirement accounts (IRAs). Using the *IS-LM* model, analyze the likely effects of the legislation on interest rates and GDP.

6 In 1986, Congress revoked an investment tax credit that had been in place for several years. Using the *IS-LM* model, analyze the consequences for interest rates and output.

7 Using the *IS-LM* framework, carefully analyze the way in which a change in velocity induced by technological changes underlying the payments process influences the equilibrium level of income and interest rates.

8 The early 1980s witnessed stimulative fiscal policy actions (income tax cuts) coupled with relatively restrictive monetary policies. Use the *IS-LM* framework to explain the implications for income and interest rates. Were those implications borne out in the real world?

9 Suppose that in order to meet a promise to balance the budget by the year 2002, Congress takes drastic fiscal measures in 1998. What would those actions be? In the context of the *IS-LM* model, analyze the implications of such actions for output and interest rates.

10 In 1994, the United States arranged for a massive loan to Mexico to help it out of a deep financial crisis. Suppose that in 1998 a surprise announcement is made that Mexico will default on the loan. Using the *IS-LM* model, analyze the consequences of the announcement for the U.S. economy.

11 Using *IS-LM* analysis, explain the consequences of a new law that prohibits the use of credit cards.

SUGGESTIONS FOR ADDITIONAL READING

For more coverage on the basics of the *IS-LM* model, consult an intermediate macroeconomics textbook. Examples include Rudiger Dornbusch and Stanley Fisher, *Macroeconomics,* 6th ed. (New York: McGraw-Hill, 1993); Robert J. Gordon, *Macroeconomics,* 6th ed. (Glenview, Ill.: Scott, Foresman, 1993); and N. Gregory Mankiw, *Macroeconomics,* 2d ed. (New York: Worth Publishers, 1994). A critique of the *IS-LM* model is presented in Robert G. King, "Will the New Keynesian Macroeconomics Resurrect the *IS-LM* Model?," *Journal of Economic Perspectives,* Winter 1993, pp. 67–82. The same issue of that journal contains discussions of Keynesian economics by Greg Mankiw, David Romer, James Tobin, and Bruce Greenwald and Joseph Stiglitz.

■ **The *IS-LM* Model: Implications for Monetary and Fiscal Policy**

n Chapter 23, we developed the *IS-LM* model of the macroeconomy. We demonstrated how various monetary (*LM*) and real (*IS*) shocks influence the equilibrium levels of output and interest rates. This laborious but essential chore completed, we can now use the model to explore some interesting issues in monetary economics and macroeconomics. In this chapter, we will use the *IS-LM* model to draw implications about the sources of economic disturbances and to study the implications of different methods of financing government expenditures. We will also use the model to examine the theoretical underpinnings that support the Keynesian and monetarist views of the appropriate roles of monetary and fiscal policy. Finally, we will employ the model to evaluate strategies for selecting intermediate monetary policy targets in an uncertain environment.

DETERMINING THE SOURCES OF ECONOMIC DISTURBANCES

The *IS-LM* model allows us to distinguish between disturbances that originate in the monetary sector (disturbances in the demand for or supply of money) and disturbances that originate from fiscal actions or other real-sector forces—that is, factors unrelated to monetary factors. As we shall see, some disturbances are triggered by events in both sectors.

Fiscal and Other Real-Sector Disturbances

A pure fiscal action involves a change in government expenditures or taxes accompanied by a constant supply of money. An example is an increase in government expenditures financed by borrowing from the public, a case illustrated in Figure 24-1.

Assume that the product and money markets are in equilibrium at point *A,* with the interest rate at i_1 and a GDP level of Y_{E_1}. Now suppose the equilibrium is disturbed by

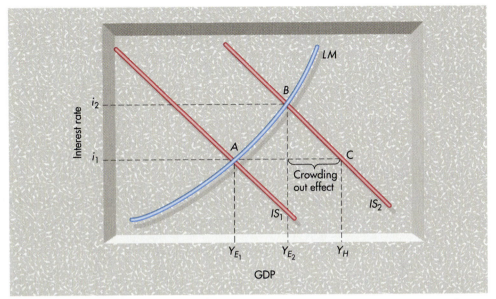

Figure 24-1   An Expansionary Fiscal Measure. An increase in government expenditures or a cut in taxes that is accompanied by a constant money supply is a pure fiscal stimulus. Such an event shifts the *IS* curve rightward, boosting GDP and interest rates.

an increase in government spending financed by the sale of bonds to the public. As recipients of the increased government spending deposit their checks in banks, buyers of the newly issued bonds reduce their deposits as they write checks to the government. Thus the money supply remains constant. However, aggregate expenditures and GDP increase as a result of the increase in government expenditures. The resulting increase in the demand for money (for transactions purposes) puts upward pressure on interest rates, releasing money from speculative holdings to finance the higher level of expenditures. We move from point *A* to point *B* in the figure.

Other real-sector events unrelated to fiscal actions of government might also shift the *IS* curve rightward, producing results similar to those illustrated in Figure 24-1. Examples include an increase in consumer or business confidence; an increase in wealth attributable to rising stock, bond, or real estate prices; and an increase in investment due to the development of new technologies. In addition, a depreciation of the U.S. dollar on foreign exchange markets or an increase in income in foreign nations tends to boost U.S. exports, shifting the *IS* curve rightward.

Conversely, if government expenditures are reduced or taxes increased, the *IS* curve shifts leftward, and both GDP and interest rates decline. A decline in consumer or business confidence, a decrease in wealth, or an appreciation of the U.S. dollar would have the same effect. Note that, in all these examples, *interest rates and GDP move in the same direction,* whether up or down.

Note in Figure 24-1 that the increase in equilibrium output stemming from a rightward shift in the *IS* curve ($Y_{E_2} - Y_{E_1}$) is significantly *smaller* than the horizontal shift in the *IS* curve ($Y_H - Y_{E_1}$). This outcome differs from that of the simple Keynesian income expenditures model, whose multiplier implies a larger increase in output. The Keynesian model essentially assumes that the *LM* curve is horizontal. In that event, as the fiscal stimulus boosts output, the ensuing increase in the transactions demand for money does not raise interest rates or reduce interest-sensitive expenditures, such as investment. The more realistic *IS-LM* model indicates that as output and income begin to increase, the demand for money rises, placing upward pressure on interest rates. As interest rates rise, investment is reduced, and we move back along the IS_2 curve from point *C* to point *B* in Figure 24-1.

Thus the multiplier that links the increase in government expenditures to the increase in equilibrium output is reduced by rising interest rates and the associated decline in investment. The increase in government expenditures *crowds out* some investment expenditures, partially negating the expansionary effect of increased government expenditures on equilibrium GDP. The **crowding-out effect** is shown in the figure as $Y_H - Y_{E_2}$. Note that the strength of this effect depends on the slope of the *LM* curve. The steeper the *LM* curve, the stronger is the crowding-out effect.

Pure Monetary Disturbances

A pure monetary disturbance involves a change in the supply of money unaccompanied by a change in *G* or *T* or any other real-sector disturbance. In this case, the *LM* curve shifts and the *IS* curve remains fixed, as illustrated in Figure 24-2.

Federal Reserve purchases of securities from the public are an example of a pure monetary expansion. The *LM* curve shifts rightward, the interest rate declines, and the level of GDP rises. Starting from equilibrium at point *A,* the money balances pumped in by the Fed create an immediate excess supply of money in the hands of the public. The excess money balances are spent on securities, pushing up bond prices and reducing interest rates. Finally, the decline in interest rates stimulates interest-sensitive expenditures and GDP.[1] In the event of a contraction in the money supply, interest rates rise and GDP declines. *Note that in the case of a pure monetary disturbance, interest rates and GDP move in opposite directions.*

Combined Fiscal and Monetary Disturbances

In the real world, we do not typically observe pure monetary or fiscal actions but rather a combination of monetary and fiscal measures. More often than not, fiscal and monetary policies *reinforce* each other. For example, in times of fiscal stimulus arising

---

[1]Again, this is a Keynesian view. Monetarists believe that the *IS* curve also shifts, because consumer demand (and hence aggregate demand) is thought to be influenced not only by income and interest rates but also by money holdings.

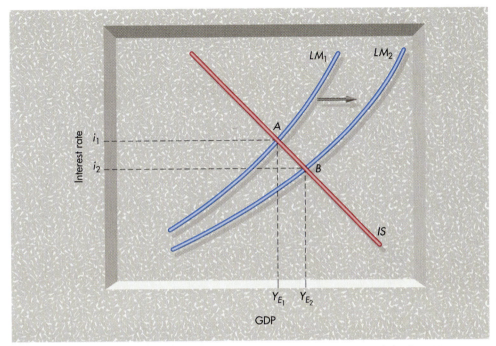

Figure 24-2   A Monetary Expansion. A pure monetary expansion shifts the *LM* curve rightward, reducing interest rates and raising equilibrium GDP.

from tax cuts or expenditure hikes, the money supply often expands at an above-trend rate.[2] The effects of combined monetary and fiscal disturbances are illustrated in Figure 24-3.

Figure 24-3 illustrates the impact of an increase in government expenditures financed by the sale of securities by the Treasury to the Federal Reserve System. This combined monetary and fiscal expansion shifts both the *IS* and *LM* curves rightward. Given the initial money supply (and LM_1), the fiscal expansion by itself would move the equilibrium from point *A* to point *B*. That would raise interest rates and increase equilibrium output from Y_{E_1} to Y_{E_2}. But the increase in the money supply shifts LM_1 to LM_2, further raising equilibrium output from Y_{E_2} to Y_{E_3} and exerting downward pressure on interest rates. The final position, point *C,* is one in which equilibrium output has clearly increased. The impact on interest rates is, however, uncertain. In the new equilibrium, interest rates may be higher or lower than, or the same as, those which prevailed at point *A.*

---

[2]Historically, the Federal Reserve has usually acted to resist interest rate movements. Because fiscal expansion tends to raise interest rates, it often induces the Fed to purchase securities to limit the upward movement in yields. Because Fed security purchases increase the money supply, a fiscal stimulus (a rightward *IS* shift) is often accompanied by a monetary stimulus (a rightward *LM* shift). On this, see Exhibit 24-1.

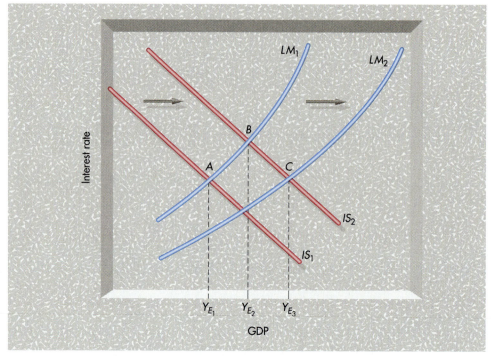

Figure 24-3   Combined Monetary and Fiscal Expansions. When both the *IS* and *LM* curves shift rightward, the equilibrium level of GDP increases. The effect on interest rates is uncertain.

FINANCING AN INCREASE IN GOVERNMENT EXPENDITURES

The foregoing analysis indicates that the method of financing a given increase in government expenditures may have important implications for GDP and interest rates and, by extension, for employment and inflation. We will now use the *IS-LM* model to analyze the implications of three different methods of financing an expansion in government spending: a tax increase, the sale of government securities to the public, and the sale of government securities to the Federal Reserve.

Tax Increase

A tax hike is the least stimulative, or least expansionary, method of financing increased government spending. Because the money balances pumped in by government spending are recouped by the tax hike, the money supply is held constant. Furthermore, the magnitude of the rightward shift of the *IS* curve is significantly reduced by a tax hike. The increase in government expenditures does shift the interest rate–$(I + G)$ relationship rightward (lower-right-hand quadrant underlying the *IS* curve). However, the impact of that shift on the *IS* curve is partially counteracted by a leftward or upward shift of the $(S + T)$–GDP relationship (upper-left-hand quadrant) resulting from the tax increase.[3] The *IS* curve shifts slightly rightward, the *LM* curve remains fixed, and both interest rates and GDP rise only modestly. Because this method is the least stimulative, it is also the least inflationary of the three methods of financing increased government spending.

Sale of Government Securities to the Public

The effect of an increase in government expenditures financed by the sale of government securities to the public was examined earlier (see Figure 24-1). This pure fiscal expansion shifts the *IS* curve rightward due to the rightward shift of the interest rate–$(I + G)$ relationship (quadrant 1 underlying the *IS* curve). The money supply remains constant because the money balances placed in the public's hands by the increased government expenditures are recovered by the sale of securities by the Treasury to the public. Thus the *LM* curve remains fixed. Because this method produces a larger rightward shift of the *IS* curve, equilibrium GDP and interest rates increase more than in the case of a tax increase. And because it is more stimulative, this method of financing government expenditures has greater inflationary implications.

Sale of Government Securities to the Federal Reserve

Increased government expenditures financed through the sale of government securities to the Federal Reserve involves a combined monetary and fiscal stimulus, as illustrated in Figure 24-3. In this case, money balances pumped into the public's hands by the expansion in government expenditures are not recouped, because the Treasury sells the new bonds to the Federal Reserve rather than to the public. As a result, the money supply increases. In the parlance of economists, the Fed has "monetized" the deficit—that is, created new money to finance the deficit. Both the *IS* and *LM* curves shift rightward, and equilibrium output expands by a relatively large magnitude. Needless to say, this method of financing government spending carries the most severe implications for inflation. Exhibit 24-1 examines the monetization issue in the United States.

---

[3]Because the income tax increase reduces saving as well as consumption, it shifts the $S + T$ function (quadrant 3 underlying the *IS* curve) up by less than the full amount of the tax hike (and government expenditures increase). A net increase in aggregate expenditures and a rightward shift in the *IS* curve result from the equal increase in government expenditures and taxes.

EXHIBIT 24-1

Does the Federal Reserve Monetize Government Budget Deficits?

Of all the potential consequences of a large budget deficit, undoubtedly the most feared is the entrapment of the central bank into purchasing a large portion of newly issued debt. Countries with fragile political structures, unable to find sufficient buyers for their government bonds, often resort to selling them to a politically subservient central bank. To the extent they do, the money supply escalates and inflation arrives with a vengeance.

In the United States, the Federal Reserve is likely to monetize a federal deficit at least partially if the deficit threatens to undermine a short-run Fed policy of stabilizing interest rates. Larger deficits are likely to push up interest rates. To stabilize interest rates, the Fed may step up its open market purchases of securities, increasing the growth rate of the monetary base and the monetary aggregates (M1 and M2). If the budget deficit is expected to have no effect on interest rates, or if the Fed ignores interest rate fluctuations, the Fed will not be likely to monetize the deficit.

What evidence is there of monetization in the United States? Is there any systematic relationship between the magnitude of the federal budget deficit and the propensity of the Federal Reserve to purchase securities on the open market and expand the monetary base? The literature on the subject is mixed. Some students of the subject report a significant positive association between the magnitude of budget deficits and the growth rate of monetary variables such as the base, M1, and M2. Others claim such results hold only during wartime or that the relationship is tenuous, depending on the measure of the deficit employed or the political party in power at the time the deficit is incurred. Still others claim that any positive relationship is spurious—attributable to seasonality in the data or to econometric problems.

The accompanying graph shows the historical relationship between the magnitude of the federal budget deficit, expressed as a percentage of GDP, and the growth rate of the monetary base. The slope of the regression line indicates the extent to which the Fed has monetized budget deficits in the period since 1959, on average. The results may be summarized as indicated by the regression equation:

$$\%\Delta \text{Base} = 5.02 + .87 \text{ Deficit/GDP}, \qquad R^2 = .39$$

This equation indicates that over the period 1959–1994, on average, the growth rate of the monetary base accelerated by 0.87 percentage point for each 1 percentage

---

KEYNESIAN VERSUS MONETARIST VIEWS IN THE *IS-LM* MODEL

Keynesians and monetarists disagree about the relative effectiveness of monetary and fiscal policy. The *IS-LM* model is an effective means of conveying the sources of these different views. In the next several sections, we will explore these differing viewpoints in the context of the model.

EXHIBIT 24-1   (CONTINUED)

point increase in the ratio of the deficit to GDP. This suggests that if the nation moves from a balanced budget to a deficit of 3 percent of GDP, the Fed will step up the growth of the monetary base by nearly 3 percentage points (2.61, to be precise). The R^2 of .39 indicates that variation in the magnitude of the federal budget deficit relative to GDP accounts statistically for 39 percent of the variation in the growth rate of the monetary base.

   This finding supports the view that the Fed has partially monetized government budget deficits over the past 35 years—though the scatter diagram shows that the relationship has not been a tight one.

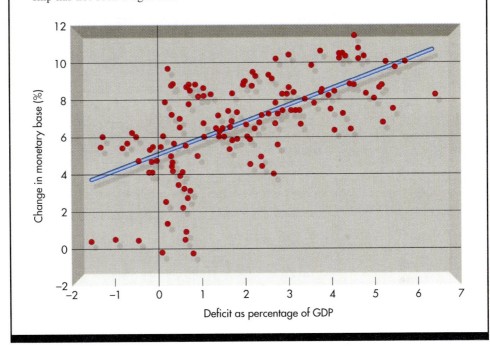

The Interest Sensitivity of Velocity Expressed in the *IS-LM* Model

Focus your attention for a moment on the interest-sensitive portion of the demand for money, or the speculative demand for money, function, L_S. The nature of this function is central to the issue of crowding out and the debate over the relative strength of monetary and fiscal policies. We will demonstrate that the steeper the L_S curve, the stronger is the crowding-out effect and the less powerful is fiscal policy relative to monetary policy. Figure 24-4 shows three alternative shapes of the L_S curve, together with the corresponding *LM* curves they imply (shown below each L_S curve).

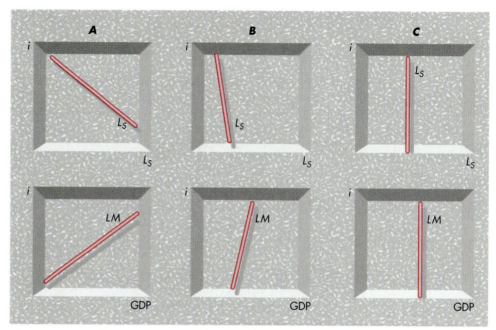

Figure 24-4   Alternative Money Demand Relationships and *LM* Curves. If the demand for money is highly sensitive to interest rates, the *LM* curve is relatively flat (panel *A*). If the demand for money is inelastic with respect to interest rates, the *LM* curve is steep (panels *B* and *C*).

In panel *A*, L_S is shown as relatively flat, meaning that the effect of fiscal stimulus on money demand and velocity and therefore on aggregate expenditures and GDP is large. The accompanying *LM* curve is relatively flat, indicating that fiscal policy is relatively effective, and the crowding-out effect is relatively modest. In panel *B*, L_S is relatively steep but not vertical. Thus higher interest rates will exert only a small effect on money demand and velocity. Because the velocity response to higher interest rates is small, a fiscal stimulus will have only minor effects on aggregate expenditures and GDP. Most of the potential expansion of GDP associated with the fiscal stimulus is crowded out by the negative effect on investment of higher interest rates. In panel *C*, with a vertical L_S curve, the *LM* curve is also vertical. In this case, crowding out is complete and fiscal policy is totally ineffective in boosting output. The rightward shift in the *IS* curve boosts interest rates but has no effect on money demand or velocity.

In terms of our MV_Y framework, a pure fiscal stimulus (increased G or reduced T) will boost aggregate expenditures and GDP only to the extent that it stimulates the velocity of money (V_Y). To increase velocity, the fiscal stimulus must reduce the demand for money relative to income. Suppose government spending increases, raising interest rates. As long as the L_S function is not vertical, the demand for money will decline as interest rates rise. The flatter the L_S curve, the larger the response of the demand for money (and velocity) to higher interest rates induced by a fiscal stimulus. A vertical L_S curve implies that money demand, velocity, and MV_Y (aggregate expenditures) will be unaffected by a fiscal stimulus. That is, the effect of the increase in government expenditures is fully negated by a contraction in investment and/or other interest-sensitive expenditures. Crowding out is complete, and fiscal policy has no effect on output. In the $MV_Y \equiv PY$ framework, because the increase in G failed to reduce the demand for money and increase its velocity, aggregate expenditures (MV_Y and PY) failed to increase. In this instance, fiscal policy is totally ineffective in influencing GDP.[4]

Position, Slope, and Stability of the Curves

Keynesian economists believe that frequent and significant exogenous shocks to consumption and investment spending cause considerable instability in the *position* of the *IS* curve. They also believe that the *LM* curve is relatively flat because they view the demand for money as being relatively interest elastic. Thus, Keynesians view the L_S and *LM* curves as being as shown in panel *A* of Figure 24-4.

Given a relatively flat *LM* curve, shifts in the *IS* curve should produce significant fluctuations in the equilibrium level of output and employment. To avoid potential instability in output and employment, Keynesian economists espouse a philosophy of monetary and fiscal policy activism aimed at stabilizing aggregate demand and equilibrium output. In their view, when consumption and investment soften, stimulative monetary and fiscal actions should be implemented to compensate for the shortfall. When consumption and investment threaten to become excessive, restrictive monetary and fiscal measures should be implemented.

Monetarists generally believe the factors underlying the *IS* curve (consumption, investment, government purchases, net exports) are relatively stable; because the *IS* curve is relatively stable, monetary and fiscal policy activism is unnecessary and potentially damaging to economic stability. Furthermore, monetarists think the *LM* curve is quite steep, because they view the speculative demand for money as either nonexistent or highly interest inelastic. Thus, monetarists believe the L_S and *LM* functions look like those shown in panel *B* or *C* of Figure 24-4.

Because monetarists believe that the *LM* curve is quite steep, they conceive of the monetary sector as a shock absorber, inhibiting the effects of disturbances originating in

---

[4]Actually, we have ignored several other effects that may reinforce or counteract any crowding out attributable to increased money demand, higher interest rates, and lower investment. An initial shock to the *IS* curve may influence expenditures through additional channels, leading to additional crowding out or crowding in of expenditures. For example, as the government issues securities to the private sector to pay for increased expenditures, wealth in the private sector may increase. If the public perceives that its wealth has increased, and if securities and money are complementary goods, the demand for money will increase and the *LM* curve will shift left, reinforcing the crowding-out effect. On the other hand, if securities and money are viewed as substitutes, the increased government debt held by the private sector will reduce money demand and shift *LM* rightward, partially attenuating any crowding out. Also, as government spending rises, boosting interest rates, the U.S. dollar is likely to appreciate. The rise in the value of the dollar stimulates U.S. imports and reduces exports, reducing the U.S. GDP and reinforcing the crowding-out effect. Finally, if people view an increase in deficit spending as implying higher future taxes, they may increase their saving. This increase in saving shifts the *IS* curve left, partially or perhaps even fully negating the effect of the increase in government expenditures. In the latter event, an increase in the deficit has no effect on output or interest rates.

the real sector of the economy on output and employment. For example, if consumer confidence were to increase strongly, thereby threatening to trigger excessive aggregate demand and boost inflation, rising interest rates would reduce interest-sensitive expenditures (chiefly investment and net exports), stabilizing economic activity. In the view of most monetarists, the best policy is a stable government budget accompanied by a steady, slow growth of the money supply.

Recommended Policy Measures

Suppose that in an unusually severe recession, both monetarists and Keynesians agree that stimulative policy measures are called for. In this event, monetarists will call for an expansion in the growth rate of money, while Keynesians will prefer fiscal measures such as tax cuts or an increase in government expenditures. The rationales for these differing views are shown in Figure 24-5.

In the monetarist scheme of things (left-hand panel), the *LM* curve is quite steep because monetarists see the demand for money as being highly inelastic with respect to the interest rate. Their *IS* curve is relatively flat, reflecting the alleged sensitivity of investment spending to interest rates. Thus stimulative fiscal measures which shift IS_1 to IS_2 will move the economy from point *A* to point *B*, resulting in only a modest expansion in equilibrium output, from Y_1 to Y_2. In this case, the interest rate rises considerably, crowding out an important amount of investment spending. In fact, if the

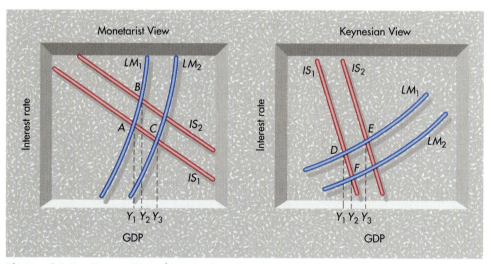

Figure 24-5   Monetarist and Keynesian Views. Monetarists view the *LM* curve as being relatively steep and the *IS* curve as relatively flat. Keynesians typically believe the opposite. This controversy has important implications for the relative strength of monetary and fiscal policies.

LM curve were vertical (because the demand for money is totally inelastic with respect to the interest rate), crowding out would be complete. With a constant money supply, the increase in government expenditures would crowd out an equivalent amount of investment expenditures, so that total expenditures would remain unchanged; output would remain at Y_1.

In the $MV_Y = PY$ framework, because the demand for and velocity of money do not respond to higher interest rates in this extreme case, a fiscal stimulus cannot boost equilibrium expenditures or GDP. Thus, fiscal policy is totally ineffective.

On the other hand, in the monetarist view, expansion of the money supply will stimulate output powerfully. Given a constant government budget and the *IS* curve shown as IS_1, expansion of the money supply shifts the *LM* curve from LM_1 to LM_2. The economy moves to point *C,* and GDP rises from Y_1 to Y_3. Though the rightward shift of the *LM* curve reduces interest rates, this does not appreciably increase the quantity of money demanded or reduce its velocity. In terms of the $MV_Y = PY$ framework, because V_Y remains nearly unchanged, the increased money supply is translated into an approximately proportionate change in MV_Y and PY—that is, GDP.

In the Keynesian view (right-hand panel), the *LM* curve is relatively flat because the demand for money is highly interest elastic. The *IS* curve is steeper than in the monetarist scheme because investment is thought to be relatively inelastic with respect to interest rates. Given the existing monetary conditions as indicated by LM_1, if fiscal expansion shifts the *IS* curve from IS_1 to IS_2, the economy moves from point *D* to point *E* and output expands considerably, from Y_1 to Y_3. The relatively flat *LM* curve implies that interest rates are boosted only modestly as GDP rises. And the increase in the interest rate exerts only a small impact on investment because of the steep *IS* curve. Thus only a modest crowding out of investment, if any, occurs in the Keynesian framework. Because these considerations minimize the exposure to crowding out, fiscal measures are powerful instruments.[5] (Exhibit 24-2 examines some empirical evidence on the crowding-out phenomenon.)

In this Keynesian scheme, monetary policy is not as potent as fiscal policy. Given a particular fiscal posture (IS_1), the expansion in money moves LM_1 to LM_2 and reduces interest rates as the economy moves from *D* to *F* in Figure 24-5. However, because of the interest inelasticity of the *IS* curve, GDP is not stimulated powerfully. As the increased money supply reduces interest rates, the demand for money rises and its velocity falls appreciably. Hence, much of the potential increase in aggregate expenditures (MV_Y and GDP) flowing from an increase in the money supply is negated by the decline in velocity, and output increases only from Y_1 to Y_2. Thus, Keynesians view monetary policy as having a weaker influence on aggregate expenditures (MV_Y and GDP) than fiscal policy does.

---

[5]In fact, Keynesians sometimes argue that we might even experience *crowding in,* a phenomenon in which increased government spending actually boosts investment. If the increase in *G* occurs in an economy with significant excess capacity, and if investment spending is favorably influenced by the resulting increase in the nation's capacity utilization rate, the increase in *G* may outweigh the negative influence of higher interest rates, producing a net increase in investment expenditures in spite of higher interest rates.

EXHIBIT 24-2

Crowding Out: The Evidence from a Macroeconometric Model

Macroeconometric models are essentially sophisticated extensions of the *IS-LM* model presented in this book. In constructing such models, economists first use historical data to estimate such key parameters as the interest elasticity of investment expenditures, the income and interest rate elasticities of the demand for money, the marginal propensity to consume, and so forth. With the help of modern high-speed computers, such estimates are incorporated into macroeconometric models and used to generate estimates of the impact on GDP of shocks to the *IS* or *LM* curves.

Consider the DRI macroeconometric model of the U.S. economy. This model, constructed by Data Resources Incorporated, simulates the effect of increased government expenditures on GDP under two different conditions. One is that the Fed holds the money supply constant while *G* increases. The second is that the Fed monetizes the deficit, increasing the money supply at a rate sufficient to hold interest rates constant. The multipliers that link the increase in government expenditures to the *first-year* expansion of GDP generated by the DRI model are as follows:

Monetary Policy Assumption	Size of Multiplier
Money supply held constant	0.6
Interest rate held constant	1.9

In the case of a pure fiscal expansion, in which increased government spending is accompanied by a constant money supply, the DRI model indicates a 1-year multiplier of only 0.6. This indicates that an increase in government expenditures of $50 billion would increase output by only $30 billion after one year. This figure suggests a strong (but not complete) crowding-out effect in the first year.

In the case in which the Fed monetizes the deficit, holding interest rates constant while government expenditures increase, the 1-year multiplier is estimated to be 1.9. A $50 billion increase in government spending would increase GDP by $95 billion after 1 year. The difference between these two multipliers suggests that crowding out is a powerful effect and that the bulk of the potential increase in GDP associated with a pure fiscal expansion is negated by a decline in investment and/or other components of aggregate expenditures.

Of course, macroeconometric models differ in both the details of their construction and their implications for policy. Because different models employ different interest elasticities of money demand and other key parameter estimates, they exhibit different crowding-out propensities and therefore different multipliers for government expenditures. But the DRI model yields support for the monetarist view that crowding out is a major force and that pure fiscal measures have a relatively weak impact on the nation's GDP.

SELECTION OF INTERMEDIATE MONETARY POLICY TARGETS

The *IS-LM* model can be used to demonstrate the conditions under which the money supply is the more desirable intermediate target of monetary policy and the conditions under which the level of interest rates is the preferred target. If the goal of monetary policy is to stabilize the level of output or GDP at some desired level (Y^*), the appropriate intermediate target will depend on which curve, *LM* or *IS*, is subject to greater uncertainty—that is, to larger and more unpredictable shifts.

The Case of *LM* Uncertainty

Assume initially that the *IS* curve is known with certainty—that is, that we are never fooled by unexpected shifts in its position. Also assume that consumption, investment, and net export behavior are quite stable. At the same time, let's suppose that the *LM* curve is subject to significant random shifts attributable to unpredictable changes in the demand for money and/or the money supply multiplier. These conditions are illustrated in Figure 24-6. We will assume the Federal Reserve's ultimate goal is to achieve the output or GDP

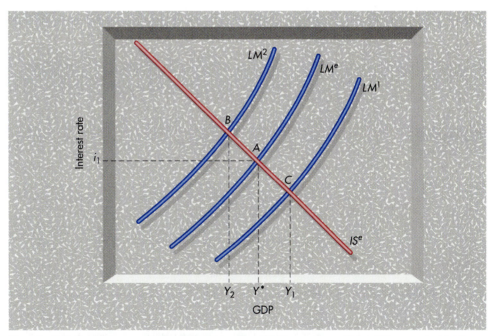

Figure 24-6   Monetary Policy Targets under *LM* Uncertainty. If the *LM* curve is highly uncertain but the *IS* curve is not, the Fed will minimize output errors if it targets the interest rate.

goal Y^*, which will yield a low level of unemployment accompanied by an acceptable inflation rate.

Suppose initially that the economy is operating at point A, the intersection of IS^e and LM^e, the expected IS and LM curves, so that the Fed is achieving its output goal of Y^*. An unexpected shift in either the demand for money or the money supply multiplier will shift the LM curve away from LM^e. Let's assume that the Fed is targeting the money supply. If money demand is unexpectedly strong, or if any of the variables underlying the money supply multiplier (k, r_r, or r_e) unexpectedly increase, the LM curve will shift leftward unexpectedly, from LM^e to LM^2.[6] The economy moves to point B in the figure, and output falls from Y^* to Y_2. In this case, use of the money supply target may result in a recession.

On the other hand, if the demand for money or the variables underlying the money multiplier decline unexpectedly, efforts to hit the money supply target will result in a shift in the LM curve from LM^e to LM^1. The economy then ends up at C in the figure. Output is Y_1 rather than Y^*—an excessive level of aggregate demand and economic activity that leads to an undesired acceleration of inflation. Hence, if the potential range of LM uncertainty is LM^1 to LM^2, the use of a money supply target will produce a potential range in GDP of Y_1 to Y_2; significant deviations from Y^* will occur.

If the Fed targets interest rates in the face of unpredictable shifts in the LM curve, the output goal of Y^* will always be achieved. Suppose the demand for money rises unexpectedly, shifting LM^e to LM^2. As the figure shows, such a shift would normally increase interest rates and reduce output. However, if the Fed is targeting interest rates at i_1, it will inject reserves into the banking system, increase the money supply, and shift the LM curve back to LM^e in order to maintain the interest rate at its target i_1. In doing so, the Fed hits the output goal of Y^* precisely. The increase in the money supply counteracts the unexpected decrease in velocity, so that MV_Y remains unchanged and GDP remains on target. We conclude that if there is reason to expect instability in money demand but not in the real forces underlying the IS curve, the Fed should employ interest rate targets rather than money supply targets.

Your Turn

In 1980, Congress passed the Depository Institutions Deregulation and Monetary Control Act (DIDMCA). Among other things, this legislation removed the statute prohibiting payment of interest on checking accounts by depository institutions. It also removed statutory ceilings on rates payable on various types of savings and time deposits. Suppose you were a member of the Federal Open Market Committee at the time Congress passed DIDMCA. What implications would you keep in mind while choosing intermediate target variables for monetary policy?

---

[6]The Federal Reserve does not have continuous data on the money supply; on a given day, it does not know the magnitude of M1 and M2. By forecasting the money supply multiplier and setting the monetary base at an appropriate level, the Fed can attempt to hit M1 and M2 targets. To the extent that k, r_r, and r_e are uncertain, however, both the money supply multiplier and the LM curve are uncertain.

The Case of *IS* Uncertainty

Now let us reverse assumptions and assume that the monetary sector of the economy is very stable and predictable, so that the central bank is never fooled by shifts in the demand for money or the money multiplier. In other words, the *LM* curve remains at LM^e unless the Fed deliberately changes the money supply. The *IS* curve, however, is highly unstable, owing to unpredictable shifts in consumption, investment, and other components of aggregate demand. Figure 24-7 illustrates these assumptions.

Suppose the economy is initially operating at *A*, the intersection of LM^e and IS^e, with output precisely at the desired level, *Y**. If the Fed is targeting the money supply and the *IS* curve unexpectedly shifts to IS^1, we move to point *B* in the figure. Equilibrium output moves to Y_1, which is somewhat higher than the *Y** objective. On the other hand, if activity in the real sector is weaker than expected, the *IS* curve shifts down to IS^2. The economy moves to point *C*, and output drops to Y_2. We see that in the context of *IS* uncertainty, the use of money supply targets produces an unavoidable but relatively small output error.

However, if the Fed were targeting interest rates in the face of *IS* uncertainty, the output errors would be considerably larger. To hold the interest rate at an i_1 level as the *IS* curve shifts up to IS^1, the Fed would purchase securities on the open market, thus

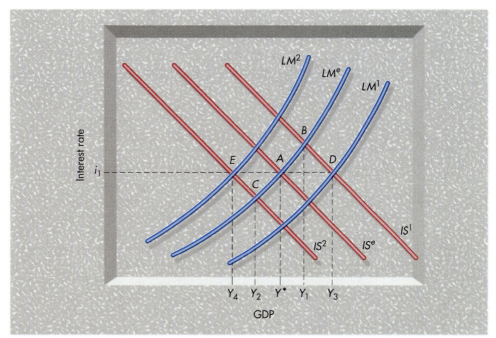

Figure 24-7   Monetary Policy Targets under *IS* Uncertainty. If the *IS* curve is highly uncertain while the *LM* curve is not, the Fed will minimize output errors by targeting the money supply.

increasing the money supply and shifting the *LM* curve to LM^1. The economy would move to point *D* in the figure, producing a gross output error of $Y_3 - Y^*$. Under such circumstances, severe inflation is likely to occur.

On the other hand, if activity in the real sector is unexpectedly weak, IS^e will shift down to IS^2, depressing output and interest rates. In order to stay on its i_1 interest rate target, the Fed would pursue a restrictive policy of open market security sales, thereby reducing the money supply and shifting LM^e to LM^2. The economy would end up at point *E*, and output would fall to Y_4, substantially below the Y^* goal. A severe recession would be likely to occur under these circumstances.

Thus, by targeting interest rates when the *IS* curve is shifting, the Fed becomes a destabilizing force. The lesson is clear: If the Fed has reason to expect instability in the *IS* curve due to unpredictable changes in consumption, investment, or net exports, it must abandon its interest rate target.

Assuming that the ultimate objective of monetary policy is to stabilize output and income, we see that the debate over the selection of the appropriate intermediate target hinges on the relative stability of the monetary sector (*LM* curve) and the real sector (*IS* curve). Monetarists believe that the demand for money is more stable than aggregate expenditures ($C + I + G$) and that the money supply multiplier is relatively stable and predictable. These monetarist views imply that shocks to the *LM* curve are likely to be smaller and more predictable than shocks to the *IS* curve. It follows logically that the money supply is their preferred target.

Nonmonetarists believe that the demand for money is unstable or volatile and that the variables underlying the money supply multiplier are unstable and unpredictable. They are therefore inclined to believe that shocks to the monetary sector are at least as important as shocks to the real sector. For this reason, nonmonetarists are more inclined to favor the use of interest rates as an intermediate monetary policy target. They are wary of the monetarist prescription of sticking rigidly to money supply targets.

Uncertainty in Both the *IS* and *LM* Curves

We have demonstrated that if the *LM* curve is uncertain while the *IS* curve is not, the Fed will minimize output errors by targeting interest rates. On the other hand, if the *IS* curve is uncertain while the *LM* curve is not, the Fed will minimize output errors by targeting the money supply. But what about the case in which *both* the *IS* and *LM* curves are uncertain and the Fed has no reason to expect either to be more stable than the other? In that event, the Fed might be wise to adopt a strategy aimed at minimizing the chances of gross policy errors of the types discussed earlier.

Suppose the Fed notes upward pressure on short-term interest rates but has no idea what the source of the pressure is; it could be caused by either a leftward shift in the *LM* curve (due to increased money demand) or a rightward shift in the *IS* curve (due to increased consumer or business confidence or other factors). Remember that while information on yields is available to the Fed continuously, data on the national income accounts are released only quarterly and data on the money supply only weekly (and are then subject to extensive later revision). Thus, when the Fed observes upward yield pressure in the money market, it frequently does not know the source.

If the Fed is targeting interest rates and the source of the upward pressure on yields is a rightward-shifting *IS* curve, the Fed will commit a gross policy error. The Fed will likely overstimulate the economy and contribute to an acceleration of inflation. On the other hand, if the Fed is targeting the money supply and the upward pressure is attributable to increased money demand (a leftward-shifting *LM* curve), output will fall well short of Y^*, and a recession may occur. Figure 24-8 illustrates the choices open to the Fed.

Initially, the economy is at *A*, the intersection of LM^e and IS^e. Output is on target at Y^*, and the interest rate is i_1. Now the Fed notes upward pressure on yields but is uncertain about its source. If the pressure stems from a rightward shift in the *IS* curve (to IS^2) and the Fed is targeting interest rates at i_1, the economy will end up at point *B*. In boosting the money supply and shifting the *LM* curve to LM^3, the Fed will have committed a gross policy error because output will expand to Y_H and inflation will accelerate. If the yield pressure stems from a leftward shift of the *LM* curve (to LM^2) and the Fed is targeting the money stock, the economy will end up at point *C*. As the interest rate rises to i_2, output falls to Y_L, and the Fed's policy error contributes to a recession.

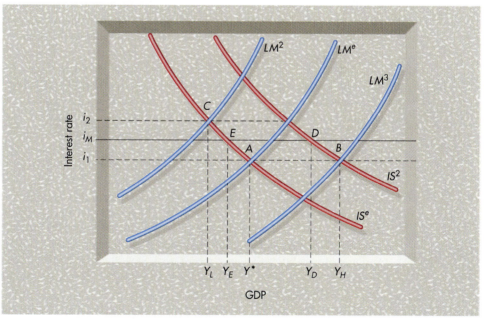

Figure 24-8   A Strategy for Avoiding Gross Policy Errors. By targeting an interest rate midway between the initial rate, i_1, and the new equilibrium rate, i_2, the Fed will avoid committing gross policy errors.

A policy that avoids these two extremes would be targeting an interest rate midway between the original interest rate and the new equilibrium interest rate. Suppose the Fed sets an interest rate target at i_M, midway between the original interest rate (i_1) and the equilibrium rate after the yield pressure is manifested (i_2). This scheme reduces the potential damage done by monetary policy. If the pressure stems from an increase in the *IS* curve and the Fed increases the money supply to hit its new interest rate target, i_M, the economy ends up at point *D*. Output (Y_D) exceeds Y^* but is significantly lower than Y_H. If the yield pressure stems from an increased demand for money and the Fed increases the money supply to hit i_M, the economy will end up at *E*. Output Y_E is lower than Y^* but higher than Y_L. Thus by targeting the interest rate at an intermediate level, the Fed reduces the potential range of output from Y_H–Y_L to Y_D–Y_E, thus eliminating the possibility of extreme output errors (Y_H and Y_L).

In sum, if the Fed is totally uncertain about the nature of an economic disturbance that is placing pressure on interest rates, it may be wise to abandon strict targeting of *either* monetary aggregates *or* interest rates and adopt a compromise scheme.

MONETARIST VERSUS KEYNESIAN POLICY VIEWS: SUMMARY

Monetarists and Keynesians express diametrically opposing viewpoints about the relative strengths of monetary and fiscal policy, the appropriate degree of policy activism, and the choice of intermediate target variables. Their differences are based on differing views of the economy, as expressed in the shapes and stability of the *IS* and *LM* curves.

Monetarists view the position of the *IS* and *LM* curves as being relatively stable in the absence of aggressive monetary and fiscal policies. They believe the *LM* curve is especially stable because of the alleged stability of the demand for money. Because they view the *LM* curve as being quite steep (reflecting interest inelasticity in the demand for money), they view the monetary system as a built-in stabilizer, inhibiting the impact of shifts in the *IS* curve on the nation's output and employment. An exogenous increase in consumer expenditures, for example, will shift the *IS* curve right, boosting interest rates. But the increase in interest rates reduces interest-sensitive expenditures, attenuating much of the potential expansion in output and employment. For this reason, monetarists believe that active use of monetary and fiscal policies is unnecessary. In fact, because the economy is likely to be stable on its own accord, discretionary policy actions are likely to be a source of instability. Because monetarists view the *LM* curve as being more stable than the *IS* curve, they are especially wary of targeting interest rates, preferring instead to set low and stable money growth targets.

Keynesians view the *IS* curve as inherently unstable, largely because of frequent, significant changes in investment and consumption expenditures. Because they view the *LM* curve as being even more unstable (because of high variability in the demand for money), they believe that, in the absence of government intervention, the economy is likely to be unstable. Keynesians picture the *LM* curve as relatively flat because they think the demand for money is sensitive to interest rates. That belief implies that the monetary system does *not* serve as an effective shock absorber in moderating the effects of shifts in the *IS* curve on output and employment. For these reasons, they view the economy as inherently unstable and advocate monetary and fiscal policy activism in order to promote economic stability. Because they view the *LM* curve as even more unstable than the *IS* curve, Keynesians are wary of adhering to money supply targets; they typically prefer interest rate targets instead.

SUMMARY

The *IS-LM* model is a convenient framework for distinguishing monetary and fiscal disturbances. A pure fiscal disturbance involves a change in government expenditures and/or taxes accompanied by a constant money supply; a pure fiscal expansion, for example, shifts the *IS* curve rightward, boosting output and interest rates. A pure monetary disturbance involves a change in the money supply while government expenditures and taxes remain constant; a pure monetary expansion, for example, shifts the *LM* curve rightward, increasing output and reducing interest rates. While increased government expenditures financed by taxes or bond sales to the public are an example of a pure fiscal expansion, increased government expenditures financed by bond sales to the Federal Reserve represent a combined fiscal and monetary expansion. The interest elasticity of the demand for money determines the slope of the *LM* curve, thereby helping determine the relative

effectiveness of monetary and fiscal policies. If the demand for money is highly sensitive to the interest rate, the *LM* curve will be relatively flat, implying that fiscal policy is relatively powerful. If the demand curve for money is highly insensitive to the interest rate, the *LM* curve will be quite steep. This means that monetary policy will be more powerful than fiscal policy. The *IS-LM* model indicates that if the position of the *IS* curve is more uncertain and volatile than the *LM* curve, the Fed will minimize output errors if it targets the money supply. On the other hand, if the *LM* curve is more uncertain and unstable, the use of interest rate targets will produce smaller output errors. If the *IS* and *LM* curves are equally uncertain and unstable, the Fed's best strategy may be to adopt a compromise scheme in which it targets an interest rate at a level midway between the initial level and the new equilibrium level implied by the disturbance.

Answer to Your Turn (p. 574)

Clearly, one would expect this legislation to have important implications for the demand of money and therefore the stability of the LM *curve. Assuming that banks were expected to respond to deregulation by paying an attractive interest rate on demand deposits, the demand for M1 would be likely to increase significantly. To the extent that banks were expected to boost the interest rates paid on savings and time deposits, the demand for M2 would also be likely to increase. This reasoning suggests a leftward shift in the* LM *curve, the magnitude of which would be highly uncertain and difficult to predict. That in turn indicates that targeting the monetary aggregates would likely produce undesired fluctuations in output and employment. You would advise your colleagues on the FOMC to deemphasize the monetary aggregates as targets and place a higher priority on interest rates.*

KEY TERM

crowding-out effect

STUDY QUESTIONS

1 Using the *IS-LM* model, explain the relative strength of the expansionary effects of a $20 billion increase in *G* if financed by

   a An equivalent personal income tax hike

   b The sale of securities to the public

   c The sale of securities to the Fed

2 Using the *IS-LM* framework, show why the elementary, or naive, fiscal multiplier overstates the actual consequences of shifts in government expenditures for equilibrium output.

3 Use the *IS-LM* framework to illustrate and explain the crowding-out phenomenon, in which an increase in government expenditures, accompanied by a constant money supply, reduces investment expenditures.

4 Monetarists believe that the demand for money is stable and that the interest elasticity of the demand for money is very low. Using the four-quadrant approach, derive the *LM* curve under such conditions, and compare it to the *LM* curve derived under the assumption that money demand is highly interest elastic.

5 Keynesians believe that investment is relatively inelastic with respect to the interest rate. Derive the *IS* curve under such an assumption, and compare it to an *IS* curve derived under the assumption that investment is highly sensitive to interest rates.

6 In the 1970s, OPEC's actions resulted in a dramatic increase in the price of oil. Analyze the effects of that event on U.S. output using the *IS-LM* framework. Then, assuming that the Fed is more concerned about recession and unemployment than inflation, use the framework to arrive at appropriate monetary and fiscal policies.

7 Suppose that the speculative money demand function is perfectly elastic with respect to interest rates. What policy prescription would be most effective in curing a recession under those circumstances? Explain *intuitively* why this is so.

8 The early 1980s witnessed several economic changes that can be analyzed in the context of the *IS-LM* model. First, personal and corporate income taxes were reduced. Second, an unprecedented peacetime defense buildup resulted in a rapid expansion of government expenditures. Third, a restrictive monetary policy was put into place to bring down high and entrenched inflation. Illustrate these events graphically using the *IS-LM* framework. What would you expect to happen to output? To interest rates?

9 Using the *IS-LM* framework, analyze the effect on output and interest rates of a Republican proposal to balance the federal budget by the year 2002.

10 "Crowding out will be greater the less elastic money demand is with respect to the interest rate." Explain *intuitively* whether this statement is true or false.

11 In the early 1990s, the Fed abandoned M2 in favor of interest rates as an intermediate policy target. Assuming that the Fed acted wisely, what does this imply about the stability of the demand for money and of velocity? Is your conclusion supported by the empirical evidence presented in Chapters 20 and 21?

12 What happens to the composition of national output when we experience

   a A tax-financed fiscal expansion?

   b A fiscal expansion financed through bonds sold to the private sector?

   c A fiscal expansion financed through bonds sold to the Federal Reserve?

13 Suppose consumer optimism increases sharply. Using the *IS-LM* framework, demonstrate the implications for total output, investment, consumption, and interest rates.

14 Suppose the U.S. stock market crashes and stocks lose 40 percent of their value in the next 6 months. Use the *IS-LM* framework to examine all the implications of the event that you can think of.

15 Why does the strength of monetary policy depend heavily on the sensitivity of investment to interest rates? Explain intuitively, using the *IS-LM* model as your framework.

SUGGESTIONS FOR ADDITIONAL READING

On the interest rate-sensitivity of the demand for money and its implications, see Chapters 7 and 11 of David Laidler, *The Demand for Money: Theories, Evidence, and Problems* (New York: HarperCollins, 1994). An excellent source on the issue of crowding out is Benjamin Friedman, "Crowding Out or Crowding In? Economic Consequences of Financing Government Debt," *Brookings Papers on Economic Activity,* 1978:3, pp. 593–654. Also, see Alex Chrystal and Daniel Thornton, "The Macroeconomic Effects of Deficit Spending: A Review," Federal Reserve Bank of St. Louis *Review,* November/December 1988, pp. 48–60. A classic paper on monetary policy targeting under uncertainty is William Poole, "The Optimal Choice of Monetary Policy Instruments in a Simple Macro Model," *Quarterly Journal of Economics* 84 (1970), pp. 192–216. A simplified presentation by Poole is "Rules of Thumb for Guiding Monetary Policy," in *Open Market Policies and Operating Procedures* (Washington, D. C.: Board of Governors of Federal Reserve System, 1971).

C H A P T E R

25

■ ## The Transmission of Monetary Policy

B y now you are familiar with the fact that the Federal Reserve's monetary policy actions influence economic activity principally by shifting the nation's aggregate demand (*AD*) curve. An increase in the money supply shifts the *AD* curve rightward, stimulating real output and boosting the nation's price level. A reduction in the money supply shifts the *AD* curve leftward, reducing real output and tending to reduce the price level. While almost all economists agree that monetary policy has important influence on aggregate demand and economic activity, there is considerable uncertainty about *how* monetary policy influences the economy.

In this chapter we will move beyond the simple notion that a change in the money supply triggers a shift in the *AD* curve to look in some depth at the **transmission mechanism** of monetary policy. We will examine the different ways in which changes in Federal Reserve policy alter aggregate demand and economic activity. We will see that while there is broad agreement that monetary policy has a strong effect on economic activity, the manner in which its influence is transmitted is not clear. Different models attribute different degrees of influence to the various channels of monetary policy. Those channels are also subject to change over time in response to institutional, regulatory, and technological changes. Today, for instance, monetary policy influences the economy in different ways than it did in the 1970s. For these reasons, the monetary policy transmission mechanism is the subject of active research; over the past decade, numerous papers have been published on the subject.

Aggregate expenditures consist of four components: consumption (*C*), investment (*I*), government purchases of goods and services (*G*), and net exports of goods and services (*X − M*). Monetary policy influences all four components, especially consumption and investment spending and net foreign demand for U.S. goods and services (*X − M*).[1] Figure 25-1 shows the shares of U.S. GDP constituted by *C, I, G,* and *X − M* in recent decades. Note that, in the past decade, consumer expenditures have made up more than

---

[1] By influencing interest rates, monetary policy probably also influences local government expenditures, a component of *G*. For example, lower interest rates engineered by the Fed encourage municipalities to issue bonds to finance expenditures for schools, swimming pools, and so forth. In our discussion in this chapter, however, we will ignore the potential effect of monetary policy on *G*.

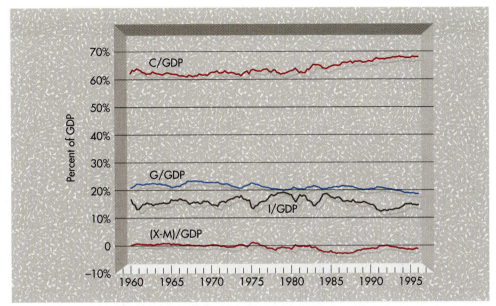

Figure 25-1   GDP Shares Contributed by the Four Components, 1960–1996. Consumer expenditures make up more than two-thirds of aggregate expenditures. Investment expenditures, government purchases, and net exports constitute the remainder.   *Source:* Data from *Citibank Economic Database.*

two-thirds of the nation's total expenditures. Government purchases make up the second largest component, constituting approximately 20 percent of total expenditures in recent years. Investment expenditures, which include residential and nonresidential construction as well as expenditures for producers' durable equipment and the change in aggregate business inventories, are the most volatile component. Total investment expenditures typically contribute about 15 percent of aggregate expenditures. Net exports (exports minus imports) have been consistently negative since the early 1980s. Although the share of total expenditures constituted by net exports is small, economists believe that the international sector is a very important part of the transmission process of monetary policy.

Theories of the transmission mechanism have evolved over time. We will first sketch the relatively simple early Keynesian and monetarist views of how a change in the money supply affects economic activity. Then we will look in more detail at the various avenues through which money derives its influence and examine newer theories and developments involving the details of the transmission mechanism.

EARLY VIEWS OF THE TRANSMISSION MECHANISM

In this section, we will look at some early Keynesian and monetarist viewpoints on the mechanism by which Fed policy influences the economy. This discussion will lay the groundwork for our discussion of more recent views.

Early Keynesian Views

In Keynes' original analysis, investment expenditures are determined by the interest rate and the **marginal efficiency of investment (MEI)**—that is, the rate of return expected from an additional unit of investment expenditures. The MEI schedule shows how this expected rate of return declines as the volume of investment increases. Investment is profitable as long as the MEI exceeds the market rate of interest. When the interest rate is placed on the vertical axis alongside this expected rate of return, the MEI schedule can be viewed as an investment demand function. In this framework, by changing the interest rate and moving along the MEI schedule, monetary policy is capable of influencing investment expenditures. This simple Keynesian scheme is illustrated in Figure 25-2. According to Keynes, the interest rate is determined by the supply of and demand for money. An increase in the supply of money from S_{M_1} to S_{M_2} reduces interest rates from i_1 to i_2 (panel A). The reduction in interest rates means that some investment projects that were unattractive at higher interest rates are now profitable. Businesses move down the MEI function from point A to point B in panel B, increasing their investment spending from I_1 to I_2.

Keynes believed that the interest rate elasticity of investment demand is relatively low. That is, he thought that the MEI function is relatively steep, as shown in the figure. In the Keynesian framework, that belief, coupled with the very limited breadth of the monetary transmission mechanism, suggests that monetary policy exerts a moderate influence on aggregate expenditures. Keynes believed that fiscal policy actions—changes in taxes and government expenditures—exert a more powerful influence over economic activity than do changes in the money supply.

As we will soon discover, however, the transmission mechanism in Keynes' model is unrealistically narrow. Keynes neglected to consider many alternative ways in which

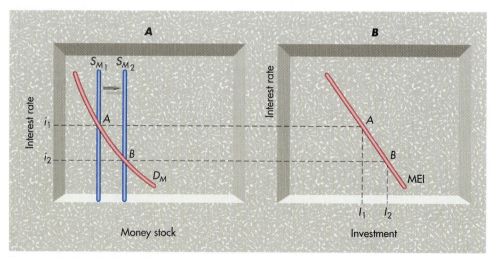

Figure 25-2   The Early Keynesian Monetary Policy Transmission Mechanism. In Keynes' scheme, an increase in the money supply reduces interest rates (panel A). By doing so, it increases the number of profitable investment projects and stimulates economic activity (panel B).

monetary policy might influence aggregate expenditures. Thus he may have underestimated the strength of monetary policy. Empirical evidence indicates that money has a strong effect on economic activity.

Early Monetarist Views

Early monetarist views were based on a stable link between money and other assets. In this view, individuals and firms maintain a broad portfolio of assets, both financial and real. Such assets include money, certificates of deposit, government bonds, common stocks, physical capital, durable goods, and even human capital. Based on the returns expected at the margin on such assets, together with their liquidity, individuals and firms maintain a *portfolio equilibrium.*

Now assume that the Federal Reserve upsets this equilibrium by increasing the stock of money. Initially, individuals and firms discover they are holding more money than they desire relative to stocks, bonds, physical capital, durable goods, and so forth. This disequilibrium triggers a round of asset substitution, in which individuals rid themselves of their excess money by acquiring nonmoney assets—stocks, bonds, cars, houses, and so forth. Only when the holdings of these nonmoney assets resume their relative importance vis-à-vis money holdings does the economy reach a new equilibrium. By that point, stock and bond prices have increased, as have the stocks of housing and consumer durable goods. In this way, money influences economic activity.

In the monetarist transmission mechanism, changes in the money stock may influence economic activity even if interest rates are unaffected.[2] Whereas the early Keynesian transmission mechanism was *indirect*—running from money to interest rates to investment expenditures—the monetarist mechanism was *direct*—running from money to expenditures on goods and services as well as financial assets.[3]

The effect of money on stock and bond prices is an important part of modern theories of the transmission mechanism. Let us look more closely at how monetary policy affects stock and bond prices.

STOCK AND BOND PRICES

We have seen that monetarists view the impact of a change in the money supply on stock and bond prices as being quite direct. An increase in the money supply creates a disequilibrium among holdings of money, stocks, and bonds. This prompts individuals to use

---

[2]In terms of the *IS-LM* model presented in Chapters 23 and 24, an increase in the money supply shifts not only the *LM* curve but also the *IS* curve rightward. In the monetarist view, money influences economic activity *directly,* apart from any influence it has on interest rates.

[3]The difference in the two transmission mechanisms explains why Keynesians are more skeptical than monetarists about the general efficacy of monetary policy. In the Keynesian transmission mechanism, two factors can cause the potential influence of money on economic activity to break down. First, the Federal Reserve may at times find it difficult to push interest rates down. Second, if the MEI function is highly interest rate inelastic, interest rate changes will have little impact on investment and aggregate expenditures. Such breakdowns in monetary policy effectiveness are much harder to rationalize in the monetarist transmission mechanism.

their excess money to purchase more stocks and bonds (as well as goods and services). In doing so, they bid up stock and bond prices. Thus an increase in the money supply raises stock and bond prices, while a decrease in the money supply lowers stock and bond prices.

To see other ways in which a change in the money supply can influence stock and bond prices, we need to review the present value formula presented in Chapter 5. Consider the following equation:

$$(25\text{-}1) \qquad PV = \frac{R_1}{1+i} + \frac{R_2}{(1+i)^2} + \frac{R_3}{(1+i)^3} + \cdots + \frac{R_n}{(1+i)^n}$$

In this expression, PV is the present value (and price) of an asset such as a stock or bond. The R's are the returns currently expected from the stock or bond in the year indicated by the subscript. For example, R_3 is the return currently expected from the asset 3 years from now. In the denominator, i is the current interest rate used to discount the future returns. The present value of any asset that is expected to yield a flow of returns in the future is calculated by summing the discounted present values of the individual returns expected in each future year.

In the case of corporate, municipal, and government bonds, the R's are fixed contractually. Barring insolvency of the issuer, there is no uncertainty about the returns to be received each year from bonds. Because the R's earned on bonds are fixed, monetary policy influences bond prices entirely through its effect on market interest rates. If the Fed reduces interest rates, bond prices must rise; if the Fed increases interest rates, bond prices must fall.

Common stocks, however, do not offer a specific dividend or other return to stockholders. The R's expected from stocks are therefore highly uncertain. Expected returns are revised frequently as new information about the economy and individual companies comes out. If a corporation is successful and is growing over time, the R's anticipated from its common stock are likely to be positive and to be sequentially increasing—that is $R_2 > R_1$, $R_3 > R_2$, and so forth.

We see from this formulation that if monetary policy is to influence stock prices, it must do so by influencing either the expected returns (R's) or the interest rate (i). If an increase in the money supply consistently stimulates economic activity, it will also be likely to increase the expected returns from stocks (the R's), thereby increasing stock prices. Even if the increase in the money supply fails to boost expected returns, it is still likely to increase stock prices (as well as bond prices) by reducing interest rates.[4] We conclude that, given other factors, an increase in the money supply increases stock and bond prices and that, holding other factors constant, a decrease in the money supply reduces stock and bond prices.

---

[4]However, one must be cautious in advancing the proposition that stimulative monetary actions can systematically increase stock and bond prices. The outcome probably depends on the economic environment at the time of the monetary stimulus. In an environment in which economic agents are highly attuned to inflation, an acceleration in money growth may trigger an increase in expected inflation—which may lead to *higher* nominal long-term interest rates through the Fisher effect. In that case, stock and bond prices will fall unless the positive effect of the monetary stimulus on expected returns (R's) offsets the effect of higher interest rates. Most economists agree that, in an environment of subdued inflation, the Fed is capable of lowering long-term interest rates through stimulative monetary policy measures.

Table 25-1

Shares of GDP by Component

	1950s	1960s	1970s	1980s	1990s
Consumption (C):	**64.2%**	**63.5%**	**63.9%**	**65.9%**	**67.6%**
Durables	9.0	8.7	8.9	8.4	8.2
Nondurables	31.7	27.8	25.4	23.2	20.9
Services	23.5	27.0	29.6	34.3	38.5
Investment (I):	**16.2**	**15.8**	**17.0**	**17.0**	**13.7**
Residential building	5.6	4.8	5.1	4.5	3.8
Nonresident structures	3.8	3.8	4.0	4.6	2.9
Producer's durable equipment	5.9	6.2	7.1	7.5	6.7
Change in inventories	0.9	1.0	0.8	0.4	0.3
Government purchases (G):	**19.3**	**20.4**	**19.5**	**19.0**	**19.6**
Net exports (X − M):	**0.2**	**0.4**	**−0.4**	**−1.9**	**−0.9**
Exports	4.5	5.0	7.4	8.7	10.3
Imports	4.3	4.6	7.8	10.6	11.2

Note: Figures for each decade are averages of quarterly data. Figures for 1990s include data from 1990 through 1995.

Source: National income accounts data from *Citibank Economic Database.*

CONSUMPTION, INVESTMENT, AND NET EXPORTS

Before analyzing the ways in which monetary policy influences consumption, investment, and net exports, let us examine the relative importance of those various components of GDP. Table 25-1 illustrates the proportionate share of GDP of each of the components of consumption, investment, and net exports from the 1950s through the 1990s.

By far the largest component of GDP is consumer expenditures. Government purchases constitute approximately 20 percent of GDP—a share that has decreased slightly since the 1960s.[5] The investment share of output, which consists chiefly of producers' durable equipment and residential and nonresidential structures, has declined in the 1990s; it now represents about one-seventh of total GDP expenditures. Net exports

---

[5]Government purchases include expenditures for goods and services by federal, state, and local governments. They do *not* include government transfer payments—expenditures by government for which no concurrent good or service is rendered (which make up about half of total government expenditures). Because government transfer payments are reflected in such GDP components as consumption, residential building, and imports, to include government transfer payments in *G* in the national income accounts would be to engage in double-counting.

$(X - M)$ have been negative since the 1970s. Note, however, the sustained uptrend in the shares of GDP constituted by exports and imports. The role of international trade in the U.S. economy has increased persistently since the 1950s.

Consumer Expenditures

In recent years, consumer expenditures have accounted for nearly 70 percent of aggregate expenditures in the United States (see Table 25-1). Note that this category consists of expenditures on durable goods (cars, TV sets), nondurables (food, clothing), and services (health care, entertainment). Because the income elasticity of demand for consumer services is significantly higher than that for consumer durables and nondurables, the share of the nation's output going into consumer services has increased sharply as incomes have risen since the 1950s. The share of nondurables has declined correspondingly, while the share of durables has remained relatively stable. Note that, in the 1990s, consumption accounted for a significantly higher share of the nation's output than it did in earlier decades.

Monetary policy is believed to influence total consumer expenditures through several channels, including the effect of a change in interest rates on durable goods expenditures; the effect of a change in wealth on all categories of consumption; and the effect of a change in liquidity on durable goods expenditures.

Interest Rates and Consumer Durable Goods

Table 25-1 shows that consumer expenditures on durable goods typically make up between 8 and 9 percent of aggregate expenditures. Consumer durables such as cars and major appliances are often purchased on credit. For example, about 60 percent of new automobile purchases are financed by borrowing. When the Fed pursues stimulative policies that reduce interest rates, monthly payments on new consumer loans are reduced accordingly. Thus stimulative monetary policies encourage increased purchases of consumer durable goods. This channel of influence may be summarized as follows:

$$M \uparrow \ \rightarrow i \downarrow \ \rightarrow \text{Consumer durable goods expenditures} \uparrow \ \rightarrow \text{GDP} \uparrow$$

The consensus in the empirical literature on this subject, however, is that this effect is relatively small.[6]

---

[6]Traditionally, economists have regarded the interest rate as a measure of the incentive to abstain from current consumption—that is, to save. In making the decision to save, individuals substitute *future* consumption for *current* consumption. A change in interest rates sets off two effects on consumption which tend to pull consumption in opposite directions. Assume that real interest rates increase. This change raises the opportunity cost of current consumption by increasing the amount of future goods that can be enjoyed by saving an additional dollar today. Hence, a *substitution effect* occurs, in which consumers substitute future consumption for current consumption. When interest rates rise, individuals step up their current saving. On the other hand, the increase in interest rates boosts the flow of income earned from savings. In doing so, it triggers an *income effect,* which tends to increase the fraction of current income spent on consumer goods. In other words, the income effect of higher interest rates works to reduce saving. If the income effect is as powerful as the substitution effect, the net effect of an increase in interest rates is to leave consumption unchanged. Only if the substitution effect is stronger than the income effect (which is normally assumed in economic analysis) can we conclude that an increase in interest rates reduces consumption (increases saving).

Wealth and Consumption Expenditures

A consensus exists in macroeconomics that consumer expenditures depend not only on *current income* but also on *wealth* or *expected average future income*. Holding current income constant, an increase in wealth implies an increase in expected future income. Thus an increase in wealth stimulates current consumption.

Stocks and bonds are an important component of financial wealth. By influencing stock and bond prices, monetary policy affects wealth. For example, if the Fed pursues a stimulative policy and reduces interest rates, both stock and bond prices are likely to rise, increasing wealth and stimulating consumption. This channel may be summarized as follows:

$$M \uparrow \; \rightarrow \text{Stock and bond prices} \uparrow \; \rightarrow \text{Wealth} \uparrow \; \rightarrow \text{Consumption} \uparrow \; \rightarrow \text{GDP} \uparrow$$

Many economists believe that this mechanism contributes appreciably to the power of monetary policy.[7]

Liquidity and Consumer Durable Goods Expenditures

Assume that an individual owns a portfolio of financial and real assets. Those assets differ in their *liquidity*—the ease with which they may be converted to cash on short notice without appreciable cost. In general, financial assets such as money market mutual fund shares, bonds, and stocks are more liquid than real assets such as houses, cars, and land. If you experience an unexpected need for cash, you will find it easier to raise the cash if your portfolio is weighted heavily with such liquid assets as savings accounts, money market mutual fund shares, and Treasury securities.

It follows that big-ticket consumer durables expenditures are likely to be influenced by the liquidity of the asset portfolios of individuals and firms. The likelihood of financial distress influences consumer confidence and, by extension, consumer purchases of these expensive, potentially postponable items. Suppose the Fed tightens monetary policy significantly in an effort to combat escalating inflation. As interest rates rise, bond prices fall. Stock prices are likely to follow, reducing the value of financial assets held by individuals, as well as the *share* of liquid assets in their portfolios. As the likelihood of financial distress is revised upward, individuals may postpone expenditures on consumer durables.

When the Fed eases its monetary posture, interest rates fall. Stock and bond prices rise, and the liquidity of portfolios increases. As the prospect of financial distress is reduced, consumer confidence increases. Expenditures on consumer durables increase, and GDP rises. This channel of monetary influence may be summarized as follows:

$$M \uparrow \; \rightarrow \text{Portfolio liquidity} \uparrow \; \rightarrow \text{Likelihood of financial distress} \downarrow$$
$$\rightarrow \text{Consumer durables spending} \uparrow \; \rightarrow \text{GDP} \uparrow$$

This effect applies equally well to the purchase of new homes, which is counted in the national income accounts (somewhat arbitrarily) as a form of investment rather than consumption. Like consumer durable goods, houses are highly illiquid; they are difficult to sell quickly at full value. An increase in stock and bond prices boosts wealth, improves consumers' balance sheets, reduces their prospects of financial distress,

---

[7]In the Federal Reserve's econometric model, this channel of influence is very important. In this model, the influence of monetary policy on consumption through the wealth effect exerts about the same influence as the money–residential construction channel and four times as much influence as the money–interest rate–plant and equipment expenditures channel.

and increases their willingness to invest in new housing. This channel is quite similar to the previous example.

$$M \uparrow \rightarrow \text{Portfolio liquidity} \uparrow \rightarrow \text{Likelihood of financial distress} \downarrow$$
$$\rightarrow \text{Investment in new housing} \uparrow \rightarrow \text{GDP} \uparrow$$

In sum, monetary policy influences aggregate consumer expenditures (as well as investment expenditures) by altering interest rates, wealth, and liquidity. It is important to keep in mind that consumer expenditures constitute a very large share of GDP. For this reason, even fairly modest percentage changes in consumption induced by changes in interest rates, wealth, and liquidity can result in significant changes in total consumption and GDP.

Monetary Policy and Investment Spending

Table 25-1 indicates that the components of investment expenditures, in order of magnitude, are producers' durable equipment (computers, tractors), residential structures (houses, apartments), nonresidential structures (factories, business buildings), and changes in business inventories. It is likely that monetary policy influences each of these categories of investment spending.

We can identify four channels through which monetary policy influences investment spending. They include interest rates, the availability of bank credit, the role of stock prices in inducing firms to issue new shares of stock, and the role of stock prices in influencing banks to lend money. We will discuss each of these channels in the sections that follow.

Interest Rates and Investment Spending

To a significant extent, the simple Keynesian investment framework outlined earlier in this chapter (the interest rate–marginal efficiency of investment framework) captures this channel. This is especially true for investment in producers' durable equipment and nonresidential structures. In this MEI framework, firms undertake all investment projects for which the (risk-adjusted) expected rate of return exceeds the current rate of interest. By altering the current rate of interest, monetary policy influences the number of investment projects that firms view as profitable. If the Fed reduces interest rates, for instance, more projects appear profitable, so firms undertake more of these projects, and investment increases.

In the case of new owner-occupied homes (a major share of residential structures), interest rates determine the mortgage payments and therefore the affordability of new homes. If the Fed reduces interest rates, monthly mortgage payments are reduced and more families can afford to purchase a new home. Because the purchase of a new home can often be postponed, new home construction is particularly sensitive to interest rates.

The change in the nation's inventories is counted in the national income accounts as a form of investment. Changes in inventories may be either voluntary or involuntary. Firms may voluntarily (deliberately) build up inventories if they are optimistic about future sales growth. Or they may suffer unplanned increases in inventories if sales forecasts are too optimistic.

There are costs and benefits involved in holding inventories. The cost is the interest expense incurred to finance the inventory—that is, to purchase and hold the goods.[8] The benefit associated with holding larger inventories is the additional sales and customer goodwill that may be achieved by maintaining a full complement of goods in stock. If the Fed reduces interest rates, the cost of holding inventories is reduced. Other things being equal, reduced interest rates lead to a deliberate buildup of inventories—a voluntary increase. That, in turn, stimulates aggregate expenditures and GDP.

In summary, the interest rate channel of monetary policy influence may be described as follows:

$$M \uparrow \ \rightarrow i \downarrow \ \rightarrow I \uparrow \ \rightarrow \text{GDP} \uparrow$$

Availability of Bank Credit

Large firms with well-established credit ratings may typically choose from alternative sources of funds to finance their purchases of equipment, structures, and inventories. They may issue commercial paper, bonds, or shares of stock, or they may borrow from banks. But many small firms have no alternative to banks. They are not sufficiently large or well enough established to issue paper, bonds, or stock. Thus, bank loans are "special" in the sense that small firms and individuals may have no substitute source of funds.

When the Fed tightens monetary policy, banks respond by tightening their credit standards. As a result, many smaller firms are cut off from funds. Rather than rationing the limited amount of funds through market forces by allowing the interest rate to move up to market-clearing levels, banks simply deny loans to some smaller firms. Because many such firms have no alternative source of funds, the banks' action causes a reduction in investment. This phenomenon has been confirmed in several recent studies.[9]

Conversely, when the Fed eases monetary policy, say, by purchasing securities on the open market, banks find themselves with additional reserves. They relax their credit standards and extend loans to firms to which they had previously denied credit. The mechanism may be summarized as follows:

$$\text{Fed securities portfolio} \uparrow \ \rightarrow \text{Bank reserves} \uparrow \ \rightarrow \text{Bank lending} \uparrow \ \rightarrow I \uparrow \ \rightarrow \text{GDP} \uparrow$$

Of course, rather than being induced by Federal Reserve actions, the amount of bank credit can change at banks' own initiative. For an example from the early 1990s, see Exhibit 25-1.

---

[8]Instead of borrowing, some firms finance inventories with internal funds. In that case, the opportunity cost of holding additional inventory is the rate of return on the best alternative use of the firm's funds. That is frequently taken to be the current yield on safe, short-term securities—that is, the interest rate. Hence, an increase in interest rates reduces the incentive to hold inventories, whether financed with internal or external funds.

[9]See, for example, the article by Mark Gertler and Simon Gilchrist cited in the "Suggestions for Additional Reading" at the end of this chapter.

EXHIBIT 25-1

The Credit Crunch of 1990–1992

A credit crunch may be defined as a sharp reduction in banks' *ability* or *willingness* to lend at each possible interest rate. It may be shown graphically as a leftward shift in the supply curve of bank loans. Historically, most credit crunches have been brought on by restrictive Federal Reserve actions. But there is evidence that the 1990–1992 crunch was due largely to a sharp increase in caution on the part of banks. In that crunch, banks elected to tighten their lending standards, holding a smaller portion of their assets in loans and a larger portion in safe, short-term securities.

Survey results indicate that bank loans became more difficult to obtain in 1990. The spread between bank lending rates and the cost of funds to banks increased. For example, the spread between the banks' prime loan rate and the federal funds rate increased significantly. If the decline in bank lending had resulted from reduced demand for loans by bank customers, one would expect such spreads to have declined. Instead, banks appear to have tightened their credit standards.

Several factors probably contributed to the increase in banks' nervousness. First, both individuals and business firms had taken on an unprecedented amount of debt in the 1980s. This increased level of leverage clearly signaled an increase in risk. Banks were also concerned about the balance sheets of their prospective borrowers. The late 1980s had witnessed a boom and bust in the real estate sector, resulting in big losses to banks. Bank failures were on the rise, and regulatory authorities had tightened capital standards in response to banks' deteriorating financial condition. The recent S&L debacle was fresh in bankers' minds, as were memories of the sharp stock market sell-off in October 1987 and the shocking bankruptcy of the investment banking firm Drexel Burnham Lambert in February 1990.

The accompanying figure indicates the dramatic slowdown in the growth of bank lending in this period and the corresponding increase in the holding of securities by banks. In spite of stimulative actions by the Federal Reserve, bank lending was essentially flat for about 2 years (in contrast to an average growth of 9.8 percent per year during 1960–1989). This severe slowdown in bank lending contributed to the recession of 1990–1991 (shaded area) and the unusually sluggish recovery in the 2 years following the end of the recession.

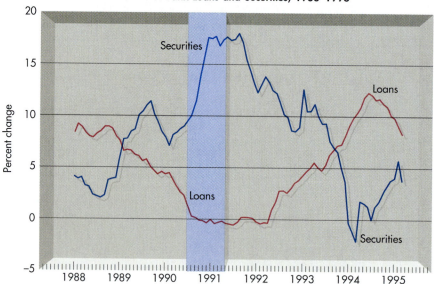

Growth Rates of Bank Loans and Securities, 1988–1996

Stock Prices and Firms' Incentive to Issue Shares

James Tobin has developed a theory of investment known as the **q theory.** Tobin defines q as follows:

$$q = \frac{\text{Market value of firms}}{\text{Replacement cost of capital}}$$

In this expression, the market value of a firm is the value the stock market places on the firm's stock. The replacement cost of capital is what it would cost to buy the machinery and tools, erect the buildings, and so forth, to replicate the firm.

If the stock market has placed a high valuation on firms, so that q is high, firms can issue new shares of stock and get a good price for them relative to the cost of equipment and buildings they are considering replacing or supplementing. In this case, investment levels will be high. If q is low because stock prices are depressed, firms will be reluctant to issue new shares to finance new investment, and investment levels will be low.[10]

In this theory, monetary policy influences the investment decision by influencing stock prices. Stimulative monetary policy reduces interest rates, boosts stock prices, raises q, and stimulates investment expenditures. Schematically:

$$M \uparrow \; \to \text{Stock prices} \uparrow \; \to \text{Tobin's } q \uparrow \; \to \text{Investment} \uparrow \; \to \text{GDP} \uparrow$$

Adverse Selection, Moral Hazard, and Bank Lending

Monetary policy also influences investment spending in more subtle ways. We saw in Chapter 11 that adverse selection occurs when those most in need of loans due to financial difficulties are the ones who seek and are granted loans. An increase in firms' net worth reduces the problem of adverse selection. Higher net worth essentially means that firms have more collateral to support loans. That reduces the likelihood of default and makes banks more willing to grant loans.

Higher net worth also reduces the moral hazard problem by increasing the cost of failure to a borrowing firm. With higher net worth, a firm has more to lose if things go wrong. Thus higher stock prices, by increasing firms' net worth, reduce the incentive to undertake highly risky or desperate ventures financed by borrowing. In this way, monetary policy reduces the moral hazard problem.

In sum, by influencing stock prices, monetary policy influences the wealth and the net worth of firms. That in turn reduces adverse selection and moral hazard problems, inducing banks to extend more loans. Hence, we have the following rather complicated scheme:

$$M \uparrow \; \to \text{Stock prices} \uparrow \; \to \text{Net worth} \uparrow \; \to \text{Adverse selection and moral hazard problems} \downarrow$$
$$\to \text{Bank loans} \uparrow \; \to I \uparrow \; \to \text{GDP} \uparrow$$

---

[10]Suppose a firm is bent on expansion. It can expand either by purchasing an existing firm or by purchasing new plant and equipment. If stock prices (and q) are low, it will likely choose to purchase an existing firm. If stock prices are high, it is more likely to expand through building new facilities. Only in the latter case does the nation experience an increase in investment spending.

Net Exports ($X - M$)

Until about 20 years ago, economists thought monetary policy exerted almost all its effect on aggregate expenditures through its influence on consumption and investment spending. The lessons of the past 20 years have radically altered that view. Table 25-1 shows that the share of U.S. output constituted by exports and imports more than doubled between the 1960s and the 1990s. In recent decades, the U.S. economy has become more open (in the sense that X/GDP and M/GDP have increased), though still significantly less so than Japan and many European nations. Thus the implications of monetary policy for export and import behavior cannot be ignored. Indeed, some economists believe that the net export channel may be the most powerful channel of monetary influence today.

The key to understanding the influence of monetary policy on the net foreign demand for U.S. goods and services ($X - M$) is to remember the fundamental fact that each nation's total transactions with the rest of the world must net out at zero. If the United States imports more goods and services than it exports, it must transfer money and securities to the rest of the world. Phrased in reverse, if the United States sends more securities and money to foreign nations than it receives from them, it must exhibit a deficit in its international trade balance—that is, U.S. imports must exceed exports. Holding actual flows of money (demand deposits and currency) constant, if net holdings of U.S. financial assets by foreigners increase by, say, $40 billion in a given year, the U.S. trade deficit must also increase by $40 billion.

For the most part, monetary policy influences the net foreign demand for U.S. goods and services ($X - M$) by influencing the desire of U.S. and foreign individuals and firms to hold U.S. and foreign securities. A huge pool of financial capital exists worldwide. These funds can be shifted instantaneously to the financial center that offers the most attractive rates of return. By influencing such *capital flows,* monetary policy influences the exchange rate, which in turn alters net exports ($X - M$).

Suppose the Federal Reserve tightens its monetary policy, and interest rates rise. The foreign demand for interest-bearing U.S. financial assets will then increase. Also, as domestic securities become relatively more attractive, U.S. demand for similar foreign assets (and foreign currencies) declines. To purchase American financial assets, foreigners must now purchase dollars. The increased foreign demand for dollars (and decreased U.S. demand for foreign currencies) causes the U.S. dollar to appreciate in foreign exchange markets. The value of the dollar, expressed in units of foreign currencies, rises. That in turn makes U.S. goods more expensive in foreign markets and foreign goods less expensive in the United States, decreasing U.S. exports and increasing U.S. imports.[11] The U.S. trade balance ($X - M$) deteriorates, and the aggregate demand for U.S. goods and services declines.

Conversely, if the Fed reduces interest rates, the net demand for U.S. financial assets declines. The dollar depreciates, making U.S. goods relatively more attractive to both foreigners and Americans. The decline in the value of the dollar stimulates U.S. net

---

[11]This is partially attenuated by a wealth effect that inhibits imports. As the Fed tightens its monetary policy, interest rates rise and securities prices fall, reducing wealth. That in turn reduces imports into the United States.

exports $(X - M)$, boosting the aggregate demand for U.S. goods and services, and GDP increases. This channel of monetary policy transmission may be summarized as follows:

$$M \uparrow \ \rightarrow i \downarrow \ \rightarrow \text{Exchange rate} \downarrow \ (\text{Dollar depreciates}) \rightarrow (X - M) \uparrow \ \rightarrow \text{GDP} \uparrow$$

Because the U.S. economy has become more open to international trade since the 1960s, changes in $X - M$ are today a more important element in the transmission process of monetary policy. However, the expansion in the worldwide pool of financial capital may have weakened the impact of the Fed's monetary policy. As the Fed pushes up interest rates to restrict the aggregate demand for U.S. goods and services, inflows of foreign capital moderate the magnitude of the interest rate response. Similarly, when the Fed seeks to reduce interest rates via open market securities purchases, outflows of capital from the United States inhibit the downward movement of U.S. interest rates. Because of the increasing integration of global capital markets, the Fed may have to pursue more vigorous monetary policy actions to achieve a given change in the aggregate demand for U.S. goods and services than was the case in earlier times. Exhibit 25-2 discusses the ways in which the channels of monetary influence have changed.

THE MONEY VIEW VERSUS THE CREDIT VIEW

Picture an aggregate bank balance sheet of the commercial banking system. On the asset side, we have cash, deposits at the Federal Reserve, loans and securities. The liability side is dominated by demand deposits and other checkable deposits (DDO) and time deposits (TD). Also listed are large negotiable CDs issued by the nation's larger banks. Under current regulations, banks are required to maintain reserves (cash and deposits at the Fed) in the amount of a certain percentage of DDO. There are currently no reserve requirements on non-DDO bank liabilities.

All Commercial Banks

Assets	Liabilities
Cash	DDO
Deposits at Fed	TD
Loans	Large CDs
Securities	

Almost all economists believe that changes in this balance sheet induced by Federal Reserve policy actions lead to changes in aggregate expenditures, output, and the price level. However, economists disagree about the details of the process. They disagree about whether, in evaluating the impact of monetary policy, we need to look only at the liability side of the balance sheet or the asset side as well. Here, we examine two views of the monetary policy transmission process: the "money view" and the "credit view."

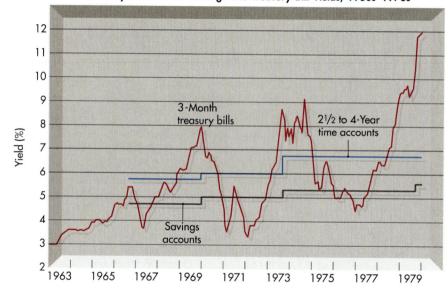

EXHIBIT 25-2

The Changing Channels of Monetary Policy

One phenomenon that complicates the conduct of monetary policy is the fact that the ways in which monetary policy affects economic activity can change significantly over time. A good example is the changing role of residential construction in the monetary policy transmission mechanism. In the 1960s and 1970s, whenever the Fed moved to tighten credit, much of the impact was transmitted through a contraction in homebuilding. Statutory interest rate ceilings limited the ability of savings and loans and other housing-lending institutions to attract deposits in periods when short-term yields moved up significantly (see the accompanying figure). The slowdown in the flow of funds into S&Ls produced a sharp contraction in the availability of funds for new houses. Thus an increase in interest rates sharply curtailed housing activity, accomplishing the desired slowdown in aggregate expenditures. Credit crunches in 1966, 1969, and 1974 served this function.

Statutory Interest Rate Ceilings and Treasury Bill Yields, 1960s–1970s

The Money View

In the traditional **money view,** the information about the nation's monetary aggregates (M1, M2) gained from the liability side of the bank balance sheet is sufficient to predict the impact of monetary policy on aggregate spending and GDP. Suppose the Fed desires to pursue restrictive policy actions for the purpose of reducing aggregate expenditures. The Fed sells securities on the open market. Essentially, the general public writes checks to the Federal Reserve to purchase these securities. The public does not regard these securities as perfect substitutes for demand deposits. To induce the public

---

EXHIBIT 25-2   (CONTINUED)

The Depository Institutions Deregulation and Monetary Control Act of 1980 phased out statutory interest rate ceilings in the 1980s. Today, to accomplish a desired slowdown in expenditures, the Fed must push interest rates significantly higher than in the 1960s. The advent of adjustable-rate mortgages and the development of secondary markets in mortgages have also diminished the role of residential construction in the monetary policy transmission mechanism.

Several other events have also altered the channels of monetary influence over time. Because debt burdens increased sharply in the 1980s, consumers and businesses became more sensitive to interest rates. In other words, the interest elasticity of demand for consumer durable goods and investment goods increased. That change strengthened the power of monetary policy. In addition, the increasing openness of the U.S. economy, coupled with the worldwide movement from fixed to floating exchange rates in 1973, has likely increased the importance of the international sector in the monetary policy transmission mechanism.

On balance, is the Fed more powerful now than it was in the past, or less powerful? Benjamin Friedman believes that the declining relative importance of depository institutions (banks, S&Ls, credit unions) in the financial intermediation process has likely reduced the overall power of monetary policy. However, empirical studies yield no convincing evidence that the Fed is less powerful today than in the past.

---

to trade its money balances (*DDO*) for these securities, the Fed must accept reduced prices (offer higher yields) on the securities it wishes to sell.[12] Also, as the checks written by the public to the Fed are cleared, bank reserves decline on a dollar-for-dollar basis. Because required reserves decline only fractionally, banks find themselves short on reserves. Banks must collectively implement some combination of securities sales and loan reductions in order to satisfy reserve requirements. In this process the money supply falls and interest rates are increased further. This increase in interest rates triggered by the Fed's restrictive actions reduces aggregate expenditures by reducing interest-sensitive expenditures (investment and consumer durables expenditures) and by reducing net U.S. exports of goods and services ($X - M$).

When the Fed provides new reserves, banks create money, either by making loans or by purchasing securities from the general public. In response to restrictive Fed policy actions, banks reduce the money supply, either by reducing loans or by selling securities. In focusing only on the liability side of the bank balance sheet (*DDO* and *TD*), the "money view" implicitly assumes that the *source* of the change in the money supply is of little significance. In this view, an increase in the monetary aggregates influences economic activity in approximately the same way irrespective of whether the money is created through bank lending or through bank securities purchases. In other words, in the "money view" the asset side of the bank balance sheet is ignored.

---

[12]If people are to willingly hold fewer *DDO,* the opportunity cost of holding *DDO* must increase. This opportunity cost is the yield that can be obtained on government securities. By offering higher yields (lower prices) on government securities, the Federal Reserve induces the public to hold more securities and less money in the form of *DDO.*

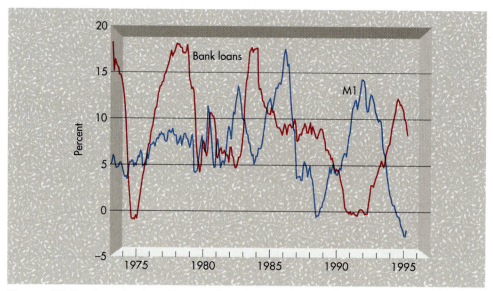

Figure 25-3   Growth Rates of M1 and Bank Loans, 1973–1996. The growth rate of bank loans frequently deviates markedly from the growth rate of money. In the credit view, the link between bank lending and GDP is stronger than the money supply–GDP link. *Source:* Federal Reserve data from *Citibank Economic Database.*

The Lending, or Credit, View

In recent years, however, this "money view" has increasingly been called into question. A debate is currently being waged over whether it is a mistake to concentrate solely on the liability side of the bank balance sheet. Many economists today believe that *bank lending,* a crucial item on the asset side of the bank balance sheet, also significantly influences economic activity above and beyond the role played by *money.* In this **credit view,** an increase in bank loans has a stronger impact on GDP expenditures and economic activity than does an equal amount of bank securities purchases, even though both events have the same impact on M1 and M2.[13]

Whenever banks grant new loans, money is created. When banks reduce loans, the money supply declines. One might therefore suspect that bank loans would track the monetary aggregates quite strongly over time. If so, ignoring bank loans and focusing on M1 and M2 would make little difference in practice even if bank loans are very important in influencing economic activity. Figure 25-3 indicates, however, that the rate of

---

[13]In terms of our $MV_Y = PY$ framework, the "credit view" asserts that money created through bank loans has a higher velocity than does money created through bank securities purchases. This follows from the fact that individuals and firms that take out bank loans are more likely to spend the proceeds on goods and services than are individuals and firms that sell securities to banks. Hence, in the credit view, aggregate expenditures (MV_Y and PY) will be stimulated more strongly by an increase in bank lending than by an equal increase in bank securities purchases, even though the two bank actions have the same effect on M1 and M2.

change of bank loans at times differs significantly from the rate of change of the money supply (M1).

Note in the figure that the rates of change of bank lending and M1 growth are not well synchronized.[14] During 1990–1992, a period of recession followed by anemic recovery, M1 growth accelerated strongly while bank loans stagnated. As the economy picked up strength in 1993 and 1994, bank lending accelerated while the growth rate of M1 declined. In these instances, bank lending provides a better indicator of economic activity than money growth.

If bank lending is to be an important channel of monetary policy, two conditions are essential. First, bank loans must be "special" in the sense that certain borrowers have a limited ability to tap alternative sources of funds. In other words, good substitutes for bank loans must be unavailable to at least some borrowers. Second, the Fed must be capable of influencing bank lending significantly. This means, from the point of view of bank asset management, that loans and securities must not be close substitutes for each other. Furthermore, from the point of view of bank liability management, nonreservable sources of funds (such as time deposits and negotiable CDs) must not be close substitutes for reservable sources of funds for banks (*DDO*).[15]

If banks view securities and loans as perfect substitutes, they may respond to restrictive monetary policy actions by liquidating their securities and leaving their loan portfolio intact. In this event, the money supply declines but bank loans do not. Also, if banks view nonreservable sources of funds as close substitutes for *DDO,* they may respond to a loss of *DDO* and reserves in periods of restrictive Fed policy by issuing additional negotiable CDs or other nonreservable liabilities (sources of funds) in order to maintain their loans. If banks react in these ways, the Federal Reserve may find it quite difficult to control bank lending. While a near consensus does exist about the "special" nature of certain bank loans, economists disagree about the extent to which the Fed can influence bank lending in the short run.

Are Bank Loans Special?

Because of informational problems in financial markets, alternative forms of finance are imperfect substitutes for individuals and many firms. In fact, alternative sources are sometimes not available to such borrowers. The expertise that banks have in evaluating and screening loan applicants and in monitoring loan performance enables them to extend credit to customers (typically individuals and small firms) who find it difficult or impossible to obtain credit on the open market. In the credit view, bank loans are special because many individuals and smaller firms are unable to find other sources of credit. Large, established firms with good credit ratings can borrow in the bond market or commercial paper market. To the extent that such sources of funds are close substitutes for bank loans, these large firms can maintain desired expenditures even when the Fed tightens credit. However, smaller firms that rely entirely on banks for

---

[14]A glance at a similar graph that employs the growth rate of M2 in place of the growth rate of M1 shows only a marginal increase in the synchronization between the loan growth and monetary growth series.

[15]By reservable deposits, we mean deposits subject to reserve requirements. Under current regulations, only *DDO* are subject to reserve requirements. Nonreservable sources of bank funds include savings deposits, small time deposits, negotiable CDs, and Eurodollar borrowing.

loans are likely to be forced to reduce their expenditures when the Fed tightens and banks respond by reducing lending. In this view, in periods of restrictive Fed policy, smaller firms absorb the brunt of cutbacks.[16]

To prevent being cut off from bank credit in times of monetary stringency, many firms obtain credit lines in advance in the form of loan commitments from banks. Banks are less willing to grant such loan commitments to smaller firms. A recent survey indicated that while 60 percent of firms with more than 50 employees had secured loan commitments, only 27 percent of smaller firms had been successful in obtaining such commitments. During a period of restrictive monetary policy, small firms without loan commitments tend to be served last or not at all. In summary, there is a fairly strong consensus that bank loans are special to a significant class of borrowers.

Can the Fed Control Bank Lending?

Even if it is universally agreed that bank loans are special, the lending or credit view breaks down if the Federal Reserve cannot influence bank lending. To the extent that banks respond to restrictive Federal Reserve actions by selling off securities and issuing nonreservable liabilities in order to maintain their supply of loans to the public, the Fed's ability to influence aggregate expenditures is reduced. Studies have shown that banks react this way, at least in part. A well-known cyclical phenomenon is that the ratio of bank loans to securities rises during business cycle expansions and declines during recessions. Systematically, when economic activity strengthens, banks accommodate the increased demand for loans by selling securities. When economic activity slows and the demand for loans falls, banks increase their holdings of securities. The rates of growth of bank loans and securities holdings during the 1973–1996 period are illustrated in Figure 25-4.

Studies also indicate that banks increase their issuance of negotiable CDs when economic activity strengthens and the Fed tightens its monetary posture. Rather than reduce loans to established customers, banks take actions to obtain funds with which to accommodate their valued customers. However, such actions taken by banks in response to restrictive policy measures do not imply that Fed policy actions fail to influence aggregate expenditures. For example, to the extent that banks must accept reduced prices in selling securities to make funds available to borrowers, they will increase their loan rates. Also, to the extent that banks are forced to pay higher interest rates to attract funds through the issue of negotiable CDs, they will boost their loan rates to customers. This in turn reduces the willingness of bank customers to borrow and spend on goods and services. Hence, while bank asset and liability responses to Federal Reserve actions may partially attenuate the effects of monetary policy actions, few would deny that monetary policy is capable of strongly influencing economic activity.

---

[16]A recent study reported that large manufacturing firms with plant and equipment worth more than $1 billion received less than 15 percent of their long-term credit from banks. Firms with capital goods valued between $100 million and $1 billion obtained about 45 percent of their long-term credit from banks. Smaller firms obtained approximately 70 percent of their long-term credit from banks. Clearly, small firms are more dependent on banks than larger firms are.

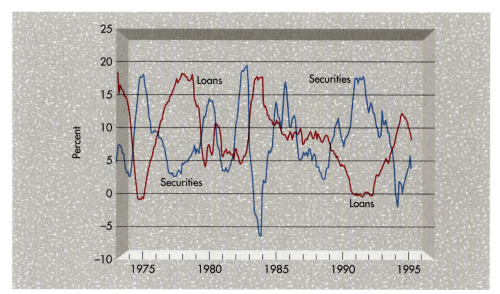

Figure 25-4   Rates of Change of Bank Loans and Securities Holdings, 1973–1996.
Loans and securities are close substitutes in bank portfolios. When economic activity
strengthens, banks sell securities and expand loans. When economic activity weakens, the
growth of bank lending slows and securities holdings increase.   *Source: Citibank Economic Database.*

SUMMARY

Monetary policy influences each of the four components of aggregate GDP expenditures—consumption, investment, government purchases, and net exports. Early Keynesians restricted monetary policy's influence to the interest rate–investment expenditures channel. Early monetarists viewed monetary policy as working by creating a disequilibrium between actual and desired money holdings. In this view, an increase in the money supply directly increased expenditures on an array of real and financial assets. However, these early monetarists failed to spell out the details of their transmission mechanism. Today, economists believe

that monetary policy also influences the economy by influencing stock prices, wealth, exchange rates, and borrowers' balance sheets. The conduct of monetary policy is complicated by the fact that the channels of monetary policy change over time. It is likely, for example, that the importance of residential construction in the monetary policy transmission process has declined in the past 15 years, while the role of the international trade balance ($X - M$) has increased. Figure 25-5 summarizes the various channels through which monetary policy is believed to influence aggregate expenditures and economic activity.

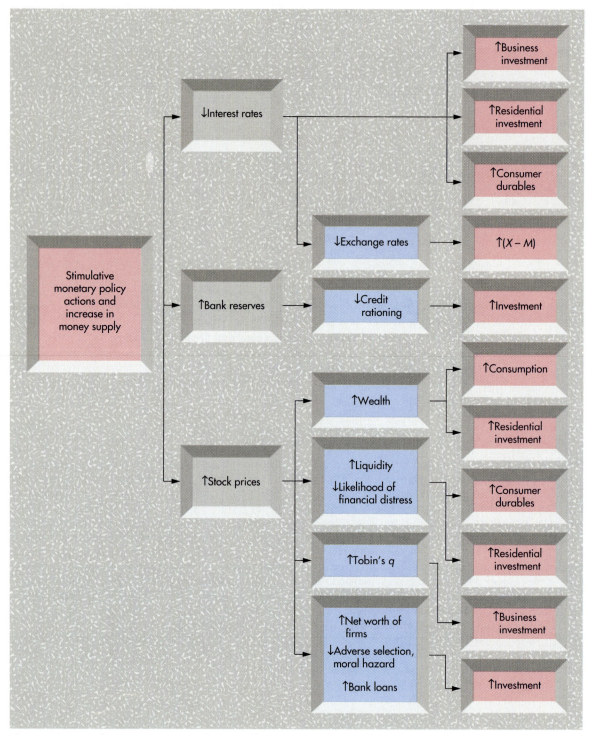

Figure 25-5 **The Transmission Mechanism of Monetary Policy.** Federal Reserve policy actions influence economic activity through many channels.

KEY TERMS

transmission mechanism
marginal efficiency of investment (MEI)
q theory

money view
credit view

STUDY QUESTIONS

1 Your company is considering an investment that will generate cash flows of $1000 per year for the next 3 years and thereafter be scrapped. The cost of the investment is $2500. If the market interest rate is 10 percent, would you make the investment? If the Fed reduces the interest rate to 7 percent, would you make the investment? Explain.

2 Following the stock market crash of October 1987, the Federal Reserve immediately engaged in large open market purchases of government securities. What was it seeking to accomplish?

3 "The stock market crash of 1929 was the principal cause of the Great Depression of the 1930s." On what foundations does this argument rest? Explain.

4 Explain all the ways you can think of in which Federal Reserve policy is capable of influencing consumption expenditures.

5 Suppose the Fed sharply reduces the money supply in an effort to combat rising inflation. List and briefly explain all the ways in which this might influence investment expenditures.

6 Why might monetary policy actions influence small firms differently than large firms? Explain.

7 Your firm is experiencing tremendous growth in sales, and a major expansion of your firm is being planned. Before your final commitment, suppose the Fed implements restrictive monetary actions. In terms of Tobin's *q* analysis, discuss your firm's alternatives and how they might affect your firm's investment decision.

8 In the early 1970s, the United States and other nations moved from a system of fixed exchange rates to a floating-rate system. How do you suppose this move affected the relative importance of the various channels of monetary transmission? How do you suppose it influenced the overall strength of monetary policy? Explain.

9 Suppose the stock market falls by 25 percent during the next year. Explain how the following components of GDP expenditures would be affected.

 a Consumer durables

 b Consumer nondurables

 c Consumer services

 d Residential investment

 e Nonresidential investment

 f Inventory investment

 g The international trade balance $(X - M)$

10 Explain how a change in interest rates initiated by the Fed affects

 a Consumer durables expenditures

 b Consumer services expenditures

 c Consumer nondurables expenditures

 d Residential investment

 e Nonresidential investment

 f Net U.S. exports $(X - M)$

SUGGESTIONS FOR ADDITIONAL READING

Much of the literature on the topics covered in this chapter is quite recent. For discussions of the channels of monetary policy and how they have changed over time, see Eileen Mauskopf, "The Transmission Channels of Monetary Policy: How They Have Changed," *Federal Reserve Bulletin,* December 1990, pp. 985–1008, and Benjamin Friedman, "The Role of Judgement and Discretion in the Conduct of Monetary Policy: Consequences of Changing Financial Markets," in Federal Reserve Bank of Kansas City, *Changing Capital Markets: Implications for Monetary Policy,* 1993, pp. 151–196. Also, the entire May–June 1995 issue of the Federal Reserve Bank of St. Louis *Review* is devoted to an analysis of the channels of monetary policy. An excellent survey on the role of credit is Ben Bernanke, "Credit in the Macroeconomy," Federal Reserve Bank of New York *Quarterly Review,* Spring 1993, pp. 50–70. Work supporting the view that credit is an important determinant of economic activity is presented in Ben Bernanke and Alan Blinder, "The Federal Funds Rate and the Channels of Monetary Transmission," *American Economic Review,* September 1992, pp. 901–921, and Anil Kashyap, Jeremy Stein, and David Wilcox, "Monetary Policy and Credit Conditions: Evidence from the Composition of External Finance," *American Economic Review,* March 1993, pp. 78–98. Evidence that money dominates bank credit as an indicator of forthcoming economic activity is presented by Stephen King, "Monetary Transmission: Through Bank Loans or Bank Liabilities?," *Journal of Money, Credit, and Banking,* August 1986, pp.

290–303, and by Christina Romer and David Romer, "New Evidence on the Monetary Transmission Mechanism," *Brookings Papers on Economic Activity,* 1990:1, pp. 149–213. See also Valerie Ramey, "How Important Is the Credit Channel in the Transmission of Monetary Policy?," *Carnegie-Rochester Conference Series on Public Policy* 39 (1993), pp. 1–45. An excellent discussion of the role of bank lending is Charles Morris and Gordon Sellon, "Bank Lending and Monetary Policy: Evidence on a Credit Channel," Federal Reserve Bank of Kansas City *Economic Review,* 2d quarter, 1995, pp. 59–75. Evidence supporting a strong effect of bank credit on small firms is demonstrated in Mark Gertler and Simon Gilchrist, "Monetary Policy, Business Cycles, and the Behavior of Small Manufacturing Firms," *Quarterly Journal of Economics,* May 1994, pp. 309–340. A good source on the credit crunch of the early 1990s is Federal Reserve Bank of New York, *Studies on Causes and Consequences of the 1989–1992 Credit Slowdown,* published in February 1994. The hypothesis that a bank capital shortage resulted in a credit crunch in 1990–1992 is advanced in Ben Bernanke and Cara Lown, "The Credit Crunch," *Brookings Papers on Economic Activity,* 1992:2, pp. 205–239. See also Ronald Johnson, "The Bank Credit Crumble," Federal Reserve Bank of New York *Quarterly Review,* Summer 1991, pp. 40–51. Finally, a collection of papers on the role of bank lending in the transmission mechanism is published in Joe Peek and Eric Rosengren, "Is Bank Lending Important for the Transmission of Monetary Policy?," Federal Reserve Bank of Boston, 1995.

■ **Monetarism and the New Classical Macroeconomics: Skeptical Views of Discretionary Monetary Policy**

Most economists today support activism in the conduct of monetary policy because they believe that output sometimes departs significantly from full employment levels and because they are confident in the effectiveness of discretionary monetary policy. However, many economists are dubious of the proposition that the Fed can contribute to economic stability through discretionary policy. In this chapter, we will examine the problems that monetary policymakers confront. And we will examine the positions of two groups of economists who believe the Federal Reserve should abandon discretionary monetary policy. These schools of thought include monetarism and new classical macroeconomics, or rational expectations macroeconomics. Some of the best-known monetarists of recent decades include Milton Friedman, Karl Brunner, Alan Meltzer, and William Poole. Prominent new classical macroeconomists include Robert Lucas, Neil Wallace, Thomas Sargent, and Robert Barro.

THE SELF-CORRECTING MECHANISM AND THE AGGREGATE DEMAND–AGGREGATE SUPPLY MODEL

In Chapter 20, we saw that the nation's equilibrium output and price level are determined by the aggregate demand (*AD*) and aggregate supply (*AS*) curves. We also pointed out that the resulting equilibrium output level frequently differs from the economy's **natural,** or **full employment, output level**—the output level that is produced when the prevailing unemployment rate is equal to the economy's natural unemployment rate.

Recall that the full employment output level is the level corresponding to the lowest rate of unemployment that can be maintained without igniting an acceleration in the nation's inflation rate. The equilibrium output level—the level toward which the economy gravitates—fluctuates as the *AS* and *AD* curves shift over time. For example, an increase in aggregate demand (a rightward shift in the *AD* curve) increases equilibrium output, as does an increase in aggregate supply (a rightward shift in the *AS* curve).

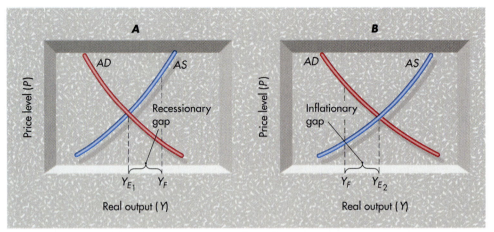

Figure 26-1   **Equilibrium Output versus Full Employment Output: Recessionary and Inflationary Gaps.** A recessionary gap occurs when equilibrium output falls short of full employment output (panel A). An inflationary gap exists when equilibrium output exceeds full employment output (panel B). Discretionary monetary policies seek to reduce or eliminate such gaps by shifting the AD curve.

Figure 26-1 summarizes these concepts. In panel A, equilibrium output (Y_{E_1}) lies below the full employment output level (Y_F). In this instance, there exists a *recessionary gap* ($Y_F - Y_{E_1}$), as aggregate demand is not strong enough to create full employment. In panel B, the equilibrium output level (Y_{E_2}) exceeds the full employment output level (Y_F), creating an *inflationary gap* ($Y_{E_2} - Y_F$); excessive aggregate demand is putting upward pressure on the nation's inflation rate.

On the face of it, the appropriate prescription for these two situations looks straightforward. When a recessionary gap prevails, why not adopt a simulative monetary and/or fiscal policy and shift AD rightward, boosting equilibrium output and getting people back to work? When the economy is overheated and an inflationary gap prevails, why not use monetary and fiscal policies to apply the brakes, shifting AD leftward, reducing equilibrium output, and arresting the inflationary pressures? In the context of Figure 26-1, the problem looks simple and unambiguous. In reality, however, it is not so simple. For one thing, economists and policy makers are uncertain about the shapes and positions of the AD and AS curves, as well as the direction and strength of the nonpolicy forces that are currently shifting the AD and AS curves. And they are uncertain about the *dynamics*—that is, the speed with which the curves shift in response to policy actions and the speed with which output responds to shifts in the AD and AS curves. Finally, economists are even uncertain about the natural unemployment rate and the output level that would generate full employment (Y_F). Given all these uncertainties, it is inevitable that the Federal Reserve will make mistakes.

Those who advocate abandonment of discretionary monetary (and fiscal) policies defend their position on two grounds. First, they believe that the economy contains powerful self-correcting mechanisms, which, in the absence of Federal Reserve efforts to stabilize the economy, will *automatically* return output to full employment levels. Second,

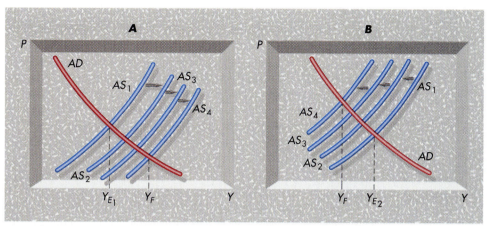

Figure 26-2   Automatic Correction of Recessionary and Inflationary Gaps. When a recessionary gap occurs (panel A), wages and other input prices fall, shifting the AS curve rightward. In the case of an inflationary gap (panel B), these input prices rise, shifting the AS curve leftward. Such forces tend automatically to eliminate output gaps, restoring Y_E to Y_F.

they believe that discretionary efforts to manage the AD curve will be ineffective, both because of the uncertainties just mentioned and for other reasons. Indeed, they believe that discretionary monetary policies are likely to destabilize output and employment and lead to significantly higher rates of inflation. We will look first at the view that stabilization policies are *unnecessary.*

The Self-Correcting Mechanism

In theory, the economy exhibits an inherent tendency toward self-correction that should automatically eliminate recessionary and inflationary gaps over time. This mechanism, which stems from wage and price level flexibility, is illustrated in Figure 26-2.

Assume, in panel A, that output is at Y_{E_1} and that the nation's unemployment rate is 7 percent—well above its natural rate of perhaps 5.5 percent. The existence of involuntary unemployment implies disequilibrium in the labor market. Because there is an excess supply of labor at the existing wage, wages will tend to fall. The decline in wages shifts the AS curve rightward, from AS_1 to AS_2, a process that will continue as long as the unemployment rate exceeds the natural rate—that is, as long as an excess supply of labor exists. As the AS curve shifts right, the price level declines, and the economy moves down the AD curve.[1] Given time and competitive labor markets, the recessionary gap will automatically self-destruct.

---

[1]Recall from our discussion in Chapter 20 the factors that contribute to the negative slope of the AD curve: Falling prices boost wealth, stimulating consumer expenditures. Lower prices are also likely to reduce interest rates, stimulating investment expenditures as well as spending on consumer durables. Finally, to the extent that lower prices make U.S. products more attractive in international markets, net exports $(X - M)$ will be stimulated. In sum, falling prices stimulate real expenditures; the process continues to boost output until Y_F is reached.

A similar process causes an inflationary gap to correct itself without assistance from monetary and/or fiscal policy. In panel *B*, equilibrium output (Y_{E_2}) exceeds full employment output (Y_F). At prevailing wages, the quantity of labor demanded exceeds the quantity supplied. The shortage of workers and materials means that wages and raw material prices will rise. As long as Y_E exceeds Y_F, these forces persistently shift the *AS* curve leftward. Over time, rising prices reduce wealth and unleash the other effects that move the economy upward to the left along the nation's *AD* curve. The equilibrium level of output finally moves to Y_F, and the inflationary gap self-destructs.

The Viability of the Self-Correcting Mechanism

Monetarists and new classical macroeconomists advocate reliance on the self-correcting mechanism. They believe that private-sector expenditures are relatively stable, so that, given a stable budgetary and monetary policy, the discrepancies between equilibrium and full employment output levels should be small. They also believe that the self-correcting mechanism is powerful. Thus these economists support measures to ensure that wages and other input prices are fully flexible in both directions, to allow full scope for the self-correcting mechanism to function effectively.

Keynesians believe that, in the short run, wages and other prices tend to be "sticky," particularly on the downside. In other words, the self-correcting mechanism may take an intolerably long time to function, particularly in the case of recessionary gaps. This stickiness is due to the existence of contracts, minimum wage statutes, and other forces that impede the downward flexibility of wages.[2] Even in the severe 1981–1982 recession, when the unemployment rate in the United States topped 10 percent, average wages did not decline. Thus, Keynesians and many other economists call for the implementation of stimulative monetary and/or fiscal measures when the unemployment rate exceeds the natural unemployment rate appreciably. And they advocate monetary and fiscal restraint when aggregate demand is excessive and the unemployment rate threatens to fall below the natural rate.

Both monetarists and new classical macroeconomists believe that, *at best,* discretionary monetary policy is likely to be ineffective. More realistically, they believe that such policies are likely to be *counterproductive;* that is, that such policies are likely to destabilize economic activity, amplifying the swings in the business cycle. Interestingly, the two camps arrive at this pessimistic conclusion via totally different routes. They believe that discretionary Federal Reserve monetary actions are doomed to failure for entirely different reasons. Monetarists believe that discretionary policies are counterproductive because of political considerations that influence Federal Reserve behavior and

---

[2]Keynesians also view the *AD* curve as being relatively steep, which reduces the efficacy of falling wages as a self-correcting mechanism. If the wealth effect (through which falling wages and prices stimulate real expenditures) is relatively weak, it takes a big decline in the price level to produce a large enough effect to return output to full employment levels. But deflation (falling prices) introduces other serious problems, for example, debt defaults and the resulting economic disruption. Hence, to a Keynesian, even if prices were perfectly flexible on the downside, the so-called automatic correction mechanism would not represent a viable mechanism for returning the economy to full employment.

because of technical problems that arise from the uncertainties discussed earlier. New classical macroeconomists attribute the alleged ineffectiveness of monetary policy to the role played by the public's expectations. In the remainder of this chapter, we will examine both the monetarist and new classical macroeconomics positions in depth.

THE ARGUMENT FOR ABANDONING DISCRETIONARY MONETARY POLICY

Monetarists typically call for the abandonment of efforts to stabilize economic activity through discretionary monetary measures. Instead, this group would substitute a "rule" which would require the Federal Reserve to ignore other considerations and devote all its attention to increasing the supply of money at a slow, constant rate, year in and year out. Milton Friedman suggests that while the exact money growth rate that is chosen is not of overriding importance, the avoidance of instability in money growth is essential.

What is the appropriate growth rate of M in a constant money growth regime? One might attempt to arrive at an answer on the basis of the *trend* behavior of the variables in the equation of exchange, $MV_Y \equiv PY$. Over a period of years, because of growth in the labor force and productivity, real output (Y) growth has averaged about 3 percent annually. Thus, if we desire a stable price level in the long run, aggregate GDP expenditures (MV_Y and PY) should grow at approximately 3 percent annually. The optimal growth of M therefore depends on the trend behavior of V_Y. Friedman argued many years ago that, over the long haul, V_Y would probably *decrease* at an average annual rate of approximately 1 percent. In that event, an annual growth rate of M of 4 percent would be required to accomplish a 3 percent annual growth rate in aggregate GDP expenditures.[3]

Friedman anticipated the possibility that the trend of velocity might depart from his estimate of a 1 percent annual rate of decline when he advanced the suggestion of a 4 percent constant rate of money growth. But he argued that velocity moves smoothly over time and emphasized that any inflation (or deflation) resulting from unexpected trend behavior in the income velocity of money (or in real output growth) would be relatively *steady* over time. What Friedman and other advocates of the fixed monetary rule abhor, and hope to eliminate via implementation of the rule, is not mild or steady inflation but economic instability of the sort exhibited by double-digit inflation on the one hand and severe recession on the other. In the monetarists' view, the U.S. economy can adjust to a steady 4 percent rate of inflation in such a way as to render it fairly harmless. Such is not the case when the economy is subjected to alternating episodes of high inflation and severe recession. A constant 5 percent inflation rate is much more desirable than a volatile

---

[3]If we convert the equation of exchange, $MV_Y \equiv PY$, into its dynamic version for examining behavior *over time,* we get $\%\Delta M + \%\Delta V_Y = \%\Delta P + \%\Delta Y$. If we set $\%\Delta P$ equal to zero in line with Friedman's objective of zero inflation and solve for the appropriate growth rate of money, we get $\%\Delta M = \%\Delta Y - \%\Delta V_Y$. Now, if we plug in Friedman's estimates of the trend growth rates of Y (3 percent) and V_Y (-1 percent), we get $\%\Delta M = 3\% - (-1\%) = 4\%$.

inflation rate ranging from 0 to 10 percent. (This is a natural implication of the proposition that many of the adverse effects of inflation will disappear if the inflation rate can be anticipated accurately.)

The Federal Reserve as a Destabilizing Influence

Monetarists believe that much of the historic instability exhibited by the U.S. economy can be directly attributed to instability in the supply of money. It follows in their view that avoidance of instability in the money supply would have prevented much of the economic instability. Hence the case for the monetary rule. Friedman believes that if the Fed had employed a constant money supply growth rule since its inception in 1914, the U.S. economy would have been spared all major episodes of inflation and depression, and some of the less severe fluctuations as well. It is alleged that, on balance, the Fed has destabilized the U.S. economy, serving as a negative factor in post–World War I U.S. economic history. This proposition is controversial.

To provide a crude test of the proposition that the Fed has destabilized the U.S. economy, we might examine the average annual growth rates of M1 and M2 in the expansion and recession phases of each of the 14 full business cycles since 1920. If the Fed has imparted a *stabilizing* influence to the economy, we might expect to observe that the supply of money has increased more rapidly during recessions than during expansions.[4] Table 26-1 shows the cyclical pattern of M1 and M2 over time. During each of the first seven expansions listed in the table, the growth rates of both M1 and M2 exceeded those in the ensuing recessions. In three instances, the *level* of M1 and M2 decreased during the recession phase of the cycle. During 12 of the 14 business cycles, the growth rate of M1 was higher in the expansions than in the ensuing recessions. The M2 results are similar: during 11 of the 14 business cycles, M2 grew more rapidly during the expansion phase than during the ensuing recession.

The difference between the money growth rates during expansions and contractions is also notable. Over the 14 cycles, M1 expanded on average more than *twice as fast* during expansions as during recessions. On average, M2 expanded 2.5 percentage points faster during expansions than recessions. Many economists consider this type of evidence to be indicative of a poor record on the Federal Reserve's part.

But because money growth is generally believed to influence aggregate expenditures, GDP, and employment with a significant time lag, the findings reported in Table 26-1 do not constitute proof that historically the Fed has destabilized economic activity.

---

[4]In order for this proposition to be valid, three assumptions are required: First, that the Fed was responsible for the observed money supply behavior; second, that the money supply exerts significant influence on economic activity; and third, that the influence is experienced with a relatively brief time lag. If the Fed is incapable of controlling the money supply, one cannot criticize (or praise) its performance. If the money supply exerts no influence over economic activity, one cannot be critical of the Fed for the behavior of the money supply even if our central bank was responsible for rapidly increasing M1 and M2 during business expansions and sharply reducing M1 and M2 during recessions. Finally, if long and variable lags occur between the time that the money supply changes and the time the economy responds, specifying the appropriate (i.e., stabilizing) cyclical behavior of M1 and M2 becomes quite difficult.

Table 26-1

Annual Rates of Growth in M1 and M2 during Business Cycles, 1920–1996

Expansion Phase			Recession Phase		
Trough to Peak	%ΔM1/Year	%ΔM2/Year	Peak to Trough	%ΔM1/Year	%ΔM2/Year
July 1921–May 1923	+5.4	+7.6	May 1923–July 1924	+2.6	+4.6
July 1924–Oct. 1926	+4.0	+5.5	Oct. 1926–Nov. 1927	+2.5	+4.8
Nov. 1927–Aug. 1929	+0.2	+0.8	Aug. 1929–Mar. 1933	−7.1	−7.5
Mar. 1933–May 1937	+12.1	+10.3	May 1937–June 1938	−3.4	−2.2
June 1938–Feb. 1945	+19.4	+16.3	Feb. 1945–Oct. 1945	+11.5	+14.9
Oct. 1945–Nov. 1948	+2.6	+3.4	Nov. 1948–Oct. 1949	−0.9	−0.5
Oct. 1949–July 1953	+4.1	+4.1	July 1953–Aug. 1954	+1.5	+3.3
Aug. 1954–July 1957	+1.7	+2.7	July 1957–Apr. 1958	+0.1	+3.7
Apr. 1958–May 1960	+1.2	+2.5	May 1960–Feb. 1961	+1.2	+6.6
Feb. 1961–Nov. 1969	+4.2	+7.3	Nov. 1969–Nov. 1970	+5.0	+6.0
Nov. 1970–Nov. 1973	+6.9	+11.1	Nov. 1973–Apr. 1975	+4.1	+7.1
Apr. 1975–Jan. 1980	+7.3	+10.4	Jan. 1980–July 1980	+3.7	+8.9
July 1980–July 1981	+8.4	+9.2	July 1981–Nov. 1982	+7.9	+9.5
Nov. 1982–June 1990	+7.3	+7.2	June 1990–Mar. 1991	+4.2	+3.8
Average	+6.1	+7.0	Average	+2.4	+4.5

Sources: Calculated from data in *Federal Reserve Bulletin*, various issues, and Milton Friedman and Anna J. Schwartz, *A Monetary History of the United States, 1867–1960* (Princeton, N.J.: Princeton University Press, 1963), Appendix A-1. Business cycle turning points are National Bureau of Economic Research classifications.

An average of numerous empirical estimates of the lag suggests that the time lag may be approximately 1 year. Figure 26-3 illustrates the relationship between the growth rate of M1, lagged 1 year, and the nation's output gap—that is, the difference between actual real GDP and trend real GDP, expressed as a percentage of trend real GDP. In the figure, a positive output gap occurs when real GDP exceeds trend GDP. A negative gap prevails in periods of depressed economic activity—that is, when output falls below trend.

Assuming that a 1-year lag correctly captures the dynamics of the money supply–GDP expenditures relationship, a *stabilizing* monetary policy would be one in which the two series in the figure are mirror images of each other. The (lagged) money growth rate would accelerate when output was below trend, reaching a peak when the output gap was largest. It would slow when output exceeded trend, reaching a trough when this negative output gap was largest. A *destabilizing* monetary policy would be one in which the two series tend to move together over time—that is, in parallel.

Note in the figure that the series seem to fit the latter description through much of the 1960s and 1970s. This pattern suggests that monetary policy may have destabilized economic activity during that period. But note the change in the pattern after the early 1980s. The Fed accelerated money growth to combat the huge recessionary gap of

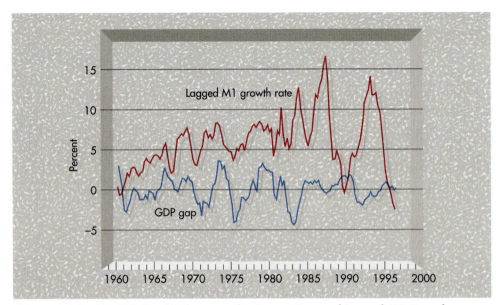

Figure 26-3   The Relationship between the Output Gap and Lagged M1 Growth, 1960–1996. Before the 1980s, money growth appears to have destabilized output, stimulating GDP when it was strong and retarding it when it was weak. After 1980, the Fed's performance looks much better.   *Source:* Data from *Citibank Economic Database.*

1982–1983 (although it was somewhat late in doing so). It did the same thing to avert a recession in 1986. In the late 1980s, the Fed slowed money growth dramatically to head off incipient inflation, then accelerated it to minimize the severity and duration of the 1990–1991 recession. In the mid-1990s, the Fed again slowed money growth as the economy moved into the fourth and fifth years of an economic expansion. Thus the figure suggests a marked improvement in the Fed's performance over the past 15 years relative to that of earlier times.

Monetarists remain convinced of the Fed's destabilizing influence, however. According to advocates of the constant money growth rule, two factors have contributed to the destabilizing character of Fed policy. One is the Fed's propensity to change priorities from time to time in response to political forces and other factors. The other involves the Fed's inability to achieve a given goal due to uncertainty about the structure of the economy, to the long and variable lags in monetary policy, and to shortcomings in the art of economic forecasting. We will examine both of these questions.

The Federal Reserve's Tendency to Change Objectives

In Friedman's and other monetarists' view, the Federal Reserve really has only *one legitimate objective:* to attempt to stabilize aggregate expenditures on goods and services. Throughout its history, however, the Fed has often been diverted from that objective.

For example, the Fed implemented restrictive policy measures in 1929 to counter excessive stock market speculation even though the aggregate demand for goods and services was not excessive and prices were stable. In the early 1930s, the Fed seemed to ignore such important domestic considerations as the double-digit unemployment rate, instead conducting policy largely in response to international pressures such as those touched off by England's abandonment of the gold standard in 1931.[5] During the bond-pegging era of 1942–1951, the Fed abdicated its control over the money supply in order to hold down interest rates and assist the U.S. Treasury in its debt-funding efforts. The resulting expansion of the money supply was highly inflationary. The same basic phenomenon occurred on a much smaller scale during the Vietnam War buildup from 1965–1968. In the monetarists' view, all these examples serve to indicate that the Fed tends to forget its primary responsibility of stabilizing aggregate expenditures. Implementation of the constant money growth rule would alleviate the problems caused by the Fed's inability to remember its chief function and its propensity to be influenced by political considerations.

Lags of Monetary Policy

The other major problem that confronts monetary policymakers is the rather long and variable lags which characterize the economy's response to policy changes. The problem is compounded by the state of the economic forecasting art, which, in the monetarists' view, is so poor that it poses major problems for the conduct of effective countercyclical monetary (and fiscal) policies. Three lags complicate the active use of monetary and fiscal policy: the recognition lag, the implementation lag, and the impact lag.

The Recognition Lag

The **recognition lag** encompasses the time that elapses between the point at which policy actions would ideally have been implemented (discovered only with hindsight) and the point at which policy-making officials become aware of the need for action. Given the fact that key economic data (on industrial production, GDP, and so forth) become available only periodically rather than continuously, together with the imperfect and conflicting nature of our economic indicators, such a lag is inevitable.

The Implementation Lag

The **implementation lag** is defined as the time that elapses between the date on which a need for a policy change is recognized and the date on which the policy is implemented. In the case of monetary policy, this lag is normally quite brief, as the Federal Open Market Committee meets approximately every 6 weeks for decision-making purposes and emergency meetings may be called if needed. The chairman of the Board of Governors is sometimes given the authority to make inter-meeting adjustments in monetary policy as new developments arise. Monetary policy actions are therefore capable of quick implementation.

---

[5]In September and October 1931, the Federal Reserve Bank of New York raised the discount rate by 2 full percentage points in response to England's decision to suspend the convertibility of foreign currencies into gold. At the time of this massive discount rate increase, the U.S. unemployment rate stood at more than 15 percent (see Chapter 16).

In this aspect, monetary policy is considered far superior to fiscal policy. The implementation lag of fiscal policy tends to be considerably longer because congressional action and serious political obstacles are often involved.[6]

The Impact Lag

The **impact lag** is defined as the time that elapses between the point at which policy action is implemented and the point at which it begins to influence GDP. Monetary policy influences GDP with a significant lag because, in order to influence GDP, it must first influence such variables as interest rates and wealth. Business investment spending, housing construction, and state and local government spending respond to interest rate changes with a lag. Consumer demand responds to changes in wealth and interest rates with a lag. And aggregate demand is likely to influence production (and GDP) with a slight lag. Monetarists emphasize the point that monetary policy impinges on GDP with a rather *long* and fairly *variable* lag. The length of this lag has been estimated at anywhere from 6 to 24 months.[7]

An Example of Monetary Policy Lags

Let us illustrate the problems posed by the three lags for the effective use of counter-cyclical monetary and fiscal policies. Consider the case of the anti-recession policy illustrated in Figure 26-4. In the figure, the economy peaks at time t_0, when a recession begins. *In retrospect,* we can see that an economic stimulus would have been helpful at that time.[8] However, owing to the conflicting evidence of the various indicators and the fact that GDP figures are tabulated only quarterly, the need for a stimulus does not become firmly established until time t_1. The time elapsed between t_0 and t_1 constitutes the recognition lag.

Unfortunately, stimulative policy measures may not be instituted immediately at time t_1. Differing philosophies concerning the propriety of economic intervention, political considerations, or even sheer bureaucratic inertia may postpone the implementation of stimulative policies until time t_2.[9] The time elapsed between t_1 and t_2 constitutes the implementation lag. Note that the economy is approaching the trough of the business cycle when stimulative policy measures are finally implemented.

---

[6]A good example of the implementation lag in fiscal policy occurred during the Vietnam War. In late 1965, President Lyndon B. Johnson was informed by his economic advisors that a general tax hike was needed to counter the inflationary consequences of expanded military expenditures. Partly because of the looming 1966 congressional elections, President Johnson deferred requesting the tax legislation until January 1967. Congress then deferred passing the legislation until July 1968. The implementation lag in this case was nearly 3 years.

[7]See the references to literature in the "Suggestions for Additional Reading" at the end of this chapter.

[8]Because of the impact lag, stimulative policies would ideally be implemented even *before* t_0. That would require that the Fed implement actions on the basis of economic forecasts rather than actual economic phenomena. Such a move could prove highly unpopular, because it might involve implementation of restrictive policy actions during a period of fairly high unemployment—in the middle phase of an expansion, for example.

[9]Political biases may result in different lengths of implementation lags in expansions and contractions. During a recession, the short-run political implications of expansionary fiscal and monetary actions are conducive to their implementation; the implications of tax hikes and monetary restraint during an expansion are not. One might therefore guess that implementation lags tend to be shorter on average for expansionary measures than for restrictive actions. The implementation lag associated with the tax cut of 1981, for example, was much shorter than the implementation lag associated with the tax increase of 1968.

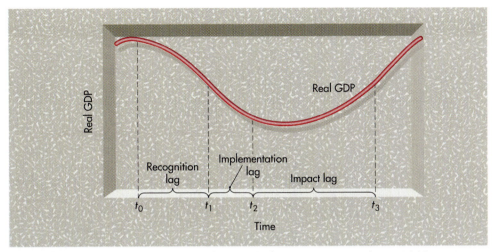

Figure 26-4 Monetary and Fiscal Policy Lags. Ideally, monetary policy would boost output immediately when it is deficient and reduce output immediately when it becomes excessive. In reality, the existence of time lags makes such an ideal difficult or impossible to achieve.

By the time the stimulative policy actions begin to influence GDP at time t_3, considerably more time has passed. This impact lag is represented in the figure as the length of time between t_2 and t_3. Note that the expansionary policies begin to take effect at a time when the cyclical trough is past history and has given way to a solid economic expansion. At this point (t_3), the economy is gathering plenty of momentum on its own and the need for additional stimulus is dubious. Further stimulus to the economy at time t_3 will merely accelerate the pace of the economic advance, perhaps cause a rapid climb to capacity output, and trigger inflationary bottlenecks and an ensuing recession. In this way, the monetary policy stimulus may actually endanger the life of the economic expansion. Good intentions may produce perverse policy!

We can now see the problems posed for the effective use of countercyclical monetary (and fiscal) policies. There is a genuine possibility that discretionary policies may end up being *procyclical* instead of *countercyclical*. The longer and especially the *more variable* the policy lags, the greater are the problems involved in trying to "fine-tune" the economy. Given the fact that the median post–World War II recession has lasted only 11 months and the median expansion only 40 months, even a modest error in the timing of monetary policy could destabilize the economy.

Monetarists conclude that the problems are sufficiently formidable that, on average, the use of a monetary rule would significantly outperform human discretion in the conduct of monetary policy. They believe such a rule would be superior even if the Federal Reserve learned to correct its alleged tendency to be sidetracked from its purpose of providing overall economic stability. And monetarists believe that discretionary fiscal policy should be abandoned anyway, because of their view that fiscal actions have little effect on aggregate demand and economic activity.

THE DEBATE OVER THE FIXED MONEY GROWTH RULE

We have considered the monetarist claim that discretionary policy actions are destabilizing and should be abandoned. We will now examine the pros and cons of the proposed constant money growth rule.

Arguments for a Fixed Money Growth Rule

Several arguments can be made for the adoption of a fixed rate of growth of the money supply. They include elimination of the Fed's alleged adverse influence, creation of an improved economic climate, reduced government intervention in economic affairs, and ending the Fed's role as a political scapegoat. We will briefly look at each argument.

Elimination of a Destabilizing Agent

In the monetarists' view, Federal Reserve policy has contributed to the history of instability in the U.S. economy. This point is, however, subject to dispute. Those who believe it are logically led to the advocacy of the fixed money growth rule, provided that they believe the Federal Reserve cannot improve on its past performance.

A Climate of Confidence

Proponents of a fixed money growth rule claim it would promote a climate of confidence and stability, thereby facilitating long-term planning and investment decisions. Friedman has demonstrated that all the major inflations in U.S. history have been associated with relatively rapid monetary expansion. Likewise, all the severe cyclical contractions have been accompanied by either an absolute contraction in the money supply or a significant slowdown in its rate of growth. Adoption of the fixed money growth rule would eliminate the specter of volatility in the money supply. In doing so, it might lead business executives to anticipate a more stable economic future, devoid of episodes of double-digit inflation and severe recession. Business firms, foreseeing only relatively mild "peaks and valleys," might stabilize their investment expenditures, increasing the stability of the economy as a whole.

The key issue here is whether economic agents believe that changes in the *supply* of money are more important sources of instability than are changes in the *demand* for money (and V_Y). If they believe that instability in the demand for money (and in velocity) is less damaging than are changes in the money supply, the case for the monetary rule is enhanced.[10] On the historical instability of velocity, see Exhibit 26-1.

A Reduced Role for Government

Proponents allege that adoption of the fixed money growth rule would result in less government intervention in economic affairs. In the view of its advocates, adoption of the monetary rule would reduce the pressure on the executive and legislative branches

---

[10]Friedman and Schwartz point out that in 78 out of 91 years, the annual change in income velocity was less than 10 percent. The authors seem to regard this as a point in favor of monetarism. However, given a 4 percent constant growth rate of *M*, one must note that a 10 percent rise or fall in V_Y is likely to be associated with an 8 to 12 percent inflation rate on the one hand and a rather severe recession on the other hand. See *A Monetary History of the United States, 1867–1960,* p. 682.

EXHIBIT 26-1

The Lucas Critique, Velocity Behavior, and the Constant Money Growth Rule

The velocity of money varies significantly from year to year. The accompanying figure shows the 12-month rates of change in M1 and M2 velocity in the United States in the period after 1960. Note that changes in M1 velocity have ranged from approximately +8 percent to −11 percent. Changes in M2 velocity have ranged from +7 percent to −6 percent.

A critic of the constant money growth proposal might be tempted to use the data in the graph as ammunition to shoot down the proposal. The M1 graph suggests that, given a constant 4 percent money growth (M1) regime, the range of fluctuation in MV_Y (nominal GDP) would have been from +12 percent to −7 percent. At the positive extreme, that would have resulted in severe inflation; at the negative extreme, in extremely deep recession. Using M2 as the measure of money to be fixed at 4 percent annual growth, the implied range of nominal GDP growth runs from +11 percent to −2 percent—a result only slightly less troublesome. On the surface, historical experience seems to suggest that a constant money growth rule would yield unsatisfactory results.

In a famous 1976 article (see "Suggestions for Additional Reading" at the end of this chapter), Robert Lucas warned economists against drawing conclusions from past data if the policy regime in place has changed. If a constant money growth regime had been in place years ago, the behavior of velocity would likely have been significantly different. Monetarists would argue that velocity would have been far more stable: the inflation of the 1970s would have been far less severe, and the 1973–1975 and 1981–1982 recessions would have been tempered. Interest rates would have been more stable, and uncertainty would have diminished. Indeed, many of the variables that influence velocity might have been more stable. In short, the Lucas critique warns that one should be very cautious in using the past experience of velocity to make a case for rejecting the fixed money growth rule.

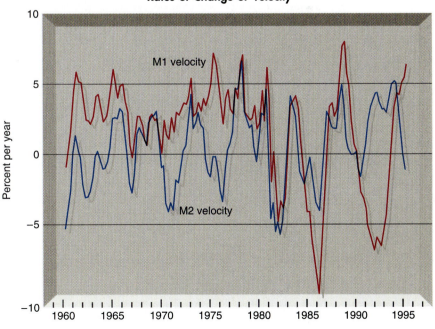

Rates of Change of Velocity

of government to implement changes in federal taxes and expenditures to influence the economy. This follows from the presumption that adoption of the monetary rule would stabilize the economy and thereby render the active use of fiscal policy unnecessary. If the implementation of the fixed money growth rule would indeed eliminate episodes of severe inflation and deep recession, the role of several government agencies could be reduced. For example, if bank failures were reduced because of a more stable economy, the authority and power of the banking regulatory agencies might be reduced. In short, if the use of the constant money growth rule would in fact improve our overall economic performance, the government bureaucracy might be trimmed back and economic freedom enhanced. For this reason, political conservatives tend to be attracted to the proposal.

Elimination of Political Scape-goating

Implementation of the rule might also improve budgetary policy, ending the scapegoat role in which the Fed is sometimes cast by those responsible for the budget. When the economy turns sour, those in charge of the federal government's budget have a tendency to point the finger at the Federal Reserve. Often the finger should in fact be pointed at Congress and the president.

A good example of this phenomenon occurred in the late 1960s, the years of the Vietnam War military buildup. Large budget deficits were incurred in response to increased military spending unaccompanied by a tax hike—a hike recommended by independent economic advisors. Unemployment declined below 4 percent, inflation began to accelerate, and the combination of heavy government borrowing and increased inflationary expectations resulted in a persistent bidding up of market interest rates. The Fed could have maintained interest rates at low, pre-Vietnam levels at least temporarily, through heavy open market security purchases. However, such measures would have caused excessive monetary expansion, adding to the mounting inflationary pressures. The Fed did in fact allow the money supply to expand at an above-normal rate, though not fast enough to prevent a sharp upsurge in interest rates. As a result, the housing market plummeted and many small businesses and local governments found borrowing difficult.

As complaints from the public escalated, many Washington politicians blamed the Federal Reserve for being overly restrictive in its credit policies. In reality, the upward pressure on interest rates stemmed from the Vietnam expenditures and the budget deficits. The rising budget deficits, incurred during a period of full employment and excessive aggregate demand for goods and services, placed the Fed in an impossible situation. Suppose the Fed had pursued an "easy money" policy and purchased much of the new debt issued by the Treasury during 1965–1968. The resulting rapid monetary expansion, while temporarily holding down interest rates, would have contributed considerably to the inflationary forces already in place. Congress would probably then have blamed the Fed for the massive inflation. Any way you look at it, the Fed comes out the villain!

What does all this have to do with the proposal for a monetary rule? If the Fed were committed in advance to constant money supply growth and the public and Congress were aware of it, there would be no possibility of politicians leaning on the Fed as a scapegoat. Because Congress would be more accountable, it would have more incentive to put its budgetary house in order. Hypothetically, if the 4 percent money supply growth rule had been in effect during 1965–1968, the public would have seen more clearly that the budgetary process, not the Fed, was the source of the escalating inflation and the associated increase in interest rates. In that event, Congress might have looked more favorably on the recommended tax hike, which was clearly needed several years before 1968.

Arguments Against a Fixed Money Growth Rule

Those who defend the active use of monetary policy to combat the adverse forces of the business cycle do not accept the monetarist critique of the Fed. They argue that the Fed's policy actions contribute to economic stability and that it is necessary for the Fed to have multiple objectives. They point out that the velocity of money is unstable and that implementing a fixed money growth rule is itself a discretionary policy.

The Fed as a Contributor to Economic Stability

Many students of the subject take issue with the charge that the Federal Reserve has been a destabilizing influence, particularly in recent decades. Admittedly, the Fed has made numerous mistakes. However, supporters of the Fed believe that, on balance, it has been a beneficial force. In their view, human discretion is capable of outperforming the fixed money growth rule. And even if the Fed has been a destabilizing factor in the past, one could argue that improvements in the quality of economic data, forecasting techniques, and monetary theory, as well as the benefit gained from the "learning experience," should allow the Fed to improve upon its past performance. Indeed, one can argue that the Fed's performance has improved appreciably over time. Figure 26-5

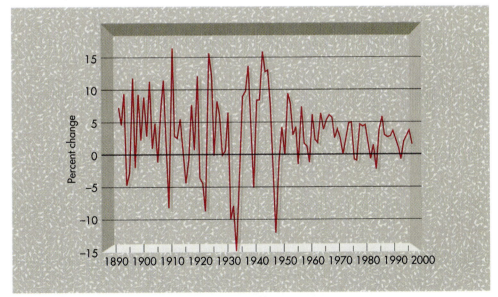

Figure 26-5   Annual Rate of Change in Real GDP, 1890–1995. The rate of growth in real GDP fluctuates from year to year. In the period after World War II, the annual rate of output growth became more stable and economic contractions less severe. *Source: Historical Statistics of the United States* and *Citibank Economic Database.*

shows the annual rates of change in real GDP since 1890. The figure suggests that fluctuations in real output have been smaller since Congress created the Federal Reserve System (1914). This is particularly true for the period after World War II. A cursory glance at the figure indicates that since the early 1950s, when the Federal Reserve first began to employ discretionary monetary policy actively, economic stability has increased. Of course, the apparent increase in stability may well have been the result of other factors.[11] However, the evidence in the figure does raise questions about the monetarist characterization of the Fed as a perverse force that has increased economic instability in the United States.

Instability of Velocity

Most economists are wary of a constant money growth rule. If income velocity (V_Y) and real output (Y) cannot be projected smoothly into the future, one cannot specify the appropriate growth rate of money in advance. Suppose that V_Y declines by 5 percent in a given year while aggregate productive capacity increases by 3 percent. In that event, a 4 percent prescribed increase in M would produce a 1 percent contraction in aggregate GDP expenditures—that is, in MV_Y and PY. Given the existence of downwardly rigid wages and prices, output would fall and unemployment would increase considerably. Discretionary monetary policy offers the possibility of providing the above-normal expansion in the money supply which is needed in this instance. In 1986, when M1 velocity fell by approximately 10 percent, the Fed stepped in and aggressively accelerated the rate of money growth, averting a serious economic downturn.

Also, the inability to arrive at a clear consensus regarding the appropriate measure of money raises questions. The various monetary aggregates are not scalar multiples of one another. A 3 percent growth rate in M1 might be consistent with a 6 percent or zero growth rate in a broader measure of money, such as M2 or M3. It is conceivable that liquid assets not currently included in our measures of money may become much more important in the future, further clouding the definition of the money supply. Tobin makes the point effectively:

Sometimes Friedman and his followers seem to be saying: "We don't know what money is, but whatever it is, its stock should grow steadily at 3 or 4 percent per year."[12]

---

[11]The view that the U.S. economy has become more stable since World War II has been challenged in a series of papers by Christina Romer (see "Suggestions for Additional Reading"). Romer argues that faulty construction of the early GDP and industrial production series overstates the volatility of economic activity before 1945. If it *is* true that the economy has become more stable, there are several potential explanations that have nothing to do with monetary policy. For example, the economy's built-in stabilizers have increased in power since the 1930s because of a larger (relatively stable) government sector, higher income tax rates, and other forces. Higher tax rates effectively reduce the income multiplier, resulting in smaller changes in equilibrium output for any shift in expenditures. Also, as the (relatively stable) service sector of the U.S. economy has increased relative to the (more unstable) manufacturing, agricultural, and mining sectors, overall economic stability has tended to improve. On the causes of increased economic stability in the post–World War II era, see the work by Robert Gordon cited in the "Suggestions for Additional Reading" at the end of this chapter.

[12]James Tobin, "The Monetary Interpretation of History," *American Economic Review,* June 1965, p. 647.

The Fixed Money Growth Rule as a Discretionary Policy

Some economists point out that setting a rule calling for a precise, constant money growth rate is itself a powerful act of discretion. If humans are so fallible that their efforts to stabilize the economy via discretionary policy generally have perverse consequences, how can we hope to devise one rigid, all-encompassing rule to be adhered to hereafter? Paul Samuelson, who (like Friedman) is the recipient of the Nobel Prize in economics, has observed that

when men set up a definitive mechanism which is to run forever afterward by itself, that involves a single act of discretion which transcends, in both its arrogance and its capacity for potential harm, any repeated acts of foolish discretion that can be imagined.[13]

When viewed in this light, the proposal for a constant money growth rule seems hard to defend. In fairness to Friedman, however, it must again be stressed that his basic contention is not that the merit of the monetary rule proposal lies in a claim that it specifies a single precise, appropriate growth rate for the money supply. Friedman's position is that the stability of the money supply growth rate, whether it be 2 percent, 4 percent, or 6 percent, is crucial. Friedman believes that 6 years of 4 percent monetary growth are to be preferred over 3 years of no growth and 3 years of 8 percent growth.

The Legitimacy of Multiple Objectives

Advocates of discretionary monetary policy argue that, in the real world, the Fed must sometimes pursue more than one objective. Besides its primary goal of contributing to the stability of aggregate expenditures and output, the Fed does have to concern itself with other matters. Some economists feel that the Fed should attempt to react to money market pressures. That implies that the Fed should purchase significant quantities of government securities in times of heavy Treasury borrowing and liquidate many of those acquisitions in times of light Treasury borrowing. Strict adherence to a fixed money growth rule would prevent the Federal Reserve from responding to money market pressures as well as to periodic financial crises. For example, when the stock market plummeted more than 20 percent in October 1987, the Fed pumped liquidity into the financial system and successfully headed off major ripple effects. A rigid money growth rule would handcuff the Fed, preventing such discretionary actions in time of crisis.

THE CHALLENGE OF RATIONAL EXPECTATIONS MACROECONOMICS

In combining the flexible-price, market-clearing tenets of classical economics with certain fairly strong assumptions about the way in which economic agents form expectations, disciples of **new classical macroeconomics,** or **rational expectations macroeconomics (REM)** arrive at the same conclusion about policy activism as do monetarists—that is,

---

[13]Paul Samuelson, "Reflections on Central Banking," in Joseph Stiglitz, ed., *The Collected Scientific Papers of Paul Samuelson* (Cambridge, Mass.: MIT Press, 1966), Vol. 2, p. 1362.

because discretionary monetary policies are likely to be ineffective at best, such policies should be replaced with strict monetary rules.

Like monetarists, members of this group believe the economy has a powerful self-correcting mechanism. They believe that deviations from the natural, or full employment, output level set up forces which eventually return the economy to full employment. Like monetarists, they emphasize the likelihood that discretionary policies will cause instability. Unlike monetarism, however, REM implies that *systematic* and *predictable* changes in the money supply have *no impact* on real output and employment. Only surprise or unanticipated changes in the money supply can influence these important real variables. Thus, they conclude that discretionary monetary policy is ineffective and probably counterproductive—but for a different reason from the monetarists'. Let's take a closer look at the reasoning behind their conclusion.

Assumptions of Rational Expectations Macroeconomics

A fundamental building block of REM is the assumption that economic agents (both individuals and firms) have **rational expectations.** In other words, economic agents take into account *all available information* and use it *efficiently* in forming their expectations. That is not to say that agents have perfect foresight or that they always make accurate forecasts. Their forecasts are frequently incorrect. However, they do not make *systematic* mistakes—continually underestimating inflation, for example. In rational expectations, forecast errors are assumed to be *random*—sometimes too low, sometimes too high—because people learn from past mistakes and take steps to avoid repeating them.

This assumption departs from earlier economic analysis and research, in which agents were assumed to exhibit **adaptive expectations**—that is, to change their expectations gradually in response to recent phenomena. For example, if expectations are formed adaptively, economic agents will consistently underestimate inflation in periods in which it is rising and consistently overestimate inflation in periods in which it is falling.

Proponents of REM assume that economic agents are quite sophisticated in economic matters. They assume that individuals and firms understand the structure and workings of the economy—for example, that they are aware of the linkage among money growth, inflation, and nominal interest rates. They know that an acceleration of money growth will boost inflation and lead to higher interest rates. If a **political business cycle**—a tendency for the economy to be stimulated as elections approach—exists, economic agents are aware of it, too. And they know about the threshold inflation and unemployment rates that will trigger compensatory Federal Reserve actions. Essentially, these agents act as if they are tuned in to a state-of-the-art economic model.

Suppose the inflation rate has been declining slowly over the past 5 years. Given *adaptive expectations,* agents will slowly revise their expectations of future inflation downward in response to the decline in actual inflation. If *rational expectations* prevail, agents will basically ignore the recent trend in inflation. Instead, they will make their forecast based on the recent and current behavior of variables incorporated into a modern model of inflation. In other words, they will look at the recent behavior of the monetary aggregates, government expenditures, exchange rates, oil prices, wage rates, and so forth.

If these variables indicate that inflation will rise, economic agents will revise their forecasts of inflation upward in spite of the fact that it has recently been trending downward.

Supporters of REM also believe that product and resource markets are quite competitive. They believe that the prices of resources (including wages—the price of labor) change quickly in response to changes in supply and demand. Economic agents quickly process new information. This leads to rapid shifts in supply and demand curves, causing wages and prices to respond quickly. Markets clear quickly and are almost continuously in equilibrium.

Policy Implications of Rational Expectations Macroeconomics

REM has important implications for the efficacy of countercyclical monetary and fiscal policy. Figure 26-6 illustrates those implications. Assume that output is Y_{E_1}, the intersection of AD_1 and AS_1. This output is significantly lower than the full employment output level, Y_F, which means that the nation's unemployment rate exceeds the natural rate of unemployment. Because a recessionary gap exists, Keynesians and other policy activists advocate stimulative actions to boost the AD curve to AD_2. The economy would move to point B in the figure, and equilibrium output would rise to the full employment level. In

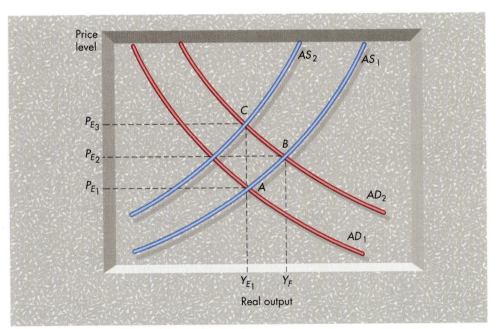

Figure 26-6   Impact of an Anticipated Policy Stimulus on Output and Employment. Proponents of policy activism believe that a monetary stimulus can boost the AD curve and move the economy from point A to point B. However, if the policy stimulus is fully anticipated, the AS curve shifts leftward, the economy moves to point C, and the potential effect of the stimulus on output is nullified

this case, discretionary monetary policy successfully stimulates real output and reduces the unemployment rate, though the nation's price level increases from P_{E_1} to P_{E_2}.

According to REM, however, the economy will end up at point *B* in the figure *only* if the public is caught totally by surprise by the policy stimulus. Suppose instead that economic agents can foresee the stimulus. In that case, wage demands will be higher than they would otherwise be, and the increase in wages will shift the *AS* curve leftward, to AS_2. If the policy stimulus is fully anticipated, the economy will end up at point *C* in the figure. Note in this case that equilibrium output remains at Y_{E_1}, while the price level increases to P_{E_3}. The stimulative monetary policy has increased the price level but left real output and employment unchanged. The recessionary gap is not eliminated by stimulative policies.

Thus, a corollary of REM is the **policy ineffectiveness theorem,** which states that anticipated monetary and fiscal policy actions will have no effect on real variables such as output and employment. Such actions affect the price level but not real economic variables. Only *unanticipated* policy actions can influence output and employment. In a discretionary regime, economic agents will inevitably learn to anticipate actions of the Federal Reserve. In times of recession, they will correctly expect stimulative monetary policy actions. Because only unanticipated policies have real effects, and because the public inevitably learns to anticipate policies, discretionary monetary policy is inherently ineffective. It should therefore be abandoned and replaced with a monetary rule.

If the policy ineffectiveness theorem is valid, it yields both good and bad news. The bad news, as indicated, is that discretionary monetary and fiscal policies do not systematically influence output. The good news is that a *credible* anti-inflation program can lead the economy out of a period of high inflation without an accompanying loss of output and increase in unemployment.

Suppose inflation has become entrenched in the 6 to 8 percent range in recent years and the Fed is determined to eradicate it. The Fed announces that it will immediately reduce the growth rates of M1 and M2 from the recent 6 to 10 percent range to zero and will maintain a zero rate of money growth over the next 5 years. To the extent that the public is convinced the Fed means business, wage hikes will be dramatically curtailed or even terminated because of the anticipated monetary stringency, and the *AS* curve will shift rightward as wage demands are sharply reduced. This means that the output loss associated with the downward shift in the *AD* curve (induced by monetary stringency) will be reduced dramatically. Under strong assumptions about total credibility surrounding the policy, rational expectations, and instantaneous clearing of labor and product markets, inflation is eliminated without *any* cost in the form of lower output or higher unemployment. The policy ineffectiveness theorem then becomes a blessing rather than a curse! See, however, Exhibit 26-2.

Implications for the Phillips Curve

The policy ineffectiveness theorem is an interesting idea. However, most economists believe there is a short-run trade-off between inflation and unemployment. That is, most economists believe that the Federal Reserve can reduce unemployment for a period if it

EXHIBIT 26-2

The "Monetarist Experiment" of 1979–1982: A Fair Test of REM?

One of the implications of rational expectations macroeconomics (REM) is that if the intentions of the monetary authorities are clearly and *credibly* conveyed to the public, their policy will have no effect on real output, employment, and unemployment. This implication becomes a blessing in the event the Federal Reserve desires to eradicate inflation.

In the period beginning in the mid-1960s and running through the 1970s, the U.S. inflation rate ratcheted higher and higher. From an annual inflation rate of less than 2 percent in the first half of the 1960s, the rate escalated to 12 percent by summer 1979. In August 1979, President Jimmy Carter appointed Paul Volcker chairman of the Board of Governors of the Federal Reserve System. Approximately 6 weeks later, in a clear and dramatic effort to reduce the public's inflation expectations, the Fed announced a major change in the way it would conduct monetary policy in the future. It announced that it would no longer seek to maintain short-term interest rates within a narrow target range. Instead, it would target the growth of the monetary aggregates (M1 and M2) at rates significantly lower than those that had prevailed in recent years. The Fed's objective in announcing the policy change was to reduce inflation expectations, slow the resulting leftward shift of the *AS* curve, and reduce the cost of bringing down inflation. The announcement itself was testimony to the increased influence of rational expectations theory on the conduct of monetary policy.

Rational expectations theory asserts that if the public correctly anticipates a severe tightening of monetary policy, the ensuing downward shift in the *AD* curve engineered by the Fed can knock out inflation without knocking out jobs. Critics of the theory claim that Volcker's announcement provides a clear test of the validity of the proposition that anticipated policies have no effect on output and employment. During the 3-year period of "the monetarist experiment" (October 1979 to August 1982), the U.S. inflation rate came down sharply, as predicted by the theory. But during those years the nation also experienced two back-to-back recessions. A severe reduction in industrial production and real GDP occurred in 1981–1982. The unemployment rate reached double-digit levels and did not fall below 7 percent again until 1986. Clearly, the short-run Phillips curve is not vertical. Critics of rational expectations theory argue that this historical experience indicates that anticipated as well as unanticipated policies affect output and unemployment. In this episode, a clearly announced disinflation policy separated some 6 million Americans from their jobs.

Supporters of rational expectations macroeconomics deny that the public correctly anticipated the severity of the Federal Reserve's disinflation policy. They think the public underestimated the Fed's resolve. After years of accommodative monetary policy, the public simply was not convinced that the Fed meant business. For Fed policy to gain true credibility, the nation would perhaps have to return to a gold standard, or the Fed would have to adopt a constant money growth rule.

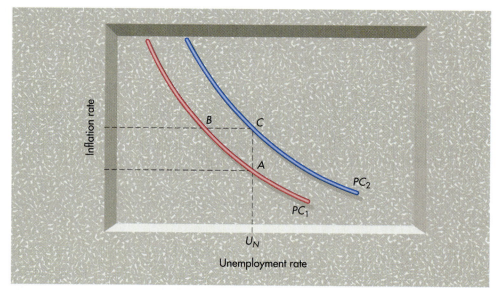

Figure 26-7 **The Short-Run Phillips Curve.** Most economists believe there is a short-run trade-off between inflation and unemployment and that a stimulative economic policy boosts inflation, reduces real wages, and increases employment. In an REM world, however, because the policy is fully anticipated, real wages do not fall and output and employment do not increase. The short-run Phillips curve is then vertical, and there is no short-run trade-off.

is willing to accept an increase in inflation. This notion is encompassed in the **Phillips curve,** the graph illustrating the alleged inverse relationship between a nation's inflation rate and its unemployment rate. The Phillips curve is illustrated in Figure 26-7.

Before the rational expectations revolution of the 1970s, almost no one disputed the assertion that the Fed could routinely reduce unemployment for a period of time through stimulative monetary actions if it were willing to accept a higher rate of inflation. Most economists believed that the Fed could move us from A to B in the figure through stimulative policy actions. Given stimulative policies, the inflation rate would tend to rise, reducing real wages, boosting profits, and inducing firms to step up employment. Hence, conventional analysis suggested a negatively sloped short-run Phillips curve.

In a strong-version REM world, there is no trade-off between inflation and unemployment, even in the short run. In other words, the short-run Phillips curve is vertical. Suppose we are initially at point A in the figure, with an unemployment rate of U_N. The Fed implements stimulative actions, and the inflation rate rises. However, because economic agents anticipate the Fed's actions, wages immediately accelerate. Because the increase in price level inflation is accompanied by a similar increase in wage inflation, real wages fail to decline. Output and employment fail to increase, and the unemployment rate remains constant at U_N. Rather than moving from point A to point B in the figure, we move to point C. After the smoke clears, we note that the unemployment rate remains unchanged but inflation has risen. Thus monetary policy is ineffective; there is no trade-off between inflation and unemployment, even in the short run.

In fact, not only is monetary policy ineffective, it is actually counterproductive! Because inflation is higher at point *C* than at point *A* while the unemployment rate is unchanged, we would have been better off if the Fed had remained on the sidelines. By entering the fray, the Fed has only increased the nation's inflation rate and misery index.

THE ACTIVIST CRITIQUE OF RATIONAL EXPECTATIONS MACROECONOMICS

During the past quarter century, rational expectations theory has had a considerable impact on macroeconomic thinking. Nevertheless, only a very small minority of professional economists believe that the policy ineffectiveness theorem is valid. Most economists believe that the doctrine exaggerates the awareness and economic insight of consumers, workers, and firms. Do thousands of economic agents *really* understand the workings of the economy? Do they really understand monetary and fiscal policies? Do they really form expectations rationally?

Although it is naive to suppose that people form their expectations only adaptively, it seems likely that past events do have some impact, given uncertainty about the future. Our expectation about next year's inflation is likely to be influenced by this year's inflation, as well as by developments that a macroeconomic model suggests are important determinants of inflation. Studies have demonstrated that people's expectations of inflation are sluggish, changing only modestly in response to changes in variables included in models of inflation. When the inflation rate was ratcheting higher and higher in the period 1965–1980, inflation expectations consistently lagged behind actual inflation. Contrary to rational expectations theory, forecast errors were *not* random. And as inflation rates came down in the 1980s, inflation expectations again lagged behind.

Furthermore, contracts, minimum wage statutes, and other impediments prevent wages from adapting immediately to changes in expected inflation. Three-year contracts that were written in the early 1980s prevented wage inflation from slowing as fast as the decline in actual and expected inflation. What had seemed rational when the contracts were written no longer appeared rational a year or two later. Of the many studies that have been conducted of the formation of inflation expectations, only a few demonstrate rationality on the part of economic agents. Numerous studies demonstrate that *expected* as well as *unexpected* policies influence real output and employment.

Nevertheless, rational expectations theory has made major contributions to economic analysis. Though few economists take the theory seriously in its extreme version, most agree that it contains an important element of truth. As people come to anticipate a change in policy, they take actions which reduce the policy's impact on output and employment. With the post–World War II advent of Keynesian policy, people have learned to expect stimulative policies whenever economic activity weakens significantly. This expectation has probably contributed appreciably to the inflationary propensity that has characterized industrial nations in recent decades. Rational expectations theory has provided an alternative way of thinking, which has stimulated consideration of aggregate supply as well as aggregate demand. By focusing on the role of expectations in macroeconomic analysis, REM has yielded major insights into economic theory and policy.

SUMMARY

Efforts by the Federal Reserve to employ discretionary monetary policy for the purpose of stabilizing economic activity at levels close to full employment have come under attack from two well-known groups of economists. Monetarists charge that discretionary actions by the Fed are likely to fail because of political factors and the Fed's historic propensity to change its goals periodically. Furthermore, monetarists believe that even if the Fed were to focus strictly on trying to stabilize the economy, it would be bound to fail because of the various uncertainties about the structure of the economy and because of the long and variable lags that characterize the response of economic activity to changes in the Fed's policy tools. For these reasons, monetarists have long proposed that the Fed abandon efforts to conduct discretionary policies and instead simply increase the money supply each year by some slow, constant rate. Critics of the constant money growth proposal dispute the allegation that the Fed is a destabilizing influence and argue that implementation of the rule would handcuff the Fed, preventing it from responding to periodic crises. Proponents of new classical macroeconomics also charge that the Federal Reserve is ineffective, though they reach this conclusion via a totally different route than monetarists. They argue that, in a discretionary policy regime, economic agents inevitably learn to anticipate Federal Reserve policy and that the reactions of these agents to expected Fed policy actions negate the effect of such policies on real economic variables such as output and employment. For this reason, they believe that discretionary policies are ineffective and should be abandoned.

KEY TERMS

natural, or full employment, output level
recognition lag
implementation lag
impact lag
new classical macroeconomics, or rational expectations macroeconomics (REM)

rational expectations
adaptive expectations
political business cycle
policy ineffectiveness theorem
Phillips curve

STUDY QUESTIONS

1 How would an advocate of the fixed money supply growth rule arrive at an appropriate growth rate for *M*?

2 Why do you suppose that the growth rate of the supply of money, illustrated in Table 26-1, has typically been significantly more rapid during expansions than during contractions? Does this fact prove that the Fed has destabilized the economy? Explain.

3 How do lags in economic policy enter into the rules-versus-discretion debate?

4 Evaluate the argument that a fixed money growth rule would promote a "climate of confidence" among business executives, thereby contributing to economic stability.

5 Why are political conservatives often attracted to the fixed money growth proposal?

6 In what way would the implementation of a fixed money growth rule impose more "discipline" on the congressional budgetary process?

7 "If V_Y and Y cannot be projected into the future with any degree of confidence, the case for the fixed money growth rule breaks down." Evaluate this statement.

8 "All one has to do to refute the claims made by supporters of a fixed money growth rule is to look at the historical behavior of velocity. Its documented variability implies that the monetary rule would result in similar volatility of aggregate expenditures and GDP." Critique this statement.

9 Name the three lags involved in monetary and fiscal policies. Would the length of the lags be the same for fiscal policy and monetary policy? If not, why?

10 Explain why, in a REM world, the same forces that render discretionary monetary policy ineffective in combating a recession become a blessing in fighting inflation.

11 Suppose you sell leather to manufacturers of gloves and coats. Assume that you are fully aware that the economy is entering a recession. In setting prices for the leather, how would your behavior differ in a constant money growth regime as compared to a discretionary monetary policy regime?

12 Analyze the operation of the self-correcting mechanism in eliminating recessionary gaps. What real-world factors inhibit this mechanism? Were these inhibiting factors present 100 years ago?

13 By examining Table 26-1 and Figure 26-3, evaluate the Fed's performance in the recessions of 1969–1970, 1973–1975, 1981–1982, and 1990–1991.

14 Suppose Milton Friedman is appointed chairman of the Board of Governors of the Federal Reserve System. Given his monetarist stance, what should we expect to observe immediately if rational expectations theory is strictly valid? Explain.

15 While campaigning for president in 1988, George Bush stated, "Read my lips: No new taxes." Two years later, the economy entered a recession following a Bush-approved tax increase. If rational expectations theory is strictly valid, was Bush a believable fellow in 1988? Can we reach the same conclusion if expectations are not rational?

SUGGESTIONS FOR ADDITIONAL READING

For a more in-depth discussion of the self-correcting mechanism, see any intermediate macroeconomics textbook. A good example is N. Gregory Mankiw, *Macroeconomics* (New York: Worth Publishers, 1994). Two excellent works by Thomas Mayer analyze the viewpoints of monetarists: *The Structure of Monetarism* (New York: Norton, 1978) and *The Political Economy of American Monetary Policy* (New York: Cambridge University Press, 1990). The seminal article proposing a constant money growth rule is Henry Simons, "Rules versus Authority in Monetary Policy," *Journal of Political Economy,* February 1936, pp. 1–30. Milton Friedman's position is set forth in "A Monetary and Fiscal Framework for Economic Stability," *American Economic Review,* June 1948, pp. 245–264, and *A Program for Monetary Stability* (New York: Fordham University Press, 1960). Opposing viewpoints on the constant money growth proposal include Franco Modigliani, "The Monetarist Controversy or, Should We Forsake Stabilization Policies?," *American Economic Review,* March 1977, pp. 1–19, and Paul Samuelson, "Reflections on Central Banking," in Joseph Stiglitz, ed., *The Collected Scientific Papers of Paul Samuelson,* Vol. 2. (Cambridge, Mass.: MIT Press, 1966), pp. 1361–1386. On the issue of the lags in monetary policy, Friedman's views are set forth in "The Effects of a Full-Employment Policy on Economic Stability: A Formal Analysis," in Milton Friedman, *Essays in Positive Economics* (Chicago: University of Chicago Press, 1953), and in "The Lag in the Effect of Monetary Policy," in Milton Friedman (ed.), *The Optimum Quantity of Money and Other Essays* (London: Macmillan, 1968). Also, see Chapter 12 of the Friedman and Schwartz classic cited in the references at the end of Chapter 22. Christina Romer's hypothesis that early estimates of U.S. industrial production and GDP overstated the degree of output instability are presented in "The Prewar Business Cycle Reconsidered: New Estimates of GNP, 1869–1908," *Journal of Political Economy,* 1989, pp. 1–37, and "Is the Stabilization of the Postwar Economy a Figment of the Data?," *American Economic Review,* June 1986, pp. 314–334. On the alleged increase in postwar economic stability, see the viewpoints of Robert J. Gordon, Arthur Okun, and Herbert Stein in Martin Feldstein (ed.), *The American Economy in Transition* (Chicago: University of Chicago Press, 1980), pp. 101–182. The "Lucas critique" is presented in "Econometric Policy Evaluation: A Critique," in Karl Brunner and Allan Meltzer (ed.), *The Phillips Curve and Labor Markets,* Carnegie-Rochester Conference Series on Public Policy 1 (1976), pp. 19–46.

P A R T

7

The International Financial System

Economists have long debated whether fixed or floating exchange rates provide the more desirable international monetary arrangement▮ From World War II until the early 1970s, world trade was conducted under the Bretton Woods system▮ In this system, governments were obligated to intervene directly in foreign exchange markets to maintain their exchange rates at fixed levels for an indefinite period▮ This system collapsed in the early 1970s▮ For the past quarter century, such major currencies as the dollar, yen, and deutsche mark have been floating against each other, although many smaller nations have fixed their exchange rate with a major trading partner such as the United States, France, or Germany▮ Some important limitations of floating exchange rates have become apparent in recent years, including short-term volatility and persistent misalignment of exchange rates▮ Several European nations today are moving toward adoption of a single currency and establishment of a single European central bank▮

C H A P T E R

27

■ **The International Monetary System**

n earlier chapters, we examined the role of money in economic activity. We have seen the important role that money plays in a nation's economy, especially as a medium of exchange and as an asset, a way of storing wealth. Much of this text has been devoted to these topics.

Because the world's nations use different currencies, and because those nations exchange goods, services, and assets, it is important to see how their currencies interact. Chapter 8 introduced the foreign exchange market, in which currencies are exchanged, and the foreign exchange rate—that is, the price at which currencies exchange for each other. That chapter discussed how the foreign exchange market operates and analyzed the factors that determine the exchange rate in both the short run and the long run. This chapter will refer when necessary to points made in Chapter 8, and it assumes that you are familiar with that chapter.

Exchange rates link the prices in one country with prices in other countries. When a country's exchange rates change, the prices of its goods, services, and assets change relative to the prices of goods, services, and assets in other countries. Because these price changes influence decisions about producing, importing, exporting, and investing, exchange rates are clearly important.

The objective of this chapter is to introduce and analyze the international monetary system in which exchange rates are determined. We will look at the international monetary system over the last 50 years—the period since the end of World War II. For the first half of that period, nations cooperated in the Bretton Woods system, which had as its objective keeping exchange rates fixed over long periods of time. The fixed exchange-rate system lasted until the early 1970s, and we will see why it ended. We will then discuss the exchange rate arrangements used by countries since the early 1970s. Some major exchange rates have been floating, but about half the world's countries still keep their exchange rate fixed. We will see that the European Union countries decided to keep their own currencies fixed in relation to one another while permitting them to float jointly relative to currencies outside Europe. We will discuss the exchange rate movements of the dollar since 1973, point out some problems that have emerged, and look at some proposed solutions to these problems.

An important point needs to be made at the beginning. The past 50 years have seen enormous economic progress compared to all previous periods of equal length. The developed capitalist countries have experienced rapid growth, and there has been substantial movement toward convergence of living standards as the poorer developed capitalist countries closed the income gaps relative to the richer developed capitalist countries. In most of the less developed countries, real output has grown faster than their rapidly growing populations, so their average economic well-being has improved. A number of less developed countries in Asia have made such striking economic progress in recent decades that they should rightfully now be counted among the developed countries. The precise contribution of the international monetary system to this widespread economic progress is uncertain, but it is obvious that the international monetary arrangements of the past half century have been, at the least, compatible with tremendous economic progress.

THE BRETTON WOODS EXCHANGE RATE SYSTEM

In 1944, as it became clear that the Allied countries were eventually going to be victorious in both the European and Pacific theaters of World War II, an international conference was held at Bretton Woods, New Hampshire. The conference created the institutional framework for the postwar world economy. The intention was to create a framework for international economic cooperation that would avoid some of the disastrous economic policies, such as competitive currency devaluations and dramatic increases in tariffs and other barriers to international trade, that had been put into place in the 1920s and 1930s. These destructive policies had contributed to the catastrophically poor worldwide economic performance in the 1930s, thereby contributing to the political turmoil that led to World War II.

Establishment of the International Monetary Fund

The Bretton Woods conference led to the establishment of three institutions that have played important roles ever since. The International Bank for Reconstruction and Development (now called the World Bank) was created for the purpose of repairing the devastation that had occurred during World War II. In recent decades the World Bank has been a major source of capital for economic development programs and projects in less developed countries. The General Agreement on Tariffs and Trade (GATT) created the rules and regulations concerning international trade and contributed greatly to the reduction of tariffs and other barriers to international trade.[1] The third institution, the **International**

---

[1]The Bretton Woods conference also recommended the formation of an International Trade Organization, but that was not established, and the General Agreement on Tariffs and Trade (GATT) emerged in its place. The latest round of GATT negotiations resulted in the formation of a World Trade Organization (WTO), which replaced GATT in 1995.

Monetary Fund (IMF), was created to ensure a stable international monetary environment. That environment is our topic in this chapter.

The International Monetary Fund established a system that attempted to maintain fixed exchange rates between major currencies. The system it established is referred to as the **Bretton Woods system,** which came into operation in the late 1940s and lasted essentially unchanged until 1971. As mentioned, that period witnessed enormous economic growth in the developed capitalist countries and most of the rest of the world. A robust expansion of international trade in goods and services and a particularly large increase in international investment took place. It is widely agreed that the Bretton Woods system contributed importantly to the expansion of international trade and to economic growth in general in the first quarter century after the war. It is important to see how the system operated and why it came to an end in the early 1970s.

The Bretton Woods (Fixed Exchange-Rate) System

The purpose of the system was to maintain **fixed exchange rates** among the different currencies.[2] In part this was a reaction against the competitive **devaluations** that had occurred in the 1920s and 1930s, when countries had changed their exchange rates to raise the price of foreign currency—that is, to reduce the number of units of foreign currency per unit of domestic currency. By raising the prices of foreign goods relative to domestic goods, devaluation of a country's currency reduces imports and increases exports. This in turn stimulates domestic production and employment. In part, the prevailing sentiment in the 1940s was that international trade would flourish better under fixed exchange rates than in a system of floating rates. Fixed exchange rates simplify international transactions. With fixed exchange rates it is easier for importers and exporters to predict import payments and export receipts, and it is easier for investors to estimate the costs and returns associated with international investments. In other words, it was believed that the costs of making international transactions would be lower in a fixed exchange-rate system than in a floating-rate system. Thus, a fixed-rate system would lead to a greater volume of international economic transactions, thereby conferring the benefits of trade more fully.

The United States, which had by far the largest and strongest economy, played a central role in the fixed exchange-rate system. The United States agreed to buy and sell gold to the governments of other members of the IMF at $35 per ounce upon their request. In the late 1940s, the U.S. government owned $25 billion worth of monetary gold, a total that far exceeded the total stock of dollars that had been accumulated by other member governments, and there was no question that the United States could honor its obligation to redeem dollars with gold at the request of other members, as specified by the IMF.

Each of the other member countries determined a central exchange rate of its currency relative to the U.S. dollar, called its **par value.** For example, the Bank of Japan set its par value exchange rate at 360 yen to the dollar. The central bank (or monetary

---

[2]In practice, the system operated differently than had been planned at Bretton Woods (see the article by Ronald I. McKinnon cited in "Suggestions for Additional Reading" at the end of the chapter). The account provided here discusses how the system actually operated.

authority) of each IMF member committed itself to maintain the exchange rate within a band 1 percent either side of its par value through direct intervention in the foreign exchange market—that is, by purchasing or selling foreign currency. The other IMF members used dollars as their *foreign exchange reserves,* or *international reserves.* Thus the U.S. dollar played a central role in the Bretton Woods system as the **intervention currency**—the currency in which other nations held their international reserves. The dollar was frequently referred to as the *key currency* of the Bretton Woods system.

Note that under the Bretton Woods system the United States did not in fact determine its own exchange rate—that is, the exchange rate of the dollar relative to other currencies. Once each other member of the IMF had established the par value of its currency relative to the dollar and stood ready to intervene in the foreign exchange market to maintain that exchange rate, this determined the dollar exchange rate. For example, when the Bank of Japan established its par value exchange rate at 360 yen per dollar and committed itself to maintaining that exchange rate by buying and selling U.S. dollars at the price of 360 yen to the dollar, that fixed the yen-dollar exchange rate for everyone, including the United States. Another way of making this point is to note that between any two currencies there is only *one* exchange rate.

Upon joining the IMF, each member was assigned a *quota,* determined essentially by the size of its economy (its GDP) and the volume of its international trade. Each member country contributed funds to the IMF in an amount determined by its quota. One-fourth of each member's quota contribution was to be in gold or dollars, and three-fourths in its own currency. In this way, the IMF established a large *currency fund.* IMF members were entitled to borrow dollars or other foreign currencies from the IMF's currency fund in the event such funds were needed in order to maintain the fixed exchange rate near its par value through direct foreign exchange market intervention.

How the Bretton Woods System Operated

Figures 27-1 to 27-3 illustrate the way the system worked. If the pegged (fixed) exchange rate determined by a member nation happened to be a market-clearing (equilibrium) rate, there would be no need for its central bank to intervene in the foreign exchange market. The quantity of dollars demanded and supplied at the par value exchange rate by private foreign exchange market participants would be equal. Assume that the German central bank (the Bundesbank) has agreed to peg the price of the dollar at *OA* marks. If the market's demand for and supply of dollars happen to be as shown in Figure 27-1, no action (that is, no intervention) by the Bundesbank is needed because the private market clears at exchange rate *OA*. Given these circumstances, the exchange rate would be *OA* even under a system of floating exchange rates.

But these supply and demand curves do not remain fixed over time. Instead, because of changing price levels, income levels, interest rates, expectations, and so forth, they are continually shifting. Given the normal fluctuations in the supply of and demand for dollars, it is certain that in any given period of time the equilibrium exchange rate will deviate from the level at which the government is pegging the exchange rate. Figure 27-2 shows the case in which, at the pegged (fixed) exchange rate of *OA,* the quantity of dollars supplied exceeds

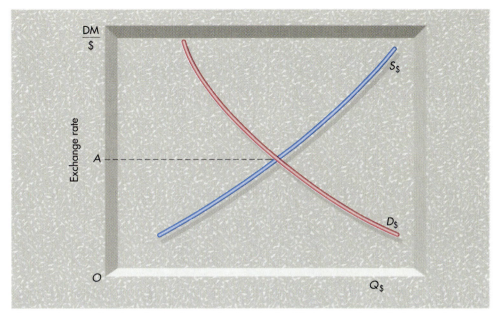

Figure 27-1 Pegging the Exchange Rate at Its Equilibrium Level. With the supply and demand curves for dollars as shown, and with the dollar fixed at an exchange rate of *OA*, there is no need for government intervention. In this case, the exchange rate happens to be pegged at its equilibrium level.

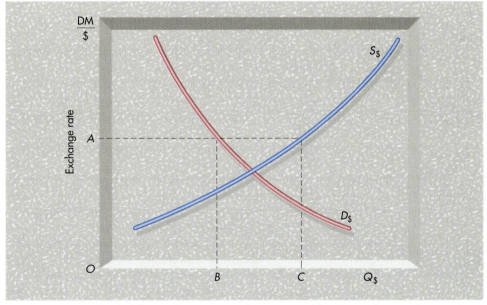

Figure 27-2 Pegging the Exchange Rate above Its Equilibrium Level. With the supply and demand curves for dollars as shown, if the German central bank is to maintain the exchange rate at *OA*, it must intervene to purchase *BC* dollars with deutsche marks each period. These dollars are added to Germany's foreign exchange reserves.

637

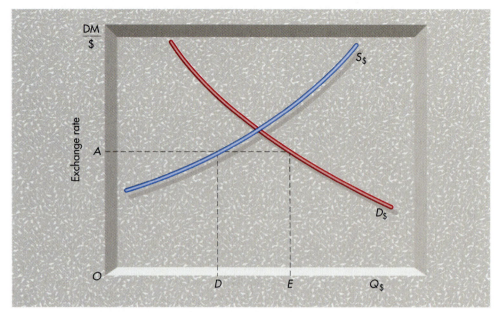

Figure 27-3 Pegging the Exchange Rate below Its Equilibrium Level. With the supply and demand curves for dollars as shown, the German central bank must intervene to sell *DE* units of dollars each period. That is, it buys deutsche marks with dollars, reducing its foreign exchange reserves of dollars.

the quantity of dollars demanded. To keep the exchange rate at *OA,* the Bundesbank must intervene in the market to purchase *BC* dollars each period, paying for these dollars with deutsche marks. These dollars purchased by the Bundesbank will be added to the bank's foreign exchange reserves. In this situation, the dollar is said to be an **overvalued currency**—that is, the dollar is being maintained at an exchange rate above its fundamental equilibrium level.

In contrast, at the pegged (fixed) exchange rate of *OA,* there will be periods during which the quantity of dollars demanded exceeds the quantity supplied. Figure 27-3 shows this case. Because the free market exchange rate exceeds *OA,* the German central bank must sell dollars to maintain the exchange rate at *OA.* In this situation, the dollar is said to be an **undervalued currency**—that is, it is being maintained at a level *below* its equilibrium level. The Bundesbank would then sell *DE* dollars from its foreign exchange reserves each period—that is, it will purchase marks with dollars. If a country's own international reserves were inadequate to continue such operations, it could borrow foreign currency from the IMF. Borrowing from the IMF was intended to allow a country to maintain its exchange rate at the declared par value despite a short-term inadequacy of reserves.

As mentioned earlier, an enormous growth in international trade took place during the first quarter century after World War II, in large part due to the reduction of trade barriers (tariffs, quotas, exchange controls, etc.) around the world as a result of the multilateral trade negotiations sponsored by GATT. In addition, countries gradually reduced their restrictions on the mobility of capital, thus allowing their citizens to make investments abroad more freely. To finance the rapidly growing volumes of international trade and investment, the volume of foreign exchange transactions increased enormously during this period. In terms of Figures 27-1 to 27-3, both the demand and supply curves were persistently shifting outward—that is, to the right.

Over time, the various exchange rates established at the beginning of the Bretton Woods period inevitably became disequilibrium rates. Given the enormous economic changes taking place, this ought not to have been surprising. Some countries found that their established exchange rate resulted in their having an overvalued currency. Because this caused foreign products to be artificially inexpensive, such countries persistently imported more than they exported—that is, they experienced persistent *international trade deficits.* Other countries had exchange rates that chronically undervalued their currency. These countries persistently exported more than they imported—that is, they exhibited persistent *trade surpluses.* And this is where the Bretton Woods system proved brittle. *In design,* the "adjustable-peg" system allowed a country whose exchange rate had become a disequilibrium rate to change its par value—that is, to "repeg" the exchange rate at a new level. *In practice,* however, the system did not operate as its designers had intended because countries were reluctant to change the par value of their currency. Thus, changes in par values were very rare. Of the countries possessing the major currencies, Germany had two small revaluations (in 1961 and 1969), France devalued once (in 1969), the United Kingdom devalued twice (in 1949 and 1967), and Japan kept its exchange rate with the dollar unchanged throughout the entire Bretton Woods period.

Why Exchange Rate Realignments Were Rare

Why would a country be reluctant to change its exchange rate? Consider the case of a country such as Japan, whose unchanging par value had caused its currency to become undervalued and the U.S. dollar overvalued vis-à-vis the yen. This case is illustrated in Figure 27-4. Perhaps at the time the currency's par value was originally established, the demand for and supply of dollars were $D_\$^1$ and $S_\$^1$ and the par value (¥360/$) was an equilibrium value. But over time demand and supply shift to $D_\$^2$ and $S_\$^2$. The original and unchanging par value now undervalues the yen (overvalues the dollar). The dollar, at 360 yen per dollar, is being maintained above its equilibrium level. An undervalued yen causes imported items to appear artificially expensive in Japan, thereby limiting Japan's demand for imports. Undervaluation of the yen also causes Japan's exports to be priced artificially low in foreign countries, resulting in a robust volume of exports. Undervaluation thus implies, in the foreign exchange market, that the quantity of dollars supplied to Japan exceeds the quantity of dollars demanded by Japan. At the pegged exchange rate, an excess supply of dollars exists. To maintain the exchange rate, the Japanese central bank must intervene to purchase *AB* dollars each period, and Japan's foreign exchange reserves increase persistently.

Because those firms and individuals engaged in the export sector and the import-competing sector of a country benefit from currency undervaluation, the producers of export- and import-competing goods find it in their interest to resist any attempt by their government to eliminate the undervaluation by changing the par value—that is, by revaluing its currency. Because the country is accumulating dollars (all or some of which can be used to purchase gold from the United States), there is no great political pressure to

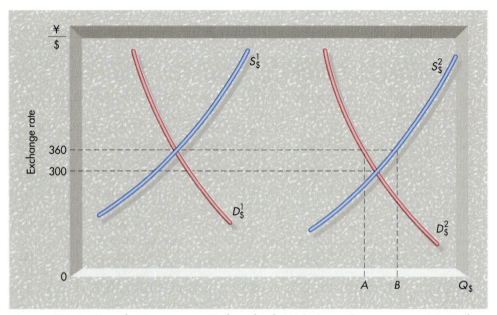

Figure 27-4   How the Yen Became Undervalued. With the exchange rate at ¥360/$, assume the supply and demand curves shift to the right as shown. In this situation, the pegged rate of ¥360/$ undervalues the yen and overvalues the dollar. To restore equilibrium, the exchange rate needs to be repegged at ¥300/$, thus devaluing the dollar.

revalue the currency.[3] Many observers believe that this describes the situation in Japan and Germany in the later years of the Bretton Woods system. Both nations had persistently undervalued currencies, were persistently accumulating dollars, and were reluctant to revalue their currencies.

In contrast, consider a country whose par value was fixed at a level that overvalued its currency relative to the dollar. This country would experience artificially low-priced imports. Its exports would appear expensive in foreign markets, thus reducing its ability to export. The nation's high demand for imports and the low foreign demand for its exports would imply that the demand for foreign currency would exceed the supply of foreign currency. The country's central bank would have to intervene in the market to provide the foreign currency from its reserves. This could be done only as long as the reserves lasted. To meet its *temporary* shortfalls, the country would be able to borrow some foreign currency from the IMF under increasingly onerous conditions. But any country whose par value *chronically* overvalued its currency came under pressure to implement fundamental and sometimes costly measures to stem the loss of reserves. The Bretton Woods system, as envisioned in 1944, indicated that a member country (other than the United States) in this situation should devalue its currency—that is, reduce the

---

[3]Of course, Japanese consumers were hurt by the high cost of imported goods associated with the undervalued yen. However, it proved difficult to organize the millions of consumers to form an effective political coalition for currency revaluation.

number of units of foreign currency per unit of domestic currency. Some countries were reluctant to devalue; it was politically difficult because national pride was at stake, and a country was often reluctant to acknowledge that it was a weak-currency nation and admit that its currency was not as valuable as before.

Problems with the Bretton Woods System

We have seen why currency realignments were relatively rare. Countries with undervalued currencies and persistent trade surpluses were content to maintain the status quo. They were unwilling to implement measures to eliminate the undervaluation of their currencies. The burden of adjustment therefore fell almost entirely on weak-currency nations—that is, nations with overvalued currencies, such as England, Italy, and France. Because such nations were reluctant to devalue their currencies, however, they were forced to implement other methods to remedy the overvaluation.

Looking once again at Figure 27-2, note that a nation with an overvalued currency is obligated to purchase its own currency with foreign exchange in order to defend the par value exchange rate. Because a given country has only limited supplies of foreign exchange, this process can be maintained only for a limited period. Therefore, the nation finds it necessary to implement measures to boost the demand for its currency (shift the demand curve rightward) or reduce the supply of its currency (shift the supply curve leftward), thereby restoring the equilibrium exchange rate to the par value level. For example, countries like England and France sometimes implemented restrictive monetary policy measures in an effort to attract foreign capital and push down their domestic price level to make their products more competitive in world trade. By boosting demand for a country's currency and reducing the supply, such measures could potentially increase the equilibrium exchange rate, thereby reducing the magnitude of intervention required to support the currency. Such contractionary policies often triggered recessions, appreciably increasing the unemployment rate. Other countries imposed trade restrictions, such as tariffs and quotas on imported goods, in an effort to reduce the supply of domestic currency on the foreign exchange market, thus shifting the supply curve leftward and fortifying the exchange rate. The destructive consequences of such actions taken by countries with overvalued currencies—increased unemployment and reduced trade—constitute the chief shortcomings of the Bretton Woods fixed exchange-rate system.

Toward the end of the Bretton Woods period, the United States found itself with an overvalued currency and chronic balance-of-payments deficits. Unlike other IMF members with overvalued currencies, the United States could not unilaterally change its exchange rate. However, it did occasionally implement restrictive monetary policy actions to drive up interest rates for the purpose of defending the dollar exchange rate.

This brief summary of the Bretton Woods system reveals the unique role of the United States and the U.S. dollar in the system. In one sense, the United States was in an advantageous position. Throughout most of the Bretton Woods period, it could focus its monetary (interest rate) policy on domestic objectives. Because the dollar was the key currency used in international transactions and because the dollar was used as reserves by the rest of the world, the United States was able to run persistent balance-of-payments deficits for most of the Bretton Woods period. The rest of the world wanted and needed dollars. But there was an important disadvantage for the United States: it had no control over the dollar exchange rate. If, for example, the Japanese or German central bank maintained a chronically undervalued currency, these countries would run chronic trade surpluses and their trading partners, including the United States, would experience chronic trade deficits. The United States could not unilaterally change its exchange rate to reduce its trade deficit.

The Breakdown of Bretton Woods

In the later years of the Bretton Woods period, the large U.S. balance-of-payments deficits led to major increases in the stock of dollars held by other nations. Some of these dollars were exchanged for gold, and the U.S. gold stock steadily decreased. Starting from about $25 billion in 1947, the U.S. gold stock was reduced to about $12 billion by 1971. Meanwhile, because of the persistent U.S. balance-of-payments deficits, the stock of dollars held by foreign countries increased. The holdings of dollars by foreign governments came to exceed the value of the U.S. gold stock by far. In 1947, it had been clear that the United States could live up to its obligation to convert dollars into gold at $35 per ounce upon the request of foreign governments. But over the years the U.S. balance-of-payments deficits led to a situation in which it became obvious it could no longer do so. This came to be termed the *confidence problem.* Speculators, sensing that the United States would be forced to devalue the dollar to reduce the balance-of-payments deficit, began selling dollars in large quantities.

The United States' position was that exchange rate realignments were needed. Countries with undervalued currencies, such as Japan and Germany, should revalue their currencies to more realistic levels in order to reduce their trade surpluses (and thereby to reduce the U.S. trade deficit). In contrast, the German view was that the United States should "put its house in order"—that is, it should use its monetary policy and fiscal policy tools to maintain price level stability, thereby making its goods more competitive in foreign markets and alleviating the overvaluation of the dollar.

In August 1971, the United States announced it would no longer honor its commitment to exchange its gold for dollars until the major surplus countries had revalued their currencies. An agreement was reached that resulted in some limited realignment of exchange rates, and the United States increased the price of gold (that is, devalued the dollar relative to gold and foreign currencies). However, this was an unsuccessful solution, and in 1973 the Bretton Woods system collapsed. Since 1973, the world's major currencies have not been linked in a fixed relationship with one another.

In retrospect, we now understand why the Bretton Woods system ended. We know there are three policies which are *mutually incompatible*—that is, policies which countries cannot choose to follow simultaneously. These policies are a fixed exchange rate, monetary (interest rate) policy autonomy, and free international movement of capital (flows of funds to purchase financial assets). A country can choose at most only two of these three policies. For example, a country can fix its exchange rate and have an autonomous monetary policy, but it cannot simultaneously allow the free international movement of capital. Otherwise, if the nation sets its interest rates relatively low because of domestic considerations, a capital outflow would place downward pressure on its currency, forcing it to use up its international reserves to defend its exchange rate. To prevent persistent loss of these reserves and an ultimate devaluation, a country with an overvalued currency would have to impose restrictions on international capital movements.

Alternatively, a country can choose to maintain a fixed exchange rate and free international movement of capital if it is willing to forgo selecting its desired monetary policy, adopting instead the monetary policy and interest rates of its strong-currency trading partner. Finally, a country can choose to determine its own monetary policy and permit free international movement of capital, and forgo having a fixed exchange rate in favor of a floating (flexible) exchange rate.[4]

At the beginning of the Bretton Woods period, most countries did not allow the free movement of capital. Also, the volume of international transactions was small relative to the world's stock of international reserves. For these reasons, countries could choose fixed exchange rates and monetary policy autonomy. Over time, as the volume of world trade increased and nations removed their controls on capital, it became increasingly essential for countries with fixed exchange rates to adopt the same basic monetary policy employed by the United States. Their unwillingness to do so was one of the principal reasons for the demise of the Bretton Woods system.[5] Instead, the major countries chose to have an autonomous monetary policy and freedom for international capital movements; consequently, they abandoned the fixed exchange rate and the Bretton Woods system came to an end.

INTERNATIONAL MONETARY ARRANGEMENTS SINCE 1973

International monetary arrangements in the quarter century following the end of Bretton Woods are more difficult to summarize. Countries have chosen from a wide variety of possible exchange rate arrangements, or regimes. These arrangements can be described as falling along a spectrum from fixed exchange rates at one extreme (close to the way in which the Bretton Woods system operated), all the way to freely floating exchange rates at the other.

The key fact is that since 1973 the three major currencies—the dollar, the yen, and the deutsche mark—have not been fixed in relation to one another. Simply put, the Bundesbank and the Bank of Japan do not intervene in the foreign exchange market to keep the exchange rate of the mark and the yen fixed relative to the dollar. The mark-dollar and yen-dollar exchange rates float, based on market forces of supply and demand. While the central banks do not intervene on a day-to-day basis to maintain a specified exchange rate as they did under the Bretton Woods system, they do intervene occasionally to prevent the exchange rate from moving too far in one direction.

While the international monetary system since Bretton Woods has been described as a floating exchange-rate system, this wording applies strictly to only about half the world's currencies. Because a fixed exchange rate has many advantages—reduced transactions costs of international trade, better predictability of future prices of imports and

---

[4]This last combination is the choice preferred by Milton Friedman; see his classic article advocating flexible exchange rates, cited in the "Suggestions for Additional Reading" at the end of the chapter.

[5]As we will learn shortly, the desire for monetary policy autonomy is a major consideration that causes some European nations today to be hesitant to relinquish control over their monetary policy to a proposed European central bank.

exports, and so forth, many countries fix the exchange rate of their currency relative to the currency of their major trading partner. This is especially true of smaller countries whose international transactions are predominantly with one trading partner.

Table 27-1 shows the IMF's exchange rate classification scheme. It indicates the various exchange rate arrangements in place and the countries using each arrangement as of the end of 1995. At first glance, the existing structure seems complex and hard to describe. In reality, it is not so complex if we keep in mind that the three major currencies are floating in relation to one another but that many countries have chosen to maintain a fixed exchange rate of their currency to one other currency.

Approximately half of the world's central banks still intervene in the foreign exchange market to fix the exchange rate of their currency. The countries in the first five categories of Table 27-1 have chosen to maintain a fixed exchange rate. More than 20 countries peg their currency to the dollar; others (mostly former French colonies), peg to the French franc; a few small neighboring African countries peg to the South African rand, while still other countries peg to the German mark. We will see shortly that many European countries (IMF category 7) participate in an arrangement that keeps their exchange rates mutually pegged—that is, fixed in relation to one another. We saw earlier that a country that chooses to fix its exchange rate must make a choice between establishing its own monetary policy (thus sacrificing free international movement of capital), and allowing its citizens free international movement of capital (thus sacrificing its autonomy in the conduct of monetary policy). Most of the countries that maintain fixed exchange rates today (the first five categories in the table) still impose controls on capital movements.

Because the three dominant currencies—the dollar, mark, and yen—float against one another, the currency of any fourth country acting to maintain a fixed exchange rate with one of the three also floats relative to the other two. For example, the Saudi Arabian Monetary Authority fixes the riyal-dollar exchange rate. This means that the riyal is fixed not only relative to the dollar but also to all other currencies that are fixed relative to the dollar; it floats relative to the yen, the mark, and all other currencies that float relative to the dollar. Saudi Arabia fixes the riyal-dollar exchange rate and allows its citizens free international movement of capital. Consequently, it has no autonomous monetary policy; it adapts its monetary policy to that of the United States.

Studies indicate that a country's choice of exchange rate arrangements is not random or unpredictable. Four factors influence a country's choice: the size of its economy, the relative importance of international trade to the nation, the concentration of its trade among other countries, and the inflation rate. At one extreme, a small country whose international trade is a relatively large proportion of GDP, whose trade is concentrated predominantly with a single important trading partner, and whose inflation rate is similar to that of the trading partner is very likely to choose to maintain a fixed exchange rate with the currency of the major trading partner. At the opposite extreme, a large country whose international trade represents a small proportion of its GDP, whose trade is spread among several countries, and which desires to conduct monetary policy on the basis of domestic considerations will likely choose to float its currency; it will choose not to fix its exchange rate. The exchange rate arrangements of countries with other combinations of these factors are harder to predict.

In the remainder of this chapter, we will focus attention on two very important aspects of the current international monetary arrangements: the U.S. dollar and the problem of misaligned exchange rates, and the European Monetary System.

Table 27-1

Exchange Rate Arrangements as of December 31, 1995

Category	Countries
Pegged to U.S. dollar	Antigua and Barbuda, Argentina, Bahamas, Barbados, Belize, Djibouti, Dominica, Grenada, Iraq, Liberia, Lithuania, Marshall Islands, Federated States of Micronesia, Nigeria, Oman, Panama, St. Kitts and Nevis, St. Lucia, St. Vincent and the Grenadines, Syria, Venezuela, Yemen.
Pegged to French franc	Benin, Burkina Faso, Cameroon, Central African Republic, Chad, Comoros, Congo, Equatorial Guinea, Gabon, Ivory Coast, Mali, Niger, Senegal, Togo
Pegged to a single other currency (indicated in parentheses)	Bhutan (Indian rupee), Bosnia and Herzegovina (deutsche mark), Estonia (deutsche mark), Kiribati (Australian dollar), Lesotho (South African rand), Namibia (South African rand), San Marino (Italian lira), Swaziland (South African rand)
Pegged to the SDR	Libya, Myanmar, Seychelles
Pegged to other composite ("basket")	Bangladesh, Botswana, Burundi, Cape Verde, Cyprus, Czech Republic, Fiji, Iceland, Jordan, Kuwait, Malta, Morocco, Nepal, Slovak Republic, Solomon Islands, Thailand, Tonga, Vanuatu, Western Samoa
Flexibility limited in terms of a single currency (U.S. dollar)	Bahrain, Qatar, Saudi Arabia, United Arab Emirates
Cooperative arrangements (European Monetary System)	Austria, Belgium, Denmark, France, Germany, Ireland, Luxembourg, the Netherlands, Portugal, Spain
Flexible according to a set of indicators	Chile, Nicaragua
Other managed floating	Algeria, Angola, Belarus, Brazil, Cambodia, People's Republic of China, Colombia, Costa Rica, Croatia, Dominican Republic, Ecuador, Egypt, El Salvador, Eritrea, Georgia, Greece, Guinea-Bissau, Honduras, Hungary, Indonesia, Iran, Israel, Korea, Kyrgyz Republic, Latvia, Macedonia, Malaysia, Maldives, Mauritius, Norway, Pakistan, Poland, Russia, Singapore, Slovenia, Sri Lanka, Suriname, Tunisia, Turkmenistan, Turkey, Ukraine, Uruguay, Uzbekistan, Vietnam
Independently floating	Afghanistan, Albania, Armenia, Australia, Azerbaijan, Bolivia, Bulgaria, Canada, Ethiopia, Finland, Gambia, Ghana, Guatemala, Guinea, Guyana, Haiti, India, Italy, Jamaica, Japan, Kazakstan, Kenya, Lao People's Democratic Republic, Lebanon, Madagascar, Malawi, Mauritania, Mexico, Moldova, Mongolia, Mozambique, New Zealand, Papua New Guinea, Paraguay, Peru, Philippines, Romania, Rwanda, São Tomé and Príncipe, Sierra Leone, Somalia, South Africa, Sudan, Sweden, Switzerland, Tajikistan, Tanzania, Trinidad and Tobago, Uganda, United Kingdom, United States, Zaïre, Zambia, Zimbabwe

Source: International Monetary Fund, *International Financial Statistics,* April 1996, p. 8.

The U.S. Dollar since 1973

In contrast to the period of the Bretton Woods system, when exchange rates remained stable for long periods, exchange rates have moved considerably in the period of floating rates. We can usefully limit our discussion to the relationship between the dollar and yen, and the dollar and mark. Figure 27-5 shows the yen-dollar and mark-dollar exchange rates from 1967–1996. It is useful to distinguish among three categories of exchange rate movements: long-term trends, short-term day-to-day movements, and intermediate-term movements about the long-term trends.

Long-Term Movements

Chapter 8 analyzed the factors determining long-term exchange rate movements, including the role of national price levels. The purchasing power parity (PPP) theory of exchange rate determination states that if the rates of inflation in two countries differ over a long period of time, the exchange rate between their currencies will change. The theory predicts that if the U.S. price level increases more rapidly than the German price level, the dollar will depreciate (buy fewer marks) and the mark will appreciate (buy more dollars). Figure 27-5 shows the long-term depreciation of the dollar relative to both the deutsche mark and the Japanese yen since the early 1970s. Because U.S. inflation has exceeded Japanese and German inflation in this long period, the PPP prediction that the dollar would depreciate relative to the mark and yen has proven correct. And largely because the U.S. inflation rate has been lower than that experienced in England and Italy, the dollar has appreciated vis-à-vis the British pound and Italian lira over the past quarter century.

Short-Term Movements

Since 1973, the exchange rates between the U.S. dollar and other major currencies have been extremely *volatile*. An exchange rate is said to be volatile when it changes greatly from one day to the next. Under Bretton Woods, the maximum variation in exchange rates within any given *year* was in most cases not more than 1 or 2 percent. Recall that for 20 years the exchange rate between the dollar and the yen was fixed by the Bank of Japan at 360 yen to the dollar. Since 1973, the yen-dollar exchange rate has sometimes changed more from one day to the next than it did within *any* interval in the entire 20-year period. This is demonstrated in Figure 27-6, which shows the closing mark-dollar and yen-dollar exchange rates for *each day* during 1984. Note that it was not uncommon for exchange rates to change by 5 percent or more within a 2-week period.[6]

One possible reason for exchange rate volatility is what economists call **overshooting,** a phenomenon in which a change in a nation's money supply causes its exchange rate to change more in the short run than in the long run. A change in a nation's money supply (and interest rates) can cause a large change in exchange rates. Suppose the Federal Reserve increases the money supply. Short-term interest rates will then decline temporarily because of the increased liquidity of the financial system. This leads to a depreciation of the dollar because investing funds in U.S. financial instruments is now somewhat

---

[6]In 1984, a relatively volatile year in the foreign exchange markets, the largest 1-day change in the mark-dollar exchange rate was 2.99 percent, while the *average* daily change was 0.65 percent. The corresponding figures for the yen-dollar exchange rate were 2.30 percent and 0.34 percent, respectively. Because exchange rates tend to move in the same direction for several consecutive days, it was not uncommon to witness a 5 percent exchange rate change in a 10- or 15-day trading period.

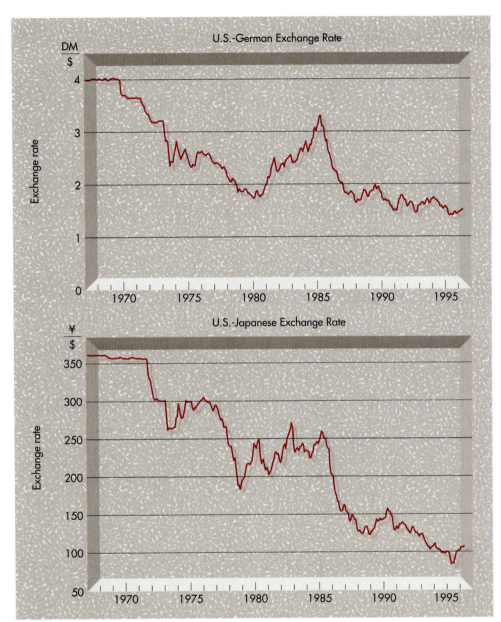

Figure 27-5 Key U.S. Exchange Rates, 1967–1996. In a system of floating exchange rates, these rates exhibit day-to-day fluctuations as well as intermediate and long-term trends. The dollar has experienced long-term depreciation against the deutsche mark and yen.

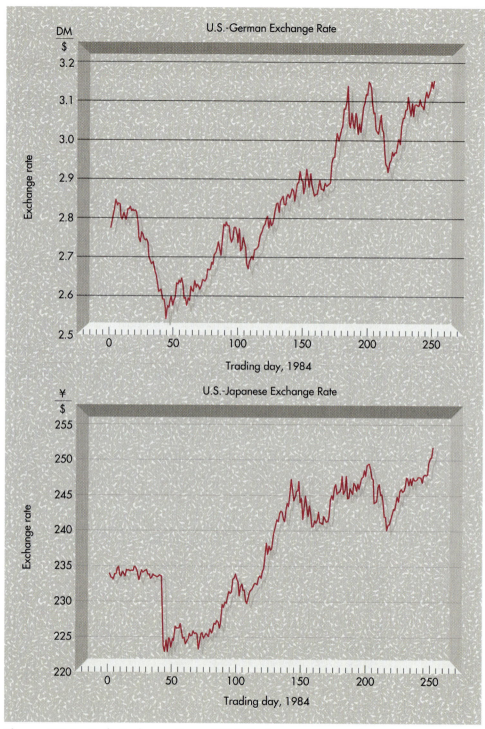

Figure 27-6 Daily Exchange Rates, 1984. Exchange rates can be volatile, sometimes changing by more than 1 percent in a given day and 5 percent or more in a 2-week period.

less attractive. In addition, foreign exchange market participants anticipate that the increase in the U.S. money supply will lead to an increase in prices of U.S. goods and services over a period of months. The increased U.S. price level, in turn, is expected to justify a longer-run depreciation of the dollar, as indicated by the PPP theory of exchange rates. Anticipating this chain of events, the foreign exchange market adjusts *immediately,* producing a short-run change in exchange rates that goes too far. That is, the depreciation of the dollar *overshoots* the expected long-term exchange rate. After a period, the strengthening of U.S. economic activity resulting from the Fed's stimulative actions begins to pull U.S. interest rates up. This arrests the depreciation of the dollar and terminates the overshooting phenomenon, and the dollar begins to appreciate as the exchange rate moves toward its long-term equilibrium level.

Actual or expected interest rate changes can trigger an enormous volume of foreign exchange transactions. The currency transactions in the foreign exchange market related to these short-term financial flows are vastly larger than the fundamental flows related to trade in goods and services and long-term international investment. To reduce the undesired exchange rate volatility these transactions produce, some prominent economists have advocated implementation of measures to reduce the volume of international financial transactions induced by small interest rate differentials among countries. Exhibit 27-1 explores one such proposal—taxing foreign exchange transactions.

Chapter 8 discussed the spot and forward foreign exchange markets. We have learned that the forward market allows a person to lock in a price today at which currencies will be exchanged at some given future date. Since 1973, the forward market and other types of markets have become increasingly important for dealing with the uncertainties caused by fluctuating exchange rates, including day-to-day volatility.

Intermediate-Term Movements

While the dollar has trended downward (depreciated) relative to the yen and the mark over the long run, there have been subperiods of considerable duration in which exchange rate movements have been contrary to the long-term trend. In particular, we need to take a careful look at the swings in exchange rates in the period from 1980–1987. In the first part of that period, the dollar experienced an enormous appreciation (review the mark-dollar exchange rate in Figure 27-5). From early 1980 to early 1985, the dollar appreciated from 1.73 marks to 3.30 marks, an appreciation of almost 100 percent. During this period of dollar appreciation, the U.S. inflation rate exceeded the German inflation rate, so any test of the PPP theory of exchange rates limited to this subperiod would lead to the conclusion that PPP theory is invalid.

The high levels of U.S. interest rates in the early 1980s can explain some, perhaps a great deal, of the dollar's appreciation in this period. An increase in U.S. interest rates increases the demand for dollars to purchase U.S. financial assets. This in turn produces appreciation of the dollar. The high U.S. interest rates were caused in part by the expansion of the federal budget deficit and the consequent increased need for funds at a time of relatively slow growth of the money supply. In the early 1980s, the Federal Reserve maintained a relatively restrictive monetary posture in a successful bid to eradicate a severely entrenched inflation.

But economists now generally agree that toward the end of the period of dollar appreciation in 1984 and early 1985, economic fundamentals were no longer determining the

---

EXHIBIT 27-1

Should Foreign Exchange Transactions Be Taxed?

The volume of transactions on the world's foreign exchange markets each day exceeds $1 trillion. Only a small portion of these transactions stems from the most important elements of international trade—the exporting and importing of goods and services, and long-term international investment. The predominant proportion is related to extremely short-term financial flows. Indeed, many of the transactions involve movement into a foreign currency and back into the domestic currency within a few hours. Many students of exchange rates believe these financial flows have an undesirable impact on exchange rates, accounting for much of the volatility in the foreign exchange market. Misbehaving financial markets can have adverse real consequences. For example, they can increase the cost of conducting international trade and reduce its volume. And they can divert the attention of central banks from important domestic problems.

James Tobin, winner of the 1981 Nobel Prize in Economics, has proposed imposing a tax on foreign exchange transactions. This tax would have the effect of sharply reducing the volume of foreign exchange transactions related to short-term financial flows. A small tax, Tobin argues, would have an undesirable but negligible impact on export and import activity and on long-term international investment, the really important international transactions. But the tax would have a large deterrent effect on transactions aimed at taking advantage of small interest rate differentials between countries. Consider a tax of 0.5 percent on all foreign exchange transactions. Purchasing a foreign currency and selling it for the domestic currency a short time later (a "round trip") would bear a total tax of 1 percent (0.5 percent each way). To make a 90-day round trip profitable, the interest rate differential between two countries would have to exceed 4 percentage points. Thus the small tax on foreign exchange transactions would dramatically reduce the enormous volume of foreign exchange transactions related to small interest differentials and speculative motives.

Tobin's proposal has been criticized mainly for its administrative difficulties. To be effective, the tax would have to be applied in every foreign exchange market. Any country that was willing to host the foreign exchange market but not impose the tax would attract all the transactions. For this reason, all nations would have to agree to levy the tax in order for it to be effective in reducing short-term capital movements.

---

direction of exchange rate movements. In contrast to theories of exchange rate movements which claimed that free markets and speculators would lead exchange rates toward their fundamental equilibrium values, a speculative bubble had taken hold in the foreign exchange market, and the appreciating dollar was persistently moving away from its fundamental equilibrium. Sometimes market participants know that market fundamentals indicate that a currency is moving away from its equilibrium exchange rate and that an adjustment toward the equilibrium rate must occur at some time in the future. A *speculative bubble* occurs when the market participants conclude that the adjustment is not likely to take place in the *immediate* future, so they take actions that cause additional movement away from equilibrium in the short run. In the case of the dollar in 1984 and early 1985, market participants realized that the dollar was overvalued and would eventually depreciate to a lower level, but they took actions that caused additional appreciation of the dollar in the short run. Of course the additional appreciation was taking the dollar still further away from its fundamental equilibrium, creating an even more overvalued dollar. Some have argued that in the late stages of this dollar appreciation, exchange rates had become seriously misaligned. A **misaligned exchange rate** is an exchange rate that is not consistent with the satisfactory performance of the economy, either internally or externally. Internally, the exchange rate is inconsistent with the goal of high employment and low inflation. Externally, the exchange rate is inconsistent with an appropriate export-import balance with major trading partners.

The Plaza and Louvre Agreements

The sustained appreciation of the dollar from 1980–1985 and its misalignment (overvaluation) in the later stages are not matters of mere academic interest. The overvaluation of the dollar led to a surge of imports into the United States, causing acute competitive difficulties in major import-competing U.S. industries such as autos and steel. Such industries were placed at an unfair disadvantage in international trade by the overvalued dollar. These industries sought relief from import competition by requesting "protectionist" action by the U.S. government. Simultaneously, of course, the overvalued dollar acted to reduce U.S. exports, and the U.S. trade deficit widened sharply in the mid-1980s. The United States' commitment to free trade was threatened by these developments.

Early in 1985, it finally became clear that the foreign exchange market had created a serious overvalued dollar and that some corrective action was needed. Central bank intervention to stop the appreciation of the dollar took place in February 1985. In September 1985, the Plaza Agreement among Britain, France, Japan, the United States, and West Germany formally acknowledged that the dollar was overvalued and that central banks would intervene to drive it down. The dollar depreciated sharply over the next year and a half, and in February 1987 the Louvre Agreement among the Group of Seven (G-7) countries (the five named above plus Canada and Italy) concluded that the dollar had fallen enough and that exchange rates were now roughly appropriate. But no formal mechanism was established to coordinate future international action.

The experience of the mid-1980s, when the dollar became seriously overvalued and threatened to produce serious adverse real-world consequences, has led some informed observers to conclude that the current informal system of ad hoc international stopgaps is inadequate to solve such problems. These observers propose a formal international agreement to keep the exchange rates of the dollar and other major currencies confined to **target zones** through coordinated international action.[7] Exhibit 27-2 summarizes the target zone proposal for international cooperation, designed by John Williamson. The debate over proposed measures to reform the international monetary system promises to continue in the years ahead.

---

[7]Some observers have suggested that a speculative bubble caused the Japanese yen to become seriously overvalued in 1994 and 1995, as the dollar had become seriously overvalued a decade earlier. In 1995, the dollar was quoted as low as 80 yen. Look in the paper and compare today's yen-dollar rate with that of 1995. How much has the dollar appreciated since it exchanged for 80 yen in 1995?

EXHIBIT 27-2

A Proposal to Prevent Exchange Rate Misalignments

John Williamson, in collaboration with a number of other scholars, has designed a system of international policy coordination that would prevent major currency misalignments while taking advantage of flexible exchange rates. The proposal assumes that participating countries seek both *internal balance* (full employment and minimal inflation) and *external balance* (an appropriate balance between exports and imports) and that a set of internationally consistent export/import balances could be estimated. The proposed system would work as follows:

1 A set of *fundamental equilibrium exchange rates (FEER)* of participating countries would be determined, consistent with the established set of export-import targets. The calculated FEERs would change over time to reflect inflation differentials among countries.

2 The goal would be to keep exchange rates within a *target zone*—that is, a range of plus or minus 10 percent around the FEER. Participating governments would intervene in the foreign exchange market to keep the exchange rate within its target zone.

3 If, in spite of intervention, an exchange rate threatened to move outside the target zone, monetary policy actions would be implemented to maintain the exchange rate within the target zone. Depending on the growth of world expenditures, either the interest rate in the weak-currency country would be increased, or the interest rate in the strong-currency country would be reduced.

In principle, this system would manage exchange rates in a way that would prevent large misalignments of exchange rates, including both those of the sort experienced under Bretton Woods as a result of the failure to adequately adjust the fixed exchange rates which had become misaligned and those of the type that occurred in the mid-1980s due to speculative bubbles in the foreign exchange markets.

Some critics of target zone proposals believe that activity in the foreign exchange market is so enormous that central banks would not be able to maintain exchange rates within the target zones. Williamson argues, on the basis of recent studies of exchange market intervention, that coordinated intervention can be effective in moving exchange rates back toward their fundamental equilibrium levels. Williamson argues that such coordinated policy action will succeed so long as governments are attempting to move exchange rates toward the FEER rather than away from it.

Williamson's proposal has been criticized by Richard Cooper and other economists on two grounds: that participating countries will not be able to agree on a consistent set of export-import targets (thus preventing determination of the FEER) and that democratic governments are not likely to subordinate their domestic considerations to the achievement of exchange rate targets.

The European Monetary System

Since the end of World War II, European nations have been engaged in promoting economic and political cooperation and integration. The largest and most important group is the **European Union** (previously named the European Common Market and European Community), which in mid-1996 contained 15 members.[8] The European Union has long been the foremost example of economic integration. Over the 40 years of its history, barriers to the movement across international borders of goods, services, people, and capital have been greatly reduced or eliminated. There has been a very large increase in intra-European trade and investment since the movement toward integration began in the 1950s. In 1986, the European Community adopted a formal program to complete the removal of barriers, thereby eventually creating what was termed the *single market*. Border controls on the movement of goods and people were eliminated at the beginning of 1993.

European leaders have long envisioned moving still further toward political and economic integration through monetary cooperation and integration. The advantages of fixed exchange rates among countries of highly integrated economic regions have led the Europeans to seek to limit the fluctuations of exchange rates among their currencies. European policies such as the Common Agricultural Policy, with its large agricultural subsidies and consequent large subsidy payments among European nations, required essentially fixed exchange rates for their subsidy calculations. Even during the Bretton Woods period of fixed exchange rates, the two small revaluations of the German mark and the single devaluation of the French franc threatened the very existence of the agricultural policy and its subsidy system. So even before the collapse of Bretton Woods in the early 1970s the Europeans were establishing agreements to keep their mutual exchange rate fluctuations within very narrow limits. Following the breakdown of the Bretton Woods system, Germany, Belgium, the Netherlands, and Luxembourg attempted to fix exchange rates among themselves and to float their currencies as a group relative to the dollar. The United Kingdom, France, and Italy participated intermittently in this informal system.

Formation of the EMS

In 1979, the Europeans implemented a formal agreement, the **European Monetary System (EMS).** At its heart is the **Exchange Rate Mechanism (ERM),** in which each participating country is assigned a **central exchange rate** against the **European Currency Unit (ECU).**[9] This central exchange rate is analogous to the par value concept of the Bretton Woods system, discussed earlier. Each participating country intervenes in the foreign

---

[8]The group began in 1957 with six members: Belgium, France, Germany, Italy, Luxembourg, and the Netherlands. The first enlargement added Denmark, Ireland, and the United Kingdom; the second added Greece, Portugal, and Spain; and the most recent, in 1995 added Austria, Finland, and Sweden. Many countries have applied for membership, including Estonia, Latvia, Lithuania, Poland, the Czech Republic, Slovakia, Hungary, Slovenia, Romania, Bulgaria, Cyprus, and Turkey.

[9]The ECU is a currency unit defined in terms of specified quantities of various European currencies. The ECU is not a currency one can hold in one's hand. It does not circulate as a medium of exchange. Because each of the constituent currencies in the ECU has an exchange rate relative to the dollar, the ECU itself has an exchange rate relative to the dollar, which is reported daily along with other exchange rates (see the exchange rate table on page 166).

exchange market to maintain its exchange rate within a narrow margin around its central rate. Until mid-1992, most participating members attempted to keep their exchange rates within 2.25 percent of the central rate, although some established wider margins. In essence, the Europeans established and maintained what, for practical purposes, was a "Bretton Woods" system for Europe. The ERM was a system of fixed exchange rates to be maintained among European currencies by means of central bank intervention in the currency markets, with the deutsche mark playing the same central role in the ERM as the U.S. dollar had played under Bretton Woods.

One of the necessary conditions for a successful fixed exchange-rate system is that countries maintain similar rates of inflation. In fact, one of the arguments sometimes made on behalf of fixed exchange rates is that maintaining a fixed exchange rate with the currency of a low-inflation country imposes needed discipline on a nation's monetary authorities to contain inflation. Inflation rates among the European nations differed greatly in the early 1980s, so there were a number of realignments of central rates in the EMS in the period 1979–1987. But after most of the countries' inflation rates had converged on the low German inflation rate, there were significantly fewer realignments.

We saw earlier that another necessary condition for a viable fixed exchange-rate system when international capital mobility exists is that nations maintain similar interest rates. Countries attempting to maintain a fixed exchange rate cannot have independent monetary policies.[10] As exchange controls on capital movements in Europe have gradually been removed, countries participating in the EMS have in effect had to follow the monetary policy set by the Bundesbank in Germany. Some countries, however, have been reluctant to do so.

The Maastricht Treaty

The convergence of Europe's inflation rates during the 1980s, together with the absence of exchange rate realignments after 1987, encouraged the notion that Europe was headed in the direction of a single currency, to be adopted by all members of the European Monetary Union. The **Maastricht Treaty** of December 1991 created a timetable for the emergence in Europe of a European central bank and a single European currency. The Maastricht Treaty established conditions that countries were required to meet to be entitled to membership in the European Monetary Union (EMU). These conditions concerned upper limits on permissible inflation rates, government budget deficits, government debt, interest rate differentials, and exchange rate movements. Exhibit 27-3 discusses the conditions imposed by the Maastricht Treaty.

Progress toward the EMU, with one central bank and a single currency for all the European Union's members, has not been smooth. In the early 1990s, German reunification and its monetary consequences caused Germany to implement a restrictive monetary policy. It boosted interest rates to combat inflation at a time when other members

---

[10]If everyone believes that the exchange rate 1 year from now will be the same as today's rate, and if everyone is free to purchase foreign currency today in order to earn interest on a foreign asset, the interest rate on assets with comparable risk in the two countries will have to be the same. Otherwise, there would be a one-way flow of financial capital out of the low-interest-rate country into the high-interest-rate country, eventually forcing the low-interest-rate country to devalue. Effectively, in a (permanently) fixed-exchange-rate world with capital mobility, interest rates in all participating countries must be equal.

EXHIBIT 27-3

The Maastricht Treaty on European Union

In December 1991, at Maastricht, the Netherlands, the members of the European Community agreed to move to a "deeper unity." This deepening of the integration of the economies of the existing members was to be achieved before commencing the prospective widening of the community. The prospective expansion was to include the many nations of Eastern Europe expected to apply for membership following the collapse of the USSR. The key part of the Maastricht Treaty was the planned creation by 1999 of an Economic and Monetary Union (EMU), the centerpiece of which would be a new European central bank with a common currency replacing the existing national currencies of the member countries. As one consequence of Maastricht, the European Community was renamed the European Union on November 1, 1993.

The Maastricht Treaty established certain conditions known as *convergence criteria,* which members would be required to meet before being eligible to belong to the monetary union. These conditions included the following: limiting budget deficits to not more than 3 percent of GDP; limiting the national debt to not more than 60 percent of GDP; reducing the rate of inflation to not more than 1.5 percentage points above the average inflation rate of the three members with the lowest inflation rates; and achieving long-term interest rates of not more than 2 percentage points above the average rate of the three members with the lowest interest rates. (The use of the actual budget deficit rather than the high-employment deficit has evoked criticism from knowledgeable individuals who point out that this measure is likely to prevent the use of countercyclical fiscal policy to fight recessions.) These criteria are quite demanding. In fact, as of mid-1996, no prospective major member of the monetary union (France, Germany, Italy, or the United Kingdom) had satisfied all the criteria.

To some extent, the Maastricht Treaty was negotiated by political leaders who were ahead of public opinion. Maastricht faces substantial grassroots opposition. Danish voters, for example, rejected Maastricht in a referendum in June 1992 before finally accepting it in a second referendum in May 1993. French voters narrowly accepted Maastricht in September 1992. The opposition to European Union bureaucrats in Brussels is reminiscent of the widespread discontent in the United States with bureaucrats in Washington that was expressed in the November 1994 elections.

Following the turmoil in the European currency markets in September 1992 and August 1993 caused by high German interest rates (a by-product of German reunification), the prospects for the achievement of a European central bank and a common currency dimmed, at least temporarily. But there clearly remains substantial momentum in the direction of monetary union, possibly including only a few members in the beginning. In July 1993, the decision was made to locate the European Monetary Institute, intended to be the core of the future European Central Bank, in Frankfurt, Germany. In December 1995, the prospective single currency was given the name "Euro," and the timetable for its introduction was extended to the year 2002. The final decision on which countries will be eligible to participate is scheduled for January 1998.

wanted to fight their recessions with stimulative monetary policies and lower interest rates.[11] Unwilling to boost interest rates at a time of high unemployment, Italy and the United Kingdom left the ERM in September 1992.

In August 1993, continuing high interest rates in Germany triggered a large movement of funds out of the French franc and some other European currencies into deutsche marks. Massive intervention by the Bank of France and the Bundesbank failed to stop the depreciation of the franc. The speculative attack ended when the ERM's permissible band of fluctuation was widened to 15 percent either side of the central exchange rate.

In spite of these recent setbacks there seems to be substantial support, at least at the leadership level in Europe, for adhering to the Maastricht timetable for the establishment of a single central bank and single currency. A fascinating episode in political and economic history is presently being played out in Europe. Giving up one's national currency, central bank, and control over monetary policy clearly means sacrificing a portion of national sovereignty. This issue has played a major role in the politics of Europe in recent years. In Britain, controversy within the ruling Conservative Party over Britain's role in Europe led to a change in leadership in 1990. Debate about whether Britain should participate in a single-currency Europe continues even today. The other side of the sovereignty issue stresses that a European central bank controlling the Euro currency and conducting monetary policy for all of Europe will effectively enhance the power of every other European country relative to Germany, whose Bundesbank currently dominates European monetary policy. As a consequence, many Germans are having second thoughts about yielding some control of Europe's monetary policy to those Europeans less concerned about inflation than themselves.

SUMMARY

Exchange rates link prices in one country with prices in other countries. Movements in exchange rates influence decisions about producing, importing, exporting, and investing. This chapter examined the evolution of the international monetary system over the past 50 years, a period of enormous growth in worldwide production and international trade. For the first half of the period the Bretton Woods system remained in place as nations attempted to keep exchange rates fixed. Under Bretton Woods, a country's central bank was obliged to keep the exchange value of its currency very close to its

fixed par value relative to the dollar. It did this by buying and selling dollars, thereby either adding to or drawing down its foreign currency reserves. If a country's exchange rate became chronically overvalued or undervalued, the country was deemed to have a "fundamental disequilbrium" and was permitted by the IMF to adjust the rate. During the Bretton Woods period, different inflation rates among nations and other changes in economic fundamentals combined with the increasing international mobility of capital to cause exchange rates that may originally have been equilibrium rates to

---

[11]Exhibit 27-2 mentioned Richard Cooper's criticism that Williamson's target zone proposal was politically unrealistic. Cooper argued that major participating countries will not often willingly subordinate their national monetary and fiscal policies to the achievement of exchange rate targets. Cooper's examples of this include the United States in the early 1980s (when the burgeoning budget deficits and restrictive Federal Reserve actions resulted in interest rate increases, triggering the huge dollar appreciation) and Germany in the early 1990s (when German reunification led to fiscal deficits and interest rate increases, and the subsequent breakup of the ERM).

become significantly under- or overvalued. Despite each country's freedom to adjust its rate, they actually went unchanged for years at a time. This caused some countries to experience chronic international trade surpluses while others experienced chronic deficits.

The Bretton Woods system collapsed in the early 1970s. Since then, various nations have employed a variety of approaches to exchange rates. At least half of all countries still maintain a fixed exchange rate with at least one of the major currencies. The major currencies—the dollar, yen, and mark—float. Central banks do not intervene to keep these exchange rates fixed. The exchange rates among these major currencies sometimes fluctuate appreciably from day to day and have changed considerably over the long run. There have been periods of years when exchange rates

trended predominantly in one direction or another. To the extent that exchange rates become misaligned, important adverse consequences occur. Proposals have been advanced for a new international monetary system to modify the floating-rate system by confining these major exchange rates within flexible target zones, but no formal agreements have been reached. The European Union, recognizing the convenience of exchange rate stability among its highly integrated economies, has long operated its own mechanism for keeping European exchange rates stable in relation to one another while permitting them to float relative to the dollar and the yen. The nations belonging to the European Union are in the process of moving to a single central bank and a single currency within the next few years.

KEY TERMS

International Monetary Fund (IMF)
Bretton Woods system
fixed exchange rates
devaluation
par value
intervention currency
overvalued currency
undervalued currency
overshooting

misaligned exchange rate
target zone
European Union
European Monetary System (EMS)
Exchange Rate Mechanism (ERM)
central exchange rate
European Currency Unit (ECU)
Maastricht Treaty

STUDY QUESTIONS

1   Under the Bretton Woods system, who determined the U.S. dollar–German mark exchange rate, the United States or Germany? Who had to take the initiative to change it?

2   Consider the exchange rate between the U.S. dollar and the German mark. Construct a supply-demand diagram with the quantity of dollars on the horizontal axis and the mark price of one dollar (DM/$) on the vertical axis. Draw hypothetical demand and supply curves for dollars that would produce a free market equilibrium price of 4 marks per dollar. Now assume that the German central bank, the Bundesbank, has pegged the price of the dollar at 3.6 marks. At that pegged

exchange rate, is the mark overvalued or undervalued relative to the dollar? To maintain the exchange rate at 3.6 marks per dollar, what kind of intervention in the foreign exchange market must the Bundesbank undertake? What change in Germany's international reserves would take place as a result of the intervention?

3   Returning to question 2, what would happen to the demand and supply curves if, over time, the U.S. inflation rate were consistently higher than the German inflation rate? If the exchange rate were maintained at the original pegged exchange rate of 3.6 marks per dollar, would the different inflation rates make the mark undervalued or

overvalued? If the Bundesbank decided to adjust the exchange rate to restore equilibrium, would it have to devalue or revalue the mark?

4 Look at Figures 27-2 and 27-3, where the fixed exchange-rate level is not in equilibrium and central bank intervention is required to maintain the exchange rate at its fixed level. In which of these two situations would a central bank be under more pressure to adjust the fixed rate toward its equilibrium rate? (Hint: What is happening to the nation's foreign exchange reserves in each situation?)

5 Look at Table 27-1. What kind of exchange rate arrangement was being used by each of the following countries at the end of 1995?

a Venezuela

b Estonia

c Latvia

d Lithuania

e Japan

6 Table 27-1 shows that Argentina (in IMF category 1) is attempting to keep the exchange rate of its currency, the peso, fixed in relation to the dollar. How would we describe the exchange rate relationship of the peso to the *yen*? (Hint: What is the relationship of the *dollar* to the yen?)

7 What kind of exchange rate arrangement would you predict would be chosen by a small country whose international trade is predominantly with one, much larger economy? Do you think the rate of inflation in the larger country would

be an important factor in the small country's choice?

8 Look at Figure 27-5, which shows the mark-dollar exchange rate. The overall appreciation of the mark relative to the dollar over the entire period is prominent. The dramatic appreciation of the dollar (depreciation of the mark) in the period 1980–1985 stands out. Do you think it likely that economic fundamentals (inflation rates, consumption preferences, productivity behavior) could possibly have changed enough in that short period to warrant such a change in exchange rates?

9 Why must a nation that desires free international movement of capital and chooses to maintain a fixed exchange rate sacrifice control over its conduct of monetary policy? Explain.

10 Why must a country that wishes to maintain its sovereignty over domestic monetary policy and maintain fixed exchange rates place restrictions on international capital flows? Explain.

11 Discuss the advantages and disadvantages of fixed exchange rates and floating exchange rates.

12 Focusing on the roles of inflation, national pride, and international reserves, explain the forces that produced the collapse of the Bretton Woods system in the early 1970s.

13 Why might a country desire to have an undervalued currency? An overvalued currency?

14 Explain why a tax on foreign exchange transactions would help reduce exchange rate volatility without having a major adverse effect on imports, exports, and long-term capital flows.

SUGGESTIONS FOR ADDITIONAL READING

For alternative analyses of the topics in this chapter, consult an undergraduate textbook in international economics or international finance. Good examples include Michael Melvin, *International Money and Finance,* 4th ed. (New York: HarperCollins, 1995); Paul Krugman and Maurice Obstfeld, *International Economics: Theory and Policy,* 3d ed. (New York: HarperCollins, 1995); and Dennis R. Appleyard and Alfred J. Field, Jr., *International Economics,* 2d ed. (Homewood, Ill.: Irwin, 1995). A lucid and classic paper that advocates floating exchange rates over fixed rates is Milton Friedman, "The Case for Flexible Exchange Rates," in Milton Friedman, *Essays in Positive Economics* (Chicago: University of Chicago Press, 1953). An especially useful book is Peter B. Kenen (ed.), *Managing the World Economy: Fifty Years after Bretton Woods* (Washington, D.C.: Institute for International Economics, 1994). See especially Chap. 1, by Barry Eichengreen and Peter B. Kenen, entitled "Managing the World Economy under the Bretton Woods System: An Overview." Chap. 2,

"Managing the Monetary System" by John Williamson and C. Randall Henning, is a detailed summary of the target zone proposal. The comments on these papers by others in the Kenen book are also very useful. Ronald I. McKinnon, "International Money in Historical Perspective," *Journal of Economic Literature,* 31(1) (March 1993), pp. 1–44, contains a useful analysis of Bretton Woods and the European Monetary System. See also Barry Eichengreen, "European Monetary Unification," *Journal of Economic Literature,* 31(3) (September 1993), pp. 1321–1357. A very comprehensive analysis of the experience with floating exchange rates is contained in Maurice Obstfeld, "International Currency Experience: New Lessons and Lessons Relearned," *Brookings Papers on Economic Activity,* 1 (1995), pp. 119–220. Also, a convenient and up-to-date summary of this experience is provided in Jeffrey A. Frankel, "Recent Exchange-Rate Experience and Proposals for Reform," *American Economic Review,* 86(2) (May 1996), pp. 153–158.

G L O S S A R Y

A

Adaptive expectations: Method of forming expectations in which agents gradually change their expectations in response to recent phenomena. **26**

Adjustable-peg exchange rate system: See Bretton Woods exchange rate system. **8, 27**

Adjustment credit: Discount loans granted to banks by the Federal Reserve in response to routine, but unexpected, reserve deficiencies. **18**

Adverse selection: The tendency for those persons with the highest probability of experiencing financial problems to seek out and be granted loans or insurance. Arises *before* a transaction occurs, due to asymmetric information. **4**

Aggregate demand (AD) curve: The relationship between a nation's price level and the amount of real output demanded, other factors being held constant. **20**

Aggregate supply (AS) curve: The relationship between a nation's price level and the amount of real output firms collectively desire to produce, other factors being held constant. **20**

Appreciation: An increase in the value of one nation's currency relative to another currency in a floating exchange rate system, such that each unit of the nation's currency buys more units of the other nation's currency. **1, 8**

Asset: A material possession or financial claim that is a store of value, owned by an individual, firm, government or other entity. **9**

Asymmetric information: Condition in which the two parties to a transaction possess differing information concerning the intentions of the other party and the likely risks and returns associated with that transaction. May lead to the problems of moral hazard and adverse selection. **4**

Automatic transfer service (ATS) account: Type of account in which funds are automatically transferred from savings account to checking account as checks are presented for payment. Legalized nationwide by the Depository Institutions Deregulation Act of 1980, and are included in M1. **9**

B

Bank: Financial institution which accepts various types of deposits and uses the funds attracted primarily to grant loans and purchase relatively safe debt instruments. The term is used generically to encompass commercial banks, savings and loan associations, credit unions, and mutual savings banks. **1**

Bank Holding Company Act of 1956: Legislation which prohibited bank branching via acquisition of banks by shell corporations called bank holding companies. **10**

Bank liquidity trap: Potential situation in which bank demand for excess reserves becomes perfectly elastic with respect to the interest rate, thus rendering the central bank incapable of increasing the money supply. **16**

Bank of the United States: The first national bank chartered in the United States, formed to finance Revolutionary War debt and to provide stability to the financial sector. **10**

Bankers' acceptance: A check, usually written by a firm, which is guaranteed ("accepted") by a major bank and is payable at some future date. They are tradable in a secondary market at a discount from face value. **3**

Banking Act of 1933 (Glass-Steagall Act): Legislation separating commercial banking from investment banking, and separating banking from industry. Other provisions in the Act established deposit interest rate ceilings and federal deposit insurance, and regulated the nature of permissible bank assets. **10, 11**

Board of Governors of the Federal Reserve System: Seven person board, appointed by the U.S. president, which dominates the conduct of monetary policy. This board sets reserve requirements and the discount rate, and constitutes the voting majority of the Federal Open Market Committee. **12**

Bond: A long-term debt instrument issued by a firm, government, or agency; a contractual agreement to make a certain stream of payments at specified future dates.   **1**

Bretton Woods exchange rate system: International financial arrangement in place during 1944–1973 in which each nation's government agreed to directly intervene in the foreign exchange market to peg exchange rates at specified levels.   **8, 27**

Brokered Deposits: A financial innovation in which brokerage firms divide multi-million dollar blocks of funds into $100,000 units and sell them to depository institutions as fully insured certificates of deposit.   **11**

Budget deficit: The amount by which government expenditures exceed tax revenues.   **1**

C

Capital accounts (capital):   The net worth of a bank, or the equity claim of the bank's owners on the bank's assets; total assets minus liabilities of a bank at a given point in time.   **9**

Capital market: Market in which long-term debt instruments and equities are traded. Instruments include bonds, mortgages, preferred stock, and common stock.   **3**

Capital standards: Minimum required ratio of a depository institution's capital accounts to its total assets, established and enforced by the banking regulatory authorities.   **11**

Central bank: A nation's monetary authority or agency charged with conducting monetary policy, along with other duties. In the United States, the central bank is the Federal Reserve System.   **1**

Central Exchange Rate: A specified exchange rate, around which the members of the European Monetary System agree to maintain the actual exchange rate within a narrow band through direct government intervention; analogous to par value exchange rate in the Bretton Woods system.   **27**

Certificate of deposit (CD):   A form of time deposit issued by a depository institution, which entitles bearer to receive interest payment plus principal at a specified future date.   **3**

Clearing House Interbank Payments System (CHIPS):   A private telecommunications system through which banks can transfer funds internationally to one another via electronic impulse.   **2**

Commercial paper: A short-term debt instrument issued by financial and nonfinancial firms of excellent credit standing. Usually denominated in units of $1 million, these money market instruments are traded by dealers.   **3**

Common stock: Equity or ownership claim on a firm's real capital assets which has no maturity date and which entitles the owner to share in the profits of the firm.   **3**

Comptroller of the Currency: An agency of the government (an office within the Treasury Department) charged with chartering, supervising, and examining national banks.   **10**

Corporate bond: A long-term debt instrument issued by a corporation; a debt claim against a corporation's assets which may be collateralized (secured) or unsecured. (*See also* **Bond.**)   **3**

Countercyclical monetary policy: A (successful) monetary policy which smoothes or reduces the fluctuations in economic activity over the course of the business cycle.   **18**

Coupon rate: Rate of return on bond, expressed as annual interest payment divided by the face value of the bond.   **3**

Credit View: Hypothesis that bank lending more strongly influences economic activity than bank security purchases. Hence, one must look not just at the *money supply*, but rather the *source* of money in order to predict its impact on economic activity.   **25**

Crowding-out effect: Propensity for a debt-financed increase in government

spending to cause a compensatory decrease in another form of spending—particularly investment or net exports.   **24**

Currency ratio (*k*):   The ratio of currency held by the public to demand deposits and other checkable accounts. An important variable, determined by the public, which influences the money-supply multiplier and the nation's money supply.   **15**

Current yield: A measure of the rate of return on an asset, which consists of the yearly return on the instrument divided by the price of the instrument, but which does not include the return stemming from price appreciation or depreciation of the asset during its holding period.   **3**

D

Debt instrument: A contractual agreement by a borrowing party to pay a specific amount of money (the face value) at a specified future date. The contract may also contain provisions for periodic interest payments over the life of the contract.   **3**

Debt management: Management or decision making concerning the maturity structure of newly issued U.S. government debt; a responsibility of the U.S. Treasury.   **3**

Default risk: Risk that some portion of principal or interest on a debt instrument or other claim will not be repaid by the borrower.   **3**

Defensive open market operations: Buying or selling securities in the open market by the Federal Reserve for the purpose of defending bank reserves and the monetary base against undesired changes caused by factors outside of the Fed's control.   **17**

Deflation: Process of negative inflation or a falling general price level, experienced in the United States during pre-World War II business cycle contractions, including the Great Depression of 1929–1933.   **16, 20**

Demand deposits: Deposits which can be withdrawn in currency or transferred by check to a third party at the initiative of the owner; constitutes the bulk of the narrow money supply, M1. **9**

Demand for Money: Amount of wealth that an individual (or the nation collectively) prefers to maintain in the form of money. **21**

Depository Institutions Deregulation and Monetary Control Act (DIDMCA): 1980 legislation that provided for the phase-out of all interest rate ceilings, the phase-in of uniform reserve requirements for all depository institutions, and generally moved in the direction of deregulation of depository institutions' asset and liability structures. **11**

Depreciation: A decline in the value of one nation's currency relative to another currency in a floating exchange rate system, so that each unit of the nation's currency buys fewer units of the other nation's currency. **1, 8**

Desired excess reserve ratio (r_e): Ratio of desired aggregate excess reserves to aggregate checkable deposits; an important variable, determined by bank managers, which influences the money supply multiplier and thus the nation's supply of money. **15**

Devaluation: An exchange rate adjustment in a fixed or adjustable-peg exchange rate system, in which the value or price of the nation's currency expressed in units of foreign currency is reduced. **27**

Directive of Federal Open Market Committee: Formal statement indicating the intended posture of Federal Reserve policy, drawn up and voted upon during FOMC meetings. **12**

Discount rate: Rate of interest charged by the Federal Reserve to depository institutions which borrow reserves at the Federal Reserve Banks. **9, 14, 15**

Discount window: Term used to refer to the mechanism in place for deposi-

tory institutions to borrow reserves from the Federal Reserve Banks. **18**

Discounts and advances: Loans in the form of reserves made by the Federal Reserve Banks to depository institutions. **9, 12, 17, 18**

Diseconomies of scale: Cost structure characterized by rising costs per unit of output as output expands. This phenomenon is attributable to duplication and bureaucratic confusion inherent in very large organizations. **10**

Disintermediation: Withdrawal of funds from depository institutions by lenders in order to purchase direct claims issued by deficit spenders. Occurred in 1966, 1969, and 1974, but is less likely to occur in the future due to dismantling of interest-rate ceilings. **6**

District Federal Reserve bank: The Federal Reserve System consists of twelve regional districts, each of which has a Federal Reserve District Bank. **12**

Divisia aggregate: An alternative measure of the money supply which consists of a *weighted average* of currency, checkable deposits, and other short-term financial claims that influence aggregate expenditures. **2**

Dual banking system: System in which both the federal government and individual state governments are granted authority to charter commercial banks. **10**

Dynamic open market operations: Open market security transactions by the Federal Reserve System which are intended to push key variables such as the unemployment or inflation rate in a direction perceived by the Fed to be in the national interest. **17**

E

Economies of scale: Cost structure characterized by declining cost per unit of output as output expands. This phenonemon is attributable to existence of certain large fixed and overhead costs, which can be spread over more units as output expands. **10**

Economies of scope: Condition in which a variety of goods or services may be produced at lower average cost when produced as a group than they can be individually. **10**

Electronic funds transfer system (EFTS): Use of computer technology to make payment by debiting and crediting bank deposits by electronic impulse rather than by use of checks. **2**

Emergency Credit: Loans by the Federal Reserve to individuals or firms (other than depository institutions) whose financial impairment may cause serious economic repercussions. Authority to grant such loans has not been exercised since the 1930s. **18**

Equation of exchange: A mathematical identity or truistic equation which sets forth the relationship between the supply of money, income velocity of money, the price level, and real output. $MV_y \equiv PY$. **21**

Equity: A financial claim representing ownership in a business entity; gives the bearer a right to share in the net income of the instrument's issuer, and consists chiefly of common stock. **3**

Equity multiplier: Ratio of a firm's total assets to its equity capital; it is indicative of the magnitude of leverage applied to its rate of return on assets. **9**

Eurodollars: Deposits denominated in U.S. dollars held in banks located in foreign nations. **3**

European Currency Unit (ECU): A currency unit defined in terms of specified quantities of various European Community currencies; the currency unit of the European Monetary System; serves as unit of account but not as medium of exchange. **27**

European Monetary System: An organization of European nations, initially formed in 1979, which agree to fix their mutual exchange rates while allowing their currencies to float against currencies of nonmember nations. **27**

European Union: Organization of European countries promoting economic integration via removal of barriers to trade, labor mobility, and capital movements. Formerly known as the European Common Market. **27**

Excess reserves: Depository institution reserves (cash and deposits at the Fed) held above and beyond the amount that is required. **9, 13, 15**

Exchange rate: See Foreign Exchange Rate. **1**

Exchange Rate Mechanism: System in which exchange rate fluctuations among the currencies of cooperating European nations are limited by mutual agreement. **27**

Expected or ex-ante real interest rate: Effective interest rate after adjusting nominal interest rate for expected inflation; calculated by subtracting expected inflation rate from the nominal interest rate. **6**

Extended credit: Long-term loans from the Federal Reserve to depository institutions experiencing serious liquidity problems. **18**

F

Federal Banking Commission: Proposed body that would assume responsibility for chartering national banks and thrift institutions; would also regulate all federally insured depository institutions. **10**

Federal Deposit Insurance Corporation Improvement Act of 1991 (FDICIA): Legislation designed to improve the system of federal deposit insurance; included provisions to recapitalize the FDIC, establish tighter capital standards, and establish risk-based deposit insurance premiums. **11**

Federal funds: (*See also* **Federal funds market.**) **3**

Federal funds market: Market in which excess reserve balances of depository institutions at the Federal Reserve are traded on an overnight basis. **9**

Federal funds rate: The rate of interest prevailing on overnight loans of deposits at the Federal Reserve; a widely quoted, sensitive barometer of money market conditions. **9**

Federal Home Loan Bank Board (FHLBB): Organization established by Congress in the 1930s to regulate the Savings and Loan industry. Its subsidiary, the Federal Savings and Loan Insurance Corporation (now defunct), was responsible for insuring S&L deposits. **11**

Federal Open Market Committee (FOMC): Committee which formulates the general posture of monetary policy. Consists of the 7 members of the Board of Governors and the 12 presidents of the district Federal Reserve banks, 5 of which serve as voting members on an alternating basis. **12**

Federal Reserve Act of 1913: Legislation which created the Federal Reserve System; drafted in response to recurrent financial panics in the 19th and early 20th centuries. **12**

Federal Reserve System: The central bank of the United States, charged with conducting monetary policy and other duties associated with our financial system. **1**

Federal Savings and Loan Insurance Corporation (FSLIC): Subsidiary of FHLBB, created to insure deposits of savings and loan associations (now defunct). **11**

Fedwire: An electronic system through which financial institutions that maintain accounts at the Federal Reserve can transfer funds to one another. **2**

Fiat money (credit money): Money which has little value in nonmoney purposes (i.e., as a commodity), instead usually deriving its value by government decree. All of our currency and coins today are fiat money. **2**

Financial Institutions Reform, Recovery, and Enforcement Act (FIRREA): 1989 legislation drafted in response to the savings and loan and commercial banking crises of the 1980s; abolished the FHLBB and the FSLIC, created the Resolution Trust Corporation to liquidate failed banks and S&Ls, and created the Office of Thrift Supervision, the Bank Insurance Fund, and the Savings Association Insurance Fund. **11**

Financial intermediary: An institution which issues various types of secondary claims, such as savings deposits, and purchases primary claims issued by deficit-spending units; it thereby serves the function of assisting in the transfer of funds from savers to deficit-spending units. **1**

Financial intermediation: The flow of funds from savers to deficit spenders by way of financial intermediaries. **4**

Fisher effect: The tendency for the level of interest rates to be influenced by the magnitude of expected inflation. Named for Irving Fisher, one of the first economists to intensively study the phenomenon. **5**

Fisher Hypothesis: Theory which asserts that nominal interest rates move in a point-for-point fashion with changes in the expected rate of inflation. **5**

Fixed exchange rates: International financial arrangement in which governments directly intervene in the foreign exchange market to prevent exchange rates from deviating by more than a very small margin from some specific central or parity value. (*See also* **Bretton Woods exchange rate system.**) **1, 27**

Float: Difference between cash items in the process of collection in the banking system and deferred availability cash items; essentially an interest-free loan of reserves from the Federal Reserve to the banks, arising from check collection procedures. **14**

Floating exchange rates: International financial arrangement in which exchange rate levels are allowed to change continuously in response to market forces. Arrangement may vary from *free float,* i.e., absolutely no government intervention, to a *managed float,* i.e., limited but sometimes aggressive government intervention in the foreign exchange market. **1, 8**

Forbearance: Practice of allowing technically insolvent savings and loan associations to continue operations in hopes that better financial conditions will return them to solvency. **11**

Foreign exchange market: The market in which national currencies are exchanged for one another. **1, 8**

Foreign exchange rate: The price at which one nation's currency is traded for the currency of another nation. **1, 8**

Forward exchange rate: The exchange rate in a contract for receipt of and payment for foreign currency at a specified date, usually 30 days, 90 days, or 180 days in the future. **8**

Forward exchange transaction: Purchase and sale of a foreign currency for delivery and payment at a specified future date at a price specified in advance. **8**

Forward interest rate: Hypothetical future short-term interest rate that equalizes average returns that investors earn by purchasing a long-term security or a succession of short-term securities. **7**

Fractional reserve banking system: A form of banking system in which banks are required to hold reserves, i.e., cash and deposits at the central bank, only in the amount of some fraction of their deposit liabilities. **12**

Free Banking Era: Period from 1836–1863, characterized by minimal supervision of banking activity. **10**

Full-bodied money (commodity money): Form of money such as gold coins, tobacco, or fishhooks, whose value in exchange (as money) is equivalent to its value as a commodity. The gold standard (1880–1914) was an example of a commodity money system. **2**

G

Garn-St. Germain Act of 1982: Legislation which implemented significant deregulation of thrift institutions; granted thrifts authority to engage in additional activities to enable them to compete with money market mutual funds. **11**

I

Impact lag: Time that elapses between the date on which a policy change is implemented and the date on which that policy change begins to influence economic activity. **26**

Implementation lag: Time that elapses between the date on which a need for policy change is recognized and the date on which the needed policy is actually implemented. **26**

Income: The flow of earnings, measured as dollars per unit of time. **2**

Income effect: The effect that a change in the money supply exerts on interest rates via its prior effect on the nation's income. **5**

Income elasticity of demand for money: A measure of the responsiveness of money demand to changes in income; the percentage change in demand for money divided by the percentage change in income. **22**

Income velocity of money: Ratio of the flow of GDP to the stock of money; a multiplier that links the money supply to aggregate GDP expenditures. **21**

Inflation: Persistent increase in the general price level, or persistent reduction in the value of the monetary unit, e.g., the dollar. **1, 20**

Inflation expectations effect: The effect on interest rates stemming from the announcement of a change in the money supply. **5**

Inflation neutrality: Condition in which inflation is fully anticipated and compensated for by economic agents, fully attenuating the potential redistributive effects of inflation. **5**

Inflationary gap: The magnitude by which the equilibrium output level exceeds the full-employment output level; occurs in an overheated economy, when aggregate expenditures exceed the nation's capacity to produce output. **20**

Insolvency: State of financial condition in which the value of an entity's assets is less than the value of its liabilities. **9**

Instrument or tool of monetary policy: A mechanism used by the central bank to implement changes in reserves, interest rates, credit availability, and the supply of money. The primary instruments are open market operations, discount policy, and reserve requirement policy. **17**

Interest parity condition: Condition in which, in a world of perfect capital mobility, expected returns on assets are equal across countries. **8**

Interest rate: The cost of borrowing or the return from lending, expressed as an annual percentage. **1**

Intermediate target of monetary policy: A variable in the transmission linkage of monetary policy which lies in between the Federal Reserve instruments and the ultimate goals of policy, and which the Fed attempts to control in order to achieve the ultimate goals. Includes such variables as reserves, the monetary aggregates (M1, M2, M3), and short-term interest rates. **19**

International capital flows: Transfers of funds internationally in the form of acquisition of bank deposits, securities, or real assets. **8**

International Monetary Fund: Organization created by the 1944 Bretton Woods Agreement for the purpose of promoting a stable international monetary environment. **8, 27**

Intervention currency: In a fixed exchange rate system, the currency in which participating nations hold their international reserves. Under the Bretton Woods system, the U.S. dollar served as the intervention currency. **27**

IS curve: Locus of all combinations of interest rates and aggregate income levels which are consistent with equilibrium in the product market. **23**

IS-LM model: Macroeconomic model incorporating product market and money market equilibria to determine the equilibrium level of output and interest rates. **23**

J

Junk bond: Corporate or municipal bond judged to bear a high risk of default; a bond rated Ba or lower by Moody's. **7**

L

Law of one price: Fundamental economic principle asserting that, under conditions of free trade and zero transportation costs, a homogeneous good's price will be the same whether purchased at home or abroad. **8**

Legal reserves: (*See also* **Reserves.**) **9, 12**

Legal tender: Currency which, by law, cannot be refused if offered as payment. In the United States, currency and coins are legal tender. Demand deposits and other checkable deposits are not legal tender (though they are redeemable in legal tender on demand). **2**

Lender of last resort: Function of the central bank in providing funds to depository institutions in time of panic or widespread severe financial distress. **12**

Liabilities: Financial claims on an individual, firm, government, or other entity, held by external entities. **9**

Limited branching: Restrictions imposed by state banking commissions which limited banks to a certain number of offices. **10**

Liquidity: The ease with which an asset can be converted to money. The lower the transactions costs and risk of depreciation of principal, the greater is the liquidity of the asset. **2, 3, 9**

Liquidity effect: The short-term effect that a change in the money supply exerts on interest rates by altering the liquidity of the financial system. **5**

Liquidity preference schedule: A schedule depicting the inverse relationship between the level of interest rates and the quantity of money held for speculative purposes. **21**

Liquidity premium theory: Theory of term structure of interest rates which asserts that the long-term interest rate is equal to the average of current and expected future short-term interest rates plus a premium to compensate lenders for the additional market risk embodied in long-term securities. **7**

LM curve: Locus of all combinations of interest rates and aggregate income levels which are consistent with equilibrium in the money market, i.e., the combinations that equate the demand for money with the existing supply of money. **23**

Loanable funds model: An interest rate model in which the interest rate is viewed as the price which equates the flow supply of loanable funds with the flow demand for loanable funds. **5**

M

M1: The transactions or narrow measure of money; consists of currency held by the public, traveler's checks, demand deposits and other checkable deposits such as NOW and ATS accounts and credit union share draft accounts. **2**

M2: A broader measure of the money supply; consists of M1 plus several highly liquid financial assets, such as overnight repurchase agreements and Eurodollars, noninstitutional money market mutual fund balances, money market deposit accounts, and savings and small time deposits, i.e., time deposits of less than $100,000. **2**

M3: A very broad measure of money; consists of M2 plus large denomination time deposits, institutional money market mutual fund shares, term repurchase agreements and term Eurodollars. **2**

Maastricht Treaty: 1991 treaty among European Community members; called for creation of a single European central bank and a single currency, and established criteria that prospective members must meet in order to join the monetary union. **27**

Manager of the System Open Market Account: The individual (a vice-president of the Federal Reserve Bank of New York) who receives and implements the directive of the Federal Open Market Committee. This individual carries out open market operations by purchasing and selling U.S. government securities. **12, 17**

Margin requirements: Minimum percentage of the value of a purchase of securities which must be paid for with the buyer's own funds (as opposed to borrowed funds); set by Board of Governors of the Federal Reserve System. **12**

Marginal efficiency of investment (MEI): The expected rate of return from an additional unit of investment in capital goods. The MEI schedule depicts the expected rate of returns from investment in capital goods as a downward-sloping function of the volume of investment. **25**

Marginal productivity of capital: Rate of return expected from an additional unit of capital goods. **6**

Market risk: The risk that the principal value (or price) of a financial asset will fluctuate as a result of changes in expectations, interest rates, and other phenomena. The higher the market risk of a financial asset, the lower its liquidity. **3, 7**

Matched sale-purchase transaction (reverse repurchase agreement, or reverse RP): Arrangement in which the Federal Reserve sells securities under the condition that the buyer re-sells them to the Fed at a specified future date and price. **17**

McFadden Act of 1927: Federal legislation prohibiting national banks from operating outside the borders of the home state, and compelling national banks to abide by state laws governing intrastate branching. **10**

Misaligned exchange rate: An exchange rate that is inconsistent with achievement of such domestic goals as high employment or low inflation and external goals such as absence of an international trade deficit. **27**

Misery index: An indicator of a nation's overall economic hardship, calculated as the sum of the rate of inflation and the unemployment rate. **20**

Monetary Aggregates: The various measures of the money supply used by the Federal Reserve; includes M1, M2, M3, and L. **2**

Monetary base: Those financial assets which can potentially be used as bank reserves for purposes of meeting reserve requirements; consists of depository institutions' deposits at the Federal Reserve plus all currency and coin outside of the Treasury and Federal Reserve. **14**

Monetary policy: Measures implemented by the central bank to change the supply of money, the level of interest rates, or the availability of credit in order to seek to achieve ultimate goals of policy such as stable prices and high employment. **1**

Monetary theory: Analysis of the relationship between the nation's money supply and economic activity. **20**

Money: Anything widely or universally accepted as payment. Usually defined to consist of all legal tender (currency and coins) plus various transactions accounts and other short-term financial assets. The most commonly used measure of money is M1, defined above. **1, 2**

Money illusion: The propensity to judge value only in nominal terms rather than in real or price-adjusted terms, and therefore to be fooled by changes in the nation's price level. **6**

Money market: Market in which short-term, highly liquid financial instruments are traded in large quantities. Money market instruments include Treasury bills, bankers' acceptances, commercial paper, Eurodollar deposits, federal funds, and negotiable CDs. **3**

Money market deposit accounts (MMDA): Accounts authorized by the Garn-St. Germain Act of 1982; they require an initial balance of $2,500, are not subject to interest rate ceilings, and have limited check writing features. Included in M2, but not in M1. **9**

Money supply: A stock of financial assets which serve the medium of exchange function or are easily convertible into such media. The narrow measure of money (M1) consists of demand deposits and other checkable deposits plus currency held by the public, and thus emphasizes the medium of exchange function of money. Broader measures (M2, M3) include other highly liquid assets easily convertible into M1. **1, 2**

Money supply multiplier: Ratio of the money supply to the monetary base; this variable encompasses the role of the portfolio behavior of the public and depository institutions in influencing the money supply. **14**

Money view: The view that bank lending and bank security purchasing have similar effects on economic activity; in this view, one need only look at change in the money supply rather than changes in the amount of bank loans to effectively forecast economic activity. **25**

Moral hazard: The risk, arising from asymmetric information, that the borrower may engage in activity that is undesirable from lender's point of view; stems from lender's difficulty in monitoring borrower's activity after loan is granted. **4**

Mortgage: A loan-term loan to finance the purchase of real property, secured by a lien on that property. **3**

Mortgage-backed security: A financial claim which separates the financing and servicing of mortgages. Banks package groups of mortgages, which are sold in security form to large investors. The banks continue to service the mortgages, and pass the payments on to the buyers of the security. **3**

Municipal bond: Debt instrument representing a claim on a municipality such as country or city, which may be backed by a specific revenue source (industrial revenue bonds) or by the taxing power of the issuing entity (general obligation bonds). **3**

N

National Banking Act of 1863: Legislation which permitted the chartering of national banks; drafted to moderate the excesses of Free Banking Era, and to create institutions to hold debt issued to finance the Civil War. **10**

Natural or full employment output level: Highest level of output consistent with the existing rate of inflation. (*See also* **Potential GDP.**) **20, 26**

Natural unemployment rate: The lowest unemployment rate that could be sustained without triggering an acceleration in the underlying or existing rate of inflation. **19, 20**

Negative externality: Situation in which the cost of an event (such as a bank failure) to society exceeds the costs incurred by the entity experiencing the event (the owners of the bank). **11**

Negotiable CD: A certificate of deposit in a denomination of $100,000 or more, which may be traded prior to maturity in a well-developed secondary market. **3**

Negotiable order of withdrawal (NOW) account: Interest-bearing savings account, on which limited check writing privileges are permitted. Included in M1. **9**

Net free reserves (NFR): The difference between aggregate excess reserves in the banking system and the volume of bank borrowing from the Federal

Reserve (discounts and advances). This variable was formerly used by the Federal Reserve as an intermediate target of monetary policy.   **19**

Net worth: The amount by which total assets exceed total liabilities. When related to financial institutions, net worth is also known as "capital accounts."   **9**

New Classical Macroeconomics, or Rational Expectations Macroeconomics (REM):   Modern school of thought that asserts that economic agents take all available information into account in forming expectations, and utilize the correct economic model in making forecasts; therefore, only *unanticipated* macroeconomic policies affect such real economic variables as output and employment. (*See also* **Rational Expectations theory.**)   **26**

Nonborrowed base ($B - A$):   The monetary base (bank reserves plus currency held by the public) minus the volume of discounts and advances. Sometimes used as an intermediate target of monetary policy.   **19**

Nonborrowed reserves ($R - A$):   Total bank reserves minus the volume of discounts and advances. Sometimes used as an intermediate target of monetary policy.   **19**

O

Open market operations: The principal tool of Federal Reserve Policy; consists of purchases and sales of securities in the open market by the Federal Reserve.   **12, 17**

Overshooting: Phenomenon in which a change in the money supply causes the exchange rate to change more in the short run than in the long run.   **27**

Overvalued currency: A currency whose foreign exchange value is greater than that justified on the basis of such economic fundamentals as price-level and productivity behavior.   **27**

P

Par Value: A specific exchange rate in the Bretton Woods system, around which each nation agreed to maintain

the actual exchange rate within a narrow margin.   **27**

Permanent income: Long-run average expected future income.   **22**

Phillips curve: A graph depicting existence of an alleged trade-off or inverse relationship between the unemployment rate and the rate of inflation.   **26**

Policy directive: (*See also* **Directive of the Federal Open Market Committee.**)   **17**

Policy ineffectiveness theorem: Theory which states that anticipated monetary and fiscal policy actions will have no effect on real variables; proposition that only unanticipated policy actions can influence output and employment.   **26**

Political business cycle: Deliberate manipulation of economic activity for political purposes; tendency for the economy to be stimulated by discretionary monetary or fiscal actions as elections approach.   **26**

Potential or natural GDP: The level of GDP which would hypothetically prevail if the economy were maintained at the high level of output corresponding to the natural rate of unemployment.   **20**

Precautionary demand for money: Money held as a contingency to protect against an unexpected increase in expenditures or an unexpected decrease in income.   **21**

Preferred habitat theory: Theory of term structure that asserts that borrowers and lenders have strong preferences for particular maturities, but may be induced to switch maturities if returns on alternative maturities are particularly large.   **7**

Present value: The value today of the right to receive a certain payment or stream of payments in the future.   **5**

Primary claim: Financial claim issued by the ultimate deficit spending or equity-issuing unit. Examples include commercial paper, bonds, and shares of stock.   **4**

Primary market: Market in which newly issued securities are exchanged.   **3**

Prime loan rate: A benchmark interest rate that banks establish for large borrowers with excellent credit ratings. Most other loan rates are linked to the prime rate by a positive margin.   **1**

Principal-agent problem: A moral hazard problem that occurs because the managers in control (agents) act in their own interest rather than in the interest of the owners (principals). This phenomenon arises due to differing sets of incentives on the part of managers and owners.   **11**

Productivity of Capital: Positive rate of return associated with acquisition of capital goods; one of the reasons why expected real interest rates are positive.   **6**

Purchasing power parity theory (PPP):   Hypothesis that relative price level behavior in two nations is the predominant determinant of changes in the exchange rate between those two nations, and that exchange rates adjust fully in the long run to offset the effects of different rates of inflation between those nations.   **8**

Pure expectations theory: Theory that the term structure of interest rates is determined by the expected future level of interest rates relative to current interest rates. The long-term rate is viewed as the geometric mean of the current and expected future short-term rates.   **7**

Q

q Theory: Theory that treats investment spending as a function of q, the ratio of the market value of firms to the replacement cost of firms' capital. Developed by James Tobin, the theory emphasizes role that stock prices play in influencing investment spending.   **25**

Quota: An explicit and specific restriction on the volume of imports a nation permits in any given period.   **8**

R

Rational expectations theory: Theory premised on the assumption that economic agents formulate their expectations after using all available relevant information as well as the knowledge of how economic variables interact in the appropriate model of economic behavior. **6, 26**

Real aftertax interest rate: Effective interest rate after adjusting for both taxes and expected inflation. Calculated by subtracting expected inflation from the aftertax nominal interest rate. **6**

Real interest rate: Interest rate after adjusting the nominal interest rate for expected inflation. **1, 6**

Realized or ex-post real interest rate: Real interest rate calculated after the fact by subtracting the actual inflation rate from the nominal interest rate. **6**

Recessionary gap: The magnitude by which the equilibrium output level falls short of the full-employment output level. Occurs when aggregate expenditures are insufficient to purchase output that would be produced in conditions of full employment. **20**

Recognition lag: Time that elapses between the date on which policy action would ideally be implemented and the date on which policy-making officials become aware of a need for action. **26**

Representative full-bodied money: Paper money that attests to ownership of an underlying commodity. **2**

Repurchase agreement (RP): Transaction in which a security is sold under agreement to repurchase it (at a higher price) at a specified future date. **3, 1**

Required reserve ratio (r_r): The ratio of required reserves to *DDO* (demand deposits and other checkable deposits). **15**

Required reserves: Dollar amount of reserves (cash and deposits at the Fed) which depository institutions are required to hold, based on percentage reserve requirements set by the Fed and the magnitude of deposits. **13, 15**

Reserve requirement: Percentage figure specified by the Federal Reserve, which depository institutions are required to hold in reserves to support deposit liabilities. **9, 13**

Reserves (R): Cash on hand and deposits at the Federal Reserve maintained by depository institutions. **9, 13, 15**

Ricardian Equivalence Proposition: Theory which asserts that agents anticipate the future tax liabilities associated with larger budget deficits, and increase their savings rates to compensate. This renders fiscal policy impotent and negates any potential crowding out effects. **5**

Riegle-Neal Interstate Banking and Branching Efficiency Act of 1994: Federal legislation which gradually eliminates branching restrictions from interstate banking. **10**

Risk premium: Additional yield embodied in financial claims to compensate lenders for increased default risk. May be measured as difference between yields on risky assets and on government bonds with similar maturity, marketability, and tax treatment provisions. **7**

S

Seasonal credit: Loans in the form of reserves made by the Federal Reserve to small depository institutions that are subject to strong seasonal fluctuations in loan demand. **18**

Second Bank of the United States: The second national bank to emerge in the United States, chartered in 1816 to provide financial stability following the War of 1812. **10**

Secondary claim: Financial claim issued by a financial intermediary, the proceeds of which are used largely to purchase primary claims. Examples include deposits, money market mutual funds shares, and insurance policies. **4**

Secondary market: Market in which securities are traded after they have been issued. **3**

Secondary reserves: Highly liquid short-term financial instruments held by depository institutions as a safeguard against possible loss of funds or increase in loan demand. Consists chiefly of Treasury bills, bankers' acceptances, federal funds sold, and excess reserves. **9**

Segmented markets theory: The proposition that various potential issuers and purchasers of securities are rigidly committed to a particular maturity. For this reason, there is alleged to be little scope for substitution among maturities by market participants. **7**

Share: Claim of ownership in a corporation. (*See also* **Equity**.) **1**

Sources of the Base: Factors that produce changes in the monetary base; includes ten factors, the Federal Reserve security portfolio being the dominant factor. **14**

Speculative demand for money: Money held so that a speculative opportunity can be undertaken and financed in the event it should arise. **21**

Spot exchange rate: The foreign exchange rate for "on-the-spot" or immediate delivery and payment. **8**

Spot transaction: An exchange of currencies for immediate, or "on-the-spot" delivery and payment. **8**

Stagflation: Economic environment characterized by the simultaneous existence of economic stagnation or recession and strong inflationary forces. **20**

Supply-side economics: Macroeconomic policies designed to increase saving, investment, and work incentives, thus enhancing the nation's productive capacity and shifting the aggregate supply curve persistently outward. **20**

T

T-account: A device showing the *change* in a balance sheet resulting from a given action or event. **9**

Target Zone: A modern-day proposal for government intervention in foreign exchange markets for the purpose of maintaining exchange rates within certain (flexible) target zones.   **27**

Tariff: A tax on imported goods.   **8**

Tax and loan accounts: Deposits maintained in commercial banks by the U.S. Treasury, managed by the Treasury for the purpose of minimizing its infringement on bank reserves, the monetary base, and the money supply.   **12**

Tax illusion: The propensity of economic agents to judge value and make decisions on the basis of pretax considerations; failure to fully account for the effects of taxes in forming decisions.   **6**

Term premium: Additional yield embodied in long-term debt instruments to compensate investors for the increased market risk inherent in long-term securities relative to short-term securities.   **7**

Term structure of interest rates: Relationship between length of time to maturity and the level of interest rates, holding constant other factors such as default risk and tax treatment.   **7**

Terms of trade: Ratio of the price of a country's exports divided by the price of its imports, both prices being measured in units of domestic currency.   **8**

Time preference: The human propensity to exhibit preference for current goods over future goods; a factor explaining prevalence of positive real interest rates.   **5, 6**

Too-big-to-fail policy: Regulatory policy of systematically bailing out large, troubled institutions whose failure might touch off major financial repurcussions such as a financial panic.   **11**

Trade deficit: The amount by which the total value of a nation's imports exceed the total value of the nation's exports.   **1, 8**

Transactions (checkable) deposits: Deposits whose primary function is to make transactions; deposits on which checks may be written. Includes demand deposits, NOW accounts, ATS accounts, and credit union share drafts.   **9**

Transactions costs: Costs associated with making a financial transaction; generally includes a brokerage or other explicit fee plus the value of time spent in dealing with the transaction.   **4**

Transactions demand for money: Money held for the purpose of financing transactions in a world in which imperfect temporal synchronization between receipts and disbursements exists.   **21**

Transactions velocity (of money):   Ratio of the flow of total expenditures (including financial transactions and purchases of new and used goods and services) to the stock of money.   **21**

Transmission mechanism: The process through which monetary policy actions ultimately affect total expenditures, real output, and the price level.   **25**

Treasury bills: Short-term IOUs issued by the U.S. government in minimum denominations of $10,000. They are traded at a discount from face value in a well-developed secondary market through a network of about 40 government securities dealers. Original maturities are 1 year or less.   **3**

Treasury bonds: IOUs issued by the U.S. government which have an original term to maturity of 10 to 40 years, and a face value of $1,000. Treasury bonds typically pay interest at regular intervals, although some are tradable as zero-coupon bonds.   **3**

Treasury notes: IOUs issued by the U.S. government which have an original term to maturity of 1 to 10 years. Treasury notes have a face value of $1,000 and pay interest at regular intervals.   **3**

U

Undervalued currency: A currency whose foreign exchange value is less than that justified on the basis of such economic fundamentals as price-level and productivity behavior.   **27**

Unit banking: System in which a bank is permitted to have only one office, with no branching permitted.   **10**

Uses for the base: Ways in which the monetary base is allocated or held. Consists of bank reserves (deposits at the Fed and cash holdings) and currency held by the public.   **14**

V

Velocity (of money):   Average number of times per year that each dollar of money is spent, either on final goods and services (income velocity), or on all transactions (transactions velocity).   **21**

W

Wealth: The value of assets, including money and other financial and real assets, minus the value of liabilities, measured at a given point in time; a synonym for net worth.   **2**

Wealth effect: The effect of a change in real wealth owned by the private sector on aggregate expenditures; a declining price level, by increasing the real value of money and certain other assets, increases wealth and stimulates the quantity of real output demanded.   **20**

Y

Yield: The rate of return on an earning asset, expressed as percent per year.   **1, 3**

Yield curve: A graph illustrating the term structure of interest rates, that is, the yields available on differing maturities of a particular type of debt instrument.   **7**

Yield to maturity: A measure of the rate of return on an asset, encompassing both the annual income stream and the capital appreciation or depreciation of the asset.   **3**

Z

Zombie institutions: Term referring to insolvent savings and loan associations which were permitted to continue operations during the 1980s.   **11**

I N D E X

Special Text Features

Exhibits